SOUNDTRACK AVAILABLE

Essays on Film and Popular Music

Edited by

Pamela Robertson Wojcik

and Arthur Knight

DUKE UNIVERSITY PRESS

Durham and London 2001

© 2001 Duke University Press
All rights reserved
Printed in the United States of
America on acid-free paper ⊚
Designed by Amy Ruth Buchanan
Typeset in Scala by Tseng
Information Systems, Inc.
Library of Congress Cataloging-
in-Publication Data appear on
the last printed page of this book.

Contents

List of Illustrations

Acknowledgments

Editing a collection of essays is a collaborative effort, much like making a film or cutting a record. From this book's inception to its release, we have been fortunate to have the assistance and contributions of many people and institutions.

This project's origins go back to our days as graduate students. We met through the Mass Culture Workshop at the University of Chicago, where we found a community of scholars interested in film and popular music. At the University of Chicago we had two particular mentors who deserve thanks: Gerald Mast and Miriam Hansen. In very different ways, they inspired us to examine popular film music.

The Chicago Recorded Music Reading Group at Northwestern University provided a then sorely needed forum for thinking about popular music and introduced us to new friends and colleagues. Students from courses in film and popular music at the University of Newcastle and the University of Notre Dame, from "Multicultural Media Representations" at DePaul University, and in a variety of American studies, film, literary and cultural studies, and English courses at the College of William and Mary provided direct inspiration for this book, and sometimes road-tested essays for the collection. Our colleagues at the University of Notre Dame, the College of William and Mary, and the University of Newcastle in Australia provided welcome support over the course of this project.

Ken Wissoker has encouraged this project from the beginning. Thanks to Ken and the anonymous readers at Duke University Press for their advocacy and their advice. For help with illustrations, we owe thanks to Carbon and Josh Yumibe at the University of Chicago Film Studies Center, Cheryl Kelly in Multimedia Services at the University of Notre Dame, and Dorinda

Hartmann at the Wisconsin Center for Film and Theatre Research. We owe the Institute for Scholarship in the Liberal Arts at the University of Notre Dame a special thanks for funding many of the costs associated with illustrations.

Our contributors have been patient and conscientious throughout this process. We're delighted to have had this opportunity to work with established scholars whose work has influenced us, as well as new talents whose work we were pleased to discover.

Finally, we thank Rick Wojcik, Martha Howard, and Nora and Djuna Knight. Their love and support provides the "unheard melody" that shapes our work.

Overture

ARTHUR KNIGHT & PAMELA ROBERTSON WOJCIK

I think we are starting to think in soundtracks. —Alan Rudolph

Increasingly, it seems, we think in soundtracks. Popular music, in particular, governs our thoughts. Filmmakers, whether due to their own inclinations or market demands, conceptualize scenes in relation to popular song, and the mixing board becomes a storyboard. As viewers, we recall movies through song. Who can any longer hear "Stuck in the Middle with You" without seeing Mr. Blonde's chilling dance of torture in *Reservoir Dogs* (1991)? Songs used in films recall us to our past, or they conjure up a past we never experienced and, through the familiar language of popular music, make it ours. Witness the spate of seventies pop soundtracks, whether for films set in the seventies—such as *Dazed and Confused* (1993), *Boogie Nights* (1997), and *Dick* (1999)—or for films set in the present but with nostalgic or deliberately outdated camp soundtracks—as in *Reservoir Dogs* (1994), *Muriel's Wedding (1994)*, or *The Adventures of Priscilla, Queen of The Desert* (1994). In the worst cases, the songs are inserted cynically and clumsily, booming over montage sequences and credits as if they are Pavlovian advertisements for synergy. In the best cases, the soundtrack is a product of thought, and, more than mere triggers for soundtrack sales, the songs become essential components of the film experience.

Consider the soundtrack for *Wayne's World* (1992). The film includes thirty different songs, ranging from Tchaikovsky's "Romeo and Juliet: Fantasy Overture" to the theme from *Mission Impossible,* and including music by Jimi Hendrix, Eric Clapton, the Red Hot Chili Peppers, and Alice Cooper. Song cues move seamlessly between diegetic and nondiegetic, subjective and objective. Often, songs cue us to characters' subjectivity, as

1   Author's photo of some soundtracks available. [Author's collection]

when we hear Tchaikovsky as an internal diegetic soundover for Garth's fantasy girl, Donna Dixon. In a similar moment, "Dream Weaver" subjectively marks Wayne's experience of love at first sight. The theme from *Mission Impossible* plays nondiegetically as ironic commentary on Garth's self-perception as he prepares to avenge a bully by strapping on a high-powered stun gun.

The characters in *Wayne's World* frequently perform with the music in what could be seen as a reinvention of the musical. For instance, Garth lip-synchs "Foxy Lady" in a subjective fantasy when he imagines himself seducing his fantasy girl rather than just dreaming about her. Wayne sings "Happy Birthday to You" in a parody of Marilyn Monroe's famous Madison Square Garden birthday serenade for JFK, and Garth whistles the theme from *Star Trek* as he and Wayne watch airplanes taking off. In a moment of pure postmodern referentiality, the film launches Wayne and Garth into a full-blown imitation of the opening credit sequence for *Laverne and Shirley* when they see a road sign for Milwaukee. And, in one of the film's most memorable moments, Wayne, Garth, and friends sing-a-long with head-banging abandon to Queen's "Bohemian Rhapsody" as it plays on their AMC Pacer's 8-track tape deck.

Both by virtue of its postmodern credentials and the phenomenal sales of its soundtrack, *Wayne's World* may be a particularly privileged example of the successful soundtrack.[1] It is, however, by no means unprecedented. As Jeff Smith's *The Sounds of Commerce* details, *Wayne's World* has many varied antecedents, including such notable commercial successes as the soundtracks for *A Man and a Woman* (1966), *A Star Is Born* (1976), *Saturday Night Fever* (1977), *Fast Times at Ridgemont High* (1982), and *Pretty in Pink* (1986). In stylistic and aesthetic terms, *Wayne's World* exists alongside such critically acclaimed compilation scores as Martin Scorsese's *Mean Streets* (1973) and *Goodfellas* (1990), Spike Lee's *Do the Right Thing* (1989), or Quentin Tarantino's *Pulp Fiction* (1994). These scores have their roots in works of the American avant-garde like Kenneth Anger's *Scorpio Rising* (1964) or Bruce Connor's *Marilyn Times Five* (1973). Thinking beyond compilation scores, the popular score can trace its family tree to European directors like Jean-Luc Godard, Wim Wenders, and Rainer Werner Fassbinder who, rather than simply spotting songs for soundtrack sales, create various alienation effects through their use of global popular music.

The popular score is not, as many seem to suggest, exclusively a post-1950s, rock-and-roll-era phenomenon. Popular music of all kinds has been a crucial component of film from the beginning. It reaches back to the silent era, when phonographs, player pianos, or live musicians would accompany films, and early exhibitors would include song slides, "musical illustration" films, live singers, and sing-a-longs as key elements of the film program. The silent film industry even had its own brand of synergy as exhibitors sold sheet music for movie tie-ins.[2] To accompany feature films, live orchestras would play familiar standards in a kind of proto-compilation score. In the case of *The Birth of a Nation* (1915) D. W. Griffith specified what the musical accompaniment should be and so audiences heard such familiar folk and patriotic songs as "Dixie," "Home Sweet Home," and "Bonnie Blue Flag" along with Wagner's "The Ride of the Valkyries" and, from Grieg's "Peer Gynt" suite, "In the Hall of the Mountain King."[3]

In the classical Hollywood era, of course, the musical synchronized—or in industry parlance, "married"—the sounds of Tin Pan Alley, Broadway, and Harlem to film. While musicals emphasized singing and dancing as key components of the mise-en-scène, other films incorporated musical performance consistently but seemingly transparently. To fully appreciate the expressive weight of such transparent uses of popular music in Hollywood film, imagine *Casablanca* (1942) without Dooley Wilson's repeated performances of "As Time Goes By." Or consider what a Marlene Dietrich or Mae West film would be if they didn't include song. Beyond these specialty numbers by musical performers, nonsingers too were somehow always called upon to sing in Hollywood. Recall Jimmy Stewart's drunken

2 "You must remember this . . ." Dooley Wilson, Humphrey Bogart, and Sydney Greenstreet on the set of *Casablanca*. [Author's collection]

crooning in *It's a Wonderful Life* (1946) or Katherine Hepburn and Cary Grant singing "I Can't Give You Anything But Love" to a leopard in *Bringing Up Baby* (1938).

Popular music becomes a key aural component of the mise-en-scène in genre films. The western, for instance, seamlessly integrates scenes of country dances and cowboys strumming guitars. In a John Ford western like *My Darling Clementine* (1946), for instance, the dance takes on ritualistic significance. In a different vein, film noir seems to take any excuse it can to enter a jazz joint or a nightclub, giving rise to such musical moments as the wild orgiastic drum solos of Elisha Cook Jr. in *Phantom Lady* (1946). A screwball comedy might include a song for comedic effect, as in *The Awful Truth* (1937) when Ralph Bellamy bellows "Home on the Range" or Irene Dunne, impersonating a tacky southern showgirl, sings the hilariously inappropriate, pseudosexy "My Dreams Are Gone with the Wind." In various genres, the piano bar has provided the setting for romance and, crucially, enabled African American specialty acts to steal into nonmusical films. Remember Humphrey Bogart and Gloria Grahame listening to Hadda Brooks at a chic piano bar in *In a Lonely Place* (1954), or

Rock Hudson and Doris Day singing "Roly Poly" with Perry Blackwell in *Pillow Talk* (1959).

These examples signal the degree to which film has incorporated popular music and the variety of roles it has assigned this music. In addition to serving as nondiegetic score, popular music enters the soundtrack by way of musical performance, source radios, and record players. In films, people sing, sing-along, lip-synch, dance, and play to popular music. These examples also highlight how wide-ranging and flexible the broad category of popular music is. It includes folk, country, Tin Pan Alley, Broadway, jazz, disco, pop, rock-and-roll, rap, selections and adaptations of "classical" music, and more. We—both film scholars and music scholars—need to think more deeply about soundtracks to consider fully the range and variety of popular musical moments in film. Rather than erect a false barrier between musical and nonmusical films, or between post-1950s compilation soundtracks and diegetic performance in nonmusical film, we need to consider how these various practices are related. Instead of dismissing popular soundtracks as signs of cinema's waning integrity, or the public's being suckered by synergistic marketing practices, we need to consider how fundamental popular music is to the cinematic experience and, often, how fabulous.

Soundtrack Available seeks to capture this broader sense of pop music's relationship to film. The impetus for this volume came from a belief that most writing on film music has not adequately described popular music's role in film or people's experience of it (in the theater or outside). We believe, nonetheless, that serious thinking about soundtracks—in their many varied manifestations—is crucial to our understanding and experience of film and music.

Heard Melodies

Until recently, film music criticism has largely ignored popular music in favor of analyzing the classical nondiegetic film score. Film music histories, whether coffee table books for buffs or serious academic works by musicologists, have tended to treat film music history as a series of great works by great composers. Typical in this regard are Mark Evans's, *Soundtrack: The Music of the Movies,* and Roy M. Prendergrast's *Film Music: A Neglected Art.*[4] Emphasizing Hollywood's debt to Romantic traditions, these works, for the most part, quarantine film music away from film and focus on presumably pure musical patterns and structures without any consideration of how those patterns and structures are placed in film or how they relate to filmic patterns of narration, character, editing, framing, or mise-en-scène.

Since the late 1980s, film theorists and critics have increasingly turned their attention to the film score, thus avoiding some of the pitfalls musicologists face by emphasizing the nondiegetic score's importance for film narrative. The major texts in this vein are Claudia Gorbman's groundbreaking *Unheard Melodies: Narrative Film Music*, Caryl Flinn's *Strains of Utopia: Gender, Nostalgia, and Hollywood Film Music*, Kathryn Kalinak's *Settling the Score: Music and the Classical Hollywood Film*, and Royal S. Brown's *Overtones and Undertones: Reading Film Music*.[5] Approaching film music from within a film studies perspective, these theorists have written about the semiotics and ideology of film music, stressing its power to simultaneously be "invisible" or "unheard," produce spectacle, and enhance the narrative in its utopian or affective dimension. This approach, however, still tends to laud the work of a coterie of great composers, like Bernard Hermann, Max Steiner, and David Raksin, and to have an auteurist bias in its selection of films. In addition, most work on classical nondiegetic scores ignores the nondiegetic soundtrack's existence outside the cinema—its circulation through phonograph recordings, sheet music sales, Academy Awards, and so forth. Overall, then, rather than simply electing to discuss the Romantic tradition in film scoring instead of popular traditions, this work privileges the Romantic nondiegetic film score over popular traditions in a familiar high/low split.

In part, this work on the classical nondiegetic score, especially in its early manifestations, needs to be understood as a response to the effusive fan discourse that grew up around the Hollywood musical, a genre dedicated to ensuring—to invert Claudia Gorbman's famous and influential formulation—that its melodies were emphatically heard. The problems with the musical, from the perspectives of many of its critics, were that it was too clearly tied to its theatrical forebears and that it did not respect the apparent "natural" primacy of the visual over the acoustic experience of cinema. In Gorbman's more subtle analysis, "songs require narrative to cede to spectacle, for it seems that lyrics and action compete for attention."[6] What Gorbman doesn't say is that for many critics the problem of the musical spectacle is that it is either not spectacular enough (a singing head) or it is too spectacular (Busby Berkeley) when considered against the classical—and classically scored—narrative cinema.

Roughly congruent with the rise of film scholarly work on the classical score, which was one flavor of reaction to "low" Hollywood, came a wave of serious film scholarship on the musical genre, which worked to complicate fan discourse while still taking the musical seriously. The key works in this wave were Rick Altman's edited collection, *Genre: The Musical,* Jane Feuer's *The Hollywood Musical,* Altman's *The American Film Musical,* and Gerald Mast's *Can't Help Singin': The American Musical on Stage and Screen.*[7] Together these books are the first works of film criticism to examine popular music in film, and in important regards they are a cornerstone of *Soundtrack Available.* They opened the door for many of us to finally *hear* the movies we cared about.

At the same time, this work on the musical developed across the 1980s and is limited, from our present vantage, by being produced as the musical was becoming the music video and by having to do the hard, ground-clearing work of, in Feuer's formulation, "peel[ing] away the tinsel . . . [to] find the real tinsel underneath" the genre. With the partial exception of Mast's book, the work on the musical focuses on the genre's structuring tension between narrative and musicalized spectacle and it skirts specific, extended analyses of music. Because of this focus, musicals that at least tend toward formal "integration" are favored objects of analysis, displacing more fragmented, less narrative-driven films like the extraordinarily popular *This Is the Army* (1943) and less fully musicalized films like *She Done Him Wrong* (1933). In the paradoxical critical archeology of the musical, many of the cultural (and scholarly) values, like coherence and inflexible hierarchies, that the genre seems to abjure, sneak in the back way.[8] For instance, Mast's book does spend considerable time with the popular music of the musicals and with the notion of popular music's portability and multiple media, but opts to tame pop's profusion through recourse to a familiar "masterworks" schema organized around composers and lyricists.

A pair of more recent works, Jonathan Romney and Adrian Wootton's collection, *Celluloid Jukebox: Popular Music and the Movies since the 50s,* and our contributor Jeff Smith's *The Sound of Commerce: Marketing Popular Film Music,* both served as inspirations for *Soundtrack Available,* and this book may be profitably read and used in the classroom with one or both.[9] Both books extend the work on both the classical narrative score and the musical by focusing on the nondiegetic popular music score. For its part, *Celluloid Jukebox* displays the virtues and limits of the program catalog, which was its original function. On the one hand, it contains accessible overviews of a number of pop-rock film subgenres, an interesting filmography, and helpful interviews with film directors about how they conceptualize their uses of popular music. On the other hand, it is still entirely focused on the United States and England, on rock and roll, and on the near-present. By contrast, Smith's excellent study offers a much broader sense of the popular in popular music, a useful history of the film and music industry nexus in the United States, and particularly detailed and sensitive close readings of three crucial pop scores. Nonetheless, a single volume cannot cover the panoply of popular music's wedding with popular cinema, especially in that relationship's full historical scope and international reach.

Track List

While previous work on nondiegetic film scores, musicals, and popular music has informed and inspired us in our own efforts, the limitations of the treatments available prompted us to create this anthology. As teachers interested in film and popular music, but frustrated by the lack of books and essays available to teach, we wanted to produce a reader that could be used in graduate and undergraduate courses on film and popular music, and that could inspire new courses. At the same time, we envisioned a book that more casual readers would pick up and enjoy, a book for fans and scholars alike. Our goal was to gather fresh new essays that would explore previously unexplored terrain and open up new ways of thinking about popular music in film. In particular, we wanted to expand the range of analysis to include a more complex sense of the variety of functions pop music performs in film, including diegetic and nondiegetic music, title songs, uses of playback technology, and modes of performance in musical and nonmusical films. Therefore, we sought specific textual analysis along with broad overviews to encourage more in-depth analysis of the specific ways in which songs are used in films. In addition, in order to offer a more far-reaching and comparative range of popular music, we sought essays on different kinds of music, from country to disco, jazz to rock and roll. We especially wanted to include essays that dealt with popular music in film from before 1950 and from countries outside the United States, and we aimed to include essays dealing with popular music's extratextual functions. Because we understand popular music to be an overloaded cultural signifying system, we felt that an anthology on popular music and film would, by necessity, deal with issues of cultural identification and ideology, including sex, gender, race, ethnicity, and national identity.

Still, when we developed a call for papers, we did not know exactly what to expect. We were not sure how many writers and scholars we would find who were interested in popular music and film, or how many would venture into unpredictable territories. We were surprised and delighted with the response we got. It was exciting to discover that there were so many people writing about film and popular music and that they were working on such a variety of topics. We got exactly what we wanted and more than we could have hoped for.

The essays in *Soundtrack Available: Essays on Film and Popular Music* deal with films and music from India, France, England, Australia, and the United States. Essays cover material from the silent era to the present, in illustrated song slides, musicals, dramatic films, documentaries, rockumentary, and biopics. Writers consider the functions of diegetic songs in dramatic films, nondiegetic scores, uses of and representations of playback technology, and extratextual and intertextual relationships between film and radio and film and soundtrack albums. Categories of popular music discussed include country, teenybopper pop, disco, swing, jazz, classical, Bhangra music, French cabaret music, and showtunes; music by composers Henry Mancini and George Gershwin, and by artists Johnny Hartman, Duke Ellington, Louis Armstrong, the Monkees, Bing Crosby, and Loretta Lynn.

The first four essays, grouped together under the heading "Popular vs. Serious," each in different ways explore the often false distinctions between popular and classical music, low and high culture, commercialism and art. In "Cinema and Popular Song: The Lost Tradition," Rick Altman recovers the lost history of illustrated song slides to suggest the origins of popular song-oriented accompaniment practices of early cinema, practices that carried over into Hollywood's sound era and still operate today. Altman's essay sorts through the differences and points of overlap between popular and classical film scores and provides a backdrop for the essays that follow.

Priscilla Barlow complicates our understanding of what counts as "popular" and offers a key example of "classical" music being appropriated as "popular" in the 1930 film *L'Age d'or*, a collaborative work by Luis Buñuel and Salvador Dali. Barlow argues that Buñuel used "the most irreproachably bourgeois music one can imagine"—familiar classical music such as Beethoven's Fifth Symphony—to scandalize and shock bourgeois audiences and break down distinctions between high and low culture. Nonetheless, she claims, Buñuel unwittingly reinforced artificial hierarchical divisions between upper and lower classes and between "serious" and popular music.

Addressing the frequent dismissal of much popular music as frivolous, Murray Pomerance's essay elaborates on the importance of the seemingly disposable song "Que Sera, Sera (What Will Be, Will Be)" in Hitchcock's *The Man Who Knew Too Much* (1956). Superficially, "Que Sera, Sera" seems simple, both in its content and its function in Hitchcock's film, but Pomerance's writerly essay convinces that the song reflects the film's labyrinthine structure and captures the film's dynamic movement.

Analyzing the tensions between popular, commercial pressures and avant-garde stimulus, Paul Ramaeker assesses the 1968 Monkees vehicle *Head,* jointly created by Bob Rafelson, Bert Schneider, and Jack Nicholson. Exploring the discourse around *Head*'s "failure," Ramaeker finds the film juggling seemingly contradictory impulses. On the one hand, it aims to capitalize on the success of the prefabricated teenybopper quartet among preteen audiences and, on the other hand, it makes a bid for cultural credibility among mature adults by deconstructing the Monkees' image and presenting the group as countercultural figures.

In the next section, labeled "Singing Stars," Allison McCracken, Kelley Conway, and Neepa Majumdar analyze the role of the singer in such diverse historical contexts as the early sound period in Hollywood, 1930s France, and recent Bollywood. Taken together, these essays provide a fascinating cross-cultural comparison of how singing has been gendered in different historical and national contexts. In "Real Men Don't Sing Ballads: The Radio Crooner in Hollywood, 1929–1933," McCracken argues that due to his artificial amplification, his female fan-base, and his "effeminate" voice, the figure of the crooner "challenged traditional notions of the integrity of embodied white masculinity." Arguing that the masculinity of the crooner is ultimately, if uneasily, established in Hollywood through the early films of Bing Crosby, McCracken suggests that the crooner reveals how imbricated popular song, musical film, and changing conceptions of white masculinity are.

Kelley Conway's essay on the *chanteuse réaliste* in 1930s French cinema examines the prevalence and popularity of popular songs and singers in French film of this era. Looking at a range of films featuring the singers Fréhel and Damia, along with actress Louise Brooks, Conway finds embodied in the chanteuse réaliste a rich constellation of meanings associating the popular song mode with changing constructions of femininity and class, while also reflecting the film's preoccupation with gendered public spaces.

Neepa Majumdar's essay, "The Embodied Voice: Song Sequences and Stardom in Popular Hindi Cinema," challenges conventional notions of stardom through an examination of the unique aural stardom of playback singers in Hindi cinema. In contrast to Hollywood's concealment and vilification of dubbing as an inauthentic mode—notably in *Singin' in the Rain* (1952)—Majumdar describes the use of playback singing in Indian

Notes

1 For example, Jeff Smith also uses *Wayne's World* to situate the aesthetic and commercial aspects of post-1950s soundtracks. See *The Sounds of Commerce: Marketing Popular Film Music* (New York: Columbia University Press, 1998), 1–2.

2 On silent film music, see Martin Miller Marks, *Music and the Silent Film: Contexts and Case Studies, 1895–1924* (New York: Oxford University Press, 1997), and Charles Merrell Berg, *An Investigation of the Motives for and the Realization of Music to Accompany the American Silent Film, 1896–1927* (New York: Arno Press, 1976). On early "synergy," see Smith, *Sounds of Commerce,* 28–29.

3 See Harlow Hare's review of *The Birth of a Nation,* reprinted in *The Birth of a Nation: D. W. Griffith, Director,* ed. Robert Lang (New Brunswick, N.J.: Rutgers University Press, 1994), 186–89.

4 Mark Evans, *Soundtrack: The Music of the Movies* (New York: Hopkinson & Blake, 1975); Roy M. Prendergrast, *Film Music—A Neglected Art: A Critical Study of Music in Films,* 2nd ed. (New York: W. W. Norton, 1992). See also William Darby and Jack Du Bois, *American Film Music: Major Composers, Techniques, Trends, 1915–1990* (Jefferson, N.C.: MacFarland, 1991).

5 Claudia Gorbman, *Unheard Melodies: Narrative Film Music* (Bloomington: Indiana University Press, 1987); Caryl Flinn, *Strains of Utopia: Gender, Nostalgia, and Hollywood Film Music* (Princeton, N.J.: Princeton University Press, 1992); Kathryn Kalinak, *Settling the Score: Music and the Classical Hollywood Film* (Madison: University of Wisconsin Press, 1992); and Royal S. Brown, *Overtones and Undertones: Reading Film Music* (Berkeley: University of California Press, 1994).

6 Gorbman, *Unheard Melodies,* 20.

7 Rick Altman, ed., *Genre: The Musical* (London: Routledge & Kegan Paul, 1981); Jane Feuer, *The Hollywood Musical,* 2nd ed. (Bloomington: Indiana University Press, 1993); Rick Altman *The American Film Musical* (Bloomington: Indiana University Press, 1989); and Gerald Mast, *Can't Help Singin': The American Musical on Stage and Screen* (Woodstock, N.Y.: Overlook Press, 1987).

8 Several more recent works by film scholars on genres and forms that are tributary to the musical help to complicate these tendencies when held adjacent to the work on the musical and, indeed, on the classical score: Henry Jenkins, *What Made Pistachio Nuts? Early Sound Comedy and the Vaudeville Aesthetic* (New York: Columbia University Press, 1992); Robert C. Allen, *Horrible Prettiness: Burlesque and American Culture* (Chapel Hill, N.C.: University of North Carolina Press, 1991); Rick Altman, *Film/Genre* (London: British Film Institute, 1999), and "The Silence of the Silents," *Musical Quarterly* 80.4 (1996): 648–718.

9 Jonathan Romney and Adrian Wootton, eds., *Celluloid Jukebox: Popular Music and the Movies since the 50s* (London: British Film Institute, 1995); Smith, *The Sounds of Commerce.* Krin Gabbard's collection, *Representing Jazz* (Durham, N.C.: Duke University Press, 1995), dedicates half of its essays to jazz and film and would also be useful as a companion to these works and *Soundtrack Available.*

POPULAR VS. "SERIOUS"

Cinema and Popular Song: The Lost Tradition
RICK ALTMAN

Most writing on film music has concentrated on the practice in early cinema of underscoring a film segment's narrative or emotive content with light classical music in the European tradition. Historiographically, this approach to film accompaniment falls short on three separate counts: (1) It neglects the auditory practices of early cinema, thereby failing to recognize cinema's investment in a competing popular song tradition. (2) It unjustifiably limits our notion of the principles operative in musical accompaniment to those characterized by European-inspired light classical music. (3) It oversimplifies the complex dialectic between disparate musical traditions that undergirds the history of film music.

Illustrated Songs and Nickelodeon Accompaniment

Traditional accounts of silent film sound have assumed that early film exhibition borrowed its sound practices directly from the nineteenth-century theater, and thus featured accompaniment like that of the later silent period.[1] Treating nickelodeons as the first theaters specifically dedicated to films, critics typically assimilate nickelodeons and their music to later purpose-built film theaters. However, a closer look at nickelodeon programs suggests radically different conclusions.

As facade photographs readily attest, the highlight of many nickelodeon programs was the illustrated song, a live entertainment featuring a popular song illustrated by colorful lantern slides. Accompanied by the piano, the singer would typically warble two verses and two choruses, then the audience would join in while the chorus-lyrics slide was projected. First invented in the mid-1890s, illustrated song slides grew rapidly in popu-

3 1902 Sears catalog ad for a song slide outfit "made up with a special view to the after addition of moving picture effects." [Author's collection]

larity as sheet music publishers recognized their publicity value, exhibitors exploited their hand-colored brilliance, and audiences appreciated the chance to participate. With the rise of nickelodeons, illustrated song slides became a standard part of the program. Since the projectors of the period served double duty for moving pictures and lantern slides, song slides offered a convenient and inexpensive manner to occupy audiences while the film was changed. In fact, the enormous popularity of song slides suggests that films offered respite for the singer between song slides, rather than vice versa. Song slides held their popularity until around 1913, when a second film projector was installed in most projection booths, allowing films to alternate with films rather than with slides.

The typical illustrated song slide set included a title slide made from the sheet-music cover, twelve to sixteen live-model slides corresponding to two verses and two choruses, and a chorus-lyrics slide that remained on screen while the audience belted out the chorus, often many times over. Initially distributed gratis by music publishers as a form of publicity, slide sets were eventually sold or rented for modest sums. Ads for song slides appeared regularly in trade journals like *Views and Films Index* and *Moving Picture World and View Photographer*. Produced by small, undercapitalized companies with names like Chicago Transparency Company, A. L. Simpson, DeWitt C. Wheeler, or Scott and Van Altena, song slides featured many actors and actresses who would become familiar silent film figures (Francis X. Bushman, Alice Joyce, Mabel Normand, Anita Stewart, Norma Talmadge, Florence Turner, Lillian Walker). Sung on the vaudeville stage by big-name "song illustrators" like Ada Jones and Meyer Cohen, or teams like Maxwell and Simpson, song slides would later give their first chances to the likes of George Jessel and Al Jolson. In nickelodeons, however, the singer would often be the owner's wife, daughter, or niece.

There are many reasons why illustrated song slides have been neglected. Even when they weren't broken by the intense heat of projection, the extremely fragile $3 \frac{1}{4}$" × 4" glass slides were often simply thrown away like yesterday's publicity. Considered as a different medium, song slides have been ignored by film archives and film scholarship, and are almost never shown as part of a film program. Conversely, the few heroic collectors who have preserved song slides — people like John W. Ripley and Margaret and Nancy Bergh — are not film scholars and thus tend to show song slides within a lantern-slide context rather than in conjunction with films. Our ignorance of illustrated song slides and their relationship to film exhibition has seriously compromised our ability to make sense of the nickelodeon period.

The active presence of illustrated song slides in nickelodeon programs suggests many different avenues of research. What effect did the illustrated song preference for ballads and other narrative forms have on film's mid-aughts turn toward narrative? Was the contemporary songwriter Charles K. Harris right to claim that song slide scenarios provided the basic model for "the moving picture play scenario"?[2] Before Hollywood "invented" background projection and long before television devised the blue screen process, song slides had blazed the trail with a black background technique for combining studio-shot interiors with location exteriors. How did the compositing techniques developed by the song slide industry influence Hollywood's constitutive foreground/background separation? The early teens have been seen as a watershed, with the spread of large purpose-built theaters, the installation of a second projector, and the rise of feature films, but what of the active repression of a cinema of attractions through industry criticism of song-slide-spawned audience participation? These and other basic questions are raised by the intermediality of nickelodeon programs.

When considered from the standpoint of sound practice, illustrated songs suggest a totally different set of issues. Close inspection of the

lantern-slide images that song slide manufacturers accepted as appropriate matches for song lyrics suggests that nickelodeon accompaniment
standards may have been very different from later criteria. As *Film Index*
insists, "it is to be questioned whether a picture of a bird on its nest truly
illustrates a line to the effect that the hero will return when the birdies
nest again, but usually the slide gets a hand, the women murmur 'Ain't it
sweet' and the slide maker makes some more of the same sort because he
is in business to fill a demand, not to furnish an art education with each set
of slides."[3] Unlike later practice, which emphasizes the emotive value of
musical texture, song slides and early accompaniment often stress verbal
matches. A deaf man could make song slides, since only the lyrics count.
In fact, a deaf man did: Edward Van Altena's partner John D. Scott had
been deaf since the age of four.

A closer look at prewar sound practices suggests that early accompaniment may have been directly influenced by illustrated songs, film's audiovisual partner in the nickelodeon business. Repeatedly, we find producers
recommending popular songs to accompany their films. Edison suggests
the following familiar tunes to accompany *A Western Romance:* "If a Girl
Like You Loved a Boy Like Me," "School Days," "I'm Going Away," "On the
Rocky Road to Dublin," "Pony Boy," "Temptation Rag," "I'm a Bold Bad
Man," "Wahoo," "So Long, Mary," and "Everybody Works but Father."[4] As
late as 1912 a forward-looking showman like S. L. Rothapfel (Roxy), even in
an upscale theater like Chicago's Lyric, would lace his program with such
old favorites as "Auld Lang Syne," "A Hot Time in the Old Town Tonight,"
"He's A Jolly Good Fellow," "Tramp, Tramp, Tramp," "Oh You Beautiful
Doll," "Annie Laurie," "Rosary," and "Good-bye."[5] As Clyde Martin confirms in 1910, "half of the musicians in the country . . . will pick up a publisher's catalogue and get *names* of songs that correspond with the scenes
portrayed [my emphasis]."[6]

To connect the music to the image, nickelodeon accompaniment depended not only on popular songs, but on their titles and lyrics. One particularly adept house pianist, affirms Martin, "kept the house in laughter
with his selections in accompaniment to pictures of a flirtation. He made
the Lothario say: 'There's something about you dear that appeals to me;
my wife's gone to the country—won't you come over to my house? You're
just my style. I like you. How'd you like to spoon with me?' The fellow's
wife broke in upon the flirtation, then left him in a rage. The piano sym-
pathized. 'Gee, I Wish I Had My Old Girl Back Again.'"[7] Nearly a century later, we still recognize in this account the titles of no less than eight
popular songs, evoked seriatim to reinforce the narrative presented by the

image. Far from simply recycling nineteenth-century melodrama music and prefiguring the accompaniment style typically applied to silent features, nickelodeons depended heavily on popular song.

The Structure of Popular Songs and "Classical" Music

For decades, scholars have neglected illustrated songs and the nickelodeon's popular song aesthetic. In order to revive that tradition, and to understand its continuing role throughout the history of cinema, we must first highlight the differences separating popular songs from the music used for late silent films and through-composed sound films. For simplicity's sake, I will adopt Royal S. Brown's use of the term "classical," in quotation marks, to designate the various types of music included in the latter category.[8] I thus am using the term "classical" to designate not two centuries of musical tradition, but only the styles commonly employed in late silent film accompaniment and in through-composed sound cinema. The category of classical music, without the quotation marks, would include art song and opera; my "classical" category, with quotation marks, does not include those forms, since they are not regularly used in film music.

Film music critics typically stress the Wagnerian tendency of "classical" film music to employ repeated leitmotifs and themes in connection with specific characters or situations.[9] While not denying the importance of this technique, I will here concentrate instead on more basic aspects of "classical" music. For the purposes of a comparison with popular song, it is essential to recognize the fundamental muteness, indeterminacy, inconspicuousness, and expansibility of "classical" music, along with the effects that these characteristics have on listeners.

> *muteness.* Though "classical" pieces sometimes have titles, they achieve audiovisual matching by generalized parallelism between the emotive connotations of particular musical textures and the content of specific image sequences, rather than through verbal content.
>
> *indeterminacy.* Whereas the title and lyrics of a popular song usually overdetermine meaning, the signification of "classical" music is far more dependent on the images and situations to which it is linked.
>
> *inconspicuousness.* By this term I do not mean simply that "classical" music is "unheard," as Claudia Gorbman says of narrative film music. Gorbman's point relates to the way "classical" music is deployed in the cinema, whereas I am referring to a fundamental dif-

ference in saliency between wordless music and popular songs. Language is processed differently from instrumental music (even when only a reminiscence of that language remains, as with an instrumental version of a popular song); "classical" music is thus by its very nature inconspicuous, even before being inconspicuously applied to Hollywood films.

expansibility. In terms of its difference from popular song, "classical" music's expansibility looms large. Variable phrase length and delayed closure contribute heavily to this feature. "Classical" music's expansion methods include development by variation, modulation, minor or modal treatment, and change of instrumentation, register, or volume. To delay closure, "classical" music employs deceptive cadences, where a v–vi harmonic structure extends the piece rather than closing it off through the expected v–i "authentic" cadence. The multilayered nature of "classical" music offers multiple opportunities for extension, any separate layer potentially justifying continuation, even when the others have reached closure.

quiet listening and mental involvement. Though "classical" music depends on the same drive toward tonic resolution as does popular song, its lack of repetitive and predictable closure diffuses rather than unifies audience reaction. Because it operates on multiple levels, "classical" music rarely offers a separable hummable melody, and never provides singable lyrics, thus encouraging quiet and attentive listening rather than active participation. As such, "classical" music involves audiences mentally more than bodily, inviting them to internalize rather than externalize their reactions. The convention of silent listening to concert music, established well prior to "classical" music's debut in film exhibition, provides strong cultural reinforcement for this tendency.[10]

In contrast, popular song depends on language, and is predictable, singable, remememberable, and physically involving in ways that "classical" music usually is not.

linguistic dependence. The musical aspects of popular songs may suggest emotive or narrative connotations just as "classical" music does, but musical modes of meaning-making are typically overwhelmed by popular song's tendency toward direct linguistic communication. Titles and lyrics so dominate public evaluation of a popular song's emotive or narrative content that a song rarely signifies separately from its linguistic content.

predictability. Built out of standard four- or eight-bar units, popular songs at regular intervals reach rhythmic closure, reinforced by linguistic structures, such as the placement of rhyming lyrics at the end of phrases. Based on regular melodic repetition, popular songs establish and satisfy audience expectations of return to familiar melodic material. Because they systematically employ standard iv–v–i harmonic progressions, popular songs also establish and satisfy audience expectations of predictable harmonic closure. Not only do popular songs privilege repetition and regularity, but they align linguistic and musical systems to take advantage of multiple simultaneous closure cues.

singability. Popular songs are hummable because they imply reducibility to their melody, which is restricted to an accessible frequency range. They are singable because they have easily pronounced lyrics arranged in convenient and readily understandable breath groups reproducing common speech patterns. Careful matching of music and lyrics further reinforces popular song's singable nature.

rememberability. Composed of short, standardized, repeated components, popular songs are easy to remember, both musically and linguistically. Through repetition of verse and refrain, the song is easily taught to even the most unmusical audiences. This return to familiar material generates anticipation of further repetition that popular songs amply satisfy.

active physical involvement. Predictable, singable, rememberable, apparently reducible to melody and lyrics, and often based on familiar dance rhythms, popular songs typically inspire toe-tapping, whistling, humming, singing along, and other types of active participation.

Of course "classical" music at times borrows elements from popular song. When a studio arranger like MGM's Roger Edens needed bridging music, he would often create it by applying the principles of "classical" music to melody material derived from one of the film's songs. In other words, neither the principles of "classical" music nor popular song strategies should be seen as insulated from each other. By and large, however, the tendencies presented here are strong and clearly differentiated.

When they are used in association with images, "classical" music and popular song reveal yet another important difference. Because it has an obvious coherence, with each line clearly connected to the overall structure and a universally expected musical cadence and linguistic conclusion,

popular song never allows listeners of the song's individual parts to escape from the whole. As such, the popular song always remains a coher-
ent block that appears to be authored separately from whatever images it
accompanies, whereas "classical" music's meandering capacity often con-
ceals overall structure, implying that the music is generated not by some
global vision, but by the image at hand. "Classical" music thus more easily
convinces us that it is authored not by a composer, but by the image. In
this sense, the popular song aurally recalls the discursive nature of an early
cinema of attractions, while "classical" music fits especially well into the
impersonal narration of classic Hollywood cinema.

Popular Song and the History of Film Music

Film music scholarship has concentrated almost exclusively on "classical"
music. Yet the influence of the nickelodeon's song-oriented accompaniment practices is visible throughout the history of film music. From the
theme song craze of the mid-twenties to the compilation soundtracks of
the last two decades, popular song has continued to share cinema sound
space with "classical" music. Several genres depend wholly or primarily on
the song mode. These include early sync sound camera and disc recordings; 1930s animation series based on popular songs available through
recently acquired music publishers; Soundies and other pre-TV attempts
to provide an audiovisual version of popular songs; and music videos
spawned by MTV and its imitators.

More complex, and in the long run more interesting, are the many feature film attempts to take advantage of popular song's ability to perform
certain operations better than "classical" music. Two of these in particular
stand out. While "classical" music is particularly able to provide routine
commentary and to evoke generalized emotional reactions, popular song
is often capable of serving a more specific narrational purpose. Thus John
Ford regularly used folk songs to establish a specific mood in his westerns,
historical films often employ period songs to signify specific historical moments, and film noir regularly interrupts loveless male-dominated narratives with nightclub songs offering an oasis of romance or female power.
From *High Noon* to *Miller's Crossing,* nondiegetic popular song lyrics provide a unique opportunity to editorialize and to focus audience attention.
Theme songs used over initial credits constitute a particularly common
example of this strategy.

A second capacity not fully shared by "classical" music is popular song's
separate marketability. By virtue of its reproducibility by a piano and ama-

4 1925 *Film Daily* ad for Cameo Music's "Thematic Music Cue Sheet" service, featuring a typical example mixing popular songs drawn from Victor Herbert operettas with classical favorites by Schubert and Rachmaninoff. [Author's collection]

5 As Twentieth Century Fox's most precious commodities, stars and song titles share top billing on this 1939 poster for *Rose of Washington Square*. [Author's collection]

teur singers, popular song for decades carried on an intense symbiotic relationship with the sheet music industry. Short, inexpensive, and easily
distributed, popular songs also made ideal auditory commodities when
recorded on cylinders, discs, or tape. Since the American cinema is a
for-profit industry, films regularly renew attempts to take advantage of
the commercial opportunities associated with popular song. Even before
sound, orchestra leaders understood the benefits of this strategy, privileging certain music cues and building them into potentially lucrative theme
songs. By the fifties, the film and recording industries were so tightly intertwined that theme songs were often released as singles in advance of the
film's opening. With the triumph of albums and the development of compact discs, the single theme gave way to the compilation soundtrack built
entirely out of popular songs.

```
                "TRAILER TO WAR NURSE"


        1.
        Open's with 1st. slide while Playing Introduction and half Chorus of
        Madelon - (Open Curtain on last 8 Bars of Madelon -


        2.
        Last bar of Modulation to Rose of No Man's Land - buzz for slide,
        while singer, sing using a P. A . system. - ( The Chorus of No
        Man'sland has four slides.


        3.
        When Chorus is over buzz for slide of Mother Nurse, while singer
        recites, Orchestra continue playing chorus PP - until talking trailer
        goes on.


        4.
        For last two frames of talking trailer, buzz the booth to have it
        silent so that the singer can pick up last half chorus of Rose of
        No Man'sland. Build up the last two Bars and close curtain.


            PLEASE REHEARSE THIS VERY CAREFUL, SO EVERYTHING BLEND'S TOGETHER.



                        H. L. SPITALNY.
```

6 Extraordinary internal document in which Balaban and Katz musical director
H. L. Spitalny explains to local conductors how to combine song slide techniques
with a talking trailer in order to feature *War Nurse*'s theme song. [Chicago Public
Library]

One of the film music problems most requiring attention involves the
interaction between "classical" music and popular song in films that include both. Is a song melody thematized and turned into a leitmotif? Is
part of a song expanded, developed, and used according to "classical" principles? In short, is the popular song made to change colors and participate
in the work of the "classical" soundtrack? Or are lyrics and a title imposed
on "classical" material? Is a "classical" theme so often repeated in conjunction with a particular structure and cadence that it emulates a popular
song? In short, is the film's "classical" accompaniment forced into accom-
plishing popular song goals?

When we consider these questions historically, we recognize the important role played by the sound component of early exhibition practices.
Nickelodeons established many expectations and techniques that would
ultimately either be overtly adopted by Hollywood or repressed and carried
covertly within dominant filmmaking practice. In order to understand

Hollywood sound more fully, we must begin to address the dialectic that simultaneously relates and separates "classical" music and popular song. We must also recognize the extent to which this relationship serves as a vehicle for essential oppositions between spectacle and narrative, between *discours* and *histoire,* between static dual-focus forms and dynamic single-focus modes, between bodily reaction and mental processing, between film as participatory mode and as spectator form, between European inspiration and American pragmatism. None of these important dichotomies can be properly understood independently of the ongoing and complex relationship between "classical" music and popular song.

Notes

1 For a critique of this position, and for several other points of particular relevance to the subject of this article, see Rick Altman, "The Silence of the Silents," *Musical Quarterly* 80.2 (1997): 648–718.

2 Charles K. Harris, "Song Slide the Little Father of Photodrama," *Moving Picture World,* 10 March 1917, 1520.

3 "Unique Effects in Song Slides," *Film Index,* 6 May 1911, 12.

4 *Kinetogram,* 15 March 1910, 11.

5 Reported by Clarence E. Sinn in "Music for the Picture," *Moving Picture World,* 9 July 1912, 49.

6 "Playing the Pictures," *Film Index,* 19 November 1910, 27.

7 Clyde Martin, "Playing the Pictures," *Film Index,* 22 April 1911, 13.

8 Royal S. Brown, *Overtones and Undertones: Reading Film Music* (Berkeley: University of California Press, 1994), 38–39.

9 See for example Claudia Gorbman, *Unheard Melodies: Narrative Film Music* (Bloomington: Indiana University Press, 1987), 26ff.

10 For European audiences' turn toward silence in the early nineteenth century, see James H. Johnson, *Listening in Paris: A Cultural History* (Berkeley: University of California Press, 1995). For the silencing of American audiences in the latter half of the nineteenth century, see Lawrence W. Levine, *Highbrow/Lowbrow: The Emergence of Cultural Hierarchy in America* (Cambridge: Harvard University Press, 1988), esp. 179 ff; and John F. Kasson, *Rudeness and Civility: Manners in Nineteenth-Century America* (New York: Hill & Wang, 1990), 215 ff.

Surreal Symphonies:
L'Age d'or and the Discreet Charms
of Classical Music

PRISCILLA BARLOW

In their 1930 film collaboration, *L'Age d'or,* Luis Buñuel and Salvador Dali aimed at surpassing the scandal they had attempted to create with their first film, *Un Chien Andalou,* released the previous year. *Un Chien Andalou* was an enormous *succés de scandale* and enjoyed an eight-month run in Paris. Buñuel ended up earning seven or eight thousand francs from the film. Following the surprise critical and commercial success of this first collaboration, Buñuel must have been gratified at the response to *L'Age d'or,* which was screened for packed houses at Studio 28 for six days. At that point, a right wing claque disrupted a screening, set off stink bombs, shouted "Death to the Jews," and slashed Surrealist paintings that were on display in the lobby. Eventually the police confiscated the film.

Whereas the film became infamous almost immediately, one aspect of it has received very little attention, and that is its soundtrack. At first glance, or rather, first listen, the music might appear to be merely an assortment of pieces from the classical and Romantic symphonic repertory, selected primarily for the ironic contrast between what one hears and sees. However, Buñuel's decision to use this music must be understood in the context of his desire to outdo the shocking effect of *Un Chien Andalou.* Because he aimed to shock the bourgeoisie, he used the most shocking music possible, which was the most familiar and irreproachably bourgeois music one can imagine. The soundtrack is comprised primarily of music by Mozart, Beethoven, Mendelssohn, and Wagner. Ironically enough, jazz, the "popular" choice, would have been less familiar and association-laden to his cultivated European audience than the supposedly elite classical music he selected.

The resulting juxtapositions are startling, to say the least: Mozart's "Ave Verum Corpus" accompanies the sight of decaying bishops' bodies, a broken down bunch of bandits travel across the countryside to the first movement of Beethoven's Fifth Symphony, two scorpions battle to the strains of Mendelssohn's Hebrides Overture, and Lya Lys sucks the toe of a statue to the "Liebestod" from Wagner's *Tristan und Isolde*. In comparison to Buñuel's trademark off-putting narrative techniques, obscenity, and anticlericalism, these juxtapositions might appear merely ironic. However, part of the effect of his film depended on its play with intertextual associations, on the way it shocks by juxtaposing the known and familiar with the dreamlike and strange. By using music that his highly cultured audience could be expected to know, Buñuel in effect bridged the supposed gap between serious and popular music. As a result, *L'Age d'or* both explodes and reinforces the artificial, hierarchical divisions between mass and "class," serious and popular music.

Popular versus Classical Music

A discussion of this kind naturally begs the question: what is popular music? The answer is clearly more complicated than one would think at first. "Popular" music is generally defined in opposition to what many people refer to as "classical" or "serious" music.[1] For the most part, during the last century of mass communications, these oppositions have become stronger, through a process of accretion. The music publishing and recording industries have made the distinctions between types of music of paramount importance, since these distinctions are crucial to their marketing efforts. The cross-over work of composers like George Gershwin and Leonard Bernstein, or of performers like Wynton Marsalis and Benny Goodman, are the exceptions to a tacitly understood rule.

Despite common conceptions of the distance between classical and popular music, the categories are not as fixed and immutable as they appear to be. With increased audience exposure, these categories blur and shift. A case in point is the music of Richard Wagner. Once considered avant-garde, certain frequently excerpted segments of Wagner's operas, such as "The Ride of the Valkyries" from *Siegfried,* composed in 1857, have become so familiar that they can be deployed as musical jokes. In 1915 when D. W. Griffith worked on the score to *The Birth of a Nation,* he selected music with an eye toward impressing the film's mostly rural or small-town audiences that were unfamiliar with a great deal of classical music. He used the "Ride of the Valkyries" to underscore the heroism of the Ku Klux Klan. However, by 1938 the same music was used to ironic effect in *Daffy Duck in Hollywood* (Warner Bros., 1938), an animated short in which Daffy Duck uses a combination of stock footage from the studio library to produce "a goofy newsreel compendium of absurd live-action shots with mis-matching narration," including a brief segment where a shot of strip mining is accompanied by the strains of none other than "The Ride of the Valkyries."[2] In the space of twenty-three years, music that was unfamiliar to D. W. Griffith's audience had become a complete cliché. As a piece of music becomes increasingly familiar, it continues to acquire intertextual associations. Another well-known Warner Bros. short, *What's Opera, Doc?* (1957) effectively put a stop to any possible subsequent serious use of the "Ride of the Valkyries," since anyone familiar with the short would associate it with Elmer Fudd singing "Kill the wabbit." (The accumulated weight of all these uses underscores its ironic deployment in *Apocalypse Now.*) For a 1970 screening of *The Birth of a Nation*, therefore, Charles Hofmann accompanied the film with "the topical period tunes of the Civil War Period, songs from Lincoln's day and the songs of Stephen Collins Foster," because the pieces Griffith and Carl Breil had selected—Wagner's "Ride," Grieg's "Peer Gynt," and the overture from Rossini's *Guillaume Tell*—were all too well known and would strike a contemporary audience as ludicrous.[3]

A category of music currently being marketed as "light classical" is classical music that has become accessible and popular by means of mass communications. Light classical music is both well known and widely dispersed through such venues as "pops" concerts, restaurants and shops that play background music, radio stations specializing in this music, advertisements, and film soundtracks. Occasionally a piece is resurrected and becomes popular in unforeseen ways, like Pachelbel's Canon in D and the Gregorian chants on the "Chant" compact discs. The "Three Tenors" concerts, compact discs, television broadcasts, and videos have exposed huge numbers of listeners to operatic music. Ravel's *Bolero*, which musicologist Donald Grout had called "the musical equivalent of a best-seller" before it was included in the soundtrack to *10* (Blake Edwards, 1979) attained a new level of mass popularity after the release of the film.[4] People who don't usually listen to classical music make an exception for music of this sort. As a result, enormous numbers of people are familiar with these pieces, which ordinarily would be considered a somewhat esoteric taste. Once highbrow and esoteric, light classical has become well known and therefore middlebrow. Thus, in some way, this kind of light classical music can be considered popular, because it has become classical music for the masses. The result is a hybrid category that shares characteristics of both classical and popular music, and which has existed, uneasily at times, for approximately a century.

Not surprisingly, classical music purists find "light classical" anathema for reasons of intellectual and social snobbery. In the late nineteenth century, the same period that classical music became increasingly familiar because of the ubiquity of pianos, piano rolls, and inexpensive sheet music, many great cultural institutions were also founded, among them some of the world's greatest symphony orchestras.[5] These orchestras and opera companies performed in halls that seated literally thousands of people. During this period, symphony going became an expected part of the bourgeois lifestyle. As a result of the wider availability of classical music, the late nineteenth century was also characterized by a rush to establish cultural hierarchies. The social elite managed to find ways to separate themselves from the herd, either physically, by sitting in much more expensive seats, or intellectually, by cultivating their increasingly sophisticated taste. As Lawrence Levine argues, when too many people crowded to hear Italian opera, Italian opera lost favor among the cultural elite, who turned to Wagnerian opera and symphonic music. As early as 1889, Theodore Thomas, the founder of the Chicago Symphony Orchestra, vigorously resisted attempts to establish any kind of "pops" repertoire, arguing that "one does not buy a Krupp cannon to shoot sparrows."[6]

As the seminal work of Pierre Bourdieu has made clear, in a culture of consumption, discriminating taste becomes the hallmark of superior social or intellectual status.[7] The more the average person was exposed to classical music, the more rarefied became the tastes of the pure devotees. While large cities were establishing orchestras, ostensibly to entertain large crowds of music lovers, their joint, mutually exclusive missions became to entertain educated listeners and educate any listener who could afford to purchase a ticket. When one purchased a ticket to a performance of a symphony orchestra, one was purchasing not just an evening's entertainment but entrance into a nexus where either one's cultivated taste or one's income, or perhaps both, served to exclude anyone who lacked the money or the necessary cultural education to enjoy listening. One's knowledge of the classical symphonic and operatic repertory becomes, in short, a badge of one's membership in the haute bourgeoisie. In E. M. Forster's 1910 novel *Howard's End,* the lower-middle-class identity of clerk Leonard is made clear instantly when in conversation with the highly cultured Schlegel sisters, he decides not to mention the Wagner opera he has in mind, because he is unsure about the correct pronunciation of "Tannhäuser."

The development of the modernist movement in music served to promulgate classical music's hierarchical structure. Modernist music was characterized by increasingly further forays away from the tonal system and musical structures that characterized the music of Bach, Mozart, Beethoven, and Brahms. Popular reaction to this music was overwhelmingly negative. For example, in 1913 audiences rioted at the premiere of Stravinsky's *The Rite of Spring*. Beginning in 1921 with the publication of Schoenberg's *Twelve Note System of Composition*, modernist music broke away from traditional Western harmony, relying instead on the twelve-tone scale for its harmonic structure. The resulting dissonant compositions led to a hierarchy in which the less melodic and the more intellectual, abstract, or atonal a piece is, the more value it attains as a serious work of art. Thus high-art musical purists might listen to the music of Schoenberg, Webern, Harry Partch, and other composers who reject standard tonalities. A little further down the hierarchy might come the music of living composers such as Pierre Boulez—pieces that are difficult because they are not structured or orchestrated in ways that symphony audiences have come to expect. Next, one would find the pieces that comprise the standard repertory for chamber music, piano, symphonic, and operatic performances—the pieces that established the norms from which the aforementioned two groups diverge. Finally, one would find the "light classical" music described above.

Film scores have undoubtedly played an important role in helping to create the category of "light classical" music, because for years film music was derived from well-known classical pieces. As the score to *The Birth of a Nation* indicates, this practice began during the silent film period. Filmmakers preferred to use classical music for three reasons. Because of the pace of production, a lot of music was needed quickly, and it was easier to use classical pieces than to compose original music for every film. In 1912 Max Winkler, a clerk in the Carl Fischer music store in New York, originated the idea of producing musical cue sheets, but the sheer volume of music that was needed was overwhelming. According to Winkler:

> In desperation we turned to crime. . . . We began to dismember the great masters. We began to murder the works of Beethoven, Mozart, Grieg, J. S. Bach, Verdi, Bizet, Tchaikovsky and Wagner. . . . Extracts from great symphonies and operas were hacked down to emerge

again as "Sinister Misterioso" by Beethoven, or "Weird Moderato" by Tchaikovsky. Wagner's and Mendelssohn's wedding marches were used for marriages, fights between husbands and wives, and divorce scenes: we just had them played out of tune, a treatment known in the profession as "souring up the aisle."[8]

In addition, using previously written music in the public domain avoided problems with copyrights. The third reason was undoubtedly to add a veneer of cultural respectability to their films. In all respects, the score Carl Breil and D. W. Griffith developed for *The Birth of a Nation* in 1915 was both groundbreaking, in that it was prepared in great detail by the filmmakers themselves, and exemplary, in that it was comprised of a combination of original music, fragments of nineteenth-century symphonic and operatic pieces, and well-known older popular songs like "Dixie."

Clearly, the process of familiarization that started in the nineteenth century with the production of inexpensive sheet music, piano rolls, and the phonograph continued as more and more people were exposed to classical music by means of silent film accompaniments. This process would only continue with the introduction of sound film. The changeover to sound made it necessary to develop a new aesthetic of film accompaniment. Originally, sound filmmakers were uncomfortable with the inclusion of any kind of nondiegetic music. However, this situation didn't last long; almost immediately the need was felt for musical accompaniment. In other respects, however, the customary frantic pace of silent film production was now exacerbated by the need to produce musical accompaniments synchronized to what was shown on the screen. Silent film accompaniment practices also influenced sound film scoring in their reliance on the sonority of the late-nineteenth-century symphonic orchestra. Even when a film score didn't use music by actual nineteenth-century composers, film composers deliberately employed a musical vocabulary inherited from them. Again, what had thrilled the packed houses that saw the first run of *The Birth of a Nation*—the sound of a full symphony orchestra used to accompany a film—quickly became an expected part of the film-going experience.

Production and Reception of L'Age d'or

Before discussing the use of classical music in *L'Age d'or*, let us consider the immediate context for the film's production. When Luis Buñuel and Salvador Dali collaborated on their first Surrealist film, *Un Chien Anda-*

lou, Buñuel didn't expect the film to be particularly well received and was surprised at the response:

> The opening of *Un Chien Andalou* took place at the Ursulines, and was attended by the *tout-Paris*—some aristocrats, a sprinkling of well-established artists (among them Picasso, Le Corbusier, Cocteau, Christian Berard, and the composer Georges Auric), and the Surrealist group *in toto*. I was a nervous wreck. In fact, I hid behind the screen with the record player, alternating Argentinean tangos with *Tristan und Isolde*. Before the show, I'd put some stones in my pocket to throw at the audience in case of disaster. . . . I expected the worst; but, happily, the stones weren't necessary. After the film ended, I listened to the prolonged applause and dropped my projectiles discreetly, one by one, on the floor behind the screen.[9]

Buñuel was amazed and then distressed at audience and critical reaction to *Un Chien Andalou*. Not only was his film playing to packed houses, but three journals were interested in publishing the scenario. Buñuel would have preferred to publish the screenplay in *Variétés* but he had already promised it to *La Revue du Cinéma*. When he tried to back out of his agreement, it was too late; copies were already circulating. André Breton felt that Buñuel should have offered the scenario to *La Révolution Surréaliste* before letting it be published elsewhere. As a result, the Surrealist group became offended with Buñuel and held a trial. As Buñuel recalled in his autobiography: "Aragon was the prosecutor, and in violent terms he accused me of selling out to a bourgeois publication. Moreover, there was something suspect about the commercial success of my film. How could such a scandalous film draw such an enormous public?"[10]

At a loss to defend himself or rectify the situation, Buñuel decided to send his screenplay to *Variétés*, so that it would be published in the journal he preferred, and wrote an explanatory prologue for both publications calling his film "a desperate appeal to murder."[11] He also sent letters to several Parisian journals protesting the publication of his screenplays and claiming that he was a victim of a bourgeois plot. The results were less than satisfactory, however. At the same time that he was being acclaimed as "Paris's hottest new talent"[12] the Surrealists were viewing Buñuel as a sell-out.

Audience reception of *Un Chien Andalou* also disturbed Buñuel because, rather than being viewed as a revolutionary document, his film was perceived primarily as a work of art. Buñuel was disturbed by the tendency of bourgeois and aristocratic filmgoers to regard Surrealism as just

another branch of the avant-garde, and to aestheticize everything they saw
on the screen. To some extent, this tendency resulted from audience exposure to Dada filmmakers. Whereas the goal of the Dadaists had been
merely to "try the spectator's patience," the Surrealists wanted to create
a scandal.[13] Surrealism regularly brought subjects previously considered
untouchable to the fore. Magazine articles included questionnaires asking
the readers "Do you masturbate?" At a talk he was giving on avant-garde
cinema at the students' residence in Madrid, Buñuel suggested that they
"announce a menstruation contest and award prizes after the lecture."[14]
Surrealism was no mere attempt to shock the bourgeoisie, however. While
both Dada and Surrealist filmmakers wanted to burst through their audience's complacency, the Surrealists wanted to move past absurdity to revolution.

   For Buñuel, Surrealism was characterized by an "aggressive morality."[15]
In Buñuel's autobiography, he explained the movement's life-long hold on
him: "Although the Surrealists didn't consider themselves terrorists, they
were constantly fighting a society they despised. Their principal weapon
wasn't guns, of course; it was scandal. Scandal was a potent agent of revelation, capable of exposing . . . all the secret and odious underpinnings of
a system that had to be destroyed. The real purpose of Surrealism was not
to create a new literary, artistic, or even philosophical movement, but to
explode the social order, to transform life itself."[16] Keeping these goals in
mind, it becomes clear why Buñuel was distressed at the great success of
Un Chien Andalou. Writing in December 1930, Léon Moussinac summed
up Buñuel's purpose in making *L'Age d'or:* "Clearly . . . the authors wanted
to make sure that the snobs and smart audiences who had gratuitously admired *Un Chien Andalou,* thereby insulting them, should make no mistake
this time about their meaning and should feel the disgust in which they,
the authors, hold them."[17] *L'Age d'or* can therefore be viewed as Buñuel's attempt to create a greater scandal than he had in *Un Chien Andalou,* if only
to regain his stature in the Surrealist camp.

   L'Age d'or was commissioned by Charles de Noailles, a wealthy aristocrat
and well-known art patron. The film was intended as a birthday present
for de Noailles's wife Marie-Laure, a painter, poet, and the granddaughter
of the wife of the Marquis de Sade. By far the more adventuresome of the
two, she embraced all that was modern, whereas her husband's tastes ran
to antique furniture and eighteenth-century paintings. The de Noailles developed an interest in film in 1928, and had a mirrored salon in their mansion in Paris's 16th arrondissement transformed into a screening room.

For a four-year period, beginning in 1928, the Vicomte de Noailles commissioned a film every year as a birthday present for Marie-Laure. In 1928 Marcel L'Herbier filmed *Biceps et Bijous* (Biceps and Jewels) and in 1929 Man Ray created *Le Mystère du Château de Dé* (The Mystery of the Chateau of Dice.) Both were filmed at the the de Noailleses' summer house at Hyères, and the couple and their friends appeared in both films as themselves.

Charles de Noailles invited Buñuel to dinner in his mansion in Paris, and *Un Chien Andalou* was screened after the meal. Afterwards, de Noailles asked Buñuel to make a two-reel film like *Un Chien Andalou,* but with the addition of a soundtrack. The only creative control the de Noailleses appeared to want to exert was over the soundtrack. They wanted to combine Buñuel's film with another commission they had in mind, which was for a piece by Igor Stravinsky. However, Buñuel refused to use Stravinsky's music. He told the Vicomte that he "didn't want to work with geniuses" and de Noailles agreed, telling Buñuel "make the film anyway you want, with or without music. Whatever you want." [18] Buñuel traveled to Cadaque, a seaside village in Spain where Dali was staying, and worked on the scenario with him. However, the perfect harmony in which they had collaborated on *Un Chien Andalou* had disappeared. Dali had just met his muse, mistress, and eventual wife Gala Eluard, and had for the most part lost interest in filmmaking. It is unclear how much of the finished film owed to Dali, but we know that Buñuel completed the screenplay at the de Noailles summer house in Hyères. Every evening he would read what he had written that day to the de Noailleses, and they invariably pronounced it "exquisite and delicious." [19]

L'Age d'or revolves around the impossible love of a government official, played by Gaston Modot, for an aristocratic woman, played by Lya Lys. Their story occupies the middle third of the film, and it is surrounded by segments depicting various battles—of scorpions, bandits, and Modot himself being attacked by the bourgeois citizenry. In addition to the battles, Buñuel shocks his audience by violating the space/time continuum, juxtaposing segments in a seemingly random order, and employing explanatory intertitles that only confuse or amuse the spectator. In a final affront to bourgeois respectability, Buñuel cast Lionel Salem, an actor noted for his resemblance to Jesus Christ, as the Duc de Blangis, a Marquis de Sade type. The availability of sound film technology gave Buñuel a new way to scandalize the bourgeoisie: the film's soundtrack. The music was an important weapon in Buñuel's war against respectability, a war against hierarchy in general. In *L'Age d'or* Buñuel used the hierarchical nature of popular and serious music to expose the "odious underpinnings" of the equally hierarchical class system, thereby offending "the snobs and smart audiences" that had admired *Un Chien Andalou* too much.

The first screening of *L'Age d'or* took place at the de Noailleses' house in Paris, at the time the only screening facility equipped with a sound projector. The de Noailleses then arranged for a screening at the Panthéon for the whole city to attend. They greeted people as they came in, and stood by the doors as the audience filed out, as though they were expecting to be congratulated on the film. However, the day after the first public screening Charles de Noailles was expelled from his club and threatened with excommunication. Following the riot that occurred a few days later, the police shut down the theater and the film was confiscated. When he wrote his autobiography in 1982, Buñuel hadn't seen his own film in over fifty years. If his goal had been to create a scandal, it must be said that the film was an unqualified success.

Before it inspired a riot, *L'Age d'or* had received mixed reviews. While one critic singled out Buñuel's use of sound and dialogue for special praise, saying, "the role of sound and speech in the film indicates in Buñuel a surprising sense of the new possibilities in the cinema,"[20] Jean-Paul Dreyfus commented that people reproached Buñuel for the film's "technical poverty."[21] Dreyfus defended the film, not by contradicting these claims, but by stressing their relative unimportance in the larger scheme of things:

> Once and for all, let's not go on worrying about technique! Let's grant it its place, which is completely mechanical and artificial. It's not the unsurpassed technical perfection of American films that, to my mind, determines the quality of the American cinema; and, for that reason, it has never touched me very deeply. Once more *L'Age d'or* verifies this opinion—that one willingly overlooks a deficiency in technique in order to follow a wonderful "story" impatiently. If it's true of certain parts (notably, the soundtrack added after the shooting), if it's true that *L'Âge d'or* smells of cardboard, if the photography is poor, if the silent scenes follow the sound scenes in the disagreeable style of *Sous les toits de Paris*, . . . none of that can harm or prejudice the spiritual perfection of the film.[22]

Dreyfus maintains that you can either accept the technical "deficiencies" of *L'Age d'or* or remain "here below" with "the talkies."[23] When he opposes "technical" versus "spiritual perfection" he is oversimplifying the matter. Sophisticated sound recording techniques would not make *L'Age d'or* an unspiritual film. Even if he had had access to superior technology, it was quite likely that Buñuel would have refused to use it. After all, he had deliberately used jarringly different film stocks when he included the stock footage of the scorpions and exterior shots of Rome in his film. It was not technical perfection or even realism that interested Buñuel, but Surrealism, and his soundtrack contributes to the film's Surrealistic qualities. Dreyfus's inability to "get" aural Surrealism proves that in 1930 sound film aesthetics were still nascent. Even Dreyfus, who praised the film's "implacable logic of the absurd,"[24] expected the sound of *L'Age d'or* to mimic reality and remain consistent when he expected no other attempts to create a straightforward narrative. He "got" the scrambled intertitles and space-time *dis*continuum but did not "get" Buñuel's play with music, dialogue, and sound effects. He could "explain" *Un Chien Andalou* but was stumped by *L'Age d'or*, and his praise was reserved for the film's visual imagery.[25]

Music in Dada and Avant-Garde Films

When Buñuel selected the music for *L'Age d'or*, he was undoubtedly influenced by a tradition of avant-garde and Dada silent films. It was extremely rare for an avant-garde or Dada filmmaker to use music specifically composed for a film.[26] Like commercial films, these films were for the most part accompanied by European popular music or well-known classical music, although the filmmakers were fond of using recordings of American jazz, as well. If we examine the music used to accompany Dada films as well as the way music is portrayed in Dada and Impressionist films, we find that filmmakers like Germaine Dulac and Man Ray held rather standard beliefs regarding music. They appeared to feel that popular music and classical music were very different; that classical music is hierarchical in nature. Unlike commercial filmmakers, however, Dulac and Man Ray played on these commonly held beliefs to add a wealth of intertextual meanings to their films.

Music plays an important role in the films and critical writings of Germaine Dulac. For the most part, Dulac was concerned only with highbrow, high-culture music, and in explaining her intentions she used musical analogies to convince her readers that the cinema could achieve a similar high-culture position. In Dulac's view, the symphony was the greatest height serious music could reach, and the goal to which film should aspire: "There is the symphony, pure music. Why should the cinema not have its symphony as well?"[27] It is clear that some of her thinking about film was colored by the programmatic, highly emotional, and impressionistic music she clearly preferred. She describes Chopin's "Raindrop" prelude and Debussy's "Le Jardin sous la Pluie" (Garden in the Rain), as metaphorically "expressions of a soul pouring forth." In preferring composers like Chopin and Debussy, Dulac reveals her musical tastes as both upper-middle-class and upper-middle-brow. Dulac was no revolutionary; she shared the hierarchical outlook of the highly cultivated bourgeois and aristocratic filmgoers that would view her films.

Dulac's 1923 film *La Souriante Madame Beudet* illustrates Dulac's hierarchical point of view with regard to classical music. In this film, Madame Beudet's husband receives a pair of opera tickets as a gift, and is pleased with the idea of hearing Gounod's *Faust,* a very well known crowd-pleasing opera. In one shot, Dulac shows Beudet smiling and "singing" along with costumed characters from the opera. Dulac dramatizes the couple's fundamental incompatability by showing Madame Beudet involved in a different kind of musical moment—playing Debussy on the piano. As she plays, Madame Beudet has a vision of light shimmering on a pond—imagery clearly designed to complement Debussy's impressionistic style of composition. More important, Dulac's musically educated spectators would gain insights into the characters as they saw what kinds of classical music the characters prefer. The sides are clearly delineated: on the one hand, Gounod's *Faust,* on the other Debussy's preludes. Not only is going to the opera more expensive, status-ridden, yet more passive than actually playing the piano oneself, but the crowd-pleasing *Faust* is definitely middlebrow in contrast to the high-brow Debussy. What we see and don't hear spoken speaks intertextual volumes about these characters.

The Dada films of Man Ray illustrate how both popular music like jazz and widely known light classical music could be used alternatively and fruitfully to produce new intertextual meanings. For his 1926 film *Emak Bakia,* Ray alternated shots of a woman dancing the Charleston and a man playing the banjo, two immediately recognizable images of American jazz. For musical accompaniment at the film's first screening, he alternated recordings of jazz with live musicians playing tangos and popular French music, as well as the "Merry Widow Waltz," which accompanied the shot of the collar sequence, where a pearl necklace is shown.[28] *The Merry Widow,* a comic operetta that tells the story of a Ruritanian wealthy widow beset by suitors who have plans for her fortune, has been described as "delightful but essentially 'Palm Court'" with a "light Hungarian flavour."[29] It certainly qualifies as the lightest of light classical music. In addition, the waltz itself was so well known that its inclusion in *Emak Bakia* accompanying a shot of a pearl necklace would provide an intertextual and ironic commentary on wealth itself.

Ray had originally planned to have live musicians alternate playing American jazz with the "Merry Widow Waltz," which would emphasize the contrast between American popular music and European light classical music in a straightforward manner. However, he decided that jazz pieces "were beyond the house musician's repertory." From this remark we can extrapolate that in the Paris of the 1920s, American jazz was too new and unfamiliar for the average small orchestra to play easily. For subsequent screenings of the film, Ray maintained that "any collection of old jazz will do," which makes it clear that he expected people to use records—again, an indication that American jazz was too difficult and exotic for French musicians.[30]

To accompany his next film, *L'Etoile de mer* (1928), Ray eschewed jazz altogether, and instead selected pieces from the popular and light classical repertory. Some of the pieces were instantly recognizable pieces of traditional music, such as "Plaisir d'amour" (The Pleasure of Love), a French love song, the Neopolitan traditional song "O Sole Mio," and the Carmagnole, a traditional French dance. *L'Etoile de mer* also used "Dernier tango" (Last Tango), a popular dance tune, Strauss's "Beautiful Blue Danube" waltz, and a Bach aria.[31] The Bach aria is the only piece not specifically identified, and may have been difficult for the spectators to place. The ironic commentary that the rest of the music provides is clear: "Plaisir d'amour" is heard during the man and woman's first encounter on the street; "Dernier tango" is played when they go to her bedroom and she undresses; the intertitle saying "How beautiful she is" is accompanied by the music of the "Beautiful Blue Danube" waltz.

From these examples, it becomes clear that Dada and Impressionist filmmakers depended on well-known classical and popular music to provide commentary, either straightforward or ironic, on what we see. The music chosen by the Dada and Impressionist filmmakers often highlighted the contrast between past and present, stuffy and modern. Images of jazz musicians and dancers or of someone playing Debussy underscored the modernity of the cinema itself. In addition, the effect of their films depended in part on their spectators' knowledge of both classical and popular music. Buñuel and Dali continued this practice for their Surrealist films. As accompaniment for *Un Chien Andalou*, Buñuel selected two of the most association-laden kinds of music he could choose, the "Liebestod" from *Tristan und Isolde* and tangos. The tango took the world by storm in the teens and 1920s, in part because of its association with Rudolph Valentino's performance in *The Four Horsemen of the Apocalypse* (1921). *Tristan und Isolde* was equally well known, having achieved a cultlike following among "Wagnerites." Both *Tristan und Isolde* and Argentine tangos were therefore easily recognizable at the time as the high- and low-culture pinnacles of musical sensuality.

Classical Music in *L'Age d'or*

As we can see, in selecting well-known classical music for the soundtrack of *L'Age d'or*, Buñuel was in part continuing a trajectory that Dada filmmakers like Man Ray had established and that he and Dali had continued in *Un Chien Andalou*. These films all used some classical music as accompaniment, and the music they used was both well known and heavily laden with associations. For *L'Age d'or*, Buñuel selected an assortment of pieces from the classical and romantic repertory whose one common denominator is their widespread popularity. Mendelssohn's "Hebrides" Overture and "Italian" symphony, Mozart's "Ave Verum Corpus," Beethoven's Fifth Symphony, the "Liebestod" from Wagner's *Tristan und Isolde*, and Schubert's "Unfinished" Symphony were all part of the standard symphonic repertoire. One difference between *L'Age d'or* and its predecessors is its relative dearth of popular music. Except for the final sequence of the film, a shot of a cross covered with women's scalps, which is accompanied by "Gallito," a *paso doble* specially composed for the film by Georges van Parys, the soundtrack includes nothing resembling popular music. Classical music has a triply privileged role in *L'Age d'or:* it has its complex intertextual role in the soundtrack, which I will discuss below; a filmed performance of the "Liebestod" from Wagner's *Tristan und Isolde* occupies a long segment; and this performance is the subject of the longest dialogue in the film.

The original audience for *L'Age d'or*, like the original audience for *Un Chien Andalou*, was composed primarily of artists and aristocrats. Buñuel, who played several musical instruments and at one point had wanted to become a musician, probably understood more about classical music than most of the people in the room. However, aristocrats like the de Noailleses and members of the bourgeoisie like Buñuel himself could be expected to have some knowledge of the standard symphonic repertoire. This audience would have been aware and appreciative of at least some of the ironies that resulted from Buñuel's combination of image and music.

While Raymond Durgnat argues that Buñuel's "use of classical music is conspicuously ironical," he doesn't discuss the matter in any depth.[32] However, we need to understand how musical irony works if we are to understand the forces operating in *L'Age d'or*. The ironic use of classical music in film depends on the music's associational qualities. For example, in

Wayne's World (Penelope Spheeris, 1992) when Garth (Dana Carvey) sees the doughnut shop waitress (Donna Dixon), we see a point-of-view shot of the waitress, filmed in slow-motion, her hair obviously being moved by a wind machine. This shot is accompanied by the strains of the love theme from Tchaikovsky's "Romeo and Juliet." The ironic effect is achieved even if the members of the audience don't recognize the Tchaikovsky as such, because the lush sonority of a full orchestra playing nineteenth-century Romantic music is at humorous odds with what they see: a heavy metal fan in a doughnut shop in Aurora, Illinois. This kind of ironic use of music in film can be considered a kind of direct address to the film spectator, because rather than aiding the narrative, the music disrupts it by calling attention to itself. By disrupting the narrative, irony effects a break with realism and calls the spectator's attention to the film's own status as artwork. This kind of irony depends, therefore, on the spectator's acceptance and understanding of decorum, as the term was understood in the eighteenth century, when it was considered of primary importance that substance and style complement each other. Any understanding of decorum depends on an implicit acceptance of a mutually understood and accepted hierarchy. In effect, irony both resists and supports hierarchy by trading on our perceptions of high and low. The humor of the scene in *Wayne's World* is in part derived from the indecorous mismatch of high-art Tchaikovsky, on the one hand, and a constellation of popular culture icons on the other: Donna Dixon, Dana Carvey, and doughnuts.

Like the Dada filmmakers, Buñuel selected well-known classical music that provided an ironic commentary on the film's images, but in *L'Age d'or* he surpassed his predecessors in the rich variety of intertextual associations that come into play. Following the Dada lead, in almost every piece he selected, Buñuel's choice creates a rather broad gag. For example, he uses the overture to Mendelssohn's "Scottish" Symphony for the scorpion sequence—the "overture" of his film. In the next scene, he juxtaposes a group of broken-down, disreputable bandits with music from Beethoven's Fifth Symphony. According to musicologist Donald Grout, the opening motif of Beethoven's Fifth has often been called "Fate knocking at the door." [33] Fittingly enough, the first sound effect in this scene is the returning bandit's knock on the door. For the scene with the dead bishops Buñuel selected Mozart's "Ave Verum Corpus," an anthem sung during the mass. Sometimes the gag involves a pun on the name of the piece. For example, Buñuel uses a long portion of the minuet of Mendelssohn's "Italian" Symphony as the background to the founding of Rome and the travelogue that follows. The Mendelssohn fades out after a series of shots of Rome, and a violin solo begins while a man is shown walking down the street kicking a violin—again, a rather broad musical joke. Finally, the frustrated attempts of the lovers to consummate their relationship are accompanied by Schubert's "Unfinished" Symphony and the "Liebestod" or "love/death" theme from Wagner's *Tristan und Isolde*.

In some cases, the music Buñuel chose has only a tenuous relationship to what is seen, and any ironic commentary implicit in the choice is the result of the piece's actual sound rather than its name or reputation. Mendelssohn's "Hebrides" overture was inspired by a trip to Fingal's Cave in the Hebrides Islands. The widespread sonorities and arpeggios of the piece were supposed to evoke the strangeness and remoteness of this cave at the edge of the sea. Perhaps they do, but the music is at rhapsodic odds with the dry, hot weather we see on the screen, as well as the poisonous and fierce nature of the scorpions.

Although the actors do not move across the screen in strict time to the music as Mickey Mouse did in the early Disney shorts, the action on the screen is choreographed quite tightly to the music, to the extent that it could be considered a live-action, ironic kind of mickey mouse-ing. Rather than using existing recorded versions of the pieces he selected, Buñuel hired an orchestra to perform the pieces, which were then dubbed onto the soundtrack. Buñuel expressed concern regarding the synchronization of the music with the visuals. For example, in the scene depicting the two lovers in the garden during a performance of Wagner's "Liebestod," his scenario notes indicate that he thought it would be "necessary for the orchestra to find a measure to repeat" in case the footage used to shoot the love scenes was longer than the footage used to record the concert.[34] He was willing to alter Wagner's music to make it fit the action on the screen more exactly. Buñuel stresses that the lovers' "paroxysms must be in phase, even at the price of repeating certain musical phrases" and concludes that the "cinematic effect takes precedence" over the musical effect.[35]

Another example of the tight synchronization of the music with the action occurs in the bandit sequence. Here Buñuel uses the third movement from Beethoven's Fifth Symphony, which opens with an arpeggiated figure in the bass, followed by an answer in the strings. The arpeggio has a tentative quality and seems to echo the way the men are moving. Then the woodwinds and brass enter in an energetic dotted-note rhythm, based on the symphony's famous four-note opening. As if on cue, the captain raises his eyes and looks off screen right. This is the film's first close-up, so the moment is doubly energized. It then appears that two bandits with pitchforks are pulling ropes in time to the music. In addition, a bandit with a

"Liebestod" with six musicians, no matter how closely miked they are. In addition, the reference to miking has a self-referential tongue-in-cheek quality, reminding Buñuel's spectators of his film's status as an early talkie. Although Buñuel's simultaneously straightforward and ironic use of classical music afforded the spectator a wealth of intertextual materials, the final and most shocking scene in the film breaks from the norm that Buñuel had established throughout the rest of the film. This final sequence, which depicts the end of an orgy by the Marquis de Sade protagonist, the Duc de Blangis, uses original music composed by film composer George van Parys. Van Parys wrote a *paso doble,* a traditional Spanish dance piece, and Buñuel used it to accompany the shot of women's scalps affixed to a cross. In this scene, Buñuel's anti-Catholicism reached new heights. He couldn't have come up with a better way to shock his audience. Making use of Lionel Salem's identification with the role of Jesus Christ, Buñuel, after a long series of strongly worded intertitles, cuts to a shot of the duc leaving his chateau, and the similarity to images of Christ is quite clear. On top of that, it was well known that Buñuel's patroness, Marie-Laure de Noailles, was the granddaughter of the wife of the Marquis de Sade. In addition, the French were in general shocked by the Spanish tendency to blasphemous remarks such as "I spit in the chalice." Given the right-wing French hatred of *métèques,* or foreign residents, there could be no more provocative climax to a film by a Spanish director than a blasphemous scene accompanied by identifiably Spanish-sounding music.

The anticlericalism that shocked his audience resonated even more strongly for Buñuel. His background, while bourgeois, was also provincial. Buñuel was born in 1900 in Calanda, a large village about one hundred miles west of Barcelona, where, as he writes in his memoirs, "the Middle Ages lasted until World War I." [40] Buñuel's father had made a fortune in Cuba and, having married a young woman of good family, retired to enjoy a life of leisure. According to Buñuel, village society was very hierarchical, with "clear and unchanging distinctions among the classes. The respectful subordination of the peasants to the big landowners was deeply rooted in tradition, and seemed unshakable." [41] Religion was central to everyone's life, and for Buñuel religion and music went together: "I . . . sang and played the violin in the Virgin of Cermen choir, along with one of my friends, who played the double bass, and the rector of Los Escolapios, a religious institute in Alcaniz, who played the cello." [42] At about the same time that he was considering a career in music, Buñuel broke away decisively from the Catholic Church.

The fascination and then repulsion that Buñuel felt for bourgeois society and religion were to inform his filmmaking for the rest of his life. Although his sympathies were always aligned with the more revolutionary aspects of Surrealism, Buñuel could never completely depart from that underlying sense of social and cultural hierarchies that informed his choice of music in *L'Age d'or*. In his memoirs, Buñuel writes: "Most Surrealists came from good families; as in my case, they were bourgeois revolting against the bourgeoisie. But we all felt a certain destructive impulse, a feeling that for me has been even stronger than the creative urge. The idea of burning down a museum, for instance, has always seemed more enticing than the opening of a cultural center or the inauguration of a new hospital."[43] *L'Age d'or* brilliantly dramatizes the Surrealist concept of *l'amour fou*, and pokes violent fun at anything that contributes to the separation of the two lovers, including the twin pillars of church and state revered by the bourgeoisie. But some of Buñuel's most scathing criticisms are inaudible to anyone who lacked his knowledge of classical music. Buñuel succeeded in creating a scandal and in shocking the bourgeoisie, but in using classical music as one of his tools, he unknowingly and unconsciously reinforced the very hierarchical social structures he despised.

Notes

This article started as a paper written for Corey K. Creekmur's course on avantgarde film at the University of Chicago. No end of thanks are due to him for his inspiring teaching, as well as his encouragement. I would also like to thank James Lastra for his helpful presentation on Buñuel at a mass culture workshop at the University of Chicago. I gave a version of this paper at the 1999 Society for Cinema Studies conference, and would like to thank Gerard Dapena for organizing the Buñuel panel. Finally, and most important, my heartfelt thanks to Peter Bloom and Hans Vaget for the course they co-taught on Wagner at Smith College. Imperfect Wagnerite as I am, the knowledge gleaned from their course still colors my scholarship like a leitmotif.

1 For a musicologist, the word *classical* is defined more narrowly, referring to music written during the late eighteenth and early nineteenth centuries by composers such as Haydn and Mozart. However, for the purpose of this discussion, I will use the term *classical music* to denote works otherwise referred to as "serious" or "art" music. For a discussion of the use of the term *classical* to characterize music employed in silent and sound cinema as nondiegetic film soundtrack, see Rick Altman's essay in this volume and Royal S. Brown, *Overtones and Undertones: Reading Film Music* (Berkeley: University of California Press, 1994), 38–39.

2 Jerry Beck and Will Friedwald, *Looney Tunes and Merrie Melodies: A Complete Illustrated Guide to the Warner Bros. Cartoons* (New York: Henry Holt, 1989), 81.

3   See Charles Hofmann, *Sounds for Silents,* with a forword by Lillian Gish (New York: Drama Book Specialists, 1970), n.p.

4   Donald J. Grout, *A History of Western Music* (New York: W. W. Norton, 1973), 658.

5   The Royal Albert Hall, which seats ten thousand people, was built in London in 1871. The new Paris Opera was built in 1875. The Berlin Philharmonic Orchestra was founded in 1882; New York's Metropolitan Opera in 1883; the Boston Symphony Orchestra and the St. Louis Symphony Orchestra in 1881; the Chicago Symphony Orchestra and the Royal Scottish National Orchestra in 1891; and the Philadelphia Orchestra in 1900.

6   Lawrence W. Levine, *Highbrow/Lowbrow: The Emergence of Cultural Hierarchy in America* (Cambridge: Harvard University Press, 1988), 118.

7   See Pierre Bourdieu, *Distinction: A Critique of the Judgement of Taste,* trans. Richard Nice (Cambridge, Mass.: Harvard University Press, 1984).

8   For more on music for silent films, see Martin Miller Marks, *Music and the Silent Film: Contexts and Case Studies, 1895–1924* (New York: Oxford University Press, 1997); Roy M. Prendergast, *Film Music—A Neglected Art: A Critical Study of Music in Films,* 2nd ed. (New York: W. W. Norton, 1992), 8–10; Gillian Anderson, *Music for Silent Films: 1894–1929* (Washington, D.C.: Library of Congress, 1988); and Charles Merrell Berg, *An Investigation of the Motives for and the Realization of Music to Accompany the American Silent Film, 1896–1927* (New York: Arno Press, 1976).

9   Luis Buñuel, *My Last Sigh,* trans. Abigail Israel (New York: Random House, 1984), 106.

10 Ibid., 108.

11 Raymond Durgnat, *Luis Buñuel* (Berkeley: University of California Press, 1977), 23.

12 John Baxter, *Buñuel* (New York: Carroll & Graf, 1998), 88.

13 Judi Freeman, "Bridging Purism and Surrealism: The Origins and Production of Fernand Léger's Ballet Mécanique," in *Dada and Surrealist Film,* ed. Rudolf E. Kuenzli (New York: Willis Locker & Owens, 1987), 32.

14 Buñuel, *My Last Sigh,* 103.

15 Ibid., 107.

16 Ibid.

17 Quoted in Francisco Aranda, *Luis Buñuel: A Critical Biography,* trans. and ed. David Robinson (London: Secker & Warburg, 1975), 72.

18 José de la Colina and Tomás Pérez Turrent, *Objects of Desire: Conversations with Luis Buñuel,* ed. and trans. Paul Lenti (New York: Marsilio Publishers, 1992), 21.

19 Buñuel, *My Last Sigh,* 116.

20 "L'affair de *L'Age d'or,*" reproduced in Pedro Christian Garcia Buñuel, *Recordando a Luis Buñuel* (Zaragoza: Sansueña, Industrias Graficas, 1985), n.p.

21 Jean-Paul Dreyfus, "'*L'Age d'or,*'" in *French Film Theory and Criticism, 1907–1939,* ed. Richard Abel (Princeton, N.J.: Princeton University Press, 1988), 70.

22 Ibid.

23 Ibid.

24 Ibid., 69.

25 Modern critics also ignore the film's sound in favor of its imagery. See Allen
Weiss, "Between the Sign of the Scorpion and the Sign of the Cross: *L'Age d'or*,"
Linda Williams, "The Critical Grasp: Buñuelian Cinema and Its Critics," and
Rudolf E. Kuenzli's "Bibliography: Dada and Surrealist Film," in *Dada and Sur-
realist Film* ed. Rudolf E. Kuenzli (New York: Willis Locker & Owens, 1987),
159–75, 199–206, and 220–36.

26 Composer George Antheil wrote a piece for anvils, automobile horns, bells,
machines, percussion, and player pianos to accompany Fernand Léger's *Ballet
Méchanique*, but the score wasn't ready for the film's first screening in September 1924.

27 Germaine Dulac, "The Essence of the Cinema: The Visual Idea," in *The Avant-
Garde Film: A Reader of Theory and Criticism*, ed. P. Adams Sitney, Anthology
Film Archives Series, no. 3 (New York: Anthology Film Archives, 1987), 41.

28 See Steven Kovacs, *From Enchantment to Rage: The Story of Surrealist Cinema*
(Cranbury, N.J.: Associated University Press, 1980), 124–34.

29 Geoffrey Hindley, ed., *The Larousse Encyclopedia of Music* (Secaucus, N.J.: Charwell Books, 1977), 413.

30 Kovacs, *From Enchantment to Rage*, 152–53.

31 See "Robert Desnos's and Man Ray's Manuscript Scenario for *L'Etoile de mer*,"
in Kuenzli, "Bibliography: Dada and Surrealist Film," 218–19.

32 Durgnat, *Luis Buñuel*, 51.

33 Grout, *A History of Western Music*, 526.

34 Buñuel quoted in Dominique Haas, "*L'Age d'or*," *L'Avant-Scène Cinema*, November 1983, 26.

35 Haas, 26.

36 Buñuel, *My Last Sigh*, 104.

37 This is true even in the United States. Note that the orchestral piece included
in the first Vitaphone program was the overture from Wagner's *Tannhäuser*—
another previously shocking opera which became hugely popular with the bourgeoisie. See Mary Lea Bandy, ed., *The Dawn of Sound* (New York: Museum of
Modern Art, 1989), 44.

38 Grout, *A History of Western Music*, 615.

39 Ibid., 617.

40 Buñuel, *My Last Sigh*, 8.

41 Ibid.

42 Ibid., 12.

43 Ibid., 107.

"The Future's Not Ours to See":
Song, Singer, Labyrinth in Hitchcock's
The Man Who Knew Too Much

MURRAY POMERANCE

Any art form in which young people cannot freely participate is doomed from the start. —Jean Cocteau, "En faveur du 16 millimetres," 1948

In conceiving a remake of *The Man Who Knew Too Much* early in 1955, it had not been Alfred Hitchcock's plan to include a popular song, but constraints of business inspired him. His agent Lew Wasserman (president of MCA Beverly Hills), who also represented James Stewart, Doris Day, Ray Evans, and Jay Livingston, made it clear that from his company's perspective Hitchcock should have the much-desired Stewart only if he took the others.[1] And Livingston and Evans already had a song.[2] It was their working method always to have materials available for call, and when they were summoned to meet Hitchcock and his associate producer Herbert Coleman in the office of Louis Lipstone at Paramount, "Que Sera, Sera (What Will Be, Will Be)" was ready for performance.[3] "I've worked it into the plot so that it makes sense," understated Hitchcock, according to Livingston. "I want a song that is sung to the little boy. It would be nice if it had a foreign title, because Jimmy Stewart is a roving Ambassador." Having heard it, however, he was swept away: "I told you I didn't know what kind of a song I wanted. That's the kind of song I want."[4]

It was not the only song by Livingston and Evans that was available to him. Another was "Holy Gee," submitted for consideration for this film but ultimately rejected in favor of "Que Sera, Sera." Sent for the censor's

7 Jo Conway McKenna (Doris Day) singing "Que Sera, Sera" at the embassy soiree. Hank can be saved only if the song in performance can be continued. [digital frame enlargement]

clearance on May 18, 1955 (the same day as "Que Sera, Sera"), "Holy Gee" had these rather sucrose words:

> Holy gee! What a wonderful world for you and me!
> Holy gee! Did you ever imagine this?
> Holy cow! I don't know what you did but do it now!
> Holy cow! What-cha puttin' into that kiss!
> I go right into space when I feel your embrace
> There's a new sensation runnin' thru it,
> Addin' to it, how do you do it!
> Holy gee! You're the sugar that's in my cup o' tea!
> I thank your mother and your dad
> For havin' that wonderful kid they had!
> You're everything good and that ain't bad!
> Holy! Holy! Holy gee!
> What a beautiful world for you and me![5]

Without access to the melody, we are, of course, in no position to judge the merits of the song itself; yet it is clear the words seem empty and un-melodic, philosophically unprepossessing, in this artificial context. As alluring as the music might have been, however, the intended vocalist, Doris Day, found the title a little too similar to "Holy Jesus,"[6] and so the song was rewritten within the following eleven days as "Holy Cow":

Holy cow!
I don't know what you did, but do it now!
Holy cow!
Whatcha puttin' into that kiss?

Holy smoke!
When you opened my eyes, my heart awoke!
Holy smoke!
Who could ever imagine this!

I went right into space
When I felt your embrace;
There's a new sensation runnin' through it,
Addin' to it,
How do you do it?

Holy cats!
What a beautiful day for waving hats!
I thank your mother and your dad
For havin' that wonderful kid they had!
You're everything good, and that ain't bad!
Holy! Holy! Holy cow!
Hey, whatever we did, let's do right now![7]

A little more conviction is provided in the second version, yet the message of the piece, denuded of its music, is still simplistic and rather corny. The insinuation that had bothered Doris Day was now gone, but in the meantime Hitchcock had heard and immediately accepted "Que Sera, Sera." That Livingston and Evans were prepared with an alternate song is not, perhaps, surprising; it was their working style always to "present two songs for every project."[8] The producer, Herbert Coleman, was called to hear "Que Sera, Sera" and was so confounded by its dissimilarity to what he had been expecting, for a song that Doris could sing in the film, he insisted Hitchcock come up to hear it as well. On one hearing, Hitchcock accepted it.[9]

"Que Sera, Sera (Whatever Will Be, Will Be)," as it is formally known, is a controversial bonbon that has provoked a wide range of vocal responses.

For example, the author Bharati Mukherjee reports that her father, who owned a pharmaceutical company in Calcutta, would sing it "on jerky drives through the crowded city, in between yelling at the chauffeur to be more cautious and at the two bodyguards cramped in the back of our conspicuously large Dodge station wagon to be more alert for bomb-tossing, acid-splashing, communism-inspired thugs." "Que Sera, Sera," she says, "became for him more a mantra than a song; it synthesized a New World pleasure in risk taking with a fatalistic Hindu acceptance of disastrous outcomes."[10] Doris Day, by contrast, insisted the piece was for children, and after recording it for Columbia (in an arrangement by Frank De Vol) in one take, insisted, "That's the last time you're gonna hear this song."[11] Bernard Herrmann, who had signed a contract on July 12, 1955, to "compose, arrange, orchestrate and conduct" the music for the film, was sufficiently disenchanted when he heard it to carp, "What do you want a piece of junk like that in the picture for?"[12] The critic George Perry suggests sarcastically that it was an "anodyne lullaby" that Day's playing a retired musical comedy actress "gave her sufficient excuse to warble."[13] And Jonathan Coe goes so far as to pronounce her "a woman who sang too much."[14]

But, as I will attempt to show, this deceptively simple and very popular little song plays a role of the most profound significance in a very complex film. Indeed, to understand "Que Sera, Sera" as a filmic entity, which is what popular songs become when they are embedded in films, it is first necessary that we should consider the nature of the film's complexity. *Man-much* (as Hitchcock affectionately called it) has as much to do with secrecy and obscurity as with the lambent innocence that "Que Sera, Sera" purports to convey. We must follow a brief diversion into a kind of maze before we can ask whether the future is sufficiently illuminated to be, as Jo McKenna sings it, "ours to see."

The Man Who Knew Too Much can be understood as an arabesque, for an understanding of which intriguing form we may read Guy Davenport's explosive title essay in *The Geography of the Imagination:* "Arabesque clearly means the intricate, nonrepresentational, infinitely graceful decorative style of Islam, best known to us in their carpets, the geometric tilework of their mosques, and their calligraphy."[15] Coiling, twisting, secretive, intestinal darknesses; mysterious passions; incomprehensible turnings. Passages that wind back upon themselves, both hiding and revealing. And, thus, futures that look like pasts. Such artful convolvement is reproduced in a typical Moroccan restaurant, such as the one replicated for a key sequence in the film. The floor is relatively plain, even undecorated (here it is a kind of chess or draughts board), while the upper area, walls and ceiling, are fitted with myriad tiles configured in delicate and intriguing patterns. The tiles are each a little different, because they have been shaped by hand. By contrast with the Persian style, in which earth is pictured as complex and wildly variant while heaven is serene, the Moroccan decor posits a stable and knowable lower world (the present), and a heaven (a future that resembles a past) of great richness and diversity. This may be interpreted to mean there is more after life than in it, or certainly more after the present moment—an idea given some potent recapitulation in the many key scenes set in the *souks,* the market, of the Place Djemaa el Fna (which means "return of the dead souls"). Mythically if not orthographically, then, the labyrinthine nature of the Moroccan segment of the film—the segment in which "Que Sera, Sera" is introduced—reflects not the mundane world but the unpredictable, complex future, the "whatever-will-be" that will be.

Labyrinthine forms are everywhere in this film. If we consider the route of the murder chase in the marketplace in the geography of the screen— the construction of the shots, their placement, the cutting, and the way the camera's "consciousness" follows or leads that of the fleeing man— we find a labyrinth. A similar labyrinthine structure organizes the marketplace entertainments Hank (Christopher Olsen) observes with the Draytons (Bernard Miles, Brenda de Banzie); the movement of Ben and Jo McKenna (James Stewart, Doris Day) around the Royal Albert Hall during the symphony concert; the movement (in a baroquerie) of Ben at the embassy in London; the conversational movement of the McKennas and the Draytons at the Moroccan restaurant; Ben's hunt for Ambrose Chappell; the snail-slow passage of the Casablanca-Marrakech bus into Marrakech; the anatomy of the snails Hank McKenna jovially invites Louis Bernard (Daniel Gélin) to come home to Indianapolis to eat; and—the many-chambered "Que Sera, Sera (What Will Be, Will Be)" which is in many ways the heart of the film. As we give serious consideration to both the song and the singing, we may recall those apparently insignificant escargots of Hank's: if they are labyrinthine, so—and elaborately—are the workings of the human ear.

Visual space and acoustical space are different, and the space of hearing is the secret chamber. As Lacan and others have shown, the heard space constitutes for us a very early concept of the world.[16] And so every hearing divorced radically from sight returns us to that primary moment when reality comes thundering through the caverns of the Minotaur. In his trilogy *La Voix au cinéma, Le Son au cinéma,* and *La Toile trouée,* and in *Audio-Vision,* Michel Chion explores the many kinds of acoustical space possible in film and introduces the concept of the acousmetron:

> When we speak of a "structural" game, we mean by that a certain syntax governing conceivable relations between the cinematic image and the voice — relations in which the shapes and combinations seem limited in number. But just as Occidental music has worked for centuries with twelve notes, film is far from having exhausted the possible variations of these arrangements. And the richest, certainly, is not the one which consists of *making the speaker visible;* it's the one in which we do not see the person we're hearing, at the same time as her voice flows out from the center of the image by the same means as the other sounds in the film. This is the *invention of the acousmetron.*[17]

Essentially a voice disembodied and truncated from visual space. If we examined some of the voices that inhabit *The Man Who Knew Too Much* independent — from a viewer's perspective — of the realistic visualized world given to the eyes, we could find in the Moroccan part of the film alone several instances of labyrinthine, acousmetric sound, but the most provocative of these, the most complex in meaning, and the most popular with audiences around the world, is "Que Sera, Sera."[18]

We begin in an enchanting, and shocking, mise-en-scène on the evening of the McKennas' arrival in Marrakech. They have agreed to be guided to dinner by the gallant, if taciturn, Frenchman, Louis Bernard, who will join them for apéritifs in their hotel room. But first:

> [Marrakech, exterior, night]
> 76.   LS: *The distant sounds of bells and drums can be heard. Before a twilit sky streaked with luminous white clouds and glowing with a crescent moon the dark shapes of minarets, towers and buildings are seen. Jo's voice fades in, singing.**

The vision is a concrete and pure romantic condensation of our stereotype and idealization of the arabesque world. The characteristic shape of the minarets establishes geography, even as the haunting indigo of the sky alludes to a time between day and night, a liminal hour when we are susceptible to cocktails and to transformations, to visitations, to sensuality.

---

*All descriptions and shot numbers come from a continuity script prepared by the author.

This shot, produced on Stage 1 at Paramount August 5, 1955 with the aid of a painted matte optically printed in,[19] is also technically rich in an interesting cultural and linguistic way. In the Moslem religion that governs this area, the portrait the shot delivers is of the time of day called "el Maghrib," the early evening and time for prayers. On the following night, of course, we will be in this room again, in sadness, and we will hear the muezzin calling Moslems to pray; but tonight the muezzin is only anticipated, perhaps yearned for. El Maghrib, however, is also the Arabic name for Morocco.[20] So, the shot makes reference to the two sanctities that suffuse all of the action in the film—the religious sanctity of prayer, fervency, devotion, and belief in the divine; and the secular sanctity by which geography becomes transcendental.[21] The shot is a symbol for the land. The moon, crescent, is also a sheik's scimitar flashing across a desert; it calls up in a synopsis our own susceptibility to romance, luring us to remember the Hollywood that conjured it for us even as we hope it is in fact real. We hear bells and drums that are unmistakably local, vague, stirring; and at the same time, moving into acoustical presence, the sound of a woman's soothing, entrancing— but also clearly performing—voice in song.[22]

In a single shot we are thus handed the key to the distinction between geographical realism and cinematic illusion, metaphorized as the gap between two environments as tropes—the Moroccan evening and the surrounding family. First we encounter the singing voice as lambent and encompassing, part of el Maghrib; but soon, focusing, arranging meaning for ourselves, we identify it as Jo's, realize that we are very near to her, and make ourselves into the vulnerable child she is singing to. Truffaut has alluded to Hitchcock's technique of establishing from the farthest to the nearest.[23] The surround is given before the detail of plot, even if it is only by means of ancillary details that the surround is composed. In this case, the tropic of place precedes the tropic of biography as Morocco comes in to color the voice before Jo's position in the family (of the plot) does. But the setting from which we move into the tunnels of the action is, even from without, a pleasantly confounding one: we look upon a Moroccan cityscape at twilight, but we hear an American inscape; the world we conceive is thus hybrid. The phallic Arabian towers are framed by the low, guiding, Western female voice.

We now move directly in, skipping the middle steps which could have identified the hotel among all the buildings, and the door of the McKenna suite among all the doors in one of its corridors (middle steps, I should make clear, which will emphatically *not* be skipped later, as we hunt on the stairwell of the embassy to the sound of the same song). We have entered the suite, and are in the foyer near the door:

[McKenna Hotel suite, interior, night]

77. *Beginning in LS, the camera tracks forward through the inner door of the McKennas' suite. Jo is out of sight, singing "Que Sera, Sera." Ben is at screen-left, fixing his tie in a mirror. At the rear, framed in the double doors that lead to the balcony, Louis Bernard is casually sipping a drink. The camera tracks right, past the twin beds with the bedside lamps turned on, to an open doorway into a second room. Jo is in the doorway in MS, just out of Bernard's line of view, adjusting the shoulder straps of her evening gown. Hank can be heard in the room behind her, singing a verse of "Que Sera, Sera."*

Here the acoustic effect is doubled. Jo is out of sight as the shot begins, but by the time we have traveled far enough to discover her she is no longer singing and Hank, out of sight, is continuing the song. The gist of the lyric, "What will be, will be," is a reference to a subjunctive condition that is out of sight, beyond prediction; and in fact her very words are out of sight as we hear them. In this respect, they stand as perfect representations of the deliberate and exquisite unfoldingness of cinema itself, and the developing, and to some extent unforeseeable, character of much situated action in general.[24]

However Jo's words are not hidden in an unforeseeable future; they are rooted in a discernible past. This is because the condition referred to by the lyrics of her song—we are prone to call it the "future"—is in fact a deep memory. "When I was just a little girl / I asked my mother, 'What will I be?'" the song begins. The second verse: "When I was just a child in school / I asked my teacher, 'What should I try?'" The third verse: "When I grew up and fell in love / I asked my sweetheart, 'What lies ahead?'"[25] The time of being just a little girl or boy, of being just a child in school, even of growing up and falling in love, is for Jo already an aboriginal time, what Mallarmé called "l'heure fauve," to which she strives to return, because now she is past deciding "what to be," "what to try," "what road to take ahead." This song will eventually *become* performance in the film; but when first we encounter it, it draws up not a sense of presence (as performances relentlessly do: presence and impending absence) but a sense of absence and loss. And it paints the scene for us not as a playing out of motives in a hotel room in a foreign land, but as a reenactment of childhood scenarios—family unities—that could be cherished if they had not been lost. At the end of the film Jo will sing of lost unities tragically, but already now she invokes losses, preparing us for what is to come.

If the labyrinthine space of Morocco is invoked for us prior to the family space as conceived through the lyric of the song, it is oddly true that the immediate surround of the hotel room is not. But our introduction to the space is exactly in our moving to follow the passage of the song, so that the song is always ahead of our consciousness; the song comes before the space in which we hear it; the space is born out of the song. Therefore, the song is always in the deep past, prior to the shot we are watching. To put this more technically: Hitchcock has conceived a scene in which the soundtrack is synchronized with the film, but simultaneously precedes it.

We have been placed, then, into an acoustic labyrinth. Indeed, what labyrinth is not acoustic, shapelessly echoing, temporally dislocating and alluring? The deep past time out of which the song emanates is related to a deep past space, so the song sung in *this current* space is produced here but exists somewhere else. And, too, the lyrics we now hear are situated, through a past tense, in a *before*. We are moving forward cinematically as we hear the words, one could say jogging ahead of them, so that each phrase comes up as a memory not only of the deep past in which it is configured but also of the immediate past moment in which, before moving to the present moment, we heard it. Everything in the scene, then, is not so much *about* memory as *constituted of memory itself*. (In the embassy reprise, singing the same lyrics, Jo allows her vocalization to blatantly overshadow the meaning so that the voice is more important than the message. And the camera is static. We have a distinct sense of being *here*.)

The song has the appearance of being simple, but if we pay it close attention we are immediately sunk in a confounding and evocative marsh of temporality. Hank now recapitulates the song, but the temporal play emitted in his "little boy's" voice has become ironic, because every question *sung* in the past tense seems diegetically *meant* in the present—as do Jo's answers:

77. *(Cont'd.)* HANK:
When I was just a little boy
I asked my mother, "What—
Jo looks toward Ben with a smile.

78. MS: *Ben turns, working with his tie, to acknowledge her.*
HANK: —will I be?"

BEN: He's gonna make a fine doctor. *He turns back toward the mirror,*
but gives her a reassuring double-take.
HANK: "Will I be—

79.   MS: *Jo is smiling into a mirror off-camera right, as she does in 77.*
HANK: "—handsome, will I be rich?" *She smoothes her hair.*

We must try to understand "Que Sera, Sera" not in its own terms but *as*
Hitchcock shows it to us, since the song exists for Hitchcock's purposes. It is
notable that the song makes a knot of time. In this scene, Ben is getting tied
(becoming a man wearing a tie), even tied up. He takes considerable time
at the vanity in this sequence, as though tied into the occupation of tying
himself for dinner. He feels tied up with Bernard, certainly, and we will
notice soon, if we have not already, that he is tongue-tied generally. The ele-
mental mother-son relationship—the tie that binds—is being introduced,
and we are identifying with the child who sings. It is our childhood that
is being reconstituted in this hotel room, with loving parents dedicated
to domestic tasks that comfort us on a journey and assure us all that our
defining relationships are stable. Bernard, the amicable stranger—like a
warm uncle—keeps his distance and enjoys the scene from without, not
really unlike the viewer. We look at what we are, and remember wondering, as children, what we would be; and in this composition, the wondering
and the self-evaluation are laminated upon one another. "I asked (when
does one stop asking this?) my mother, 'What will I be?'" To which the
father replies, "He's gonna make a fine doctor." But Ben is the doctor. So
Hank is Ben, who once wondered if he would become what he has become
now (and probably asked his mother, in a song). All time is wonder: wondering, and then wondering what we might once have wondered. And it is
somehow the presence of the mother, not the male technique implied by
Ben at the mirror, that binds the past to the present musically, producing a
sense of fluid time in which movement is possible. Movement, of course,
means death, but also life. Life in which we turn. "Turning and turning in
the animal belly," wrote Norman O. Brown, "the mineral belly, the belly of
time. To find the way out: the poem." [26]
   However, now a confounding and disturbing conception of time is
introduced because though Hank *is* a little boy—we hear his small voice—
he sings a song written for an adult reminiscing. The rhetoric is thus self-
parody, the child singer pretending to be grown up already, and not what
he is. This is generally one of the strategies of human development, of
course—socialization anticipates—and yet here the strategy of pretending
to be an adult is twisted back upon itself in a labyrinthine way since the

adult that Hank is pretending to be as he sings is "remembering" what it was, "once," to be the little boy he in fact now incontestably is.[27] To remember is to be. To remember is to cause. By singing of the past, *in this shot*, with his father reacting to his mother, Hank becomes Ben (the man in the family, who would once have been a little boy); or, more crucially, by reacting to Hank's voice off-camera, Ben becomes — at least in sympathy — his own past, and the future he projects in his comment is, in truth, his present.

For McKenna is, I would argue, the "fine doctor" he purports his son will be. If he is cynical about having paid for his trip with his patients' afflictions, he puts no blemish upon his professional competence. Middle-class morality and respect are laid aside in favor of a certain kind of technical efficiency; and Ben, advocate of efficiency, is suggesting Hank will grow up to be what he is, an efficient operator, not a moralist. In his folksy sweetness, his sure-handed knowledge, his amicable skepticism, Ben McKenna typifies the midwestern farm boy made good: practical, earthy, starry-eyed, capable, direct — and not particularly comfortable with women.[28] He is lifted from a painting by Thomas Hart Benton; or certainly generated by parents who were.

Yet at the instant Ben hears Hank singing this song, there has been no action from the boy that could justify the father's comment. It is a comment, to be sure, befitting a man who is contented with his life and proud of his son. Were such a man to say of Hank, generally, "He's gonna make a fine doctor," he would be implying, "I can see that he's just like me," and also, "Perhaps the boy will turn out to have a talent for medicine in him," or even, more simply, "This is certainly a very bright kid." At this point, and in this situation, however, all the evidence we have from Hank that could inspire such a claim — indeed all the evidence we have from Hank that could inspire anything — is his singing, singing that may well seem to have little to do with medicine. Nor is it the case that we are to regard Ben's observation as having been made in general time and in general reference to a general relation between himself and Hank — "I always think of my son as someone who will make a good doctor when he grows up" — since there was plenty of that sort of definition, and quite explicitly, back on the bus. Ben's observation now is being made specifically, carefully insinuated at the end of a bar as Jo and Hank sing this particular song, and as he tightens this particular tie, in front of this particular mirror, in this particular room. The singing is a little striven for, eager, dedicated, true. Since it is music, it therefore has melody and rhythm. Hank can also be seen in this sequence as serenading Jo as she prepares to go out for the evening with her "other man," Ben. Thus the boy is being timely, courtly, romantic, and protective of his mother, at least symbolically. All of these — and no others — constitute the characteristics that lead Ben to conclude he would be a fine doctor. If romanticism and courtliness are removed from the technical proficiency we associate with medicine — and assume Ben associates, too — then perhaps it is a different kind of "doctoring" Hank shows promise for here. The boy possesses the finest qualities of each of his parents, energetic practicality, music, romance, starry eyes, and grace, and these will "doctor" for us when we need them. It is a foreshadowing of the winning capability of Ben and Jo when they work together against indeterminate odds. It is also a foreshadowing of the boy's ability to "doctor" the marriage, to heal the rift that has been created between Ben and Jo because she is two people — Jo Conway the famous (and former) singer now become (now playing) Josephine McKenna, his wife — but he believes he has married only one.

The song "Que Sera, Sera" thus introduces twisting, labyrinthine time formally to the film, in part (and significantly) because to some extent it is sung off-screen and therefore seems to come from around and before. Through it we learn about children and parents, time, generations, becoming: all the stuff of mortality. The only adult who will sing it in the film is Jo, and she was never a little boy, so in her solo later the lyric will change. But if we take the present lyric very directly and simply, we see that Hank is asking in song what is going to happen in his future, and his mother's only answer is that the future will determine itself. Alfred Hitchcock will determine the boy's future, however. Indeed, he did so in advance: visualizing the entire construction before a single frame was committed to stock. The power of the "future," of "fate," sung out in the script thus euphemizes the veiled power of forces not operating openly — creative and directorial forces. Whatever will be, will be what some people determine should be. One can see this logic as a dictum for comprehending not only this film but all films. There is an unwapping that the director effects. Hitchcock here spells it out in the greatest possible kind of articulation, song.

I am treating with straightforward seriousness a piece of music that has been received in the popular arena, since that recording of Day's, in a derogatory, much lighter spirit.[29] Indeed, "Que Sera, Sera" can be as sucrose as it is reassuring, especially and distinctively in the choreography through which it is realized — Nick Castle was responsible for it — when finally it is embodied on the screen.[30] This happens in the middle of a shot.

79. *(Cont'd.)* HANK *(Off-camera):* Here's what she said—*Jo steps away,
looking at her dress. She enters the boy's room, reaches out a hand.*
JO: Come on, darling.
HANK: *Singing:*—to me. *She goes to his bed and in his pajamas he
follows. Hank sits at the foot of the bed as she draws back the spread,
singing.*
JO: "Que sera, sera, whatever will be will be,
   The future's not ours to see
   Que sera, sera,
   What will be will be." *She dances to him and kneels in front of him,
bowing a little and touching his nose with her finger. Second verse—:
They sing together, and she gets up and dances to his closet.*
JO and HANK: When I was a just a child in school—
She opens the closet, brings out his slippers.
HANK: I asked my teacher, "What should I try?"
JO *(Softly, tossing him the slippers):* Catch.
HANK: "Should I paint pictures? Should I sing songs?" *Jo laughs,
and turns back to the closet for his bathrobe as he puts on the slippers.*
   This was her wise reply: *She shuts the closet.*
JO: "Que sera, sera, *He whistles along as she sits and does up his robe.*
   Whatever will be will be,
   The future's not ours to see, que sera sera"—oops!
JO and HANK: "What will be will be."
JO: May I have this next dance?
HANK: Yes. *He bows slightly.*
JO: All right. *She gets up in a half-curtsey. As she hums the chorus again,
they waltz as the camera pulls back to the doorway.
A knock is heard at the door.*

In this strikingly delicate and sensitive sequence we learn the depth of
the intimate relationship between Jo and Hank. He is the gentleman in his
houserobe, she the elegant woman of society and the stage. "Should I paint
pictures?" he wonders leisurely, and we might surmise, "Like this picture,
painted for us?" Then: "Should I sing songs?" To this, Jo gives an amicable
laugh. Hank is envisioning following his mother, not his father, and we
can hear that he has the voice to do it; she has been teaching him, and is
teaching him even as we watch. It's a game in which attitudes and skills are
developed, a game in which he will learn not only to vocalize but to detect
vocalizations.[31] Thus he is preparing now to participate in his own salvation in the embassy. And he is preparing, too, a rhetorical skill that will

mirror Jo's and dwarf Ben's. He is a mother's boy, not, perhaps, in some ways unlike Bruno Anthony in *Strangers on a Train*, Maxim de Winter in *Rebecca*, or Roger O. Thornhill in *North by Northwest*. He is learning the legacy of artistry and performance, but also the value of the human voice, and from an expert in the field who can "throw" the lessons deftly enough for him to "catch" them, as with his (dancing) slippers:

> HANK: I asked my teacher, "What should I try?"
> JO *(Softly, tossing him the slippers):* Catch.

Because the focus of the scene is acoustic, the actual dance routine is carefully arranged to be visually interesting without disturbing the continuity of the sung lyric or the harmonic development. Thus, when the duet is abruptly interrupted by an invisible rap at the door, heard from off-scene, we experience a purely acoustical override of an acoustic development. This knock functions in this scene much as the bus horn functioned before the swerve that got Hank into trouble "snatching" the Arab woman's veil in the opening sequence. It brings into a picture of routine tranquility—in this case the blissful duet between mother and son—an ominous, thunderous note from both *off* and *before*. It suggests the tranquility—the happy singing—is a problematic, because discontinued, state of affairs. The interruption further suggests that in this unified peacefulness is the root of all terror, that in these happy lyrics is the essence of discord. "When I grew up and fell in love / I asked my sweetheart, 'What lies ahead?'" At a terrifying question such as this, the song must stop.

Ironically, viewers cloyed by the simplicity and pop quality of the musical composition wonder in irritation through this rather long development when, if ever, the song will end so that the action of the film can pick up. But the song is the action. Later, in the Albert Hall, a song will be action once again. The cynical, and oft-expressed, view that the song is nothing but a commercial hack job, and that it loses in elegance, subtlety, and profundity because of the slick veneer brought to it in the singing sequences, leave a great deal to be heard, and experienced, in *The Man Who Knew Too Much*. Many present-day viewers of the film churlishly turn aside from the simplicity, the essential and central sweetness shown as possible in this family. Thus they deeply wish for the discord that brings about the turn of the plot. And therefore their attitude toward the McKennas reflects that of the Draytons. For those of us jaded in the face of the song's innocence, the kidnapping of little Hank takes on a twist as we posit to ourselves that he is undoubtedly better off away from these hokey parents who sing—and enjoy—such musical drivel. Edward Drayton, for a contrast that will please the viewer discontented with "Que Sera, Sera" (and may well have tickled so exemplary a member of this group as Bernard Herrmann), has symphonic taste, brandished in the assassination rehearsal scene.[32] There, we *ultimately* understand that Drayton is coaching the assassin to a piece of classical symphonic performance; but our *introductory,* and *immediate* sensation as the scene begins, is that Drayton is *listening* to music, not teaching it. The listening precedes the conspiracy, and the music the plotters are listening to is certainly "tonier" than what Hank McKenna typically has to put up with: it has more cachet but not more music.

And the "Storm Cloud" Cantata does not inspire dance. "Que Sera, Sera" (in the same key as the cantata, C major) is a waltz and Jo and Hank utilize it as such. While Ben watches, Jo is inculcating old-world values and an old-world style in a child not quite old enough to cut his own meat. When at the end of the film she treats the guests at the embassy (which is to say, us) to a beautiful rendition of Livingston and Evans's "We'll Love Again," a thoroughly American torch song, we recognize that the siren song Jo and Hank share is fundamentally different, pre-American, a rejection of life in Indianapolis in favor of something grander and prior—indeed, more eastern.[33] In this way, all of the deep meaning of "Que Sera, Sera" is itself a voice from a world before this world.[34]

The compositional simplicity of "Que Sera, Sera" is in many ways at the heart of the dynamic movement of *The Man Who Knew Too Much.* When Hank has been kidnapped (Hitchcock is ensuring in the duet scene) the sensitive viewer will quickly enough wish for that tepid, reassuring little song again. Further, if the film is to be a temporary interruption of family life (and an interruption that counts dramatically), the family life that is interrupted has to be shown as being warm, vibrant, glowing, assured, easy, natural, intense, and worth reconstituting. In the astonishing and very long sequential shot 79, Hitchcock shows all of these aspects of the McKennases' family life without once breaking for angle or reference. Everything is continuous and fluid—which can reassure the viewer that in the long run it will be. The smoothness of this shot is analogous to the evenness of the emotional ground from which the film arises and to which it will return in rest at the conclusion.

But most disturbing about the "Que Sera, Sera" duet is another feature of the staging which contains it. Popular music, already by the 1930s in the United States, had become so professionalized and commercialized an activity that most people expected, most of the time, to listen to songs rather than to sing them. Songs were sung, in fact, typically by relatively highly paid and specialized "new minstrels" established on elevated stages, accompanied by organized background ensembles, alienated from the participatory engagement of ordinary folk. Jo McKenna, indeed, is just such a performer in her professional life, or was; and because she is on her way out to dinner, on a holiday, in a strange place, she is dressed to the hilt—much as she would have been at the Palladium, stepping out in front of a band to sing a song very much like this one. Now, however, as she moves gracefully around Hank, it is clear that she is giving a command performance for an audience of one, and the audience participates.

Normally, such a folksy rendition of popular music would be diegetically assimilated: the scene would fade into only a snatch of it; the action would swallow it up. Here, however, we are given the whole song—as we would be in a live stand-up performance—in a staging which demystifies, reduces, normalizes, and thus galvanizes the event. We are intruders, like Bernard; and we are in no position to do anything but enjoy this; yet Jo's elegant voice and Hank's charm ensure that we really do; but it is too lifelike to be filmlike, and so we are embarrassed into wishing the tenderness will be wiped away. (And when it is, we will be mortified into wanting it back.) Our fondness for popular music is in part based on a desire to be regaled by the pretense of friendliness in strangers who don't mean what they sing, in short, by our theatrical need to suspend disbelief and go along. To the extent that this is a "bad" performance (Hank is no professional singer, but he is heartily engaged in projecting a voice) our very attitude to popular music is highlighted and questioned, our theatrical engagement threatened, our pose of innocence thrown in our face. Highly abstracted popular music—an industry unto itself—is unrelated to the real life of the listening populace, after all, and must be, because that laborious life fuels it; but in this strange scene the disingenuously popular lyrics Jo sings are at one and the same time profound realities for Josephine the mother. But all through this film, Jo is torn between her career in the music industry and her down-to-earth family life. Hitchcock's way of showing us the passion in her conflict—this passion is a central element—is to present a very simple song in a performance that is both "pop" and real at the same time.

In the embassy at the film's conclusion, Jo must sing "Que Sera, Sera" again, this time for a crowd of diplomatic hangers-on in tuxedoes and long gowns and in a rendition, appropriate for the scene, that is all cabaret. She is perfectly stagey, of course, but unbeknownst to her listeners there is method to her crooning style; and the "artificial" pantomime of complaint[35] embedded in her vocal act—exactly the stuff of theater—is more practically a desperate yodel for her lost son.[36] The apparent entertainment, an impression of a navigational call, is in truth a navigational call.

"Will there be rainbows . . . day after day . . . ," means, "Will he hear me and signal that he has, *right now?*" Hank does hear and whistles along—but half a beat off—from a room far, far away. And he whistles loudly—because he doesn't know where she is; and he whistles off-key, because that is what happens when you whistle, as sympathetic Lucy Drayton urges him to, "just as loud as you can":

957. LUCY *(Craftily, with a little smile, looking at Hank and raising her head):* Hank. Can.you whistle that song?
   JO *(Off-camera, singing):* "The future's not ours—

958. CS: *Over Lucy's shoulder, looking down at Hank. Timidly he looks up.*
   JO *(Off-camera, singing):* —"to see—
   HANK: I guess so.

959. CS: *As at the end of 957, from behind Hank. Lucy lowers herself to his level and the camera drops, picking up Hank's head at the right.*
   JO *(Off-camera, singing):* "Que sera, sera—
   LUCY *(Softly, lovingly):* Then go on. Whistle it!

960. CS: *Reverse shot, over Lucy's shoulder. Hank is looking at her with opened eyes.*
   LUCY *(Feelingfully):* Whistle it as loud as you can!
   JO *(Off-camera, singing):* "What will be, will be."
   Hank is incredulous, staring at Lucy. She nods.

But now Hitchcock has us:

What are we to do? As lovers of professional performance, advocates of the popular music industry—in short, as industrialists—should we wish this irritating whistling to stop? It is surely ruining the performance and as advocates of the entertainment industry we are bound to maintain that performances are more important than anything.

Or should we be glad she has heard him—that is to say, that he has been (as Stephen Sondheim might put it) "singing too loud"?

While our middle-class sentiments lead us to hope the commonplace person in Jo will triumph over the performer, the mother will leap up from the keyboard and cut off the popular song to establish the popular mother-child reunion in its place, Hitchcock in fact establishes the scene in such a way that Hank can only be saved *if the song in performance can be continued, too.* Ben and Jo McKenna are on the embassy premises on false pretenses, merely pretending to be guests of the prime minister whose life Jo has saved; merely pretending to be gracious in bowing to a request for Jo's act. Should it become openly known that they are hunting for a captive secreted in an upper room, they will be trespassing. And so, just as in any other entertainment, the song must press forward to its end. The melody that rises must fall.

Or que sera sera, what will be, will be. That key phrase is trenchant. The first "will be" is a simple future tense; that which we project as occurring in time beyond the present. But the second "will be" is a testament of intention and definition of what can be predicted with absolute confidence. "Que sera sera" doesn't mean merely, "We won't know what will happen until it happens." It means instead, "Whatever it is that must happen *will in fact happen*." The resolution of the film will arrive, because that preparation for an arrival leading to an arrival is what film is. Time will move, or appear to move, because the appearance of movement is time. The music will reach its conclusion, even as the cymbal crash in the Albert Hall had to follow the opening notes of the cantata, in order, as the film's epigram put it, to "rock the lives of an American family." Speaking through this simple but profound little song, Hitchcock is telling us the secret of film itself: the future's not ours to see, but it will come.

Notes

I am especially grateful to Bob Bornstein, Christopher Husted, Jay Livingston, Randy Talmadge, and Eldridge Walker for their generous assistance to me in writing this essay.

1 Jay Livingston's recollection, recounted to me September 18, 1995. Arthur Park was in fact Doris Day's agent at MCA at the time. It is rather likely that Wasserman formed Filwite (the production company on record for the film) on behalf of his clients, Hitchcock and Stewart, who were partners in it. By March 29, 1955, both Stewart and Day had been set, according to a Paramount casting memo. (Margaret Herrick Library, Academy of Motion Picture Arts and Sciences, Beverly Hills. I am also grateful to Saul Cooper.)

2 Written one night after they saw *The Barefoot Contessa*, in which Rosanno Brazzi says near the end, "Che sera sera." Livingston jotted the words down in the dark and they "knocked off the song" afterward. Two weeks later the call from Hitchcock came through. (Conversation with Jay Livingston, September 18, 1995.)

3 From 1939 until his death on March 18, 1954, when he was succeeded by Roy Fjastad, Lipstone had been head of Paramount's music department. Livingston's memory may have been faulty as he recalled these events; or the music department head's office may still have been thought of, by him or others, as Louis Lipstone's. (I am grateful to Douglas Gomery.)

4 Personal conversation with Jay Livingston, September 18, 1995.

5 "Holy Gee," music and lyrics by Jay Livingston and Ray Evans. Text from

the Margaret Herrick Library, Academy of Motion Picture Arts and Sciences, Beverly Hills, Calif.

6 According to Jay Livingston, "Holy Gee" was played for Doris Day and she rejected it on the ground that it sounded too much like "Holy Jesus." The rewritten song was rejected as well, but not by her. (Communication from Randy Talmadge, September 19, 1995.)

7 "Holy Cow," music and lyrics by Jay Livingston and Ray Evans. Text from the Margaret Herrick Library, Academy of Motion Picture Arts and Sciences, Beverly Hills, Calif.

8 Communication from Randy Talmadge, September 19, 1995.

9 Conversation with Herbert Coleman, September 26, 1995.

10 "Love Me or Leave Me," in *The Movie That Changed My Life,* ed. David Rosenberg (New York: Penguin, 1991), 109.

11 Personal conversation with Jay Livingston, September 18, 1995.

12 Production files, Margaret Herrick Library, Academy of Motion Picture Arts and Sciences, Beverly Hills.

13 George Perry, *Alfred Hitchcock* (London: Macmillan, 1975), 91.

14 Jonathan Coe, *James Stewart: Leading Man* (London: Bloomsbury, 1994).

15 Guy Davenport, *Geography of the Imagination* (San Francisco: North Point Press, 1981), 3 ff.

16 Jacques Lacan, *Écrits* (Paris: Éditions du Seuil, 1966), 817.

17 Michel Chion, *La Voix au Cinéma* (Paris: Éditions de l'Étoile, 1982), 19. (My translation.)

18 In addition to the mise-en-scène of the duet scene, (1) the off-camera blast of the bus horn before Hank is sent careening into the Arab woman who wears the veil; (2) an off-camera conversation between a man and a child (in French) about wearing hats, as the McKennas arrive at the Hôtel de la Mamounia; (3) Louis Bernard's furtive phone call from the McKenna hotel room (also in French), with his back to the camera; (4) the death of Louis Bernard, as we watch Ben McKenna's face while he listens to Bernard's dying words; and (5) the mysterious telephone call McKenna receives at the Commisariat de Police, are all constructed on film through a stunning and central use of the acousmetron.

19 I am grateful to Henry Bumstead for this observation.

20 I am grateful to Abdel Khalig Ali for this observation.

21 On the "spirit of place" see D. H. Lawrence, *Studies in Classic American Literature* (New York: Viking, 1964).

22 The scene was shot with direct sound, which is to say, Doris Day and Christopher Olsen were actually singing "Que Sera, Sera" live on the set as the camera turned, August 5, 1955, on Paramount's Stage 1. Later, at the studio's insistence, and for commercial release, Day recorded the song again (in the single take mentioned above). But she enjoyed "rehearsing" it openly, for example at a soirée given by Jimmy Stewart at his home on North Roxbury Drive in Daniel Gélin's honor, where Stewart accompanied her at the piano as she sang to a gathering including Billy Wilder and Merle Oberon. Effective 9:30 P.M. on September 24,

1968, her voice was heard on CBS television singing the song yet again, as the theme intro to "The Doris Day Show." By that time it had become "Doris's favorite song." See Christopher Young, *The Films of Doris Day* (Secaucus N.J.: Citadel Press, 1977), 88.

23 François Truffaut, *Hitchcock* (New York: Simon & Schuster, 1985), 266. In the "el Maghrib" shot of *The Man Who Knew Too Much* we have distal perception before proximal, reiterating the history of modern art from the quattrocento, in José Ortega y Gasset's view. See Ortega y Gasset, "On Point of View in the Arts," in *The Dehumanization of Art and Other Essays* (Princeton N.J.: Princeton University Press, 1968), 110 ff.

24 Much, but perhaps not all. In staged action, at least for those who collaborate in the staging, what outcomes may be hard for an audience to predict are rehearsed in advance, and typically played out according to the rehearsal. Though unforeseen outcomes are not utterly restricted—the onstage death of Leonard Warren is a chilling case in point—rehearsed action does tend to differ from spontaneous action in at least the relative certainty some members have as to what other members will experience in the future. See, for much more elaborate discussion, Erving Goffman, *Frame Analysis: An Essay on the Organization of Experience* (Cambridge Mass.: Harvard University Press, 1974), chap. 5.

25 These lyrics were sent to the M.P.A.A. for clearance of censorship, April 18, 1955.

26 Norman O. Brown, *Love's Body* (New York: Random House, 1966), 56.

27 For insight into anticipatory socialization I am grateful to John Long.

28 Ben is contrasted, then, with the suave Louis Bernard, the oily but exceptionally graceful assassin, and the theatrical producer Val Parnell, a ladies' man, whose presence in a suite at the Savoy anchors all of the action in London exactly as Bernard's presence echoed the action in Marrakech.

29 "Que Sera, Sera (Whatever Will Be, Will Be)" first appeared on Billboard's "Top 100" chart July 7, 1956. It rose as high as number two on that chart and remained in that position for three weeks, staying on the chart altogether for twenty-two weeks. It was number two on the Disk Jockey list, and number three on the best seller list and the juke box list. At the same time, people were avidly listening to Elvis Presley's "Don't Be Cruel," Guy Mitchell's "Singing the Blues," Gogi Grant's "The Wayward Wind," and Dean Martin's "Memories Are Made of This." See Billboard Books, *Top 40 Hits* (New York: Billboard/Watson-Guptill, 1992).

30 William Meiklejohn's memorandum to Sidney Justin of July 5, 1955, directs an agreement be drawn up for Castle's services to "stage and create one number." Castle was to start that day and be paid $3,000 for one week and one day, not necessarily consecutive. Filwite Productions would have no obligation to give him a credit billing, and he did not get one. (Margaret Herrick Library, Academy of Motion Picture Arts and Sciences, Beverly Hills.)

31 A useful approach to the importance of production and recognition in the ethnomethodology of situated action is A. Lincoln Ryave and James Schenkein's "Notes on the Art of Walking," in *Ethnomethodology*, ed. Roy Turner (Harmondsworth: Penguin, 1974).

32 In his impatience with the hopelessly commercial "Que Sera, Sera" there is

doubtless a preparation of sorts for the earnestness Bernard Herrmann displayed in dissociating himself from the Alfred Hitchcock who rejected his "serious" score for *Torn Curtain* at the Goldwyn Studios in March 1966. (Donald Spoto, *The Dark Side of Genius: The Life of Alfred Hitchcock* [New York: Ballantine, 1984], 520–21.) Hitchcock's will to make use of popular music, therefore, was not born in the mid-1960s as a response to pressure from insensitive executives at Universal Pictures.

33 Day was apparently crying when she recorded "We'll Love Again" in England. (Jay Livingston, personal conversation, September 18, 1995.) For an eloquent discussion of the American cultural meaning of "eastern," see Leslie A. Fiedler, "Boxing the Compass," in *The Return of the Vanishing American* (New York: Stein & Day, 1969). East of Indianapolis are New York and then Europe.

34 Which is to say, what Michel Chion called an "acousmetron" (*La Voix au cinéma*).

35 See Jonathan Miller, *The Body in Question* (London: Jonathan Cape, 1978).

36 On "downkeying" and "upkeying," two concepts that very handily explain (a) Jo's belief in the hotel room that she is giving a performance when in fact she is addressing the condition of her own life; and then (b) her knowledge at the embassy that she is addressing the conditions of her own life while others believe she is giving a performance, see Goffman, *Frame Analysis*, 312–14.

"You Think They Call Us Plastic *Now* . . .": The Monkees and *Head*

PAUL B. RAMAEKER

Anyway, the idea is this: by-products! Imagine the tie-ins! Blonde wigs for kids! Swords! The whole phallic thing is happening! I mean, why don't we use classic things? Millions! I'm tellin' ya, millions! [The band walks away.] — Lord High 'n' Low, speaking to the Monkees, in *Head*

Freaking out [is] a process whereby an individual casts off outmoded and restricting standards of thinking, dress, and social etiquette in order to express CREATIVELY his relationship, to his immediate environment and the social structure as a whole. — Frank Zappa

"Hey, Hey . . ."

For the last decade and a half, the Monkees have experienced a steady increase in their cultural stock. Their television series, produced by Bob Rafelson and Bert Schneider's Raybert Productions, enjoyed a brief run on MTV in the mid-1980s, kicking off a long period of intermittent cable syndication. Collections of episodes have been released on videotape by Rhino, along with their TV special *33 1/3 Revolutions Per Monkee,* and their lone feature film, *Head.* All of their recordings, including some albums even original fans may not remember (*Changes,* for example, recorded by Micky Dolenz and Davy Jones after the departures of first Peter Tork, then Michael Nesmith), have been reissued on compact disc by Rhino with the remastering and bonus tracks that bespeak prestige. There have been numerous reunion tours featuring Dolenz, Jones, Tork, and on occasion even Nesmith (who generally wants nothing to do with the nostalgia surround-

8 The Monkees.
[Author's collection]

ing the big hits for which he had little but contempt at the time). Two new albums have emerged from these reunion tours: *Pool It!* in 1986, and *Justus* in 1996.

The sixties-rock nostalgia circuit may be enough by itself to sustain interest in the band, but not to fully account for the elevated critical reputation the original Monkees projects (both televisual and musical) have enjoyed in the recent period. In the 1960s, the nascent rock press, and much of the countercultural community that it served, made much sport of reviling the band as "prefabricated" and "plastic." The band's success was greeted with, at best, bitter resignation and bemusement from the rock underground, as demonstrated by this line from *Crawdaddy:* "The amusing thing about all this is its supreme unimportance. After it's all over and they've outsold everyone else in history, the Monkees will still leave absolutely no mark on American music."[1] Thanks in part to a younger generation of music critics raised in the post-punk era, and to cultural studies' embrace of popular pleasures, pop music (as opposed to the more serious "rock" of the era) has enjoyed a critical reappraisal from which the Monkees have benefited.

Even in such circumstances, however, *Head* remains obscure: little watched, less discussed, its place in music and film history uncertain. *Head* has been underexamined both as a statement by a rock band and as a film that is an immediate precursor to the "Hollywood Renaissance" of the 1970s. Following its release, Rafelson and Schneider would divorce themselves from the Monkees, form BBS Productions, and produce *Easy Rider,* arguably the most influential studio film of its era. Jack Nicholson, who wrote the script for *Head,* would begin his ascent to fame through his performance in *Easy Rider.* Indeed, long after *Head*'s box office failure, Rafelson, who directed the film, would say this about the origins of the project: "Well, I'll tell you, having been responsible—for better or worse—for putting the Monkees together, for having created that sort of bizarre phenomenon, I then felt it was only deserved to de-mythologize the whole thing. I didn't expect the film to be seen by anybody, but I felt I was entitled to make it."[2] Some critics have responded that this is merely a rationalization for the film's commercial failure.[3] Both stances, however, obscure the industrial and cultural context in which *Head* was actually produced. In fact, *Head* may well not have been motivated by commercial concerns in any *uncomplicated* way, and the film is certainly among the least conventional ever released by a Hollywood studio. But I will argue that it is precisely the unorthodoxy of the film that demonstrates the bid for cultural credibility that the project represented for Rafelson, Schneider, Nicholson, and, most importantly here, the Monkees themselves. The continued economic viability of the Monkees (as well as the ambitions of the Rafelson/Schneider partnership) was dependent upon precisely the kind of prestige they attempted to gain through this project, specifically, prestige in the eyes of the counterculture that had always rejected them as plastic teenyboppers.

They failed. With *Head,* the Monkees not only continued to alienate their preteen audience, but they also failed utterly to tap into the radicalized collegiate (and teen) audience that had become so important to the success of those musical artists who had opted for "rock" authorship instead of "pop" stardom. In order to understand why the Monkees and their creators attempted a project like *Head,* and why it failed, it is necessary to examine the history of the Monkees as a multimedia commercial phenomenon; the changing musical and film marketplace in the late 1960s and the ways in which Raybert and the Monkees adapted to this; and finally the context provided by a counterculture that increasingly fueled that marketplace, and thus motivated the Monkees' (failed) metamorphosis. *Head* can be seen as a crucial part of the Monkees' ongoing project to reconfigure the group's cultural identity by explicitly interrogating the terms by which it had come to be defined. Simultaneously, *Head*'s creators appropriated musical, visual, and narrational strategies to align the film and its soundtrack (and themselves) with developments in the late-sixties experimental arts culture. Finally, just as a historical examination of the countercultural discourses informing its production may reveal much about *Head*, so its failure may reveal much about the student marketplace and its preferences. Noting *Head*'s strategies for countercultural acceptance may bring into relief the strategies that other films adopted in order to succeed precisely where *Head* failed.

"And People Say We Monkey Around"

The Monkees was perceived as unorthodox television before it even reached the air, which caused immediate commercial vexations for its producers. After a disastrous comic performance by the "group" at a reception for NBC affiliates in June of 1966, five key stations refused to carry the show, which *TV Guide* later claimed resulted in "national ratings that did not accurately reflect its true popularity."[4] Produced for NBC by Raybert Productions and Columbia Pictures' television arm, Screen Gems, *The Monkees* premiered on NBC in September of 1966. While the show received some positive press initially, it never cracked the top twenty-five rated Nielsen shows. Indeed, the first episode came in sixty-fifth on the Nielsen scale.[5]

What mattered, however, was that the show seemed to reach the audience for which it had been intended—preteens and teenagers. If the ratings may not have reflected the actual size of the show's following, the group's record sales provided a corrective. Nesmith is undoubtedly accurate in his perception that "those records were designed as ancillaries to the television show."[6] But it is also the case that the records provided exactly the index of commercial success that the show's ratings did not, and proved to advertisers that the show targeted a demographic with money to spend. The Monkees' single "Last Train to Clarksville" topped the Billboard Hot 100 singles charts in October of 1966, after the show had been on the air for one month. The subsequent LP *The Monkees* sold three million units, higher than any individual Beatles album to that date. The follow-up LP, *More of the Monkees*, released in January of 1967, sold five million units. At the same time, Monkees merchandising experienced a comparable bonanza. It is estimated that Monkees merchandising had earned twenty million dollars by the end of 1966, only a few short months after the show premiered in September of that year.[7]

Publicity for the show (and, consequently, for other Monkees products) targeted the youth audience in *opposition* to older viewers. For example, the show's unconventionality was consistently foregrounded in press coverage of the show. From the beginning, this was a selling point for the act, and thus both consistent with and part of its attempt to target a youth demographic. As Aniko Bodroghkozy has discussed, "initial critical response to *The Monkees* . . . focused on the fact that adults would hate the show but kids would love it."[8] For example, Lawrence Laurent of the *Washington Post* wrote, "Adults will scream in outrage . . . [but it] will delight the young."[9] The reviewer for the *Dallas Times-Herald* wrote, "Some adults may not understand the Monkees, but I think the teenagers will get the message loud and clear."[10] However unorthodox the show may have seemed to these critics, however, they also made it clear that *The Monkees* was treading ground that had proven commercial appeal. *Variety* identified the show as working in "a dramatic genre created by 'A Hard Day's Night' and 'Help.'" The review noted that both groups seemed to be "four youngsters with a good rock sound and lively personalities." Like the Beatles, in other words, they were basically "nice kids."[11]

The boys' comic antics and musical interludes formed the center of the show's teen appeal, but additionally, a high degree of play with visual style was equated with its address to young viewers. However much *The Monkees* diverged from the televisual norms of its era, its techniques were clearly derived from the conventions of contemporaneous rock and roll movies.[12] A typical *Newsweek* review isolated the stylistic quirks of the show:

> The four mopheads bound along the beach with the quick jerkiness of speeded-up film. Jump-cut to the same four, floating in a slow-motion gallop across the lawn of a baronial estate, then an instantaneous change of clothes and they're in a helicopter circling a city. And always the strum-thump rock beat in the background: a syncopated pandemonium. . . . Such cinematic kinetics are really the property of Richard Lester, director of the Beatles' films, 'A Hard Day's Night' and 'Help!' But television is a medium that thrives on thievery, and there Beatlemania has been exchanged for Monkeeshines.[13]

In fact, the reviewer notes, "plot lines are marginal — simple old-time melodrama or situation-comedy gimmicks. Emphasis is on treatments — wild camera work and ad-libbing. . . . For director James Frawley [the show's regular director], it's a chance to make trick shots; for film editors, who must sort out the crazy footage, it's cause for dyspepsia."[14]

In its stylistic play, then, *The Monkees* had a ready form of product differentiation from virtually everything else on the air in 1966 and 1967.

It is partly because the show so easily stands apart from other situation comedies that in "*The Monkees* and the Deconstruction of Television Realism," Laura Goostree claims that the show "subverts the realistic system [of television]."[15] But she also makes a crucial qualification: such visual play, she writes, is mostly confined to the "music clips" within each episode, and therefore is easily contained within an internally consistent diegesis. It should be noted, however, that this was not always the case in the first season of the show, when breaking the diegetic coherence was most typical. For example, the pilot episode, "Here Come the Monkees" (actually the tenth episode to be aired) often recalls Warner Bros. cartoons in this regard. Intertitles are used frequently (e.g., "But inside, all is not well," as we move to a new scene), lampooning whatever melodramatic narrative conventions the show borrows at any given juncture. Elsewhere, titles are superimposed over freeze-frames. For instance, a shot of a young female extra dancing features the title "A typical teenager?"; when we return to her, another title reads: "No, a friend of the producer!" Another cartoon convention often utilized in the first season was the sudden jump-cut to a comic transformation. In "The Picture Frame," the police show Davy, Mike, and Micky in a film, shot by a hidden camera, of the three of them robbing a bank; when Peter enters with popcorn, however, the squad room is suddenly transformed into a movie theater complete with several other "typical" audience members (two teenagers necking, etc.).

Certainly, during the second season, a tendency toward stylized visuals would be continued and extended, but mostly in the musical segments. "Hitting the High Seas" features a performance of "Star Collector" filmed in a quasi-psychedelic style. The number, featuring jittery handheld camerawork and quick cutting, takes place on a stage filled with smoke and surrounded by lights supplemented with gels in primary colors. At the end of "Monkees in Texas," Micky performs "Goin' Down" alone on a stage, accompanied, through optical printing, by identical images of himself, each one tinted a different color. But while such sequences demonstrate the kind of extreme stylization that would become central to *Head,* otherwise the episodes in which they appear feature conventional, consistent diegeses, with more or less standard sitcom plot devices. These scenes occur at the end of their respective episodes, completely isolated from the narrative action. Thus, while the visual style becomes more "experimental" in musical sequences in the second season, the limits of the musical interludes are more tightly circumscribed. The show would include unconventional stylistic techniques, but utilize them in a highly conventionalized way.

If these aspects of the show's visual style were central to its appeal to a younger audience, and anticipate *Head,* the same claims can be made for the reflexivity that would be routine throughout the series. In "Double Barrel Shotgun Wedding," the boys whip out their scripts to check on what they should do next. In still another, "Dance Monkee Dance," Micky consults with the screenwriters to write them out of a predicament, only to trash the new script, complaining, "Man, this is terrible. Those guys are really overpaid." In addition to such instances wherein the boys break the fourth wall (it is noteworthy that only very infrequently does any other character get to do so), another recurring feature of the series was the interview segment at the end of the episode. Here, we were supposed to see the true Monkee, the real person behind the make-believe and skits. Goostree remarks on the play of identity that results from this, the sense given that "the character does not subsume the actor, and the actor does not subsume the character." In such instances, she argues, "elements of the boys' personalities emerge that totally contradict what the audience knows about the characters the boys portray," such as Nesmith's "anti-authoritarian feelings and somewhat pompous avant-garde aesthetic," Dolenz's thoughtfulness, Tork's "intelligence and political awareness," and Jones's "wit and working class background."[16] But, on the contrary, one may note the degree of congruence between such impressions and the characterizations presented within the narrative segments. Jones is typically portrayed as the pluckiest Monkee, Nesmith as the most serious, Tork the most sensitive, and Dolenz the one who most easily thinks on his feet. Here, too, then, while the show seems to experiment quite freely with standard televisual characterization, the interviews only present those aspects of the Monkees' personalities that do not contradict their character traits in the narratives of *The Monkees.* Star personae and character may have been made consistent to reinforce the viewer's sense of the boys' authenticity, but, of course, to detractors, would function in exactly the opposite manner.

Despite the carefully cultivated appearance of rebelliousness and nonconformity surrounding both the characters and the series itself, from the very beginning, media coverage never failed to comment upon the prefabrication of the act. *Variety,* for example, notes that the group was "virtually manufactured for this show."[17] *Newsweek* criticizes the Monkees for being "as calculatingly manufactured a product as a TV Dinner" and quotes Davy Jones to the effect that "'This isn't a rock and roll group. . . . It's an act.'"[18] While concessions of this sort may have looked forward to the baring of the marks of construction in *Head,* Raybert soon took a different tack in promoting the Monkees project. A *TV Guide* cover story on the show, from January 1967, notes that these so-called "kids" were actually in their twenties, but also quotes Bob Rafelson to the effect that the governing idea in casting the Monkees was " 'not to find four actors to *play* The Monkees, but to find The Monkees.' " The article goes on to claim that of all the Monkees, Micky (who had the most flamboyant onscreen persona) was "the only one who seem[ed] to be acting," and moreover that this was "probably only natural" since his father was an actor, and he himself had been a child-actor.[19]

Clearly, however, this approach could not satisfactorily answer questions concerning the authenticity of the band. The criticisms faced by the Monkees over their prefab status are amply discussed in the many histories on the band available. By the time that the Monkees appeared on the recording scene, they exemplified a model for pop music construction that, while never commercially outmoded, was certainly falling out of favor in the rock intelligentsia and the press. The rock community had begun to adopt two distinct, but complementary, discourses of artistic production and the relationship of artist to audience.

The folk ideology of musical production of, for, and by a community had begun shaping the development of rock "scenes" in cities such as San Francisco. At the same time, Bob Dylan, the most important artist of the American folk scene, had begun to turn away from the restrictions of that genre. By 1965, his songwriting had shifted from the likes of "Blowin' in the Wind," which embodied the optimism and romanticization of the country and "America's continuing past" of the folk revivalist movement, toward the more complicated, and, crucially, personal allegories of "Desolation Row" and "Highway 61 Revisited."[20] As Iain Chambers writes, with Dylan's turn to introspection, " 'Protest' turns into proseity, and the 'truths' of the individual 'artist' replace and refine vague populist sentiments. It was to be this later existential radicalism, this 'uncharted journey into the rebellious imperatives of the self' (Norman Mailer), as much as the sharpened impact of race and student politics on American campuses, that ended up woven into the cradle of the alternative 'society' and its counterculture."[21] Following the example of Dylan's turn to more subjective lyrics, the Beatles, whom the Monkees were so clearly modeled on, had , by 1964's soundtrack to *A Hard Day's Night,* moved from covering R&B and Brill Building standards on their earliest albums to recording only songs they themselves had written. Lennon would recall that, inspired by Dylan, he departed from "a professional songwriter's attitude to writing pop songs," and from his own methods of working within pop conventions: "Instead of projecting myself into a situation, I would just try to express what I felt about myself."[22] In this way, through the influence, not of folk music as a genre, but rather of certain folk musicians, a model of the rock artist as author began to take hold. Unlike the folk performer who is one with his audience, this kind of rock musician is the classic Romantic artist, whose work is essentially personal, and only secondarily for public consumption. As Simon Frith puts it, "Music was thus defined as self-expression and social commentary, as a matter of truth rather than popularity."[23]

For all the extent to which their television image as irreverent "kids" gently poking fun at the establishment was based on the personae of the early Beatles, particularly as presented in *Help!* and *A Hard Day's Night,* the Monkees, as a musical group, in fact represent a continuation of Brill Building production practices. They were dependent on songs by the likes of Carole Bayer, Gerry Goffin and Carole King, Neil Diamond, Cynthia Weil and Barry Mann, and newcomers Tommy Boyce and Bobby Hart. Their records were produced by Don Kirshner, head of Screen Gems Music, a businessman who had long worked with such professional songwriters. From the contemporary perspective, the Monkees' reliance on the output of professional songwriters alone would seem to be indicative of their manufacturedness. But in that period, a degree of reliance on outside songwriters was not at all unusual, not only in mainstream pop but within more prestigious rock circles as well. While the Beatles had turned decisively to original compositions by 1964, with other British Invasion groups soon to follow, the Byrds, one of L.A.'s most prestigious bands, released their first two albums, mainly comprised of cover songs, in 1965. Only starting with *Fifth Dimension,* in 1966, did their own compositions dominate their albums. Yet their repertoire continued to feature Dylan compositions, traditional songs, and covers even of the likes of Brill Building writers Goffin and King, throughout their career.

Despite the wide variety of sources the Byrds tapped for their compositions, "what makes their eclecticism so interesting," Jon Landau argued in *Rolling Stone* in 1968, "is that the style they have concocted out of all these musical sources is very un-eclectic, and is, in fact, a style of incredible consistency. . . . It all comes out with the unmistakable imprimatur of the Byrds."[24] Here, then, was an alternative model of rock authorship— the band that has developed such a strong, and unmistakable, musical "sound" that *any* source material is transformed by their touch. Another L.A. band, Love, would, in 1966, turn Bacharach and David's "My Little Red Book" into garage-punk that recalls their beginnings and "street" identity. Several of the new British "progressive" rock bands would prove their individual identity and instrumental dexterity via this route, on singles as well as album tracks: in 1968, the Nice released a cover of "America" from *West Side Story*; in 1969, Yes covered "Something's Coming" from the same musical, and their first and second albums would also include covers of songs by the Byrds, Ritchie Havens, and the Beatles. The apex of this tendency, though, was the 1967 debut album by Vanilla Fudge, which contained long, slowed-down, "heavy" versions of songs that had been performed or written by artists like Donovan, Cher, the Beatles, and the Supremes.

But if songwriting constituted only one possible mode of authorship in rock of the late sixties, its chief alternative, taking others' compositions and radically altering them through a distinctive personal style, was dependent upon two factors. First, for artists like Yes, the Nice, and Vanilla Fudge, it was crucial that the songs they performed were covers of instantly recognizable songs. This allowed the application of their own musical innovations to the source material to stand to the fore. Secondly, the instrumental abilities of the musicians themselves became crucial as a corollary of this. These were musicians who were able to choose what songs they would perform, and control how they would perform them.

The Monkees fell short of both these criteria. None of the Monkees' early recordings were cover versions (which was, in fact, rather unusual for 1966–67). Instead, as with the Brill Building at its height, all of their songs were written for them by professional songwriters working with an eye on the market. There would be no original version from which theirs could stand apart; there would only be these songs supplied to them, and written in conventional, then-popular styles. Second, it was revealed to the press that not only did the Monkees have no role in writing their early hits, but they also did not actually play any instruments on those records. In fact, Don Kirshner had assembled a crew of studio musicians to perform all but the vocals on their early recordings. Such a practice was perhaps more common than is well known. Except for Roger McGuinn's guitar playing, no instrumental work on the first Byrds album, *Mr. Tambourine Man*, was performed by a member of that band. But the Byrds still had control over their own repertoire and, more importantly, sound. The Monkees had no involvement in the making of their first two albums beyond vocal performance. The revelation that they had so little to do with their recordings would prove especially damaging to the group's credibility within musical circles. Though Michael Nesmith would remark that the controversy over the issue of whether or not the Monkees were a "real" band was "tantamount 'to a flap that the Starship Enterprise [was] not really going to outer space,'" it nonetheless earned them the enmity of rock bands everywhere.[25]

Somewhat ironically, given the recording history of *Mr. Tambourine Man,* the Byrds' Chris Hillman and Jim McGuinn wrote their "So You Want to Be a Rock and Roll Star" (1967) to protest the rise of just such manufactured groups.[26] By this point, rock was increasingly coming to differentiate itself, as a mode of musical practice, from the pop marketplace and bands who were so unarguably prefabricated as the Monkees.[27] As Frith writes,

> By the late 1960s, musicians on both sides of the Atlantic were distinguishing rock as art from rock as entertainment: rock was a complex musical form; it could not be constrained by the pop tradition of singles, package tours, and reproduced hits. Pop meant groups put together, like the Monkees, to satisfy a fad, anonymous players bought—their personalities and all—to meet a need. In pop, even when the musicians themselves were responsible for how they pleased their public, they had to take account of the public's demands, and the youth market was as constraining as any other. Rock, by contrast, was a means of self-expression; it could not be subordinated to any market.[28]

Against the backdrop of this controversy, frustrated by their status as hired hands in the face of the increasing self-consciousness of the rock community, Nesmith, Tork, Jones, and Dolenz, with the support of Bert Schneider, staged their well-publicized takeover of the Monkees music machine. *TV Guide* documented this in September of 1967, as the second season of the show began, billing the development as "The Great Revolt of '67." The article claims that, whereas they had once seemed to be "corporate pawns," any notion that they were mere cogs in a multimillion dollar machine was a "dream . . . built on a house of cards. The TV Establishment is not ready for The Monkees; worse yet, The Monkees are not ready for the Establishment."[29] As proof of this change, the group was quoted: "'The music on our records has nothing to do with us,' the spokesman for the group, intense young Mike Nesmith, had said once and was ready to say again. 'It's totally dishonest. We don't record our own music. Tell the world we're synthetic because, dammit, we are! We want to play our own.'"[30] Thus the band, "tired of being 'corporate pawns,'" took over, becoming a real group at last.[31] *Headquarters,* their third album, released in June of 1967, would feature the instrumental as well as vocal performances of all the Monkees, and this fact would be heavily promoted. This suggests that the Monkees had become willing, even eager, to puncture their own myth, and that such a step might have been perceived as necessary to their artistic growth. This logic would be carried to its apex in *Head.* Indeed, their problematic relationship with their own position within the industry would become their primary cinematic subject.

"Wait 'Til I Tell Them How We Do It!"

From an industrial standpoint, the Monkees phenomenon is noteworthy precisely for its simultaneous and combined "attack upon the American consumer" from television *and* music *and* merchandising.[32] But the group first and foremost existed as performers on a weekly television show. Their exposure through that medium was crucial for their performance in other commercial domains. Therefore, the Monkees faced a serious threat when, in the 1967–68 season, CBS moved its powerhouse *Gunsmoke* from the Saturday night slot it had occupied since 1955 to a Monday night slot, opposite *The Monkees*. While *Gunsmoke* had slipped from the Nielsen Top 25 in the years immediately preceding this rescheduling, it seemed to pick up steam in its new time slot. *Gunsmoke* managed to become the fourth-rated show of the season, with a 25.5 percent share. *The Monkees* could not withstand the competition, and the show was canceled at the end of the 1967–68 season, following a two-season run. The Monkees remained active as a musical group, but album sales had already begun to drop. *Headquarters* sold only two and a half million copies, half that of its predecessor.[33] *Pisces, Aquarius, Capricorn, and Jones, Ltd.*, released in November of 1967, sold one million copies.[34] *The Birds, the Bees, and the Monkees*, released in April of 1968, sold less still. Without the exposure provided by the television show, which had so prominently featured their music, album sales could only get worse. Their popularity with teens and preteens seemed to be on the wane, and, especially without the promotion provided by the television show, they had no new audience available to replace them.

Against this backdrop, Raybert Productions convinced Columbia Pictures to invest in a Monkees feature film, *Head,* to be directed by Rafelson, written by then up-and-coming screenwriter Jack Nicholson, and produced by Schneider, Rafelson, and Nicholson.[35] It is unclear what expectations Columbia had for the film, but if they expected a "ninety-minute version of the television series,"[36] they would be disappointed. *Head* represents a turning point in the Monkees project, an attempt to radically reconfigure the terms by which the Monkees had come to be defined as both comedic and musical performers.

While some elements and episodes of the television show can be seen as attempts to expose the image-making process that produced the Monkees, the opening of *Head* presents a far more radical critique: namely, astonishingly, suicide. The film opens on a ceremony dedicating a bridge, a stiff "Establishment" affair disrupted by the sudden appearance of the Monkees, running frantically as if chased. With no explanation, Micky climbs onto the railing, then jumps, while the rest of the band looks on. This metaphoric suicide is followed by a musical sequence, accompanying "Porpoise Song," depicting Micky floating in the water, each shot slowly dissolving to the next. Each image is optically printed with a polarization effect so that the positive and negative areas of the image are dyed with different, and highly saturated, colors—blue and green, red with green, etc. Micky is joined by mermaids, who frolic in the water with him; he kisses one of them, and the polarized shot dissolves to an unprocessed image of Micky kissing a woman, seen from the other side of an aquarium.

These opening sequences perform two crucial functions for the film's discourse about the Monkees and their relationship to their own pop stardom. First, the "suicide" provides a vivid manifestation of the rejection and negation that is at the heart of the film. The effect of the opening is shocking, though what *exactly* is being rejected is not yet clear. The images of Micky swimming with the mermaids contextualize and qualify interpretation of the suicide gesture. This imagery, with its free, almost abstract play of color and form, strongly recalls that which had become associated with cinematic representations of the psychedelic experience, in films ranging from American experimental works like Kenneth Anger's "Sacred Mushroom" version of *Inauguration of the Pleasure Dome,* Jordan Belson's *Samadhi,* and Scott Bartlett's *Off/On,* to youth exploitation films like Roger Corman's *The Trip* (all 1967).[37] It is telling that in *Head* this imagery becomes aligned with the image of death. One may recall Ken Kesey's assertion that "the first drug trips were, for most of us, shell-shattering ordeals";[38] or, more significantly, Timothy Leary's adaptation of the Tibetan Book of the Dead for his 1964 *The Psychedelic Experience,* a guidebook for the LSD trip.[39]

By the time that *Head* was produced, Leary had become a totemic figure within the counterculture, and references to his work saturate lyrics from the cycle of "psychedelic" rock then gaining popularity, from bands as obscure as the Third Bardo (so named after one of the stages of the "trip" that Leary describes) to the Beatles ("Tomorrow Never Knows," of course) and the Moody Blues ("Timothy Leary's Dead"). None of these, however, would pursue a connection with his work to extent that *Head* did. The stages that Leary outlines revolve around one's relationship to the self and reality games, and the liberatory ways that these relationships can be altered during the LSD experience. The first stage involves transcendence of the self, with the onset of the drug; the second, facing up to and dealing with the self; the third, return to the self, but a self that can, he wrote, be radically transformed. During the "trip," if one approaches it correctly, one's entire relationship to the self and the culture that surrounds and helps to comprise it may be altered; the consciousness can be freed from "the games that comprise 'personality.'"[40] On the way back from this journey, the consciousness will reconstitute the personality, in the process allowing one to freely choose a new identity, one that has been liberated from the deadening oppression of Establishment culture.

Head, in fact, mimics, or at least approximates, the structure and characteristics of these three stages. As Micky jumps off the bridge into a psychedelic fantasia, he does not die: he transcends. Subsequently, the film does not develop any real narrative arc, but instead follows a number of threads, digressions, wherein events may be connected only by graphic matches, or discontinuous spaces may be united by matches on action. The film departs completely from the relatively stable, conventional linear narrative structures that the television series had employed. Shortly after these opening scenes, the screen splits into twenty separate images, each shaped like a television set. "Ditty Diego," written by Rafelson and Nicholson, commences on the soundtrack to provide a primer of *Head*'s experimental structure for the viewer, and to highlight the subversiveness of that structure:

> We hope you'll like our story
> although there isn't one
> That is to say there's many
> That way there is more fun
>
> . . . .
>
> We know it doesn't matter
> 'cause what you came to see
> is what we'd love to give you
> and give it 1-2-3
> But, it may come 3-2-1-2
> or jump from 9 to 5
> And when you see the end in sight
> the beginning may arrive

Bridging all of the episodes in the film's complex, circular structure is the recurrent motif of a television set, its channels being switched. Each of the individual narrative units, however causally disconnected, are unified by thematic content. Apart from the musical sequences, each concerns the Monkees being manipulated, trapped, hunted, chased, questioned by authority, and, in the midst of all this, searching for answers, spiritual or otherwise, to their predicaments. Finally, the narrative takes us back to the bridge where we began. Only now, all the Monkees leap into the psychedelic void. As with the circular trajectory of the LSD trip, we literally return to the beginning—here, the promise of escape from constraints. Both *The Psychedelic Experience* and *Head* are concerned with freedom: one with freedom from the personality and the Establishment, and one with freedom from star personae and the image-making machine.

Leary had written that personality, in Western culture, was imposed from without, the result of the elaborate, essentially meaningless "game structure" of Western life, and that psychedelic drugs were important insofar as they provided an efficient way to cut through this mental conditioning and clear it away.[41] *Head*, however, is crucially concerned with wiping away all the manipulation, the "conditioning," that had been "imposed" on the Monkees in and through their televisual roles (though, ironically, Rafelson and Schneider retain responsibility for both the manipulation and this attempt to rid them of it). In this way, *Head* attempts to tap into the cultural discontent that fueled so much oppositional rhetoric in the late sixties.[42] A representative figure for sixties countercultural politics, Leary claimed that for any real change "the first thing you have to do is completely detach yourself from anything inside the plastic, robot Establishment."[43]

Throughout, *Head* addresses the popular conception of the Monkees as manufactured, so as to eventually contradict it with evidence of their jumping off of that bridge for good. The opening of "Ditty Diego" establishes this as a theme in the film:

> Hey, hey, we are The Monkees
> You know we love to please
> A manufactured image
> with no philosophies
>
> . . . .
>
> You say we're manufactured
> to that we all agree
> So make your choice and we'll rejoice
> in never being free
> Hey, hey, we are the Monkees
> We've said it all before
> The money's in
> We're made of tin
> We're here to give you more

The "Ditty" provides a concise version of the accusations the Monkees would direct toward themselves and their existence.

From this point, the filmmakers at once acknowledge and contradict the "no philosophies" admission. It is quite difficult to attempt to summarize the plot events in *Head*, but I will attempt to do so while recognizing that if one hasn't seen the film, this description may seem obscure. The film first goes into a parody of war dramas, followed by a concert sequence. The band plays Nesmith's "Circle Sky," a Vietnam protest song. The young female audience, however, screams nonstop throughout the song. At the song's conclusion, these fans rush the stage and tear apart the band members, who are revealed to be mannequins. On the one hand, this invokes the contempt for the young female pop fan found throughout the hippie subculture.[44] But its harshest accusations are reserved for the band themselves. The scene, like so many in the film, tries to dramatize, simultaneously, divergent responses to the Monkees' vilification: on the one hand, the mannequins seem to reinforce the criticism that the band doesn't play its own music; on the other, it features handheld camerawork (as well as superimpositions and other optical effects) which depicts an unaccompanied, musically accomplished live performance by the band playing a serious, self-written song. The scene thus both embodies and contradicts accusations that the band is "made of tin." The band is revealed to be a manufactured teen-pop act, certainly, but one that also has an acute sense of their own irrelevance in wartime: the protest lyrics of the song refer back to our first view of the screaming fans at the conclusion of the "Ditty Diego" segment, when they had been juxtaposed with the famous footage of a Vietcong soldier being shot in the head by a South Vietnamese officer. The act of making such a connection, and singing about the war, begins to correct the impression that they indeed have "no philosophies."

The filmmakers then establish the motivic image of the switching channels on the television set. This is used as a transition between some scenes, and thus at once contains the action and reinforces the film's critique of the television Monkees. Throughout the film, the Monkees will rebel against their roles as actors within the narrative of "the Monkees." The film constantly returns to the studio lot, and to meta-parodies of the genre narratives that the tv show itself had parodied. While shooting a western, for example, Micky storms off the set in disgust. Mike follows, and together they walk up the steps of a tenement past Davy, who is playing the violin for the residents. Once they get past an encounter with Lord High 'n' Low, who tries out some new marketing ideas on them to no response, they make their way to the commissary. There they find Peter, but are harassed by the waitress. Finally, the waitress punches Davy. There is a graphic match on the punch, and Davy is now inside a boxing ring; he has a flashback of himself playing the violin on the steps, an action that is now completed. This becomes part of a parody of the melodramatic cliché of the conflicted boxer whose girlfriend (played by Annette Funicello, her tears carefully dabbed on by a not-very-surreptitious makeup man) wants him to remain a violinist. In the climax of the boxing scene, Davy won't throw the fight after all. Micky, his manager, calls him a "dummy." A gangster, played by Mike, replies "No, *you're* the dummy." This provokes Micky to climb onto the stage, repeatedly yelling "I'm not the dummy!" He punches Davy, Mike, and others, knocking them out. When he is apprehended by the police, Peter appears: "*I'm* the dummy, Micky. I'm *always* the dummy." Within this narrative circle, then, are both parodies of generic conventions and of Monkees conventions themselves (Peter *is* always the dummy).

Elsewhere, they will find themselves trapped in another western (in a face-off against Lord High 'n' Low), in a Cormanesque horror film, a jungle drama, a foreign-legion drama, and, most nightmarishly, in a commercial wherein they play dandruff on Victor Mature's head, and are sucked into a "real" vacuum cleaner. The television series, too, featured parodies of genre conventions, but in *Head* the deconstruction is less lighthearted, and more cynical—e.g., the violence of the boxing scene, and the hand dabbing tears onto Annette Funicello's face. The film contains numerous asides that call our attention to the Monkees as performers. At one point, speaking to the rest of the band, whom he suspects of hiding and playing a practical joke on him, Mike says, "You think they call us plastic *now*, you wait 'til I tell them how we do it!"

The film also expands upon the "backstage" moments in the series. After Davy explains to Annette that he won't quit the fight, that they will pick the round and he will pick the fighter, he abruptly leaves the set. The camera, now handheld, its image nearly out of focus, struggles to follow him as he picks the other fighter for the scene. Later, after a scene that ends with Peter hitting the commissary waitress, there is a similar instance of a cut to a handheld camera shot, as we see Peter complain to Rafelson about the scene. Rafelson pays little attention to Peter's complaints that the action isn't "right." Nicholson confers with Rafelson, as Dennis Hopper and Peter Fonda walk past. Rafelson assures Peter that if the scene isn't right, they will cut it. Peter replies, "That's what you always say, man, and it never happens." The intrusion of jerky, handheld camerawork seems meant to cement the notion that the illusion is being broken here, and indeed such segments acknowledge the realities of the Monkees' existence more than the series ever had ("Millionaires at 25!" gloats Peter in a later scene). But, ultimately, there are limitations to the revelations on display here. This is still the same Monkees as in *The Monkees*, living together in a house on Beechwood Drive, inseparable friends. The deconstruction of their star image in *Head* is finally bound by the limits of that image, however contested. The subject of the film, then, is that contestation, and its project is to destabilize the image rather than to demolish it.

In form and subject, *Head* plays with, and blurs, the distinctions between the reality and illusion of the fiction of the Monkees. At one point, when they become trapped in a windowless black box for the second time, Peter shares the teachings of a guru whom he has just encountered, to help the others see past the limits of the box itself.[45]

> Psychologically speaking, the human mind, or brain, or whatever, is almost incapable of distinguishing between the real and vividly imagined experience. Sound and film, music and radio, even these manipulated experiences are received more or less directly, and uninterpreted, by the mind. They are catalogued and recorded, and either acted upon directly, or stored in the memory, or both. Now this process, unless we pay it tremendous attention, begins to separate us from the reality of the now.

This monologue offers yet another possible approach to the stardom dilemma, a reconciliation with manipulation and illusion. For a moment, the movie comes as close as it ever will to endorsing a single point of view, as Peter's monologue is presented with all the solemnity befitting pearls of wisdom from the Master. Yet the band's response to this is to reject it and *fight* their way out of the box, past their captors, and off the studio lot until finally they all jump off the bridge.[46] We return to the beginning here, and to the possibility of a way out of the image and the manipulation that it offers. But just when the Monkees seem to have finally escaped everyone into the psychedelic images of their ocean fantasy, they are revealed to be trapped in another box, an aquarium, under the watchful eye of Victor Mature, who plays "The Big Victor" (a reference to RCA Victor, overseas distributors of Monkees recordings).[47] Again, they are trapped by the corporate structure to which they are contracted. As the Columbia logo is shown, the film appears to slip and burn in the gate. In this final gesture, even the film's negation of the Monkees' escape is itself negated.

"Can You Dig It?"

The narrative (such as it is) of *Head* does not present a Monkees that have found their way through the labyrinth of image manipulation into a new artistic life. With no evidence of any authentic existence beyond media manipulation within the narrative of the film, one might instead look to the musical, visual, and narrational strategies embodied in the form of the film itself. The six songs used in *Head* provide a succinct representation of the musical directions the band members pursued once they had gotten control of their own output. Half of these were written by the Monkees themselves. Nesmith had written "Circle Sky," and Tork wrote "Can You Dig It?" and "Do I Have to Do This All Over Again?" The other half was composed by long-time members of their songwriting stable: Harry Nilsson wrote "Daddy's Song," while Gerry Goffin and Carole King wrote "Porpoise Song," and King and Toni Stern wrote "As We Go Along." The band had become increasingly fragmented by this point, and all were pursuing different musical directions, but each of the songs on the soundtrack represents the ambitions toward rock relevance that the entire band shared. While "Daddy's Song" was certainly consistent with the Broadway direction that Davy Jones-sung numbers always took (to match his vocal capabilities), it may also be compared to Paul McCartney's music-hall influenced compositions for the Beatles, such as "Your Mother Should Know" (Nilsson was a regular Beatle companion by this point). Peter Tork had been an aspiring folk musician prior to membership in the Monkees, and this background is evident in "Do I Have to Do This All Over Again?" Nesmith had also been a folk musician, though with rather more experience; in fact, in his pre-Monkees period, one of his compositions, "Mary Mary," had been covered by the Paul Butterfield Blues Band. But Nesmith was now moving in a country-oriented direction, and his efforts just predated the Byrds' more celebrated work on *Sweetheart of the Rodeo* (1968). Evidence of the country influence, along with a Byrds-influenced folk-rock sound, can be seen in "Circle Sky," though subsequent band efforts like "The Only Thing That I Believe Is True," "Listen to the Band," and "Good Clean Fun" would more fully prefigure the series of six country-rock albums Nesmith recorded from 1970, the year he left the band, to 1973.

The Goffin/King and King/Stern compositions, despite being Brill Building product on some level, are also very clearly part and parcel of the band's gestures toward the musical developments of their contemporaries. "Porpoise Song" was the lone single released to promote the *Head* soundtrack. Considering the band's struggle for credibility, it may seem poorly judged to release a Goffin/King composition to promote such efforts. While a band like the Byrds could use a Goffin/King for an album track with no impact on their reputation, the Monkees had relied upon such professionals throughout their recording career; another Goffin/King single would seem par for the course for a "manufactured" band. But while "Porpoise Song" is certainly a product of the mainstream pop establishment, it also demonstrates the extent to which experimental musical styles like psychedelic rock had affected the output of the record industry, and is a prime example of pop songwriters adapting to a new marketplace that had assimilated countercultural tastes and preferences.

Recorded in February 1968, the song has more in common with British psychedelia than the American San Francisco sound; the former had always been more conventionally pop-oriented in its compositional style, and generally less blues based. The track centers on a lazy organ riff, echoed vocals from Dolenz, cello and string-bass backing, with woodwinds and horns winding in and out throughout. The simplicity of the melody, use of strings against a slowed-down tempo, horns, organ, and vocal effects recalls the Beatles' 1967 "I Am the Walrus" most obviously (and, to a lesser extent, "Strawberry Fields Forever," "Blue Jay Way," and "Flying"). Simon Dupree and the Big Sound's "Kites," and in particular the Troggs' "Love Is All Around," both released in the fall of 1967, make comparable use of ballad tempos along with distant, tonally flattened, effects-laden vocals and psychedelic lyrics. The orchestration, melody, and rhythm of "Porpoise Song" can also be compared to tracks by the British band Nirvana, such as "Rainbow Chaser" and "Tiny Goddess," released the same year. Besides adapting psychedelia's musical techniques, instrumentation, and use of studio technology, "Porpoise Song" featured the kind of oblique, hallucinatory lyrical visions found throughout that genre. If anything, however, the lyrics are more easily subjected to a fully formed thematic interpretation than those of most contemporaries of Goffin, King, and the Monkees ("My, my the clock in the sky is pounding away / There's so much to say / A face, a voice, an overdub has no choice / And it cannot rejoice / Wanting to be, to hear and to see / Crying to the sky / But the porpoise is laughing good-bye, good-bye"), expressing as it does the theme of desire for an escape to freedom that resonates through so many other aspects of the film.

Of the other tracks on the album, only Tork's "Can You Dig It?" pursues a comparably psychedelic style, here with a vaguely Middle-Eastern-accented use of guitar and percussion. The lyrics here, such as the couplet "To sing that you can dig it / Is to make your summer fly" and chorus "Can you dig it? / Do you know? / Would you care to let it show?" are simpler than those of "Porpoise Song," and rather more similar to those of the majority of psychedelic numbers of the period. Like many such songs, its lyrics obliquely demonstrate a knowledge of drugs, and by doing so stake a claim for membership in a psychedelic, countercultural fraternity, and the credibility in the student marketplace that such a membership implied. In the film, Rafelson accompanies the song with visuals of the band lazing about a harem tent, watching women belly-dance, and incessantly puffing on hookahs, in case audience members had somehow ignored the lyrics entirely.

Elsewhere, Rafelson utilizes less didactic, but far more daring, visual devices to accompany the songs. In terms of visual style, I have already noted the debt owed by the visuals in "Porpoise Song" to the kind of psychedelic imagery used by the likes of Scott Bartlett and Jordan Belson. Rafelson uses polarization effects during "Porpoise Song," and later in conjunction with a party scene to accompany "Do I Have to Do This All Over Again." The visuals in this latter case resemble those used for "Porpoise Song" in both the distortion and emphasis on color, but with some differences in the mise-en-scène, camerawork, and cutting. The effects of the optical printing are altered by the use of filtered lighting and projected op-art patterns in the profilmic space. To add to the disorientation, the scene features shaky handheld camerawork and fast cutting. Certainly the visual effects of the "Porpoise Song" and "Do I Have to . . ." segments are analogous to those from the "Star Collector" and "Goin' Down" segments from the series, but in the former two, the distortion is more thorough, and the segments themselves are integrated into the flow of the narrative, not isolated in an entirely separate context. Because they must still perform some narrative function, however, the images in these scenes in *Head* retain some narrative function and realist component. In this sense, *Head*'s closest visual comparison may be to *The Trip*, a film that had used a narrative of a TV commercial director's first LSD experience as motivation for a number of optical-effects-dominated sequences. These musical sequences in *Head* not only evoke psychedelic avant-garde works, but also rock concerts. Under the influence of Ken Kesey's Acid Test and such events as the Trips Festival, more and more "hip" rock promoters like Bill Graham were incorporating elaborate lighting effects, projected film loops and op-art patterns, and the like, into the concerts of psychedelic rock bands to evoke the psychedelic effect in concert attendees.

If the visual effects in the "Porpoise Song" and "Do I Have to . . ." segments of *Head* manifest this psychedelic, experimental influence, then the narrational techniques recall art cinema. In *Head*'s highly digressive narrative action only the chase sequence at the end can be said to present a linear trajectory. This diminution of narrative as a salient component recalls David Bordwell's notion that in art cinema narrational systems are destabilized so as to create uncertainty about the status of the events. This throws the viewer into an interpretational mode, wherein the uncertainty can be resolved with reference to the figure of the author, and speculations about his or her intended "message."[48] In *Head,* the author is present literally and physically, as well as metaphorically: Rafelson can be seen allaying Peter's concerns about hitting the "waitress," and is visible shooting dancers during the birthday party scene. Some of *Head*'s symbology, as in art cinema, is assertively ambiguous. The black box, in particular, has provoked some uncertainty over interpretation. Within the film, Micky offers the notion that the box "right now represents our universe," while in later years Davy would opine that the box "represented life."[49] Patrick McGilligan reads the box as the titular "head," which represented "all the rules and straitlaced conventions inside one's head that inhibit[s] enjoyment of life."[50] Still another interpretation might see the box as representing simply the rules and straitlaced conventions of show business.

Head's absurdism and antirealism, however, resemble little else in the European art cinema (with the possible exception of Godard's work, which is typically more rigorous and materialist than anything in *Head*). Some comparisons may be made here, again, to *The Trip,* in which Nicholson and Corman extensively utilized symbolism and oneiric imagery. But the most persuasive comparisons may be found outside the realm of film entirely. In its comic tone, as well as its constant and parodic use of conventional genres, and quality of assemblage, the film resembles nothing so much as a filmic analogue of Frank Zappa's version of musique concrete. Zappa had been a long-time member of the young, countercultural Hollywood scene that had also included Rafelson and Nicholson, as well as associates like Peter Fonda and Dennis Hopper. Zappa appears in *Head* as "The Critic," a figure who leads a cow by a rope, telling Davy that he "should spend more time on [his music], because the youth of America depends on [him] to show them the way." (There is nothing sincere in his line reading.)

In *Frank Zappa: The Negative Dialectics of Poodle Play,* Ben Watson analyzes Zappa's variations on the highly edited compositions of musique concrete, in particular his emphasis on strongly contrasting blocks of sound (comparable to the Beats' cut-ups). Zappa's version of this involves a heavy use of pop song constructions. Watson asserts that "Zappa is trying to educate his listeners in the representational nature of pop music, the fact that it is a construct, not real life." Part of his mode of composition, then, involved "surprise as an aim." For Watson, Zappa's early work does not merely anticipate postmodernist pastiche, but rather, and crucially, "draw[s] attention to the material provenance of the elements." Moreover, analyzing 1968's *Lumpy Gravy,* Watson writes that Zappa's montages work by "abutting various modes of representation," thus seeking to "drama-tize their shortcomings, create dissatisfaction with limits."[51] Zappa, evi-dently unlike the Monkees, vehemently disapproved of psychedelia, and drugs in general. In fact, in 1968, the year of *Head*'s release, Zappa and the Mothers of Invention also released *We're Only In It for the Money,* an album-length attack on the psychedelic hippie counterculture. None-theless, Zappa's strategies in this period strongly resemble those used in *Head,* in particular the genre parodies and assemblage structure of both the film and the soundtrack album.[52]

The tortured reflexivity of the narrative components of *Head* interrogate and destabilize the Monkees' star image, but ultimately refuse to present an alternative. The Columbia logo may burn in the gate, but back in the diegesis, the Monkees are still being carted off in a giant aquarium. What is refused on the explicit level of story action, though, is demonstrated all over the film on the level of form. In the musical choices, the narra-tional choices, and the visual choices, the makers of *Head* paid reference to experimental developments in pop and rock music (psychedelia, mu-sique concrete) and cinema (art film, the avant-garde), and sought credi-bility within those fields by doing so. At the very least, they certainly moved past their original indebtedness to Richard Lester. In 1968 interviews, the Monkees seemed confident that precisely due to these innovations, the project would distinguish them as serious artists, and consequently win them a more serious youth audience than their old one. Just as the pub-licity for the television show had predicted, "the kids" would understand. Nesmith insisted that "our film is going to astound the world. . . . Gone is the soft-spoken, puppy dog, pattable Monkee image of yesterday. What you will see is the natural extension of where we were headed in our TV series. . . . Even the Beatles wouldn't be able to duplicate what we're doing in our film."[53] Micky would add, "It's our rebellion thing. The kids are going to love this movie because they are going to *understand* it. The adults will walk out and say, 'I wonder what that was all about?' but kids will know *exactly* what it is about. It's fast, surprising, and totally kooky. It flashes from one scene to another without any continuity. The truth is that our movie *Head* is the movie of tomorrow."[54] However great their ambitions, though, their work in *Head* would not prove enough to overcome the cultural politics so firmly in place surrounding the Monkees phenomenon.

"Do I Have to Do This All Over Again? Didn't
I Do It Right the First Time?"

Even in the context of a steep decline in the Monkees' commercial performance, the *Head* project stands out as disastrous. Its marketing probably didn't help; motivated by the Monkees' gradual commercial decline, Rafelson and John Brockman, an associate of Marshall McLuhan, concocted an advertising campaign for the film wherein the Monkees themselves would never be mentioned. Advertisements would feature only a picture of Brockman's face, along with the title.[55] Only weeks into the film's release would it be advertised as a Monkees vehicle.

This did nothing to improve its commercial fortunes. The film opened in New York in the first week of November 1968. Because the film did not open in a Broadway venue, it did not show up on *Variety*'s box-office reports until it opened in Philadelphia, Boston, San Francisco, and Los Angeles during the last week of the month. Then, its grosses were reported as between "OK" and "sad."[56] By the following week, grosses had dropped by 75 percent in LA, and 50 percent in San Francisco and Philadelphia.[57] The following week, it had all but disappeared. In fact, its performance was so poor that in mid-December Columbia rereleased it on a double bill with *The Love-Ins*, a "lurid"[58] exploitation melodrama, set in Haight-Ashbury and depicting evil hippie demagogues. While *Head* never dented the list of top box office performers, *Yellow Submarine*, released one week later, consistently came in near the top. When it emerged in December of 1968, the *Head* soundtrack became the worst-selling Monkees album to date.

A commercial flop, *Head* also failed to raise critical opinion of the band. Film reviewers maintained their view of the Monkees as prefabricated products, "ersatz Beatles." Renata Adler, in the *New York Times*, calls the film a union of "pot and advertising," writing that "the use of pre-packaged stars gives the movie a kind of brand-name respectability — like putting Jim Dooley (of the 'come on down' commercial) on display in a hashish crowd," and that the film "takes subversive styles . . . and covers them with famous mediocrities."[59] Stanley Kauffmann was the most generous of the national periodical reviewers, claiming that the film "would not exist" had it not been for the Lester-Beatles films, and that unlike the "Liverpool quartet," the Monkees are "virtually devoid of charm . . . but they are vigorous and willing."[60] Pauline Kael, on the other hand, was among the harshest, claiming that the advertising campaign suggested "some sort of turned-on movie about the drug scene," but that the movie itself was "designed for the sub-teens," and that "this is the kind of material, taken from all over, that the Monkees have already worn out on television, only much worse."

> The movie might have worked for bored kids at kiddie matinees, but the filmmakers got ambitious. The by-now standard stuff of girls squealing as pop idols perform is not even convincing when they're squealing for the Monkees, and when this is intercut with documentary footage of the suffering and horror or war, as if to comment on the shallowness of what the filmmakers are manufacturing and packaging and desperately trying to sell, the doubling up of greed and pretensions to depth is enough to make even a pinhead walk out.[61]

The fledgling rock press were no kinder. In February of 1969, *Rolling Stone* published its end-of-the-year wrap-up. "The Non-News Story of the Year Award" went to "the Monkees in general, for their record albums, their imitation-Beatles movie (*Head*) . . . and finally, for the fact that Peter Tork . . . is leaving the group . . . which news was not even carried by the trade papers, let alone the New York Times."[62]

It might have been expected that *Head*'s formal innovations would prove unsuccessful at the box office, and that their preteen fans would be unhappy enough with their psychedelicized musical directions to provide commercial support to either the "Porpoise Song" single or the *Head* soundtrack. But the film had also failed to win over their fiercest critics, who still only saw them as "imitation-Beatles." To some degree, the Monkees were unable to shake their prefabricated image. But perhaps, ironically, *Head* was too cynical and not "imitation Beatles" enough. *Head* never offered the audience a way out of the conundrum of image construction and manipulation. The Monkees never escaped within the film. The only possibility presented was in jumping off the bridge, and that finally was revealed to be an illusory escape. *A Hard Day's Night, Help!,* and *Yellow Submarine,* by contrast, innocently offer us a Beatles who are, apparently, quite genuine. The films make every effort to blur the distinctions between the performers and their star personae, offering us people who appear to be genuinely rebellious, irreverent, kind-hearted, fun-loving, etc.—in short, everything that had been the foundation of the original Monkees image, the one they later tried so persistently to destroy. The Dave Clark Five vehicle, *Catch Us If You Can,* likewise, focuses on the possibility of its heroes' escape from a life of enslavement to the image-makers, here of advertising, and while in the end that escape is not presented unproblematically, the band themselves successfully leave it all behind.

Head's cynicism does not resemble other films with countercultural themes. Other films that could be broadly construed as dealing with countercultural themes, if not necessarily explicit subject matter, present their subversive antiheroes as doomed, and therefore authentic. *Bonnie and Clyde* and *The Wild Bunch,* while period genre pieces, present outlaws who are ennobled by their fate at the hands of the corrupt and powerful. *Easy Rider,* which of course does deal with the counterculture, pursues a similar course. It depicts its lead characters as genuine heroes on some level, and while Captain America may have believed they "blew it"—though they may have ended up dead—there was a sincere romanticism to this downbeat ending. America may have killed them, but they were free and noble cowboys to the last. *Head* leaves no room for such ease of identification with heroic archetypes, no recourse to the stable ground of an American mythology of the outlaw.

"Goin' Down"

The Monkees' commercial decline and failure to win over the student audience seems to prove the inertia of star images and their resistance to such an attempt at radical alteration as *Head*. The film's failure may in part be attributed to the confusion it engendered among both the Monkees' old audience and their new target audience (prepubescents and hippies, respectively), as well as to the commercial decline that had already begun. The rejection of *Head* by the teen and collegiate audience may reveal more to us than simply that those groups could not get past who they had always thought the Monkees to be, however. The myth of authenticity that was so central to the counterculture now looks remarkably Romantic, even traditional in some ways. In refusing to grant the Monkees either a heroic escape or doomed martyrdom at the film's end, *Head* provides a critique of the counterculture's romanticism. But *Head's* brand of cynical response to the counterculture would not become commercially viable until the 1970s, with such cultural artifacts as *Fear and Loathing in Las Vegas,* Frank Zappa's later works, and indeed Rafelson's later films, including *Five Easy Pieces.* In this respect, while the film was reviled for being ersatz subversion, it may be that in fact its subversion was simply too cynical, arguably even too sophisticated, for its moment.

Notes

1. Quoted in *Monkeemania*, by Glenn A. Baker, assisted by Tom Czarnota and Peter Hogan (London: Plexus, 1986), 83
2. Bob Rafelson, in *A.F.I. Seminar on Bob Rafelson* (Glenrock, N.J.: Microfilming Corp. of America, 1977), 5.
3. Patrick McGilligan, *Jack's Life* (New York: W. W. Norton, 1994), 192.
4. Dwight Whitney, "The Great Revolt of '67," *TV Guide*, 22 September 1967, 6.
5. *Newsweek*, 24 October 1966, 102.
6. Michael Nesmith, quoted in McGilligan, *Jack's Life*, 192.
7. Baker, *Monkeemania*, 35, 37, 45, 47.
8. Aniko Bodroghkozy, "'We're the Young Generation and We've Got Something to Say': A Gramscian Analysis of Entertainment Television and the Youth Rebellion of the 1960s," *Critical Studies in Mass Communication*, June 1991, 218.
9. Lawrence Laurent, "Critics View of Hits, Misses," *Broadcasting*, 19 September 1966, 63.
10. *Television magazine*, November 1966, quoted in Bodroghkozy, 219.
11. TV review, *Variety*, 14 September 1966.
12. See, for example, *Catch Us If You Can* (1965), starring the Dave Clark Five, and later *Mrs. Brown, You've Got a Lovely Daughter* (1968), starring Herman's Hermits.
13. *Newsweek*, 24 October 1966, 102.
14. Ibid.
15. Laura Goostree, "*The Monkees* and the Deconstruction of Television Realism," *Journal of Popular Film and Television*, summer 1988, 52.
16. Ibid., 52.
17. TV review, *Variety*, 14 September 1966.
18. Newsweek, 102.
19. Leslie Raddatz, "More Fun Than . . . a Barrel of the Originals," *TV Guide*, 28 January 1967, 19, 21.
20. Robert Shelton qtd. in Greil Marcus, "Theatre of Hate," *Mojo Magazine*, July 1996, 72, 76.
21. Iain Chambers, *Urban Rhythms: Pop Music and Popular Culture* (New York: St. Martin's, 1985), 89.
22. *Rolling Stone*, 4 February 1971, 28.
23. Simon Frith, *Sound Effects* (New York: Pantheon, 1981), 72.
24. Quoted by David Fricke in "The Chimes of Freedom," liner notes to Columbia reissue of the Byrds' *Mr. Tambourine Man*, 1996.
25. McGilligan, *Jack's Life*, 187.
26. Baker, *Monkeemania*, 82–83.
27. Other such prefab bands include the likes of the Peanut Butter Conspiracy, the Rotary Connection, and the Chocolate Watchband, as well as such studio groups as the Millenium and Sagittarius.
28. Frith, *Sound Effects*, 73.

29 Dwight Whitney, "The Great Revolt of '67," *TV Guide*, 23 September 1967, 5.

30 Ibid., 7.

31 Ibid., 8.

32 Micky Dolenz quoted in Baker, *Monkeemania*, 37.

33 Ibid., 57.

34 Ibid., 74.

35 Columbia's president, Abraham Schneider, was Bert's father.

36 Baker, *Monkeemania*, 92

37 Not coincidentally, Nicholson wrote *The Trip* as well.

38 Ken Kesey, *Ken Kesey's Garage Sale* (New York: Viking, 1973), 175.

39 Timothy Leary, with Ralph Metzner and Richard Alpert, *The Psychedelic Experience: A Manual Based on the Tibetan Book of the Dead* (New York: Citadel, 1995).

40 Ibid., 12.

41 Jay Stevens, *Storming Heaven: LSD and the American Dream* (New York: Harper & Row, 1987), 158.

42 For more on 1960s countercultural rhetoric, see Todd Gitlin, *The Sixties* (New York: Bantam, 1993), and Theodore Roszak, *The Making of a Counterculture: Reflections on the Technocratic Society and Its Youthful Opposition* (New York: Doubleday, 1969).

43 Quoted in Martin A. Lee and Bruce Shlain, *Acid Dreams, The Complete Social History of LSD: The CIA, the Sixties, and Beyond* (New York: Grove Weidenfeld, 1985), 166.

44 For example, note the oft-quoted story of Ken Kesey and the Merry Pranksters' encounter with Beatles fans, found in Stevens, *Storming Heaven*, 297–98, and Tom Wolfe, *The Electric Kool-Aid Acid Test* (New York: Bantam, 1969), 178–86.

45 Possibly a reference to the black "box" constructed for the Monkees as a recreation center on the Columbia backlot.

46 In this respect, the ending of *Head* anticipates the ending of Mel Brooks's *Blazing Saddles* (1974).

47 Baker, *Monkeemania*, 94.

48 See, for example, David Bordwell, *Narration in the Fiction Film* (Madison: University of Wisconsin Press, 1985).

49 Harold Bronson, ed. *Hey Hey We're the Monkees* (Los Angeles: Rhino, 1996), 143.

50 McGilligan, *Jack's Life*, 188.

51 Ben Watson, *Frank Zappa: The Negative Dialectics of Poodle Play* (New York: St. Martin's, 1995), 43–44, 68–69, 91, 92.

52 Watson, in fact, mentions that the *Head* soundtrack album, put together by Nicholson, interweaves music and dialogue in a manner that resembles *We're Only In It for the Money*. Watson, *Frank Zappa*, 120.

53 Quoted in Baker, *Monkeemania*, 99.

54 Ibid., 99.

55 Bronson, *Hey Hey We're the Monkees*, 147.

56 *Variety*, 27 November 1968, 10.

57 *Variety*, 4 December 1968, 9.
58 Bosley Crowther, film review, *New York Times*, 19 August 1967.
59 Renata Adler, "Head," in *New York Times*, 7 November 1968, 51:1.
60 Stanley Kauffmann, "Head" review, *New Republic*, 7 December 1968, 24.
61 Pauline Kael, "Head" review, *New Yorker*, 23 November 1968, 202.
62 *Rolling Stone*, 1 February 1969, 18.

SINGING STARS

Real Men Don't Sing Ballads:
The Radio Crooner in Hollywood, 1929–1933
ALLISON McCRACKEN

Nobody can tell a man by the pitch of his voice. — Rudy Vallee, *New York Tribune,*
31 January 1932

Although historically Bing Crosby has been awarded the title of "America's
Crooner," from the years 1929 to 1931 radio crooner Rudy Vallee was not
only the nation's most famous singer but its biggest star. Vallee was the
first national star created by radio and the first performer to become a star
in all three forms of mass media: radio, records, and films. His tender,
pleading love songs, sung softly into a closely held radio microphone, defined the romantic crooner image of the day and made the term *crooning* a
household word in 1929. Vallee was largely acknowledged to be the most
popular performer since Rudolph Valentino, and, as with that other Rudy,
his female fans were credited with rocketing Vallee to stardom. Vallee's
booster clubs numbered in the thousands, and his appeal was considered
to transcend boundaries: women old and young, regardless of class, tuned
in to hear him and flocked to his live performances, causing riots at the
height of his popularity.[1] Husbands and lovers might come and go, but as
the New York periodical *The Judge* noted wryly, "Girls can just twist a knob
and they have Rudy."

For three years, Rudy Vallee enjoyed unparalleled success for a singer
and made crooning the most popular form of singing in the country. As
Vallee became more famous, however, he also began to incite public criticism. His singing's intense romanticism, its continual and invasive presence within the home circle via radio and its strong emotional effect on

9 Rudy Vallee, the golden-haired boy, in 1929. [Photo courtesy of Eleanor Vallee, and Rudy Vallee Archives, American Library of Radio and Television.]

listeners were new phenomena that many in positions of cultural authority found threatening. By the early 1930s, crooners had become the objects of widespread condemnation by critics, who referred to them most frequently as "emasculated, effeminate whiners."[2] Attacks came not only from those who associated themselves with moral leadership or "high art" forms, such as religious leaders and music critics, but from within the realm of popular culture as well. Popular songs, cartoons, and films ridiculed crooners, characterizing them as narcissistic dopes whom women would be fools to desire.

Such broadly based and intense public scrutiny seems more significant in retrospect, given that by the mid-1930s crooners like Bing Crosby, Dick Powell, and Fred Astaire were churning out so-called crooning songs by the dozens in musical films with little fuss. In a remarkably short time, crooning became an accepted and even celebrated part of American popular culture. This naturalization, however, has obscured the crooner's early controversial history, a history that reveals larger concerns about the mass media's power to define and shape social life, in this case the sound of white masculinity.

The development of mass-culture industries like radio and the motion picture had transformed the country from a production to a consumption-based economy; entrepreneurs therefore concentrated on attracting a mass rather than a class market and looked for ways to unify and assimilate the masses of immigrants. Middle-class moralists, educators, and politicians also shared the same goal, but for different reasons; they worried about protecting white (Anglo-Saxon) ideals and standards of behavior in an increasingly diverse culture. This concern resulted in increased nativism, as evidenced by the immigration quotas of the 1920s, as well as a new emphasis on identifying and promoting an "American" character in literature, history, and culture.[3] The introduction of jazz in the 1920s set off a fevered debate about what should be considered "American" music; the formation of national radio networks and the emergence of sound films in the late 1920s brought even more urgency to these discussions. When vaudeville and the record industry were crippled by the crash of 1929, radio and sound films became the primary means of entertainment for Americans and thus vehicles of extraordinary influence.[4]

In this context, the popularity of crooners became a cause for concern. Crooners challenged traditional notions of the integrity of embodied white masculinity. At a time when a white man's masculinity was defined by his physical vigor and muscularity, radio offered a disturbingly disembodied, artificially amplified male presence, one that competed with traditional patriarchal authority for the attention of the family. The fact that it was largely female listeners who supported crooners also indicated the disturbing power of this new domestic audience.[5] The intense criticism of crooners indicated the society's discomfort with having issues of cultural representation decided by the "feminine" consuming majority, although at the same time the patronage of these stars was clearly vital to the American economy. Broadcasting technology had invented a new kind of male performer in the radio crooner, one whose popularity and influence necessitated a renegotiation of white masculinity that would address objections to the crooning voice while continuing to satisfy an increasingly heterogeneous consumer base.

Hollywood was eager to capitalize on the popularity of crooners during the costly transition to sound film without taking on crooning's critics, and it is Hollywood, I will argue here, that was eventually able to mitigate the threat posed by the disembodied radio crooners. The early short films of Bing Crosby, specifically, became the key site of negotiation; through them, Hollywood was able to forge an acceptably masculine crooner persona that retained enough qualities of the crooning voice to satisfy both critics and the public. My examination of Rudy Vallee and Bing Crosby's early films traces the development of the "sound" of white masculinity through the figure of the radio crooner — from Vallee's woman-made, radio-born star and Crosby's movie playboy to the crooning everyman that Crosby would become. This period of transition is crucial because the gender codes established for sound and image in these few years do much to determine the evolution of both American popular song and the American musical film through the classical period and beyond.

Muscles vs. Microphones: The Development of Male Popular Singing

Singing is healthful; it develops the lungs and purifies the blood by emptying the lungs more completely of used air and filling them deeply with fresh air. . . . Singing increases poise and self-confidence, and develops character through difficulties overcome. — American Academy of Teachers in Singing, "Reasons for Studying Singing," 1931

Back in the 1920's, lads — or even grown up men — who sang with bands did so at the risk of having their manhood suspected. It was a time when tennis players or men who wore wrist-watches were given the hand-on-hip and the burlesque falsetto-voice routine. — Bing Crosby, *Call Me Lucky*, 1953

As scholars like Gail Bederman, John Higham, and Gaylyn Studlar have argued, traditional white Protestant masculinity took a "defensive stance" during the period from 1880 to 1920.[6] Because of the increasing occupation of traditionally male public space by women and immigrants, white middle-class men needed to distinguish themselves from others in ways that were no longer simply spatial or institutional but physical; white masculinity needed to be defined as a physical attribute, identifiable on the body.[7]

Middle-class singing was constructed along similar masculine and moral lines during this period. Singing manuals clearly define the purpose of singing as "healthful exercise." According to the American Academy of Teachers in Singing, singing should not be primarily for enjoyment or as a means of personal expression, but for the pleasure and erudition of others. It should first be thought of not as an art or entertainment form but as a way to preserve one's physical and emotional well-being through the productive and controlled "release" of the singer's "pent up emotions." Like other forms of exercise, singing was supposed to make one mentally and physically healthy and morally good. Singing is described in these manuals very much like a sport, an activity one can master that will develop "strong muscles."[8]

The middle class emphasized and defined "principles of singing" for the same reasons it so defined white masculinity—namely, as a way of protecting white social dominance against cultural homogenization. Nevertheless, this period in American music saw the collapse of distinctions between "high" and "low" forms and the creation of new forms of popular song that combined elements of both. As popular song became more accessible to larger groups through simplified lyrics and melodies and deemphasized ethnic content, it also became increasingly star driven, sexually suggestive, and emotionally charged.

Tin Pan Alley publishers, who had begun to dominate the industry before the turn of the century, offered audiences a more homogenous style of music than ever before.[9] Its second generation of songwriters, mostly Jewish immigrants best typified by Irving Berlin, were influenced by vaudeville's ethnic songs; as a result, the moral lessons of popular middle-class ballads from the late nineteenth century like "After the Ball" (Harris, 1894) and "She's Just a Bird in a Gilded Cage" (Von Tilzer, 1900) began in the early years of the twentieth century to give way to the more permissive tone and lyrics of vaudeville novelty songs, creating a new genre of popular song that celebrated the glamour and excitement of big city life, including its romantic and erotic possibilities.[10]

Increased homogenization in popular entertainment meant that urban, ethnic entertainment would impact the middle class, and vice versa. For example, the increased presence of middle-class women in vaudeville audiences accounted for the increased centrality of the romantic ballad and the presence of solo male singers. Historically women fans had been especially devoted to male opera tenors and blackface ballad singers, but these men had always been parts of ensemble casts, and female audiences a minority.[11] Vaudeville changed this situation by combining individual musical attractions, revue-style, in an attempt to offer something for everyone. Vaudeville entrepreneurs who wanted to attract a "family" audience especially catered to women. Because ballad singers were sold as individual acts, their popularity with women was more significant to their success. At the same time that the Boy Scouts were urging boys to lead the "strenuous" outdoor life and build their muscles,[12] ballad singing positioned boys and young men as objects of desire for vaudeville audiences. The ballad singer's youth, innocence, and beauty could be emphasized in their presentations because blackface was not a factor. There was thus a new directness about the relationship between audience member and performer that had not been possible before, and which set the stage for crooners' mass reception as objects of desire.[13]

While crooning has its roots in Tin Pan Alley's homogenized music and vaudeville singers, it was most directly a product of the microphone age and jazz, specifically white "sweet" or "syncopated" jazz. The first singers to be widely known as "crooners" were "sweet" jazz dance band leaders like Rudy Vallee and Will Osborne or band singers like Bing Crosby. By the mid-1920s, jazz bands and jazz-inspired dances like the fox-trot were the nation's most popular entertainment and also sources of great controversy. The "strong feelings" jazz provoked in its audiences were associated with the emotional and sexual excesses of black culture, and therefore considered morally degenerate by the dominant culture.[14] The biggest male singing stars of this time were minstrel singers like Al Jolson and Eddie Cantor, Jewish singers who used blackface as a way to express intense emotion without being stigmatized for it.[15] This situation began to change, however, as jazz band crooners became increasingly popular.

Music historian Will Friedwald cites the years between 1925 and 1935 as marking a "gradual transformation of singers and their public. The evolution of vocal music pivoted upon the development of the jazz influenced dance band, and the two forms grew up as non-identical twins in the jazz family." Friedwald argues that while black orchestra leaders were the great innovators in music, white bandleaders originated the use of band singers.[16] These singers were not originally regarded as important players in a dance band and certainly not as stars themselves. Bandleaders wanted to develop their names through their music and star musicians, not through their singers. Like the Broadway shows of this period, jazz bands emphasized dancing over singing; Andre Millard claims that at this time all recorded jazz was meant for dancing.[17] In the early to mid-1920s, singers appear to have been regarded as a necessary evil to "sweet" bandleaders, who wanted to focus more on musicianship than on vocalizing. However, since music publishers at that time made most of their money from sheet music sales rather than records, they found singers valuable for popularizing the lyrics of songs.[18]

Band singers were therefore most often employed for recording rather than for performing songs before live audiences.[19] In fact, when Bing Crosby and his partner Al Rinker joined Paul Whiteman's orchestra in 1926, they were used primarily as backup singers for the musicians. According to Friedwald, Crosby and Rinker may have been the first full-time

band singers hired in the business, since "the mere act of signing someone who did nothing but sing seemed strange enough in those days."[20] In
his autobiography, *Call Me Lucky*, Crosby notes that he didn't get a solo
with the band for months, and Whiteman tried to disguise the fact that
he and Rinker were only singers by having them hold instruments "so the
audience wouldn't wonder why we were doing nothing."[21]

The band singer was an awkward presence. A man who did "nothing"
but croon into a microphone in the natural, easy fashion of these singers
had the potential to undermine the standards of white masculinity established by a band's hard-working, professionally trained musicians (even
Jolson worked up a sweat when he sang).[22] Yet by the late 1920s, band
singers were becoming popular attractions in their own right, the result
primarily of advances in recording technology. Three technical developments are crucial to the advent of the crooner of the late 1920s: amplification, the microphone, and electronic recording. Amplifiers, developed
during the 1910s, made it possible to magnify weak signals without significant distortion.[23] The sensitive condenser microphone (a word that literally
means "small sound") appeared in 1922; it helped give clarity and smoothness to the singer's voice while further reducing the noise level or distortion.[24] Finally, the development of electrical as opposed to acoustic recording in 1924–25 made it possible to reproduce the range and complexity
of sounds heard by the human ear much more accurately. These advances
fundamentally changed popular singing, making it possible for soft or untrained singers to be heard over large distances while conveying a much
more conversational and intimate tone than had been heard before in performance. That sound soon became commonly known as "crooning."[25]

Previously, the term *crooning* had been used only to refer to characters in
popular songs who "crooned" to *each other*. A singer could not "croon" until
technology made it unnecessary for singers to project their voices. The
first use of the term *crooning* in American popular song is in minstrelsy,
used from the late nineteenth century onward to describe mammies who
"crooned" to their charges (like the one made famous by Al Jolson in his hit
song "Rock a Bye Your Baby with a Dixie Melody"). By the 1910s, the term
had moved beyond minstrel music and was used to describe the romantic
way lovers sang to each other. When microphone technology permitted the
live embodiment of the crooner, the first singer to be called such was radio
singer Vaughn DeLeath, a generously proportioned white woman with a
motherly, asexual persona. She had more in common with the crooning
mammy of minstrel songs than a romantic lead, and thus her soft, inti-

mate singing style did not elicit the strong emotions that the male crooners who followed her would.[26]

In its etymology as in many other ways, crooning represented a major shift in popular music. Crooning songs were sung largely by "unmarked" white jazz band singers, depended more on technology than any previous song style, were mass marketed through radio and records, and exemplified the new homogenized popular song: crooning combined the intense romanticism of the high-class ballad, the amorality of the vaudeville novelty song, the emotionalism of minstrelsy, and the sensuality and accessibility of jazz. This new sound was the beginning of what we now think of as "classic pop," but at the time its singers were considered embarrassingly feminine, not only because of their emotional intensity but because of the smallness and the softness of the sounds they made.[27] It is not surprising, therefore, that these singers were initially marginalized within their bands.[28]

Even so, crooners became enormously popular during the late 1920s when the demand for singers grew as a result of radio, sound pictures, and the burgeoning record industry. All three of these industries utilized electronic reproduction of sound, and crooning best suited the new technology. "Sweet" band crooners Dick Powell and Gene Austin and vaudeville singers "Whispering" Jack Smith and Cliff Edwards (who were now labeled "crooners" because of their soft singing styles) swiftly became star attractions and their recordings began to sell as well as those of stars like Al Jolson.[29] It wasn't until crooners began to take over radio, however, that they became the focus of wide public concern.

Radio crooning was different from these earlier instances of male singing in a number of ways, not the least of which was that it erased everything except the sound of the voice. In previous performance contexts, male singers could rely on certain signifiers to mitigate the emotionalism of a particular song and thus protect them from charges of effeminacy: masculine banter with band members, the use of blackface, or a focus on dance or the playing of an instrument rather than the lyrics of a song. In addition, the physical fact of the performing space and the presence of the audience in a nightclub, Broadway theater, or a vaudeville house also diverted attention away from the performer and the sound of his voice. Radio crooners created a new intimacy with their listeners by evaporating these physical boundaries. With no band to mitigate their small sound and literally nobody to ensure some kind of masculine presence, these crooning voices began to provoke much more intense reactions from their fans and detractors.

The Rise and Fall of Rudy Vallee, 1929–1932

Rudy Vallee has become a national figure and in some respects, almost a national problem—the joy of the wife, the despair of the husband, the idol of the flapper and the envy of the young man.—*The Radio Revue,* December 1929

After the crash of 1929, radio became the premier source of popular music, and therefore the most important source of revenue for the music industry.[30] National radio networks formed during the late 1920s, creating the possibility for the establishment of national radio stars. The first such star was crooner Rudy Vallee, whose New York broadcasts in 1928 and 1929 became so popular that he was given his own national program on NBC, sponsored by Fleischmann's Yeast. It debuted in October of 1929 and was an immediate sensation.

Although Vallee was not the first radio crooner, he was the most famous and he epitomized the crooner image of his day. Vallee's nightclub performances already had made him stand apart from other crooners because he was his band's leader as well as its singer: he made the crooner the central figure of the band. Like "sweet jazz" bandleaders, he was very much interested in making jazz a mass, democratic art form, but he differed from most in that he privileged the "democratic" over the "art." Vallee was a calculating crowd-pleaser; he fashioned his nightclub programs to address particular audiences and relied on their feedback in making decisions about what to play. He was especially concerned about "pleasing the ladies," and felt that "a woman's likes and dislikes are always to be considered first."[31] Since romantic ballads pleased his audiences, Vallee worked to infuse his songs with however much "emotion and feeling" the lyrics seemed to warrant, and he sang mainly choruses so the words would be easier for his listeners to remember.[32] He focused on giving each note "the idea of fullness and sustained tone," making the emotion in his songs resonate even longer, and he was one of the first crooners to emphasize the use of vibrato to express emotion in popular song. Vallee adapted the "live vibration" he could make with his saxophone to his vocal instrument, and found that it was particularly effective in conveying emotional involvement.[33] Crooning, as Vallee defined it, was high pitched, breathy, and intense; in structure, Vallee's crooning songs reflected the accessible melody and simple language of the homogenized popular ballad as well as the syncopated rhythm of the "sweet" jazz tune.

Most significantly for his fans, Vallee gave the voice sex; he held the microphone close to him and yearned into it. Radio pluggers put it more bluntly, calling him "the guy with the cock in his voice."[34] He took advantage of radio's "intimate" potential and redefined radio's domestic space as a romantic, sexualized space. Where Al Jolson was declarative, Vallee was insinuating. His songs, like those of other crooners of his day, spoke longingly of love desired, love unrequited, love supreme. Crooning songs from this period generally are very distinctive because traditional gender roles are redefined; although men still desire women, it is the crooners who are portrayed as passive and their girls as aggressive. The crooner is most often dependent on his love, melancholy and hopeless. What is unique to the early male crooner is that he is not suspicious of his love while she is with him, and he does not blame her if she leaves. In fact, crooning songs revere the independent woman and frequently idealize her in their lyrics, offering defenses of her behavior to her supposed critics.[35]

Crooners' lyrics often refer to their own tears and depict themselves as constantly crying, excessively emotional: "For all these years I've cried out my heart in tears without measure, but with you to treasure, I'm living in dreams." The lyrics are romantic in standard cliché ways, with frequent references to "dreams," "gardens," and "flowers," again references more associated with women than men: "I'll spend all my hours arranging fragrant flowers—then I'll be reminded of you."[36] By appearing both to desire young women and identify with their feelings, crooners defied traditional masculine norms and allied themselves with the cultural and social feminine.

What is most sexually suggestive and characteristic of crooning songs is that crooners can't quite reach the higher notes; the effort is almost too much for them and they seem constantly on the verge of expiring, always on the edge of attainment (always, therefore, on the brink of orgasm). In fact, what Vallee's live audiences found most exciting about him was that "he closes his eyes when he sings," suggesting that he is so overcome with emotion he cannot remain conscious.

Press coverage of Vallee tried to mitigate his passivity by suggesting that he was simply an adolescent, in much the same way as the boy vaudeville singers, a "boy" who had not yet achieved "mature" (phallic) sexuality. In profiles of Vallee, he is constantly referred to as a "boy" or a "youth"; he's a Peter Pan figure, a college boy, a playboy with blond curly hair and deep blue eyes. He's the antithesis of muscular masculinity; his "softness," gentleness, and passivity are constantly emphasized with derision in the press, and with adoration by his fans. *Literary Digest* reports that women prefer to see Rudy relaxed, for "in repose, he's more enchanting than ever," and *Outlook* equates his effect with the "joys of a plate of fudge."[37]

For his fans, Vallee indeed provided a kind of erotic and romantic pleasure that was forbidden because it wasn't procreative, not vaginal sex; it
did not require a "real man." As Miriam Hansen writes regarding Valentino's appeal, "It's a different kind of sexuality, different from the norm of
heterosexual, genital sexuality." Like Valentino, Vallee "articulated the possibility of female desires outside of motherhood and family."³⁸ But Vallee
was an even more valuable and significant figure because he privatized
mass entertainment for women, giving them access to these urban pleasures within their own homes for the first time.³⁹

At first, the film industry was primarily interested in capitalizing on
Vallee's appeal to women as a "novelty," the radio crooner. Vallee's film
appearances were clearly meant to appeal to women, framing him as a
romantic love interest for them alone. In 1929, he appeared in two Vitaphone musical shorts, *Radio Rhythm* and *Rudy Vallee and His Connecticut
Yankees,* had a cameo appearance in the Ziegfeld Follies variety film *Glorifying the American Girl,* and played the lead role in *The Vagabond Lover,* a
film meant to capitalize on the popularity of his song "I'm Just a Vagabond
Lover." What's remarkable about these roles, and what makes them different from Crosby's short films a couple of years later, is that they in no
way attempt to establish Vallee as a film actor; they instead attempt to reproduce the effects of his radio and concert performances. *Radio Rhythm,*
for example, begins with a close-up of a young woman caressing the radio
dial while the broadcast voice promises her that "for the next few minutes,
you will be entertained by Rudy Vallee and His Connecticut Yankees." The
girl smiles as the camera closes in on the initials "RV" on the radio, and
the screen fades to Vallee and his band, suggesting that Vallee is inside the
radio itself and therefore associating him with radio rather than film as a
medium. In *Glorifying,* Vallee has a bit part as himself and is framed by
a theatrical stage, in what's meant to be a Ziegfeld Follies show. Both appearances do nothing to mitigate his highly emotional presentation style,
thus reinforcing current attitudes toward the singer.

Vallee's first dramatic role did little to change this pattern. In *The Vagabond Lover,* released in December 1929, Vallee plays a would-be jazz bandleader who achieves success as a crooner and sings his way into the heart
of a middle-class girl, played by Sally Blane. Although he's called "Rudy
Bronson" here, Vallee is playing himself, and he performs a number of
his well-known ballads. Although today we would probably label the film
a "romantic comedy," *Vagabond Lover* lacks the snappy pace and witty dialogue that came to be associated with this genre in the 1930s. It is remarkably slow paced, and more romantic and melodramatic than comic; while

the story involves a case of mistaken identity (Vallee takes on the persona of a famous bandleader to avoid arrest), it is played for pathos rather than comedy. For example, Rudy feels immensely guilty that the girl he loves believes him to be someone else; at one point, after singing to her about how happy he would be if they could be together forever, he bursts out with "I've just got to tell you the truth!" There is a gravity in his performance and in the general tone of the film that suggests the lovers' depth of feeling and emotional vulnerability toward one another.[40] Vallee's love scenes with Blane are lengthy and slow paced; they always involve long takes of Vallee holding her hands, singing a love song to her while she gazes at him, her breathing heavy and her eyes full of tears. In these scenes, Vallee is the object of Blane's adoration; she is given the only close-ups in the scene and we are, therefore, encouraged to view Vallee through her eyes. These scenes also privilege Vallee's voice over his body, thus referencing Vallee's radio persona. As in his short film appearances, Vallee is not given any close-ups, and he is not a man of action; his body remains perfectly still so the audience can focus on the movement of his voice.[41]

Critics received *The Vagabond Lover* as a woman's film, made to capitalize on Vallee's appeal to women but having little crossover appeal. Critics felt that Vallee was a wooden actor and most of them were unable to understand his popularity. The reviewer for *Variety*, for example, acknowledges that "New York gals, young and old, are nuts over this boy" but claims to be mystified as to why and finds it difficult to evaluate the film because of it: "Who can figure the feminine tangent? They threw flowers at him at the Riverside [a vaudeville theater]. So, upon that deduction, this release classifies as an oddity."[42] As Vallee's popularity intensified with the release of the film, he went from being an "oddity" to being widely referred to in the press as "the Vallee Peril," and attacks on his masculinity began in earnest.

The first well-documented complaint registered against crooners occurred when a male student threw a grapefruit at Rudy Vallee during a 1931 concert. In his 1962 autobiography *My Time Is Your Time*, Vallee said he recognized at the time that the attack had come because "my vocalizing had been lacking in virility and masculinity."[43] However, his significance as a national figure is reflected in the prestige of the attackers who took up the student's cause. In a much publicized address in January 1932, Cardinal O'Connell of Boston attacked the effeminacy of the crooner and objected to the song style's sexual implications: "Crooners make the basest appeal to sex emotions in the young. Their songs are not true love songs; they profane the name. They are ribald and revolting to true men. No true American would practice this base art."[44] The New York Singing Teachers

Association agreed, calling crooning "debased" and "a corrupter of youth" because "its devitalized tone robs the voice of its ability to express higher emotions and deprives it of its inherent devotional quality."[45] They also felt crooning was detrimental to the vocal "instrument," the first of several equations of crooning with the dangers of masturbation.

The potential threat of radio crooners was even more substantial than that of previous stars because their virility could not be as easily attacked as actors whose bodies were continually on display. Crooners are defined by their intimacy with the microphone and hence with their listeners, who largely inhabit private rather than public spaces. Crooning is untrained, natural sounding, jazz influenced, and therefore unpredictable in contrast to the "good and even tone, correct enunciation and expression" of the trained singer.[46] Most significantly, crooning is constructed as a means of personal expression for the singer, and a means of emotional involvement and identification on the part of the individual listener. The crooner's purpose is not to enlighten but to move and arouse, and, far from being unselfishly motivated, is a product of his own supposed emotional need and desire for sexual pleasure. The crooner's autoeroticism is what most separates him from embodied, public performers. He is not directly working for the approval of an audience through exhaustive physical labor. Instead, the crooner persona is relaxed, passive, at play, acting on instinct, spending his emotions for his own pleasure instead of working for the money. Crooners are deviants because their suggested sexualization of the body indicates a lack of emotional and physical control, which strikes at the heart of standards of masculinity ("no true American"). It also clearly connects them with sexually uncontrolled blacks and immigrants whose "spending" in terms of reproduction does not increase property and is, indeed, a drain on the welfare of the state and a threat to white racial purity.

The crooner's dependence on technology was disturbing to a male public not equally able to artificially amplify its virility. While Vallee's lack of sexual aggression was very appealing to women, his male critics clearly felt threatened by the sexual competition, continually situating the debate in terms of sexual virility and size. Significantly, the voice is made the sexual signifier in place of the absent body in these attacks. Critics claimed that crooners had small, almost nonexistent voices. Colin O'More, a program supervisor for CBS, reported in *The Musician* that crooners in fact "have no voices," that they were solely the products of amplification: "In the studio, they are actually inaudible."[47] Crooners' use of technology made it possible for disembodied men to have more sexual power and effect on women than "real men."

While crooning represents an important step in the homogenization of American music, the preceding argument suggests that it must also be seen as culturally disruptive. Vallee and other national crooners appropriated and erased other kinds of singing styles over the airwaves, including more local ethnicity-based singers and black singers. I would argue, however, that given their open identification with typically feminized, passive positions, these early crooners actually did represent an alternative white masculinity and a more inclusive music form than has been recognized. This singing style was genuinely disturbing to many; its threat is perhaps most evident in the way in which crooning was culturally reconfigured and contained through the persona of Bing Crosby.[48]

Crosby and Containment, 1932–1933

Popular singing can quite literally be divided into two periods: B.C. and A.C.: Before Crosby and After Crosby.—Larry Carr, singer and record producer, quoted in *Discovering Great Singers of Classic Pop,* 1991

Bing Crosby has won more fans, made more money than any entertainer in history. Today he is a kind of national institution.—*Life Magazine,* June 1945

While Vallee's crooner has been historically remembered as a "transitional figure," Crosby is remembered as "America's Crooner," the defining male singer of his time. In 1931, however, Crosby's persona was very much that of the playboy crooner and his career, like Vallee's, was also threatened by public attacks on his masculinity. Within a couple of years, though, both Crosby's singing and his public image had changed in ways that made him seem acceptably masculine. A growing public perception formed that crooning could become a "truly American art form" and a big money maker for the radio, music, and film industries if its more unsettling aspects, especially its links with masturbation and effeminacy, could be eliminated.

In 1931, Crosby hardly seemed like a good bet. He had become a star that summer with the release of his first short film, *I Surrender, Dear* (made in part to promote his hit single by the same name) and debuted his nightly fifteen-minute radio program on CBS that fall. But his public image was controversial. He missed the debut of his New York radio show because of his drinking, and he was regarded in the industry as unstable. His widely publicized marriage to Fox star Dixie Lee in September of 1930 was in trouble by March 1931, when she left him in a shower of publicity, charg-

10 Bing Crosby, the
playboy crooner, at CBS.
[Author's collection]

ing "mental cruelty." Although Dixie eventually returned to him (in part,
apparently, to help his career), Crosby was very vulnerable to the attacks
on crooners in 1931; by 1932, however, his image had begun to undergo
significant change.

During the attacks on crooners, Crosby denied that he was one. Instead, Crosby tied his type of singing to public rather than private space:
"I wish I could croon . . . it would be a lot easier on my throat than the
way I sing now. I tried it once or twice—in private—when I had a throat
breakdown, but I was not satisfied with it."[49] He also tried to distance
himself from crooning by suggesting that his own work ethic was properly in place; no slacker Crosby, he argued that crooning was easy but his
singing took real "work"; it was not masturbation. Crosby's repertoire and
style of singing also changed; although he sang romantic songs with pleading crooner lyrics during the early 1930s ("Please," "I Surrender, Dear"),
Crosby lowered the pitch of his crooning songs in 1931 and did not visibly
strain to reach high notes as those before him had done.[50] He also sang
in a more noticeably jazz-influenced manner; he "scatted" and whistled
during his songs rather than emphasizing his vibrato, and his early record-

ings are more improvisational than Vallee's. Most importantly, Crosby's performances were far less emotionally intense than those of Vallee.

Crosby also began recording and performing other types of popular music in addition to crooning ballads: folk songs, nostalgic minstrel tunes, hymns and popular songs that spoke on behalf of the common (white) man, most notably the huge hit "Brother Can You Spare a Dime?" (1932). "Dime" became an anthem to unemployed men of the 1930s and its success proved that crooning could have valuable crossover appeal to a male audience. The changes in Crosby's musical repertoire are largely credited to music producer Jack Kapp, of Decca Records. Crosby worked with Kapp on and off from 1931, and he moved permanently from the Brunswick to the Decca label in 1934. Kapp believed that Crosby could be a type of "musical everyman," and he encouraged him to sing a variety of different types of music in an attempt, as Will Friedwald suggests, to "turn him into all things for all people."[51]

Well-publicized changes in Crosby's private life also served to distance him from his playboy crooner image. His marriage stabilized and the birth of his first child, Gary, in 1933, established him as a "family man"; his virility and masculinity were no longer in question.[52] Profiles of Crosby from that point on, although they emphasize his "boyish" appearance, portray him as a devoted husband and father who, unlike Vallee, enjoyed traditionally male pursuits such as sports, horseracing, fishing, and making money.[53] One immediate result of the changes in Crosby's image and the general worry about crooning's effeminacy was that Crosby's fans increased: booster club members largely switched their allegiance from Vallee to Crosby in 1932, claiming that "he is more masculine."[54] The politics of the Depression supported notions of a democratic song style which would bond white men from different classes by reinforcing rather than challenging their traditional masculine roles, and Crosby began to be seen more and more as the standard-bearer of the new American popular song.

Although Crosby is chiefly thought of as a singer, his crooner persona is a product of both the radio and film industries. Unlike Vallee, whose disembodied, bedroom voice paralyzed listeners across the country, Bing Crosby caused no such shock when he began his radio career. His persona had already been narrativized by Hollywood, chiefly through a series of film comedy shorts he made for Mack Sennett between 1931 and 1933 and his first feature film, *The Big Broadcast*. The Mack Sennett shorts are very different from Vallee's early film work as star spectacle.[55] Crosby's persona on radio was almost nonexistent when he began his film work, since he did not have his own program until the fall of 1931. He was known chiefly for being a member of the Rhythm Boys, as well as a few recordings and his nightclub appearances at the Coconut Grove in Los Angeles. While Vallee's film appearances suggest a radio singer on film, a spectacle that does not fit easily into conventional narrative forms, Crosby made his name in film as a comedian as well as a crooner.

Unlike *The Vagabond Lover*, Crosby's "crooner-gets-girl" romantic comedy shorts emphasize comedy over romance. He does not begin his film career playing the romantic leading man; his love scenes are rarely played for pathos and are much faster paced than similar scenes in the Vallee film. Crosby's films also forgo the emotional connection of the central couple and the centrality of the ballad in favor of lots of action and familiar comic characters and situations: madcap heroines, car chases, cross dressers, zoo animals, and, especially, "sissy" men. The presence of the "sissy" is especially vital to Crosby's persona, and marks an important difference from Vallee; in *The Vagabond Lover*, all the other male characters are more "masculine" than the sensitive Vallee. In Crosby's films, the more effeminate men buttress Crosby's own masculinity, making him the obvious choice for the desired girl's affection without his actually having to make love to her or, indeed, display any of the crooner's characteristic emotional vulnerability toward women. Crosby's short films typically contain at least two "sissy" men, one the friend of Crosby who helps him win the girl, the other his rival (usually played by familiar 1930s "sissy" actor Frank Pangborn). While Crosby defeats his rival through wit and brains rather than physical strength, because his rival is a sissy, there is no need for Crosby to physically prove himself the more masculine of the two.

These early films do not abandon the identifying characteristics of the crooner so much as they reframe and reshape them through comedy and Crosby's more confident, aggressive persona. Unlike the passive Vallee, the object of women's affections, Crosby is the active pursuer of the women in his films; he's the confident playboy who picks up women easily and uses his singing as a way to seduce rather than romance them. Unlike Vallee's crooner, Crosby's attachment to particular women is competitive and possessive rather than romantic; he is emotionally much less vulnerable than Vallee, and he enjoys figuring out how to get a girl away from her fiancé or overprotective parent. In *I Surrender, Dear*, the first of these short films, Crosby is described as a "masher" on three separate occasions, and the description fits; although these films typically end in marriage, this denouement seems more a convention than any sense of commitment or intense desire on Crosby's part. Crosby does not seem to really need (much less love) the women he pursues, nor do they in turn seem as attached to him as Sally Blane was to Vallee in *Vagabond*.

In addition, Crosby's characters do not identify with the traditionally feminine point of view about love affairs; even the performances of his ballads in these shorts rarely involve his singing directly to his girl. The romanticism of Crosby's ballads is instead mitigated by sight gags involving radio broadcasts of the song or by Crosby's own slapstick performance of them. In *I Surrender, Dear*, for example, Crosby makes fun of his own rendition of "You Came out of Nowhere" when it comes on the radio, suggesting the silliness of the sentimental song and its emotional excess. While Vallee pokes fun at masculinity in his performances, it is femininity that gets ridiculed in Crosby's films, the most obvious indication of this being the frequent use of cross-dressing men as comic elements in these films.

Yet the tensions between the Vallee and Crosby crooner are subtler and more playful in Crosby's early films than they will be later in his career. While these short films posit a masculinity much more in keeping with traditional gender roles, Crosby's crooners are hardly moralists, and they come down solidly on the side of sexual freedom and high spirits versus parental authority and social convention. The crooner is allied with the impulsive youth of the jazz age, with the college kids who celebrate mass culture over high culture and are optimistic about the future. The frivolity and hopeful tone of these shorts does much to undercut Crosby's emotional blankness and the hints of homophobia and misogyny in their narratives: a cross-dressing college boy, for example, pairs up happily with Crosby's sissy pal at the end of *Billboard Girl* instead of being punished for his gender deviance. The variety of attitudes toward gender represented in these films reflects in part the instability of the film industry's position on the representation of gender during the transitional period after the dawn of sound and before the Production Code, as well as, in a larger sense, instabilities in public attitudes as a result of the Depression.

This uncertainty regarding proper gender norms is especially evident in Crosby's first full-length feature film, the lively and popular musical satire of radio broadcasting, *The Big Broadcast*. Because it was made during this transitional period, this film offers a portrait of the radio crooner that is more complex and interesting than later films. In *Big Broadcast*, Crosby plays himself as a drunk, undependable radio crooner (a characterization that mirrored his real life situation). His first scene encapsulates perhaps better than any other the publicized appeal of the radio crooner for women; as Crosby steps out of his taxi, young and old women begin shouting "Bing!"; they then surround him and tear at his clothes. When he finally makes it to the studio microphone, his face is covered with lipstick, his clothes are torn, and he has only enough energy in him to barely get out the words "I Surrender, Dear." Women's adulation of Crosby is shown to be as widespread within the studio as outside of it; the telephone operators and secretaries are equally infatuated with Bing, whose lack of responsiveness is attributed to his drunken bewilderment rather than a lack of interest in women. In fact, we soon learn Bing is happily in love with an ambitious young woman named Mona Low (Sharon Lynne), and he has paid little attention to his work because he is so excited about their impending marriage.

In these first few scenes, Crosby's crooner has much in common with the crooner so despised by critics. He has a poor work ethic, he drinks, and he is more interested in love and romance than he is in earning a living. At the same time he is much more friendly and generous than the masher-crooner of the short films; after his radio performance at the film's beginning, he goes immediately to a local bar, where he meets and befriends a Texas oilman who has just been jilted by his girl. Stuart Erwin, who plays the oilman here, is another of Hollywood's best-known sissy actors, and his presence is in keeping with the Crosby crooner as developed in the film shorts. But Crosby's relationship with Erwin in the *Big Broadcast* is much more complicated than in the short films. The friendship he forms with Erwin is mutually affectionate and respectful. In fact, after Crosby finds out that his own girl has jilted him, the two friends decide to go home together. There, after an aborted suicide pact, they decide that they are both through with women and they plan instead to live together, looking at women as "only the toys of an idle hour." After spending the night on their side-by-side twin beds, Erwin gets up and offers to make breakfast, already the good wife to Crosby's crooner. In this and in many other instances throughout the rest of the film, Erwin's character performs routine "sissy" shtick: he puts on women's clothes by mistake, he indicates a degree of knowledge of women's clothes unusual for a man, and he fusses over Crosby.

What makes Crosby's relationship with Erwin in this film different from his films before and after it is the mutual affection and caring the two men exhibit for each other. The same comic business that in Crosby's later films will be used to ridicule "sissy" men in a very mean-spirited way (most obviously in Crosby's "Road" pictures with Bob Hope), is here made much more complex because of the emotional bond between the two men. They are in no way competitive with each other. When they become involved in a love triangle with an office secretary, played by Leila Hyams (she loves Crosby, Erwin loves her, Crosby is fond of both), it is remarkable how affectionate and generous they all are toward each other. They agree to all remain friends ("one for all and all for one") rather than hurt each other. At one point, Crosby even promises to get Erwin a job at the studio where the other two work "so we can be together, pal." The triangle continues to get more complex, as Hyams realizes she is attracted to both men in different ways, while they try to find ways of making the other happy without hurting her.

The Big Broadcast is unique among crooning films because it was made as attacks on crooners were just beginning. Although it reproduces the situations that most worried crooning's critics—the crooner's effeminacy and his poor work ethic—it complicates them in unexpected ways. While the film clearly allies the crooner with effeminacy in the pairing of Erwin and Crosby, it also attempts to reassure the audience that Crosby is still a man's man despite his voice. An exchange between Erwin and Hyams makes this point plain:

> HYAMS: "It's funny, there's something about Bing that reminds me of you. . . . It's that funny little catch in his voice when he sings."
> ERWIN: "I'll have to practice that."
> HYAMS: "You do it, anyway, sometimes, when you talk."

Here, Hyams indicates that it is indeed the emotional vulnerability of the crooning voice that she responds to, and it is an emotionality she associates with "sissy" men like Erwin, although not with Crosby as a man. The "catch" in Crosby's voice is significantly not indicative of his overall masculinity, especially in comparison to the "sissy." This is one of the clearest indications that in Crosby's case it will be possible to reconcile a crooning voice with a masculine body. One would expect, in this case, that Crosby would be the more acceptable love interest for Hyams and that the ending of the film would have Crosby paired off with her to acknowledge that he is the "real" man. The film throws the audience a curve, however, when, in the conclusion of the film, Hyams is paired with Erwin, while Crosby is reunited with his old girlfriend, Sharon Lynne. Lynne is a fairly demanding woman who spends her time with Bing getting into fistfights. Her lack of femininity would seem to suggest that she would not be the appropriate mate for even the more manly of the two men, but this film stumps expectations, suggesting that the conventions that it appears to reverse have not yet been established in the films of 1932. "Sissy" men can still be appropriate and desirable mates for women, and the more aggressive female may get the goods (although the battle may leave her a bit bloody).

While *The Big Broadcast* plays more loosely with gender roles than any other crooning film, it does reinforce many of the patterns Crosby set in his shorter films and which will continue throughout his career, especially in the "Road" films with Bob Hope: crooning is linked with comedy over romance; Crosby is paired with a "sissy," this time one who doubles as both "buddy" and rival; and he prefers the company of men to women. There are no love scenes between him and Lynne; in fact, in the only semiromantic scene between them, the film's conclusion, Lynne appears brandishing a black eye apparently given to her by Crosby as she tried to prevent him from going to the studio. His promise to Erwin to perform (Erwin now owns the studio) is obviously more pressing and important to Crosby than Lynne's wishes, a reversal of his feelings in the opening of the film. It is a roundabout way for the film to endorse the work ethic and masculine aggression, but it succeeds in doing so at the expense of Crosby's female "true love." The crooner image certainly did not change overnight (a *Newsweek* review of Crosby's 1933 film *Too Much Harmony* refers to him as "the almost bearable crooner"), but Crosby's films for Paramount in the 1930s reflect a strategy similar to Jack Kapp's at Decca: Crosby plays a variety of parts, from crooning cowboys to college professors, thus promoting the idea of him as a musical "everyman" rather than a crooner with limited appeal.[56]

The predominant way of presenting the crooner for the next few decades was as an arrested adolescent (think of a grown-up "Alfalfa" from *The Little Rascals*, a popular crooning figure from the mid-1930s). Men who sang romantic songs to women in the 1930s and 1940s were almost always constructed as college boys (Dick Powell, Ozzie Nelson, Dick Haymes) or idealistic, innocent young men (Frank Sinatra, Kenny Baker, Dennis Day) who would presumably someday grow up and grow out of their childish crooning phase. In the meantime, their mooning about and emotionality was not to be taken seriously. This portrayal of the crooner as adolescent suggests how culturally ingrained the association between emotion, pitch, and masculinity was by the mid-1930s.[57]

While Crosby was able to attain some level of masculine maturity and still croon, he did so by evacuating emotion and desire from the crooning body. Although he pursues the heroine in his films with the intention of marrying her, there is nothing remarkable about her or his attachment to her. He is often nonchalant to the point of indifference or meanness, using his singing to seduce women without suggesting his sincere devotion to them or reverence for them (this is usually accomplished by scenes in which Crosby does not look directly at his intended while he sings). Although he is more comfortable in a homosocial environment, Crosby shows very little strong feeling for his male buddies, either (unlike his early film *The Big Broadcast*).[58] While the presence of the mature crooner like Astaire or Crosby necessitates the presence of "sissy" men to reinforce their masculinity, the bonds between the crooner character and the sissies are not strong, especially not in Crosby's case.[59]

Crosby also more clearly aligned himself with country over city living as the 1930s advanced; he claimed to be uninterested in nightclubbing and instead celebrated the traditional values of small-town living (religion, hard work, family centeredness). These values came to be reflected more and more in his films, which also built on the idea of him as "America's supreme musical patriarch"[60] through their increasingly conservative politics, "exotic" locations and women, and the regular presence of blacks, children, and animals in addition to or instead of "sissy" characters. These tendencies are most obvious in the series of "Road" pictures Crosby made with Bob Hope beginning in 1940, but they are notably present in 1935's *Mississippi*, set in the antebellum South, and in 1937's *Waikiki Wedding*, set in Hawaii. *Mississippi* reinforces Crosby's patriarchal whiteness by having him sing "Swanee River" with a black chorus, while *Wedding* sets Crosby's whiteness and more masculine singing against a group of "natives" whose musical performances are more spectacularized and feminized.

Although Crosby did not perform in blackface in *Mississippi*, he occasionally used it, first in the 1932 short film *Dream House*, and more famously in the later feature films *Holiday Inn* (1942) and *Dixie* (1943). Unlike Jolson, however, Crosby did not use blackface as a vehicle for expressing emotion, but rather in order to ally himself with traditional values and symbols of homogenized "Americana."[61] Crosby was a well-known church-going Catholic, and his religion further helped to mitigate his playboy-crooner persona when he put crooning in the service of religious praise; his devotional albums sold very well, and his two best-selling records were Christmas songs, "Silent Night" and "White Christmas." These songs became Crosby's signature tunes (as much as his folksy straw hat and pipe) and they are indicative of just how far away from the Vallee crooner he had come by the early 1940s. Crosby's Academy Award-winning 1944 film *Going My Way*, in which he plays a priest, represents the ultimate Crosby crooning image: the crooner as cultural and even religious icon, disinterested and devoid of human passion. *Going My Way* thus serves as the final repudiation of the Vallee crooner on behalf of white patriarchy; Crosby's Father O'Malley is father to all, husband to none. Crosby's crooner thus effectively disciplines the body to the degree that it is no longer human: expressionless, unfeeling, undesiring.

Conclusion

The musical standards Crosby established both ensured the dominance of crooning songs in national culture and set the narrow gender norms against which subsequent male singers would be measured. Crosby's crooner did not offer an alternative masculinity, as previous crooners like Vallee had, but instead sought to legitimize crooning by connecting it to traditional tropes of masculinity: a good work ethic, patriarchy, religious belief, whiteness, and contained emotions. The balance that Crosby achieved, however, would not be as easily maintained by the singers who followed him. Society's continued unease regarding the crooner—most notable in the lack of artistic value awarded their music and the belittlement of their fans—suggests that the ideals and pleasures Vallee offered his listeners remain both potent and disruptive. By making the crooner more central to the history of music and film, we can better understand the gendered nature of the relationships between sound and image, voice and body, that constitute our mass culture.

Notes

Portions of this essay previously appeared in Allison McCracken, "'God's Gift to Us Girls': Crooning, Gender, and the Re-Creation of American Popular Song, 1928–1933," *American Music* 17. 4 (1999): 365–95. My deepest thanks to archivists Ellen Gartrell at Duke University and Brad Bauer at the American Library of Radio and Television for their assistance in researching this essay. My gratitude also to Eleanor Vallee, for sharing her memories with me and allowing me to publish Vallee's photo. Finally, thanks to the friends and colleagues whose feedback was invaluable: Rick Altman, Jay Beck, Corey Creekmur, Clark Farmer, Taylor Harrison, Michele Hilmes, Arthur Knight, Martti Lahti, Melanie Nash, John Peters, Lauren Rabinovitz, Doris Witt, and Pamela Robertson Wojcik.

1   See, for example, *Variety*, 4 December 1929, 15, and Martha Gellhorn, "Rudy Vallee: God's Gift to Us Girls," *New Republic*, 5 August 1929, 310–11. Vallee also had a substantial number of male fans; they are nowhere mentioned in contemporary news reports, but men frequently wrote letters praising him to radio fan magazines, as well as to Vallee himself. See Rudy Vallee, *Vagabond Dreams Come True* (New York: E. P. Dutton, 1920), 87 and 160, and the fan magazine

Radio Guide, "Voice of the Listener," column 1931–34. Rudy Vallee letters, Special Collections, The American Library of Radio and Television, Thousand Oaks Library, Thousand Oaks, Calif.

2 Dean Harold Butler of the Hill College of Fine Arts, quoted in the *New York Times,* 11 January 1932, 32. This attack opened the floodgates of public criticism.

3 Warren Susman, *Culture as History: The Transformation of American Society in the Twentieth Century* (New York: Pantheon Books, 1984), 158.

4 Philip H. Ennis, *The Seventh Stream: The Emergence of Rock 'n' Roll in American Popular Music* (Hanover, N.H.: Wesleyan University Press, 1992), pt. 1, and Andre Millard, *America on Record: A History of Recorded Sound* (New York: Cambridge University Press, 1995), 158–75.

5 For detailed discussions of the importance of female consumers to radio advertisers, see Michele Hilmes, *Radio Voices: American Broadcasting, 1922–1952* (Minneapolis: University of Minnesota Press, 1997), and Susan Smulyan, *Selling Radio: The Commercialization of American Broadcasting, 1920–1934* (Washington, D.C.: Smithsonian Institution Press, 1994).

6 For discussions of white masculinity and nativism during the late Victorian period and the early part of this century, see Gail Bederman, *Manliness and Civilization: A Cultural History of Gender and Race in the United States, 1880–1917* (Chicago: University of Chicago Press, 1995); John Higham, *Strangers in the Land: Patterns of American Nativism, 1860–1925,* 2nd ed. (New Brunswick, N.J.: Rutgers University Press, 1988); Michael S. Kimmel, *Manhood in America: A Cultural History* (New York: Free Press, 1996); E. Anthony Rotundo, *American Manhood: Transformations in Masculinity from the Revolution to the Modern Era* (New York: Basic Books, 1993); Joseph Pleck and Elizabeth H. Pleck, eds., *The American Man* (Englewood Cliffs, N.J.: Prentice-Hall, 1980). For a thorough synthesis of many of the above sources, including primary sources, see Gaylyn Studlar, *This Mad Masquerade: Stardom and Masculinity in the Jazz Age* (New York: Columbia University Press, 1996), intro. and chap. 1. For a good general analysis of whiteness and masculinity, see Richard Dyer, *White* (New York: Routledge, 1997), esp. chaps. 1 and 4.

7 The need for this change in the construction of masculinity was the result of a number of complex historical factors. The Victorian separation of public and private spheres became less secure in the last part of the nineteenth century. Increased transportation opportunities made it possible for women to go back and forth between downtown and home more easily, and the department store emerged to take advantage of women's new mobility and to encourage their presence as consumers. Previously domestic middle-class women also began to take a more public role in politics and social work. Equally, the emergence of mass culture meant that public entertainments were no longer solely the province of men; mass entertainments like pulp fiction, vaudeville, film, and amusement parks targeted the family audience in order to increase their sales. Finally, increased immigration and the growth of cities meant more nonethnically "pure" whites occupying public spaces; the need for white men to emphasize their ethnic and racial purity and manliness necessitated increased atten-

tion to their bodies as the source of their superiority. For more on this transition, see Susan Porter Benson, *Counter Cultures: Saleswomen, Managers, and Customers in American Department Stores, 1890–1940* (Champaign: University of Illinois Press, 1986); Lauren Rabinovitz, *For the Love of Pleasure: Women, Movies, and Culture in Turn-of-the-Century Chicago* (New Brunswick, N.J.: Rutgers University Press, 1998); M. Alison Kibler, *Rank Ladies: Gender and Cultural Hierarchy in American Vaudeville* (Chapel Hill: University of North Carolina Press, 1999); Lewis Erenberg, *Steppin' Out: New York Nightlife and the Transformation of American Culture, 1890–1930* (Chicago: University of Chicago Press, 1981), esp. chap. 3; Robert Allen, *Horrible Prettiness: Burlesque and American Culture* (Chapel Hill: University of North Carolina Press, 1991), esp. 185–93.

8 The American Academy of Teachers in Singing, "Reasons for Studying Singing," *Etude*, July 1931, 510. See also Wayne Kostenbaum's discussion of early singing manuals in *The Queen's Throat: Opera, Homosexuality, and the Mystery of Desire* (New York: Vintage Books, 1993), 167–75.

9 Charles Hamm, *Yesterdays: Popular Song in America* (New York: W.W. Norton, 1979), 290.

10 For more general histories of Tin Pan Alley, see David Ewen, *The Life and Death of Tin Pan Alley: The Golden Age of American Popular Music* (New York: Funk & Wagnall's, 1964); Isaac Goldberg, *Tin Pan Alley: A Chronicle of the American Popular Music Racket* (New York: John Day, 1930); and David Jansen, *Tin Pan Alley* (New York: Donald I. Fine, 1988). For more on the early career of Irving Berlin and the evolution of early American popular song, see Charles Hamm's excellent *Irving Berlin, Songs from the Melting Pot: The Formative Years, 1907–1914* (New York: Oxford University Press, 1997).

11 Women fans' fondness for opera tenors and minstrel ballad singers is entertainingly recorded in John J. Jennings's *Theatrical and Circus Life* (St. Louis: M. S. Barnett, 1882), 296–302, 355, 371–74. For a history of the minstrel ballad singer and his influence on popular music, see Edward Marks, *They All Sang: From Tony Pastor to Rudy Vallee* (New York: Viking Press, 1935), 60–70.

12 For a thorough survey of "boy culture" material from this period, see Studlar, chap. 1.

13 For the use of boys as song pluggers, see the Tin Pan Alley books noted above, as well as Marks, *They All Sang*, 3–5, 129, and 152. For a personal account of the evolution of song slides presentations in vaudeville, the preference for adolescent boys and girls as singers, and their perception as desirable objects, see Charles Harris, *After the Ball: Forty Years of Melody* (New York: Frank-Maurice, 1926), 254. What vaudeville did to promote male singers, cabarets did for male dancers. The "tango pirates" who headlined the cabaret scene in the 1910s presented themselves quite aggressively as objects of desire for female patrons, for which they received much bad press and public condemnation. The intimacy of the cabaret also permitted closer contact between performers and audience members, anticipating the "close-up" style of the radio broadcast. For an excellent detailed study of these cabarets and their place in urban nightlife, see Erenberg, *Steppin' Out*, chap. 4.

14 Millard, *America on Record*, 105. For a more detailed analysis of "hot" and "sweet" jazz, see Kathy J. Ogren, *The Jazz Revolution: Twenties America and the Meaning of Jazz* (Oxford: Oxford University Press, 1989); Burton W. Peretti, *Jazz in American Culture* (Chicago: Ivan R. Dee, 1997); Burton Peretti, *The Creation of Jazz: Music, Race, and Culture in Urban America* (Chicago: University of Illinois Press, 1992); and Neil Leonard, *Jazz and the White Americans: The Acceptance of an Art Form* (Chicago: University of Chicago Press, 1962).

15 Jolson's performance in the first "talking" film, *The Jazz Singer* (1927) as a blackface singer and his subsequent blackface films promoted the association of emotionality with blackness, which made the arrival of crooners that much more jarring. For an analysis of Jewishness and blackface in Jolson's early films, see Michael Rogin, *Blackface, White Noise: Jewish Immigrants in the Hollywood Melting Pot* (Berkeley: University of California Press, 1996).

16 Will Friedwald, *Jazz Singing: America's Great Voices from Bessie Smith to Bebop and Beyond* (New York: Scribner's, 1990), 50–51.

17 Millard, *America on Record*, 104–5. Although Fred Astaire was a big star during the mid to late 1920s, he and his sister Adele were famous primarily for their dancing. The ballads in their shows were divided among several singers (including well-known crooners like Cliff Edwards). Fred's singing did not begin to get noticed by reviewers until Adele retired and he began a solo career in the 1932 Broadway show *The Gay Divorce*. See Larry Billman, *Fred Astaire: A Bio-Biography* (Westport, Conn.: Greenwood Press, 1997).

18 Ennis, *The Seventh Stream*, 67.

19 Ibid., 42–70.

20 Friedwald, *Jazz Singing*, 30.

21 Bing Crosby, *Call Me Lucky* (New York: Da Capo, 1953), 83.

22 As opposed to black musicians' perceived lack of training, spontaneity ("instinct") and sense of play. See, for example, "King Jazz and the Jazz Kings," *Literary Digest*, 30 January 1926, 37–42; Paul Whiteman, "Jazz," *Saturday Evening Post*, 27 February 1926, 3–5+; "The Anatomy of Jazz," *Harper's*, April 1926, 578–85.

23 Michal Chanan, *Repeated Takes: A Short History of Recording and Its Effects on Music* (New York: Verso Press, 1995), 38–39.

24 Rick Altman, "The Technology of the Voice," *Iris* 3.1 (1985): 6, and Chanan, *Repeated Takes*, 56 and 75.

25 Millard, *America on Record*, 143. See also Chanan, *Repeated Takes*, chap. 4, and Al Bowlly, *Modern Style Singing ("Crooning")* (London: Henri Selmer, 1934), 10–11.

26 Kate Smith, whose radio career took off in 1931, took over DeLeath's role as "the first lady of radio"; her persona, like DeLeath's, was that of a mammy, an asexual, soothing mother-figure. For this reason, she was often called a crooner, especially in her early days.

27 My description of crooning has been distilled from a number of histories of "classic pop," among them Friedwald, *Jazz Singing;* Roy Hemming and David Hadju, *Discovering Great Singers of Classic Pop* (New York: Newmarket Press, 1991), 9; Henry Pleasants, *The Great American Popular Singers* (New York: Simon

& Schuster, 1974); Gene Lees, *Singers and the Song* (New York: Oxford University Press, 1987); and Gary Giddins, *Jazz and American Pop* (New York: Oxford University Press, 1981).

28 It is difficult to say whether these singers were considered to be homosexual in the current sense of the term. As scholar George Chauncey has shown, although the present connotation of homosexual was becoming much more prevalent in the 1920s and 1930s, it is more likely that these singers were thought of mainly as "gender inverts," or "fairies," since at that time, one's identity was primarily based on one's gender identity rather than one's sexual identity (this distinction made effeminacy no less of a problem for the middle class, of course). The latter would seem to be Crosby's position, according to the quote that begins this section. For a discussion of homosexuality in this period, see George Chauncey, *Gay New York: Gender, Urban Culture, and the Making of the Gay Male World, 1890–1940* (New York: Basic Books, 1994), chap. 2.

29 Gene Austin's 1927 recording of "My Blue Heaven," for example, was the most popular recording of the day; its success was not equaled until Bing Crosby's "White Christmas" in 1942.

30 Ennis, *The Seventh Stream*, 99.

31 Vallee, *Vagabond Dreams Come True*, 55.

32 Ibid., 256.

33 Ibid., 41. The material on "vibrato" comes from a talk Rudy Vallee gave at the J. Walter Thompson Company, his program's sponsor, on March 31, 1930. Staff Meeting Minutes, J. Walter Thompson Archive, Duke University.

34 Rudy Vallee, interviewed by Ronald L. Davis for the *Southern Methodist Oral History Project* (122), 4 October 1975, 16.

35 In Whispering Jack Smith's hit song from 1929, "A New Kind of Old-Fashioned Girl," he asserts that the flapper is really "a saint under the paint / as wise as her brother / and as good as her mother. Nothing is wrong with the girl of today / Blame the parents who misunderstood," 'Whispering' Jack Smith with the Victor Orchestra, Rose, BE-51659-1, 1929.

36 Russ Columbo and his orchestra, "Living in Dreams," Green, BS-73019-1, 1932, and Rudy Vallee and the Connecticut Yankees, "I'll Be Reminded of You," Smith & Heyman, BE-57125-1, 1929.

37 See *Vanity Fair*, July 1929, 47; *Literary Digest*, 19 October 1929, 46; *Outlook*, 11 September 1929, 58.

38 Miriam Hansen, *Babel and Babylon: Spectatorship and American Silent Film* (Cambridge, Mass.: Harvard University Press, 1991), 292–93.

39 For more on the relationship between Vallee and his early fans, see Allison McCracken, "'God's Gift to Us Girls': Crooning, Gender, and the Re-Creation of American Popular Song, 1928–1933," *American Music* 17.4 (1999): 365–95.

40 Vallee described his part in the film this way in 1930: "I conceived of the part as a shy, embarrassed boy in a group of orchestra boys who considered themselves superior to him, a boy whose high idealistic principles caused him to be conscious-stricken throughout the entire picture due to the deception he was practicing." Vallee, *Vagabond Dreams Come True*, 148.

41 Vallee recognized that he got the part in the film solely on the basis of his radio fame, and at the time he saw voices as being privileged over bodies in the mass media: "Photography used to be the paramount thing but in the talkies today, the voice cares [sic] for a tremendous amount of things and that is why I got my break in making my picture—my vocal thing was the main thing." Address to the J. Walter Thompson agency, 31 March 1930, J. Walter Thompson Archive, Duke University.

42 *Variety*, 4 December 1929, 15.

43 Rudy Vallee, *My Time Is Your Time* (New York: Ivan Obolensky, 1962), 91.

44 *New York Times*, 1 January 1932, 32.

45 *New York Times*, 23 February 1932, 19, and *The Musician*, March 1932, 3.

46 The American Academy of Teachers in Singing, "Reasons for Studying Singing," 510.

47 *The Musician*, January 1932, 17.

48 Crooning permanently emasculated Vallee, turning him into a cultural "sissy" at a time when the common man was the real man. The films he made in the late 1930s and early 1940s, especially those with Preston Sturges, confirmed his new "sissy" status, pitting him as the undesirable male competing for the girl with the likes of Tyrone Power, Joel MacRae, Rex Harrison, and Cary Grant. In these roles, Vallee is most famous for his pince-nez glasses, his prissiness, and his fastidious habits, characteristics that remained tied to him for the rest of his life, eclipsing and erasing memories of him as a romantic idol. Vallee's career trajectory provided a cautionary tale for the crooners who followed, suggesting the difficulty in maintaining one's masculinity after exhibiting an unmanly amount of emotion and identifying too much with women.

49 Ted Crosby, *The Story of Bing Crosby* (New York: World Publishing Company, 1946), 200.

50 In *Call Me Lucky*, Crosby claims that he lost his voice for a time in 1931, and that when it returned it was "a tone or two lower" than before (113). Other biographies make no mention of this, and in fact, refute the story, suggesting that Crosby's drunkenness accounted for the lost time performing.

51 Friedwald, *Jazz Singing*, 38.

52 In 1939, *Liberty* magazine's review of Bing Crosby's career credits the birth of his boys with deflecting charges of effeminacy: "It hasn't always been easy to be a crooner. Remember that song, 'Crosby, Columbo and Vallee'? It wasn't a very complimentary song. At the time, it sounded like the funeral dirge for all three of them. Something had to be done about it. Russ got Carole Lombard to fall in love with him. Bing Crosby had twins" (*Liberty* 25 March 1939, 57).

53 Vallee, in contrast, claimed to enjoy urban nightlife and the company of women; see Vallee, *Vagabond Dreams Come True*, 101–2. Crosby and his wife, former Fox star Dixie Lee, had four sons: Gary (1933); twins Phillip and Dennis (1934); and Lindsay (1937).

54 Noted in *The Judge*, 23 January 1932, 14. Any hint of Crosby's questionable masculinity disappeared thereafter; stories about him ten years later refer to his

early playboy days as the time when "he sowed his wild oats." See, for example, *Saturday Evening Post,* 31 October 1942, 36–39.

55 See *I Surrender, Dear* (Mack Sennett 1931), *Just One More Chance* (Sennett 1931), *Billboard Girl* (Leslie Pearce 1932), *Dream House* a.k.a. *Crooner's Holiday* (Del Lord 1932), *Blues in the Night* (Leslie Pearce 1933), *Sing, Bing, Sing* (Babe Stafford 1933), and *Bring on Bing* (Sennett 1933). His first Paramount feature was *The Big Broadcast* (Frank Tuttle 1932).

56 The film that marked the final stage in the evolution of the "Crosby crooner" and the most serious attack on and repudiation of the Vallee crooner in filmic terms is Crosby's 1933 film *Goin' Hollywood.* For a detailed analysis of this film in these terms, see McCracken, " 'God's Gift to Us Girls,' " 387–88.

57 For example, tenor voices became so connected with crooning young men that "boy crooner" Dennis Day on *The Jack Benny Program* remained an adolescent character for years after the real Dennis Day had married and had several children; grown-up men could not *sound* like Dennis Day sounded.

58 Crooner films are the first to establish the double bind of musical men in Hollywood cinema: in order not to seem too effeminate or narcissistic as performers, they must surround themselves with sissies, but they cannot show too much interest in the heroine either, lest they seem too emotionally vulnerable. This problem can result in love triangles like those in Gene Kelly's films wherein the leading men end up ultimately spending much more time with other men and seem to have much closer emotional bonds with them. In Crosby's films, however, the relationship between him and the other men is competitive rather than mutually supportive, and homosexual attachment is made fun of through constant ridicule of the effeminate. See Mark Rappaport's 1997 film *Silver Screen: Color Me Lavender* for a lengthy discussion of the homosexual allusions in Crosby's "Road" films.

59 Significantly, Crosby's lack of emotional intensity was applauded by critics who gave him credit for "not acting" in his films; Bosley Crowther, long-time reviewer for the *New York Times,* was a big fan of Crosby. In one typical review, he praises Crosby's screen presence: "One thing about Bing, you never catch him acting. He is always himself." Comments like this suggest the extent to which Crosby had successfully naturalized the contained emotions of traditional white masculinity.

60 Friedwald, *Jazz Singing,* 190.

61 As Michael Rogin points out, blackface musicals of the 1930s and 1940s, like other musicals of the time, were about national unity, the coming together of white and black (blackface numbers frequently included black participants) rather than ethnic, generational, or romantic conflict, as in Jolson films. Rogin writes, "The blackface musical offers regression as national integration." Rogin, *Blackface, White Noise,* 14.

Flower of the Asphalt: The *Chanteuse Réaliste* in 1930s French Cinema

KELLEY CONWAY

In a French film made in the early 1930s about the love affair between a detective and a prostitute, Jean Gabin plays a petty gangster who negotiates the dance floor of a working-class dance hall, boasting of his erotic exploits with a woman who, because of her prodigious sexual dexterity, is dubbed the "Rubber Kid." Without warning, a woman steps in to claim the sobriquet for herself, appropriating the song and identifying herself as the legendary "Môme Caoutchouc." She proceeds to relate her own story with great relish. "I can tell you, just between us / The rubber kid is yours truly / Oh yes, that's what they call me."[1] It makes no difference that the singer is an aging, unshapely prostitute; she nevertheless wants it known that the exploits were hers. The singer is *chanteuse réaliste* Fréhel (1891–1951), the comeback queen who reinvented herself in the 1920s after years of self-exile and drug addiction. She would have been instantly recognizable to viewers of Anatole Livak's *Coeur de Lilas* (*Heart of Lilas*) (1932).

The incorporation of songs and singers in French films of this era is an important phenomenon in both French film and popular music. In the early years of sound cinema, feature films were preceded by three, four, or five short films, some of which were *chansons filmées* (filmed songs). The *chanson filmée*, which persisted until the 1950s, featured the performance of a song either in a recording studio or on the stage of a music hall, sometimes with an audience and an orchestra in view.[2] This musical use of film is reflected in the prevalence of songs in French feature-length films of the 1930s, as confirmed by an invaluable discography published by the Bibliothèque Nationale. Compiled through the analysis of the commercial catalogs published by record companies, the discography reveals that the majority of films made during this decade contain at least one song; the average number of songs per film is two to three.[3] Films designed as vehicles for singers and adaptations of operettas tend to contain more songs, of course. *Naples au Basier de feu* (Augusto Genina, 1937), a vehicle for tenor Tino Rossi, contains six songs. The Paramount-produced operetta *Un Soir de réveillon* (Karl Anton, 1933) contains sixteen songs. But even films that are neither adaptations of operettas nor set in an entertainment milieu frequently contain several songs. *Tumultes* (Robert Siodmak, 1931), for example, featuring Charles Boyer as a petty criminal and Florelle as his unfaithful girlfriend, contains three songs. The quantitative importance of songs in 1930s French film invites us to explore the meanings they create within the narratives.

One explanation for the prevalence of popular songs in 1930s French film is that throughout the decade, but especially in the early years of sound film, French cinema absorbed performers and performance styles from live popular entertainment such as the music hall.[4] Indeed, many of the most prominent film stars of the 1930s—Jean Gabin, Florelle, Albert Préjean, Raimu, Georges Milton—performed in variety theater, the *café-concert*, and/or the music hall before acting in films. One particularly compelling crossover figure from live entertainment to the French cinema is the *chanteuse réaliste*, the realist singer.[5] Edith Piaf is the most famous *chanteuse réaliste*, but the genre has a rich history which precedes Piaf's reign as the *grande tragédienne* of French popular song from the late 1930s to her death in 1963.

The genre of the realist song emerged in the late 1880s in the *café-concert* and in the cabarets of Montmartre. Aristide Bruant (1851–1925) was among the first to compose and perform the realist song in his cabarets, but these narratives of poverty and prostitution quickly became associated almost exclusively with female performers. These singers, as we shall see, cultivated public images as women whose lives were as tumultuous and tragic as those of the female characters they sang about. The flamboyant public personae of the *chanteuses réalistes*, combined with the songs' customary commentary on the plight of its female characters, invite us to scrutinize the particular cultural construction of femininity suggested by the figure of the *chanteuse réaliste*.[6]

The realist song is almost always about loss and tends to be intensely cynical about the possibility of romantic love and domestic stability. Sometimes called the *chanson vécue* ("lived" or "true to life" song), it typically chronicles the plight of a woman facing heartbreak and poverty. The song

"Je t'aime d'amour" in the film *Paris la nuit* (Henri Diamant-Berger, 1931), for example, chronicles a young, innocent girl's initation into prostitution by the man she loves. Her lover is now tired of her; she threatens suicide. "L'Amour des hommes" (Hugon/Koger/Scotto, 1938), performed in *La Rue sans joie* (André Hugon, 1938) is about prostitutes who walk the streets in rain, snow, and wind. We have souls, we seek love, the *chanteuse* tells us, but men are all the same, blasé and vicious. Frequently, the realist singer's person is submissive and fatalistic. The songs often tell the stories of passive, dependent women incapable of escaping their brutal men. Yet the realist singer is more than the mere victim her songs and film appearances might imply. She expresses frankly her sexual desires and the hope that true love is still possible. "Tu m'fais chaud, j'ai la fièvre" ("You make me hot, I have a fever"), the singer moans in *Paris la nuit*. Moreover, the singers' deep, powerful, and imperfect voices (admiring critics described them as *"véritable," "naturale,"* and *"brutale"*), their frequently large bodies, and their public images as transgressive women mitigate the surface meaning of the songs' lyrics. Indeed, for all its pessimism, the realist song represents one of the few forums for the expression of female subjectivity and validation of women's experience in its era.

The popularity of the *chanteuse réaliste* persisted well into the early 1960s, as evidenced by Edith Piaf's career, but it was especially intense in the period between the wars. The realist song could be heard in the streets and courtyards of Paris—it was a mainstay of the street singer's repertoire—as well as in the neighborhood *cafés-concerts* and the opulent music halls like the Casino and the Folies-Bergère. Fréhel, Damia (Marie-Louise Damien), and Edith Piaf were the most famous *chanteuses réalistes*, but there were also Eugénie Buffet, Yvonne George, Marie Dubas, Andrée Turcy, Germaine Lix, Berthe Sylva, Lucienne Boyer, and many others. The film industry did not hesitate to capitalize on the appeal of this figure right from the beginning of the sound era. Not only did actual *chanteuses réalistes* perform in films, but the *chanteuse réaliste* functioned as a cultural "type" in her own right, appearing as a character in many 1930s films. *Chiqué* (Pière Colombier, 1931), the first sound film made entirely in France by a French crew,[7] is set in a louche cabaret on the margins of Montmartre and features a *chanteuse réaliste* and an *apache* as characters. In *Un Soir de rafle* (Carmine Gallone, 1931), Annabella, best remembered as the ingenue in *Hôtel du Nord*, plays a *chanteuse réaliste* in love with a boxer (Albert Préjean). Dressed in a black velvet sheath, the trademark of *chanteuse réaliste* Damia, she sings "Ce n'est pas drôle" ("It's Not Funny"), a song about the tough lives of prostitutes. In *Paris la nuit* (Henri Diamant-Berger, 1931), whose scenario was written by populist novelist Francis Carco, a *chanteuse réaliste* sings in a working-class dance hall at La Villette, the neighborhood in the northeast of Paris that provides the setting for many of the songs themselves. The cultural resonance of the *chanteuse réaliste,* then, exceeded the actual singers themselves, becoming a shorthand for female transgression, for the Parisian underworld and the working class, and for the intense emotions of sexual desire, melancholy, and despair.

Several prominent film directors of the 1930s understood the cultural resonance of the *chanteuse réaliste,* as well as the value of weaving popular songs into the narratives of their films. René Clair wrote several realist songs for Damia[8] and used popular songs (both realist and otherwise) to great effect in his script for *Prix de beauté* (1930) and in *Sous les toits de Paris* (1930) and *Quatorze Juillet* (1932).[9] Julien Duvivier also wrote realist songs, including the ballad for *La Tête d'un homme* (1932), to which we will return. Jean Renoir, above all, appreciated the legacy of the realist song and singer. *Marquitta* (1927) is about a Russian prince who is humiliated by his lover, a street singer. *La Chienne* (1931) intersperses the murder of Lulu (Janie Marèse) with a street performance of one of the earliest realist songs, "La Sérénade du pavé" ("Street Serenade"), originally performed at the turn of the century by *chanteuse réaliste* Eugénie Buffet. *French Cancan* (1954), Renoir's homage to the Belle Epoque music hall, contains a number of songs popular at the turn of the century, including "La Sérénade du pavé," this time sung by Edith Piaf dressed up as Eugénie Buffet. Renoir himself wrote the lyrics to the realist song "La Complainte de la Butte" ("Montmartre Ballad"), sung by Cora Vaucaire in *French Cancan.* Lastly, in Renoir's final film, *Le petit theatre de Jean Renoir* (1969), Jeanne Moreau sings "Quand l'amour meurt" ("When Love Dies"), a song popular in the nineteenth-century *café-concert.*

At the beginning of sound cinema, the best-known *chanteuses réalistes* were Fréhel and Damia. Fréhel appeared in fourteen films in the 1930s and three more in the 1940s; Damia performed in five films in the 1930s. Edith Piaf appeared in one film in 1936 at the beginning of her career, and in nine more in the 1940s and '50s. Although the *chanteuse réaliste* was occasionally the protagonist of the films, she was, more commonly, a secondary character. Despite the size of her roles, the *chanteuse réaliste* performs a number of crucial operations: she cues spectator expectations about the fate of the film's characters and the overall shape of the narrative; she defines social spaces; and she subverts (and sometimes confirms) the prevailing cultural norms regarding gender and class. The *chanteuse réaliste's* incarnations in 1930s French cinema are well worth exploring, for she brings to films such as *Coeur de Lilas* (Anatole Litvak, 1931), *La Tête d'un homme* (Julien Duvivier, 1932), and *Prix de beauté* (Augusto Genina, 1930) a rich palimpsest of meanings relating to femininity, the working class and the underworld, urban space, and popular entertainment itself.

Coeur de Lilas

Coeur de Lilas is about the love affair between a detective (André Luguet) and a prostitute (Marcelle Rommé) who may have committed the murder under investigation. Directed by Russian émigré Anatole Litvak during his six-year sojourn in Paris, *Coeur de Lilas* constitutes one of the most intriguing examples of the hybrid nature of early 1930s French film.[10] A harbinger of poetic realism in its visual style and in its evocation of the Parisian underworld, the film also combines elements of the bourgeois music hall and even, indirectly, the boulevard theater. *Coeur de Lilas* is a "non-musical" film in which songs play a key role.

When the body of a bourgeois factory manager is found on the fortifications of Paris, Detective Lucot sets out to investigate Lilas, a prostitute who may be guilty of the murder. Lucot infiltrates the prostitute's neighborhood disguised as a working-class man. The detective and Lilas fall in love, but just when happiness seems within their reach, Lilas discovers the detective's true identity, and, devastated, turns herself in for the crime.

Coeur de Lilas appears relatively unconcerned with the motives and identity of the criminal or with police procedure, unlike other *policiers* of the early 1930s, such as *Le Chien jaune* (Jean Tarride, 1932) and *La Tête d'un homme* (Duvivier, 1932). Moreover, the importance of the film's central love relationship between the detective and the prostitute, ostensibly the narrative focus of the film, is minimized. Instead, *Coeur de Lilas* invests most intensely in the representation of the urban and aural space found in the city of Paris. This space belongs, specifically, to the working class, which coincides (in the film and in the popular imagination) with the space of the underworld, and consequently those spaces of popular entertainment frequented by or located within the milieux. The film's emphasis on space is evident in the specificity and variety of urban spaces that are explored, and, especially, by the linking of specific spaces with singing performances by three prominent music hall performers of the period: Fréhel, Jean Gabin, and Fernandel.

The locations of *Coeur de Lilas* were carefully chosen for their ability to connote a very particular space of urban poverty. Lilas lives in a working-class neighborhood, presumably La Chapelle or La Villette. (The murder, a newspaper headline informs us, was committed in La Chapelle.) The neighborhood looks distinctly pre-Haussman with its tiny, winding streets and modest, idiosyncratic apartment buildings. In a series of striking tracking shots, the camera deftly snakes through the neighborhood, exploring a café, a *bal musette,* and cheap hotel rooms, constructing in the process a space that appears intriguing and confusing to outsiders.

The first song, performed by Fréhel, is "Dans la rue" ("In the Street"), written, like all three of the songs in *Coeur de Lilas,* by veteran music hall and operetta composer Maurice Yvain and songwriter Serge Veber. True to the genre of the realist song, "Dans la rue" is a bittersweet narrative about the lives of prostitutes on the streets of Paris. This genre is noteworthy in French culture not only for the way in which it defies expectations about femininity, but in its preoccupation with marginal urban space. The realist song is typically set in the poor neighborhoods and suburbs of Paris, such as Belleville, Ménilmontant, Montmartre, and St. Denis. Like the poetic realist films of the 1930s, these songs contain a very particular decor: the rain-soaked streets of Paris and port towns, cheap, furnished hotel rooms, neighborhood cafés and bistros, and the "Zone," an area where the poor lived on the periphery of Paris.

The first tracking shot is remarkable for its attention to detail and its obsession with the evocation of a particular social space. A hand cranks a barrel organ, then we hear the music for "Dans la rue." A café shutter rises, revealing steamed windows and lace curtains. On the soundtrack is Fréhel's voice singing the words to "Dans la rue":

> As soon as we see the sun clear out
> Everyday, it's the same.
> Taking our time, we go down to the sidewalk
> To look for dark corners.
> Fleeing the cop's eye
> Hoping for cash,
> Princess of the mud, Queen of the slime
> Flower of the asphalt with a hoarse voice.
> [All song lyrics translated by author.]

The tracking shot continues through the neighborhood streets, pausing on prostitutes, their clients, and policemen. A fade provides a bridge to a medium shot of Fréhel, who washes laundry as she sings, "But if the client isn't happy / And if he grumbles on his way out / We say to him, 'Little one, next time, I'll put on silk stockings.'" She makes a sarcastic face: these streetwalkers can't afford silk stockings. Through her song, Fréhel personifies this urban space and its inhabitants, in particular the lives of the prostitutes we see on the street. But her song, and indeed her very presence, is part of a discourse that transcends this sequence and this film, as we shall see, bringing to the film specific meanings that circulated well beyond the narrative of *Coeur de Lilas*. These additional connotations concern specifically the construction of urban space drawn from both the genre of the realist song and Fréhel's star image.

Critics noticed the film's deliberate representation of urban space. *La Cinématographie française* observed that *Coeur de Lilas* is "obviously a special film" and praised its "images of the fortifications, of the [working class] suburb, of the street with its [popular dance halls with] accordion bands."[11] The film opens on the fortifications, located on the periphery of Paris. After the dead body is discovered, onlookers are shown racing up and down the steep slopes of the fortification in a series of pans. There is a great deal of attention to the graphic elements in this sequence, such as the pattern of a bridge's iron bars, and the angles of the landscape itself. Onlookers, residents of the Zone, gather, and the camera pans slowly around the circle, taking in the details of their weathered faces. A newspaper headline screams "A Crime in La Chapelle: A Cadaver on the Fortifications."[12] The evocation of the "Zone" was seen as one of the film's strengths. Short for "zone *non-aedificandi*," the term refers to the ring of land approximately three hundred meters wide just beyond the masonry defense completed in 1845 around the city of Paris.[13] Permanent buildings were prohibited in the Zone in order to ensure a clear view of enemy approaches, but low, temporary structures were allowed. The area became a shantytown when the poorest Parisians were pushed to the margins of the city as a result of high rents and demolitions. The Zone not only "set off the sumptuousness of Paris with a frame of filth and squalor"[14] but served as the repository of intense fantasies from the turn of the century to World War II relating to the underworld, to illicit sexuality, to marginality, and to a nostalgia over a Paris that was disappearing. Proposals for the demolition of the fortifications and the shantytowns in the Zone had been discussed since the 1880s, when the obsolescence of the fortifications was made evident by their ineffectiveness during the Franco-Prussian War. The legal acquisition of the fortifications from the army took place in 1919, but their demolition was not completed until 1932, a year after *Coeur de Lilas* was made. The redevelopment of the Zone itself would take much longer, until well after World War II. The disappearance of the Zone, with its image of working-class sexuality and frisson of danger, was actually mourned long before its actual demise, as Adrian Rifkin observes in his extraordinary study of Parisian

11 Fréhel strikes a dramatic
pose. [Author's collection]

urban space and popular culture.[15] The realist song mourned the disappearance of the Zone with particular intensity. *Coeur de Lilas*, through its setting, its visual style, and its use of the *chanson réaliste*, participates in this process of mourning and celebration.[16]

Of the three singers who perform a musical number in *Coeur de Lilas*, Fréhel brings to the film the most defined public image, since she had been performing in French music halls much longer than Gabin and Fernandel. Fréhel was enormously popular in the early 1930s, while Gabin and Fernandel were not yet the cinema stars they would become a bit later in the decade. *Coeur de Lilas* was Fréhel's first sound feature film. She plays a character named, simply, La Douleur (pain), one of the underworld cohorts of Gabin's character. The film does not tell us directly why she is called "Pain," but spectators would have understood instantly that Fréhel's "La Douleur" is a character straight out of the realist song: a broken down, disappointed prostitute who has loved and lost, but who still possesses considerable verve and an audacious sexuality.

It is particularly meaningful that Fréhel sings a song called "In the Street." The street was one of the dominant tropes of the realist song and in the discourse surrounding the singers themselves. Most of the singers were raised in poverty (Piaf, the myth goes, was literally born on the street in working-class Belleville); many worked as prostitutes before achieving success as singers. All claimed an intimate knowledge of "the street"—its hardships and its seductions. Fréhel summarized her upbringing in her memoirs published in serial form in a tabloid in the late 1940s.

> It is the street that raised me, the street that made me as I am, with my qualities and my faults. It is the street that taught me to sing. While passing by the bistros, the first phonographs sent me the fashionable refrains in their nasal voices amplified by enormous loudspeakers. I would stop short, I would stay out under a freezing rain sometimes for hours, my little skirts lifted by a gust of wind, in ecstasy for hours. The song recorded itself in me, music and words. I never forgot a song I heard.[17]

Thus, the street "produced" Fréhel, and, in turn, Fréhel brings the street to *Coeur de Lilas* and to the spectators through her songs and her persona.

The *chanteuses réalistes* were particularly adept at drawing on public knowledge of their poverty-stricken pasts, ties to the underworld, drug and alcohol abuse, and failed romances. When watching "La Douleur" in *Coeur de Lilas,* spectators would have remembered Fréhel's personal pain, information of which was circulated endlessly in the press in the 1910s, 1920s, and 1930s: her childhood of nightmarish poverty, her spectacular rise to fame, the devastating loss of her lover, Maurice Chevalier, to the powerful music hall "queen" Mistinguett, the decade of self-imposed exile in Eastern Europe, her prodigious drug use, and, finally, her comeback in the early 1920s on Parisian music hall stages. One music hall critic observed, "It was quite simple, these women brought their lives to the stage."[18] Of course, it wasn't that simple; while the *chanteuses réalistes* may have transformed autobiographical experience into performance material, they did so in a very self-conscious way, by manipulating the codes of realism and melodrama circulating in literature, film, and the music hall at the time.

Fréhel thus brought to her 1930s film roles a number of images: the strikingly beautiful, self-destructive singer of the pre–World War I years; the years of drugs, depression, and exile during and after the war; and finally, resurrection, perseverance, and nostalgia in the early 1920s. Two elements of her image stand out: she is "of the people" and she is unabashedly sexual. Music hall critic Maurice Verne observed:

> The aggressive passion of this almost virile face with large cheeks, the fleshy silhouette of a nervous massif, the invective and crass laugh-

ter, and this broken voice carry us toward the landscapes of the Zone, to these shacks that overlook ever-burning furnaces, the smoking chimneys of Saint-Denis or of muddy Aubervilliers, work, the prisons of the unlucky and their women, Madames the streetwalkers. It's Fréhel, the *chanteuse réaliste,* the misbegotten offspring of Aristide Bruant and Yvettte Guilbert early in her career. But she, she is of the people.[19]

She is not merely a symbol of a generic working class or of the vague, undifferentiated mass of the urban poor; she "is" St. Denis, Aubervilliers, the Zone, prisons. We have already observed that *Coeur de Lilas* draws on this acute sense of "place." The film's second song assumes knowledge of another facet of Fréhel's image: her hearty sexual appetite.

The second song actually begins as an expression of *male* virility. The neighborhood people have gathered at a *bal musette.* Martousse (Gabin) looks on as Lilas and the detective have a drink together. Overcome with jealousy, Martousse throws his glass on the floor and begins spitting out the lyrics to "La Môme Caoutchouc" ("The Rubber Kid"), a jaunty, vulgar tune. He moves around the dance floor, playfully shoving the dancing couples out of his way:

I have an extra-special kid

. . .

And the girl is truly fantastic
She puts her head under her feet
and her toes in her nose
Suddenly she does the splits on the bed
She spins
She does the caterpillar
Suddenly, her legs are at her neck
She winds herself up into a ball
And spins around on her knees
The rubber kid
What one can do with her
Ah! It's crazy
She takes you and [that's it]!
You're only a rag, worn out
It's no sham
She dislocates you
The rubber kid
She's a beautiful piece, a funny little thing

> One looks for her underneath
> But one finds her on top;
> The rubber kid.

The songs' lyrics conform to an important aspect of Jean Gabin's nascent star image as a virile denizen of the underworld. His movements around the dance floor, half-angry, half-playful, alternate between expressing rancor toward Lucot for having stolen Lilas away and performing for the sake of entertaining the regulars of the *bal musette*. Above all, the performance emphasizes that Martousse (as opposed to André Luguet's detective character) is part of the fabric of this community. This is confirmed especially when the crowd joins in on the chorus.[20] But Martousse is not the only character who enjoys a privileged relationship with the neighborhood "regulars."

Without a warning, Fréhel steps onto the dance floor and begins singing:

> I can tell you, just between us
> The rubber kid is yours truly
> Oh yes, that's what they call me
> Compared to me, taffy
> Is as stiff as a board
> When we beat the snake, my man,
> how I give it back
> I fan my feathers for you
> I pinch my cheeks
> I jump like a marmoset
> I ruin your household,
> but I want us to laugh about it
> The rubber kid
> That's [...] us
> When you take hold of my two bazooms
> My two big boobs, that's a chore
> The rubber kid
> When he gets hold of one of you
> It gives him biceps
> It turns him on
> The rubber kid.

This is a highly unusual performance for 1930s film, not only because women were not usually positioned in such a sexually aggressive fashion, but also because Fréhel departs significantly from the norms of 1930s beauty in terms of her large size, and brags about it, no less.[21] When Gabin sings the words of the song, it's a question of a man bragging about his sexual exploits with a certain Môme Caoutchouc. But when Fréhel declares that she *is* "La Môme Caoutchouc," she takes possession of the song and exceeds Gabin's audacity and sexual verve. It's one thing to have loved the Rubber Kid; it's quite another to *be* the Rubber Kid. Fréhel's appropriation of the song from Gabin, combined with the bawdy lyrics and body language (she struts around the dance floor and even gestures toward her breasts when singing the line "When you take hold of my two bazooms / My two big boobs, that's a chore"), constitute in themselves a transgression of the prevailing codes regarding gender. But the intertextual knowledge circulating around Fréhel heightens the transgressive nature of her performance. Fréhel's performances here and elsewhere in *Coeur de Lilas* rely for their fullest meaning upon the spectators' knowledge of the various aspects of her persona formed by her music hall performances and her star image elaborated in the press. This persona was comprised of the "loser" who lived fast and lost it all (her looks, her career, her lovers), and the ribald, sexually aggressive "comeback" woman who, against all odds, emerged from oblivion, illness, and drug addiction as an improbable star in the 1920s and 1930s.

Coeur de Lilas, it must be emphasized again, is preoccupied with issues of urban space, specifically in relation to the constraints conferred upon its characters as a result of gender norms and class barriers. "La Môme Caoutchouc" is, on one level, about woman's mobility. As the lyrics of the song tell us, the Rubber Kid can thread her way through small places and she can puff up her pectorals in the metro in order to stand her ground. Despite this, and as exhilarating as Fréhel's performance of "La Môme Caoutchouc" is, it must be noted that her character's mobility and prowess are limited. La Douleur never achieves a larger mobility; she is never shown outside of the café or the *bal musette,* and, in one early sequence, she is dressed down by Martousse for speaking out of turn. Fréhel may be the Môme Caoutchouc, but Gabin 's character is more mobile, in fact, both in his singing performance and in the fact that he leaves the milieu to search for Lilas after the detective takes her away. Of course, the bourgeois detective is the most mobile character of all, for he can slip undetected into a working-class neighborhood and then escape when necessary. The prostitute Lilas, in contrast, does not possess the ability to manipulate the signs of class, and thus lacks mobility. Though she will put on bourgeois clothing, Lilas cannot escape her working-class/criminal origins.

Issues of class difference and urban space are increasingly linked with song performance as *Coeur de Lilas* progresses. Shortly after the performances of Gabin and Fréhel, the *bal musette* is raided by the police. Lucot and Lilas flee the neighborhood, embarking on a kind of tour of Paris. In an astoundingly beautiful, oneiric sequence, they ride a city bus all night, finally alighting at dawn at Les Halles, the wholesale market in central Paris. High-angle shots capture the activity of the busy market. Close-ups linger lovingly on stalls overflowing with fruit, meat, and flowers. Next, Lucot buys Lilas a new dress and hat at an elegant boutique. They go boating and dine on the "Ile de l'amour" ("Island of Love"). Two very different urban spaces are thus contrasted in *Coeur de Lilas:* the enclosed, dangerous exotic milieu which is materially poor but rich in visual texture and in community, and the sunny, open market, the elegant dress shop and restaurant, atmospheres of abundance. The contrast occurs not only visually but musically.

A final singing performance takes place at an elegant wedding reception. Lilas and Detective Lucot dine in a private room while the wedding party enters the hall next door. Lucot hums along as the orchestra plays "Te plains pas qu'la mariée soit trop belle" ("Don't Complain That the Bride Is Too Beautiful"), and he sings a few bars to Lilas in a joyous, spontaneous fashion. It seems for a moment that the sort of life represented by the wedding party is within their reach. Next, the third singer to appear in *Coeur de Lilas* emerges. Fernandel (1903–1971) began his career in the music halls of Marseille, launching his Parisian music hall career in the late 1920s. When he started making films in 1930, he was already quite well known and would go on to have an immensely successful film career. Fernandel appeared in several of Marcel Pagnol's films, but he was primarily known as a *comique-troupier,* a singer of comic songs about military life, in films such as *Ignace* (Colombier, 1937). His performance style, which we can locate at the opposite end of the spectrum from that of the restrained, naturalistic Gabin, has been described as "a conception of acting founded on grimaces, tics, and effects." [22] When Fernandel takes up the song, he is centered in the frame, is static, and shot frontally. He sings alone and then the crowd joins him at the refrain. The performance contains little spontaneity and connotes a more staged, artificial sense of community than that of the *bal musette.* The lyrics of "Ne te plains pas que la mariée soit trop belle" contrast sharply to those of "Dans la rue," which, as we recall, sketch out with sympathy the lives of streetwalkers. Fernandel exhorts the wedding party not to complain about the bride being too beautiful. "Don't complain if we paw your woman / Don't complain if we take her from you

[. . .] / You shouldn't have chosen a woman so beautiful that she excites our desires. / If she had an ugly face we'd leave her for you alone." Here, woman is an object of exchange in the bourgeois ceremony of marriage, valued solely for her appearance. It is in this context that the relationship between Lucot and Lilas unravels. During Fernandel's performance, Lilas discovers, thanks to Martousse, that Lucot is a detective. Devastated, she flees, and the happy wedding music, now nondiegetic, metamorphoses into "La Môme Caoutchouc" in a minor key. The music of the two different cultural spaces thus melds together, becoming distorted and dissident, reflecting the impossibility of the union of Lilas and the detective.

In *Coeur de Lilas,* characters are defined by the style and location in which songs are performed. The couple's relationship cannot be sustained once Lucot takes Lilas away from her milieu. In the end, the film intimates, Lucot and Lilas cannot be together because Lilas is from the world of the *bal populaire* and Lucot belongs to the world represented in the Ile de l'amour sequence: bourgeois matrimony, the music hall, and the law.[23]

Gabin, Fréhel, and Fernandel all performed in the glamorous music halls of the 1920s and '30s, but in *Coeur de Lilas,* their performance styles are wedded to specific places. Gabin and Fréhel represent the working-class entertainment milieu by performing in a *bal musette,* and also evoke the *café-concert,* the smaller-scale neighborhood performance spaces that preceded the music hall. Fréhel, in particular, stands in for a nostalgic, affectionate vision of Paris *populaire*. Fernandel and Luguet[24] stand in for the large-scale music hall and the bourgeois, Boulevard theater, respectively, and represent an existence that is well beyond the reach of La Martousse, La Douleur, and Lilas. But the film does not mourn the impossibility of bourgeois respectability and comfort. On the contrary, *Coeur de Lilas* celebrates that which is marginal in the Parisian landscape through its visual style and its privileging of Fréhel and Jean Gabin, the key emblems of underworld sexuality and criminality in 1930s French film.

Fréhel and Gabin appear together again in *Pépé le Moko* (Julien Duvivier, 1936).[25] Here, too, Fréhel is associated with both Paris and with the pre–World War I music hall in her role as Tania, the companion of a gangster hiding out from the Parisian police in the Casbah of Algeria. Her performance of a realist song occurs when she tries to comfort the film's male protagonist, the fugitive gangster Pépé (Jean Gabin). Fréhel advises him to "change d'époque" (go back in time/change eras) when he feels depressed. In what is perhaps her most autobiographical and moving appearance in the cinema, Fréhel says pensively, "Yes, I think of my youth. I look at my old photograph and I tell myself that I'm in front of a mirror. I put on one of my old records from the time when I had so much success at the Scala on the boulevard de Strasbourg, [where I] appeared on stage in a rustic decor with a red projector aimed on my pale face and I sang!" She then puts a record on the phonograph, listens pensively, then sings along with "Où est-il donc?" (A. Decaye and Lucien Carol), a hymn to a disappearing Paris:

> Where is my Moulin de la Place Blanche
> My tobacconist, my corner bistro?
> Every day was Sunday for me.
> Where are my friends, my pals?
> Where are all my old dance halls
> Their *javas* to the sound of the accordion?

The sequence conflates Fréhel's personal history and losses with the larger phenomenon of a changing Paris, specifically the disappearance of Montmartrois popular culture. As in *Coeur de Lilas,* Fréhel is linked here to the Parisian landscape and to a romanticized underworld. She is a nostalgic emblem of the "good old days" in Paris, when a sense of community still seemed to exist. Fréhel's appearance in *Coeur de Lilas, Pépé le Moko,* and in nearly all of her 1930s film performances functioned as a kind of shorthand evocation of prewar Paris: poverty, heartbreak, but also community and solidarity. Here, the female singing voice is not a siren or an obsession; it is a nourishing, nostalgic voice that binds together a community, even as that sense of community is seen to be disintegrating.

La Tête d'un homme

Whereas Fréhel and other *chanteuses réalistes* can be seen as symbols of a Paris characterized by a strong sense of community among the *petit peuple,*[26] other singers project a darker image in their 1930s film appearances. Damia (1892–1978) began singing in music halls in 1911. Like Yvette Guilbert and Eugénie Buffet before her, Damia sang both literary songs written by poets (Maurice Boukay's "La Grande Chasse," Jules Jouy's "La Veuve," and Verlaine's "D'une prison," for example) and the populist repertoire ("Le Grand Frisé," Daniderff/Ronn, 1931). Damia, along with Yvonne George, was also known for her performances of authentic sailor songs, such as "Sur le pont de Morlaix," "Pique la bleine," and "La Mauvaise prière."[27] Her biggest hit was "Les Goélands" (Lucien Boyer), a haunting song about the death of sailors at sea. She was praised for her sculptural body, her muscular, expressive arms, and her powerful voice. Unlike Fréhel, Damia kept her private life out of the press and appears to have func-

12 Damia (Marie-Louise Damien) in her trademark black sleeveless dress. [Author's collection]

tioned as a kind of screen onto which her audience could project their diverse desires: she was revered by everyone from conservative war veterans to homosexuals.[28] She is credited with bringing the principles of mise-en-scène to the *tour de chant* (song turn), applying the lessons she learned about lighting while touring with dancer Loïe Fuller during World War I. Damia's use of high-contrast lighting in her music hall performances, combined with her trademark black velvet sleeveless dress which revealed her long white arms, produced a stark, dramatic mise-en-scène. Like Fréhel, Damia brought to her films vivid connotations. "She is the Eve whose sin gave birth to our punishment, she is the sentimental, lovesick milliner, she is the girl from the fortification walls whose male terrifies her, she is the criminal haunted by remorse, she is the bar fly, she is a Nana with genius. She is all of that because she believes herself all of that, because she believes in all of that."[29]

Damia's cinema roles were few, but most of them drew effectively on her considerable magnetism, attributing to her voice and her persona a quasi-hallucinatory power that reveals much about male anxieties in the face of new cultural roles for women. In both *Sola* (Henri Diamant-Berger, 1931) and *La Tête d'un homme* (Julien Duvivier, 1932), she plays a singer whose voice, heard largely offscreen, triggers an obsession in a man.

La Tête d'un homme, an adaptation of an Inspector Maigret mystery by Georges Simenon about murder and sexual obsession, tells the story of Radek, a poor and embittered foreign medical student with a terminal illness. Damia, listed in the credits as *une femme lasse* (a weary woman), is a broken-down woman abandoned in the shabby furnished room next door to Radek's. In a plaintive voice, she sings a song in the *réaliste* tradition written by Duvivier himself for the film.[30] Damia's character itself was created specifically for the film and, as is so often the case with the realist singer, her symbolic weight in the narrative far outweighs her actual screen time.

Damia's song reaches us in several ways and with increasing intensity in the film. We first hear her voice singing during the credit sequence. Later, the murderer and Inspector Maigret listen to her singing through the walls of the murderer's apartment. At the climax of the film, we finally see Damia perform a portion of the song. Lastly, while the murderer lies dying under the wheels of a car, we hear the song once again. The film is thus permeated with her presence, albeit it mostly aural. Throughout most of the film, Radek hears Damia, but cannot see her, which leads him to fantasize that the voice he hears is that of the rich, inaccessible woman he loves, Edna (Gina Manès), singing specifically to him. He "edits" his dream woman in his mind, "dubbing" Damia's voice onto his mental image of

Edna, his love object. Near the end of *La Tête d'un homme,* Radek kidnaps Edna and bursts into Damia's room, where she sits on her bed, singing about fog and the night. Now that he has finally managed to bring the visual and aural components of his love objects together, he goes over the brink, collapsing onto Damia's bed and laughing maniacally.

Damia's disembodied voice had already undermined a man's sanity in *Sola* (1931), in which she stars as a down-and-out singer stranded in Singapore. The film opens in a recording studio, where Sola (Damia), a music hall singer at the height of her career, records a song called "Tu ne sais pas aimer" ("You Don't Know How to Love"), about a woman who looks in vain for a soul in her lover's eyes. The modernity of the enterprise is emphasized: much attention is paid to the technical aspects of sound recording in the studio, which has a sleek, art nouveau decor. The sound technician and recording equipment are shown and the sequence even contains a quasi-documentary in which the process of mass-producing records is shown. Sola then embarks on a world tour and eventually finds herself alone and penniless in Singapore, where she sings at a cabaret in order to pay for her return trip to Paris. Meanwhile, her voice becomes an obsession for a French plantation manager living in Malaysia. He listens repeatedly to Sola's "Tu ne sais pas aimer" as he becomes increasingly homesick and ill. He goes to see her at the cabaret, but when, drunken and heartsick, she doesn't behave in a way that corresponds to his fantasy, he strangles her. When the police come to arrest him, he shoots himself offscreen, while her voice on the phonograph continues to sing. Just as in *Pépé le Moko,* the female voice is associated with the heartbreak of exile and with a disappearing sense of community in Paris, but here, just as in *La Tête d'un homme,* the female voice connotes male madness and anxiety.[31]

Prix de beauté

Prix de beauté has much in common with *Sola.* Not only do we see, once again, a link between male anxiety and the singing voice of the "modern woman," but the mechanically reproduced female voice "outlives" its "original" voice here, as well. René Clair wrote the initial drafts of the screenplay, but *Prix de beauté* was turned over to Italian director Augusto Genina after a dispute between Clair and SOFAR, the film's producer.[32] Louise Brooks, appearing in her only French film, plays Lucienne, a secretary who wins a beauty contest. With her bobbed hair, her cloche hats, her women's fashion magazines, and her job as a secretary, Brooks provides a sharp contrast to Fréhel and Damia. No longer a denizen of the underworld, this *chanteuse* is an ambitious member of the modern work force. If Damia's film appearances in *Sola* and *La Tête d'un homme* constitute the beginning of a shift in the representation of the *chanteuse* from nourishing voice of nostalgia to alienation, exile, and madness, Louise Brooks's character in *Prix de beauté* goes even further in evoking the anxiety associated with the modern, post–World War I woman.[33] Lucienne sings a song that plays a crucial role in marking the modern woman's transgression and in commenting upon the shift in the nature of popular entertainment from community-based, neighborhood experience to that of the mass media.

Against the wishes of her boyfriend, André (Georges Charlia), Lucienne enters the "Miss France" beauty contest organized by a film company looking for new talent. When she wins the title of Miss France and then Miss Europe, André is outraged and insists that she choose between him and her new life as a celebrity. She returns to him, but soon tires of her monotonous life and leaves him for good. Just as she is on the verge of stardom, André fatally shoots her.

Lucienne sings a song entitled "Je n'ai qu'un amour, c'est toi" ("I Have Only One Love, It's You") (W. Zeller, R. Sylvianon, J. Boyer, 1930) in the first and the final sequences in the film. The first performance occurs at a public beach, remarkable for its documentary-style realism. Lucienne, in high spirits, does calisthenics on the beach, oblivious of the attention she attracts from the men around her. When her boyfriend chastises her for making a spectacle of herself, Lucienne sings the song in an attempt to neutralize his jealousy:

> Don't be jealous, be quiet
> I have only one love, it's you
> You must be reasonable
> You must forgive me
> When another tells me that I am beautiful
> The most flattering confessions
> Have never troubled my heart
> I remain faithful to you,
> It's stronger than I am.
> I have only one love
> It's you.

Prix de beauté shares with *Coeur de Lilas* and *La Tête d'un homme* an emphasis on realism in its portrayal of the *petit peuple* of Paris. The film's sequences at a public beach, a fair, a bistro, and in the typography workroom and the secretary pool of a daily newspaper all possess an astonishing documentary texture. However, unlike in *Coeur de Lilas,* specific neighborhoods are not identified; rather, a generic, modern, urban "working class" is presented. Outside the newspaper office, high-angle shots reveal crowds moving down a large, busy boulevard. The people pause, listening to a voice on a loudspeaker urging women to enter the beauty contest. Inside, tracking shots linger on the rows and rows of identical typewriters and linotype machinery. When *Prix de beauté* zeroes in on individual, idiosyncratic faces, it is not with the aim of valorizing the milieu of marginalized people, as in *Coeur de Lilas.* Instead, the stifling crowds at the fair elicit disgust in our protagonist, with whom we are invited to identify. For example, we see a black man in a tight close-up eating a hot dog. Lucienne looks on in disgust as he eats hungrily, with his mouth open, laughing. Next, she is repulsed by a man brutally kissing a woman. Later, when Lucienne and André have their photograph taken, Lucienne is unresponsive, even catatonic, when the photographer arranges the couple in a stiff position and exhorts her to smile. This milieu is something to escape; it's a crowd instead of a community. What Lucienne desires is social mobility and the pleasures of consumption that accompany it. These desires are represented as specifically feminine in *Prix de beauté.* Lucienne gazes longingly at the pages of a fashion magazine, a pleasure that her boyfriend disdains. She parades up and down for André in the luxurious dresses and furs she receives upon winning the Miss France contest. Numerous shots of Lucienne gazing appreciatively at her image in a mirror emphasize her narcissistic pleasure in her new appearance. This is a new kind of woman, *Prix de beauté* asserts, who wants more than a traditional working-class or petit bourgeois marriage and the ordinary pleasures of an urban fair.

The second performance of "Je n'ai qu'un amour, c'est toi" occurs in the film's extraordinary final sequence. Lucienne has, by now, left André for a career in film and a liaison with a producer/prince. Lucienne and the producer are in a screening room viewing her screen tests, which feature Lucienne singing. The song's context has changed from a private message to a public address, just as Lucienne herself is no longer the possession of a single man, but the property of the public through the miracle of mechanical reproduction. André creeps into the dark screening room and, after gazing at the film image and noting that Lucienne is holding hands with the producer, he shoots her. The film continues to run through the projector, and, in a breathtaking moment, the reflection of Lucienne's film image flickers across her lifeless face, creating a stunning homage to Brooks's beauty. Her mechanically reproduced voice and image sing on, while Lucienne the woman (and female spectator, as it were) dies.

As in the opening sequence, the performance of the song is associated with male rage, but this time the machines of modern media are also indicted, in the sense that Lucienne has been "consumed" by the cinema. The cinema is implicated in her death in several ways. It is an indirect cause of death in that its star-making function facilitates Lucienne's autonomy and thus fuel's André's rage. On a less literal level, the cinematic apparatus "consumes" Lucienne by turning her face into a screen onto which the film projects her own image. Lucienne, the desiring female consumer, is consumed by the very apparatus that facilitates her class rise. This final sequence comments uncannily on the difficulty of female spectatorship elaborated by feminist film theory when Lucienne, diegetic female spectator (of her own image), literally becomes part of the apparatus that objectifies her. Lucienne becomes a spectacle at the cost of her own activity as a spectator. Her desiring look is denied in the interest of the male gaze.

In many ways, *Prix de beauté* is about the new urban space of the late 1920s and early 1930s: a machine-filled, media-saturated space.[34] The film expresses ambivalence not only about the new woman, but about other cultural shifts. Just as Lucienne's song shifts from private performance to mass-produced commodity, the older forms of leisure represented in the film, such as fairground attractions and the neighborhood bistro, give way to mass circulation magazines, international beauty contests, and the cinema. An important component of this new urban space was, of course, the increased visibility and mobility of women, which is reflected in *Prix de beauté*. Lucienne works (for a mass-circulation daily newspaper, no less), is ambitious, and acts against her more traditional boyfriend's wishes. Just as Fréhel's mobility in *Coeur de Lilas* is limited, and just as Damia pays the price for her hypnotic powers in *Sola*, the trajectory of Brooks's character in *Prix de beauté* is contained.[35]

The *chanteuse réaliste* functions, then, in a multifaceted way in 1930s French cinema: as a mark of authenticity in the representation of the underworld, as a symbol of transgressive female sexuality, and as the repository of anxiety over new cultural roles for women. The *chanteuse réaliste* also represents different cultural spaces of Paris: in *Coeur de Lilas* and other films, she defines working-class and underworld neighborhoods and functions as the glue that binds their inhabitants together; she functions also as a link to Paris for the exile. In other films, such as *La Tête d'un homme, Sola,* and *Prix de beauté,* she is a sign of the disintegration of that sense of community, an emblem of the alienation that accompanies the transformation of Paris as a community to a modern media space.

The realist song does more than provide "atmosphere" or participate in the romanticization of the criminal milieu. It often structures the very narrative logic of the film, adopting its circular structure, its narrative pattern of hope and then heartbreak, and its linking of cultural space and social origins with the characters' destinies. Above all, crucial cultural shifts can be read through the changing narrative functions of the *chanteuse réaliste:* she is a symbol of both the resilience and the disintegration of the Parisian working-class community; she is an emblem of both the exhilaration and the apprehension around the figure of the increasingly independent woman; and she symbolizes, through her recorded voice, the atomized culture brought about, in part, by the technology of modern media.

Historians of French film are beginning to acknowledge that songs are important in 1930s French film, not only in quantitative terms but also in terms of the meanings they create within narratives.[36] One historian argues that, because the *chanson* belongs to the realm of popular culture in France, songs in French film are "more or less the involuntary reflection of the daily lives of the French" which "miniaturize, with charm and truth, the cares and the joys of the moment."[37] Songs in films accomplish this not by reflecting simplistically their times, but by generating specific (and sometimes contested) meanings around gender, class, and cultural spaces. In *Coeur de Lilas, La Tête d'un homme, Prix de beauté,* and many other films of the 1930s, songs and the *chanteuse réaliste* are crucial to the films' central preoccupations with place, with changing constructions of femininity, and with challenges to conceptions of class.

Selected Filmography: The Chanteuse Réaliste *in French Cinema*

DAMIA (1892–1978)
Sola (Henri Diamant-Berger, 1931)
Tu m'oublieras (Henri Diamant-Berger, 1931)
La Tête d'un homme (Julien Duvivier, 1932)
Les Perles de la couronne (Sacha Guitry, Christian-Jaque, 1937)

FRÉHEL (1891–1951)
Coeur de Lilas (Anatole Litvak, 1931)
La Rue sans nom (Pierre Chenal, 1933)
Amok (Féodor Ozep, 1934)
Gigolette (Yvan Noé, 1936)
Pépé le Moko (Julien Duvivier, 1936)
Le Roman d'un tricheur (Sacha Guitry, 1936)

L'Innocent (Maurice Cammage, 1937)
Le Puritain (Jeff Musso, 1937)
La Maison du Maltais (Pierre Chenal, 1938)
L'Entraîneuse (Albert Valentin, 1938)
Une Java (Claude Orval, 1938)
La Rue sans joie (André Hugon, 1938)
Berlingot and Cie (Fernand Rivers, 1939)
L'Enfer des anges (Christian-Jaque, 1939)
L'Homme traqué (Robert Bibal, 1946)
Maya (Raymond Bernard, 1949)
Un homme marche dans la ville (Marcel Pagliero, 1950)

LYS GAUTY (1908–)
La Goualeuse (Fernand Rivers, 1938)

FLORELLE (1901–1974)
Tumultes (Robert Siodmak, 1931)
Le Crime de Monsieur Lange (Jean Renoir, 1935)

EDITH PIAF (1915–1963)
La Garçonne (Jean de Limur, 1936)
Montmartre-sur-Seine (Georges Lacombe, 1941)
Etoile sans lumière (Marcel Blistène, 1945)
Neuf garçons, un coeur (Georges Freedland, 1947)
Paris chante toujours (Pierre Montazel, 1951)
Si Versailles m'était conté (Sacha Guitry, 1953)
Boum sur Paris (Pierre Montazel, 1954)
French cancan (Jean Renoir, 1954)
Les Amants de demain (Marcel Blistène, 1958)

ADDITIONAL PERFORMANCES OF THE REALIST SONG
Prix de beauté (Augusto Genina, 1930, with Louise Brooks)
Faubourg Montmartre (Raymond Bernard, 1931, with Odette Barencey)
Paris-Béguin (Augusto Genina, 1931, with Jane Marnac)
Un soir de rafle (Carmine Gallione, 1931, with Annabella)
Dans les rues (Victor Trivas, 1933, with Charlotte Dauvia)
Battling Géo (or *Toboggan*) (Henri Decoin, 1934, with Arlette Marchal)
Vénus Aveugle (Abel Gance, 1942, with Viviane Romance)

Notes

I would like to express my gratitude to David Gardner, whose thoughtful comments and translations were enormously helpful in the writing of this essay.

1 "La Môme Caoutchouc," lyrics, Serge Veber; music, Maurice Yvain.

2 Jean-Pierre Jeancolas, *15 ans d'années trente: Le Cinéma des Français, 1929–1944* (Paris: Stock, 1984), 93.

3 Giusy Basile and Chantal Gavouyère, *La Chanson française dans le cinéma des années trente: Discographie* (Paris: Bibliothèque Nationale de France, 1996). The discography also lists the recordings made of songs by those not connected with the film, information that indicates the cultural resonance of a particular song beyond the context of the film. Many films now completely forgotten or at least disdained by film historians contain songs that went on to be recorded by scores of singers. For instance, *Sola*, an all-but-forgotten film directed in 1931 by Henri Diamant-Berger, contains five songs, one of which, "Tu ne sais pas aimer," was recorded by no less than ten different performers by ten different record companies. *Capitaine Craddock* (Vaucorbeil/Schwartz, 1931) contains a song called "Gars de la marine," which was recorded by nineteen different singers. Conversely, the discography reveals that the songs in canonical films often experienced a surprisingly minimal afterlife. Not a single person recorded "A la belle étoile," after it was sung by Florelle in Renoir's *Le Crime de M. Lange*, for example.

4 For a perceptive analysis of the relationship between music hall and 1930s French film, see Ginette Vincendeau, "French Cinema in the 1930s: Social Text and Context of a Popular Entertainment Medium" (Ph.D. diss., University of East Anglia, 1985).

5 A more general discussion of the *chanteuse réaliste*, illustrated by the Bibliothèque Nationale's rich collection of posters and photographs, appears in Kelley Conway, "Les 'goualeuses' de l'écran," in *Le cinéma au rendez-vous des arts: France, années 20 et 30*, ed. Emmanuelle Toulet (Paris: Bibliothèque Nationale de Paris, 1995), 162–71.

6 For another analysis of the *chanteuse réaliste*, see Ginette Vincendeau, "The *Mise-en-Scène* of Suffering: French *Chanteuses Réalistes*," *New Formations* 3 (1987): 107–28.

7 Raymond Chirat, *Catalogue des films français de long métrange: Films sonores de fiction, 1929–1939* (Brussels: Cinémathèque Royale, 1981), 260.

8 Pierre Billard, *Le Mystère René Clair* (Paris: Plon, 1998), 55.

9 For an excellent analysis of René Clair's use of popular song in his early 1930s films, see Giusy Basile, "Une esthétique neuve de la chanson à l'écran," in *René Clair, ou le Cinéma à la lettre*, ed. Noël Herpe and Emmanuelle Toulet (Paris: Association Française de Recherche sur l'Histoire du Cinéma, 2000), 139–52.

10 Litvak (1902–1974) was born in Kiev. He spent much of the 1920s in Berlin, working as an editor on G. W. Pabst's *Joyless Street* (1925) before becoming a director at UFA in 1930. He left Nazi Germany and settled in France, where he directed *Coeur de Lilas* (1932), *Cette Vieille Canaille* (1933), *L'Equipage* (1935), and *Mayerling* (1936), an international hit starring Charles Boyer and Danielle Darrieux. *Mayerling* earned Litvak an invitation to Hollywood, where he made films until the late 1950s, including *All This and Heaven Too* (1940), the "Why

We Fight" series, which he co-directed with Frank Capra, *Sorry Wrong Number* (1948), *The Snake Pit* (1948), and *Decision before Dawn* (1951).

11   *La Cinématographie française* no. 694, 20 February 1932.

12   La Chapelle, a neighborhood located immediately to the east of Montmartre, is in the eighteenth *arrondissement* in the northeast corner of Paris. Directly to the east of La Chapelle in the nineteenth *arrondissement* is La Villette, the location of the dead man's factory. Both La Chapelle and La Villette are working-class neighborhoods steeped in urban lore. Aristide Bruant wrote songs entitled "A la Villette" and "A la Chapelle." *Dans les rues: chansons et monologues,* vols. 1 and 2 (Paris: Aristide Bruant, 1889). Léon-Paul Fargue (1876–1947)—like Pierre Mac Orlan and Francis Carco a connoisseur of marginal Parisian sites—claims La Chapelle as his own in an essay entitled "Mon Quartier" ("My Neighborhood"): "La Chapelle . . . this crawling and sonorous circus where iron mixes with man, train with taxi, and cattle with soldier. A country more than a district, formed by canals, factories, the Buttes-Chaumont, the Port de la Villette dear to the old watercolorists." *Le Piéton de Paris* (1932; Paris: Editions Gallimard, 1995), 20. La Chapelle was thus no ordinary poor neighborhood. Its sense of melancholy, its texture, and its décor fascinated a number of *flâneur*-writers in the period between the wars.

13   For a full discussion of the protracted process of the destruction and redevelopment of the military fortifications and the Zone, see Norma Evenson, *Paris: A Century of Change, 1878–1978* (New Haven: Yale University Press, 1979), 206.

14   Ibid.

15   Adrian Rifkin, *Street Noises: Parisian Pleasure, 1900–40* (New York: Manchester University Press, 1993), 28.

16   The connection between the realist singers and the geographical margins of Paris continues to be elaborated. An exhibition on the architectural history of the Parisian suburbs entitled "Paris des Faubourgs," held at the Pavillon de l'Arsenal in Paris from October 1996 to January 1997, featured a jukebox offering songs by Fréhel, Damia, Mistinguett, and other popular singers.

17   *Point de Vue-Images du Monde* no. 31, January 1949.

18   Maurice Verne, *Les Amuseurs de Paris* (Paris: Les Éditions de France, 1932), 175.

19   Ibid., 182.

20   Jean Gabin would go on to become the icon of the Parisian underworld and working class in French cinema. But before that, his career was quite typical in terms of his movement from music hall to cinema. He began performing in music halls and in variety theaters in 1923, appearing in bit parts in operettas and musical comedies. His big break came in 1928, when Mistinguett hired him as one of her "boys" for a Moulin Rouge revue called *Paris qui tourne.* Gabin experienced difficulty establishing a performance style different from that of Maurice Chevalier and began acting in sound films in 1930. *Coeur de Lilas* was Gabin's fifth film. His *mauvais garçon* image, so familiar to us from the 1930s poetic realist films, had already been established from his third film, the 1931 *Paris-Béguin,* in which he plays a thief who seduces a music hall star. Likewise,

his performance of songs within films had already begun; he sang in the 1931 *Chacun sa chance* and would go on to sing in *Zouzou* (Marc Allégret, 1934), *La Belle Equipe* (Duvivier, 1936), and *Pépé le Moko* (Duvivier, 1936). For a thorough analysis of Gabin's star image, see Ginette Vincendeau and Claude Gauteur, *Jean Gabin: Anatomie d'un mythe* (Paris: Nathan, 1993).

21 The standard of female beauty in 1930s French cinema is best exemplified by petite, usually blond women such as Florelle, Annabella, Dita Parlo, Anny Ondra, and Danielle Darrieux.

22 André Sallée, *Les Acteurs français* (Paris: Bordas, 1988), 124.

23 Marcelle Romée, who plays the prostitute Lilas, was an up-and-coming actress in 1931. One film critic called her "la Marlène Dietrich française." But Romée died shortly after the completion of *Coeur de Lilas*. In a trajectory which curiously corresponds to many realist songs, Romée drowned herself in the Seine after struggling with depression. [R.M.] "La mort de Marcelle Romée," *Ciné-Miroir*, date uknown, Bibliothèque de l'Arsenal, PHO 01 106.

24 Compared to Gabin, André Luguet, the male lead in the film, is rather insipid. *La Cinématographie française* observed that the acting is "exceptional, except for Luguet, who is discreet, but without real emotion." Luguet is better re-membered for his Occupation-era films, including *Battement de coeur* (Henri Decoin, 1939), *Jeunes Filles en détresse* (Pabst, 1940), and the sparkling com-edy *L'Honorable Catherine* (L'Herbier, 1942). Luguet had acted at the Comédie-Française in the mid-1920s, then spent three years in Hollywood. He returned to the Parisian Boulevard stage and the cinema in the early 1930s, bringing to his film roles an aura of sophistication. "Dark, malicious, delicately mustached, Luguet is the prototype of the Boulevard actor with an audacity tempered by English tact." Sallée, *Les Acteurs français*, 163.

25 For a detailed and useful study of the film, see Ginette Vincendeau, *Pépé le Moko* (London: BFI, 1998).

26 For other *chanteuse réaliste* roles along these lines, see the singing performances of Florelle in *Le Crime de M. Lange* (Jean Renoir, 1935), Odette Barencay in *Fau-bourg Montmartre* (Raymond Bernard, 1931), Charlotte Dauvia in *Dans les rues* (Victor Trivas, 1933), and Lys Gauty in *La Goualeuse* (Fernand Rivers, 1938).

27 Lucienne Cantaloube-Ferrieu, *Chanson et Poésie des années 30 aux années 60* (Paris: A. G. Nizet, 1981), 46.

28 Pierre Philippe speaks of her broad appeal in an interview in the documentary *Damia: Concert en velours noir* (Juliet Berto, 1989). According to Pierre Billard, Damia was openly lesbian (*Le Mystère René Clair* [Paris: Plon, 1998], 55).

29 Gustave Fréjaville, publication unkown, 22 December 1919, Bibliothèque de l'Arsenal, Collection Rondel, Ro 15,934 (1).

30 Giusy Basile and Chantal Gavouyère, *La Chanson française dans le cinéma des années trente: Discographie* (Paris: Bibliothèque Nationale de France, 1996), 92.

31 For other treatments of the female voice and the Frenchman in exile, see *Le Grand jeu* (Jacques Feyder, 1933), *Amok* (Fédor Ozep, 1934), and *La Maison du Maltais* (Pierre Chenal, 1938).

32 For the fullest account of this dispute, see Pierre Billard, *Le Mystère René Clair* (Paris: Plon, 1998), 151–53.

33 For a wide-ranging study of the condition and representation of women in post–World War I France, see Mary Louise Roberts, *Civilization without Sexes: Reconstructing Gender in Postwar France, 1917–1927* (Chicago: University of Chicago Press, 1994).

34 In addition to the many lengthy, documentarylike shots devoted to the printing machines at the newspaper where André and Lucienne work and the attention given to the machinery of film projection during the final sequence, there is a fascination in *Prix de beauté* with public address systems: Lucienne finds out about the Miss France contest via a loudspeaker while other pedestrians mill around her on a busy boulevard. Likewise, the Miss Europe contest is emceed over a loudspeaker. Lastly, Lucienne devours women's magazines, which were a new phenomenon in the early 1930s.

35 In the René Clair papers at the Bibliothèque de l'Arsenal in Paris are numerous drafts of the screenplay for *Prix de beauté*. They provide an interesting range of the narrative possibilities imaginable at this time for a character in Lucienne's position. The film's creators had great difficulty deciding on the ending of the film, it would seem. The scenarios are similar up until the moment at which Lucienne wins the Miss Europe contest. In two of the five versions, Lucienne is revealed to lack acting and singing talent, but she manages to get her old boyfriend back at the end. In two other versions, Lucienne loses her career *and* her boyfriend, and in one of those versions, she loses her life, as well, in a car accident. In the only version of the screenplay in which she possesses talent *and* the possibility of a career—the version that was ultimately chosen—she is murdered. Archives René Clair, RC 31 (001–006), Bibliothèque de l'Arsenal.

36 For an excellent analysis of different modes of popular entertainment reflected in Renoir's *Le Crime de M. Lange* and Christian-Jaque's *Rigolboche*, see Dudley Andrew, "Family Diversions: French Popular Culture and the Music Hall," in *Popular European Cinema*, ed. Richard Dyer and Ginette Vincendeau (New York: Routledge, 1992), 15–30.

37 Alain Lacombe and François Porcile, *Les Musiques du Cinéma Français* (Paris: Bordas, 1995), 61.

The Embodied Voice: Song Sequences and Stardom in Popular Hindi Cinema

NEEPA MAJUMDAR

In 1931, soon after the introduction of sound to Indian cinema, *Alam Ara*, the first "talkie," established a trend that was to continue to the present. This was the inclusion of song sequences, frequently combined with dance, in every feature-length Hindi commercial film. The popularity of music in these "all talking, all singing, all dancing" extravaganzas is indicated by the success of *Indrasabha* (1932), which is said to have included seventy-one songs. The first film song was released on gramophone record in 1934, and since then film songs have come to be the dominant popular music of India. According to a 1985 statistic, film music accounts for about 80 percent of total record sales, in contrast to Indian classical music, which accounts for only 2 percent.[1] Similarly, songs are also of great commercial value to the films in which they appear, as Narendra Sharma notes: "On the film song depends the popularity of the film, that is, its repeat value and box office returns."[2] Film and popular music are thus the two main parallel and intersecting components of the entertainment industry in India.

Film songs and song sequences have their own circuit of distribution, both official, or industrial, and unofficial. They reach a wide circulation via radio, TV, gramophone records, and audio and video cassettes, and also through amateur singing, games such as *antakshari*,[3] brass bands, and other forms of informal appropriation. They permeate the aural environment of India's public spaces, from markets and festivals to long-distance buses and trains. But it is primarily via radio and, more recently, audio cassettes, that film songs reach a wide audience. As Alison Arnold notes, "In

both urban and rural settings, the playing of film song cassettes is sup-
planting or displacing traditional folk and religious musical performance
in many social and cultural contexts."[4] Soon after Indian independence in
1947, All India Radio (AIR) tried to ban all film music from its programming in order to promote a national identity based on the "pure" forms of
traditional and classical music. But by the mid-1950s, competition from
Radio Ceylon in Sri Lanka, which did air Indian film songs, forced AIR to
establish a separate station, Vividh Bharati, solely for the broadcast of film
songs. Since then, radio has become the most widely accessible source of
film songs and hence a standard medium of advertising for films. For example, an ad for the film *Tezaab* in the *Times of India* newspaper, October 15, 1988, starts with the sentence: "Tune in to Vividh Bharati tonight
and every Saturday night at 9:45 P.M. for the radio programme of *Tezaab*."
The importance of song sequences to the advertising of films is also evident in the prominence that billboards typically give to the name of the
music director, which is second only to that of the film's star.

Songs have become free-floating signifiers whose original narrative context is often overlooked, even while they remain attached in popular memory to particular stars. This is because they are frequently repackaged in
TV programs and video cassettes in the form of a chain of song sequences
unified by theme, era, singer, music director, or actor. According to the
music historian Ashok Ranade, film music is created with "the desire . . . to
compose an item that is self-sufficient in its melodic draw and which can
therefore be received, reproduced and remembered in isolation, i.e., irrespective of the filmic situation in which it is intended to appear."[5] Alison
Arnold notes that "radio listener request programmes and a weekly 'top
hits' chart have determined the most popular Hindi film songs on a regular basis since the 1950s."[6] Given their permeation in Indian culture, film
songs have become a major vehicle for star construction, since the song
sequence epitomizes in every way the most spectacular aspects of star performance.

Song sequences are a potent star vehicle not only because of their infinite repeatability in other contexts, but also because, as Richard Dyer suggests with respect to the Hollywood musical, they are the site of the film's
utopian impulses and therefore frequently represent the most idealized
aspects of star presence. Their utopianism derives not so much from the
actual song content, which may very well be tragic, but from the formal
construction of the scene and the emotional appeal of the music. According to Dyer, "utopianism is contained in the feelings it embodies . . . it thus
works at the level of sensibility."[7] In the Indian commercial film, "spectacu-

lar and emotional excess will always be privileged over linear narrative development."[8] This is nowhere more apparent than in the song sequences, with their capacity for "expressing every shade of emotional reverberation."[9] The emotionality of song sequences is culturally encoded through a loose association with classical Indian performance theories and the *raga* system of Indian classical music, which sees a "predetermined correspondence between musical stimulants and audience effects."[10] Furthermore, the disregard for continuities of time and place in song sequences allows for a change of location and costuming from one shot to the next, thereby producing for the spectacle an idealized setting that does not really exist within the diegesis. Thus performance techniques, the music itself, and the "artificial geography" produced by the editing all contribute to the intensified emotion that characterizes the utopianism of song sequences.

Since the mid–1940s, the songs in Hindi cinema have been sung by "playback singers." The song sequences, or "song picturizations," are then filmed with actors lip-synching to the prerecorded voice of the singer. Until the early 1990s, playback singing was the monopoly of a very small number of singers, who became stars in their own right. In the case of the female singing voice, this monopoly went to the extreme of excluding virtually all other voices except the voice of Lata Mangeshkar and, to a lesser extent, that of her sister Asha Bhosle. This has meant that, for a period of almost five decades, every major film actress has borrowed the same singing voice, that of Lata Mangeshkar. As Bhaskar Chandavarkar observes, "Today it is difficult to imagine a female voice that is not Lata Mangeshkar's."[11] Yet, given the extreme degree of voice monopoly in the case of the female playback singer, it is easy to overlook the fact that the male playback voice was the monopoly of only a slightly larger number of voices, including those of Mukesh, Talat Mahmood, Mohammed Rafi, and Kishore Kumar. If voice monopoly characterizes the mode of aural stardom in postindependence Hindi cinema, this has important consequences for the relation between aural and visual pleasures. In particular, I am interested in the implications of the repetition, one might say during the entire lifetime of the Indian nation, of the same female singing voice as the ideal norm of aural femininity across numerous female bodies. In this context, one would have to reverse Michel Chion's statement that "for a single body and a single face on the screen, thanks to synchresis, there are dozens of allowable voices."[12]

A sequence from the 1981 film *Naseeb* (Destiny), directed by Manmohan Desai, provides a convenient point of entry into the dynamics of stardom in Hindi cinema's song sequences. In this sequence, one of the heroes of the film is distracted from his daily jog by the streetside filming of a commercial for throat lozenges. In the commercial being filmed, the heroine, whose character in the film is a singer-star, is endorsing the throat lozenges. She attempts to sing, clears her throat, takes one of the lozenges, speaks about its therapeutic potency, and then sings a flawlessly executed line of melody (*"mere naseeb mein . . ."*) in which no musical accompaniment overshadows the pure tones of her voice. Shots of the singer are intercut with close-up reaction shots of the hero, whose face wears what can best be described as the direct expressions and gestures of fandom. Even at the overt level of the narrative, the subject of this sequence is clearly star power itself. The hero experiences the pleasures of recognition, desire, and identification with the star, all of which are basic to the experience of stardom. While the narrative context here draws viewers into a fictional individual's experience of star power, there is also simultaneously another level of star fascination at work. Viewers of the film would themselves immediately recognize Hema Malini, the actress who is *playing* the singing star. They would also be equally aware that the voice emerging from her throat belongs not to her but to the playback singer, Lata Mangeshkar.

Although this sequence does not develop into a full-blown song sequence, it nevertheless epitomizes the way in which Hindi cinema's song sequences function as a unique star vehicle, simultaneously drawing upon two different star texts, those of the singer and of the actor. Putting together the ideal voice with the ideal body results in a cinematic construct, a composite star who is the visual-aural equivalent of what is frequently the Kuleshovian artificial geography of the song sequence's setting. The two intersecting star texts of the singer and the actor exist in a symbiotic relationship, appealing simultaneously to two sets of pleasures, the aural and the visual. While the disembodied voice of the playback singer attaches itself to the body of the actor and thereby acquires visual presence, the actor's figural gestures also similarly acquire an aural dimension through the borrowed voice of the singer. Responding to the voice-body pairing of Lata Mangeshkar and Madhubala in the film *Mughal-e-Azam* (1960), one fan describes it as "the most beautiful voice in the world going on the most beautiful woman in the world."[13] In its ideal matching of marketable voice and visually alluring body, Hindi cinema is no different in its cinematic imperatives from the Hollywood musical of the 1950s and 1960s.[14] However, what this voice-body combination *means* in the context of Hindi film culture is strikingly different, especially with respect to two interrelated issues: the primacy of the visual over the aural, and the masking of technology as a means of conveying the authenticity of the performance.

Because of the star status of playback singers in Hindi cinema, the question of the authenticity of the song performance is cast in terms that are different from Hollywood. The Hollywood prototype is the situation in *Singin' in the Rain,* in which the film narrative is concerned with revealing the technological artifice behind the experience of a musical, making "the exposure of song dubbing the climax of the plot."[15] Yet, as Jane Feuer and others have argued, the film reclaims its status as "magic" by itself making use of such artifice in "invisible" ways.[16] Rick Altman shows how the rhetorical structure of *Singin' in the Rain* must work to reverse "the illegitimacy of a 'lying' sound track" in which "Debbie Reynolds's voice does not emanate from the mouth portrayed by the image."[17] Important to discussions of *Singin' in the Rain* is a central irony in the climactic moment. When we are supposedly shown that the "true" source of Jean Hagen's voice is Debbie Reynolds and are meant to accept this fictional revelation as a statement about the authenticity of the *actress* Debbie Reynolds's voice, this latter voice is, in fact, being dubbed by someone else who remains uncredited in the film. This vocal substitution has taken on the aura of an apocryphal tale, especially since there are multiple versions as to who dubbed Reynolds's voice.[18] Both in the film's diegesis and in the extratextual information about the film, concerns of authenticity center upon the question of the morality of voice dubbing. Thus, in Hollywood cinema, as in this example, authenticity of performance is cast in terms of the audience's assumption of an actual match of voice and body. Further evidence of this is the denial of an Academy Award nomination to Audrey Hepburn for her role in *My Fair Lady* once it was revealed in the press that she did not sing her own songs.[19]

In the sequence from *Naseeb* there are various devices that work to visually embody the voice of the singer. We literally "see" the voice as it emerges from its point of origin, as Hema Malini strokes her throat, and we also see its visceral effect on the hero as he swoons with delight on hearing her sing. Two apparently contradictory mechanisms are at work here. At one level, the sequence illustrates a basic observation of theories of film sound, that the function of sound synchronization is to mask the operations of technology so as to produce the effect of the organic unity of voice and body and of a natural, rather than a technologically constructed, performative space. The smooth transition in this sequence from the singing voice to the speaking voice and back again to the singing voice serves to reiterate the seamless conjoining of voice and body, and to mask the different sources of the two sounds. The clearing of the throat is the point of transition between the two voices and it could be coming equally from Lata

Mangeshkar or Hema Malini. While this masking of technology is similar to constructions of authenticity in Hollywood cinema, it is complicated by the viewer's recognition of, and pleasure in, the dual star reference of the song. The viewer's awareness of the true source of the singing voice tends to pull in precisely the opposite direction, becoming a *reminder* of the workings of technology. This is similar to the effect, in the film as a whole, of the extratextual mechanism of star recognition, which puts a strain on the illusion of a self-contained narrative world with its own unique characters.

The question of the authenticity of the experience of song sequences has been vital to their history in Indian cinema. Roughly speaking, there have been three, often overlapping, phases. In the first decade of sound cinema, the 1930s, song sequences were performed by actors who sang their own songs, so that the question of authenticity was cast in terms similar to Hollywood cinema. As fan magazines of the period testify, the audience's pleasure derived from their knowledge that the singer they were watching was really singing the song. Yet, technologically speaking, even in this phase there was a disjunction between voice and body, because the playback technique, which was first used successfully in the 1935 film *Dhoop Chhaon*, was already in place.[20] In the 1938 film, *Street Singer*, directed by Phani Majumdar, there is a sequence in which the two main characters, Bhulwa (K. L. Saigal) and Manju (Kanan Bala), perform a song outside the house of a theater director, who listens appreciatively to their music. There is a similar dynamic of star fascination here as in the sequence from *Naseeb*. Here, too, there is an internal audience to the song, whose awestruck response is meant to match that of the actual audience of the film. In this case, however, viewers would know that the actress Kanan Bala is actually singing the song, and furthermore, that she is being accompanied on the harmonium by K. L. Saigal, the most popular singing actor of the time and still the prototype of the ideal male singing voice in the movies. While there is no question here of the source of the singing voice, the film recasts in other terms the question of the authenticity of the performance. As in the Hollywood musical, a hierarchy is set up between the spontaneity and immediacy of the popular music of the streets and the staged performances of the theater, between amateur and professional singing.[21] This sequence is the first moment of the meeting of the two worlds. The response of the lascivious theater director, who listens to the music with approving greed, is meant to characterize the decadent values of the theater and its impulse to commercially exploit the natural talent of singers. Both musically and morally, the film shows the world of itinerant singers to be superior to that of the theater, which is clearly a stand-in for the world of cinema. Furthermore, while the film's viewers would recognize the "true" star here as K. L. Saigal, their narrative pleasure would lie in seeing the morally questionable theater director fail to notice him and pay greater (and misguided) attention to the lesser star, Kanan Bala. The actual star persona of K. L. Saigal strongly relied on a similar unspoken hierarchy between the "natural" and the "trained" voice, emphasizing his lack of formal musical training and his "natural" gift.

Related to the question of the authenticity of song performance in Hollywood cinema is the question of the primacy of image over sound. According to Marsha Siefert, "the illusion that the voice belongs to, as well as emanates from, the image on the screen requires [the] assumption of an image's natural authority." [22] In Indian cinema, by contrast, the use of the term *song picturization* to describe the production of song sequences already shows a certain tendency toward defining the image in the terms set out by the song. Likewise, even in the 1930s, when studios used actors who sang their own songs, the star's identity was primarily constructed in terms of the voice rather than the body. Indian film critic Bunny Reuben observed in 1970 that "ours is probably the only country where [in the 1930s] the ability to sing was the prime qualification for the permission to act." [23] K. L. Saigal's star status was mainly centered upon his singing ability rather than on his acting skills or physical presence. A snide reply to a letter to the editor in the fan magazine *filmindia* in January 1941 makes note of this: "[Saigal's] views on acting should not be taken seriously. New Theatres [the studio for which he worked] took him up for his voice which is a gift not a talent." [24] A fan of Saigal wrote in 1940 that although "everyone of us is his fan" because of his singing voice, "that is all [there is] about him. His face is pudding-like, his hair is always badly dressed." [25] Conversely, physically attractive actors were often derided in *filmindia* if they were not good singers. A letter to the editor in 1940 asks: "Wouldn't it be better for Ashok Kumar to stop singing in pictures? His effort doesn't sound like singing." [26] The primacy of the aural over the visual in song sequences in Hindi cinema parallels the relation of spectacle and narrative in the films themselves, which Lata Mangeshkar pithily describes as follows: "In India, cinema is an excuse for music." [27]

When playback singers began to be used in the early 1940s, there was considerable anxiety regarding the industry's deception in using what were then called "ghost voices." In the 1940s, during this second phase in the history of the relation of singing voice and acting body in Hindi cinema, studios used voice-casting, or the use of a singing voice that matched both the speaking voice and the personality of the actor. Yet, despite voice-casting, the audience's knowledge of a split between singing voice and acting body was a source of discomfort. For example, in the December 1944 issue of *filmindia*, a reader asks, "Isn't the system of using ghost voices harmful? The film-goer soon finds out the trick and the song loses its charm." The editor's attempt at a reassuring reply is that, although this system "lends to the crow a cuckoo's voice, [it] is an artistic fraud which the producers practice on the film-goers with the good intention of giving them maximum entertainment. Though this procedure does interfere considerably with the emotional worship of the average film-fan, it is still a blessing."[28] Similarly, the tendency to repeat the same "ghost voices" receives an extremely negative response because of the obvious disjunction between voice and face and the technological impression made by such a voice: "These wholesale singing machines like Rajkumari and Amirbai get on people's nerves. . . . They have been repeated too often and whosoever's the face, experienced film-goers spot the voice as belonging to one of these two. Once the identification has been done, where is the emotional thrill in the music? . . . Everyone knows that our Madhuris and Sabitas don't sing. Where then is the sense in selling a falsehood? It is just bad business!"[29] A 1946 fan letter goes so far as to say that "we prefer to hear songs from a gramophone record or a radio instead of from the pictures because we know that the singer on the screen is not really singing."[30] At this point in the history of playback singing, the question of the authenticity of the singing voice is discussed in terms of the morality of vocal substitution and the effect this knowledge has on the viewer, terms similar to those of Hollywood cinema.

How, then, did the split between the voice and the body come to be not only accepted by the next decade, but even to be the desired norm, to the point at which voice-casting was no longer practiced? With only a handful of voices dominating the aural environment of Hindi cinema by the end of the 1950s, what mattered in this third phase was no longer whether the voice and body matched, but whether the singing voice was recognizable in and of itself. Since then, song sequences have simultaneously appealed to a seemingly contradictory set of pleasures, encompassing both knowledge and disavowal of technology. Knowledge of the use of technology enables the recognition of the singing voice as that of the playback star and not of the actress, while the willful disavowal of technology allows the pleasure of watching this well-known voice embodied in the physical presence of another star. Song performances are here authenticated precisely through knowledge of the star persona of the singing voice. The morality of vocal substitution becomes irrelevant when the dual star ref-

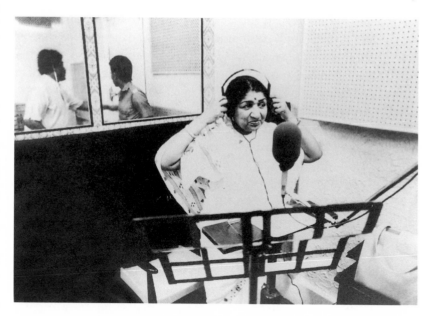

13 Lata Mangeshkar in the recording studio (from the BBC documentary "Lata in Her Own Voice"). [Photo by Peter Chappell.]

erence makes it equally a question of borrowing a body as of borrowing a voice. That song sequences address both types of pleasure is evidenced by the fact that they are marketed in two ways. One can buy audio and video cassettes titled, for example, either "Golden Hits of Lata Mangeshkar" or "Hits of Hema Malini." In the latter case, the title is legitimate even though everyone knows that Hema Malini is not, in fact, the singer of these songs, but merely embodies their performance. Similarly, the immensely popular stage shows featuring film stars can be either live performances of song sequences by acting stars, while lip-synching, or straightforward musical concerts by playback stars, who may or may not have a clearly defined stage presence.[31] Thus the marketing of song sequences caters to fan identification geared primarily either toward the aural star or toward the visual star. This is clearly unlike Hollywood cinema, in which the practice of anonymous voice dubbing "may rob the singer of the opportunity to reclaim his or her voice in live performance and may prevent the non-singing actor or actress from gaining full credit for the screen performance."[32]

The shift to the dominance of only a few recognizable voices is explained in the film industry as a monopoly engineered by shrewd individuals such as Lata Mangeshkar, who were able to take advantage of the migration of several singers to Pakistan after the partition of India in 1947. In the 1940s,

war profiteering brought large sums of money into the film industry, causing the demise of the studio system and the rise of independent producers.
Since then, there has been a general tendency toward monopolization in
Hindi cinema when it comes to the market value of stars. In the Indian
context, the "star system," or the "stardom racket" as *filmindia* puts it,[33] is
widely discussed as a pernicious system whereby freelancing stars dominate the economics of film production by signing on multiple films simultaneously and charging exorbitant fees, which can account for up to 80
percent of the cost of making a film. The heavy odds against commercial
success dictated the repeated use of "proven" stars, which translated as the
most recent box office successes, and this imperative toward a "risk-free"
production system was extended to playback singers as well.[34] While acting stars have aged over the last four decades and been replaced by others,
playback singers have continued to have commercial success, and public
taste with respect to their voices has remained unsatiated. The enduring
dominance of a mere handful of singers is also related to their shift to star
status, which is indicated in a change in the terminology referring to them:
as "ghost voices" they were unacknowledged in credits and relatively unknown to the public, but as "playback singers" they received credit and developed star personas. A further (and ironic) indication of their stardom is
their contrast with anonymous "dubbing artistes." The practice of having
dubbing artistes "record a song when the actual playback singer is not available and then dubbing it all over again when she is free to record, has been
going on for years."[35]

One of the earliest song sequences to establish Lata Mangeshkar's star
identity is "Aayega Aanewala" from the 1949 film *Mahal* directed by Kamal
Amrohi, in which she is playback singing to the actress Madhubala. In
this sequence, the hero enters an empty mansion following the sound of a
beautiful singing voice which is later revealed to belong to the ghost of the
former owner's mistress. Here, both narratively and technologically, what
we are hearing is a ghost voice, and at both levels the emphasis in this song
sequence is quite literally on the lure of the disembodied voice. This song
is now more closely identified with the star persona of Lata Mangeshkar
than with the character played by Madhubala; that is, its aural associations
are stronger than the visual or narrative context of the film in which it appeared. In the fan discourse on Lata Mangeshkar, it also provides a kind
of myth of origins to her identity as a playback star. The record of the song
was originally released with the name of the narrative character, Kamini,
credited as the singer, but it became so popular that "thousands of requests
for the song used to pour in at the radio station along with a request to

mention the name of the singer while playing the record. The radio officials approached HMV to find out who the singer of this runaway hit was. As a result of this, Lata's name began to be announced over the radio. It was only with the film *Barsaat* that names of the playback artistes began appearing on the records and on screen." [36]

In *Cassette Culture,* Peter Manuel observes that, by virtue of their association with cinema, "singers and composers of Indian popular music are not stars themselves. There is no aura of fantasy and glamour woven around the leading singers, who remain invisible voices singing for the actors." [37] Underlying Manuel's observation is a visual conception of stardom based on popular notions of what "stars" are, so that playback singers cannot be stars because they are invisible and no glamour attaches to their image. It is necessary, however, to theorize an aural conception of stardom to account for the dual pleasures and recognitions in song sequences, a concept of stardom in which even the absence of glamour and the invisibility of playback singers can be regarded as defining features of their star personas. In the context of Indian cinema, aural stardom is constituted by voice recognizability, the circulation of extratextual knowledge about the singers, and the association of certain moral and emotional traits with their voices, which then has an effect on the voice-body construct in song sequences. In a 1967 article marking the twenty-fifth anniversary of Lata's career, Gangadhar Gadgil waxes hyperbolic on her aural stardom: "To me, and, I believe, to every Indian, Lata Mangeshkar is not so much a person as a voice—a voice that soars high and casts a magic spell over the hearts of millions of Indians from the Himalayas to Kanyakumari." [38] Aural stardom is predicated upon the awareness, and even celebration, of the workings of technology and its ability to embody the star voice. Lata's song from *Mahal* may be said to mark the transition from "ghost voices" to "playback singers," a transition forced by fans. Already in 1952, the editorial in the September 19 issue of *Filmfare* magazine makes note of Lata's growing hold on the medium, even while mentioning several other popular playback singers: "In more than ninety out of every hundred films since produced, Lata Mangeshkar has given the playback for all feminine songs. Geeta Roy, Talat Mahmood, Shamshad, Mukesh, and Lata have been as much a draw at the box office as the leading stars." [39] While the tendency toward the monopoly of a few voices is unquestionable in Hindi cinema, this monopoly has itself come to constitute a defining feature of the aura of playback stardom. For fans, the numbers game of who sang how many songs is of enduring and passionate interest. The publication of the four-volume *Hindi Film Geet Kosh* (The Encyclopaedia of Hindi Film Songs) in the 1980s further added fuel to this pastime and settled many old debates, such as the controversy over Lata's entry in the *Guinness Book of World Records*.[40]

The dynamics of aural stardom are also differentiated along gender lines. The female singing voice, being limited primarily to the voices of the sisters Lata Mangeshkar and Asha Bhosle, cut across any association with a specific acting star. Remaining constant over time and across numerous bodies, the voice of Lata Mangeshkar easily lent itself to appropriation as the norm of ideal femininity, while that of her sister became associated with "oozing sensuality, . . . a compelling come-hitherness, which makes her slotted only for the cabaret and disco numbers."[41] In the case of the male voice, with at least three major playback singers between the 1940s and the 1980s, Mukesh, Mohammed Rafi, and Kishore Kumar (all since deceased), the masculine voice tended to be somewhat more varied than the feminine voice. For example, Kishore Kumar's star persona is defined entirely in terms of an eccentric, madcap genius, whose noncomformist and outright lunatic antics provide unending fodder for fan consumption. In terms of its moral traits, the male equivalent of Lata Mangeshkar's voice is that of Mohammed Rafi. The recurring motif in his extrafilmic star persona is his moral uprightness and religiosity. The traits read into male voices also often resulted from their association with specific acting stars, as in the case of the voice-body pairing of singer Mukesh with actor Raj Kapoor, who consciously cultivated a Chaplinesqe persona. The distinctions between different male voices are less gender-based than those of the two main female voices that became divided into the conventional feminine dichotomy of virgin and vamp.

While Lata Mangeshkar provides a case study in playback stardom, in a crucial sense she is more than just an example. By virtue of her five-decade dominance in Indian cinema, she has come to be regarded as synonymous with playback stardom in India. Hence any analysis of the workings of stardom in song sequences must center upon her star persona. In this regard, it is relevant that discussions of Lata's voice emphasize its affinity to the microphone. She exists only as a recorded voice, a voice mediated by technology. Music director Datta Davjekar says, "When it is time to record, you don't have to tell her how far to position herself from the mike, at what angle to hold her face, at what points to turn away slightly to avoid overemphasis, or how to tackle very high and very low notes or how to control breath. She really knows how to use the microphone. The microphone is her friend."[42] Even being in her presence makes no difference to the mediated nature of her voice, as R. D. Burman recalls. When she was recording for his famous father, S. D. Burman, he tried to listen to her: "I . . . hung around in the singer's booth. The recording started after a while, but it seemed to me that she was only moving her lips, not singing. So I went a bit closer, but it still seemed as if she was not singing at all. . . . And then, I heard the 'terrific voice', sounding exactly as it did in the records. So I asked Baba, 'She's not singing in there, so where is this voice coming from?' And Baba explained, 'That is her style—she appears to be singing so softly, but her voice carries such tremendous power and is so appropriate for the microphone, that the results take your breath away.'"[43] Given this inherent connection between her voice and the technology of playback singing, Lata has come to epitomize playback stardom in Indian cinema. Moreover, in this response to her physical presence in the studio, we see, yet again, the dominance of voice over body as she is disembodied even in the very act of recording her voice.

Implicit in the dual star reference of female song sequences is a moral hierarchy between the female *voice* and the female *body*. Unlike the voice, the body is available for visual consumption and lends itself more easily to scandalous associations. While technology allows the filmic illusion of a unity of voice and body in the song sequences, their actual division is indicative of a basic contradiction between the two star texts, which is further paralleled by an ideological contradiction in Hindi films over the issue of national and feminine identity. Just as the songs themselves are a hybrid of western and Indian musical forms, the films, too, are ideologically divided. They espouse "traditional" Indian values, while at the same time visually representing western lifestyles as desirable. This contradiction between traditional India and modern westernized India recurs at various levels, the most obvious being the simple narrative opposition between "good" (traditional) values and "bad" (western) values, as represented by characters, settings, clothing, and education. Hindi films overtly moralize about the values associated with the West, which Rosie Thomas describes as follows: "Evil or decadence is broadly categorized as 'non-traditional' and 'western,' although the West is not so much a place, or even a culture, as an emblem of exotic, decadent otherness, signified by whisky, bikinis, an uncontrolled sexuality and what is seen as lack of 'respect' for elders and betters, and (from men) toward womanhood."[44] At the same time it is precisely the visual potential of this "decadence" that is most exploited in some song and dance sequences.

The attempt of postindependence Hindi films to negotiate the contradictory values of material consumption (associated with the West) and austerity (associated with traditional Indian values) can be seen as the general principle behind the dual star text indicated in the voice-body split in female song sequences. The star image of actresses is based on their visual presence both within the films and in extrafilmic sites such as fan magazines and billboards. When it comes to the lives of acting stars, the emphasis in fan magazines is on scandal and decadence. Rosie Thomas notes that, "although the Indian audience is very conservative and easily shocked, this same audience is very eager to be shocked in certain contexts, if one is to believe the evidence of the network of gossip that surrounds the scandals in the lives and loves of film stars in India."[45] Gossip about acting stars is based on overt sexuality, the flouting of conventions of traditional Indian society, and an emphasis on conspicuous consumption. All of these are values that the narratives in the films themselves equate with the decadent West. Emphasizing public visibility and spectacle, photographs in film magazines display stars in flamboyant nontraditional clothing, visually echoing their spectacular presence in the song sequence. The female body, while made available for visual consumption in song sequences and other texts, then also becomes subject to moral and nationalist discourse. On the other hand, the female voice, as constituted in song sequences, lends itself more to notions of idealized femininity, especially because of its singular nature.

Thus, in contrast to the westernized and overtly eroticized persona of the female acting star, Lata Mangeshkar's star persona is defined precisely by the absence of physical beauty and glamour. The recurring trope here is of the ugly woman with the beautiful voice.[46] By extension, this gives rise to clichés about the beauty of the soul rather than of the body, with the implicit reference to acting stars. For example, the journalist Khushwant Singh says: "Lata is beautiful. Not in the conventional vulgar film sense, but what the word means to *me*. She is slight, dark, faintly pock-marked. She radiates an aura of goodness, humility. Her *namaskar* is a distant bow. Her eyes never rise to meet you."[47] In Lata Mangeshkar's star persona, the perceived purity of her voice is extended to her moral character. According to Gangadhar Gadgil, Lata's voice is "ageless, pure, vibrantly alive . . . [and] really belongs to a temple or ashram."[48]

Furthermore, Lata is frequently compared to the medieval singer-saint Meera, a parallel that is reinforced by Lata's own attribution of her success to *tapasya* (or religious dedication). Her first recording of Meera *bhajans* came out in 1968. But even before this, in 1967, Gadgil says, "it would have been . . . appropriate if a voice such as Lata's had sung exclusively the ecstatic bhajans of Mirabai . . . [which] are an expression of total surren-

THE EMBODIED VOICE 175

der to God. They are a quest which can only be expressed by a voice such as Lata's."⁴⁹ In keeping with her "Meera-image," fan discourse about Lata Mangeshkar emphasizes the austerity of her lifestyle, despite her fabulous wealth, while representing her in traditional familial roles. Describing a visit to her home, one reporter writes, "It is not the glittering home of a superstar which the chance visitor would expect to walk into. The last expectation for glamour evaporates when Lata enters the room. Dressed in her habitual off-white sari, peering hard through her stern reading glasses, she is mending her school-going nephew's shirt." He describes her apartment as having "an austere decor. . . . The drawing-room has no paintings, no objet d'art. The only intruder from the modern age is an electric clock."⁵⁰ One sees the clear ideological construction of her image in terms of traditional Indian religious and familial values in the fact that no sexual scandal attaches to her image, despite actual food for gossip in her life: articles about her make no more than a passing reference to her long-standing "association" with Rajasthan prince Raj Singh Dungarpur. Thus in direct contrast to the overt sexuality in the representation of visual stars, Lata Mangeshkar is completely desexualized. Describing the effect of this on individual song sequences, Partha Chatterjee says, "The picturization got past the stringent Censor Board of the time because the innocent manner in which the song was sung (in playback) . . . served to deflect the message so clearly present in the tall, shapely dancer's movements."⁵¹ Not surprisingly, a visual indicator of her public persona is that Lata Mangeshkar is invariably to be seen in a white sari. That star personas are not fixed, but develop over time, is indicated by the fact that some elements of her current public persona are taken from the early years of her career, before her separate star identity was established. For example, her visual identification with a white sari has its origins in the formative years of her career when she was often paired with the actress Nargis, who was also known as "the woman in white."

The Hindi film song sequence's ideological investment in the split between the eroticized female body and the pure female voice is well illustrated in the history of the film *Satyam Shivam Sundaram,* released in 1978. The director, Raj Kapoor, was supposedly inspired by Lata's voice to make a film about an ugly woman with a beautiful voice. Even though Lata remained the playback singer for the lead role, the actress chosen to play the ugly woman was Zeenat Aman, a fashion model and winner of beauty contests, including the 1970 Miss Asia contest. The irony of his choice of actress was not lost upon critics or upon Lata, who then failed to turn up for her recording sessions and stalled the final production of the film by months.[52] In the public eye, the film, which was a box office flop, failed to negotiate the contrary desires for a moral fable and for eroticized spectacle.

Because of the decadence ascribed to the world of cinema and the logic of the split between pure voice and eroticized body, fan discourse stops just short of denying Lata's connection with the cinema. For example, the 1967 article marking her silver jubilee observes, "It is incongruous that Lata should have almost exclusively devoted herself to singing songs for films."[53] Writing about Lata's film career in 1995, Partha Chatterjee says, "Perhaps an early exposure to the duplicity and moral degradation within the film industry made her turn away from worldliness and seek emotional sustenance in a less troubled private world. The result of this experience was startling: her singing had an innocence and naiveté that was completely at odds with the trying world she had lived in. Thus when she sang (playback) for adult heroines in films, her songs, in retrospect, were a surreal counterpoint to the amorous desires of the actresses concerned."[54] Lata has herself participated in this distancing from the world of film by repeatedly expressing regret at an aborted classical music career. In a two-part interview on Zee TV after receiving the 1999 Padma Vibhushan, India's highest national honor, she again mentioned this regret and spoke of her desire to spend the rest of her life singing religious music: "In my career this is the only vacuum which bothers me. If I would have started it earlier it would have been better as it is very tough now."[55] This aspect of Lata's star persona was reinforced by her refusal to sing songs that she considered "vulgar." Such songs often became associated with her sister's voice, which the music director Naushad described as having, in contrast to Lata's voice, a tinge of the bazaar (or marketplace) in it.[56] Between the two sisters, therefore, they met both the ideological and the commercial requirements of the entire market for the female singing voice. As Raju Bharatan puts it, "The elder [sister] picks up all the soft and lilting pieces while the younger wraps up all the hot numbers."[57]

A popular slogan, "Lata is Meera, Meera is Lata," while identifying her with the medieval singer-saint, also echoes the seventies' political slogan, "Indira is India, India is Indira." Like Indira Gandhi, Lata Mangeshkar is also perceived as a tough woman who has handled her career with shrewd business acumen. This aspect of her reputation also works to effectively reinforce the desexualized nature of her star persona. She was the first playback singer to fight for a share in the royalties to film songs, instead of a flat fee for each song. This led to a much-publicized dispute with Mohammed

Rafi and others in the film industry.[58] In the context of her shrewd career moves, most of the gossip about her is centered upon her relationship with her sister, Asha Bhosle, who is outspoken about being victim to Lata's monopolization of the female playback industry. The assumption that Lata has a monopoly is, arguably, itself something of a construct, because her dominant position in the playback industry has more to do with her place in the public imagination than with the actual number of songs she has recorded. Her star persona is also, in part, defined by her now controversial entry in the *Guinness Book of World Records* as the world's most recorded singer, a claim that was disputed by her male rival, the late Mohammed Rafi, and also by her sister.[59]

Some of these issues pertaining to the aural stardom of Lata Mangeshkar are illustrated in the continuation of the sequence from *Naseeb* with which I began this discussion. The lozenge commercial is being filmed in London and the director of the commercial tries to persuade the fictional star to wear a bikini while filming it. When he grows insistent and she continues to refuse, the hero intervenes and, reminding the expatriate director of the values of his native land, he says, "Listen, you foreign crow, the women of our country are beautiful by wearing clothes, not by taking them off." The film distances itself from its own primary mode of stardom, by making the fictional star in its diegesis a singer rather than a film actress. Furthermore, the fictional singer borrows from the known star persona of the actual singer. Here, questions of national identity are neatly conflated with norms of femininity and foreground the dichotomy between the singing voice and the displayed body. At this point, the gender connotations to the dual star text of the singer-star are also reinforced as she is "rescued" by the hero. Accompanying this is a reversal in the direction of looks with which this sequence started. Now it is actress Hema Malini who is looking at the hero, her admiring glances confirming both his masculinity and his national identity. The film's preferred mode of stardom is represented by the values given to the fictional character played by Malini. In refusing to wear a bikini, which is Hindi cinema's ultimate symbol of decadent modern femininity, both the fictional and the real-life star verbally distance themselves from associations of the body, while suggesting its erotic potential. They borrow not only the voice of Lata Mangeshkar but also traits of her star persona, specifically her identification with traditional values. The resulting construct is Hindi cinema's notion of the ideal woman whose sexuality is both suggested and contained. She is visually beautiful in accordance with the changing tastes of the time, but her familiar and unchanging voice signifies a traditional purity that transcends the female body on the screen.

In the 1990s, the voice monopoly of playback singers has given way to multiple voices, especially with the older generation of male singers all deceased. Lata and Asha now graciously "permit" new voices, the idea being that their popularity is still so enduring that nothing short of a voluntary stepping aside will make room for others. While multiple voices indicate less development of a clear-cut star persona for new singers, this has had the effect of adding new layers to the aural stardom of Lata and Asha. Since they continue to sing playback for the occasional film, with the same consistently high level of commercial success, the "ageless" quality of their voices is stressed—the over-sixty-year-old playbacking for the sixteen-year-old. With age, the moral gap between the voices of Lata and Asha is also closing, as demonstrated by many articles "reassessing" Asha's career in terms of her missed opportunities and the real affinities between her vocal qualities and those of her sister. Similarly, Lata's Meera image has acquired overtones of the elder guru,[60] as younger singers invariably make a public point of seeking her blessings, even while making veiled references to her grasping hold over the industry.[61] Music videos on MTV (and its Indian equivalents) have also changed the style of song sequences and given rise to the nonfilm music video in India. With it, the nature of the public's encounter with the singing voice has changed. The voice can no longer be the invisible, immediately recognizable, aural entity. Through the music video, the voice acquires a visual dimension over and beyond its embodiment in an actor or actress, so that now, even Asha Bhosle herself appears in music videos. While song sequences remain a central feature of Hindi cinema and playback remains its predominant technology, with all of these changes, and above all, with the multiplication of the singing voice, the female voice and body are undergoing new and varied forms of commodification.

Notes

1 Jeremy Marre and Hannah Charlton, *Beats of the Heart: Popular Music of the World* (New York: Pantheon, 1985), 141. According to Alison Arnold, the numbers were only slightly different in the 1940s and 1950s: "Record sales of film songs . . . represented an average seventy percent of a record store's business, while classical and non-classical records amounted to only thirty percent" ("Hindi Filmi Git: On the History of Commercial Indian Popular Music" [Ph.D. diss., University of Illinois at Urbana-Champagne, 1991], 258).

2   Narendra Sharma, "Half a Century of Song," *Cinema Vision India* 1.4 (1980): 58.

3   This is an alphabetical game in which participants take turns singing the opening line of a film song beginning with the last letter of the previous song.

4   Arnold, "Hindi Filmi Git," 34. For the impact of audio cassette technology on the proliferation of nonfilm popular music in India, see Peter Manuel, *Cassette Culture: Popular Music and Technology in North India* (Chicago: University of Chicago Press, 1993).

5   Ashok Ranade, "The Extraordinary Importance of the Indian Film Song," *Cinema Vision India* 1.4 (1980): 10.

6   Alison Arnold, "Popular Film Song in India—A Case of Mass Market Musical Eclecticism," *Popular Music* 7.2 (1988): 186.

7   Richard Dyer, "Entertainment and Utopia," in *Genre: The Musical*, ed. Rick Altman (London: Routledge & Kegan Paul, 1981), 177.

8   Rosie Thomas, "Indian Cinema—Pleasures and Popularity," *Screen* 26.3–4 (1985): 124.

9   Vanraj Bhatia, "Stop the Action, Start the Song," *Cinema Vision India* 1.4 (1980): 33.

10 Ranade, "The Extraordinary Importance of the Indian Film Song," 9.

11 Bhaskar Chandavarkar, "Now It's the Bombay Film Song," *Cinema in India*, July–September 1989, 22.

12 Michel Chion, *Audio-Vision: Sound on Screen*, ed. and trans. Claudia Gorbman (New York: Columbia University Press, 1990), 63.

13 Raju Bharatan, *Lata Mangeshkar: A Biography* (New Delhi: UBS Publishers' Distribution, 1995), 69.

14 Marsha Siefert discusses the Hollywood musical's matching of voice and body in "Image/Music/Voice: Song Dubbing in Hollywood Musicals," *Journal of Communication* 45.2 (1995): 57–59.

15 Ibid., 55.

16 Jane Feuer, *The Hollywood Musical*, 2nd ed. (Bloomington: Indiana University Press, 1993), 46–47.

17 Rick Altman, *The American Film Musical* (Bloomington: Indiana University Press, 1987), 258.

18 Siefert, "Image/Music/Voice," 56.

19 Ibid., 57.

20 See the entry on *Dhoop Chhaon* in the *Encyclopaedia of Indian Cinema*, ed. Ashish Rajadhyaksha and Paul Willeman (New Delhi: Oxford University Press, 1994), 244. In the playback technique, the song is recorded separately and played back when the sequence is being filmed. The singer may or may not be the same person as the actor lip-synching to the music.

21 Feuer, *The Hollywood Musical*, 3–22.

22 Siefert, "Image/Music/Voice," 46.

23 Bunny Reuben, "Hindi Screen Acting: An Assessment of Three Generations," *Star and Style* 3.4 (1970): 16.

24 "The Editor's Mail," *filmindia*, January 1941, 15.

25 Zeenath Zahara, "College Girls and Glamour Boys," *filmindia*, November 1940, 24.

26 "The Editor's Mail," *filmindia*, December 1941, 13.

27 Quoted in Sumit Mitra, "O Indisputable and Indispensable Queen," *Cinema Vision India* 2.2 (1983): 45.

28 "The Editor's Mail," *filmindia*, December 1944, 29.

29 "Ghost Voices of the Screen," *filmindia*, January 1943, 11.

30 R. N. Prasad, "Woes and Echoes," in "Reader's Forum," *filmindia*, November 1946, 74.

31 The male playback singer, Kishore Kumar, who was the only playback singer with a brief acting career, primarily in comic roles, was known for his comic performance style on stage. In contrast, both Lata Mangeshkar and Asha Bhosle are known for the absence of visual frills in their performances.

32 Siefert, "Image/Music/Voice," 57.

33 "This Stardom Racket: Overnight Glamour Products," *filmindia*, October 1942, 45–46.

34 Rosie Thomas, writing in 1985, describes the current odds against commercial success: "Over 85 percent of films released in the last two years have not made profits." She cites the *Report of the Working Group on National Film Policy* for a similar statistic for the 1970s, that "only 10% of releases made . . . profits" (Thomas, "Indian Cinema," 120).

35 Harish Bhimani, *In Search of Lata Mangeshkar* (India: HarperCollins, 1995), 154.

36 Ibid., 233.

37 Manuel, *Cassette Culture*, 48.

38 Gangadhar Gadgil, "Meet Lata Mangeshkar," *Illustrated Weekly of India*, 30 April 1967, 36.

39 "Setback for Playback," Editorial, *Filmfare*, 19 September 1952, 5.

40 Har Mandir Singh, ed., *Hindi Film Geet Kosh*, 4 vols. (Kanpur, India: Satinder Kaur, 1988, 1984, 1980, 1986 respectively). In the 1982 *Guinness Book of World Records*, Lata Mangeshkar has an entry as the most recorded voice in the world, having "reportedly recorded not less than 25,000 solo, duet and chorus-backed songs in 20 Indian languages." In a correspondence with the publishers of *Guinness*, Mohammed Rafi disputed this claim and was subsequently granted his own entry, reporting that he "claimed to have recorded 28,000 songs in 11 Indian languages between 1944 and April 1980." Rafi fans were upset over the *Guinness* choice of words, "reportedly recorded" for Lata and "claimed to have recorded" for Rafi. The controversy does not end there, as Raju Bharatan details in his chapter, "The Guinness Empress that Never Was" (Bharatan, *Lata Mangeshkar*, 275–301), because Asha fans have been quick to point out that, in the 1950s, despite Lata's greater vocal presence in the public imagination, it was Asha who actually recorded more songs, 7,500 as opposed to Lata's 5,250. In Bharatan's view, Har Mandir Singh, the editor of the encyclopaedia of Hindi film songs, has the final word when he "makes a passionate plea to all singers in India to think twice before claiming 20,000 and 30,000 songs. He points out

how ridiculous the claim is in the context of the fact that, in 60 years of Hindu-stani talkie (1932–91), the total number of songs recorded is only 50,000" (ibid., 300). In response to all the controversy, *Guinness* finally removed the category of most recorded voice, though, as far as public knowledge is concerned, Lata still has the *Guinness* pedigree of the most recorded voice in the world.

41 Mitra, "O Indisputable and Indispensable Queen," 42.
42 Quoted in Bhimani, *In Search of Lata Mangeshkar*, 211–12.
43 Quoted ibid., 235.
44 Thomas, "Indian Cinema," 126.
45 Rosie Thomas, "Sanctity and Scandal: The Mythologization of Mother India," *Quarterly Review of Film and Video* 11.3 (1989): 22.
46 When arguing that Lata Mangeshkar is not a star, Peter Manuel describes her as "portly and plain-looking" (Manuel, *Cassette Culture*, 48).
47 Quoted in Bharatan, *Lata Mangeshkar*, 85.
48 Gadgil, "Meet Lata Mangeshkar," 37.
49 Ibid., 37.
50 Mitra, "O Indisputable and Indispensable Queen," 44.
51 Partha Chatterjee, "A Bit of Song and Dance," in *Frames of Mind*, ed. Aruna Vasudev (New Delhi: UBSPD, 1995), 213.
52 Raj Kapoor explains his casting choice as follows: "When I took up the subject again, my concept of the heroine had changed. I wanted a woman with a beauti-ful voice and a beautiful body. I had Lata's voice as beautiful as ever. And Zeenat had the kind of body I wanted" (quoted in Bharatan, *Lata Mangeshkar*, 92).
53 Gadgil, "Meet Lata Mangeshkar," 37.
54 Partha Chatterjee, "When Melody Ruled the Day," in *Frames of Mind*, ed. Aruna Vasudev (New Delhi: UBSPD, 1995), 56.
55 "Melody Queen Pines for Classical Music," *India Network News Digest* 11.5, INDIA-L@INDNET.ORG, <digest@INDNET.ORG>, 22 March 1999. Archived at: <http://listserv.indnet.org/cgi/wa?A1=ind9903&L=india-l>.
56 Bharatan, *Lata Mangeshkar*, 51.
57 Ibid., 344.
58 According to Harish Bhimani, she is still "the only playback artiste who gets royalty, over and above the remuneration paid per song (wherever a royalty exists between a producer and a recording company)" (196).
59 See note 37 above.
60 In the political realm, Lata's status as elder guru was recently confirmed, in late 1999, when she was nominated as member of the Rajya Sabha, India's upper house of parliament.
61 Kavita Krishnamurty, one of the new playback singers who started as a "dubbing artiste," exemplifies this attitude in a 1996 interview: "As far as I'm concerned, I will be eternally indebted to Lataji. I started my career singing her songs which she would dub over later. . . . I owe everything to her" ("Crooning Glory," *Film-fare*, June 1996, 81–82).

MUSIC AS ETHNIC MARKER

Music as Ethnic Marker in Film:
The "Jewish" Case
ANDREW P. KILLICK

The music "track" in film has perhaps most commonly been understood as
orchestrating the viewer's emotional response to the action that is depicted
in the visual images, dialogue, and other more obviously representational
"tracks" of the film. This understanding is of a piece with conventional
thinking about musical "meaning," which holds that music is eminently
a language of the emotions, evoking and even inducing emotional sensa-
tions in the listener by means of sound patterns intrinsically congruent
with the forms of emotional experience.[1]

My intention here is not to deny that these processes operate, but to
argue that an analysis that is limited to them will often fall short of ac-
counting for the full significance of a film's music track and, worse, will
risk marginalizing music as a largely redundant "underscoring" or interpretive gloss on the film, bearing no primary information of its own. Such
an analysis is liable to reproduce the assumption, widespread in the literature on musical signification, that music (as ethnomusicologist John
Blacking suggested) merely "confirms what is already present in society
and culture, and . . . adds nothing new except patterns of sound."[2]

I take the view, to the contrary, that music can add new information
that is not otherwise apparent either in the immediate context of the film
in which it is heard, or in the broader context of the society and culture
in which the film was produced and consumed: that we can learn from
music what we would not otherwise know. I believe the unwillingness to
attribute propositional meanings to music is itself a reflection of a prevailing cultural assumption that if music has meanings at all, they are too

vague or subjective to be verbalized. This has encouraged music to become a code for precisely those meanings that are *not* expressed in more "explicit" tracks such as dialogue and visual images, and which would indeed be considered unacceptable or offensive if so expressed. I suggest that film is not an isolated phenomenon in this respect, but that its use of music for repressed or illicit meanings often derives from a stage show on which the movie is based, and carries over in turn via pop "standards" detached from musical plays and films, into independent pop songs composed purely for sale as records.

I will seek to support this view through a case study in which the "illicit" meaning is a negative ethnic stereotype, widely (and, I think, properly) considered unacceptable in explicit discourse. Using examples from very familiar movie musicals and pop songs of the 1960s and '70s, and some of their antecedents, I will show how music has been used to mark the ethnic identity of a character and/or to invoke negative stereotypes concerning the ethnic group in question. The most significant (because the least redundant) musical marking of ethnicity is likely to occur in connection with ethnic groups that are not necessarily identifiable by outwardly discernible traits such as skin color or speech style. Jews constitute one such ethnic group, often successful in "passing" as Gentiles when driven to subterfuge by anti-Semitism, and a musical style associated with Jews has been used, in film and elsewhere, to hint that the character depicted is either Jewish or is "acting like a Jew"—that is, displaying behavior that conforms to an anti-Semitic stereotype.

The most widespread anti-Semitic stereotype is perhaps the "Shylock" image of the Jew as miser, obsessed with money and unscrupulous in acquiring it. This image has been aptly described as "the cardinal one in the anti-Semitic tradition,"[3] and is of course a crux of jokes against Jews and of negative attitudes toward them. It is familiar enough to be invoked by the most implicit of allusions; and, like other stereotypes, it is reinforced every time it is invoked. We will find it invoked by musical means in narrative contexts that hinge on the ruthless pursuit of money, where the musical allusion to Jewishness implies that the character engrossed in this pursuit is either Jewish or (if the plot makes that interpretation implausible) is exhibiting typically Jewish behavior.

These musical references to "Jewishness," far from merely "underscoring" what is already present in the other "tracks" of the film, are at their most insidious when they are *not* duplicated in any other "track." That the allusion is couched only in the "implicit" code of music, I suggest, allows the stereotype to slip by the censors of explicit ideas and, potentially, to

influence the attitudes of audiences who would be shocked at the accusation of anti-Semitism. Music thus becomes the vehicle of an anti-Semitic
discourse that would, in all probability, be offensive to both producers and
consumers if expressed in a more "explicit" code.

It may seem surprising to observe the reproduction of anti-Semitic
stereotypes in a field such as musical theater and film, in which Jewish
artists and producers have been so prominent, but the dominant or hege-
monic images in a society are liable to be reproduced not only by those
whose interests they serve, but by anyone who lives in that society, such
that mothers, for example, may unwittingly impart antifeminist attitudes
to their children. Indeed, the implicitness of musical signification makes
music especially apt to encode meanings that are counter to the interests
of both composer and audience. My analysis does not, therefore, posit a
deliberate conspiracy of anti-Semitic composers, Jewish or otherwise, or
even that the composers were in every case aware of the "Jewish" connotations of the music they wrote. What it posits is that the use of this "Jewish
music" in association with lyrics expressing the desire for money can help
to reproduce and perpetuate a prejudice in the broader society without
anyone's having deliberately set out to do so.

This use of "Jewish music" can also serve the needs of the film and
music industries, regardless of the role of Jews in those industries, by projecting the pecuniary motives of the industry itself onto a group that is
represented as an "other." The entertainment industry often seems to feel
obliged to disavow its own profit motive in the effort to hide the economic
relationship of producer and consumer behind something more romantic
or utopian. Jim Collins has argued that a "displacement of value . . . is central to the musical," that "the economic success that is so highly considered
in the 'real' world is replaced in the fictional world of the musical by success
in love and the dance."[4] Jane Feuer has shown how the Hollywood musical achieved this substitution by representing its stars as amateur rather
than professional performers, and having them sing and dance for love
rather than money.[5] The profit motive is thus canceled out, and audiences
feel that they are actively participating in communal folk art instead of
passively being exploited by commercial mass entertainment.

This has been one strategy; another has been to mask the movie industry's serious goal of commercial profit by making the unscrupulous pursuit of money a subject of comedy, as in the *Gold Diggers* series of musicals
from the Depression years. A third strategy, with which I am here concerned, is the ascription of the profit motive to a marginal social element
seen as "them" rather than "us." And it should come as no surprise, given

the tenacity of the "Shylock" stereotype, when the "other" onto whom the profit motive is thus projected turns out to be the Jew.

My main examples are drawn from the 1960s and '70s, a time when opinion polls suggested that American anti-Semitism had been in decline since the Holocaust and relatively few people were openly espousing it,[6] although some Jews were anxious about its reemergence in subtler forms that were dubbed "the new anti-Semitism."[7] Britons, on the other hand, had been slower than their transatlantic counterparts to grasp the significance of the Holocaust, and continued, on the whole, to regard Jews as problematic and undesirable immigrants.[8] As late as the 1970s, the British musical *Jesus Christ Superstar* (stage version 1971, film version 1973) was attacked from across the Atlantic for retelling the Christian myth of the Jews' collective guilt in the murder of Jesus,[9] and it is probably no accident that one of my central examples comes from another British musical, *Oliver!,* and that the first objections to its anti-Semitic elements came when the show was taken to the United States. Nevertheless, on neither side of the Atlantic was anti-Semitism quite respectable when openly expressed, however widespread tacit approval it might command; and these were the conditions in which implicit allusions to the "Shylock" stereotype of the Jew could be incorporated in some of the most popular music and musicals of the anglophone world.

The songs in which these musical allusions are embedded have been so widely disseminated that one is led to ask what role they may have played in helping anti-Semitic attitudes to survive through times of apparent "political correctness" and to reemerge, as they are now doing, in such irrational forms as Holocaust denial.[10] Such a question, though no doubt unanswerable, suggests how much more there is at stake in musical signification than the mere "underscoring" or emotive inflection of meanings already present elsewhere.

Defining a Musical Sign of "Jewishness"

The show that defined Jews permanently for musical theater and film audiences was, of course, *Fiddler on the Roof* (stage version 1964; film version 1971), in which nearly all the characters are Jewish, and sympathetically portrayed. Composer Jerry Bock deliberately set out to give their music a Jewish sound throughout,[11] but especially in Tevye's solo "If I Were a Rich Man," inspired by a Hasidic folk song the composer had recently heard.[12] Joseph Swain was able to devote ten pages of his book on the Broadway musical to a sophisticated analysis of the "ethnic idiom" in "If I Were a Rich

14 In *Fiddler on the Roof,* Tevye grants his daughter's hand to the poor tailor, but she is already promised to the rich butcher—a dilemma that would never arise "if he were a rich man." [Author's collection]

Man," the song in which, he says, Bock "concentrates the greatest number of 'Jewish' commonplaces."[13]

Many of the "Jewish" musical features Swain identifies in this song will recur in our subsequent examples, and they illustrate the two main types of musical image that we will find in association with Jews: the rustic dance and the synagogue chant. Overall, the song is characterized by the rhythmic simplicity of the "rustic dance" image: the tempo is moderate, the rhythms plodding, and the articulation light; there is little syncopation, great uniformity of note values (largely limited to eighth notes and quarter notes), and many phrases begin on the first beat of a measure, without an upbeat.[14] The "dance" is, however, interrupted by passages in free, recitative-like rhythm (for instance, that beginning with the words "The most important men"), which represent the complementary "synagogue chant" image. The fermatas that occur here and at several points earlier in the song (first at the words "I'd build a big tall house") will appear in several of my further examples when the rhythmic flexibility of synagogue chant interrupts the steadier flow of danceable rhythms.

It is typically at these moments of chantlike flexibility that the most concentrated "Jewish" flavor is found, expressed not only in rhythm but in other musical parameters such as melody and word setting. Both of these are relevant in the current instance, where the nonsense syllables "boi, boi, boi" after the words, "Posing questions that would cross a rabbi's eyes," allude to the Hebrew texts of synagogue chant, unintelligible except to the initiated and often represented as gibberish. These syllables are sung to the melodic interval of an augmented second, "exotic" in the context of Broadway and Hollywood but widely used throughout the Western musical tradition (according to musicologist Susan McClary) as "the musical sign for the Jew, the Arab, the all-purpose racial Other."[15]

Such musical "Jewishisms" are not limited to the "chant" passages but are scattered throughout the song. Its word setting in general is both highly repetitive and liberally sprinkled with nonsense syllables, such as the "diga diga dum" near the beginning of the song, which perhaps evokes the textless *nign* of Jewish tradition. Melodically, the most obvious musical marker of Jewishness is the minor mode and its variants, rare in musical comedy but characteristic of a wide range of Jewish musics and of popular representations thereof.[16] Here, as often, the minor mode is flavored not only with the augmented second but with chromatically descending lines and, harmonically, with augmented sixth chords resolving directly onto the dominant (without the tonic six-four chord that more commonly intervenes) at cadences (as at the words "One more leading nowhere just for show").

Such, then, are the elements of the musical sign that we will find in association with Jews throughout our sample of popular songs and musicals. Where did this sign come from? Its most immediate antecedents might be found in a now forgotten Broadway musical of 1962, *I Can Get It for You Wholesale*, whose main characters were New York Jews, and whose songs, in the judgment of musical director Lehman Engel, were "infused . . . with a Jewish inflection."[17] That inflection is perhaps strongest in an ensemble celebrating the wholesome pleasures and values of family and home, "The Family Way," in which, for instance, plodding, unsyncopated rhythms, uniformity of note values, light articulation, a minor mode with prominent augmented seconds, and nonsense syllables ("Dye dye digga digga dye") are all present in force.

The antecedents of this "Jewish" musical sign, however, can be traced back much further than this. Its essential elements are clearly present, for instance, in the very first feature film with synchronized sound, *The Jazz Singer* (1927), not in the ragtime-style songs that Al Jolson sings but in a little tune that accompanies one of the rare moments of humor in the film.

As the Jewish elders bicker about what to do in the absence of their inca-
pacitated cantor, their bumbling is caricatured by a simple tune that Mark
Slobin has labeled the "Kibitzer's Theme."[18] And in this tune, again, we
find plodding, unsyncopated rhythms, uniformity of note values, light articulation, a minor mode containing an augmented second, and a cadence
that moves through an inversion of an augmented sixth chord directly onto
the dominant.[19]

The "Kibitzer's Theme," even if abstracted from its context, would have
been recognizable as "Jewish" because of a whole genre of "Jewish novelty
songs" that had been created for Vaudeville performers (some of whom
specialized in precisely this genre) in the earlier years of the twentieth
century, and that was still making its presence felt in the 1920s: for instance, in the descending chromatic lines of "Second-Hand Rose" as recorded by Fanny Brice (1921), or in Sophie Tucker's bilingual recording
of "My Yidishe Momme" (1925). Jewish immigrant composers and musicians themselves had taken the lead in creating the genre, drawing on
their familiarity with the music of the shtetl and of Jewish weddings as
well as the synagogue. But they made it into a sign intelligible outside
the Jewish community and capable of representing an outsider's view of
"Jewishness."

Perhaps foremost among these composers was Irving Berlin, who in the
early stages of his career wrote a large number of "ethnic novelty songs"
caricaturing German and Italian immigrants, black Americans (the so-
called "coon songs"), and rural whites ("rubes" or "hicks") as well as immigrant Jews like himself.[20] Roughly ten of Berlin's songs written between
1909 and 1913 represent Jewish protagonists and invoke "Jewish" stereotypes in their narrative frames as well as in their verbal and musical style.
"Business Is Business" for example, alludes to the stereotype of Jewish
preoccupation with money and contains many of the "Jewish" musical features already mentioned.[21] Most strikingly, while its chorus is in Berlin's
customary major-key syncopated "ragtime" style, its penultimate phrase,
sung to the words "Every little dollar carries interest all its own," reverts to
one of the unsyncopated minor-key phrases (with a prominent augmented
second) from the more Jewishly inflected verse of the song. This phrase is
evidently a Jewish "tag," for it occurs not only in the piano introduction but,
slightly modified, in the introduction to another of Berlin's "Jewish novelty
songs," "Yiddle, on Your Fiddle, Play Some Ragtime"—which also contains
the characteristically "Jewish" cadence of an augmented sixth chord moving directly to the dominant.[22]

Ultimately, the antecedents of this "Jewish" musical sign could probably be traced across the Atlantic to such popular classics as Modest Musorgsky's *Pictures at an Exhibition* for piano (1874), in which Victor Hartman's portrait of two Polish Jews, one rich and one poor, inspired a movement entitled " 'Samuel' Goldenberg und 'Schmuyle.' " Elements of the sign could even be found in the earliest preserved example of a musical caricature of Jews, Hans Neusiedler's *Der Juden Tanz* (The Jew's Dance) for lute, dating from 1544. Clearly, it is a sign with deep roots and wide distribution.

My hypothesis is that this cluster of musical features has been used in explicit association with Jews consistently enough for the same cluster to evoke the idea of "Jewishness" at some level, for some listeners, even when it is heard in contexts that make no direct reference to Jews. If this is true, an examination of some contexts in which this "Jewishness" is evoked should reveal something about the qualities by which Jews are thus represented. It will then remain to be asked why the representation is made implicitly, through music, rather than explicitly, through words.

Despite the sympathetic portrayal of the Jewish community in *Fiddler on the Roof,* especially of the central character, Tevye, who sings "If I Were a Rich Man," one is led to wonder why the "greatest number of 'Jewish' musical commonplaces" is concentrated in a song expressing the desire for money. In the context of the show, no doubt, no one will perceive Tevye as a stereotypical Jewish miser; but like other Broadway and Hollywood "standards," "If I Were a Rich Man" has often been performed outside of its original context, and in such situations, the coupling of "Jewish" musical features with a lyric expressing pecuniary longings (however benign) might inadvertently contribute to the perpetuation of the stereotype.

My purpose here, however, is not to argue that any of the examples I have so far discussed is anti-Semitic; rather, I argue that it is when the association with "Jewishness" is implicit (that is, unconfirmed by verbal elements in the context) that a "Jewish" musical sign lends itself to anti-Semitic uses. My intention in this brief sampling of music explicitly associated with Jews is merely to suggest some of the ways in which a musical sign of "Jewishness" might differ from the customary style of mainstream popular music against which it is defined, so that we will be able to identify such a sign when it occurs in "implicit" contexts.

Invoking "Jewishness" through Its Musical Sign

Lionel Bart's musical comedy *Oliver!* (stage version 1960, film version 1968) has remained unchallenged as the most popular of British musicals since its record-breaking initial run of 2,618 performances in the early

1960s. But *Oliver!* could not have achieved its reputation as wholesome family entertainment without ostensibly detaching itself from an ugly history of anti-Semitism, and it is against this background that Bart's use of a "Jewish" musical sign must be understood. In his novel *Oliver Twist* (1838), Dickens wanted to make Fagin, the evil corrupter of youth, appear as villainous as possible, and making him Jewish was evidently a device to serve that end.[23] The narrative habitually referred to Fagin as "the Jew" rather than by his name, and part of the book's "happy" ending was a gloating description of him in prison awaiting his execution (chapter 52).

Adaptations of *Oliver Twist* for stage and screen have been slow to abandon the implication that Fagin is Jewish, though they have avoided explicit verbal references to his ethnicity. In 1948, just one year after a major outbreak of anti-Semitic violence in Britain[24] (and in the same year that Hollywood launched an attack on anti-Semitism in *Gentleman's Agreement* and *Crossfire*), a British film of *Oliver Twist* directed by David Lean had Alec Guinness wear an enormous false nose to represent the stereotypical feature of Jewish physiognomy that had figured in Dickens's descriptions of Fagin and in George Cruikshank's illustrations for the original edition (e.g., chapter 42). It was not until the 1988 BBC television serialization of *Oliver Twist* that Fagin's Jewish identity would be completely erased; and in the musical, as we shall see, it was the music that furnished the principal clues.

Lionel Bart's representation of Fagin in *Oliver!* might best be grasped through two reviews of the New York production. The first, by Norman Nadel, praises Clive Revill's portrayal of the character as "funny, but never pallid" and points to "Reviewing the Situation" as "one of the most striking demonstrations of the Revill comedy."[25] A second review, by Howard Taubman, takes a more sarcastic tone, observing that "Mr. Bart nowhere identifies [Fagin] as a Jew. . . . By a strange coincidence, however, Fagin has a big number in the second act set to music that bears a close resemblance to Jewish folksong. In 'Reviewing the Situation,' he ponders the grim possibilities left open to him as retribution draws near, and a lush violin obbligato seems to stress racial strains the author obviously never meant to suggest."[26] Fagin, that is, was identified as Jewish by exclusively musical means.[27]

Taubman points to a feature of instrumentation, the "lush violin obbligato," as a musical sign of Jewishness, but there are many other features he could have mentioned, both here and in Fagin's other song, "Pick a Pocket or Two." "Reviewing the Situation" takes the old alternating verse-chorus structure of operetta and maps onto it an alternation between the "chant" and the "dance" images of "Jewish music." The verse is introduced by an improvised violin cadenza and accompanied by the "lush violin obbligato" that Howard Taubman found so distinctively Jewish. It is in free rhythm and begins and ends with long fermatas. Its mode is basically minor, but its last line contains a prominent augmented second in an unconventional position (that is, its upper note is other than the leading note of the scale), and this creates the effect of an exotic mode. The chorus shows the combination of minor mode, light articulation, and moderate tempo that we have seen so often in explicit association with Jews. Like the "Kibitzer's Theme" and "The Family Way," it stays on the same harmony for six measures before changing on the last two of the phrase. The second half of the chorus goes to an extreme in the absence of syncopation and the uniformity of note values, and its long accelerando culminates with another violin cadenza, which leads into the next verse.

In Fagin's other song, "Pick a Pocket or Two," wherein he coaxes the innocent young Oliver into the paths of crime, the mode is again minor, the tempo moderate, and the articulation light. The ad lib vamp that precedes each chorus throws great weight onto an augmented sixth chord that resolves directly onto the dominant. The lyric is characterized by repetition and nonsense syllables, with half of each chorus given over to repetitions of the title phrase, "You've got to pick a pocket or two," and the final chorus containing only this phrase plus syllables such as "Skiddle-eye-tye, Tee-rye-tye-tye" resembling those we have seen in music explicitly associated with Jews. Rhythmically, there is a complete absence of syncopation and a marked tendency to uniformity of note values and avoidance of upbeats. The melody consists initially of plodding repeated notes, and the last phrase before the refrain is delayed by a tenuto on the word "boys." In the final chorus, this tenuto is elaborated into a thoroughgoing fermata, where, in the film version, Ron Moody sings a much more ornate cadenza than is indicated in the vocal score.

In *Oliver!*, then, a particular cluster of musical features amounts to a sign that the character with whom they are associated is Jewish. It is only by assumption that the behavior of that character might then be thought to be typical of Jews in general. But if the same cluster of features appeared in association with a character who was known *not* to be Jewish, the sign would make sense only as a hint that the character was "acting like a Jew." It would thus tend to promulgate a generalized discourse about how Jews behave, potentially more insidious, though less tangible, than a portrait of a single Jewish character. It would function to perpetuate and reinforce a stereotype by giving it tacit assent.

15 "Money makes the world go round"—Liza Minnelli and Joel Grey fetishize hard cash in *Cabaret*. [Author's collection]

Such a case occurs in the film version of the musical *Cabaret* (1972). When Liza Minnelli's character Sally Bowles stumbles on an opportunity to ingratiate herself with a wealthy German aristocrat, she promptly sings the duet "Money, Money" with the cabaret emcee. Composer John Kander gave this song a Jewish accent, which, though more attenuated than in *Fiddler* or *Oliver!*, is, I think, clearly discernible. The composer's ability to use a "Jewish" musical style is evidenced by the songs of the Jewish grocer Schultz, in the original stage version of *Cabaret,* who sang a good deal of unambiguously "Jewish" music showing the features I have identified. The singing grocer disappeared in the film version, which tries to make all its songs diegetic, but traces of his "Jewish" musical accent remained in the cabaret itself.

The venue where Sally sings, the Kit Kat Klub, is a site of what the Bakhtin circle would call "carnivalesque" performances, of which "Money, Money" is one of the more extreme examples.[28] The singers flaunt their corporeality with their lustful gazes, hip thrusts, and farts; coins end up down the emcee's pants or Sally's cleavage, and body movements produce the clank of hard currency. Money is literally incorporated—absorbed into the body—and the eroticizing of money asserts the kind of hidden, indecent, or "unofficial" fact that can only be expressed in "carnivalesque" situations like the cabaret, where there is a suspension of usual prohibitions. This normally repressed message, "I Want Money," is here musically ventriloquized as the voice of an "other" that has long been associated with it: the Jew.

The syncopation characteristic of most of the songs in *Cabaret* (and indeed in Western musical comedy generally) is entirely absent in "Money, Money," and the chorus is built on fragmentary verbal and melodic repetitions, reminiscent of the repetitive and nonsensical texts we have encountered elsewhere; indeed, the title of the song is itself a repetition of the word *money*. The chromatically descending first line recalls Tevye's "All day long I'd biddy-biddy-bum," and cadences in the minor, the usual "Jewish" mode. The bridge (beginning "If you happen to be rich . . .") uses the minor consistently, and is even more repetitive.

But these clues, if they are perceived as Jewish at all, cannot be taken to mean that the characters singing are Jewish, as in Fagin's case, because we already know from the story that they are not. The use of "Jewish" music in the absence of Jewish characters makes sense only as a hint that the cynical money-grubbing philosophy expressed in the song is typical of Jews. The music of the song thus contributes a separate layer of meaning, invoking and thus implicitly reaffirming an anti-Semitic stereotype even though, on the explicit level, the story is set in Nazi Germany and presents anti-Semitism in the most negative possible light. The nature of the sign has changed from an index ("this is a Jew") to a symbol ("this is about Jews"), and it conveys a meaning that could not be deduced from the lyric alone.

The similarity between the avarice implicitly projected onto Jews by this song and the miserliness of Samuel Goldenberg or Fagin should not escape our notice, for it represents a theme that we will come across again in implicit examples of "Jewish music." We will come across it outside the world of musical theater and film, in independent pop songs that have no association with specific characters or plot, and no connection with Jews except through the history of their musical features. The wide dissemination of songs like "If I Were a Rich Man," "Pick a Pocket or Two," and "Money, Money" outside their original narrative context may have provided a musical style that was already associated with songs expressing a desire for money and that came to be used (even if its "Jewish" connotations were not always recognized) in independent songs on the same theme.

The double repetition of Sally Bowles's "Money, Money" became (in what one is tempted to call a symptom of 1970s inflation) the triple repetition of ABBA's "Money, Money, Money" (1976). It is not only in the textual repetition of its key word that this song resembles our earlier examples: the concluding line of its chorus, "It's a rich man's world," ties it thematically to Sally Bowles's maxim, "Money makes the world go round," and to Fagin's motto, "In this life one thing counts: in the bank large amounts." Its music, too, resembles these antecedents perhaps more than it resembles ABBA's own previous songs. If ABBA had sung in their own voice—that is, in their usual upbeat disco style—about scheming to get rich, it would have been an uncomfortable reminder to fans that their money was making ABBA second only to Volvo as the largest earner of foreign exchange in Sweden.[29] By treating this theme in a musical style that was, in the context of their previous songs, alien, they could express the profit motive in the voice of an "other," and thus erase the commercial relationship between themselves and their fans. Whether the composers intended it or not, the association of the profit motive with an "exotic" musical style serves to erase that motive from the "us" associated with a more "mainstream" style, by projecting it onto a marginalized "them."

The worldwide popularity of ABBA was founded to a great extent on their being pleasant and inoffensive, and the cynical lyric "Money, Money, Money" is as rare for them as the unsmiling, shadowy film noir look of the video they made to promote it. The same is true of the music, which differs from their other hit songs precisely in those features I have been identifying as "Jewish," and thus adds a layer of meaning that could not be discerned in the text alone. Foremost among these features is the minor key, combined with a descending chromatic line in the guitar during the chorus. Rhythmically, there is a striking uniformity of note values and little syncopation, especially in the verse, which contains a ritardando and fermata before the chorus begins—an exceptional rhetorical effect for a group that was normally concerned to keep a disco beat going throughout.

Even if these choices can be explained as affective devices matching a lyric of harsh realism and machiavellian ambition, they may also be overdetermined by the precedent of the earlier songs mentioned above, which had helped to normalize an association between Jewish-sounding music and themes of avarice. Such precedents can be found not only in songs of the musical stage and screen, but in autonomous pop songs such as The Who's "Silas Stingy" (1967), the opening chorus of which closely resembles that of "Money, Money, Money" both lyrically and musically. The history of extremely well known songs combining a "Jewish" musical style with lyrics expressing the desire for money, on the part of Fagin, Sally Bowles, and even Tevye, may have linked the theme of cupidity with this kind of musical setting so conspicuously that, by the time Benny Anderson and Bjorn Ulvaeus came to write "Money, Money, Money" for ABBA, they may have simply regarded this musical style as appropriate for a song about money without even being aware that it had once been associated with Jews.

It certainly could not be maintained that *all* songs about money have "Jewish" musical features: it would be far-fetched, for instance, to detect a "Jewish" accent in Pink Floyd's "Money" or the O'Jays' "For the Love of Money." But I think a historical continuity can be traced through this musical sign that once stood for Jews and that now stands for money—a continuity that rests on an anti-Semitic stereotype, even if the origins of the sign have been largely forgotten through semantic drift and few if any ABBA fans think of Jews when they listen to "Money, Money, Money." It remains to be considered whether this use of "Jewish music," even when unrecognized as such, might serve to perpetuate an anti-Semitic stereotype that is no longer considered acceptable in explicit discourse.

Conclusion: Is There a Musical Anti-Semitism?

If the "Jewish" origin of the musical features that ABBA used in "Money, Money, Money" was by that time largely forgotten, the question then arises whether the older meaning of those features still matters: whether there is a persistence, on some level, of earlier, sedimented meanings that are no longer explicitly understood. Fredric Jameson, for one, argued in *The Political Unconscious* that such a persistence would be typical of artistic genres in general, and that the most dramatic examples would come from music history: "In its emergent, strong form a genre is essentially a sociosymbolic message, or in other terms . . . form is immanently and intrinsically an ideology in its own right. When such forms are reappropriated and refashioned in quite different social and cultural contexts, this message persists and must be functionally reckoned into the new form. The history of music provides the most dramatic examples of this process."[30] If this is so, a composer need not be consciously anti-Semitic to help perpetuate, through music, an association between Jews and avarice that would be unacceptable to both composer and audience if expressed in words.

Jameson's use of the word *emergent* reminds us of Raymond Williams's distinction between the "dominant," "residual," and "emergent" elements present in a cultural system at any given time. The status of anti-Semitism in the 1960s and '70s evidently fits Williams's sense of the "residual," which, "by definition, has been effectively formed in the past, but is still active in the cultural process, not only and often not at all as an element of the past, but as an effective element of the present. Thus certain experiences, meanings, and values which cannot be expressed or substantially verified in terms of the dominant culture, are nevertheless lived and practiced on the basis of the residue—cultural as well as social—of some previous social and cultural institution or formation."[31] If music is one of the media in which this inexpressible, unverifiable cultural residue survives, this is a fact with serious social consequences, since "a residual cultural element is usually at some distance from the effective dominant culture, but some part of it, some version of it—and especially if the residue is from some major area of the past—will in most cases have had to be incorporated if the effective dominant culture is to make sense in these areas."

That an attitude such as anti-Semitism might exist even when it is not verbalized or consciously acknowledged is a possibility that cannot, perhaps, be scientifically tested; but neither can it be rashly discounted when anti-Semitic stereotypes appear to be invoked through nonverbal sign systems such as music. The interpretation of musical signs, though it must be historically informed, cannot always rely on verbal confirmation of meaning; rather, musicology can make its potential contribution to the understanding of culture only if it has the confidence to assert that we can learn from music what we would not otherwise know. The foregoing examples from music show that anti-Semitic images, even if often unrecognized as such, are more prevalent in our society than verbal sources alone may suggest.

Indeed, music may be in one respect a more powerful medium than words for persuading the listener to accept its underlying ideology, since the highly specialized and exclusive process by which the most widely disseminated music is produced enables it to persuade without argument. Susan McClary has suggested that the ability of music to influence the feelings and attitudes of its listeners—to convince them that certain culturally molded affective experiences are natural and inevitable—depends on their ignorance of the mechanisms by which music achieves its effects, their inability to "answer back."[32] It is then the business of the music analyst to expose those mechanisms along with the ideological, rather than natural, character of the models they inculcate; McClary's efforts to do so with regard to the musical modeling of gender and sexuality might well be extended to ethnicity and the self-other distinction in general.

Does music, sentimentally idealized as a symbol and gesture of social harmony, sometimes serve, on the contrary, to perpetuate and reinforce socially divisive prejudices that are no longer acknowledged in explicit speech? To address such questions, however uncomfortable, may help us to understand and respond appropriately to the effects of musical signification, not only in film but in life.

Notes

1 The most influential statement of this view has perhaps been Susanne K. Langer's *Philosophy in a New Key: A Study in the Symbolism of Reason, Rite, and Art* (New York: Mentor Books, 1948).
2 John Blacking, *How Musical Is Man?* (Seattle: University of Washington Press, 1973), 54.
3 Charles Herbert Stember et al., *Jews in the Mind of America* (New York: Basic Books, 1966), 8.
4 Jim Collins, "Toward Defining a Matrix of the Musical Comedy: The Place of the Spectator within the Textual Mechanisms," in *Genre — The Musical: A Reader*, ed. Rick Altman (London: Routledge & Kegan Paul, 1981), 141.
5 Jane Feuer, *The Hollywood Musical* (Bloomington: Indiana University Press, 1993), 13–15.
6 Stember et al., *Jews in the Mind of America*, 7–10.
7 Arnold Forster and Benjamin R. Epstein, *The New Anti-Semitism* (New York: McGraw-Hill, 1974).
8 Tony Kushner, "Immigration and 'Race Relations' in Postwar British Society," in *Twentieth-Century Britain: Economic, Social, and Cultural Change*, ed. Paul Johnson (London: Longman, 1994), 420–21.
9 Forster and Epstein, *The New Anti-Semitism*, 91–101.
10 On Holocaust denial, see Deborah Lipstadt, *Denying the Holocaust: The Growing Assault on Truth and Memory* (New York: Plume Books, 1994).
11 Mark Slobin has judged that "no systematic Jewish elements are introduced" in the music of *Fiddler*, that "many [of its] songs have no ethnic content whatsoever" (42); but this judgement is based on a comparison with works of the Yiddish theater intended for an exclusively Jewish audience, in which some form of Jewish music is the expected norm. Different criteria apply when "Jewish music" appears as an exotic style in a musical offered to a mainstream Broadway audience that is accustomed to different norms, even if that audience too has a heavy Jewish component. See "Some Intersections of Jews, Music, and Theater," in *From Hester Street to Hollywood: The Jewish-American Stage and Screen*, ed. Sarah Blacher (Bloomington: Indiana University Press, 1983), 29–43.
12 On the genesis of this song, see Richard Altman and Mervyn Kaufman, *The Making of a Musical: Fiddler on the Roof* (New York: Crown Publishers, 1971), 100.
13 Joseph P. Swain, *The Broadway Musical: A Critical and Musical Survey* (New York: Oxford University Press, 1990), 251.
14 Aron Marko Rothmuller holds syncopation to be typical of Jewish folk music, but in the context of musical comedy with its rhythmic tradition traceable to Tin Pan Alley and ragtime, it is the relative *lack* of syncopation that often marks

a song as Jewish. See *The Music of the Jews: An Historical Appreciation* (New York: A. S. Barnes, 1954), 227.

15 Susan McClary, *Feminine Endings: Music, Gender, and Sexuality* (Minneapolis: University of Minnesota Press, 1991), 64.

16 Rothmuller, *The Music of the Jews,* 226

17 Lehman Engel, *The American Musical Theater* (New York: Collier Books, 1975), 131.

18 Mark Slobin, *Tenement Songs: The Popular Music of the Jewish Immigrants* (Urbana: University of Illinois Press, 1982), 195.

19 Though Slobin construes the theme as an example of the *frigish* mode of Jewish folk music, in which an ascending scale from the tonic (D) would begin with a half-step followed by an augmented second, the insistence with which both the melody and the harmony cling to a G minor triad for six measures, before changing on the last two of the phrase, makes it difficult to hear the mode as anything but G harmonic minor, cadencing not on the tonic but on the dominant.

20 Charles Hamm, ed., *Irving Berlin: Early Songs,* Music of the United States of America II, 3 vols. (Madison: A-R Editions, 1994), 1:xxxiv–xxxviii.

21 This song is published in Hamm, *Irving Berlin,* 2:26–29.

22 Ibid., 1:86.

23 Lionel Trilling makes this point in "The Changing Myth of the Jew," *Commentary* 66.2 (1978): 32.

24 Kushner, "Immigration and 'Race Relations,'" 412.

25 *New York World-Telegram,* 14 January 1963.

26 *New York Times,* 14 January 1963.

27 I myself had grown up with *Oliver!* and participated in school performances of it without ever suspecting that Fagin was Jewish, but it was his music that first tipped me off when I returned to the show with more educated ears, initiating the line of inquiry that eventually led to the present essay. In point of fact, there are also verbal clues of Fagin's ethnicity (such as his rhetorical question "At my time of life *I should* start turning over new leaves?" and use of object-initial constructions: "*A wife* you can keep, anyway"). Professional actors who have played the role have not always suppressed the "Jewish" aspect. When Barry Humphries joined the cast of Cameron Mackintosh's revival of *Oliver!* in 1996, he explicitly played up the Jewish identity of Fagin, affecting a Yiddish pronunciation and even interpolating expressions such as "*Oy veh!*"

28 The most complete formulation of the Bakhtinian notion of the "carnivalesque" is perhaps Mikhail Bakhtin, *Rabelais and His World,* trans. Helene Iswolsky (Bloomington: Indiana University Press, 1984).

29 David J. Jefferson, "The First Step to Recovery," *Wall Street Journal Report: Global Entertainment,* 26 March 1993, R18.

30 Fredric Jameson, *The Political Unconscious: Narrative as a Socially Symbolic Act* (Ithaca, N.Y.: Cornell University Press, 1981), 141.

31 Raymond Williams, *Marxism and Literature* (Oxford: Oxford University Press, 1977), 122–23.

32 McClary, *Feminine Endings,* 53, 62.

Sounding the American Heart: Cultural Politics, Country Music, and Contemporary American Film

BARBARA CHING

"When you hear twin fiddles and a steel guitar, you're listening to the sound of the American heart," sings a young boy's faltering voice in the opening frame of Christopher Cain's *Pure Country* (1992). The words of this song ("Heartland") assure us that while we listen to this music we "still know wrong from right."[1] This opening sequence thus celebrates its viewers as it stakes a claim to both the film's and country music's power to unequivocally represent the best qualities (the "pure") of the United States (the "country"). When placed in a history of the relationship between film and country music, *Pure Country* can be read as the most recent entry in a series of cinematic appropriations of this power. In fact, the film's title indicates that it is about country music's claim to cultural significance, and its plot challenges the problematic status assigned to country music by the previous quarter century of filmmaking.

To enter into these cultural politics, the film tells the story of a country superstar's crisis of authenticity. Once the opening credits fade, we hear and see a grown man singing the same song in a huge arena, accompanied by multispectrum lights and a smoke machine. Although the song claims that songs about the heartland are also songs about the singer's life, Dusty Wyatt (played by country music superstar George Strait) no longer lives there. Tired of the corruption of his odes to purity, he deserts his band in the middle of a tour, only to find that he is easily replaced by a lip-synching member of the road crew. This crisis inspires him to return to the place where he was the naive boy of the opening credits (the young voice was supplied by Strait's son, George Jr.). He lights out for the heartland—where he cuts off his ponytail, absorbs some wisdom from his oracular granny, and meets the cowgirl of his dreams. Thanks to this immersion in supposedly unmediated experience, Dusty builds the strength to triumph over the country music machine. Paradoxically, his triumph doesn't require giving up the privileges of stardom; all it requires is "deserving" those privileges. Having earned them in the heartland, Dusty whisks his Grandma and his girl by jet and limousine to his first performance as a new man, proposes to the girl on stage, and reconnects with his adoring audience by singing about all this. "Pure country," then, is the American Dream made remarkable only by the magnitude of its achievement. Dusty Wyatt has what every American supposedly wants: a charming family, affluence, and basic decency—set to twin fiddles, a steel guitar, and fewer neon lights than when the movie started.

The first movies to feature country music and country stars similarly made the soundtrack part of the plot. Western settings and singing cowboys like Gene Autry and Roy Rogers come immediately to mind, and the "B" film era also featured "hillbilly" films with southern singers such as the Weaver Brothers and Elviry.[2] More recent films such as 1980's *Urban Cowboy* and Burt Reynolds's good ol' boy pageants celebrated the music by portraying a tight relationship between the soundtrack and the red-blooded, happily-ever-after hedonism of the plot.[3] But beginning at least as early as Elia Kazan's *A Face in the Crowd* (1957), "serious" directors used country music—the supposed bedrock of American authenticity—to sully the very images that *Pure Country* works to restore.[4] Miles Orvell has argued that the search for authenticity is a constant in American culture, and both he and Morris Dickstein note that the sixties counterculture put this issue high on its political agenda.[5] Kazan's iconoclastic approach proved particularly useful in films aimed at the hip, authenticity-seeking audience of the sixties and seventies. Art films such as Bogdanovich's *The Last Picture Show* (1971), Bob Rafelson's *Five Easy Pieces* (1970), Arthur Penn's *Bonnie and Clyde* (1967) and *Alice's Restaurant* (1969), and John Boorman's *Deliverance* (1972) use country music performance and/or country music fans to portray lonely American crowds, violence, fraud, and political corruption. Indeed, it could be argued that the films made in association with the BBS production company created the contemporary American "serious" film, and in this respect, it is crucial to note their reliance on country music.[6] Many claustrophobic moments in *Five Easy Pieces* were accompanied by Tammy Wynette songs (although Jack Nicholson's character is not ashamed to praise Vegas show music), and *The Last Picture Show* used Hank Williams songs to similar effect. So successfully has this shorthand conveyed its message that it can still be used to critique American politics and a smug, self-deceived American psyche: recent films such as Tim Robbins's *Bob Roberts* (1992) and Barry Levinson's *Wag the Dog* (1997) continue to link country music to prophecies of decay. The sound of "twin fiddles and a steel guitar" represents the kind of smug hokum that contrasts to the critical vision offered by these auteur-directors. For them, singing is deceiving but seeing is believing.

In contrast, when mainstream directors integrate country music into their narratives, they embrace the country sound. Seeing and hearing together inspire believing. But whatever their ambitions, filmmakers assume that country music bears a burden of a particularly American authenticity. A country soundtrack sounds the American heart, either affirming the purity of the "American way of life" or condemning a nation hypocritically mired in provincial materialism. In this essay I focus on four films about country music performers: Robert Altman's *Nashville* (1975), Michael Apted's *Coal Miner's Daughter* (1981), Bruce Beresford's *Tender Mercies* (1983), and Cain's *Pure Country*. In these examples country songs fuel both the art film's and mainstream film's claims to representational power, although the one casts the music as enemy territory while the other casts it as the Heartland.[7] Altman valorizes film's ability to provoke critical scrutiny by using the soundtrack and his fictional stars and fans to portray patriotic corruption; in an equally arty film, Beresford offers his audience an aura of political purification by stressing the dangers inherent in performing country music anywhere but in the heart, invisible if not for the movie camera. Apted and Cain, in films that revise the themes of *Nashville* and *Tender Mercies,* harness film to country music's supposed power to emit the "sound of the American heart." Although Apted is an Englishman and Beresford Australian, all these films stake a claim to authentic representation of value-laden American territory even as they require different sorts of audience response and construct different relations between plot and country soundtrack. Read as a series, however, all four films oppose country music to the cultural and political upheaval of the sixties, and for better or worse, all four films show (the) country's "triumph" over this upheaval.

It Don't Worry Me

To "celebrate" the bicentennial, Robert Altman's *Nashville* (1975) brought the analogy between country music and the country's culture to a zenith of critical acclaim.[8] Hal Phillip Walker's presidential campaign amplifies the analogy as it ties together the fates of twenty-four diverse characters. Appropriately, we never see this candidate but we assume we hear his voice blaring political bromides from a sound truck. Smooth Californian John Triplette comes to town to encourage the local stars to perform at a fund-raiser and rally on Walker's behalf. Several of the singers seem to be based on some of Nashville's biggest stars: Haven Hamilton was widely viewed as a blend of Hank Snow and Roy Acuff, while the black star Tony Brown was Charley Pride.[9] Barbara Jean (Ronee Blakley) and her rival Connie White (Karen Black) bear strong resemblances to Loretta Lynn and Tammy Wynette.[10] Triplette hopes to persuade Hamilton and Barbara Jean to appear at the rally, yet he also encounters the dimmest lights in the country music galaxy such as Sueleen Gay, a waitress/songwriter who imagines that she will be as big as Barbara Jean one day. Other newcomers to Nashville — such as the rock trio Tom, Bill, and Mary, the hopeful star Winifred (who wants to be known as Albuquerque), an unnamed, ominous soldier who hovers around Barbara Jean, and Kenny, a charmless young man with a violin case — orbit the country music scene. Most ubiquitous is Opal, a pompous British documentarian ("from the BBC") who misses the point of everything she sees, and who fails to see the climactic event — Kenny's assassination of Barbara Jean at the Hal Phillip Walker rally.[11]

Whereas *Pure Country* celebrates country music's devotion to American values, *Nashville* mourns America's enslavement to commercial interests. In scenes shot at the Grand Ol' Opry, the documentary-style camera and Altman's famed multitrack recording system give as much prominence to inane ads for Goo Goo clusters (a candy named from the Grand Ol' Opry's initials) as they do to the singers' performances. The movie's twenty-seven songs immediately provoked debate about whether Altman exposed the hollowness of country music or whether he and his Hollywood cohorts simply mimicked the music so poorly that they missed its message. For example, in the second of his *two* reviews of *Nashville*, the *New York Times* film critic Vincent Canby claimed the film was "brilliantly scored," while its music critic John Rockwell argued that "many of those who love country music will be bored or even annoyed with these songs."[12] Nearly two months later, the *Times* published yet another article praising *Nashville*'s

16 Haven Hamilton (Henry Gibson) on stage at the Grand Ole Opry in *Nashville*. [Author's collection]

music.[13] The film's music arranger, Richard Baskin, insisted that "it was never our intention to parody or put anyone down," and he made a point of hiring professional Nashville sidemen to provide musical accompaniment.[14] Altman himself later proved adept at handling country music when he wrote the lyrics to hard-core country singer John Anderson's 1983 number-one hit "Black Sheep." In short, while *Nashville*'s songs weren't written to be chart-toppers, they evoke the readily recognizable sounds and themes of top-forty country.

Two musical themes prove especially crucial: the political and the sacred. The movie opens during a recording session for Haven Hamilton's attempt to cash in on the bicentennial: "We Must Be Doing Something Right to Last 200 Years." While his name evokes colonial-era ideals, his message condones more recent practice.[15] What we've been doing, Hamilton sings, is gamely fighting wars to prove our rectitude: "It's up to us to pave the way with our blood and sweat and tears." Life, liberty, and the pursuit of happiness matter less to him; he twice interrupts the session, first to object to Opal's presence then to dismiss a long-haired piano player whom he asserts "doesn't belong in Nashville." In the next studio, Linnea Reese and a black chorus are recording a gospel number, "Do You Believe in Jesus." The dogged interventionism described in Haven's song, however, undercuts the trust in God evoked by the gospel group. These two themes are quickly reiterated and juxtaposed when we hear a campaign announcement attacking the national anthem. Hal Philip Walker, the unseen, wizard-of-Oz-like campaigner, proposes replacing "The Star-Spangled Banner" with an understandable, singable anthem, "something that would make a light shine in their faces." We also witness a massive fender bender and traffic jam. No injuries are apparent, and the Nashvilleans turn this event into a friendly neighborhood gathering; only Opal (the foreigner) is thrown into a panic by this stasis in the sizzling sun. She wishes she had a cameraman to document the carnage she imagines: "It's America," she asserts, "all those cars smashing into each other and all those mangled bodies." In fact, neither the accident nor the candidate make any psychic impact on the internal audience.

As talk about the national anthem fades out, strains of "It Don't Worry Me," a haunting paean to irresponsibility, drown out even the traffic snarl. "You may say that I ain't free, but it don't worry me" turns out to be the replacement for "the land of the free and the home of the brave." Even if it "don't worry" the fans who latch on to the song, it evidently does worry Altman. (Indeed, this turn of events is strangely prophetic of the "don't worry, be happy" musical politics of later campaigns.) If any of the songs we've heard so far actually serves as a reflection on the lives of the characters, this one does. In contrast, the stars and would-be stars who so convincingly mouth Nashville's musical platitudes blankly sing various hymns—gospel, southern Baptist, or Catholic—during a Sunday morning montage. Their moments of worship, like the national anthem, seem to pay lip service to various ideals rather than to express real parts of themselves or their communities, and the night before, at the Opry, Connie White, named to reveal the emptiness of her surroundings, admitted it: "I'd love to go to heaven but I forgot how to pray."[16] To introduce this emptiness, Altman begins the montage with Mary, waking from a Saturday night tryst, telling a sleeping Tom that she loves him; the camera dissolves from his unresponsive face to a stained glass window depicting Jesus.[17]

Love songs turn out to be equally loveless. Haven Hamilton's "For the Sake of the Children" explains to a mistress why the singer won't leave his wife even though off-stage Haven lives just the opposite arrangement: his wife travels in Europe while he maintains a household with his mistress and his grown son, Buddy. Tom's "I'm Easy" appears first to be about the intensity of his love for a woman but we quickly realize that it applies more readily to his promiscuity and narcissism: his tape of the song plays end-lessly in the disheveled room where he holds his trysts, and when he sings it in a bar, dedicating it to "someone special who might be here tonight," at least four women in the audience think of themselves as the special some-one. Barbara Jean's theme song, "One, I Love You," enumerates the sort of platitudes that eventually lead to her murder (One, I love you / Two, I'm thinking of you / Three, I'll never let you go, etc.). The would-be star Sueleen Gay distorts and diminishes Barbara Jean's mathematical trope so pathetically that her message is badly misunderstood: "Let Me Be the One" and "I Never Get Enough" both abjectly promise devoted monogamy although Sueleen's awkwardly explicit sexuality comes across more force-fully than her country purity. Thus the only showbiz breaks she can get require her to perform a striptease at a Hal Philip Walker fundraiser. Buddy Hamilton's blandly sweet love song leads him to a similar humiliation. Shyly singing it at Opal's coaxing, he halts mid-bar when she abandons him at the sight of a bigger celebrity. Connie White, Barbara Jean's "replace-ment" at the Grand Ol' Opry, shrinks Barbara Jean's pure and simple love songs into numb complaints of ineloquence: "I'd like to tell you how I feel but I don't know what to say."[18]

Even Barbara Jean cannot sustain a love song. When she appears at Walker's rally, she launches into the simultaneously evocative and inco-herent clichés of "My Idaho Home." Here the flaws in her lyrical vision turn fatal. While she claims that her parents' songs and laughter "would ring down the highways, on the beaches" (in Idaho?), she also hints at vio-lence and rootlessness in her verse about her father's army songs and whis-key. Mama came from Kansas, daddy obviously moved around some, and Barbara Jean lives way across the country in Nashville. The chorus, how-ever, insists, "I still love mama and daddy best, and my Idaho home." The contrast between the stated theme and the realities of family life, evidently, becomes too much for Kenny to bear, so he shoots her.[19] Kenny has al-ready experienced similar conflict: earlier we heard him arguing with his mother over the telephone, only saying that he loves her after she hangs up, expressing thereby a wish more than a true feeling. Altman makes us sense that the music itself is somehow responsible for this frustrated longing and murderous rage by frequently focusing on Kenny's "holster": the violin case that never leaves his side. Until this moment, we've be-lieved he was an aspiring musician, and if anyone scared us, it was the sol-dier who stoically endures Tom's taunts about Vietnam and Barbara Jean's indifference.

Nashville's spokespersons, then, make just as likely assassination targets as overtly political figures, and its aspiring musicians are the assassins. In fact, early in the film, the camera establishes Nashville as one vast gunman as it focuses on an airport sign warning that "all persons entering concourse are screened for weapons," and several later conversations verify this statement.[20] Haven's mistress carries a pistol even as she bemoans the assassinations of the Kennedys. As he rushes Barbara Jean off the stage, Haven Hamilton commands the crowd: "This isn't Dallas. . . . They can't do this to us here in Nashville." Nevertheless, the fact that he makes the remark indicates that a political assassination has taken place. Barbara Jean is a prisoner of a mythical American purity, and the pursuit of that mythical happiness kills her. The real impetus behind her music and her familial relations is exploitation, a fact she unwittingly reveals in a string of dotty and down-homey stage patter at a performance the day before the rally. Her "mama" bragged to a phonograph salesman that her little girl could sing. (The comparison with a machine is frightening, and Barbara Jean breaks down rapidly as she tells this story.) He promises to pay them if she learns the song on one of his records. "Ever since then I been workin'," she concludes as her husband helps her offstage. While she attributes a spontaneous harmony to her parents in "My Idaho Home," Barbara Jean knows that her singing has always been for sale. As a friend cynically warns Sueleen, who is eagerly expecting Barbara Jean to give a free performance in thanks for her homecoming ceremony, "she don't sing unless she gets paid." The one free performance she gives leads to her death. Haven, too, at the beginning of the film, was incensed to think that Opal could hear him sing "We Must Be Doing Something Right" without buying the record. They "ain't free"—we've known this since the aggressive sales pitch for the soundtrack that accompanies the opening credits—and it doesn't worry Hamilton but it destroys Barbara Jean. With her death, Altman disproves the operative premise of his country singers (and the Hollywood musical): the spontaneous expression of emotion in song.[21] Instead, country music serves as the emblem of corruption. It's about this country but this country is all show business.

Haven already knows this; that's why his songs, even the ostensibly patriotic one, are all about grim determination, and that's why he survives. His theme song proclaims that "ain't no law says you must die, keep a' goin.'" His behavior after the assassination reinforces his stage persona. He orders someone to sing, so Albuquerque picks up Barbara Jean's fallen microphone and the gospel chorus we saw at the beginning accompanies her—as if singing about Jesus or nihilism is all the same to them. In turn, at her bidding, the whole audience turns its attention away from the murder to dazedly sing, "You may say that I ain't free, but it don't worry me." Ultimately, what replaces Barbara Jean is neither the Replacement Party's candidate nor Connie White but rather the desperate Albuquerque and her star-worthy ability to mimic and incite mimicry. The political implications are chilling: if there is such a thing as the vox populi, it only repeats what is sung to it. As the closing credits roll and the internal audience fades away, the song keeps playing, insinuating itself into the external audience's mind.[22] The cynical salesmanship of the opening credits lulls the spectator into a critical smugness not so different from Haven Hamilton's self-righteous scorn for long hair, but the closing credits insist on our complicity. Stunned by the murder and mesmerized by the melody, we can easily assent to Nashville's insouciance. As screenwriter Joan Tewkesbury said in her interview with Byrne and Lopez, "the intention of the piece is for you to be a participant."[23] The first time we heard this melody, the stalled cars resumed their merry ways, and something analogous can happen to us as the melody fades. We can either leave the theater fighting to get that song out of our heads, or we can sing along with the deadly chord of business, entertainment, and politics. Criticism, refusal, authenticity, individuality, all the elements of freedom and vitality belong only to the director and to the unhappy few willing to worry along with him.[24]

So contagious is this entanglement that "It Don't Worry Me" did not even hit the airwaves as a country song. Tom, Bill, and Mary introduced it, and as rock singers they are eager to distinguish themselves from the Nashville crowd although they evidently must come to Nashville to do so. Triplette lures them to perform at the rally on this basis: they will be the only rock stars on the roster (and presumably they will sing "It Don't Worry Me"). Nevertheless, their song demonstrates the epidemic that Nashville represents. It doesn't matter who sings it; Nashville, the intersection of show business, politics, and everyday hopes, easily absorbs its competition—even, or especially—the supposedly countercultural forces represented by rock and folk stars. Only Linnea's beatific deaf children are immune to the failure of family, community, and politics that their fellow citizens experience. They strip a Carpenters' ditty of its commercial veneer, expressing a sincere wish "to teach the world to sing." Necessarily off key, they nevertheless seem to actually experience the emotional rush of the world depicted in country music. But, as Wim Wenders notes, they can't communicate this to us through music alone; listening to them re-

quires looking at them. "Suddenly it becomes evident that film is a language. There are no lies in the sign language of Linnea and the children;
that shows up the big lies around them all the more."[25] No wonder the dim
Opal claims she can't bear to hear about them or see them.

You're Looking at Country

Michael Apted's *Coal Miner's Daughter* (1981), based on Loretta Lynn's
autobiography, smoothly embodies (rather than exposes) country music's
contradictory and particularly American rhetoric of patriotism, proud individuality, lonely struggle for success, and subsequent integration into a
harmonious community. Every song we hear in the movie somehow links
these themes to the "reality" of Loretta's life (although in the book, Lynn
notes the fiction behind such an assumption: "Everyone says all my songs
are about myself. That's not completely true, because if I did all the things
I write about, I wouldn't be here, I'd be all worn out in some old people's
home").[26] *Nashville's* queen of country music, Barbara Jean, also favored
these themes although she failed to balance them so deftly. As a result,
Lynn introduced her 1977 autobiography, *Coal Miner's Daughter* as at least
partly a rejection of *Nashville's* fragile homespun diva. "If you're wondering whether that character in the movie is me, it ain't. This book is me,"
she says in her preface. Thus the movie version of this book can be seen
as a mainstream counterpoint to Altman's film; the European release title,
Nashville Lady, makes the contrast particularly clear. "If they really wanted
me, why didn't they just ask me?" Lynn wondered about Altman's production team.[27] Yet even the film *Coal Miner's Daughter* doesn't go that
far toward authenticity; instead it gestures toward authenticity by having
Sissy Spacek mimic Lynn so well that she sings Lynn's songs for the soundtrack. Spacek, in fact, won an Oscar for her portrayal of the rags-to-rustic
stardom saga that both informs and ironizes Loretta Lynn's country music
performances. The film, then, laid claim to "pure country" by portraying
a tripartite "reality": Lynn's experiences, the songs that grew out of them,
and the replication of the songs that Lynn had recorded as much as fifteen
years earlier. When Spacek sang Lynn's 1971 hit "(If You're Lookin' at Me)
You're Lookin' at Country," the film audience was supposed to assent to the
"old-fashioned" values that the song espoused and that the film portrayed
("I'll show you around if you show me a wedding band," for example). In
contrast, in *Nashville,* the nostalgic clichés of Barbara Jean's "Idaho Home"
seemed to bear no special resonance for her oddly unmoved audience. If

17 Sissy Spacek as
Loretta Lynn in *Coal
Miner's Daughter*.
[Author's collection]

anything is assented to in *Nashville*'s last scene, it is the violent disman-
tling of "pure country's" ideals, but when you look at Sissy Spacek playing
Loretta Lynn, "you're lookin' at country."

While this film does not engage political and religious issues so directly
as *Nashville,* it clearly links country music to traditional American values.
Roger Angell's review in the *New Yorker,* echoed by several other critics,
sums up the effect:

> *Coal Miner's Daughter* didn't make me feel exactly patriotic, but I did
> realize somewhere in the middle of it that an Oxford don or a Castil-
> ian winemaker would probably not share the joy I felt while watching
> Sissy Spacek astride a mule on a steep, wintry-looking Kentucky hill-
> side . . . or when I saw the fringed, shiny-white, narrow cut satin cow-
> boy shirts worn by the backup guitar-pickers at the Ryman Audito-
> rium. . . . A possessive, homebred pleasure comes to you often when
> you see this movie, and you smile in the dark, almost embarrassed
> because you have been affected so simply.[28]

The title and title track praise the work ethic and love demonstrated by
Lynn's parents, and the opening scenes in the movie beautifully evoke
the coal miner's happy family and Appalachian community. There, sing-

ing happens as part of Loretta's daily life, a natural expression of talent and femininity. We first hear her singing to comfort a young sibling; later she does the same for her own children (the first four were born before she was eighteen). Loretta's husband Doolittle, as enchanted by her voice as her children are, gives her a guitar as an anniversary gift. Soon after, he arranges for her first public appearances and recording session. To ensure that she sounds her very best in the studio, he surrounds her with her children. A little later, he makes sure that Loretta really wants a life in the limelight, cannily forcing her to shout her decision over the roar of a tractor. Unlike Barbara Jean's simultaneously overbearing and effete husband/manager, Doolittle Lynn knows how to bring out the best in Loretta. The movie critics routinely reminded the public to make the comparison. Stanley Kauffmann, for example, began his review in the *New Republic* by praising the portrayal of Lynn's childhood and early married life, and he concluded by professing that the movie "means a lot more to me than the bloated *Nashville,* with its strain to be an All-American metaphor."[29]

Although Doolittle displays a hard-drinking streak of chauvinism, Loretta successfully scolds him in her hit songs such as "Don't Come Home A-drinking (with Lovin' on Your Mind)" and "Your Squaw Is on the Warpath Tonight"; as her career flourishes, he matures into a responsible, sensitive husband and father. Her superstardom merely gives her the means to improve on this domestic bliss; she can afford a large ranch where she lives the American dream with her husband and large brood. They continue to fight, even as the movie draws to a close, but these fights keep the irony of Loretta's wealth and fame from drowning out the travails of housewifery that she sings about. Importantly, these scenes are not drawn from the book; there Lynn alludes to her tempestuous relationship with her husband as well as her gratitude for his psychological acumen but she gives few concrete details. The movie thus sharpens the contrast between the supposedly "real" Lynn and the slanderously fictional Barbara Jean. We never actually see Altman's Barbara Jean experience the family happiness that she sings about; her offstage scenes show her as bullied and brainwashed by her husband.

Likewise, the corruptions of show business leave Loretta's pure country soul untainted. While *Nashville*'s Barbara Jean and Connie White engage in nasty rivalry, Loretta and Patsy Cline (Beverly D'Angelo) become best friends. Barbara Jean and her husband collude to maintain a rustic public image, but Doolittle and Loretta never think about such things. A key scene created for the movie imagines an awkward radio interview in order to demonstrate Loretta's unmediated naturalness. She describes for

the disc jockey how she and her husband have been traveling the southern countryside, stopping at all the country radio stations they pass, and
"getting horny" in the car in between stops. Earlier, Doolittle told her that
bologna sandwiches, the mainstay of their traveling diet, had this effect,
but he refused to answer her questions about what that meant. Since they
talked and laughed a lot in the car, she concluded that getting horny meant
engaging in such banter. Without waiting for her explanation, the station
manager gets furious about her "dumb hillbilly act" and swears never to
play any of her records. Once he's out of earshot, however, the disc jockey
tells her not to worry. Since her first record now stands at number fourteen
on the *Billboard* charts, she'll have no trouble getting it played. Loretta responds with a puzzled look; evidently she's never heard of *Billboard*. "That
really isn't an act, is it?", the jockey proclaims. In the book, Lynn characterizes her encounters with the media somewhat differently: "It ain't easy
being serious on these talk shows, if the hosts just want to make fun of
your language or hear hillbilly stories."[30]

Nevertheless, Lynn experiences pressures similar to those that crush
Barbara Jean. Success entails such constant contact with fans that Loretta
loses touch with the sources of her inspiration. In the last part of *Coal
Miner's Daughter*, Lynn, too, suffers breakdowns; a slow-paced touring
montage shows her abusing prescription drugs in lonely hotel rooms while
Doolittle bathes the children and watches her on television. Appropriately,
even though she begins each show with "Lookin' at Country," she begins
to forget the words to her songs. Even more appropriately, the song that
gives her the most trouble is "One's on the Way." In theory, the lyrics contrast Loretta's life of wifely drudgery with the glamorous doings of "Liz"
(Elizabeth Taylor) and "Jackie" (Onassis), but in fact they suggest an unconscious and evidently uncomfortable similarity.[31] For Loretta to remain
completely natural and untainted by show business, she must be able to
live these words but to succeed in show business, she can't live the life of
a rural housewife. It is interesting to note that this last part of the film
was often singled out for criticism amidst the otherwise lavish praise. No
one, even film critics, wants to hear that the dream comes with a price.
Kauffmann complained that "it's probably all true, but it's certainly all
trite"; Angell called it "tedious." Lynn's audience, however, still loves her
when she's down, and in spite of a briefly sketched on-stage breakdown,
she triumphantly returns to the stage after some family time back on
the ranch.

The movie doesn't deal with assassination although Barbara Jean's assassination was the climax of *Nashville,* and in her book, Lynn claims to

have been tormented by death threats.[32] Instead, the movie concludes with Lynn introducing the autobiographical title song, "Coal Miner's Daughter." Earlier scenes from the movie reprise as the closing credits roll. These recurring images suggest that Lynn's ability to sing and to please fans comes from the same source: her rich life as wife, mother, "country girl," and "coal miner's daughter." The film, too, makes a similar claim to representing reality by repeating this "true story." Lest anyone should leave the theater thinking they'd seen a glamorized biopic, the last credits solemnly announce that Sissy Spacek and Beverly D'Angelo performed their own songs, and that this was "filmed entirely on location in Kentucky and Tennessee." In place of Altman's deadly blend of hoax and hysteria, in *Coal Miner's Daughter*, we seem to be witnessing a peculiarly American form of *history* that begins in a charming nowhere like Van Leer coal camp and ends at the top. To judge from the critical response, it's a fairy tale that all good Americans should believe. "What's different about Coal Miner's Daughter," proclaimed *Newsweek*'s David Ansen, "is that it's not about self-destruction. It's a celebration of Lynn's endurance, spunk, and heart, and yet it never feels like puffery."[33] *Coal Miner's Daughter,* particularly in the title song, inspires the audience to patriotic pride and affirmation, replacing the unpalatable options—despair or idiotic insouciance—offered by *Nashville.*

Apted's conservative technique reinforces this response. To judge from the critics, Loretta always got her message across—at least until Altman came along and garbled it. Her husband reforms when she scolds him in song, her audience buys her records, and Apted's camera and sound recorder respond with the same obedience. While Altman inundates us with noise and visual stimuli, often to the obliteration of singing, when Spacek/Lynn sings, all eyes and ears are on her. When we look at her, we are hearing and seeing country. The conventional film technique, in other words, confirms the premise of Lynn's music: hearing is believing, and seeing is, too. Altman notoriously uses as many as sixteen tracks on his sound system, thereby picking up all sorts of detracting and distracting noise. According to Altman, "it's not designed to hear every word."[34] Instead, it's a lot like noise in the "real" world, where most of our listening takes place, although we have come to associate reality with the reel world of soundproof booths and dark velvety theaters. Surely Spacek's Academy Award, and all the commentary her singing provoked, confirms this paradox. Again, Roger Angell's comments, precisely because they appeared in the avowedly urban and eastern *New Yorker,* are the most striking: "Sissy Spacek . . . is pure country and a pure pleasure to watch—most of all when she is singing. She does all her own vocal work . . . and displays a musical presence . . . that holds the entire picture together."[35] No one seemed to sense any irony in praising the acting in a story which was largely about the struggle to keep from acting.[36]

Likewise, the narrowing of Lynn's message attracted little attention: the film version of her story avoided any suggestion of unresolved political issues in the rags-to-riches story, yet in her book, she openly discusses her commitment to Native Americans, women, and coal miners.[37] In 1975, her jubilant song "The Pill" provoked great controversy and was pulled from many radio stations, because, as Lynn notes, "the men who run the radio stations were scared to death. It's like a challenge to the man's way of thinking."[38] Putting her coal-mining pride into practice, she tried to start college trust funds for the children of coal miners who died in a mining accident. Although legal difficulties kept her from maintaining the trust, she makes a point of explaining the necessity of removing the structural barriers to class mobility (rather than simply giving money): "I wanted the money to help people to break that way of living that keeps them poor and uneducated, that forces men to work in dog-hole mines and women to have too many babies and not know how to deal with lawyers and slippery little government officials."[39] In short, Lynn is proud to be a coal miner's daughter not only because she made it to the top from this lowly beginning but also because she is now in a position to question the forces that keep coal miners, women, and "hillbillies" in their place. These "worries," which aren't fully assuaged by song, make another important distinction between Lynn's vision of herself and Altman's vision of Barbara Jean; yet ironically, the movie version of *Coal Miner's Daughter* obliterates it.

It Hurts to Face Reality

Two years later, *Tender Mercies* confronted the ironies of *Coal Miner's Daughter* by driving its hero, the (fictional) washed-up country singer Mac Sledge, off the stage and the bottle and into family, hard work, and religion. Robert Duvall won an Oscar for his portrayal of Sledge. Like Spacek, he did his own singing, and like Altman's actors, he wrote several songs on the soundtrack. The hyperbolically bleak setting—what Curtis Ellison aptly calls "rural post-Vietnam Texas"[40]—is the isolated Mariposa motel, run by pretty Rosa Lee, a young widow. Mac Sledge and an unidentified friend are staying there, engaging in drunken brawls. When his friend abandons him, he asks Rosa Lee if she will let him work off his bill. She agrees, demanding only that he not drink on the job. He quickly falls in love with her, they marry and maintain the motel together, and he begins to bond with her young son (Sonny). But if Mac is to sustain this small-scale American dream, his musical talent can be of no use to him. The sound track demonstrates this point very subtly through the repetition and variation of key songs. The first song we hear (by Lefty Frizzell) provides an alcoholic's explanation for his state: "it hurts to face reality," and this refrain recurs at emotionally charged moments throughout the film, particularly when Mac is tempted to resume drinking. His new "reality," however, renders country music almost irrelevant: "I've decided to leave here forever," Mac sings as he begins to teach Sonny how to play the guitar. He turns quickly to Rosa Lee to add a reassuring "not really" lest she take the line to heart. The audience, too, like the film itself, must assume that country singers live every line. Certainly, Mac's second wife, the hysterical Dixie Scott, wallows in stereotypical country bathos, and ultimately the film will make her pay for her commitment to this career. Thus the rest of the movie is about facing not so much reality as embracing an American ideal by renouncing country performance (and alcohol with it). A newspaper reporter uncovers Mac's identity and thereby reveals it to the whole community. "Were you really Mac Sledge?," a local matron asks. "I guess I *was*," he replies. His baptism literally brings the curtain down on the hard drinking, hell raising, and country singing phase of his life: the basin is surrounded by stagy red velvet curtains that close as the preacher helps him submerge.

Nevertheless, in order to make life easier for his new family, Mac secretly tries to sell Dixie some new songs. Although she is already rich from singing his earlier songs, she cannot forgive him for his drunken abuse. (He admits that he once tried to kill her.) She sends her manager to tell him that the new songs are bad. The manager later returns and offers to buy the songs himself, but now Mac refuses to sell. Instead, he gives the songs to a struggling community band and even sings them on their first record. Dixie also refuses to let Mac see their daughter, although she secretly pays him a visit at the motel. The daughter then elopes with a shiftless musician (much like Mac in his earlier days) and is killed in an accident caused by his drunken driving. Mac learns this just as his new record is playing on the radio; he turns it off, and this is the last time we hear Mac sing in public. When Mac pays Dixie a visit in her tacky mansion, she is at once righteous and inconsolable, claiming that she gave her daughter everything she ever wanted. Her devotion to country music, we are to conclude, contributes more to their child's ruin than Mac's alcoholism, abuse, and absence. Mac thus leaves her to her lavish misery while he returns to Rosa Lee's motel. The easy irony of the dingy motel's name (Mariposa is

Spanish for butterfly) now becomes a symbol that Mac's metamorphosis is complete.

Mac is baptized with Sonny, and in many ways *Tender Mercies* is about the bond between these two. These bonds, in turn, both articulate and sublimate the political issues that a country soundtrack so often negotiates. Sonny's biological father died mysteriously in Vietnam, and the boy's questions about his father raise issues that the Reagan era worked to bury: the fate of the counterculture protest movement. Sonny repeats to Rosa Lee the schoolyard taunts that say his father died for nothing, that all soldiers did in Vietnam was learn to take dope, etc. She has little to say in reply except that his father was a good boy who would have been a good man. Mac, as a full-grown man and replacement father, somehow redeems and replaces that dead boy. In the film's final moments, Mac expresses his frustration over the injustices suffered by those close to him: Why did his daughter die while he survived his drunken escapades? Why did Sonny's father die? Likewise, Sonny questions Rosa Lee about his father's death just before the closing scene. Unfortunately, she can't give him the answers he seeks, so instead she encourages him to look at the present Mac bought him—a football. As the camera pulls away from the man and the boy tossing this ball, an almost absurdly American symbol of violence contained by domestic bliss,[41] we hear one of Mac's new songs, this time being sung by a lighter (uncredited) voice: "you're the good things that I threw away, coming back to me every day." The changed voice is crucial to the resolution. Mac can experience these emotions but he cannot sing about them in public: that way lies the domestic tragedy of drunken deaths, broken homes, and, somehow, the senseless turmoil of war and social conflict. These things no longer worry Mac and Sonny, and likewise, the film, with its relentless use of the long shot,[42] assures us that they'll stay peacefully in their desolate place, working hard and staying out of trouble. The *Nation's* Robert Hatch duly noted that Beresford "leads his hero into temptation but delivers him from evil, and the audience I was in seemed dazed by the euphoria of witnessing a miracle."[43]

Like *Nashville,* this film resolves the dilemma of the country soundtrack by substituting film for country music. Thus country music's association with both the pro-Vietnam conservatism of the sixties and the corruptions of mass-media-fueled greed is both demonstrated and evaded by the purity of the film itself. Country music is not silenced—Dixie and the unnamed final singer are still out there singing Mac's songs—but it is gracefully maligned. The audience can admire the film—the cinematography, Duvall's acting, and especially the story—without having anything to do with country music. They can applaud the troublesome class politics of the film and still feel enlightened. In fact, very few of the reviewers who commented on this film had anything to say about either the soundtrack or the politics.[44] Stanley Kauffmann concludes his glowing review by refusing to believe the movie is about country music at all: "*Tender Mercies* is more allegory than story. . . . Motels and guitars and booze are only the surface phenomena."[45] John Simon, in the *National Review,* was even more ecstatic than Kauffmann, entitling his review "Merciful Heavens, a Real Film." He, too, makes a point of severing the film from its subject matter: "The plot is almost incidental . . . the telling of it—through direction, acting, and photography—is everything."[46] *Time*'s Richard Corliss articulates the very premise of auterism in his plot summary: "Attuned to the movie's rhythm, the viewer will see wounds heal, friendships ripen, a bond sealed *between the filmmaker and the audience*" (emphasis mine).[47]

Pure Country

Restoring the cinematic bond between country music and the audience is the point of *Pure Country*. In this movie, a renunciation like Mac Sledge's or a death like Barbara Jean's would be impossible. Likewise, even though the movie is about a fictional country star, a movie star could not logically play the role, and a director could not take center stage as Altman and Beresford do in their country music films. In *Pure Country,* only the singer and his songs can convey country purity. Any other form of mediation, film excepted but movie stars included, incites the corrupting powers of sophistication. The few critics who bothered to review this unpretentious film, however, did not compare it to previous films about country performers, thus missing the full resonance of the story and its accompanying songs. Instead, they focused on star George Strait's lack of acting ability. The *New York Times*'s Janet Maslin, for example, claims that Strait "never seems the superstar he is supposed to be."[48] Of course, Strait *is* a superstar, and as Dusty his quest, like Loretta Lynn's, is to make people believe that he couldn't possibly be acting. (Doesn't the name "Strait" say it all?) As Dusty rages against the machine, he reminds his entourage that "in the early days, when it was about the music, we did it because we loved it." Now, he continues, the "fans . . . don't trust us, and I'd like to get their trust back." The media serve only to inflame the situation: once Dusty's blindly ambitious lip-synching double seeks stardom in his own right, television reporters and newspaper writers eagerly inflate his story into scandal. The cinema, however, silently exculpates itself by its alliance with country purity. Both the first song we hear ("Heartland") and the last one ("I Cross My Heart") are about telling the truth. The difference lies not only in the experiences Dusty has had in between singing them; it is the camera that proves to us that he has learned from them. If we hadn't seen what had gone on before, we wouldn't believe what we are hearing now. The camera lingers on Dusty's stolid face, showing us that he is no longer blowing smoke, that he is now who and what his songs say he is. Even the fact that this defining moment happens at the glitzy Mirage Hotel in Las Vegas, so unlike the dingy Mariposa motel of *Tender Mercies,* is unironically announced: the closing credits thank the Mirage Hotel. The country star and his songs thus triumph over the massive and malicious interests of show business, proving—at least until the next picture show goes on—that his country, no matter what "you may say," is still the land of the free.

What gives worry, though, is the hollowness of this message. Freedom, for Dusty and his fans (both internal and external) seems to lie in apolitical affirmation rather than questioning. Dusty's shorn ponytail most obviously represents his severance from show business hipness, but it's also a rejected vestige of the counterculture. His name, too, conveys a cinematic reminder of the counterculture: he's "Dusty" to his fans, but at home in the heartland, he's Wyatt. The name may echo that of western hero Wyatt Earp, but Wyatt was also the name of *Easy Rider*'s Captain America, "the man" who, according to the movie's advertising slogan, "went looking for America but couldn't find it." This Wyatt, however, heads straight to it. Evidently, all he ever wanted was to sing love songs to his wife, and the audience loves him for it. Indeed, by the time *Pure Country* hit the movie theaters, there was a vast audience making Dusty's equation between "twin fiddles and a steel guitar" and "the American heart." According to journalist Bruce Feiler, "by 1993, 42 percent of Americans were listening to country radio every week, twice the number of a decade earlier." [49] He adds that "country fans . . . were more educated than either adult contemporary or rock audiences. . . . They were also wealthier." He describes himself as a convert to the music, too, noting that Nashville "had become . . . a new patron city for the American dream. . . . Just as rock 'n' roll foreshadowed many of the changes in gender and race relations that followed in the sixties, country music in the nineties—with its themes of family and renewal—became the clearest reflection of many of the conservative ideals that were just beginning to surface in American life." [50] In this light, *Pure Country,* severed from its links with other films about country performers, is just another movie about the unremarkably American desire to have it all and feel good about it. Placed in the context of contemporary films about country performers, however, it's a story that cuts country music loose from both the cinematic worries that Altman and Beresford confront us with and the dilemmas of stardom that undermined the ending of *Coal Miner's Daughter.*

The paradoxes of screening country music show how the music's authenticity is actually negotiable territory which the American cinema can invade to construct its own grounds for representation. An art film like Altman's *Nashville* questions whether there is such a thing as pure country music, thereby tacitly constructing its own authority through a critique of an easily duped mass society. On a smaller scale, Beresford's *Tender Mercies* points to a similar conclusion: to redeem a country and a family floundering after the protest movement and the Vietnam War, country music, the opiate of some pretty nasty people, must be transcended, and *Tender Mercies* flatters its audience into just such a state of cinematic transcendence. Mainstream films such as Apted's *Coal Miner's Daughter* and Cain's *Pure Country* celebrate country music's animating (and equally paradoxical) notion of unmediated performance through triumphant explorations of how such a notion can be portrayed as an American ideal. And while *Pure Country* epitomizes such triumph, it is too soon yet to imagine that the bond between film and country music is now sealed. No film has yet to portray the country music that is associated precisely with worrying about freedom. Indeed, it is this strain of country music that American film, whether it strives for mass appeal or critical cachet, relentlessly suppresses. Lynn's life story, had it included her commitments to women, coal miners, and Native Americans, would be quite a different movie, as would Altman's *Nashville* or Cain's *Pure Country* had they sounded the complexities of a singer like Merle Haggard, who, no matter how jingoistic, sees himself as a voice of "the working man."[51] In other words, it can be argued that "authentic" country music has yet to be screened, but it is the very negotiation of these claims to authenticity that keeps the music and the movies playing.

Notes

I want to thank Allison Graham, Kevin Hagopian, Arthur Knight, and Pamela Robertson Wojcik for their helpful insights and suggestions.

1 "Heartland," written by Stephen Hartley Dorff and John Bettis.
2 See Wade Austin, "The Real Beverly Hillbillies," in *The South and Film*, ed. Warren French (Jackson: University of Mississippi Press, 1991), 83–94, for a discussion of what he calls "the Southern."

3 Bill Malone, *Country Music USA*, rev. ed. (Austin: University of Texas Press, 1985), 371.

4 The titles of two recent books, one academic and one for the general public, indicate how automatic the association between country music and national music has become: Cecelia Ticchi, *High Lonesome: The American Culture of Country Music* (Chapel Hill: University of North Carolina Press, 1994), and Nicholas Dawidoff, *In the Country of Country: People and Places in American Music* (New York: Pantheon, 1997). On the other hand, much recent work questions and/or historicizes this investment in authenticity. See Barbara Ching, "Acting Naturally: Cultural Distinction and Critiques of Pure Country," *Arizona Quarterly* 49.3 (1993): 107–25; Aaron Fox, "The Jukebox of History: Narratives of Loss and Desire in the Discourse of Country Music," *Popular Music* 11.1 (1992): 53–72; Richard A. Peterson, *Creating Country Music: Fabricating Authenticity* (Chicago: University of Chicago Press, 1997); David Sanjek, "Blue Moon of Kentucky Rising over the Mystery Train: The Complex Construction of Country Music," *South Atlantic Quarterly* 94.1 (1995): 29–55.

5 Miles Orvell, *The Real Thing: Imitation and Authenticity in American Culture, 1880–1940* (Chapel Hill: University of North Carolina Press, 1989), and Morris Dickstein, *Gates of Eden: American Culture in the Sixties* (New York: Basic Books, 1977).

6 For the most recent discussion of BBS films, see Peter Biskind, *Easy Riders, Raging Bulls: How the Sex-Drugs-and Rock 'n' Roll Generation Saved Hollywood* (New York: Simon & Schuster, 1998).

7 In his *Country Music Culture: From Hard Times to Heaven* (Jackson: University of Mississippi Press, 1995), Curtis W. Ellison discusses these films without considering them in any particular political context and without paying particular attention to the songs. Instead, his interest is analyzing stories of what he calls "personal salvation." Nevertheless, I am indebted to his analysis.

8 Benjamin De Mott provides a good summary in his "Superflick," *Atlantic* 236 (October 1975): "*Nashville* . . . looks like becoming a cultural episode, an event on the order of Woodstock, *Hair*, or the birth of streaking, about which all at once everybody on earth decides to gabble. It took off overnight from the entertainment sections to the Op-Ed page. . . . And before the box office ever opened, *Nashville* generated controversy. Pauline Kael broke a release date to cheer the show in *The New Yorker*, making other journalists natter about breaches of reviewerly ethics" (101). Kael's premature review, "Coming: *Nashville*," *New Yorker* (3 March 1975) opened with remarkable praise: "I've never before seen a movie I loved in quite this way: I sat there smiling at the screen, in complete happiness" (79).

9 Charles Michener with Martin Kasindorf, "Altman's Opryland Epic," *Newsweek*, 30 June 1975, 49.

10 F. Anthony Macklin, "*Nashville*: America's Voices," *Film Heritage* 11.1 (1975), juxtaposes remarkably look-alike photos of Connie White/Karen Black and Tammy Wynette and Ronee Blakley/Barbara Jean and Loretta Lynn (8–9). Karen Black is easy to associate with Wynette after her role as a would-be Wynette in

Five Easy Pieces. However, according to Judy Klemesrud in "Who Is Ronee Blakley and How Did She Get to *Nashville?*" (*New York Times*, 22 June 1975, sec 2, p. 19), Blakley grew "angry . . . at the suggestion that her character is patterned after that of Miss Lynn."

11 In contrast, Michael Wood, "*Nashville* revisited: The Two Altmans," *American Review* 24 (April 1976), claims that Opal "is making the same remarks as the movie itself, only in her their hollowness is revealed" (104). Altman may agree with this criticism; he claims to have instructed Geraldine Chaplin, who played Opal, "to watch me when I do my con job and then do her own take off from there. She was me, us, the outsiders who came into Nashville without knowing what the hell is going on. I don't know anything more about Nashville than she does." Joseph Germis, "For *Nashville* a Battle to Survive Early Raves," *Newsday* (Long Island), June 1975, 9A.

12 Vincent Canby, "*Nashville*, Lively Film of Many Parts," *New York Times*, 15 June 1975, sec. 2, p. 1; John Rockwell, "It's Country Music, but the Best It Isn't," *New York Times*, 13 June 1975, 24.

13 Shaun Considine, "Hollywood Can Sing Country Just Like Nashville," *New York Times*, 24 August 1975, sec. 2, p. 13.

14 Connie Byrne and William O. Lopez, "*Nashville*," *Film Quarterly* 29.2 (1975–1976): 19–20.

15 Helen Keyssar, *Robert Altman's America* (New York: Oxford University Press, 1991), 138.

16 In contrast, Keyssar argues that the churches are "a place where, even in Nashville where music is power and money, the democratization of song occurs" (156). Similarly, Robert Self, in "Invention and Death: The Commodities of Media in Robert Altman's *Nashville*" (*Journal of Popular Film* 5 [1976]) suggests that "the five-day structure of *Nashville* centers around Sunday which may represent a climax of peace and hope, or even the still center around which swirls the politics, entertainment, and death in the film" (285).

17 Norman Kagan, *American Skeptic: Robert Altman's Genre-Commentary Films* (Ann Arbor, Mich.: Pierian Press, 1982), 133.

18 Connie replaces Barbara Jean just as Hal Philip Walker is running for the Replacement Party; in fact, when Bill, of Bill, Tom, and Mary arrives in Nashville, he notices a Connie White poster with a Hal Philip Walker sticker plastered over it: "Wait a minute. Hal Philip Walker looks exactly like Connie White," he quips. Subliminally, at least, Connie White, the bitchy bearer of the truth, seems to recognize this random link with the Replacement Party since she tells the children in her audience that any one of them could grow up to be president.

19 Keyssar notes that "Kenny's target is at once the woman who remains dedicated to her parents, the virgin bride who stands as a sacrificial victim to the power that remains invisible, and the nation that raises its banners high" (171). Altman, however, says "we didn't say this guy was alone. Maybe Connie White hired him. I don't know" (Byrne and Lopez, 25).

20 Self, "Invention and Death," 277–78.

21 For discussions of Nashville as a Hollywood musical, see Rick Altman, *The*

American Film Musical (Bloomington: Indiana University Press, 1987), 323–27, and Jane Feuer, *The Hollywood Musical* (Bloomington: Indiana University Press, 1982), 112.

22 As Feuer puts it, "Just in case we don't identify with the crowd in the film, Robert Altman continues the music on the soundtrack long after the images have ended" (Feuer, *The Hollywood Musical*, 112).

23 Byrne and Lopez, "*Nashville*," 18.

24 Kurt Vonnegut's enthusiastic review in *Vogue* 165 (June 1975) underscored just this quality: "I used to think that our machines would kill all of us by and by. I now suspect that we may be rescued or at least refreshed by one of them, which is the motion-picture camera. Most of what has been done with that device so far has been as silly as a penny arcade. But now Robert Altman has used the camera to produce a ribbon of acetate which . . . projects . . . a shadow play of what we have truly become and where we might look for greater wisdom" (103).

25 Wim Wenders, *Emotion Pictures* (London: Faber & Faber, 1989), 89.

26 Loretta Lynn with George Vecsey, *Coal Miner's Daughter* (New York: Warner Books, 1977), 124.

27 Ibid., 15.

28 Roger Angell, "Butcher Holler and Hollyweird," *New Yorker*, 17 March 1980, 91. In his *The Invention of Appalachia* (Tucson: University of Arizona Press, 1990), anthropologist Allen W. Batteau argues that "in *Coal Miner's Daughter*, the special power that the Children of Nature bring to the centers of civilization (whether New York or Nashville) restates one of the most powerful stories of American society: the individual hero rejuvenating decadent civilization" (197).

29 Stanley Kauffmann, "*Coal Miner's Daughter*," *New Republic*, 29 March 1980, 27. In spite of the disparaging comments in this review, Kauffmann's review of *Nashville*, in the *New Republic*, 28 June 1975, was favorable.

30 Lynn, *Coal Miner's Daughter*, 182.

31 Although the movie doesn't mention the fact, Loretta did not write this song. It was written by Shel Silverstein, who also wrote Johnny Cash's smash "A Boy Named Sue."

32 Lynn, *Coal Miner's Daughter*, 208–12.

33 David Ansen, in "Cinderella Story," *Newsweek*, 10 March 1980, 88–89.

34 Chris Hodenfield, "Zoom Lens Voyeur: A Few Moments with *Nashville*'s Bob Altman," *Rolling Stone*, 17 July 1975, 31.

35 Angell "Butcher Holler and Hollyweird," 92; likewise, Ansen praised Spacek's "virtuoso performance that never calls attention to its virtuosity. . . . Spacek even does all her own singing" ("Cinderella Story," 88).

36 Equally ironic is the fact the Ronee Blakley had trouble getting roles after her academy-award-nominated performance as Barbara Jean. Both she and Altman ascribed this difficulty to the fact that people assumed she *wasn't* acting when she portrayed Barbara Jean. See Klemesrud, "Who Is Ronee Blakely," 19, and Bruce Williamson, "*Playboy* Interview: Robert Altman," *Playboy* 23 (August 1975): 65.

37 See Mary Bufwack, "*Coal Miner's Daughter, Honeysuckle Rose, The Night the Lights*

Went out in Georgia: Taking the Class out of Country," *Jump Cut* 28 (1983): 21–23, for another critique of the middle-class perspective of this film.

38 Lynn, *Coal Miner's Daughter,* 90. "The Pill" was written by Lorene Allen, T. D. Bayless, and Don McHan.

39 Lynn, *Coal Miner's Daughter,* 182.

40 Ellison, *Country Music Culture,* 132.

41 As Ellison puts it, "the movie ends with an image of domesticity transcending such questions" (ibid., 134).

42 As Stanley Kauffmann notes in "Tender Mercies," *New Republic,* 11 April 1983, "the distancing of the camera . . . is the tonal signature of this film" (25).

43 Robert Hatch, "Films," *The Nation,* 30 April 1983, 554.

44 Pauline Kael was a rare national critic to give the film a negative review, actually calling it "junk." "Gents and Hicks," *New Yorker,* 16 May 1983,: 120.

45 Kauffmann, "Tender Mercies," 25.

46 John Simon, "Merciful Heavens, A Real Film," *National Review,* 29 April 1983, 508.

47 Richard Corliss, "The Heart of Texas," *Time,* 28 March 1983, 62.

48 Janet Maslin, "Giving up the Glitter of Success," *New York Times,* 23 October 1992, C13.

49 Bruce Feiler, *Dreaming Out Loud: Garth Brooks, Wynonna Judd, Wade Hayes, and the Changing Face of Nashville* (New York: Avon Books, 1998), 37.

50 Ibid., 38.

51 Thus, in *Wag the Dog,* only Merle Haggard could so effectively (and self-parodically) sing such patriotic tripe. On the political complexities of hard country music, see Barbara Ching, "The Possum, the Hag, and the Rhinestone Cowboy: Hard Country Music and the Burlesque Abjection of the White Man," in *Whiteness: A Critical Reader,* ed. Mike Hill (New York: New York University Press, 1997), 117–33.

Crossing Musical Borders:

The Soundtrack for *Touch of Evil*

JILL LEEPER

Henry Mancini's score for *Touch of Evil,* which he considered amongst his best work,[1] was indeed innovative, both because of its reliance upon diegetic cues rather than the classical Hollywood practice of a continuous musical backdrop (director Orson Welles's idea) and because of Mancini's pioneering use of popular music, especially jazz and rock idioms.[2] While both of these features of the soundtrack have received some critical attention, no one has discussed the way Mancini's and Welles's soundtrack provides mutual implication within the film. By *mutual implication,* I am referring to the process Claudia Gorbman explains in her pioneering study *Unheard Melodies: Narrative Film Music:* "Whatever music is applied to a film segment will *do something,* will have an effect—just as whatever two words one puts together will produce a meaning different from that of each word separately because the reader/spectator automatically imposes meaning on such combinations."[3] Particularly with respect to the film's representation of ethnicity in a border narrative and its obsession with "half-breeds," the mutual implications provided by the soundtrack are striking. In fact, the soundtrack is as much a musical hybrid as the fictional setting of Los Robles is a culturally fractured town of wasps, Russians, and Germans, in brown-face, playing Mexicans. As such, the soundtrack is a thematic analogue of border crossings that structures the score in a direct relationship to the film's narrative organization, distorted mise-en-scène, and political ambitions. Rather than following the conventional suturing functions of a classical Hollywood soundtrack, which strive to render the spectator an "untroublesome viewing subject: less critical, less 'awake,'"[4] the music in *Touch of Evil* seeks to do the opposite. It reveals contradictions, increases the spectator's sense of discontinuity, exposes the construction of identity and ethnicity (both at the filmic level and in a broader social sense), and, in general, increases the awareness of the apparatus of film-making.

Before beginning analysis of *Touch of Evil*'s soundtrack and its contribution to the film's theme of hybridity, it must be noted that there are three release versions of the film. The first is the 93-minute version (February 1958) that is the result of Universal chief Edward Muhl's takeover of the project. According to Welles scholar Jonathan Rosenbaum, Muhl took advantage of Welles's trip to Mexico for work on *Don Quixote* by sneaking a peek at the postproduction print assembled mainly by Virgil Vogel under Welles's supervision. Rosenbaum reports that Muhl's interest was alerted by Welles's quarrel with postproduction head Ernest Nims, prior to his Mexico trip, about interfering with new editor Aaron Stell's work. Muhl was especially alarmed at the amount of crosscutting in the print, finding its innovation too arty for the expected B picture, and ordered Nims to recut it. After another screening, Muhl ordered additional footage to be shot by director Harry Keller in order to "clarify the storyline."[5] To his credit, star and producer Charlton Heston initially resisted Muhl's appropriation of the project, losing a significant $8,000 for canceling Keller's shoot. The studio quickly talked Heston into working with Keller, however.[6] The second-release version (1976) restored the scenes deleted under Muhl's directions and ran 108 minutes. It is this version that has been generally accepted as closest to Welles's original intent, though this perception is now challenged by yet a third version, which is also intended as the closest to the original Welles rough cut and runs 112 minutes.

This third-release version (September 1998) was compiled by a team consisting of Rosenbaum, editor and sound mixer Walter Murch, producer Rick Schmidlin, a photo lab team led by Bob O'Neil, and a sound crew headed by Bill Varney, working from the 108-minute print and surviving excerpts from Welles's 1957 memo to Muhl challenging his decision to take the project away from Welles. The legendary fifty-eight-page memo was written the night after Welles was allowed one last look at his reedited film, containing four new scenes shot by Keller. In this restoration, Murch reports that some fifty changes were made and that these "did not transform the film into something completely different" but instead made this final version "more in line with the director's vision, more self-consistent, more resonant, more confidently modulated, clearer." However, he is also aware that even this cannot be said to be the film Welles himself would have produced without Muhl's intervention. Notwithstanding any subsequent changes Welles might have made had he continued with the film until its completion, even the detailed memo was vague and contradictory enough at points that Murch acknowledges the restoration team's need to inter- pret some directions and also notes that Welles admits in the memo that the document does not detail every change he wanted, just what he found "significantly mistaken" in the studio's cut.[7] In Rosenbaum's excerpt of the memo, Welles demurs that "where there's simply a difference of taste be- tween your editing and mine . . . I have resigned myself to the futility of discussion, and will spare you my comments."[8]

A further complication relevant to this analysis is that as of the date this essay went to press, the third version has not been released on video or DVD. Consequently, my comments regarding significant differences in the soundtrack between the 108-minute version and the restored 112-minute "director's cut" (a dubious claim) are based upon a single viewing, Murch's description of the team's changes, and excepts from Welles's memo.

Nearly forty years later, it is in some ways more difficult to appreci- ate the innovations of the soundtrack of *Touch of Evil* than it is to ap- preciate the innovations of the film's other elements. This is because the musical genres that were new to the film industry of the late fifties have now been firmly institutionalized for at least twenty years. Neither jazz nor rock and roll strike us as "new." Yet, as Mancini himself reminds us, Hollywood practice of the fifties was firmly entrenched in the use of over- blown pseudoclassical orchestral scores: "Musically they tended to a same- ness. . . . The general musical concept was one of bigness, lushness. The large orchestra was always used as a canvas."[9] Critics agree that Mancini was one of the most influential in adding contemporary genres to the vo- cabulary of film soundtracks, especially various styles of jazz and rock and roll, and introducing a more restrained use of music in general.[10] In a lengthy interview about his career for the American Film Institute, Man- cini proudly noted that he was responsible for the first rock and roll film, *Rock Pretty Baby* (1956), and worked on early jazz biopics *The Glenn Miller Story* (1953) and *The Benny Goodman Story* (1955).[11] In his book on the main figures in film music composition, scholar Tony Thomas asserts that "Mancini brought a fresh sound to film scoring . . . a sound more in tune with the times."[12]

Yet the score of *Touch of Evil* may strike a contemporary audience as precisely the opposite, very *out* of tune with our times. As William Darby and Jack Du Bois observe in their book *American Film Music*, much of Mancini's film work had by the midsixties become "staples of easy listening and Muzak, completely assimilated within popular American culture and regarded with modest fondness as products of a happier age."[13] This is not strictly an observation from the perspective of forty years later. In fact, jazz critics in particular regarded Mancini's work with scorn very early on, accusing him of a lack of authenticity, or of creating faux jazz. Paul Kresh's comments are typical when he says Mancini creates "pastiches" that evoke little more than "wearying sterility" and are ultimately "very rarely inspired."[14]

The nature of Mancini's contribution to film scoring is important to this analysis of *Touch of Evil* because film music is by its very function an affective medium. The question of how we read the musical genres in Mancini's soundtrack—as pastiche, cliché, faux jazz, or as authentic, fresh, real jazz—influences how we see other elements of the film that are affected by the soundtrack. As Claudia Gorbman has established, "any music bears cultural associations," or "cultural musical codes," and to arrive at a consensus about the film's use of music, we must agree on what those codes signify.[15] On one hand, Mancini sought musicians outside the standard contract players usually available to him, musicians who were fluent in the particular styles he and Welles wanted in the soundtrack. Mancini believed the studio orchestra "couldn't blow like the Kenton band, which was my prototype for this," so he hired "hot players" like bongo player Jack Costanzo, who came from Dizzy Gillespie's genre-establishing Afro-Cuban jazz orchestra, and Red Norvo on vibes, an early innovator of the instrument's use in jazz.[16] On the other hand, jazz critics argue that Mancini's work is the definition of faux jazz. In light of the fact that jazz as a genre is a combination of a wide variety of earlier genres and is as much a pastiche—as much a hybrid—as any musical form can be, these arguments are highly ironic. Exactly what would constitute "pure" jazz? For the purposes of this study, it is the very *hybridity* of jazz, as well as that of rock and roll and even mariachi, which contributes to the mutual implication between the soundtrack and the other filmic elements.

The hybrid nature of the various musical genres on the soundtrack works on two levels. First, several of the genres are themselves hybrid in nature. According to *The Encyclopedia of Jazz*, "jazz is a synthesis of six main sources: rhythms from West Africa; harmonic structure from European classical music; melodic and harmonic qualities from nineteenth-century American folk music [including blues]; religious music [including Negro spirituals]; work songs and minstrel show music."[17] Furthermore, the jazz on the soundtrack is a blend of two specific varieties: Afro-Cuban and cool jazz, with Afro-Cuban being then *doubly hybrid*. Afro-Cuban, as its name suggests, is characterized by its use of African-based polyrhythms, Cuban and Latin rhythms, and instruments derived from African and indigenous Central and South American and Caribbean sources.[18] Heavily featured in the jazz selections in *Touch of Evil* are congas and bongos, which are of Afro-Cuban origin, and vibes, derived from the marimba and the xylophone and believed to be African in origin.[19] Rock and roll's origins are similar to those of jazz, and it has roots in jazz itself. A third musical genre on the soundtrack, mariachi, which most Americans may naively mistake for a native folk music, in fact has hybrid origins. According to the ethnomusicologists Gerard Béhague and E. Thomas Stanford, mariachi is a musical form developed by mestizo cultures of Mexico from both indigenous musical forms and the influences of European music introduced by the Spanish.[20] Mestizos are of mixed ethnic origin, primarily descended from indigenous peoples and Spanish colonizers. Furthermore, the instruments used in mariachi—violins, several types of guitars, and harp—are primarily of European origin, there being no evidence of stringed instruments in the Americas before the Conquest.[21] The addition of trumpets to the mariachi form is a late innovation of the 1930s, although, since there is evidence of a type of trumpet played by the Aztecs, perhaps we can consider it a native instrument.[22] Clearly, the cultural signification of jazz and rock and roll is firmly established as being hybrid in nature.

This cultural musical code that we know as viewers today was known by viewers in 1958 as well. After all, both jazz and rock and roll were then widely called "race music." Both Mancini and Welles were perfectly aware of this signification of hybridity. Welles was an accomplished pianist and violist who was raised in a musical family, and his knowledge of music was not limited to classical. He had worked on a film (never finished) about Louis Armstrong, and according to Robert Stam's account of Welles's film project on Brazil's carnival tradition, it is clear that Welles was quite knowledgeable about jazz, the role African Americans played in its development, and the cross-cultural nature of other forms of music. For example, Stam reports, Welles realized that samba was the Brazilian counterpart to jazz and that both were "expressions of the African diaspora in the New World."[23] In fact I would argue that Welles chose the genres he did for *Touch of Evil*'s soundtrack precisely for that reason: he was aware that they signified hybridity and that they would therefore comment upon the theme of hybridity in the film's casting, mise-en-scène, and narrative.[24]

The second way in which the soundtrack's musical genres provide mutual implication in *Touch of Evil* is by representing diverse cultures, as a list of those genres reveals. Mancini's music for this film includes cool jazz, Afro-Cuban jazz, Latin big band in the "Stan Kenton vein," exotica-style easy listening, rock and roll, mariachi, bluegrass, and Gay Nineties parlor music, resulting in a sound that is a strange mishmash of flavors, textures, and cultures.[25] The jarring theme in particular features Mancini's hybridization of cool jazz and Afro-Cuban jazz, with raucous horns underscored by a wild rumba beat on congas and bongos, evoking both sophistication and abandon as well as the musical contributions of Africans, Anglo-Saxons, Chicanos, Cubans, mestizos, and Spaniards. Because of this diverse mixture of genres, the soundtrack immediately lets us know that we are in a place that has no meaningful borders but is instead a truly multicultural society, a place of crossbreeding.

However the latest 112-minute version of the film presents a drastic change by eliminating the well-known Mancini theme, which is not only gone from the entire opening sequence, but is present only as a musical ghost, peeping around aural corners and snaking in and out of other motifs as diegetic source music. Of course, cutting Mancini's theme significantly reduces his contribution to the film, leaving him with credit only for the genre pieces, the possible choice of featuring rock music, and his choice of the best Latin and jazz players.

Restoration project editor Walter Murch offers several explanations for the team's striking alteration of one of cinema's most admired opening sequences. First, he refers to Welles's memo that detailed his original concept for the soundtrack during the 3-minute-20-second opening crane shot. According to the memo, "The plan was to feature a succession of different and contrasting Latin-American music numbers. Loudspeakers are over the entrance of every joint, large or small, each blasting out its own tune. The fact that the streets of these border towns are invariably loud with this music was planned as a basic device throughout the picture." Since the print the restoration team worked with had all three sound channels still intact (dialogue, music, and sound effects), when the sound engineers removed Mancini's theme from the mix the sourced sounds described above by Welles were revealed on the sound effects channel, plus ambient sounds of footsteps, sirens, the bleating of the goats, and the voices of the extras. In addition to the powerful evidence of the memo, Murch argues that having Mancini's theme dominate the opening sequence provided a misleading genre cue, explaining, "The title music told [viewers] that this was a certain kind of detective story. Around the same time, Mancini used an almost identical theme for *Peter Gunn* . . . starring Peter Graves as a debonair detective. *Touch of Evil* was actually a kind of anti-*Gunn*: Welles's Quinlan is the opposite of debonair." Thus Murch concludes that the removal of Mancini's theme creates more immediacy for viewers and provides, in Welles's use of clashing and mingling sourced music, "a soundtrack that counterpoints the visual." [26]

It is interesting that this reduction in Mancini's contribution occurs at the same time as his death and a subsequent revival of interest in his film work, though quite likely this is merely a coincidence. Also worthy of speculation is the question of whether or not Welles—if he had been allowed to complete the film in 1958—would have likely incorporated further changes, including possibly the retention of Mancini's wonderful theme in the opening sequence. After all, as this latest version shows, any music can be sourced into the scene since it features nightclubs and cars as potential audio sources. Certainly Welles could have appreciated the commercial appeal of such an original and evocative theme (although clearly Murch believes it to be neither) for his film that also cleverly raised the issue of hybridity. Thus I question this particular change as really being the only possible interpretation of Welles's notes and argue that Mancini's main contribution should not be so thoroughly tossed away.

Nonetheless, in keeping with Welles's intention to maintain only diegetic music in the film, the Murch restoration replaces Mancini's theme with strictly sourced sounds: first, a muffled, live-sounding conga beat coming from a nightclub doorway on the Mexican side, then a blaring car radio tuned to a sax-lead rock and roll instrumental (likely Mancini's influence or choice). As the camera tracks by each car, a different musical piece is faded over, up, and finally out over the previous ones. Most of these selections are boogie-woogie beat rock with saxophone or guitar leads, but some Latin and jazz sounds are included as well. Each is identifiably a different song fragment. The result is a musical cacophony of styles and rhythms, clearly emphasizing the variety of cultures, races, and classes of people listening to them. Thus this new version of the soundtrack maintains the original release's technique of using hybrid musical forms to represent the film's concerns with race. It simply does so through a clash of genres rather than a hybridized yet singular theme. One could certainly argue that this change creates more of a sense of cross-cultural tension, which is about to be manifested by the car bomb's explosion. Furthermore, where the original Mancini theme was both sexy and ominous, the new version's cacophony is more assaultive, in much the same way that the later rape and murder scenes also create viewer discomfort.

It is when we begin to consider the mutual implication between the music and the mise-en-scène that the more subtle signification of hybridity becomes evident. As the film itself repeatedly reminds us, the diegesis of *Touch of Evil* is one in which the characters either "don't look Mexican" or "don't speak Mexican," in a location that "isn't the real Mexico." The most obvious element is in the casting of the film: the characters. The casting has in fact been one of the features of *Touch of Evil* most commented upon by critics, because it is so odd. After all, this is a film in which the WASPish Charlton Heston and a very well-known German actress, Marlene Dietrich, both play Mexicans, and a Russian, Akim Tamiroff, plays an Italian Mexican American. Furthermore, their dark makeup is less than convincing, as are Heston's and Tamiroff's tiny pencil mustaches. Adding to the confusion is the fact that Heston speaks with a midwestern accent, even when he has Spanish dialogue, while Dietrich retains her own very distinctive German accent, and Tamiroff affects a Mexican accent with acceptable results. While at first this seems to strain our sense of realism, as it is of course intended to do, Naremore reminds us that at the same time the "various accents are wittily appropriate to the bordertown."[27] As if these mixed signifiers of ethnic identity aren't enough evidence that the signification of ethnicity is in question here, we have the additional narrative trope of a mysterious "half-breed" who never appears in the film but is the apparent catalyst for Quinlan's racism and subsequent ethical lapse. The narrative finally suggests that Tamiroff's character, Uncle Joe Grandi, is that half-breed, but this is not firmly established.

As with his choices of musical genre, Welles was well aware of the possible effects of his casting decisions. Once again, the critical consensus is that he was trying to create a stylized rather than realistic film. As James Naremore explains, "Welles has ignored most of the rules of movie naturalism. His idea is to make a world that is both grittily accurate and surreal, characters that are both plausible and weirdly out of key."[28] In an interview with James Delson, Heston himself discusses his initial skepticism at being cast as a Mexican. Heston says when Welles told him that he had rewritten the script and made Heston's character Mexican, Heston replied, "I can't play a Mexican detective!" Welles's response was, "Sure you can! We'll dye your hair black, and put on some dark makeup and draw a black moustache, sure you can! We'll get a Mexican tailor to cut you a good Mexican suit."[29] The authenticity or lack of authenticity of racial categories is a running joke in the film. Before meeting Vargas, a character describes him as "some sort of a Mexican," and later after meeting him, Quinlan (Orson Welles) verbalizes the spectator's thoughts about Heston as Mike Vargas when he quips, "He doesn't look Mexican" and later observes, "He don't talk like one neither." He also draws our attention to the fact that the newlywed Vargases are supposed to be read as an interracial couple when he comments, "She [Mrs. Vargas] don't look Mexican either." Later in the film there is a similar discussion of racial categories when Uncle Joe Grandi (Akim Tamiroff) has to explain to Mrs. Vargas (Janet Leigh) that she is mistaken, that his name "ain't Mexican" and then goes on to explain his mixed heritage and the fact that his family lives in both Mexico and America. He carefully insists that he himself is an American. She promptly responds with the correct ethnic insult by calling him a "Little Caesar," though "for laughs" she continues to refer to Grandi's nephew as "Pancho."

The classical Hollywood practice is to use musical motifs to help identify characters by either ethnic identity, personality traits, or moral status —that is, the Good Guy or the Bad Guy. In this way the music signals to spectators whom they are to identify with and how they are supposed to feel about each character. Gorbman explains that "commonly a motif is repeated every time its assigned character appears, creating denotation."[30] Additionally, when the ethnicity of a character is also cued by the music— in other words, the music identified with a character also carries a cultural musical code—then the given motif has "two levels of overlapping codification, and therefore becomes doubly referent."[31] This is precisely how character motifs are used in *Touch of Evil*. For example, Heston is shown listening to mariachi music while he drives with Schwartz (Mort Mills). In this way, the viewer is signaled that Heston's character is Mexican, however questionable that identity has been rendered by the deviations from filmic realism. Similarly, the teenage gang is associated with rock and roll music that signals—especially for a 1950s audience—that they are young, wild, and probably dangerous. The teenage gang, while of apparent mixed ethnic identities, is coded primarily as Mexican, and rock and roll "race music" helps emphasize their ethnic otherness. A third use of the convention of musical motifs to identify character is the music associated with Suzy Vargas. When Suzy rides in the car with her husband, he turns on the radio for her, and the radio plays a song that is identified on Mancini's score as "Something for Susan." Suzy's song, appropriately, is the sort of fluffy, easy-listening music that composer and bandleader Martin Denny called "exotica"—a music that is "self-consciously fake," an "approximation of the exotic," a fantasy representation of the South Pacific and the Orient which appealed solely to white suburbanites.[32] As a white middle-class girl from Philadelphia, Suzy also listens to appropriately sanitized rock and roll. In her hotel room, she snoozes to the sounds of a song called "Rock Me to Sleep," a dreamy pop song reminiscent of the well-known "Theme from A Summer Place." That this is the *nice* version of rock and roll is emphasized

18 Marlene Dietrich as Tana in *Touch of Evil*. [Courtesy of the Wisconsin Center for Film and Theatre Research]

by its contrast to the raucous rock that the teenage gang is associated with, and that Suzy clearly dislikes.

The last character associated in a conventional manner with a musical motif is the hotel night man, played by Dennis Weaver. He is a country bumpkin, a fact that is immediately evident when he first appears and turns on the hotel intercom to play bluegrass music. What I want to emphasize here is that, though the use of these genres to indicate characterization is quite conventional, they all contain culturally coded references to ethnic identity and are therefore doubly referent. Mariachi music is Mexican and Mike Vargas is Mexican; rock and roll music is mixed-race music and the teenage gang is racially other and mixed; easy-listening music and pop are white middle-class musics and Suzy Vargas is white and middle class; bluegrass music is white country music and the hotel night man is a white country fellow.

When we consider the leitmotif associated with Quinlan's old flame Tana (Marlene Dietrich), these cultural musical codes become even more loaded with connotations. But rather than being primarily a signifier of ethnicity, "Tana's Theme" is self-reflexive. Her music is a quaint, faintly familiar waltz straight out of the era of the cabaret, or the turn-of-the-century parlor. The music and the player piano that is its source are so old, they're new, as Tana tells us. And for the spectator with any knowledge of film or American cultural history, the music is appropriate for Marlene Dietrich herself. It *does not* fit our notion of a Mexican whore, which is the character she's playing. It is at this point that the characterization most strains the viewer's suspension of disbelief, and the musical leitmotif only emphasizes the discrepancy. As Naremore has rightly noted, Welles uses "'cameo' players [such as Dietrich] to break the surface of the illusion."[33] Who we really see in the scenes with Tana is not Tana at all, but Dietrich. Welles goes out of his way to load these scenes with codes that remind us of the Dietrich persona. Naremore argues that "Dietrich's black hair and dark skin are meant to resemble one of those fantastic costumes she wore in the von Sternberg musical numbers . . . she keeps her German accent, and when she looks at Welles and remarks, 'You're a mess, honey,' the players separate from the fiction altogether."[34] Once again the spectator is reminded that the signification is awry. Furthermore, this musical leitmotif seems to have a slippery connection to its designated character: in a later scene we hear the same tune being played on the jukebox when Quinlan is in Grandi's bar, but it is now being played in a Spanish style, with guitar as the lead instrument. So is this "Tana's Theme" or Quinlan's, since it follows him? Or has it now become connected to the "half-breed" Grandi, since it now has mixed origins too? And why has the tune's genre changed so markedly? While in general character leitmotifs are maintained in the 112-minute version, Tana's theme is modified by the inclusion of a boogie woogie passage during one scene, serving merely to complicate its nature further. What we must finally conclude is that what all these uses of music to signify character have in common is a pronounced quality of overdetermination of meanings, making viewers conscious of categories of race and ethnicity, as well as putting such categories into question.

Another function of film music is to identify setting. As has already been noted, the setting of *Touch of Evil* is Los Robles, a fictional border town between the United States and Mexico. Welles apparently put a great deal of thought into the setting of the film. When asked why he changed the setting from the novel and the original script, which followed the novel closely, Welles declared, "I never read the novel; I only read Universal's scenario. . . . It all took place in San Diego, not on the Mexican border, which completely changes the situation. I made Vargas a Mexican for political reasons. I wanted to show how Tijuana and the border towns are corrupted by all sorts of mishmash — publicity more or less about American relations."[35]

This attitude was in keeping with Welles's various other political activities centering on the problems of racism.[36] Given the border town setting, the soundtrack's main musical theme performs its duty according to classical Hollywood practices. The title theme is a combination of the minimalist cool jazz that is Mancini's signature sound and Afro-Cuban jazz influences. The Afro-Cuban influences are in fact emphasized because the first instrument we hear on the soundtrack is the conga drum, tapping out a syncopated rumba beat, an easily understood cultural musical code for Latin culture. As the horns kick in, the jazz element is emphasized, so immediately we are signaled that this is a border town in the classic sense: a place of many cultures, a place of hybridity. As discussed earlier, the changes in the 112-minute version eliminate this theme, but the substitution/restoration of the clashing yet distinct genres of music as separate pieces playing along the roadside as the camera tracks the car accomplishes the same goal, albeit in a more jarring fashion, being less mixed.

A secondary way that soundtrack music sutures the spectator into the film's setting is by creating the temporality of time and place. Gorbman says film music "rounds off the sharp edges, masks contradictions, and lessens spatial and temporal discontinuities with its own melodic and harmonic continuity."[37] In classical Hollywood narrative, the diegesis must remain consistent in a spatiotemporal sense. This continuity is accomplished by following such rules as stopping a particular piece of music playing on a radio (music with a diegetic source) in a scene as soon as we cut visually to another scene, or by maintaining a consistent volume unless some character in a given scene physically changes it. We must keep in mind, however, that classical Hollywood practice regarding soundtrack music is less than realistic in the first place. We have been conditioned to accept soundtrack music without any diegetic source as part of movie realism, what Gorbman calls a "cinematic musical code," just as when we are watching a musical we accept characters bursting into song and dance in the midst of their vacuuming. Therefore, the way Welles deviates from this practice in *Touch of Evil* suggests an even greater degree of realism. His innovative decision was to use primarily diegetic sources for the film's music. This would tend to have the effect of making an even greater connection between characters and setting. Phyllis Goldfarb's analysis of Welles's use of sound in four of his later films, including *Touch of Evil*, details the way Welles carefully uses sound effects and music to provide such continuity. She concludes, "In *Evil* almost every scene has some element to bridge the gap to the next. Grandi's son decides to call his father for instructions, and we cut away from him at the phone to Quinlan and

Grandi in a bar. A few seconds later the telephone in the background rings. We leave these two men when Grandi puts a coin in the juke box, whose music is associated with the Grandi boys, who are at the motel, where rock and roll is being piped into Suzy's room."[38] The next cut takes us to Suzy's motel room, where the volume of the music is louder due to her closer proximity to the speaker.[39]

Yet paradoxically, despite the sourced music and skillful matching of aural and visual cuts, the dominant sense of a viewer of *Touch of Evil* is not that of realism or certainty regarding location from scene to scene. Instead, as Naremore observes, viewers are aware that they are "on a deliberately hazy, shifting borderland, where the audience is prone to lose their bearings."[40] The viewer is often hard pressed to identify which side of that invisible national border we are on at any given moment in the narrative. As Quinlan says to Tana, "In a place like this you forget." This dislocation is greatest in the film's climactic scene at the bridge. As Goldfarb describes it, the scene is one in which "we have not only lost all sense of distance and direction, we are also confused about the source" of the sound itself. While Welles has taken great pains to provide a diegetic source for the music in the film, the recorded, echoed, and spoken sounds of voice and movement in the scene at the bridge become so multiple in their sources as to lose their relationship "to real filmic space, time or character."[41] And though it is carefully sourced, nonetheless the soundtrack's music provides no clues as to which country we are in, even if it does usually indicate which building or room we are in. Once again, this slipperiness of identification serves to disorient viewers, drawing our attention to the concept of identification and borders that cannot be seen or heard.

We are further disoriented by another manipulation of spatiotemporality that Welles employs. Goldfarb documents how Welles breaks the rules of spatiality in the sound effects, the dialogue, and the soundtrack music in order to manipulate "the viewer's powers of concentration, his visual and aural perception, and [disorient] . . . his spacial and temporal organization."[42] The rule most obviously broken by Welles is the rule that film music is never supposed to compete with the narrative for the viewer's attention. The first impression most viewers take away from *Touch of Evil* is that the music is at times overwhelming. Goldfarb says "our awareness of music is so intense that it takes on a ideational quality. We respond to it directly, rather than to a mood it creates."[43]

There are two instances in which this violation of convention is clearest. The first is when Suzy Vargas is aurally assaulted with the teenage gang's raucous rock and roll well before she is physically assaulted by the gang itself. In these scenes, which are unchanged in the different versions of the film, the "volume and persistence of the irritating music . . . invades our consciousness much as it does Suzy's."[44] The music's jolting effect is heightened by the sharp cuts between locations: (1) the ringing of the church bells heard through the streets of Los Robles cuts to the roar of the hot rods arriving at the motel, which then cuts to the rock and roll on the motel intercom, and (2) the match cut between the closing door of the ominously quiet, morguelike Hall of Records and the door of Suzy's hotel room, filled with the blasting rock and roll. Coupled with this immediate suturing of the viewer's aural response and Suzy's is the way the rape scene is shot and edited to connect the viewer to Suzy's point of view through the use of low-angle shots of the gang as seen by Suzy.[45] The music also dominates in the scene (likewise unchanged in the 112-minute versions) where Quinlan strangles Grandi while Suzy lies unconscious on the bed nearby. From the point when Quinlan locks the door behind him, the wild brass and congas of the music overwhelm even the sounds of Quinlan's and Grandi's struggle, the trumpets mingling with Grandi's screams and groans and the congas counterpointing his gasps for breath. The music culminates in the trumpet blasts that preface Suzy's screams at the sight of Grandi's dead, bulging eyes, and follow her to the balcony to intermingle with her cries for help. Goldfarb argues that the spatial sound is also intentionally inconsistent with reality in this scene, pointing out that sound should be different in quality when heard from inside the same room as its source than when it is heard from the other side of a door or through the floor as it is in this scene.[46] As the scene begins, the sound is such that the music is realistically playing on the jukebox in the bar below, albeit quite loudly, with a muffled quality appropriate to our aural experience. But the music's volume swells improbably rather than recedes when Quinlan locks the door. When Grandi breaks the transom in his attempt to escape, the music's increase in volume, while reasonable, is disproportionately louder than experience tells us it should be and it has lost the muffled quality appropriate to sound that has traveled through the floor and up the stairs. Its volume, as well as its quality, continues to increase beyond spatial and aural laws during the remainder of the scene. As Goldfarb concludes, when laws of sound (such as the difference between a sound within a room and outside its closed door) are broken, "the mismatch makes us vaguely uncomfortable, slightly dislocated. . . . The reaction is very subtle . . . [but the result is] a sort of floating tension . . . used . . . [by Welles] in directing audience response."[47]

Also noteworthy is the fact that though the restoration team's intention was to faithfully re-create Welles's original vision of the film, including maintaining diegetic sound throughout, there are a number of non-diegetic uses of music in the 112-minute version, just as there were in the 1958 studio-appropriated version. Some of these moments of nondiegetic music are original to this "director's cut," and thus cannot be justified as being true to Welles's alleged intent as it was articulated by the memo to Muhl. Though none of them is lengthy or jarring, they are in keeping with classical Hollywood practices: affective in intent and nondiegetic. A typical example is the scene in the jail when Vargas runs into Suzy's cell after she has been drugged and "raped" by the gang. As Vargas runs into the frame, an oboe and a low piano play appropriately evocative notes. There is no diegetic source for this music. Overall, however, the use of music to signify the film's thematic racial concerns remains notable, whether or not that music is diegetic, and both Welles's and Mancini's expertise in musical hybridities were important in its accomplishment.

These manipulations of music and sound effects in the service of characterization and mise-en-scène not only engage viewers intellectually, provoking them to question categories of identity; they also have an effect on the emotions. When characters are overdetermined by discrepancies between their real-life personas, their filmic identities, their appearances, their voices and accents, and their associated musical motifs, spectators cannot form a simple, sutured emotional identification with those characters. If Welles's goal is a "self-conscious manipulation of popular sexual stereotypes" in order to "explore the sexual psychology of race hatred," then a crucial step toward that goal is making us aware that the characters simultaneously represent and resist stereotypes.[48] If a film is set in a border town and if the location of characters and actions with respect to that border is important to the narrative but the music provides few clues as to location, the result is an uneasiness in the spectator, which is precisely the point. As William Nericcio maintains, the Los Robles of Touch of Evil is, like any border town, "*fracture* itself, where hyphens, bridges, border stations, and schizophrenia are the rule rather than the exception."[49] If the implied spectator of classical Hollywood narrative is a passive one, Welles and Mancini have done a great deal with just the soundtrack of this film, regardless of the version, to disrupt our suspended disbelief, to blur our sense of diegesis, and to dislocate our sense of a tidy, realistic space-time continuum. All of these uses of the soundtrack together send a message that something is wrong with the signification of the signs. The disparities draw attention to the constructedness of Touch of Evil's diegesis and, by implication, to the constructedness of conventional categories of race, nationality, and national borders in the real world. In examining the interpretations regarding race, Nericcio concludes, "One can find and document how Welles's *Touch of Evil* reinforces predictable stereotypes of the Mexicano subjectivity and of the Anglo subjectivity. Closer scrutiny reveals, however, that these expressionistic archetypes are mined with nuances of difference, which self-consciously derail previous Hollywood stereotypes. . . . Welles's work is a true border text; it does not hide the wounds evident at the border."[50] As Los Robles's chief of police reminds us, the whole film — the whole world — is a "mixed party."

Notes

1 See Henry Mancini and Gene Lees, *Did They Mention the Music?* (Chicago: Contemporary, 1989), 82; and Tony Thomas, *Music for the Movies* (South Brunswick, N.J.: A. S. Barnes, 1973), 199.

2 There seems to be a firm consensus on this point. See ibid., 78; Henry Mancini, *Seminar with Henry Mancini*, 13 October 1973 (American Film Institute, 1978), microfilm, reel 3, no. 118, 10; Henry Mancini Interview by Royal S. Brown, in *Overtones and Undertones: Reading Film Music* (Berkeley: University of California Press, 1994), 299; and Tony Thomas, *Film Score: The View from the Podium* (South Brunswick, N.J.: A. S. Barnes, 1979), 170–71.

3 Claudia Gorbman, *Unheard Melodies: Narrative Film Music* (Bloomington: Indiana University Press, 1987), 15.

4 Ibid., 5.

5 Jonathan Rosenbaum, "Orson Welles' Memo to Universal," *Film Quarterly* 46.1 (1992): 2.

6 Ibid.

7 All details and quotes above from Walter Murch, "Restoring the Touch of Genius to a Classic," *New York Times*, 6 September 1998, sec. 2:16 and 2:17.

8 Quoted in Rosenbaum, "Orson Welles' Memo," 5.

9 Thomas, *Music for the Movies*, 200.

10 See William Darby and Jack Du Bois, *American Film Music: Major Composers, Techniques, Trends, 1915–1990* (Jefferson, N.C.: McFarland, 1990), 465; Martin Marks, "Henry Mancini," in *New Grove Dictionary of American Music*, ed. H. Wiley Hitchcock and Stanley Sadie (New York: Grove Press, 1986), 3:166; and Tony Thomas, *Film Score: The View from the Podium*, 164ff.

11 Mancini, *Seminar*, 9.

12 Thomas, *Music for the Movies*, 195.

13 Darby and Du Bois, *American Film Music*, 463.

14 Paul Kresh, "Is There Any Music at the Movies?" in *Film Music: From Violins to Video*, ed. James L. Limbacher (Metuchen, N.J.: Scarecrow Press, 1974), 40.

15 Gorbman, *Unheard Melodies*, 3.

16 See Brown, *Overtones and Undertones*, 299; Barry Kernfeld, ed., *The New Grove*

Dictionary of Jazz (New York: Macmillan, 1988), 1:13; and Clifford Bevan, "Marimba," in *The New Grove Dictionary of Jazz*, ed. Barry Kernfeld, 2 vols. (New York: Macmillan, 1988), 2:83, 645.

17 Leonard G. Feather, *The Encyclopedia of Jazz* (New York: Da Capo Press, 1960), 23.

18 Gunther Schuller, "Afro-Cuban Jazz," in *New Grove Dictionary of Jazz*, 1:7–8.

19 *New Grove Dictionary of Jazz*, 1:242, 2:83, 645.

20 Gerard Béhague and E. Thomas Stanford, "Mexico," in *The New Grove Dictionary of Music and Musicians*, ed. Stanley Sadie, 5th ed. (New York: Macmillan, 1980), 12:232.

21 Ibid., 12:229, 232.

22 Robert Stevenson, "Mexico City," in *The New Grove Dictionary of Music*, 12:240.

23 Robert Stam, "Orson Welles, Brazil, and the Power of Blackness," in *Perspectives on Orson Welles*, ed. Morris Beja (New York: G. K. Hall, 1995), 237.

24 There is also a consensus on who chose the musical genres for *Touch of Evil*. Both Mancini and other sources clearly state that Welles already had chosen the musical styles he wanted prior to his first, and only, meeting with Mancini. See Mancini and Lees, *Did They Mention the Music?*, 78; Brown, *Overtones and Undertones*, 299; and the liner notes to the soundtrack LP (Movie Sound Records, 1993).

25 Mancini and Lees, *Did They Mention the Music?*, 79.

26 All quotes are from Murch, "Restoring the Touch of Genius," 2:16.

27 James Naremore, *The Magic World of Orson Welles*, 2nd ed. (Dallas: Southern Methodist University Press, 1989), 203.

28 Ibid., 167.

29 Charlton Heston, "Heston on Welles," interview by James Delson, *Take One* 3 (July/August 1971): 7–10; reprinted in *Perspectives on Orson Welles*, ed. Beja, 64.

30 Gorbman, *Unheard Melodies*, 28.

31 Ibid.

32 Joshua Glenn, "Cocktail Nation," *Utne Reader*, September–October 1994, 89. It should be noted that exotica is also a hybrid musical genre like jazz, rock and roll, and mariachi.

33 Naremore, *The Magic World of Orson Welles*, 171.

34 Ibid.

35 Orson Welles, interview by Juan Cobos, Miguel Rubio, and José Antonio Pruneda, rpt. in *Perspectives on Orson Welles*, ed. Beja, 59.

36 For more information regarding Welles's dedication to political causes, especially his work against racism, begin with Barbara Leaming, *Orson Welles: A Biography* (New York: Penguin Books, 1985).

37 Gorbman, *Unheard Melodies*, 6.

38 Phyllis Goldfarb, "Orson Welles's Use of Sound," in *Perspectives on Orson Welles*, ed. Beja, 113.

39 Technically the music over the intercom is what Royal S. Brown calls "phony source music" (Brown, *Overtones and Undertones*, 349) because it has much

better audio clarity and range than it probably would when played over a real intercom.

40   Naremore, *The Magic World of Orson Welles,* 149.

41   Goldfarb, "Orson Welles's Use of Sound," 110.

42   Ibid., 107.

43   Ibid., 111.

44   Ibid., 111.

45   For a more detailed discussion of the contribution of cinematography and editing to this scene, see Naremore.

46   Goldfarb, "Orson Welles's Use of Sound," 108.

47   Ibid., 108–9.

48   Naremore, *The Magic World of Orson Welles,* 123 and 157.

49   William Anthony Nericcio, "Of Mestizos and Half-Breeds: Orson Welles's *Touch of Evil,*" in *Chicanos and Film: Essays on Chicano Representation and Resistance,* ed. Chon A. Noriega (New York: Garland Press, 1992), 54.

50   Ibid., 63–64.

Documented/Documentary Asians:

Gurinder Chadha's *I'm British But . . .* and the

Musical Mediation of Sonic and Visual Identities

NABEEL ZUBERI

The evolution of British Bhangra and Bangla music marks the beginning of the end of British national chauvinism for those of us who have been born and brought up here. It has helped us define ourselves as a migrant community with a musical language of our own, created by us, for us, but open for enjoyment by all. — Gurinder Chadha

Through the patterns of belonging and distancing established in these forms of cultural production, new forms of "British" identity become available which circulate along with the records themselves in the clubs and cassette players and on the pirate radio stations. At a time when the integrity of the national culture is asserted against a common European identity, a genuinely cosmopolitan post-colonial space is opened up within and against "Englishness"—a set of identities available to all irrespective of their skin color, "rooted" in the airwaves. — Dick Hebdige

Since a British (South) Asian visual presence in photography, film, and television has long been subject to racist representation at first sight (or rather, listen) music seems to provide a partial reprieve. British Asians have had more visibility and audibility, as well as a greater degree of creative autonomy and success, in popular music culture than in film and television industries. Whereas debates about representation and discourses of black Asian identity in British cultural studies have largely focused on the media of film and television, closer attention to musical sound might suggest other ways of conceiving the relationship between black Asian subjectivity, culture, and the technologies of film/music production and consumption. Here I examine this relation through the case of Gurinder Chadha's 1989 documentary *I'm British But . . .*, a short film that uses music to signify the hybridized identities of Britain's Asians at an important juncture for black Asian cultural politics in the Thatcher era; Asians were becoming increasingly framed (and framing themselves) as distinct from the overarching political identity of "blackness" that had included African-Caribbean and other people of color in Britain since the late 1960s. *I'm British But . . .* is also shaped by the institutional and stylistic frameworks for black filmmaking at the British Film Institute, the BBC, and Channel Four, as well as an emerging youth television in the period. The final part of the essay examines the continuing problematic relationship of sound to image in some examples of British Asian music during the last decade. Fundamentally, I'm concerned with how diasporic identities are mediated through different technologies, discourses, and institutions.

British Asian Music

I'm British But . . . is dominated by bhangra music—Punjabi folk beats in old and new Afrodiasporic-influenced versions that sprang forth in Britain during the 1980s. For at least twenty years the almost hidden, yet significant, economy of music stores, grocery shops, and small businesses in Asian localities up and down Britain has supported a small music industry churning out cassettes, records, and CDS for an almost exclusively local Asian market. Radio stations, like London's Sunrise, have helped to build listening communities for bhangra and other transplanted subcontinental sounds. Thus Asian musicians have had small industry outlets for their music long before they were signed up by large recording companies.

In the 1990s, British Asian music percolated into the national mainstream media. The chart success of Punjabi-Patois dancehall DJ Apache Indian (a.k.a. the Don Raja) and dance mixologist/producer Bally Sagoo has been followed by hits for Asians working in a variety of musical styles. Groups like Babylon Zoo, White Town, and Cornershop have all topped the national singles charts. Musicians such as Sheila Chandra, Najma, DJ Ritu, Bindu, Anjali Dutt, and Sonya Madan have sharpened the musical profile of Asian women. Record labels like Nation and Outcaste have given Asians a measure of economic control over musical production in a global recording industry, and these independent companies have signed distribution deals with the majors. Thus Brit-Asian music can now be found in the rock/pop, reggae, hip hop, techno, ambient, trance, and world music sections of the typical megastore in the Western metropolis.

But such audibility and visibility disturbs the multiple silences and invisibilities perpetrated in multiracial Britain and Fortress Europe. Postmodern arguments may have reminded us that identities are fluid, open, about becoming rather than being, never complete, but regimes of representation in late capitalist commodity culture attempt to fix what it means to be a "British Asian," in order to better manage and promote identities for political and commercial purposes. Cultural racism, identity politics, the tropes of orientalism, competing notions of multiculturalism, and the vogue for hybridity-talk inform discussion of this British music.

The categorizing imperatives of "world music" and "world beat" have shaped the classification of these new sounds. During the early 1990s, pop journalists dubbed the phenomenon the "New Asian Kool." Later in the decade, booming sound systems and London club events like Bombay Jungle and Anokha have spawned the so-called "Asian Underground." Cultural studies researchers have also charted "the politics of the new Asian dance music."[1] In 1999, critics and industry watchers awarded Talvin Singh's OK the prestigious Mercury award for best U.K. album. Despite this activity on a number of fronts, Asians still play a minor role in the constitution of British popular music. And one is reminded regularly that, though South Asianness might now be fashionable in commodity form—in music, fashion, film, and television—for a lot of white Brits, we're still just "Pakis."

Asians on Film and Television

There hasn't been quite the same burst of Asian cultural production in film and television. The capital-intensive nature of film and television compared with relatively cheap music recording is the primary reason for fewer self-produced and widely distributed visual representations. Nevertheless, *My Beautiful Launderette, Sammy and Rosie Get Laid, Bhaji on the Beach, The Buddha of Suburbia,* and *East Is East* have made Asian lives visible to large British cinema and television audiences; and art photography and installations by Zarina Bhimji, Mumtaz Karimjee, Sunil Gupta, and Pratibha Parmar's filmmaking have interrogated the politics of visual representation and differences in gender and sexuality within the Asian communities.[2] Still, despite a Multicultural Commissioning Editor chair at Channel Four and ostensibly more brown bodies on the screen, Asians are still present in national film and television primarily as a "social problem." As Sarita Malik points out, "Although it is now commonplace to see black and Asian people on British television who do not necessarily function to solely 'carry' the race theme, the repertoire still remains limited. . . . There is, in addition, a lack of cultural authenticity when it comes to detail—thus, mosques are confused with Hindu temples, Black men with dreadlocks are automatically referred to as Rastafarians, Muslim characters are given Sikh names, and so on. Most importantly, however, is the fact that television, by and large, has not relinquished its investment in the slave, entertainer, social problem types, although these may have taken on more modern forms."[3]

Through the machinery of documentary realism that dominates the visual representation of Asians, the tropes of ethnography mark our institutionalization as "ethnic minorities." Common-sense English racism regularly wheels out a motley collection of stereotypes and pathologies. Asians may be passive wimps or raging vigilantes: stakhanovites of the corner shop and the late-night take-away, exemplars of Thatcherite free enterprise, fanatical fundamentalists, failed parents, wounded children, gang youths, sexist men, mysterious erotic women, and the victims of arranged marriages. These may not be the only Asians on screen but they "breed like rabbits" across media discourse. Even the moderate success of the BBC's Asian comedy skit show *Goodness Gracious Me* has resulted in television gatekeepers wanting only "funny Asians" on screen.

In response to hackneyed images of Asians, the "burden of representation" has often meant that any Asian film or program lucky enough to reach a film or television audience tends to try to cover every significant Asian "problem" and correct as many negative images as possible in its limited screen time. For example, some of us wince at Hanif Kureishi dramas in which characters speak their "positions" in heavy-handed dialogue that sounds like political speechmaking. Filmmakers invest so much effort answering back to dominant racist representations that it becomes difficult to find an aesthetic that can, as Kobena Mercer suggests, "break out of the constraints of the master code."[4]

Many of the agonistic discussions around black Asian representation have centered on the efficacy of documentary realism as a mode of counterfilmmaking. Film and television (rather than music) have been the primary sites for arguments over what should constitute an antiracist media politics. At around the same time that *I'm British But . . .* was produced under the auspices of the British Film Institute and Channel Four, Stuart Hall's article "New Ethnicities" was published with the proceedings of the Black Film/British Cinema conference at London's Institute for Contemporary Arts (ICA) in February 1988. In this influential essay, Hall argues that regimes of representation play "a constitutive, and not merely a reflexive, after-the-event role" in the construction of black identities.[5] He believes that we can reclaim the idea of ethnicity: "The term ethnicity acknowledges the place of history, language and culture in the construction of subjectivity and identity, as well as the fact that all discourse is placed, positioned, situated, and all knowledge is contextual."[6] According to Hall, a new politics of ethnicity would engage rather than suppress difference, would reveal multiple identities and identifications within the black communities (as well as draw attention to the constructedness of whiteness as an ethnicity). As Phil Cohen points out, "the notion of new ethnicities referred to myriad forms of cultural traffic generated by the process of globalization, and the convergence of transnational and transracial geographies of identification via the opening up of new diasporic networks of communication."[7]

I'm British But . . . articulates the new ethnicities of British Asians through the hybridized sounds of Asian musical forms informed by the Afrodiasporic techniques of reggae, funk, soul, and hip hop. The film's formal elements also owe a great deal to the explosion of youth television in the late 1980s. Music video and magazine programs televisually reproduced the format of "lifestyle" magazines like *The Face* and *i-D*, which regularly reported on black music and club culture in Britain's metropolitan centers. According to Simon Frith, youth television was the focus for broader debates about television and the viewer in the emerging satellite economy. He suggests that "youth" functioned as "a metaphor in the much more general attempt to redefine the TV viewer to match the new TV landscape."[8] Frith adds, "In 1988, when 'youth' became a resonant term for arguments about the future of television, the implication was that everything in broadcasting was changing, that young people were, somehow, the 'different' viewers of the future. To get youth programming right was, therefore, to provide a blueprint for the general transformation of viewing behavior."[9] These developments in national television and aesthetic debates around black-Asian visual representation set the context for the production of *I'm British But . . . .*

I'm British But . . .

The textual form of Chadha's documentary reflects the institutional conditions of film and television production in this period. The film is a combination of a typical television documentary in the Griersonian tradition, music video, and youth television. For much of its half-hour screen time, it looks and sounds like a fairly conventional talking-heads ethnographic documentary of the kind placed in the unobtrusive "ghetto slots" of Channel Four or BBC 2 schedules.

I'm British But... is a coming-of-age documentary about the children of Asian migrants. Their testimonies reveal family histories embedded in the processes and structures of colonialism and neocolonialism. From different ethnic, national, and religious backgrounds, the film's Asians include a woman from Glasgow who calls herself a "Scottish Pakistani"; a Punjabi man from the Rhondda Valleys who describes himself as "Welsh," with all the confidence that Raymond Williams might; a Bangladeshi woman who says that she has "no affiliation to any country"; and a young man from Belfast who states that he is "Northern Irish." These interviewees (not named until the film's credits) speak in their local/regional British accents and represent the four nations of the British union. Edited with the interview footage of a Punjabi DJ and a Bangladeshi rapper, they discuss the meaning of home, belonging, and unbelonging in Britain and South Asia.

The film's historiographical work connects postimperial racism and antiracist movements to a genealogy of struggle against British imperialism. For example, the Scottish Pakistani states the difficulty in pledging allegiance to the word *British* since it carries "connotations of colonialism." She recalls the 1919 Jallianwallah Bagh massacre in Amritsar, when General Dyer's soldiers mowed down nonviolent demonstrators, killing 379 and wounding twelve hundred. This event has a powerful resonance in Punjabi and South Asian collective memory. In the documentary, a photograph of the massacre cuts to black-and-white archival footage of colonial police beating Punjabi demonstrators with clubs, immediately followed by a montage of photographic stills cut to the rhythms of a bhangra track. These images include Asian women workers and trade unionists in industrial disputes during the 1970s in Britain, and men and women holding aloft the banners of antiracist groups. However, sudden silence punctuates the final chilling image in this montage. A Sikh mother grieves over the body of her son. A newspaper headline in close-up reads: "Another Asian Murdered." Significantly, this is the only moment of silence in the whole film. Then the music fades in, and for the rest of the film's short duration Asian noise fights the silencing violence of the state. *I'm British But...* presents examples of Hall's new ethnicities in formation to the beat. These Asians speak for themselves as subjects rather than as objects of documentary discourse, something rare even in 1989 when the film was made. The film has no white reporter or "native informant" interpreting Asian life on camera nor an omnipresent voice-over narration.

A decade later, the film appears to have some clear limitations. The documentary seems rather "feel-good," trying hard to affirm the meta-phorical (if invisible) hyphen between "British" and "Asian." The "But" at the end of the title covers as much as it reveals. In its positive images of Asianness in Britain, the film overlooks tensions between different ethnic, national, and religious groups *within* the South Asian diaspora. The only hint of serious conflict is generational, between the migrants to Britain (who remain silent and only appear in photographs) and their vocal, on-camera children. Politically regressive attitudes and practices within Asian communities are ignored; gender politics are left unexplored. British Asian hybridity is benign here. The film is an affirmative gesture, functioning as a statement of "unity in diversity" among Asians. Chadha privileges a Punjabi version of British Asian identity, which was, to some extent, a unifying force for second-generation Asians under the signifier of "Bhangra." Bhangra allowed for the assertion of British Asian identity for many Asians who had previously felt "lost within a scopic economy of black and white."[10] However, many musicians working in other genres routinely express annoyance that if they are Asian they are presumed to be making bhangra music. *I'm British But . . .* does feature Haroon (a.k.a KMD) of the Joi Bangla Sound (system), and Pakistani qawwali music, but Punjabi-British bhangra dominates the soundtrack. This is not to castigate Chadha for failing to make the truly "representative" British Asian docu-mentary (an impossible and pointless task), merely to point out the film's quite specific politics of location and its historical conjuncture in which Asians emerged as distinct from, but from within, political blackness.

According to Bill Nichols, *I'm British But . . .* is a "performative docu-mentary," the kind of film that stresses the "subjective aspects of a classi-cally objective discourse" and "marks a shift away from the referential as the dominant feature."[11] British national documentaries such as *Listen to Britain* (1942) and *Nightmail* (1936) themselves incorporate some "perfor-mative" techniques with musical montages and poetic commentaries, but these films, according to Nichols, are still dominated by their referential aspects. As if to emphasize the performative nature of British Asian iden-tities, Chadha introduces the video release of her documentary by stroll-ing down Southall Broadway in Asian west London in an Indian dress, a rocker's black leather jacket, and two quintessentially British appendages: an umbrella and a bulldog on a leash. Chadha remakes the national docu-mentary form, using the tropes of representing the nation common to the British documentary movement but subverting these techniques pri-marily through the use of music. *I'm British But . . .* maps a Britain of brown faces in a postcolonial update of *Listen to Britain*. Instead of Myra Hess playing Mozart to the Queen at the National Gallery, the dholak and tabla drums sound the nation into being on celluloid. In Humphrey Jennings and Stewart McAllister's 1942 musical meditation on the British at home in wartime, the empire is an absence addressed by the paternalistic announcer's voice of the BBC World Service. Chadha's film stages the return of the repressed in the bodies, voices, and musical sounds of the empire's grandchildren.

Music mashes up the cinematic nation in myriad ways. The film's titles feature the caption "British Film Institute presents" in white against a black background with an out-of-tune plinkety-plonk keyboard version of "Land of Hope and Glory" accompanying it. The words are scratched out with a white pen by a brown hand, to finally read "I'm British But. . . ." The sanctioning power of the terms "Film" and "Institute" are playfully undermined and demystified. This graffiti style detournément of the British Film Institute is accompanied by the sound of scratching vinyl, a gesture of sonic dissonance resonant with hip-hop attitude. A piano muzak version of "Rule Britannia" with the opening title screen is scratched until it mutates into a bhangra dance rhythm. The bhangra refrain in the opening of the film transforms white England into South Asian diasporic space. This music marks out the land, reterritorializes the city and nation.

Chadha's film begins with a musical and theatrical occupation of the English landscape by Asians. After a few moments of intercut talking heads, with the Welsh, Scottish, and Northern-Irish Asians introduced in conventional documentary mode, Punjabi DJ San-J from Southall states that "it's got the British groove, the Asian groove, it can even have the north African groove, it's got a bit of all five continents." The film cuts to a sequence shot that is edited like a music video. The male musical group Kalapreet, led by singer Nirmal, plays a traditional Punjabi bhangra composition on the rooftop of Ajanta Footwear on Southall Broadway. With the men dressed in blue satin shirts and white trousers, a huge banner with their record label's name, Arishma, hangs behind them. Nirmal sings "Oos Pardesh" ("That Foreign Land"), a tune addressed to the Asians who wander about on the street below. The words speak of England's desolate land, where the people are as cold as the weather. How can these Punjabis come to England? Have they forgotten what the English did to the Punjab? Southall's residents go about their daily business, shopping for groceries, now and then glancing up a little bemused at the commotion on the roof. On the pavement, several Asian girls in school uniforms dance in a circle. The Punjabi lyrics flash up on the screen in English translation.

The scene is a pastiche of the Beatles playing "Get Back" at the end of their *Let It Be* film—a rock band performing for free on a city roof is a well-worn element in the street-based mythology of rock and roll authenticity. Surely, Chadha also parodies U2's video for "Where the Streets Have No Name"—itself an homage to the famous Beatles footage—shot on a rooftop in San Diego, where the group's performance is cut short by city police, guaranteeing even more street credibility. Instead of young white male rebels taking over a public space, a bunch of unglamorous Asian musicians in dodgy outfits sing on a rooftop while teenage girls dance in the streets. A West London thoroughfare becomes the site of an Asian musical session that re-creates British space with young and old, schoolgirls in uniforms and grandfathers in turbans. Then, after the aural challenge from the group to the Asian settlers on ground level, the rest of the film responds to this provocation. Following the documentary's credits at the end of the film, the musicians are shown on a neon-lit Broadway. They emerge from an Indian take-away restaurant and pass out samosas to eat in the twilight of a Southall winter evening. Having castigated the emigrés from a great height, they are now among them. And the samosas here are as tasty as the ones back home.

The film visually and sonically deconstructs the nation, playfully traces out the British landscape and subverts the petrified poetics of space that have created this "sceptered isle," "green and pleasant land," our Albion. A bhangra soundtrack with Punjabi voices is showered over the clichés of national landscaping. The use of incongruous music disrupts the sedimented relationship certain musical sounds have with the land. An aerial shot of green fields, an iconic image of the nation that accompanies the sound of "Rule Britannia" in *Listen to Britain* and a thousand and one other films and television programs, is now overlaid with Azaad's version of the Punjabi folk tune "Gur Nalon Ishq Mitha" ("Your Love Is Sweet Like Sugar"). Instead of "Jerusalem," "Land of Hope and Glory," and "God Save the Queen," bhangra music undercuts what Benedict Anderson calls national "unisonance." [12]

Britain is glimpsed through a car window as valiant windscreen wipers swish away constant rain to the dhum-chakk-dhin-chakk rhythm of bhangra. The camera tracks past the Queen Elizabeth II ocean liner on the Thames and pans the panoramic skyline of west London, then drives past rows of identical suburban detached houses (a recurring motif of Englishness in Derek Jarman's films). Instead of Ivanhoe or any other white knight, a Welsh Asian emerges over a farmland ridge on a horse, as his voice-over affirms his Islamic faith, and Nusrat Fateh Ali Khan's qawwali "Ali Maula Ali Maula Ali Dam Dam" swells up on the soundtrack. The music adds another layer of disturbance to an image that challenges the relentlessly urban placing of British Asians in most visual representations. Stock footage of steam trains as they chug through country landscapes connects the interviews in different parts of the nation. As *I'm British But* ... cuts between the Scottish, Northern Irish, Welsh, and English interview soundbites, archival film of steam trains gives the illusion of movement between geographical locations. These anachronistic sequences bring to mind the London-Scotland train in *Nightmail,* traversing the country, joining the two ends of the nation. But the archaic train image also suggests a history of rail as the technology that mapped out and "made" British India, carving out a national infrastructure for British military and economic imperialism. Of course, the train is also a powerful and resonant metaphor for the body politic in the history of pop music. It signifies collective pleasure, migration, and social and economic mobility in popular songs like Junior Parker's/Elvis Presley's "Mystery Train," James Brown's "Night Train," Little Eva's "The Locomotion," and the O'Jays' "Love Train." The bhangra track "Rail Gaddi" (literally "Rail Car") by Chirag Pehchan plays on the soundtrack, as the film cuts between shots of train wheels and Asians on a nightclub dance floor moving in the form of a human train.

The poetics of place in *I'm British But* ... relies on a process of repetition and defamiliarization, but with the additional representational interruption of sound. Visually, Chadha's reworking of the British landscape is similar to John Kippen's photograph of Muslims at Windermere in the Lake District, in which a large group of British Muslim tourists have just finished prayers in an idyllic rural setting typical of guidebooks to Wordsworth Country. Similarly, black British photographer Ingrid Pollard's self-portraits (with text) in the Lake District register her discomfort in a landscape etched in the national consciousness as timelessly white. Familiar modes of representation—the image-repertoire of English heritage—are profanely challenged by the presence of nonwhite British people in this landscape.[13]

Pastiche, parody, and the use of incongruity are strategies through which the sound-and-image culture of Asian popular music negotiates Asian Britishness and both its proximity and distance to received ideas of nationhood. In one of the film's rhythmic montages, the brightly colored record sleeve for "Rule Britannia/Bhangra Lovers," a twelve-inch dance single by D.C.S., spins into frame and Lord Kitchener points at the viewer in the famous pose of the "Your Country Needs You" recruitment poster from the First World War. But this new version features the aristocratic minister wearing a Union Jack turban. The musical commodity itself, in its images and within the grooves of the record, contains new ways of conceiving of Britishness.

The soundtrack for *I'm British But* . . . confirms Steve Wurtzler's claim that the "nondiegetic score is evidence of the cinema's inability to speak an autonomous, centered spectating-auditing subject. Instead, films, like television and contemporary music, 'speak' a fragmented subject ever in the process of formation, multiply hailed by different discourses, representations and the events they posit." [14] The disjunction between representing the British nation and its "other" in sound and vision necessitates that the film is itself a hybridized form, made up of fragments from (at least) both.

Check the Technique/Technics: The Sound Mix

I'm British But . . . tries to visually reproduce sound aesthetics in its articulation of British Asian identity. The film uses the idea of the audio mix to stage the process of identity formation/identification. In popular dance music styles, the mix is a dialogic form, two or more elements clashing in a sound piece, with voices, music, and sound effects ricocheting off each other. Mixing makes new music through reproduction—for example, the assemblage of recorded sounds in the studio or turntables in the "live" setting of a discotheque. The studio producer or club DJ manipulates recordings for the desired effect, usually to maintain a danceable groove for the listener with enough sonic surprises and developments along the way.

Chadha uses the mix in both an audio and visual sense in a crucial scene at the center of her film. DJ San-J of the sound system X-Zecutive Soundz explains that younger Asians are changing the traditional sounds of bhangra. Cut to black and a traditional stiff-upper-lip BBC male voice announces that "this is a journey into sound." This is the well-known sampled opening of a hit twelve-inch single version of the U.S. rap group Eric B and Rakim's old school classic "Paid in Full" by U.K. remixers Coldcut. Cut to San-J in a club's DJ booth, as people groove on the dance floor. The original Eric B and Rakim version relies on the sampled heavy funk bass line of Dennis Edwards' R&B hit "Don't Look any Further." The Coldcut remix is yet another hybrid mutation. Bass line and snare beat intact, Rakim rhymes over Eric B's beats, but the sampled voice of Israeli Yemenite singer Ofra Haza floats into the mix. On the turntables, San-J cuts in a fragment of Rakim's voice from another rap classic, "I Know You Got Soul." The phrase "Pump up the volume" (itself sampled on M.A.R.R.S hit of the same name) is abruptly interrupted by the word *bhangra* pronounced with strict Punjabi accentuation. The rap utterance becomes "Pump up the bhangra," repeated several times with its ringing Punjabi retroflex "R" sound, which then segues into the bhangra hit "Pump up the Bhangra" by Pardesi. Rakim's voice is then completely replaced by a Punjabi voice. This montage of African American syncopation and orality with Punjabi diction gives an indication of the playful hybrid directions of the music. This is, of course, partly mediated by the recording of two white DJs (Coldcut) who have also brought Middle Eastern Jewish singing into this transdiasporic sound mix.

As the music plays, Chadha intercuts between San J in his booth, the dancers on the club's floor, and the sound and image of Nirmal (from the film's opening sequence) as a chiding reminder of traditional "roots" bhangra. Here, Chadha visually and sonically stages the competition between different forms of bhangra, in a simulation of the technique of the reggae sound clash or hip-hop battle. Nirmal's fragment of more traditional bhangra, his interruption of the new beat, a kind of visual equivalent to the vinyl scratch, eventually loses out in the general plenitude of the dance groove. Generic mutation triumphs over the fixity of traditional forms. New-school bhangra is victorious in its battle with old-school form. The antiphonic, dialogic call-and-response features of reggae and rap are reproduced here. Like black musical forms, bhangra itself allows for antiphony and improvisation, its lyrical couplets and drum patterns commented upon repeatedly by other musicians and other voices. Bhangra intrinsically shares some of the features of black music performance, though like many of today's popular dance music genres and subgenres, second-generation bhangra takes much from African diasporic forms.

Though the analysis of black-white relations in youth culture has generated a considerable bibliography in British cultural studies, relatively little attention has been paid to the musical exchanges and cultural affiliations between the South Asian diaspora and the African diaspora in the U.K. The black Asian musical relationship in Britain forms what Gilroy calls "communities of interpretation and sentiment," alliances which are particularly marked in youth cultures.[15] Tejinder Singh of the Anglo-Asian groups Cornershop and Clinton goes as far as to suggest that "the majority of Asian kids have an African American musical identity."[16] Kingston reggae and dancehall, East and West Coast hip-hop, soul, funk, Chicago house, as well as the U.K.'s own jungle/drum 'n' bass are powerful influences on Asian music production and consumption. Asians variously and continually recontextualize black rhetorics and poetics of anger and defiance, militancy and resistance, syncopation and "funkiness."

It is no accident that the record played in the central mix sequence of *I'm*

British But . . . is Eric B and Rakim's "Paid in Full." The track foregrounds the processes of production, labor, and commodification in popular music. The two men in the studio exchange comments about the recording of their debut album, their label 4th & Broadway, their management company Rush, and the fact that their "ladies" are put out with them for spending so much time away from home in the studio. Rakim insists they be "paid in full" for their work. Not merely an ode to conspicuous consumerism, the track delineates the material economic realities behind the record we the listeners have on the deck.

Musical recordings are commodities, but they are consumed productively. In *The Black Atlantic*, Gilroy riffs on Baudrillard's view that the work of art as commodity can become "event" rather than "object." He argues that we need "an enhanced understanding of 'consumption' that can illuminate its inner workings and the relationships between rootedness and displacement, locality and dissemination that lend them vitality in the countercultural setting."[17] Gilroy uses the example of the twelve-inch single, which developed out of record company attempts to cash in on the success of black musical genres like reggae and rhythm and blues in the early 1970s. The new musical commodity satisfied the industry's need for more formats to be sold to the consumer, but also facilitated new musical practices such as scratching, cutting, dub, talkover, and remixing in black subcultures.[18] Modes of "subcultural creativity" may vary somewhat, but the active circulation and translation of commodities is not unique to the African diaspora. *I'm British But* . . . shows us the adoption of the Jamaican sound system ethos by Joi Bangla Sound and X-Zecutive Soundz. As Paul Willis points out, the sound system or mobile disco in black culture (now an element of many dance music subcultures) is an institution "where the activities of consumption merge into and become intertwined with more conventional forms of production."[19] Through work on sound amplification, the use of electronic skills, DJ-ing, and rap/talkover, records are played and transformed in performance, and consumption becomes a kind of production.

Although political alliances between African Caribbean Britons and their Asian compatriots may have become increasingly fragile and unfamiliar in the decade since *I'm British But* . . . , at least in the popular music field Asian musicians and listeners continue to draw upon another diasporic tradition and its techniques, as well as identify with other histories marked by white racism. Their sense of both Britishness and Asianness, and the path to their own sounds and selves, are often mediated by Afro-diasporic culture.

Sound and Vision in the Black Asian Arts during the 1990s

As pointed out earlier, *I'm British But . . .* emerged at a time of considerable debate and intellectual struggle over what constituted a valid black Asian film practice. The 1988 Black Film/British Cinema conference discussed the relative merits of avant-garde technique as opposed to realism, and whether postmodernism was a more suitable way to conceptualize black cultural praxis than populist modernism. Stuart Hall argued that experimental documentaries such as *Territories* (1984/85) and *Handsworth Songs* (1986), produced by film collectives Sankofa and Black Audio respectively, broke out of a mimetic theory of representation. Their self-reflexive strategies exposed the problematic of documentary's relation to reality, opening it up for scrutiny by staging a dialogic encounter between modes of cinematic address.[20] In his review of *Handsworth Songs* in the *Guardian*, Salman Rushdie had little time for the film's Foucauldian strategies. He argued that the voices and stories of Handsworth's black and Asian residents were silenced since the film (according to its press release) "attempts to excavate hidden ruptures/agonies of 'Race'" and "looks at the riots as a political field colored by the trajectories of industrial decline and structural crisis."[21] Hall responded to Rushdie's criticism with the argument that *Handsworth Songs* was trying to "find a new language" that breaks from "the tired style of the riot-documentary."[22] Coco Fusco astutely pointed out that Rushdie's position simplistically juxtaposed authentic, unmediated voices "out there" in Handsworth against the image manipulation of the filmmakers.[23] This assumed an unmediated reality, a notion which Black Audio had precisely set about to interrogate in its filmic practice. The conference document witnessed similar impassioned arguments about *My Beautiful Laundrette*, on the one hand attacked as a realist drama that presented negative and "unrealistic" images of Asians, and on the other, defended as a film that self-consciously juxtaposes different discursive possibilities of the "real."

From the vantage point of a decade later, something more important than the old formalist fisticuffs (realism vs. avant-garde aesthetics) emerges from the conference and related discourse about black art in Britain. At the time, both Judith Williamson and Paul Gilroy brought up the issue of *audiences* for these films, suggesting that, for all their accomplishments, and though new black films did the rounds of the international art cinema and academic circuits, where they were valorized for their politics of representation, they failed to reach black working-class audiences, often the very subjects of the films. Reading avant-garde films also required the acquisition of a certain amount of cultural capital on the part of audiences, "learning to be bored" as Williamson drolly put it.[24] Gilroy argued that visual representation should maintain its links to vernacular poetics in modern black arts practice.[25] For Gilroy, music has been *the* vernacular political and utopian art form in black expressive culture. June Givanni suggested that "music is often held up as the model for mass 'crossover' success: Black music has changed the profiles of many national music and recording industries. The mass appreciation and popularity of Black music could be seen as an ideal that many filmmakers would like to achieve."[26]

The links between popular music, film, and television were raised again four years later in November 1992 at the Black and White in Color conference, a British Film Institute event that reflected film and television program makers' anxieties in a climate of television deregulation and market-friendly shifts in government broadcasting policy. Aesthetic debates were overshadowed by discussion of how black filmmakers might negotiate the new institutional frameworks and ratings imperatives of British television. What kind of access would black Asian filmmakers have to this market? What shape would multicultural programming take? The film collectives could no longer rely on Channel Four funding, and gave way to more individualistic film production. The lack of public funds for film and program production forced a retreat from formal experimentalism as filmmakers sought funding and screen time in mainstream television and cinema. Black Asian bodies had become more visible on television, but this visibility depended to a great extent on the wide success of black music culture. As Stuart Hall pointed out: "One parameter underlying this shift in visibility is the vigor, vitality and diversity of the Black cultural revolution which has exploded across the British scene in the last fifteen years, especially from Asian and Afro-Caribbean (Black British) urban cultures. Its effects can be seen, at one level in the vitality of Black music, dance, theatre, and the visual arts (with their inevitable spin-offs into television, film and video). However, its principal space of representation in television is the highly ambiguous pop music/'youth TV' sector, where Black street styles and Black bodies have become the universal signifiers of modernity and 'difference.'"[27] Black popular culture in commodified form has become increasingly central to British urban lifestyles. Soul, funk, reggae, hip-hop, house, jungle/drum 'n' bass, garage, and a score of other dance music subgenres have multiplied and thrived.

During the 1990s, Gilroy repeatedly argued that black sound practice was increasingly threatened by the hegemony of image culture. He questioned the need for visualization of black music on television: "The long-standing power of a dissident culture based on the manipulation of sound is at risk of being repudiated in the uncritical dash towards an alien regime of signification dominated by images."[28] Visual technologies eroded the dialogics and performative processes of black music production and consumption. Gilroy was convinced that sound would lose in its struggle with vision: "The protracted competition between sound and vision to define the conceptual coordinates and axiological priorities involved in Black subculture and its overground offshoots cannot be won by sound."[29] John Hutnyk has recognized that Gilroy's work "carries a nostalgia for the face-to-face relations of the local community and the dance hall scene" which are live and direct compared to film and video.[30]

The refrain that the sonic was losing out to the visual was heard in other quarters of the cultural studies field. In an article with the give-away pessimistic title "Is Anybody Listening, Does Anybody Care? On Talking about 'The State of Rock,'" Lawrence Grossberg suggested that "the ratio of sight and sound had already changed significantly. The visual (whether MTV, or youth films or even network television, which has, for the first time since the early 1960s, successfully constructed a youth audience) is increasingly displacing sound as the locus of generational identification, differentiation, investment and occasionally even authenticity. . . . As a result, the rhythms of both visual imagery and music have changed, the music as it were having adapted to television's beat."[31] While many musical forms, particularly rap and electronic genres like techno and drum'n' bass incorporate television and film soundbites and seem to echo the flow and fragmented narratives of television, the visual has always been an essential part of popular music culture since Edison's phonograph. We have always been seeing while we have been listening. John Corbett, taking a Lacanian view, suggests that "the lack of the visual, endemic to recorded sound initiates desire in relation to the popular music object."[32] So pictures have filled that "void."

Echoing Gilroy's suspicion of the visual but with greater hope for sonic redemption, Iain Chambers suggests that the "surveillance of ocular sense" and belief in the truth-value of the visual tend to limit the flexibility of the image. According to him, sound is more mobile than the image:

> The image, for all its potential ambiguity, tends towards the potential consolation of a semantic full-stop. It is sound that ultimately disturbs ocular regimes and returns images to the pleasure of surfaces, to the liberty (and limits) of the making, masking and masqueing of representations. This is to contest the triumph of the image

over the act, of the disembodied form over the corporeal flux, of the
metaphysical signature over the unruly event, of the sign over the
sound. . . . Although continually embedded in appearances, in
the visual economy, the body continually exits from this daily frame
through the migrations of sound. Memory clings to the former while
following the itineraries of the latter. In the unique instance of the
performance, sounds chafe against the constrictions of ocular hegemony—this look, that style, those bodies, that moment—constantly
threatening to break bounds and travel without regard for address or
direction.[33]

The comments of the theorists above suggest the persistence of a hierarchy
of senses in cultural theory. The human subject of theory has been defined
by looking and being looked at, rather than speaking and especially not
hearing/listening. John Mowitt argues that in the era of electronic reproducibility, subjectivities are formed in part by the technologies of reception. He suggests that popular memory will be organized around collective
listening, an outcome of digitization (the "logic of the bit"). This shift in
subjectivity will be felt first in the field of music because the production
and reception of music are mediated by the same technologies.[34] According to Mowitt, this will mean that cultural memory will be understood to
be collective and not individualized.

However, one must be cautious about what sometimes border on onto-
logical claims about the subject produced by sound rather than vision, and
skeptical about apparently immutable distinctions between the technological effects and affect of sound as opposed to vision. Technologies of
sound and vision themselves are products of representation. As Wurtzler points out, "the ideological effect of any technology also involves the
way that technology and its practice are 'known' by consumers, the way it
is itself represented and discursively produced as a science and/or commodity."[35] British Asian subjectivities are not simply determined by technologies, but also mediated by a variety of discourses and institutions.

Audio and visual technologies have been crucial to personal and collective history and memory. Videotapes and photographs are recording
Asian locatedness in Britain and are circulating across diasporic space.
The VCR has transformed Asian life in Britain, facilitating the recording
and ritualized playback of social events, like weddings, in Britain, the
subcontinent, North America, and other diasporic locations. Video also
brings Bombay's Hindi cinema culture and its Bollywood movies to domestic spaces in Britain. These films provide a repertoire of South Asian

images, music, affect, and emotion that, to some extent, produces identifications across ethnic, national, and religious barriers. In *I'm British
But* . . . a scene from a 1960s Bollywood masala movie shows a young
woman in a miniskirt as she dances among electric-guitar-toting youths
who mimic the gestures and sounds of swinging sixties Western pop performance. A female interviewee in the documentary remarks that our
mothers also wore Eastern *and* Western clothes, bouffants and beehives,
even if they were copied from Hindi movie stars. For second-generation
British Asians, this filmic/photographic evidence confirms a history of
East meeting West, and the realization that their own "hybridities" are not
uniquely freakish, that "our culture" is, in fact, not discretely partitioned
from others.

Media technologies provide images and sounds in commodity form,
but their meanings are not arrested by the fact of commodification. Aspects of "South Asianness" have slowly penetrated the everyday life of
British folks through the commodity culture of fast food, fashion, interior
decoration, and music. A rhythmically edited musical montage in *I'm
British But* . . . shows tandoori chicken and prawn tikka sandwiches being
sold under the quintessentially English department store brand of Marks
and Spencers; a Katharine Hamnett fashion collection relying on the appropriation of the shalwar kamiz and sari; and Indian rugs being sold in
boutique catalogs. Is this just United Colors of Benetton-style multiculturalism and the East as a tourist's department store, or does it suggest a
serious change in the social and cultural fabric of national life?

On the one hand, commodity culture does offer a space of representation in a predominantly white media culture. Musical products make
visible and audible an economic, political, and cultural presence. In *I'm
British But* . . . , album covers, pop charts, and record label logos bounce
across the screen, imaging Britain's Asians in commodity form. On the
other hand, visibility is never guaranteed in a racist economy; one space
frustratingly fails to lead to another, and representation is regulated by the
dominant culture's institutions. In a frustrated comment on the screening
time of Bollywood movies on British television, Alkarim Jivani remarks
that, "if Marks and Spencers can put onion bhajis on the High Street, then
Channel 4 need not bury *Movie Mahal* in an inaccessible slot for fear it
might prove an acquired taste."[36] The logic of the market cannot assure
Asians the rights to representation. British society may have the stomach
for Indian food, but is reluctant to let British Asian cultures into other
spaces. *I'm British But* . . . begins and ends on the commercially vibrant
Southall Broadway, lined with viable small Asian businesses, a backhanded

testament to Thatcherite enterprise culture in late 1980s Britain. But business and housing policies and practices in some areas of Britain still discriminate against Asians.

The market's contradictions both facilitate and block Asian representation, as well as nudging it in different directions. Asian musicians and producers have to negotiate this variegated terrain to be both seen and heard. Visibility is sought after, but the terms of visibility have to be struggled over. In the popular music market, the discourse of "world music" and "world beat" generated by record companies and media often sell orientalism in new packaging. As Steven Feld notes of this discourse, musical practices are located close to visual-graphic ones, and explained through the techniques of anthropology, the museum, and tourism.[37] For example, the ghazal and jazz singer Najma Akhtar was requested by her record company to not cut her hair because they "liked the Indian image of long hair and sari."[38] Sonya Aurora Madan, singer/songwriter with guitar group Echobelly, has found herself in a double bind: on the one hand, music publications aimed at teenage white boys want her to fit into the role of exotic "Asian babe" in their photo spreads; on the other, the British Asian press expects her to be sympathetic to the values of Asian communities vis-à-vis arranged marriage and "feminine" behavior. On a television debate about racism with Fun^Da^Mental's Aki Nawaz, her contributions were edited out: "Most of the camera angles were these very mundane, pretty girlie shots where I wasn't saying anything. You could see me and hear Aki's voice. It was typical censorship. I was totally misrepresented, made into an airhead musician."[39] Hustlers HC, a Sikh rap outfit from West London, describe how audiences expecting to see a black or white posse were bemused that "those guys with turbans" could actually rap.

The music industry cultivates and satisfies visual desire through CD covers, promotional photographs, the clothes and the artist's visual idiosyncrasies in live performance, music video, and film. British Asian musicians apply many different strategies to deal with the problem of representation in a racist cultural economy. Some artists reproduce orientalist tropes. Apache Indian's video for "Arranged Marriage" presents the kind of image of India one expects to see in a Michael or Janet Jackson video—a multicultural crowd of British good-time groovers locked on to the object of their gaze, with a lone exotic and poorly choreographed Indian dancer with the obligatory bindi on forehead marking her difference.

The New Asian Kool (early nineties journalistic jargon for some post-bhangra Asian dance music) was embraced by some Asian musicians, even though the term was premised on the view that Asians somehow used to be profoundly uncool. Talking teleology blues! Cool on whose terms? This ideology has been internalized by many Asian artists. In a television interview for Canada's *New Music,* a member of East London's Earthtribe says that there's no street credibility to be gained from too strong an association with Asian music culture (read: bhangra) because of its visual signifiers—it makes him think of "old men with Elvis suits and beer bellies." The understandable rejection of bhangra as defining Asian musical production and identity is here conjoined to a more troubling disavowal of any musical address to Asians, since only a select few Asians are deemed hip, trendy, fashionable—in short, possessing the requisite (sub)cultural capital that marks them off from the large mass of British Asians.

Another strategy for incorporating the visual is the punk-styled mimicry of black-Asian rap group Fun^Da^Mental, which aims for shock effect through an inversion of orientalist semiotics. Promotional photographs present Aki Nawaz's head wrapped in his Palestinian keffiyah. Is this Third World revolutionary chic or anti-Orientalist sartorial parody? Fun^Da^Mental's CD covers rework the melodramatic and iconic film poster styles of Bollywood to present imposing angry young men, mosques, crescent moons, and Arabic script, graphically designed to prick the perceptions of British and European Islamophobia.

Some musicians prefer invisibility. Jyoti Mishra from the East Midlands town Derby releases music under the name White Town because he grew up in "predominantly white towns." The electronic pop single "Your Woman" was recorded in his bedroom. He chose not to publicize the release with interviews or any photos of himself. The music video for the track features a white man and woman enacting the song's battle-of-the-sexes narrative. The single was a number-one hit in 1997. On the White Town website, Mishra explained that the song was written from several different perspectives: "Being a member of an orthodox Trotskyist/Marxist movement (as I was); being a straight guy in love with a lesbian; being a gay guy in love with a straight man; being a straight girl in love with a lying two-timing fake-ass Marxist."[40] Admittedly, there's no reason that listeners will perceive these different subjectivities in the tune, but it's worth considering whether an image of Mishra in the video, CD sleeve, and other media would have predisposed listeners and viewers to particular interpretations.

Though academics, critics, and musicians usually pose the visual as a "problem," sometimes sound is the issue. "Brimful of Asha" (1998) by Cornershop was supported by a colorful video in which a young black girl sits in her 1950s/1960s retro room surrounded by scores of Cornershop records. The members of the group appear as moving images on the record sleeves. Tejinder Singh's knowing wink to commodity fetishism, record collecting, and its relationship to (his and other) South Asian identities took its Velvet Underground "Sweet Jane" guitar riff to the lower reaches of the British singles charts. The track was then remixed by Norman Cook (a.k.a. Fatboy Slim), with a more muscular drum sound added to make the track more danceable. But, more interestingly, Singh's voice was speeded up considerably. The video was only slightly reedited. The remixed single went to number one.

The title of the Cornershop album *When I Was Born for the 7th Time* plays on notions of Hindu reincarnation, but also summarizes the issues raised in this essay. South Asian subjectivities in the media are mutable and re-born; their shape and development mediated by technologies of representation. But these subjectivities are also mediated by the racialized musical and nonmusical institutions and discourses of the market and the state. British Asian musical culture is formed through the intersection of these technologies, institutions, and discourses, and the spaces in between.

Notes

1 See *Dis-orienting Rhythms: The Politics of the New Asian Dance Music,* ed. Sanjay Sharma, Ashwani Sharma, and John Hutnyk (London: Zed Books, 1996).

2 See Ten.8, *Critical Decade: Black British Photography in the 80s,* 2.3 (1992); Sunil Gupta, ed., *Disrupted Borders: An Intervention in Definitions of Boundaries* (London: Rivers Oram Press, 1993); Jonathan Rutherford, ed., *Identity: Community, Culture, Difference* (London: Lawrence & Wishart, 1990).

3 Sarita Malik, "Race and Ethnicity: The Construction of Black and Asian Ethnicities in British Film and Television," in *The Media: An Introduction,* ed. Adam Briggs and Paul Cobley (Harlow: Longman, 1998), 320.

4 Kobena Mercer, "Recoding Narratives of Race and Nation," in *Black Film/British Cinema,* ed., Kobena Mercer (London: ICA Documents 7, 1988), 11.

5 Stuart Hall, "New Ethnicities," in *Black Film/British Cinema,* 27.

6 Ibid., 29.

7 Phil Cohen, "Through a Glass Darkly: Intellectuals on Race," in *New Ethnicities, Old Racisms?,* ed. Phil Cohen (London: Zed Books, 1999), 5.

8 Simon Frith, "Youth/Music/Television," in *Sound and Vision: The Music Video Reader,* ed. Simon Frith, Andrew Goodwin, and Lawrence Grossberg (London: Routledge 1993), 77.

9 Ibid., 80.

10 Gayatri Gopinath, "Bombay, U.K., Yuba City": Bhangra Music and the Engendering of Diaspora," *Diaspora* 4:3 (1995): 309.

11 Bill Nichols, *Blurred Boundaries: Questions of Meaning in Contemporary Culture*

(Bloomington: Indiana University Press, 1994), 95. Nichols erroneously states that the film is about "British Pakistanis" rather than British Asians with "roots" in various parts of South Asia.

12 Benedict Anderson, *Imagined Communities: Reflections on the Origin and Spread of Nationalism* (London: Verso, 1983), 145. Anderson describes this phenomenon: "Take national anthems for example, sung on national holidays. No matter how banal the words and mediocre the tunes, there is in this singing an experience of simultaneity. At precisely such moments, people wholly unknown to each other utter the same verses to the same melody. The image: unisonance. Singing the Marseillaise, Waltzing Matilda, and Indonesia Raya provide occasions for unisonality. . . . How selfless the unisonance feels! If we are aware that others are singing these songs precisely when and as we are, we have no idea who they may be, or even where, out of earshot, they are singing. Nothing connects us all but imagined sound."

13 See John Taylor, *A Dream of England: Landscape, Photography, and the Tourist's Imagination* (Manchester: Manchester University Press, 1994), 240–61.

14 Steve Wurtzler, " 'She Sang Live, but the Microphone Was Turned Off': The Live, the Recorded and the Subject of Representation," in *Sound Theory/Sound Practice*, ed. Rick Altman (London: Routledge, 1991), 101.

15 Paul Gilroy, *The Black Atlantic: Modernity and Double Consciousness* (Cambridge, Mass.: Harvard University Press, 1993), 201.

16 Quoted in Steven Wells, "Welcome to the Counter Culture," *New Musical Express,* November 1993.

17 Gilroy, *Black Atlantic,* 105.

18 Ibid., 106.

19 Paul Willis with S. Jones, J. Canaan, and G. Hurd, *Common Culture: Symbolic Work at Play in the Everyday Cultures of the Young* (Milton Keynes: Open University Press, 1990), 72.

20 Hall, "New Ethnicities," in *Black Film/British Cinema,* 30.

21 Salman Rushdie, "*Songs* Doesn't Know the Score," in *Black Film/British Cinema,* 16.

22 Hall, "Song of Handsworth Praise," in *Black Film/British Cinema,* 7.

23 Coco Fusco, "An Interview with Black Audio Collective," in *Black Film/British Cinema,* 61.

24 Judith Williamson, "Two Kinds of Otherness: Black Film and the Avant-Garde," in *Black Film/British Cinema,* 36.

25 See Paul Gilroy, "Nothing But Sweat Inside My Hand: Diaspora Aesthetics and the Black Arts in Britain," in *Black Film/British Cinema,* 44–46.

26 June Givanni, "In Circulation: Black Films in Britain," in *Black Film/British Cinema,* 41.

27 Stuart Hall, "Black and White in Television," in *Remote Control: Dilemmas of Black Intervention in British Film and TV,* ed. June Givanni (London: British Film Institute, 1995), 15.

28 Paul Gilroy, "Intervention for What? Black TV and the Impossibility of Politics," in *Remote Control,* ed. Givanni, 35.

29 Paul Gilroy, "Exer(or)cising Power: Black Bodies in the Black Public Sphere," in *Dance in the City*, ed. Helen Thomas (New York: St. Martin's, 1997), 32.

30 John Hutnyk, "Adorno at WOMAD: South Asian Crossover and the Limits of Hybridity Talk," in *Debating Cultural Hybridity*, ed. Pnina Werbner and Tariq Modood (London: Zed Books, 1997), 124.

31 Lawrence Grossberg, "Is Anybody Listening, Does Anybody Care? On Talking about 'The State of Rock,'" in *Microphone Fiends: Youth Music and Youth Culture*, ed. Andrew Ross and Tricia Rose (New York: Routledge, 1994), 54–55.

32 John Corbett, *Extended Play: Sounding off from John Cage to Dr. Funkenstein* (Durham, N.C.: Duke University Press, 1994), 37.

33 Iain Chambers, "Maps, Movies, Musics and Memory," in *The Cinematic City*, ed. David B. Clarke (London: Routledge, 1997), 231–32.

34 See John Mowitt, "The Sound of Music in the Era of Its Electronic Reproducibility," in *Music and Society: The Politics of Composition, Performance and Reception*, ed. Richard Leppert and Susan McClary (Cambridge: Cambridge University Press, 1987), 173–97.

35 Wurtzler, "She Sang Live," 103.

36 Alkarim Jivani "The Ghetto Hour," in *Time Out*, 26 February 1989, quoted in Stuart Hall, "Black and White in Television," 18.

37 Steven Feld, "From Schizophrenia to Schismogenesis: On the Discourses and Commodification Practices of 'World Music' and 'World Beat,'" in *Music Grooves*, ed. Charles Keil and Steven Feld (Chicago: University of Chicago Press, 1994), 270.

38 Quoted in Lucy O'Brien, *She Bop: The Definitive History of Women in Rock, Pop and Soul* (London: Penguin, 1996), 352.

39 Quoted in Amy Raphael, "Not Just an Asian Babe," in *The Guardian*, 24 August 1994, T9.

40 White Town website at http://www.white-town.com 23 January 1998.

AFRICAN AMERICAN IDENTITIES

Class Swings: Music, Race, and Social Mobility in *Broken Strings*

ADAM KNEE

The black-cast film *Broken Strings* (1940) is not particularly well known (even for a race film) and has not received much sustained critical attention — sometimes a passing reference or a paragraph in histories of blacks in film or in biographical sketches of its star, Clarence Muse. However, this melodrama about an African American classical violinist merits much closer examination as a text expressive on several levels about difficulties and dilemmas facing contemporary African American artists, as well as African Americans more generally. *Broken Strings* is no exception to the rule of clear budgetary and technical limitations befalling many black-cast films from the 1910s through the 1940s, but despite (and indeed, in some senses, by way of) such impediments, the film offers a complex image of interrelations among artistic expression, black culture, and class, with resonances on various intra-, inter-, and extra-textual levels.

Of central importance to *Broken Strings*'s narrative about a violinist whose left hand becomes paralyzed after an automobile accident is an opposition between classical music and swing, the latter being a form that the protagonist (Arthur Williams) abhors and his son (Johnny) excels in. Williams (portrayed by Clarence Muse) spends much of the film trying to inculcate in his son a reverence for the work of classical composers, whom he repeatedly refers to as "the masters," while sharply criticizing Johnny's forays into swing. The son greatly respects his father and wants to follow the man's wishes, but he nevertheless finds the discipline of classical music far too confining, and prefers the free expressivity and improvisational tendencies of swing.

While the "broken strings" of the title may initially seem to allude specifically to the protagonist's loss of musical ability, the film ultimately
works these strings into a larger allegory of African American culture,
makes them instrumental in articulating aspects of black artistic practice
under various conditions of hardship. Indeed, it is, most immediately, financial hardship—the need for funds for an operation to cure Williams's
paralysis—that motivates Johnny to play swing (for money) against his
father's wishes, and the boy's switch from classical to swing in the film's
climactic musical competition is itself precipitated by a condition of material lack—by the loss of two strings on his violin. *Broken Strings* makes
clear, however, that Johnny's real attraction to swing is hardly pecuniary at
its core. Swing, for him, represents a break from constrictions associated
here with classical music; as he explains when alone with his friend and
accompanist Mary: "I'd like to play like a bird flies—this way and that, up
and down, winging and swinging through the air. No control. Whistling,
singing, shouting: just music." It becomes clear that swing represents a
means of escape from a broader social oppression as well—alluded to,
for example, in an orchestra leader's introduction to the aforementioned
musical competition: "We are considered one of the most musical peoples
on earth, because we have suffered. Music washes away from the soul the
dust of everyday life."

Yet not all music washes away this dust in the same manner. Classical music, as a long-established form largely associated with white culture, itself becomes linked to a tradition of oppression; it is difficult not
to see this link in the sequence where Williams thunders at his son, "I'll
drill the skill of the masters into you and drive out the spirit of jazz if I
have to make you play twenty hours straight." (Note again, in the choice of
words here, the reiteration of an opposition between the practiced technical skill of classical music and the untamed spirituality of jazz.) The evident slave/master allusion becomes still stronger as we see the image of
Williams shouting "play" superimposed on that of his dutiful son, who repeats the same etude until he collapses from exhaustion. Classical music is
thus associated with social oppression as well as discipline and technique.
And in conjunction with this, in the absence of the representation of any
white people in the film, the music clearly serves as a metonymic stand-in
for the invisible but dominant/dominating white culture.

In this particular context classical music also becomes associated with
alienation: in his zeal for the "masters," Williams is unable to enjoy swing
—a form appreciated by most of those in his community, but which he
feels desecrates music. This isolation is underscored by the fact that Wil-

liams, a widower, works as a *solo* classical violinist, the only ensemble performances we see being those of jazz and swing artists. The film in fact opens with one of Williams's solo recitals, following which he tells his all-black audience, "I'm overjoyed to play for my folks. . . . It matters not if I shall play for the people of the world." He continues, gesturing to his heart, "There is a kinship tonight that strikes *here*, that will live forever in my memory. It's something that only you and I can understand." But despite this explicit expression of a profound bond to his community, moments later, when one of his "folks" invites Williams to come play for her congregation, his agent apprises her of a prohibitive performance fee and the violinist makes no offer to intervene. And when the working-class banjo player named Stringbean comes to express his true appreciation for the recital, the first of its kind he has ever heard, the violinist and his manager are most condescending. That the two of them face their automobile crash immediately after these exchanges suggests a narrative punishment for their loss of touch with some members of their community, for their evident classism, clearly linked here with the realm of classical music. Moreover, the result of the crash, the paralysis of Williams's hand, is a literal evocation of the constriction associated with the masters.

Notwithstanding the film's opposing figurations of classical music and swing, *Broken Strings* complicates any simple, race-based Manichaean dichotomy between the two musical forms. The film in no way attempts to deny the artistic merit of classical music—a form that is appreciated by all of the film's characters, with or without classical music training. Moreover, the film figures swing as a form with its roots in some sense embedded in classical music. Johnny's initial swing performances are improvisations on the classical themes he has previously learned, and Stringbean likewise offers a banjo performance based upon the classical recital he has so admired. (As Stringbean has previously told Williams, in hopes of playing a duet with him, "You sure swings a wicked bow.") In his aforementioned discussion of the significance of music, the orchestra leader at the music competition also suggests affinities between the film's differing musical forms, claiming, "There's beauty in all music—classical, swing, or jazz." The conductor goes on to demonstrate this by showing at the piano how joy can be expressed in each of the three musical realms, and his progression on a single melodic theme from classical to swing to jazz again implies that swing and jazz are elaborations or variations on something fundamentally present in classical music.[1] However, swing and jazz also operate (as represented here) by breaking free from some of these fundamentals in order to reinvigorate the music.[2]

Rather than suggesting an ideological critique (and rejection) of classical music, then, the film appears to adopt a position in keeping with certain contemporary discourses about positive black contributions to art, in
which a postulated black vitality and emotion are seen as potentially in-
vigorating traditionally white artistic forms: Swing and jazz here represent
the revitalization of white/classical music.[3] Indeed, at one point Williams
makes clear that classical music must itself be "spirited" in order to reach
its full potential. At the close of what he feels has been an unsatisfactory
private lesson, he complains that his pupil's playing has been too "cold" and
goes on to declare, while gesturing once more toward his heart, "You're
not a musician *here*. You have no soul for music. All you play is notes."
The irony in this, however, is that Williams himself is "not a musician"
owing to his paralysis. And by implication, then, his paralysis is a sign that
the musicality of his soul, too, is troubled. Moreover, the repetition of the
gesture toward his heart (previously seen at the opening of the film, in
connection to his bond with his fellow African Americans) here serves to
reiterate thematic links between having a feeling for music and having a
feeling for one's people. It would appear, then, that Williams's transgression, in musical terms, is not his partiality to classical music but his loss
of a deeper (emotional, soulful) feeling for it, as well as a related lack of appreciation for swing, a musical form that expresses its spiritedness more
freely and which all the other African Americans in the film appear to enjoy
greatly.

The figuration of swing as a vital form allowing freedom of expression
can also be related to contemporary American conceptualizations of the
idiom as emblematic of progressive New Deal politics and, more specifically, of a movement toward cultural inclusiveness. Reaching a very considerable peak in popularity at the end of the 1930s, the phenomenon
of swing allowed occasion for cross-racial cultural and social interaction
on a variety of levels, while also standing as a symbol for—indeed literally broadcasting—American ideals of democracy and opportunity.[4] At the
same time, swing was understood as having a distinctive connection to
blackness, partially owing to its (sometimes contested) lineage in African
American culture. This understanding, clearly tinged with a certain racial
essentialism, was particularly evident in the position of some music critics that African Americans played the best swing—or in more widely held
notions that black performances of jazz and swing were inevitably different from white ones.[5]

Like many other race films, *Broken Strings* is very much concerned
with positively depicting the lives of middle- and upper-middle-class

black Americans—those blacks who went unrepresented in contemporary Hollywood films—but it is implied here that the once upwardly mobile Williams, in preferring classical music alone and denigrating the distinctively African American music of swing, risks losing touch with his larger community. The 1927 race film *The Scar of Shame* makes for an instructive comparison in this regard, as it too features a central male protagonist whose class and breeding are represented in part by his involvement with classical music and who feels that less privileged blacks need to have the opportunity to develop an appreciation for "the finer things"— an appreciation figured as paramount to class mobility and racial betterment. While the earlier film does imply a critique of the detachment of the black upper class (particularly as represented in the person of the protagonist's mother), it nevertheless also appears to largely concur with the protagonist's support for individual social striving. In contrast, *Broken Strings* suggests an uneasiness with Williams's somewhat elitist cultivation of a "higher class" musical taste, because of its isolating potential.[6] This is perhaps most vividly suggested in the shots of Williams sitting in the audience for the musical contest, visibly scowling at some of the swing performances while all the other spectators smile and sway their heads in time with the music. In the film's milieu of African American artists, professionals, and businessmen, upward mobility is important—and Williams's work in classical music is in part what has allowed him such mobility— but success must not be allowed to threaten community solidarity. It is a message that would likely have been seen by audiences to have very immediate resonance, given that at the time many middle-class blacks did indeed share the fictional Williams's disdain for swing.

As presented in *Broken Strings,* Williams's distancing himself from his community—musically, socially, economically—sits in negative contrast to acts of largesse demonstrated by other successful blacks; the film's moral framework appears to support black economic and social success, so long as that success is shared with others in the community. For example, the Sorbonne-educated African American doctor who specializes in cases such as Williams's not only agrees to examine the violinist free of charge but also (after a moment of hesitation) agrees to waive his fee for the indicated surgery. (The aforementioned expenses stem from hospital costs rather than doctors' fees.) The climactic musical contest is itself sponsored as a community service by a successful local black businessman, the eponymous owner of James Stilton Products and coincidentally the employer of Williams's daughter Grace.

These gestures of community concern and support are contrasted with a number of acts of betrayal among blacks, which the film details. Stilton's son, for example, while supervising the family business in his father's absence, attempts to frame an employee (Gus) for the theft of fifty dollars — out of jealousy over Grace's romantic interest in Gus. Dickie, the young son of a prosperous grocer, likewise attempts, twice, to betray his friend Johnny, once by informing the elder Williams of his son's swing performances and then again during the musical competition, as detailed below. (By the film's resolution, however, all of these intracommunity betrayals are set right.) Broken Strings clearly positions the elder Williams's behavior at the film's opening in alignment with those of these more overt betrayers. Dickie, significantly, also shares Williams's implied class snobbery. Mary complains that "just because his dad owns a grocery store he puts on airs."

Such details link alienation to losing touch with the economic hardships of others, as well as losing an appreciation for one's musical and cultural roots, and for the spiritual bond to community. Williams's current financial difficulty thus constitutes a kind of poetic justice. The importance of this recurrent theme of material want cannot be overemphasized here; it is clearly one of the driving anxieties behind the narrative. The comfortable middle-class existence that the Williamses try to maintain is seen as most tenuous, especially in the wake of the loss of the patriarch's earnings ability; poverty always remains an uncomfortably close possibility for them, as for many blacks attempting to gain an economic foothold. Despite the violinist's evident earlier success in his field, his medical bills, we hear, are sufficient to wipe out his savings. His resultant irritability leads to the withdrawal of almost all of his private pupils, and hence the loss of his only remaining income. The news of a potential hospital bill and the loss of Grace's employment then arrive in quick succession, but the daughter insists on keeping her joblessness secret in order to avoid troubling her father. As she searches for a new job, Johnny dutifully tries to help keep the household afloat by playing swing, first at a local club and then at the musical competition. Thus many of the key narrative events in Broken Strings can be tied back fairly directly to the characters' desire to stave off economic hardship, and by implication to avoid slipping back into an earlier state of economic powerlessness (or, to engage another metaphor at work here, of enslavement). Indeed, this fear of slipping into poverty, of suddenly finding oneself financially wanting, seems to permeate the text. Even the ruse the younger Stilton plays on Gus involves his sudden discovery that he is short a fifty dollar bill.

Williams finally comes to appreciate the deeper importance of swing in watching his son's triumphant (and cash-prize-winning) performance

19   After his paralysis, violinist Arthur Williams (Clarence Muse) becomes an
increasingly harsh master to his students in *Broken Strings*. [Courtesy of the
Wisconsin Center for Film and Theater Research.]

at the musical competition. In the moments leading up to the event, we
see Dickie betray Johnny (because he fears the younger Williams's classical
violin playing may top his own) by filing two of the strings on his com-
petitor's instrument. The strings break soon after Johnny begins playing,
and, forced into a position of want, of lack, of ridicule, the boy chooses to
make do with the resources he has, to wrest from his compromised instrument a musical expression genuinely his own, to make his deficit an asset.
He abandons his sabotaged effort at a rehearsed classical performance and
instead improvises swing on the strings he has remaining. The resultant
music is so rousing, so galvanizing that the orchestra instantaneously joins
the soloist, its players feverishly improvising along with him, and all those
listening—even Johnny's betrayer and even Johnny's father—are immediately swept up in a shared enthusiasm for the music; indeed, the evidently
automatic nature of this mass response, the sudden frenzy of the musicians, quite strongly brings to mind the essentialist conceptualizations of
an *inherent* bond between blackness and swing. Whereas classical music is
linked with alienation and betrayal, swing, it is now amply clear, positively

embodies community. The solidarity engendered in swing is then under-scored as Johnny is awarded the first prize with no deliberations required, and as Johnny's betrayer confesses and receives forgiveness.

The elder Williams is so deeply stirred that he not only changes his out-look on swing, he also begins to move his previously paralyzed fingers; the open expressivity of swing has quite literally freed him from his physical and artistic bondage, miraculously succeeding where science has failed. The once and future concert violinist now declares, "My heart still belongs to the masters, but look what swing has done for me," and the film's close, in circular fashion, has Williams performing at a classical recital just as he did at the opening. Resolution comes not with the protagonist's forswear-ing of classical music but with his new appreciation of swing, his under-standing of the significance of a coexisting musical form derived under conditions of want, culled from immediate, culturally specific experience. He has now reclaimed the "soul," and by implication the community bond, that is required not only for the appreciation of swing but for the successful performance of classical. In the world of *Broken Strings*, it is this doubled musical consciousness (of both a more white-oriented musical idiom and a more black-oriented idiom), this "twoness," to use W. E. B. Du Bois's term, through which he functions as an African American artist.[7]

Allegories of Black Production

The doubled artistic consciousness that *Broken Strings* postulates (along with its corollary musical politics) clearly has resonance in the doubled career of the lead actor—who had great success (in the sense of having regular employment) both playing butlers and slaves in Hollywood films and playing leads in independently produced black-cast films. Clarence Muse, who contributed to the writing of the film, would certainly have been keenly involved with the issues of cultural expression raised therein, having worked not only as an actor but also as a screenwriter, composer, and director in contexts which were often inhospitable. Significantly, his own politics were in some ways more accommodating to Hollywood than those of many of his fellow black actors in the 1930s and 1940s. Muse thought it more efficacious to assist Hollywood (where he often worked not only as an actor but as a dialogue coach and/or advisor in the use of blacks in films) in its representations of African Americans than to protest over details of the few decent roles that existed, and, not surprisingly, he and the less compromising NAACP on occasion got into disputes over the issue. But Muse was evidently self-conscious about the need to make a positive contribution to the lot of blacks in Hollywood and did, in some instances, lodge protests against what he thought were particularly egregious representations. Thus Muse the actor-filmmaker saw himself in a real-life role very much like that of Williams the violinist—one of cooperatively working within a white-dominated idiom, even at the expense of alienating some blacks, in hopes of (in his view) improving the lives of those of his race. This particular self-awareness may have been especially strong at the time he was involved in making *Broken Strings*. The year before he had been involved not only in acting but also in co-writing, with Langston Hughes, the Hollywood B-picture *Way Down South* (1939)—a melodrama of the antebellum South (a genre that was popular in the late 1930s and continued to be so in the wake of *Gone with the Wind* [1939])— and clearly the two writers at first had hopes of imbuing the project with a more sympathetic and humane view of black life than was usually the case in the genre, whatever the ultimate outcome may have been.[8]

One way it is possible to read *Broken Strings*'s doubled consciousness is in its reference back to the white-dominated Hollywood mode of feature film production which Muse had most often worked in and which the lower-budgeted production of race films mirrored in a number of ways. *Broken Strings* refers back to Hollywood filmmaking for wider audiences not only by way of its feature film conventions but also through more specific intertextual references both to Hollywood genres and, arguably, to distinct films. The race film had, in fact, from its beginnings functioned in part as a kind of response to films targeted primarily to white audiences, with many race films offering African American versions of Hollywood genres, others referencing more specific mainstream film texts; this latter tendency can be seen as far back as Oscar Micheaux's *Within Our Gates* (1919), evidently a response in some ways to D. W. Griffith's *The Birth of a Nation* (1915).[9] One point of reference for *Broken Strings* is arguably the 1936 British-made Paul Robeson film *Song of Freedom*, as the two films share their central plot premise and some key themes: a successful classical musician of African descent encounters difficulties related to isolation from his people, and this isolation is circumvented in part through the mediation of a musical composition more deeply rooted in the black experience than any composition in the classical idiom.

In *Song of Freedom*, this composition is a tribal song the Robeson character, a London denizen, seems to know instinctively and which leads him in search of an ancestral African community. By virtue of his lineage and his knowledge of the song, Robeson is eventually able to claim sovereignty over his ancestral tribe and to use his Western knowledge to try to improve the lives of those in the community, which has evidently developed little over hundreds of years. While this in many ways far-fetched narrative thus attempts to figure a "synthesis between black spirituality and white technology," this effort "founders," as Richard Dyer has argued, "on the lack of any visualization of what the positive black contribution to that synthesis would be."[10] Once the Robeson character is accepted by the tribe, their interactions are no longer represented; there is merely a flash forward to a concluding sequence in Europe. In shifting the site of its corresponding black/white synthesis from a mythologized tribal Africa to a modern black America, *Broken Strings* does manage to more concretely represent a positive black contribution. In musical terms, this synthesis is figured as jazz and swing; as argued above, these forms are represented as more energized uses of white/classical instruments and musical frameworks. In social terms, the synthesis can be understood as occurring simply through Williams's successful promotion of classical music in a middle-class black milieu—a realm beyond the usual representational capacity of feature films for mass (primarily white) audiences.

A more direct point of reference for *Broken Strings* in mainstream film production is the wide range of films with swing music being made at the time. Given the strong popularity of the music, it is not in the least surprising that Hollywood would choose to find ways to include it in its products. As a number of scholars have noted, however, Hollywood failed to make swing music played by African Americans an integral part of its films: Swing bands on screen were segregated both in terms of their personnel and in terms of their narrative deployment. Not only were black and white musicians not generally seen playing together, sequences involving swing bands (in particular black bands) were largely superfluous to the plot, a trait that both obviated the need for further developing nonwhite characters and enabled distributors to excise black-cast sequences for southern screenings.[11] *Broken Strings* is clearly also interested in taking advantage of the contemporary swing craze in its choice of subject matter—and, as a black-cast film, its swing bands are also nonintegrated—but on several levels the film provides a distinctive opposition, if not a rebuttal, to Hollywood's use of swing. For example, although *Broken Strings*'s swing performances are generally very brief, they are also of considerable importance to the narrative; swing music, rather than providing "color" and atmosphere, goes largely unrepresented—but is nonetheless pivotal in the film's conceptual framework, its themes, its character motivations. Moreover, whereas contemporary Hollywood's black musicians were narratively expendable, having only nominal plot involvement, *Broken Strings*'s black

musicians are given a central focus, two of them serving as the key protagonists and naturally provided with full character development.

In some ways, perhaps a still more pertinent cinematic intertext is the
landmark Hollywood film *The Jazz Singer* (1927), which, as Krin Gabbard has pointed out, *Broken Strings* arguably remakes. Each film piv-
ots around a father-son conflict predicated upon differences in attitudes
toward music, in particular music identified with the family's culture and
ethnicity.[12] Michael Rogin and Gabbard have both identified some of the
ways the earlier film dramatizes Jewish protagonist Jack Robin's successful assimilation in part by taking on what are figured as certain qualities
of blackness (in addition to the obvious blackface) — specifically, a prowess
in matters musical and sexual.[13] Robin (the former Jakie Rabinowitz) manages to merge into modern mainstream America both through the popularity of his stage performance and in his romantic overtures to the Gentile object of his affections. However, in *The Jazz Singer,* as in the range
of acknowledged and unacknowledged remakes of the film, the triumph
of the jazz musician's assimilation through performance, intermarriage,
and the resolution of Oedipal tensions is a triumph consistently denied to
blacks.[14] In *The Jazz Singer* it is a blackness disconnected from any actual
African Americans (literally a masquerade of blackness) which serves as a
touchstone to allow Robin to succeed on several levels.

Rogin makes a case for the singular importance of *The Jazz Singer* in
both cultural and film-historical terms: The film articulates certain fundamental white American perceptions of race, ethnicity, and assimilation at
the same time as it marks a quantum shift in film technology and form.[15]
The film's extremely successful segregated drama of integration established the sound feature as the standard mode of Hollywood production,
and the film's structure quite clearly links assimilation with sound. Not
only is singing presented as Robin's ticket to success; as Rogin argues, the
film's structure also connects "the death of silent movies and the death of
the Jewish patriarch," the latter event allowing the resolution of the Oedipal conflict and thus paving the way for Robin's white-into-white assimilation.[16]

I would propose here that *Broken Strings* functions, on some levels, as
an African American rejoinder to the ideological project of *The Jazz Singer,*
that it fractures and reworks elements of the earlier film's narrative, as it
also fragments elements of the ascendant aesthetic decried by that earlier
film, in the service of a significantly different view of the black experience, and black potential, in America. The consistency with which *Broken
Strings* manages to invert many of the structures of the film that may have

served as its inspiration is striking indeed. Where the earlier film absents blacks (and, hence, any focus on the African American experience) from its tale of American assimilation, the later film absents whites (and thus focuses directly and entirely on black life). Where the earlier film aims for a white-dominated mass audience, the later film aims specifically for an African American audience. And where the earlier film resolves its inter-generational conflict by in effect killing off the older generation and its ethnic traditions, to allow the ascendance of the new, the later film ulti-mately resolves its conflict in the development of a greater intergenera-tional and intracommunity understanding, allowing the reaffirmation of an ethnic solidarity. *The Jazz Singer's* tale of history-negating white assimi-lation is thus converted into a tale of history-affirming black adaptation. *Broken Strings's* dramatic framework, moreover, functions to diffuse some of the more divisive Oedipal tensions built into its predecessor's struc-ture—though other tensions do operate in their place. In *The Jazz Singer's* Oedipally overdetermined narrative, Jakie/Jack's return home after being kicked out, his showdowns with his father, and his musical performances are all partially subtended by his love for his "mammy." In *Broken Strings*, on the other hand, the "mammy" is dead before the start of the film (in-deed, widower Williams is shown as an utter loner, with no romantic con-nections at all), and the father-son tensions reside centrally in differences over the potentials of swing (and even in this, the highly obedient son is generally willing to accept his father's wishes and wisdom); where Oedipal tensions most explicitly resurface is in the dramatic triangle of Williams-Grace-Gus, with Grace unwilling to marry Gus until she is certain her father can manage on his own (that is to say, without her filling in the role of the woman of the household), and even this conflict has minimal weight in the narrative. (However, in allaying *The Jazz Singer's* incestuously un-easy mother-son relationship by doing away with the mother altogether, *Broken Strings* clearly points to yet other intergenerational tensions and re-pressions, some of the ramifications of which will be discussed further on.)

What the two films' respective patriarchs have most in common is their violent reactions to their sons' musical affinities. The elder Williams sees the acquisition of "higher" musical taste as crucial to maintaining a higher social status. Johnny's excursions into the territory of swing, then, are not merely signs of disobedience, but threats to what Williams has striven to achieve for his family; just as Jack Robin's father fears that his son's music will bring social disgrace upon the family, so Williams fears that swing threatens to undermine present social refinement through a reassertion of a popular past. However, where the Jewish patriarch fears a loss of a cultural past and identity, Williams appears to fear the return of the past — one marked not by free cultural expression but by enslavement and economic marginalization. It is a past, moreover, associated with a purer blackness, as opposed to a more "whitened"/assimilated present: improved social status is linked with a traditionally white musical form.

These associations are carried over into the evident racial caste system of the film's casting as well: Stringbean, a figure negatively and comically associated with lack of refinement and with the enjoyment of swing, is played by one of the darkest-skinned actors in the film, while those exhibiting more mannered (and noncomically represented) modes of behavior — the physician, for example, and Williams's gainfully employed daughter and would-be son-in-law — are all portrayed by very light-skinned actors. Significantly, Williams and his son, as the pivotal figures in the drama of negotiating differing cultural regimes, also have somewhat darker skin, while Williams's possession of a light-skinned daughter suggests that his late wife, too, had lighter skin, that his marriage — his social coming of age — involved bringing lighter skin into his lineage. The film's other successful black patriarch, James Stilton, likewise has relatively dark skin and has fathered a very fair-skinned child (that is, Gus), by a mother whom we again do not see; and Stilton, like Williams, intends for his son to retain social status by continuing in the same line of business. Stilton's beauty products business, significantly, has only very light-skinned employees, and one of the film's most overt gags on dark Stringbean's appearance occurs when the banjo player shows up at the Stilton Products office to request assistance with his image, explaining, "Looks mean everything." [17]

Perhaps the most important divergence *Broken Strings* makes from *The Jazz Singer* is that where the earlier film achieves resolution in a movement toward assimilation (a movement predicated, as noted above, on certain markers of blackness), *Broken Strings* insists, in its pivotal moment, on a movement back away from full assimilation — a movement also predicated on a *reclamation* of certain markers of blackness. Jack Robin's act of blacking up before his triumphal final performance has its formal parallel in the breaking of Johnny's strings before *his* triumphal final performance: the breaking of the strings in effect "blackens" the violin, transforming it from an instrument of servitude under a white idiom to an instrument of free(d) black expression, an instrument damaged but paradoxically also reinvested with a lost strength and vitality. Johnny does not put on a mask, but rather removes a constriction. Arthur Williams, too, is freed from his bondage by the breaking of the strings, his literal paralysis ceasing as he realizes that the movement to swing engenders not a return to cultural and economic enslavement but a recapturing of community identity and spirit, a shift from measured solo performance to inspired group improvisation. Significantly, however, Williams goes on to use this realization as a means to enrich his own performance of classical music, rather than as the basis for a rejection of the "masters."

Krin Gabbard's observations about the way instruments serve as vehicles for a race-inflected phallic power in quite a few Hollywood films about jazz musicians (including some of the remakes of *The Jazz Singer*) allow for some interesting contrasts here. Gabbard discusses several instances in which the circulation of a phallic instrument (usually a trumpet) among a number of characters accompanies a transfer of sexual power, often from black musician to white musician and/or (in the *Jazz Singer* narratives) from father to son.[18] Williams's particular brand of musicianship—and his particular instrument—however, run counter to conventional Hollywood portrayals of black musicians; he works not in a musical idiom identified with blackness but in classical, not with a trumpet or clarinet but with a violin. A small, soft-sounding stringed instrument is hardly what would usually spring to mind as a phallic symbol, but this one is indeed clearly the source of Williams's power—his ability to command an audience and to earn both social standing and an income—at the film's opening. With the onset of his paralysis he loses his ability to hold or properly manipulate his instrument, and hence he loses this power; the frustrating sense of impotence associated with this loss is most strongly suggested in a scene in which, fed up with the lackluster playing of one of his pupils, he forgets his disability and seizes the instrument, only to remember that he cannot use his fingering hand.

While Johnny can of course still play the violin, the father imposes his authority on him in a way that prevents him from taking on a similar phallic power; Johnny is only permitted to play (white) classical music, which he can do capably, but not with passion, with power. At the musical contest, however, Williams sees the violin reemerge as phallus; the boy's swing performance (and the throwing off of the yoke of the two additional strings) reinvests the instrument with its phallic signification, with its power of blackness. Williams heads directly backstage as soon as the performance is through, and his first action upon seeing his son is to grab the violin, to reclaim his phallic authority now that Johnny has revitalized the instrument, loosened the constrictions of whiteness. Where Jack Robin's father ultimately loses his power in the struggle over tradition, Johnny Williams's father regains his.

That this scenario of the reclamation of power and racial identity is so heavily loaded with signifiers of masculinity is hardly surprising, given the importance of reclaiming *manhood* in many historical (and gender-imbalanced) conceptualizations of African American autonomy.[19] It also goes some way toward explaining the structuring absence of the mother. Whereas in *The Jazz Singer* ethnic assimilation and resolution are achieved through mother-son bonding in the absence of the father, in this film racial pride and resolution are achieved through father-son bonding in the absence of the mother. But the mirroring is an uneven one (in that the later film includes no interaction with the mother) perhaps in part because the racial ideology of *Broken Strings* needs to obviate the appearance of inter-generational, intraracial, and, most importantly, male-female conflict at the same time that it requires the reaffirmation of a specifically patriarchal lineage; the presence of the mother would threaten to reassert the significance of the matriarchal lineage, along with (in this case) its literally "whitening," assimilating influence.

This schema of patriarchal transfer alone, however, does not adequately reflect the complexity of the power dynamics of the text—a complexity, indeed a "twoness," that I would argue registers (as does the disappearance of the mother) the ambivalent politics of the film, the difficulty of its position vis-à-vis assimilation and black-white relations. When Williams loses the power of the violin, he does not lose all power; his paralyzed hand, not insignificantly, is frozen in the form of a fist, on a usually upraised arm. One phallus—one marker of power—has been replaced by another. And this fist is indeed threatening to people. It's hard to miss the aggressive implications of the frozen gesture as a hapless pupil complains that Williams is making him nervous. "So I make you nervous, ay?" the violinist responds sharply. "The pupil's going to tell the master how to teach?" In the wake of his accident, Williams gets perpetually more gruff, disagreeable, threatening—a fact which Johnny and Mary comment on privately. Even when Williams comes backstage at the conclusion of the contest, Johnny cowers out of fear that his father is angry about his having played swing. This is still real power, but power figured in negative terms, perhaps seen most clearly in the scene in which Williams implores his son to practice until he drops from exhaustion, the black patriarch himself taking on the role of the white oppressor. Yet while this negative, oppressive power links Williams with whiteness, its particular form paradoxically also threatens the social status to which Williams aspires. The angry Williams loses his gentility and manners and further isolates himself in his behavior. In this

sense the upraised fist might mark a return of a less privileged past. However, at the same time, it can be read as an image of revolt against his circumstances, a setting aside of an accommodationist posture in favor of direct protest, a return of a repressed black militancy, a reclamation of black
male selfhood. Nevertheless, Williams's anger, as figured here, does not
positively draw him to his family and community, but rather detrimentally
distances him.[20]

Again, the complexity of the paralyzed fist as a symbol and the seemingly contradictory readings it offers speak eloquently of the complexity
of the racial and political subtext. In the world according to *Broken Strings*,
revolt against the system brings hardship and alienation, but so does total
acquiescence. Assimilation can bring cultural paralysis, a loss of spirit, but
outright militancy can mean isolation and a loss of the potential benefits
of a compromise with white culture.[21] The film thus ends up appearing to
advocate a cautious mediation between black and white realms, in music
as in society. Black self-determination, black identity, distinctively African
American forms of artistic expression must not be neglected, but at the
same time the pursuit of these things is not best served through the complete rejection of mainstream, white-dominated culture. The black and
white realms, as figured here, are not fully separable; classical, jazz, and
swing are in some ways all codependant. At the same time, however, the
film subtly privileges jazz and swing as music that has an essential blackness and offers a regenerative link to community, despite the main protagonist's preference for classical. This privileging is evident, for example,
in terms of narrative structure, in that classical music is aligned with that
protagonist's difficulties, while swing precipitates the resolution of these
difficulties. It is also evident in terms of the representation of musical
performance. The classical recitals by Williams which bracket the film
(those performances which presumably show how classical music *should*
be played) are, in brief, excerpted form (in particular at the film's closing),
held on an almost empty stage and evidently not particularly inspired—an
impression fostered by both the diegetic audience's partial lack of interest
in the music and the obvious and poor synchronization of Muse's bowing
with the dubbed soundtrack. In contrast, Johnny's swing performances at
the club and at the contest get a completely positive audience response
(with the exception of Williams's), and are presented to the film's (nondiegetic) audience in their entirety, implying that these are performances
more worth listening to, more likely to have entertainment value; the musicians in the orchestra at the contest are, moreover, evidently real musicians, rather than simply actors.

The Aesthetics of Twoness

The notion of twoness and the metaphor of the broken strings can be extended here to the context of film production as well. If, as some have argued, *The Jazz Singer* allegorizes the history of Jews in film production,[22] *Broken Strings*, in its own way, allegorizes the presence of blacks in production. Like the Jewish movie moguls, Jack Robin makes use of a popular expressive form, one not technically originating with his own people, to gain a broad mass audience extending beyond his own people. On the other hand, classical musician Arthur Williams and African American filmmaker Clarence Muse each seek personal expression through an apparatus (violin/filmmaking equipment) that blacks often do not have access to and through artistic forms not previously geared toward black spectators (though nevertheless certainly counting many blacks in their number). Williams is able to continue expressing himself through the dominant idiom of classical music only after becoming revitalized (losing his paralysis) through the intervention of swing. Significantly, this intervention is able to take place because of a literal breakdown of the dominant tools of production: it is when the strings on his son's violin snap that free expression is able to surge forth. The two-stringed violin suggests a paucity of means, yet it is paradoxically precisely this instrument which allows the fullest black artistic expression. Muse, likewise, continues to work in a dominant classical mode of production in which he is marginalized, that is to say, in Hollywood. At the same time, however, with the independently produced race film *Broken Strings*, he is able to express himself more fully and freely, to deal directly with the lives of African Americans. Like Williams, and like other black American filmmakers of the time working in independent production, he is able to achieve full expression only through an alternate mode of production in which the meagerness of means is much in evidence, in a technical standard substantially below that of Hollywood; as black artists in America, Williams and Muse operate in a paradoxical, doubled context, pitting a dominant regime against a technically more "impoverished," yet culturally more fulfilling, secondary regime.

It should be noted that I am referring to Muse as a filmmaker here even though his chief credited role is that of lead actor, and I thus discuss *Broken Strings* within the context of black filmmaking, even though its director and producers were white (as was usually the case with the race film). This is not to disavow the possible importance of the artistic input of director Bernard Ray (whose directorial output consisted primarily of westerns for poverty row outfits) or the possible influence of the production company (which had been involved with other race films as well) — though these happen not to be the main interest of this particular analysis. On the other hand, to insist on granting full authorial ownership to the white director and/or producers is not only to buy into auteurist prejudices (long since theoretically discredited) about the film text tending to be bound to the director's identity, but also to deny the significance of black authorial involvement. If one wants a full picture of the history of black filmmaking in America, one cannot bracket productions in which blacks were not credited as directors, because the conditions of production were such that blacks were rarely afforded such an opportunity. While it might be imprecise to plainly label *Broken Strings* a "black film," then, a richer understanding of the film—and of the complexities historically involved in African American artistic expression—nevertheless requires that we do take heed of the mingling and interaction of black and white authorial and cultural influences.

The particular form taken by *Broken Strings*'s technical and stylistic divergence (that is, its relative "impoverishment") is itself pertinent to the argument being made here and provides another axis for comparison with Hollywood cinema generally and *The Jazz Singer* specifically. *Broken Strings* both references and diverges from the classical Hollywood style, backing away from the very aesthetic whose ascendance *The Jazz Singer* heralds (in establishing the sound feature as the standard mode of production), just as Johnny's performance backs away from the aesthetics of classical music. In this sense, *Broken Strings* itself could be said to embody a type of cinematic twoness in the very nature of its own textuality, the kinds of artistic and cultural tensions it narrativizes. While the film has a fairly tight plot structure, with clearly articulated causal relations between events and clear character motivation in the Hollywood mold, and while the film is technically adequate, there are nevertheless numerous failed references to various aspects of Hollywood rhetoric. This occurs in particular in certain establishing shots, transitional sequences, and montage sequences, that is to say, in attempts to make use of various kinds of storytelling "shorthand" that had evolved in Hollywood. Such sequences foreground *Broken Strings*'s "difference," reinscribing through their imperfection a paucity of means and a distance from dominant modes of production, while also functioning in the service of a distinct African American cinematic practice, a kind of textuality and a range of thematic concerns not to be found in the Hollywood mainstream.

One example of this divergence from the usual Hollywood syntax occurs right at the opening of the film. In order to establish the setting—a concert by Williams—the film begins with a shot of a brightly lit theater marquee advertising the musician, as we hear his violin performance in progress on the soundtrack. This is followed in quick succession by two other almost identical shots of the same marquee, at very similar distances and angles. The motivation for this particular sequencing is hardly clear—but it seems that perhaps the variety of shots of the marquee is offered in the absence of other suitable external establishing shots; there certainly would have been no budget to construct the full facade of an appropriate theater, and perhaps practical considerations also forbade scouting for locations to shoot exteriors for a nonpivotal scene. (The almost complete lack of exterior shots, in clear indication of the film's budget limitations, would strongly support this interpretation.) The result is that the film opens not with the clear establishment of the setting of Williams's concert, but with a disconcerting series of (proto-) jump cuts, held together by a classical music sound bridge, heralding up front (while also mirroring) the fragmentary nature of African American film production in the studio era. We quickly move to interior shots of Williams and his audience, but here again, the economic status of the film production impinges directly upon the filmic syntax: jarringly interspersed with other interior shots are shots with a few sets of audience members optically superimposed as they revolve around the frame at differing rates, in an evident attempt to give a sense of a larger audience (and a larger theater space) than the production could afford. The impression produced, again, is one of fragmentation and of a poverty of means. The shots thus do help establish the setting of the film, both diegetically and extradiegetically, but not via typical means.

One scene later, the major dramatic premises are established through a rapid series of stock shots intercut with images of Muse through highly conventionalized techniques, all to the accompaniment of (for 1940) very dated stock melodramatic music. A shot of Williams and his manager backstage moves, by way of a rapid diagonal wipe, to a studio shot of the two men getting into a car, followed in turn by a rapid wedge-shaped wipe to a library-stock shot of what looks like a different car on a quiet country highway. A few more studio car interior shots and stock country highway shots are followed in turn by a stock miniature shot of a car overturning, then stock shots of an ambulance rushing down crowded, neon-lit city streets (which would, quite improbably, have to be many miles away from the quiet highway). This is followed immediately by an extreme close-up shot of the leaves of a page-a-day calendar flipping by at an uneven rate, a close-up of a "quiet" sign on a hospital gate, and then, finally, a newly shot scene of Williams having bandages removed from his left hand, an event which we hear he has been awaiting for some time. A fade out from Williams's grief over the discovery of his paralysis is followed by a fade in on a close-up of another calendar, this one monthly, with about half of the days of February 1940 individually crossed out. Vague shadows play over the calendar as the pages flip forward to December, after which we move to a shot of a sign advertising "Arthur Williams Violin Instructor," and start to observe the musician's efforts to continue with his life.

The presence of such stock transitional techniques makes very clear reference to the norms of Hollywood syntax, while their striking profusion, variation, and juxtaposition within a single sequence, and the seeming clumsiness in their employment, simultaneously serve to defamiliarize this narrative shorthand and to draw attention to Broken Strings's distance from Hollywood production funding and controls.[23] It is highly suggestive that this is also the sequence in which, as noted, Williams receives narrative retribution for his alienation from his community via classical music: The foregrounding of the artifice of conventional film style at this particular juncture functions to link classical music and classical Hollywood together as alien/white forms, forms that precipitate the black protagonist's paralysis. So, again, while on one level the weaving together of mismatched stock exterior shots and clichéd and clumsy calendar shots can be taken as a lack of technical finesse, on another level the form works to underscore the uncomfortable interaction between aesthetically, economically, and socially differing realms and is hence germane to the themes of the film.[24]

One of the most striking (and expressive) of these variations on Hollywood storytelling conventions occurs in the scene in which Williams, angered by the discovery that his son has been playing swing in a local club, forces the boy to practice for hours without interruption. In a close-up, Johnny begins a steady, repetitive etude based on scales, although the musical soundtrack is plainly out of sync with his much slower bowing and fingering. Williams's face is then superimposed on the right side of the image (a little disorienting, since he was at the left side of the preceding long shot), as the father shouts "play" at regular intervals, each time successively louder; these shouts almost establish a rhythmic counterpoint to the scales, while, coming on the heels of another one of his comments about the "masters," also strongly suggesting an overseer calling orders to a rhythmically laboring slave. The image of Williams's face is then replaced with the superimposed image of a clock face. The clock's hands move forward, in the usual Hollywood convention for showing the passage of time, but the rate of this motion is visibly inconstant, and the hands occasion-

ally pause—presumably to allow the person adjusting the clock to reposi-
tion his own hands—before continuing on as before. Williams's face then
takes the place of the clock again, as he repeats his "play" commands once
more, before a shift to a long shot in which Johnny eventually collapses
from exhaustion.

Several factors distance this from the usual Hollywood montage sequences it references, as well as from the realm of more conventionally
naturalistic representation. For example, in addition to the music's being
plainly out of sync, there is a strangely cyclical nature to the sound and
image; when the etude is finished once, it then repeats by virtue of a fairly
rough sound edit about two-thirds of the way into the shot (which seems
to lop off a fraction of the first note), and Williams's series of evenly paced
commands (along with his superimposed image) is repeated as well. The
aggregate effect of the tired-looking boy's slow, asynchronous bowing, the
irregular movement of the clock hands, and the cyclicality of the music and
shouted orders is a sense of fragmentation and discomfort; it is an awkward moment but in its own way also a forceful and expressive one, suggesting at once the loss of "harmony" between father and son, the loss of
economic comfort, Johnny's "enslavement" to his father's emotional state,
and the whole family's enslavement by their material conditions (just as it
once again also recalls the industrial marginalization of the film's makers).
I do not intend to exaggerate the significance of this single shot (which lasts
only thirty-five seconds)—but I do think it exemplifies some of the distinctive dynamics of the film, the tension between Hollywood form (and goals)
and the limited resources (and differing aims) of the makers of this film.
The effect of this representational friction is that techniques that ordinarily
serve a smoothing transitional function here end up signifying discord,
financial hardship, and toil.

The sense of tension with and difference from Hollywood style emerges
as well in the sequence of the musical contest toward the end of the film—
not so much because of technical differences from the Hollywood standard
as because of a shift in performance style. Most importantly, the orchestra leader who hosts the contest (Elliott Carpenter, billed as himself) has a
relaxed, improvisational acting style markedly different from most of the
acting seen earlier in the film. While most of the lines from other actors
are delivered in a very measured, at times even stilted manner, Carpenter
speaks and performs on the piano in a relaxed fashion, some of his lines
seemingly improvised, and he also mugs shamelessly, often directly to the
camera, and grins conspiratorially; he seems to be the "trickster" figure for
this text, trying to appeal more directly and knowingly to the film audience,

while undermining a staid, classical-style framework. And as he interacts with the other performers (those playing Johnny and Mary, for example), they too seem to "loosen up," become more natural, escape the bonds of carefully measured dialogue and staging. (In relation to this, one could note as well that Carpenter's small orchestra lacks the stylistic polish and careful stage layout commonly associated with the image of swing bands at the time, sporting inconsistent attire and playing in a roughly arranged, crowded group.)

While this shift could be taken as another sign of the film's uneven nature, it does resonate with the thematic of the sequence, that of the loosening up of musical performance style, the breaking of impediments to free expression. The shifted performance style is also in keeping with the fact that much of the musical contest sequence functions not just to forward the familial drama (primarily toward its conclusion), but also, as in many other race films, to showcase black talent; the fictional chain of events, and the particular conventions of performance and verisimilitude that it implies, are suspended as we are offered performances from various African American musicians and dancers, with whom Carpenter jokes in a completely off-the-cuff manner. This break from the usual polished acting style also interestingly recalls Al Jolson's breaks from the conventions of silent acting in his sound sequences in *The Jazz Singer*, where he delivers not measured dialogue but songs with seemingly improvised verbal banter; in both films, the shift to freer expression is naturally accompanied by a shift away from a more strictly codified performance style.

In the brief backstage scene after the contest, where Johnny reconciles with Dickie and then encounters his cured father, we return to more conventional feature-film acting. We then move to a brief closing scene of Williams performing in concert once again. With remarkable economy (in both senses of the term), the filmmakers here simply recycle the opening images of the film—the three shots of the marquee followed by a shot of Williams on stage. With a cut to a second and final shot of Williams on stage, however, there is suddenly superimposed a lightning-fast montage of images from throughout the film, the pace of which picks up markedly after a one-second cutaway to one of the earlier audience collage shots; all told there are better than forty superimposed images (some of them repeated) in these final fifteen seconds of the film. This sudden barrage of images is accompanied, moreover, by an equally abrupt shift in the sound-track; the classical violin performance is roughly cut out and replaced with what sounds like the closing reprise of a very slow, mournful orchestral rendition of "Summertime" (from George Gershwin's black-influenced score for his folk opera *Porgy and Bess*).

It is hard to know precisely what to make of this final flourish. Most conventionally, it recapitulates key moments from the film (though many of the images go by almost too quickly to make out) and is perhaps intended to provide a kind of emotional culmination. But the sequence has a distinctively down-beat feel, despite the ostensibly positive ending to the narrative. Williams has, after all, regained the use of his hand, is emotionally reconciled with his son and presumably with his community, and is more appreciative of the various kinds of music enjoyed by them; as a result of the curing of Williams's ailment, moreover, the way is now paved for Grace to marry Gus. However, this montage does not emphasize the overcoming of adversity, the reconciliation, or the formation of the couple; rather, it reprises all manner of moments of the film, and so doing recalls hardships more than joy. Just as the barrage of superimposed images de-emphasizes Williams's triumphant final performance, the soundtrack also removes us from this performance, ending on a somber note rather than a joyous one, a blues-style note rather than a classical one. We are thus left recalling Williams's hardship in a black realm more than his success with a white form—and classical music is once again removed from its position of textual privilege. As elsewhere, in the awkwardness of this collage we are reminded of the difficulty and heterogeneity in the context of not only Williams's act of artistic creation but also of Muse's act of cinematic creation. Here, both in spite of and by way of their limited means, the film's makers cobble together a somewhat bizarre and yet distinctly expressive close, which resonates with both the qualified attainments and contradictory costs of black social mobility in America.

It is in part sequences such as these, so strikingly divergent from the Hollywood standard and also so strangely effective, that make *Broken Strings* such a fascinating film to watch. If one sets aside qualitative evaluations based on Hollywood technical norms and is willing to examine the film on its own terms, it clearly has much to offer, both in conceptual complexity and in theme and viewpoints. The provocativeness of the conceit of the broken strings, the careful structuring of the narrative, and the skillful scripting of much of the dialogue (some of it credited to Muse) set *Broken Strings* apart from many race films. At the same time, the acuity with which it deals with issues of black identity in America (whether we accept the film's somewhat ambivalent perspective or not), the resonance of many of its gestures, despite its surface appearance of technical deficiency, should give us pause in our examination of race films more generally. There is clearly much textual richness and cultural value in this form—both in works by the more recognized race film directors and by those largely unexamined—and we may well have a good deal further to go in appreciating its obscured sonorities.

Notes

1 This particular representation of classical music giving rise to swing appears to also allude to the contemporary phenomenon of "swinging the classics," in which melodic material from well-known classics was used as the basis for swing performances. Many classical fans were quite vocal in their revulsion at this practice, a revulsion echoed in Williams's comment to Johnny upon discovering him improvising on his (classical) lesson material: "You're desecrating a classic; you're committing a crime against music." See David W. Stowe, *Swing Changes: Big-Band Jazz in New Deal America* (Cambridge: Harvard University Press, 1994), 94–98.

2 It should be clear that the present essay is not making any claims about the *actual* historical lineage or substance of any of these musical forms (and, indeed, it is unlikely that a contemporary audience would have had a clear and consistent sense of a distinction, if any, between swing and jazz); the focus here, rather, is how the *film* figures classical, swing, and jazz as interconnected and variously white-oriented and/or black-oriented. On the murkiness of the contemporary understanding of the relationship between the terms *swing* and *jazz*, see Leroy Ostransky, *The Anatomy of Jazz* (Seattle: University of Washington Press, 1960), chap. 2. It may well be that the progression in the orchestra leader's demonstration from classical to jazz by way of swing reflects an understanding of swing as "whiter" (in terms of its influences, composers, performers, and audiences) than jazz, with jazz and classical sitting at opposite ends of a racial-musical continuum.

3 See Richard Dyer, *Heavenly Bodies: Film Stars and Society* (New York: St. Martin's, 1986), 73–77, for a brief overview of some of these discourses, especially in relation to the writers of the Harlem Renaissance. By 1940, however, many of these notions were already under attack on several fronts for their racial essentialism; see George M. Fredrickson, *The Black Image in the White Mind* (New York: Harper & Row, 1971), 327–30.

4 Lewis A. Erenberg, "Things to Come: Swing Bands, Bebop, and the Rise of a Postwar Jazz Scene," in Lary May, ed., *Recasting America: Culture and Politics in the Age of Cold War* (Chicago: University of Chicago Press, 1989), 221–45; Stowe, *Swing Changes*, esp. 13–15, 73–74.

5 Stowe, *Swing Changes*, 60–61, 78–80, 85.

6 The conclusion of Thomas Cripps's analysis of *The Scar of Shame* alludes to just such a contrast; he argues that while the film "exemplified the highest hopes

of the black generation of the 1920s who placed faith in individual aspiration as the path to group emancipation," subsequent race films (including *Broken Strings*) "grew more collectivist in keeping with the New Deal mood" of the 1930s. Cripps, " 'Race Movies' as Voices of the Black Bourgeoisie: *The Scar of Shame*," in *American History/American Film: Interpreting the Hollywood Image*, ed. John E. O'Connor and Martin A. Jackson (New York: Ungar, 1979), 52. See also Jane Gaines's important essay on the film for an analysis of its sometimes contradictory discourses on class: "*The Scar of Shame*: Skin Color and Caste in Black Silent Melodrama," *Cinema Journal* 26.4 (1987): 3–21.

7 I refer here to a passage in Du Bois's *The Souls of Black Folk* (1903; New York: Vintage Books/Library of America, 1990), 8–9, which has often been cited in studies of black literature and film. Du Bois there discusses how "the Negro is . . . gifted with second-sight in this American world—a world which yields him no true self-consciousness, but only lets him see himself through the revelation of the other world. It is a peculiar sensation, this double-consciousness, this sense of always looking at one's self through the eyes of others, of measuring one's soul by the tape of a world that looks on in amused contempt and pity. One ever feels his two-ness—an American, a Negro; two souls, two thoughts, two unreconciled strivings; two warring ideals in one dark body, whose dogged strength alone keeps it from being torn asunder." For a discussion of some of the ways Du Bois's notions have been applied in film studies, see J. Ronald Green, " 'Twoness' in the Style of Oscar Micheaux," in *Black American Cinema*, ed. Manthia Diawara (New York: Routledge, 1993), 26–48. I concur with Green's approach here in the desire to position twoness not purely as an index of social difficulty but also (and more importantly) as a source of potential value, "a knowledge worth having" (30). It should be noted, however, that the precise meanings of Du Bois's original statement and the extent of their applicability to African American culture have been the subject of some considerable contention. See, for example, the range of positions reflected in Gerald Early, ed., *Lure and Loathing: Essays on Race, Identity, and the Ambivalence of Assimilation* (New York: Viking Penguin, 1993).

8 On Muse's career and attitude toward Hollywood, see Peter Noble, *The Negro in Films* (London: Skelton Robinson, [1948]), 158–61; Gary Null, *Black Hollywood: The Negro in Motion Pictures* (Secaucus, N.J.: Citadel Press, 1975), 36, 39; Thomas Cripps, *Slow Fade to Black: The Negro in American Film, 1900–1942* (1977; reprint, New York: Oxford University Press, 1993), esp. 108–9, and *Making Movies Black* (New York: Oxford University Press, 1993), esp. 24–26; Donald Bogle, *Toms, Coons, Mulattoes, Mammies, and Bucks: An Interpretive History of Blacks in American Films*, 3rd ed. (New York: Continuum, 1994), 53–56.

9 See Jane Gaines, "Fire and Desire: Race, Melodrama, and Oscar Micheaux," in *Black American Cinema*, ed. Diawara, 49–70.

10 Dyer, *Heavenly Bodies*, 92–93.

11 Bogle, *Toms, Coons*, 118–221; Stowe, *Swing Changes*, 133–40.

12 Krin Gabbard, *Jammin' at the Margins: Jazz and the American Cinema* (Chicago: University of Chicago Press, 1996), 108.

13 Michael Rogin, *Blackface, White Noise: Jewish Immigrants in the Hollywood Melt-ing Pot* (Berkeley: University of California Press, 1996), 79–80, 90–112; Gab-bard, *Jammin' at the Margins*, 36–42, 82–83.

14 Gabbard, *Jammin' at the Margins*, 42, 66–67.

15 See, esp., Rogin, *Blackface, White Noise*, 73–81.

16 Ibid., 82.

17 I do not mean to suggest here that the filmmakers are necessarily conscious of utilizing a skin-tone cast/e system—but it nevertheless operates and is concor-dant with contemporary discourses valuing lighter skin tones (as evidence of lin-eage) within African American culture. That the genetic determinism thereby implied is at odds with the film's other (and more overt) messages about racial unity and social uplift is of a piece with the ambivalent nature of the text as pos-tulated throughout this essay. See Jane Gaines's case for a similar contradiction between an explicit uplift philosophy and a far more covert caste system in *The Scar of Shame* (in "Skin Color").

18 Gabbard, *Jammin' at the Margins*, 55–57, 71–72, chap. 4.

19 Phillip Brian Harper's *Are We Not Men?: Masculine Anxiety and the Problem of African American Identity* (New York: Oxford University Press, 1996) offers a wide-ranging look at how aspects of black identity have been culturally coded as masculine.

20 The image of the genteel Muse with the upraised fist has an interesting corol-lary in his star discourse: after playing numerous accommodating characters in Hollywood films, he appeared, in striking contrast, as a rebellious slave in *So Red the Rose* (1935).

21 In Ron Green's analysis, black filmmaker Oscar Micheaux, similarly, represents "assimilation as dangerous, as well as attractive, for his group." Green goes on to suggest that "the idea of a dangerous attraction is one reflection of the struggle with twoness in African American assimilation." Green, " 'Twoness' in the Style of Oscar Micheaux," 46.

22 J. Hoberman, "Is 'The Jazz Singer' Good for the Jews?" *Village Voice*, 7–13 Janu-ary 1981, 32; cited in Rogin, *Blackface, White Noise*, 286 n. 22.

23 Admittedly, many "B" films make heavier use of such stock techniques than do Hollywood "A" productions; the contention here, nevertheless, is that *Broken Strings* pushes their employment to a distinctive, marked extreme.

24 Green makes a similar case for the value of Micheaux's style, arguing that de-spite its "mistakes," it is "appropriate to and worthy of his situation and his issues." Green, " 'Twoness' in the Style of Oscar Micheaux," 45.

Borrowing Black Masculinity:

The Role of Johnny Hartman in

The Bridges of Madison County

KRIN GABBARD

In choosing to direct and star in *The Bridges of Madison County* (1995), Clint Eastwood once again sought to distance himself from the misogyny and iron masculinity for which most Americans—including at least one former president—have known him. When Ronald Reagan threatened Congress with the line, "Go ahead, make my day," he publicly joined those who associate Eastwood with an unyielding, even sinister assertion of phallic authority.[1] Along with the coolly murderous cowboy introduced by Sergio Leone in the 1960s, the image of Dirty Harry has dominated public perceptions of Clint Eastwood in spite of the actor's repeated attempts to change his image. Among other roles, Eastwood has "played" the mayor of Carmel, California, and the esteemed cinematic auteur honored at New York's Museum of Modern Art and at London's National Film Theatre. And in the many films released since 1970 by his production company Malpaso, Eastwood has often sought to undermine, question, and even ridicule his macho image. As many critics have pointed out, however, many of Eastwood's accommodations of feminism and revised masculinity have been disingenuous or highly provisional within narratives that ultimately restore patriarchal values.[2]

But Eastwood's role in *The Bridges of Madison County* may be something else altogether. Working with screenwriter Richard LaGravenese and playing opposite Meryl Streep, Eastwood has softened the stridently masculine Robert Kincaid of Robert James Waller's novel. Gone are the Swiss

20 Clint Eastwood
and Meryl Streep in
*The Bridges of
Madison County.*
[Author's collection]

Army knife hanging from Kincaid's belt, his self-characterization as "the last cowboy," and the suggestion that he is part gazelle, leopard, or some other "graceful, hard, male animal."[3] Furthermore, Streep, as Iowa farm wife Francesca Johnson, does not whisper in Eastwood's ear the words of the novel's Francesca, "Robert, you're so powerful it's frightening."[4] Like the Kincaid of the novel, however, Eastwood does engage in "unmanly" activities such as writing love letters, reciting poetry, peeling carrots, and shedding real tears in conversation with a woman.

Eastwood does *not* pick up a guitar and sing to Francesca as does the Robert Kincaid of the novel.[5] Although Eastwood has sung in films before, in *The Bridges of Madison County* he effectively lets the African American vocalist Johnny Hartman (1923–1983) do his singing for him. Hartman's voice, which can be heard during four of the film's most romantic and sexual moments, was an inspired choice, providing the precise musical equivalent of the nonthreatening but undeniable masculinity that Eastwood was trying to project throughout the film. More than any other singer from jazz or popular music, Hartman expressed phallic masculinity at its most unproblematic. Effortlessly displaying a deep, smooth voice, he seems to occupy his manhood with complete confidence and serenity. Just as there is no swagger or menace in his singing, neither is there whining or masochism. Anecdotal evidence suggests that the audience for *Bridges* was predominantly female, but those men who attended the film do not appear to have felt betrayed by Eastwood's lack of weaponry or by his surrender to a woman. Similarly, my survey of the various newspaper and magazine reviews of the film turned up few suggestions that Eastwood fell short of some male ideal.[6] I am convinced that the unambiguously masculine sounds of Hartman's voice helped prevent charges of emasculation in the popular press.

At least since the early 1980s, however, emasculation *has* been an important issue in the literature on Eastwood. More precisely, film scholars have observed how Eastwood's films both "arouse and contain" questions of gender, sexuality, race, and social class, often in ways that can be considered progressive when the films seem to invite different readings from different audiences.[7] Christine Holmlund, for example, has argued that *Tightrope* (1984) repeatedly exposes contradictions within received notions of masculinity and femininity.[8] Adam Knee sees the "feminization" of the Eastwood character as early as 1971 in *Play Misty for Me,* with Eastwood playing a radio disc jockey who reads poetry over the air (twenty-four years before he would again recite poetry in *Bridges*).[9] And Robin Wood has written that, as a "buddy film," *Thunderbolt and Lightfoot* (1977) comes close to acknowledging the genre's inevitable homoeroticism, most specifically when the camera cuts to Eastwood preparing to fire a distinctly phallic cannon immediately after Jeff Bridges in drag bends over and lets his dress ride up to reveal a pair of thin bikini panties.[10]

The Law of the Father

Eastwood's creation and maintenance of a powerful, if occasionally complex, masculine persona can be best understood with the help of psychoanalytic theory. In an especially useful discussion, Frank Krutnik argues that "the patriarchal order is 'mapped onto' the psychosexual development of the subject."[11] Drawing upon Freud's account of the male child's Oedipal crises, Krutnik explicates conflicting attitudes about masculinity in the "tough" films of the 1940s. Freud's male child must renounce the mother and accept the authority of the father in order to escape the threat of castration and ultimately to achieve masculine autonomy. To maintain his autonomy, the man must avoid a return to the body of the mother—or her surrogates—who hold out the promise of an oceanic feeling, a "desired image of plenitude."[12] For Freud, even "normal" heterosexual desire returns the man to his "infantile fixation on tender feelings for the mother."[13] These feelings, however, must always coexist with anxieties about castration as punishment for violating the father's law.

Krutnik singles out *The Maltese Falcon* (1941) as the purest representation of "redeemed" masculinity, especially at the climax when Sam (Humphrey Bogart) overcomes his desire for the murderous Brigid (Mary Astor) and hands her over to the agents of patriarchal law on the police force. A more masochistic scenario was regularly acted out in many of the *films noirs* of the mid- to late-1940s that reflect disenchantment with traditional masculinity in postwar America—films such as *Out of the Past* (1947) and *The Killers* (1946), in which even soon-to-be macho icons Robert Mitchum and Burt Lancaster betray their father figures and submit to the will of phallic women. Although these films tend to be moral fables about what happens to men who swerve from the true path of masculinity, the films also address male anxieties about living up to impossible standards. American films such as *Bonnie and Clyde* (1967), *Body Heat* (1982), and *Basic Instinct* (1992) have continued to offer audiences the complex experience of identifying with men who break the law on multiple levels as they submit to sexual and powerful women.[14] At the same time, however, audiences have experienced a steady stream of films about phallic heroes who refuse the infantilizing desire for female plenitude while they function as agents of patriarchal law. If a character such as James Bond acts on his desire for a woman, he does so without in any way relinquishing his autonomy or ceding control to the woman, who is almost always objectified to an extreme degree. And in spite of his sexual dalliances, Bond never betrays the patriarchs and the system they support. Much the same can be said for recent films starring action heroes such as Sylvester Stallone, Arnold Schwarzenegger, Bruce Willis, Wesley Snipes, and Jean-Claude van Damme.

With a few notable exceptions, much the same can also be said for the films of Eastwood. If one of his characters becomes sexual, it is because a woman has offered herself and the Eastwood hero can remain in control. Very often an Eastwood character has left romance behind because of a dead but fondly remembered spouse. He has also played a series of characters whose mates have simply abandoned them. *Tightrope* (1984) includes several reaction shots of the hero's ex-wife, who does little except glare at him. In *The Rookie* (1990), when Charlie Sheen asks the Eastwood character if his wife left him because she hated his passion for auto racing, Eastwood replies, "No, she loved racing—she just hated me." And in *Bronco*

Billy (1980), Eastwood plays a former shoe salesman who shot his wife after he found her sleeping with his best friend; asked why he shot the wife and not her lover, Billy/Eastwood replies incredulously, "He was my best friend."

While it is true that Eastwood's character rides off with a female love object at the conclusion of *Bronco Billy, Pink Cadillac* (1989), and a few other films, his movies have never shown him in a comfortable, stable relationship with a woman. The single exception to this custom came late in Eastwood's career when he directed himself as a happily married engineer in *Space Cowboys* (2000). (But Barbara Babcock, who was cast as Eastwood's wife, was more than twice the age of the woman to whom the real-life Eastwood was married at the time.) The trope of placing the Eastwood character's romantic encounters in the past was already present in 1964 in *A Fistful of Dollars*. Eastwood and director Leone departed from their source, Kurosawa's *Yojimbo* (1961), by giving No Name a touch of vulnerability otherwise absent from the seemingly invulnerable protagonist; when a woman asks the gunman why he risked his life to reunite her with her hapless husband, he responds, "Because I knew someone like you once, and there was nobody there to help." Like many American heroes in both literature and film, the Eastwood character seems to have overcome his Oedipal crises and renounced the need for the oceanic feeling offered by union with a woman. In what is surely a consequence of this American myth, romantic relationships tend to resist representation and can only be *referred* to as part of an impossible past. Since this is usually the case in Eastwood's films, *The Bridges of Madison County* becomes all the more remarkable.

The change represented by *Bridges* may result in part from Eastwood's attempts to confront the realities of middle age. As Holmlund has argued in "Aging Clint," although the turn-of-the-century Eastwood may simply be too old to continue playing Dirty Harry, his more recent roles do not signal resignation.[15] Like Sean Connery in *The Rock* (1996), the older Eastwood plays powerful characters with skills derived from experience, maturity, and painfully acquired wisdom. In *Absolute Power* (1997), Eastwood's master thief Luther Whitney is spry enough to outrun a group of much younger Secret Service agents, but he is even more skillful at outsmarting the president of the United States and his various operatives. In *The Bridges of Madison County*, Kincaid is a seasoned traveler who knows how to survive in Africa as well as in middle America. The film suggests that this kind of knowledge, gained only after many years of experience, lies behind Kincaid's unique and powerful love for Francesca.

Accordingly, when this love is tested, when Francesca emotionally accuses Robert of egotism and cowardice as she questions him about his "routine" with the women he romances in his travels, she learns that she is not attacking a callow seducer or a passive misogynist. Instead of snarling and tightening his fist in the familiar Clint style, the mature and sensitive Kincaid turns away and sheds tears. In another stark contrast to the usual inarticulateness of his screen persona,[16] Eastwood then eloquently reassures Francesca: "If I have done anything to make you think that what we have between us is nothing new for me, that it's just some routine, then I do apologize." In this scene Eastwood's Kincaid succeeds, at least temporarily, in convincing Francesca that what they are doing is right. Later, however, as they sit at her dinner table for the last time, his words are impotent; he cannot prevent her from staying with her husband. As Francesca explains how she would destroy her husband if she deserted him, Kincaid wanly offers assurances that her husband will recover: "People move on." Until his final assertion—"This kind of certainty comes but once in a lifetime"—Eastwood returns to his conventional reticence and frequently befuddled manner with women. Finally, looking old and helpless outside the general store after Francesca's husband has returned, Eastwood invokes Ruskin's pathetic fallacy as he stares imploringly at Francesca in a driving rainstorm, finally smiling faintly while the sky seems to weep for him. But as I will argue later, even in this scene Eastwood has not been defeated. In fact, he has preserved his autonomy by moving away from an Oedipal triangle.

One Sings, the Other Doesn't

Before Eastwood gained virtual control over his image by releasing all of his post-1969 films (with the single exception of *In the Line of Fire* [1993]) through his own Malpaso Productions, he was called upon at least once to veer dramatically from masculine autonomy. Playing the benign "Partner" in *Paint Your Wagon* (1969), Eastwood willingly enters into a *ménage à trois* with Jean Seberg and Lee Marvin. Although he eventually wins complete possession of the Seberg character, he spends a good portion of the film submitting to her desire to live—and presumably have sex—with two husbands. *Paint Your Wagon* is also the first major film in which Eastwood sings. Whenever the film shows up in the *New York Times*'s television listings, the title is followed by the comment, "Clint sings like a moose." This is an inaccurate characterization of Eastwood's vocal style. His tenor voice is scarcely operatic—in the sense of either Pavarotti or Orbison—but his singing does convey many of the same qualities that Eastwood projects as an actor, including his shyness and his discomfort with romantic expression. When he sings "I Talk to the Trees," his singing style conveys his guilelessness as well as his confusion.

In what may be his most important singing role, when he directed himself in *Honkytonk Man* (1982), Eastwood brings a degree of pathos and even lyricism to a vocal style that is entirely consistent with the role of a struggling alcoholic singer dying of tuberculosis. Unlike films such as *Every Which Way but Loose* and *Escape from Alcatraz* (1979) that fetishize Eastwood's nude or seminude body, *Honkytonk Man* almost always shows him fully clothed. Even his walk is hunched over and tentative. As in *Paint Your Wagon*, Eastwood's untrained singing voice expresses his character's suffering and romantic confusion. Earlier, in *The Beguiled*, Eastwood sings extradiegetically, winsomely intoning an antiwar ballad at both the beginning and end of the film. As the eponymous hero of *Bronco Billy*, he idly sings along with the voice of Merle Haggard on his car radio. His disembodied voice can also be heard over the opening credits of *Any Which Way You Can*, joining Ray Charles in a rendition of "Beers to You." The mise-en-scène of "Beers to You" is a barroom where men sing of the ephemeral nature of women as opposed to the reliability of male friendships and the taste of cool beer. This is also the only time that Eastwood strives to project a robustly male presence in his singing, and it may therefore be the least successful of his several vocal performances.

It is no longer a secret that masculinity is constantly being constructed and reconstructed in culture, within and across boundaries of race, class, ethnicity, and age, often in contradictory ways.[17] Not surprisingly, then, anomalies of masculinity can appear even in a figure like Eastwood who has consistently succeeded in projecting "the masculine" over the course of several decades. The more threatening aspects of Eastwood's persona are usually subdued when he sings, but "Beers to You"—in which he seems to be trying to remasculinize his voice—exposes an important gap in a supposedly complete inventory of masculinity. As a singer, Eastwood is no Johnny Hartman.

Undoubtedly, Eastwood's vocal performance of "Beers to You" suffers at least in part because of its proximity to the legendary Ray Charles, who never appears on camera and is never heard again after the opening moments of the film. Nevertheless, singing with Charles surely represented a profound wish fulfillment for Eastwood, who has been fascinated by black artists and jazz musicians at least since his childhood when his mother first played Fats Waller records for him.[18] He has told interviewers that he once worked as a jazz pianist, a role he briefly reprises in both *City Heat* (1984) and *In the Line of Fire*. In his debut as a director, Eastwood cast himself as a jazz disc jockey in *Play Misty for Me* and gratuitously included scenes from the Monterey Jazz Festival. He has employed black blues artists in *Honkytonk Man* and *Tightrope*, and the extradiegetic score for *The Gauntlet* includes several solos by jazz musicians Jon Faddis and Art Pepper.

In this context, the use of Johnny Hartman's voice in *The Bridges of Madison County* may represent the culmination of Eastwood's fascination with blacks and their music (as well as his borrowing of their cultural capital).[19] Yet when Eastwood focused most closely on black music in *Bird*, his controversial biopic of Charlie Parker, he chose to take himself out of the picture altogether.[20] (Except for the early *Breezy* (1972) and the late *Midnight in the Garden of Good and Evil* (1997), *Bird* is the only film that Eastwood directed without casting himself in a major role.) When acting alongside African Americans as Dirty Harry Callahan or some other tough cop, Eastwood has faced difficult choices about how to treat at least some blacks sympathetically without undermining his status as the guardian of the law-and-order values so dear to American conservatives, with their profound suspicion of African Americans. Eastwood and his directors and screenwriters have developed imaginative solutions such as the one identified by Dennis Bingham in *The Enforcer* (1976). When the head of a black nationalist group tells Harry that he is on the wrong side — "You go out there and put your ass on the line for a bunch of dudes who wouldn't even let you in the front door any more than they would me" — Callahan responds, "I'm not doin' it for them." "Who then?" "You wouldn't believe me if I told you." As Bingham points out, Eastwood is effectively telling the black man, "I'm doing it for you," without abandoning his tough, independent, suspicious stance.[21]

In *The Bridges of Madison County* these kinds of elaborate evasions are no longer necessary precisely because the body of the black man is not present, or because blacks are marginalized as an exotic Other, particularly during the scene when Kincaid and Francesca dance in an Iowa roadhouse with an otherwise exclusively black clientele. Regardless of whether or not audiences at *Bridges* are aware of Hartman's race—and it is likely that many are not—the gentle but unambiguous manliness of his voice seems to emanate from Robert Kincaid himself more than from a singer that few in the audience are likely to know. In *Bridges*, Eastwood has gone farther than ever before in expropriating black masculinity and sexuality for one of his own characters.

According to Bruce Ricker, who served as the film's "music consultant,"

Eastwood chose the recordings of Hartman well before he began filming *Bridges*.[22] He chanced upon Hartman's voice one afternoon in his car when the radio began playing selections from Hartman's 1980 LP *Once in Every Life*.[23] In an interview with Bob Blumenthal, Eastwood has said that he had been a fan of Hartman ever since he first heard him at a club in the late 1940s.[24] He also proclaimed his admiration for Hartman's extraordinary LP with John Coltrane, released on the Impulse! label in 1963. Although the Coltrane/Hartman collaboration would have been an appropriate choice for action that takes place in 1965, Eastwood chose to make anachronistic use of music recorded in 1980. He bought the rights to *Once in Every Life*, subsequently releasing two CDS on his own Malpaso label, combining tracks from the Hartman LP with other soundtrack recordings from *Bridges*.

In Eastwood's film the singing of Johnny Hartman seems exactly appropriate for a director/star hoping to capitalize on the unproblematic masculinity of Hartman's singing. Nevertheless, Hartman's voice might not have seemed quite so natural if the film had been released several years earlier. Johnny Hartman was never much of a success prior to his death in 1983, vacillating between the obscurity of jazz singing and the large no man's land inhabited by pop singers without a natural audience of youthful or nostalgic fans. Nor did it help that he was short and not especially attractive. In what may be his only appearance on national television, Hartman sang Rodgers and Hart's "It Never Entered My Mind" in an episode of the short-lived *Sammy Davis Junior Show* in 1966.[25] Dressed in a tuxedo, he carried himself very much in the pensive but casual style established by Nat King Cole, the last black entertainer before Davis to have his own network program. People who have listened to Hartman's records in recent years will probably find that the man in the video does not *look* like the man they seem to be hearing on the records. With an unflattering haircut and awkward gestures, Hartman possessed little charisma as a performer. The diminutive "Johnny" seems appropriate for the man in the video just as "Hart-man" seems right for the singer on the records who injects so much sexuality into romantic ballads such as "It Never Entered My Mind."

Today Hartman is substantially more popular then he ever was during his lifetime. According to discographer and producer Michael Cuscuna, Hartman's record with Coltrane has become, along with *Giant Steps* and *A Love Supreme*, one of the three best-selling albums of the saxophonist's music.[26] In 1990 media commentator Daniel Okrent celebrated the Coltrane/Hartman LP in *Esquire* magazine as "the greatest record ever made," in spite of the fact that the record received little attention from critics when it was first released.[27] We can assume that Hartman had a following both inside and outside the jazz world if only because he continued to make records and public appearances for several decades. He usually won sixth or seventh place among male vocalists when *Down Beat* magazine conducted its annual readers' polls in the 1960s, but he was mostly invisible in the magazine's more prestigious critics' polls (although *Down Beat*'s critics voted him the male vocalist most "deserving wider recognition" in 1965). Many jazz critics regarded Hartman as a mere crooner, or worse, a conventional lounge singer. Even Okrent says that Hartman sounded like "a Johnny Mathis for grownups."[28] Although the 1963 LP with Coltrane was not widely admired immediately after its initial release, reviewers in the jazz press regularly greeted subsequent Hartman records with laments about his inability to perform again at the same level he had once achieved.

Born in Chicago in 1923, Johnny Hartman made a handful of records—often with narrated passages—under his own name shortly after he left the army in the late 1940s. He can also be heard crooning awkwardly with Earl Hines in 1947 and with Dizzy Gillespie's big band in 1948 and 1949. According to an article in *Our World,* a magazine aimed at black Americans, a white booking agent told Hartman in the 1940s that he couldn't use him because "your voice is too classy for a Negro."[29] Classy or not, the early Hartman was an insecure imitator of Billy Eckstine. Especially on "You Go to My Head," recorded with Gillespie in 1949, Hartman sounds like many young singers still searching for a style they can comfortably inhabit. When he climbs into the upper register, he seems unsure of his vibrato and intonation, perhaps trying to shade his timbre and pitch but falling short of the easy mastery he would later exhibit.

Hartman came of age as a singer when he began making albums under his own name for the Bethlehem label in 1955. With these recordings he perfected the art of seeming "natural," performing like the Stanislavskian actor who seems to "live" his role rather than interpret it. This aspect of Hartman's performance persona may have led Coltrane to take the unique step of recording with the singer, insisting to producer Bob Thiele that Hartman would be the best vocalist to complement his ballad style. Most critics and the record buying public now agree that Hartman did his best work with Coltrane and the rhythm section of pianist McCoy Tyner, bassist Jimmy Garrison, and drummer Elvin Jones.

Nevertheless, Hartman seldom reached a large audience in the 1960s and 1970s, undoubtedly two of the worst decades for jazz as a popular art. For most record buyers during this period, Hartman would have been associated with bland baritones like Perry Como, whom Hartman has specifically mentioned as an influence.[30] Nat King Cole, Billy Eckstine, and Frank Sinatra had all established popularity with large audiences in the 1940s when the younger Hartman was just emerging. The rage for Swing Era vocalists was already beginning to play itself out and suffer eclipse behind rock and roll when Hartman was making his first LPs in the mid-1950s. Jazz critics, meanwhile, were more likely to canonize "hipper" stylists such as Eddie Jefferson, Mose Allison, or Jon Hendricks, who brought a degree of irony or vocal calisthenics to their performances, or gutsier singers such as Ray Charles, Joe Williams, and Jimmy Rushing, who were more profoundly based in the blues. In 1981 Hartman's *Once in Every Life* was nominated for a Grammy, but the award went to an LP by a more mercurial singer, Al Jarreau. But Hartman persevered, staying with a style that was romantic and sensual without the sexual menace one can hear in the contemporary recordings of Billy Eckstine or the masochism one hears in the records of Johnny Ray and Johnny Mathis. Even Frank Sinatra, who has sung with a "tear" in his voice as often as he has with a macho swagger, presents a thoroughly problematic male sexuality when compared with Hartman.[31] As a female colleague who recently discovered Hartman's records has told me, "Listening to his voice is like being held by two strong arms." However, Hartman did not always project precisely this persona. On a 1966 recording of "Girl Talk," he begins with a spoken introduction before singing Bobby Troupe's lyrics to Neal Hefti's tune. Adopting a jokey, lounge-singer's delivery inconsistent with his singing style, Hartman says, "A kiss doesn't mean a thing unless it comes from that special girl. That particular girl. But one thing all girls have in common is that they're all pretty long-winded. Have you ever tried to phone your wife and give her a message—a very important message—and the phone stays busy for hours and hours? And man, don't let it be a long distance call or you'll really blow your top. I know you guys wonder, 'Just what could they be talkin' about that long?'"[32] Although the women's movement in America was still in its embryonic stages when Hartman recorded this patter in 1966, not all female listeners may have found Hartman's casual misogyny amusing.

But many women have fallen in love with the Coltrane/Hartman album, recorded even earlier. On the one hand, as a kind of art music, the Coltrane/Hartman album would not have included the narration and direct appeals to audiences associated with less ambitious or more working-class entertainments. On the other hand, when placed in less austere surroundings, Hartman was capable of engaging in the kind of practice with which "pure" jazz artists are seldom associated.

As I have argued elsewhere, the claim of jazz to art status has always been subject to the whims of critics, journalists, disc jockeys, audiences, and performers at different moments in the music's history.[33] To be sure, Hartman's thoughtful but unpretentious vocal style has benefited greatly from the recent classicization of jazz that began in the 1980s. Repertory orchestras in Washington and New York—including the big band of Jazz at Lincoln Center, where Wynton Marsalis is artistic director and Stanley Crouch is his advisor—have both confirmed and promoted the perception that jazz is a legitimate peer of ballet, the opera, the symphony, and the more familiar industries of American high culture.[34] There is no question that Americans have developed a much greater tolerance for jazz, especially the smoother styles of the music that listeners once avoided as scrupulously as they did the more avant-garde or challenging genres of the music.[35] Since Coltrane was regarded as virtually a religious figure by his fans but as a purveyor of cacophony by noninitiates, the Coltrane/Hartman album was not a natural purchase for listeners with little interest in jazz. As jazz began to acquire a new cachet in the 1980s, however, the album became the ideal point of entry into jazz and, in particular, into the music of the profoundly canonical Coltrane, who was at his most restrained and accessible with Hartman. Just as Hartman's "pure" jazz recordings have acquired aesthetic gravity for many audiences, the singer's attempts at reaching a popular audience in performances such as the 1966 "Girl Talk" are likely to strike many in these same audiences as something of an embarrassment. The 1980 recordings that so impressed Eastwood and that grace the soundtrack of *The Bridges of Madison County* belong more with the "pure" jazz recordings even if Hartman sounds a bit more mannered than he did with Coltrane in 1963. Certainly the presence of revered jazz artists such as Billy Taylor and Frank Wess on the 1980 album places it well outside the domain of pop ephemera.

Bridging the Racial Gap

Regardless of where Johnny Hartman stands in old or new jazz canons, in *The Bridges of Madison County* his voice endows Clint Eastwood's actions with real masculine authority at the same time that it heightens the film's romanticism. Hartman's voice is first heard in *The Bridges of Madison County* when Robert Kincaid and Francesca Johnson are chatting innocently at her kitchen table. At the moment when Kincaid initiates a more personal level of conversation by mentioning "his dreams," the radio in the kitchen starts to play Hartman's recording of the slow ballad "Easy

Living." Thanks in part to Hartman, a man talking about his inner life—
his *feelings*—does not sound emasculated. Just minutes after Hartman's
voice first plays on the soundtrack, Francesca takes the major step of inviting Robert to dinner. Several musical numbers are heard diegetically
and extradiegetically during the next stages in the romance plot: when
Francesca looks out her window and sees Robert washing up in the back-
yard, a love theme composed by Eastwood and Lennie Niehaus is played
by an unaccompanied string section; back in the kitchen a few moments
later, Dinah Washington's "I'll Close My Eyes" emanates from the radio;
and while Robert reduces Francesca to helpless laughter with his story of
the female gorilla, the music is "Poinciana" by the Ahmad Jamal Trio.

When Hartman sings again, the plot has reached the crucial moment
on their second evening together when the freshly bathed Francesca walks
into the kitchen in her new dress. Hartman begins to sing the connoisseur's ballad by Howard Dietz and Arthur Schwartz, "I See Your Face Before Me," at the precise moment that Robert sees her.[36] This is the music
to which they will dance and then kiss for the first time. An advertisement
for *The Bridges of Madison County*'s soundtrack album that appeared in a
June 1995 issue of *The Nation* includes a characterization of the song and
its effect:

> Tell everyone you bought it because of its selection of classic 1964
> [*sic*] gems from the likes of Dinah Washington, Johnny Hartman,
> Irene Kral with the Junior Mance Trio, and Barbara Lewis.
>
> Play it during your next chess tournament or secret meeting to
> overthrow the government and delight your guests with your knowl-
> edge that Clint Eastwood (a true music connoisseur) hand-picked
> each selection and even wrote the instrumental (with Lennie Nie-
> haus).
>
> We won't tell anyone that you actually listen to it to re-live that
> scene in the kitchen where they dance and the whole world changes.
> Promise.[37]

As the ad suggests, *The Bridges of Madison County* is at its most intensely
romantic when Hartman's performance of "I See Your Face before Me"
resonates through the theater. And as the ad implies, however ironically,
Hartman's music can do what neither images nor words can do—make us
feel what the characters are feeling and somehow connect these feelings
to our own experiences. To a large extent all film music functions in this
way, but something about Hartman's voice must have convinced the adver-

tising executives at Warner Bros. that Hartman's recordings are uniquely capable of achieving this goal, even for the highly suspicious leftists and intellectuals who read *The Nation.*

At another emotional peak in the film, the couple dances among the black patrons at the roadhouse while Hartman sings still another slow love song, "For All We Know." This recording continues extradiegetically as the film cuts to the couple making love back at the farmhouse and then as the narrative flashes forward to the present, where Francesca's daughter has clearly been moved by her mother's story. Finally, Hartman sings Hal David and Archie Jordan's "It Was Almost Like a Song" at another emotional climax when the lovers eat their final meal together and Robert ineffectually tries to convince Francesca to leave with him. This is also the moment when Kincaid seems to paraphrase the first words of the song, "Once in every life . . . ," when he speaks the line, "This kind of certainty comes but once in a lifetime."[38]

In a trenchant review of *The Bridges of Madison County,* Armond White has raised the issue of the white reception of black music that is crucial to Hollywood and especially to Eastwood's career.[39] White is highly critical of the film, comparing it unfavorably to the 1948 British melodrama *Brief Encounter,* another story about a woman who reluctantly decides to send away her lover and return to her husband. Whereas the earlier film engaged in an "artfully subtle critique of bourgeois restraint," White charges *Bridges* with squeezing pathos out of the film's validation of conventional marriage and concern with what the neighbors might think. White also suggests that Eastwood and the makers of *Bridges* have condescended to black music by recruiting Hartman and other black artists to dignify a banal story at the same time that *Bridges* and most of Eastwood's films make no attempt to focus on "Black emotional experience."[40]

While I agree with White's assertion that Eastwood has consistently ignored the inner lives of black people, most especially in *Bird,* I must point out that virtually no other element of dominant American culture regularly redresses this omission. I must also resist White's argument that Hartman, Dinah Washington, Ahmad Jamal, and the rest of the soundtrack music are pulled out of a purely black cultural context. One of the more sensual voices on the soundtrack belongs to the white singer Irene Kral, whose 1963 recording of "This Is Always" can be heard during the erotic moment when Robert and Francesca lie in the bathtub drinking brandy. Eastwood has also placed Kral's version of "It's a Wonderful World" on the radio as an ironic comment on Francesca's pain when she is reunited with her family after Robert's exit. Furthermore, it is not entirely fair to associate the singing of Johnny Hartman, who admitted a debt to Perry Como, exclusively with black culture. After all, white songwriters are responsible for all four of the songs he sings on the soundtrack. In another fortuitous instance of interracial collaboration, Junior Mance, Bob Cranshaw, and Mickey Roker, all of them black, accompany Irene Kral on "This Is Always" and "It's a Wonderful World." Although there is no question that blacks have suffered from the crushing asymmetries of power that have always characterized the meeting of white and black musical traditions, it is also true that the singing style of Johnny Hartman—and for that matter jazz in general—has flourished at precisely these intersections. Since jazz has almost from the beginning relied upon mechanical reproduction for its reception, there have always been patterns of mutual influences among blacks and whites even when they have not played together in the same rooms. As Amiri Baraka has argued in *Blues People*, the beginnings of white fascination with jazz marked the crucial moment when an aspect of black culture became an essential part of American culture, when it was "available intellectually, when it could be learned."[41] And, of course, black musicians have learned a great deal from white artists, whether it is Louis Armstrong listening to arias from European operas, Lester Young listening to Frankie Trumbauer, or Johnny Hartman listening to Perry Como.[42]

There are also serendipitous aspects to Eastwood's appropriation of Hartman and other artists. Throughout his career Eastwood has been careful to emphasize interactions among the races as he pays tribute to jazz and American vernacular music. He brought together black blues singers and white country artists in *Honkytonk Man* just as he centered the relationship between Charlie Parker and the Jewish trumpeter Red Rodney in *Bird*. Eastwood told Bob Blumenthal that he shot "virtually the entire festival" at Monterey when he was directing *Play Misty for Me*.[43] That only Cannonball Adderley and Johnny Otis appear in the final film reveals much about Eastwood's understanding of jazz and "black" music. The African American saxophonist Julian "Cannonball" Adderley was leading an integrated group at this time, with the Austrian pianist Joe Zawinul composing and arranging much of the band's music. Johnny Otis, seldom regarded as a jazz artist, is nevertheless one of the most intriguing figures in the history of racial crossover. Although he was born John Veliotes in 1921 to a family of Greek immigrants, Otis regularly refers to himself in his autobiographical writings as black and characterizes African Americans as "my people."[44] In *Play Misty* Otis is the only white face on stage as his band plays one of its biggest hits, "Willie and the Hand Jive." Like the young Eastwood, Otis felt real affinity for blacks and their music as a young man growing up in California. But Otis did not simply dabble in black culture. Married to the same African American woman for over fifty years, Otis has worked in black Los Angeles as a disc jockey, record producer, and performer but also as a politician, community activist, and minister. Otis could of course reinvent himself at any moment and reassume a "white" identity, but he has never made this choice. Surely these aspects of Otis's life were important to Eastwood when he was deciding which acts to include in *Play Misty For Me.*

As Frank Dobson has pointed out, Eastwood often plays characters who treat their fascination with black culture like a coat that can be taken on and off at whim.[45] Dobson concentrates most closely on *White Hunter, Black Heart* (1990), but he also makes an important observation about an early scene in *In the Line of Fire* (1993). Coming home after a day as a Secret Service agent, Eastwood sheds his professional gear after he picks up a bottle of bourbon and turns on Miles Davis's classic album *Kind of Blue.* Recorded in 1959, *Kind of Blue* featured trumpeter Davis with Bill Evans, one of the few white musicians with whom Davis regularly worked in a small group context. (The group also included John Coltrane as well as Eastwood's old favorite, Cannonball Adderley.) The film portrays Eastwood's transformation from Secret Service agent to jazz enthusiast synecdochically: the camera holds a shot of a table on which Eastwood places a magazine full of bullets and a pair of handcuffs alongside the "jewel box" for the compact disc of the Miles Davis album. When the telephone rings, giving Eastwood his first contact with the film's villain, Eastwood turns off the music and returns to his principal identity as the protector of American presidents. As Dobson points out, Eastwood quickly snaps out of his romance with black culture when duty calls.

Wolfgang Petersen, not Eastwood, directed *In the Line of Fire.* Nevertheless, the scene identified by Dobson is emblematic of Eastwood's practice of entering the domain of black Americans only when it suits him. Eastwood may identify with a figure such as Johnny Otis, but he does not seem to understand the patronizing, even colonialist nature of many "hip" appropriations of black culture by affluent whites.[46] Nevertheless, there is no denying the sincerity with which Eastwood has regularly made jazz and black music a crucial part of his projects, bringing music to mainstream audiences that they might not otherwise hear. He must also be given credit for producing (and bankrolling) Charlotte Zwerin's ambitious documentary *Thelonious Monk: Straight No Chaser* (1988). By the same token, the odd moment in *Bridges* when Francesca and Robert find a black blues club in the middle of the Iowa cornfields can be read less suspiciously as another of Eastwood's attempts to promote interracial cooperation through music. Although the white couple seems to have stepped into an all-black universe, the group on the bandstand is integrated. Led by the black blues musician James Rivers, who also performed over the opening and closing credits of *Tightrope*, the band features the Asian American pianist Peter Choe and Eastwood's son Kyle on bass.

Armond White is correct, however, in suggesting that Eastwood has made a film that is in some ways "a yearning dramatization of white incompleteness."[47] As Eric Lott has argued in his study of blackface minstrelsy in early-nineteenth-century America, white men have long regarded black men with a profound ambivalence.[48] Although minstrelsy allowed whites to indulge their contempt and even hatred for blacks, Lott argues that whites in the early nineteenth century, especially working-class males, regarded black males as sexual role models; the minstrel shows regularly played to white obsessions with the supposed hypersexuality, spontaneity, and phallic power of black men. Lott points out that similar obsessions with blackness characterize "most American white men's equipment for living" just as much today as in the 1830s when minstrelsy was most popular.[49] Like the vast majority of white men growing up in America, Clint Eastwood undoubtedly found some part of his identity in the conduct of African American men. A large portion of that identity was surely related to their displays of masculinity through music, along with sports the most important arena in which whites have partaken of a black male mystique. Throughout his career, Eastwood has carefully maintained the image of an impenetrable, autonomous male at the same time that he has cultivated a passion for jazz and black music. For Eastwood, the two are surely related, as they have been for the last two centuries in the white American imaginary. We can celebrate Eastwood for expanding public awareness of black artists such as Charlie Parker, Thelonious Monk, and Johnny Hartman, but we can only speculate on the extent to which his understandings and misunderstandings of black masculinity are responsible for his cinematic image.

Even when he reaches out for the masculine authority as well as for the romance in Johnny Hartman's voice, Eastwood may not have drastically departed from his familiar personae by performing as Robert Kincaid in *Bridges*. Like No Name in the Leone films as well as in Eastwood's own imitations of Leone's work, Kincaid rides into town alone, bearing few similarities to and little sympathy for the townsfolk. We might even compare Eastwood's Kincaid with the intruder/redeemer in *Pale Rider* (1985), an inflated remake of *Shane* in which another lone, unnamed cowboy played by Eastwood eventually makes love to a mature woman played by Carrie Snodgress. (Snodgress was thirty-nine when the film was released, roughly the same age as the Francesca Johnson of *Bridges*.) And like all the skillful gunmen that Eastwood has played in his many westerns and *policiers,* Kincaid has solid professional competence with his phallic cameras. In one of the more unusual marketing initiatives associated with the film, Warner Books collected the actual photographs that Eastwood took while performing as Robert Kincaid and released them in a book consisting primarily of blank pages that could serve as a diary. For a price of $11.95, fans of the film could assure themselves that Eastwood was not shooting blanks when he aimed his cameras at the bridges of Madison County.

What most separates *Bridges* from the conventional Eastwood film, however, is its emphatic shift away from the phallic quest of the hero and toward the pathos of the heroine. As I have implied, the nonthreatening masculinity of Johnny Hartman's singing may be more consistent with female fantasies than with those of the male. Furthermore, Eastwood exits well before the end of *Bridges* and generously hands over the rest of the film to Meryl Streep, ultimately making a film very much like the classic woman's picture. Like many films in the genre, *Bridges* begins by closely observing the mundane details of the heroine's life and later devotes its attention to the fetishized souvenirs of her four days with her lover. And like many heroines of women's films from the forties, Francesca is not allowed to have it all; the film follows the basic patterns of the woman's film of the "sacrifice" genre by asking Francesca to give up her lover for her husband.[50] Jim Mullen, the wag at *Entertainment Weekly,* summed up *The Bridges of Madison County* with the one-liner, "Most men went to this movie only because they thought Clint Eastwood was going to blow up the bridges."[51] Like him, I cannot help associating Robert Kincaid with more familiar Eastwood heroes. Kincaid does, after all, regain his masculine independence after he has moved beyond tears and violations of patriarchal law. This would explain the striking lack of conviction with which Kincaid suggests that Francesca leave her husband even while Hartman's records play softly in the background. Thus, when Francesca is reunited with her husband at the conclusion, Eastwood is once again the autonomous male who will not take mother away from father. At one moment in *The Bridges of Madison County,* that father, Francesca's husband Richard, watches *F Troop* on television. In the mid-1960s, with *Rawhide* on television and Leone's spaghetti westerns soon to be playing in theaters everywhere, Richard may have been an Eastwood fan as well.

Notes

Many thanks to Dennis Bingham, Susan White, Louise O. Vasvari, Arthur Knight, Michael Kimmel, Michael Jarrett, Robert Eberwein, Christine Holmlund, Lewis Porter, Paul S. Machlin, Michael Cuscuna, and Will Friedwald for talking me through some of the important issues in this essay. I am especially grateful to Sandy Flitterman-Lewis for effectively rewriting whole sections and for bringing structure to some of my inchoate arguments.

1 Michael Rogin, "'Make My Day!': Spectacle as Amnesia in Imperial Politics," *Representations* 29 (winter 1990): 99–123. When Eastwood uttered the words as Harry Callahan in *Sudden Impact*, he was daring an armed black man to murder a white woman so that he could shoot him.

2 Although a film such as *Tightrope* (1984) matches Eastwood with an aggressively feminist leading lady (Genevieve Bujold), centers his fear of involvement, and repeatedly suggests equivalences between the "normal" masculinity of the hero and the pathological behavior of a killer, the film ends with a return to conventional notions of gender as Eastwood rescues Bujold and then pursues the villain to his death. See Paul Smith, *Clint Eastwood: A Cultural Production* (Minneapolis: University of Minnesota Press, 1993), and Judith Mayne, "Walking the *Tightrope* of Feminism and Male Desire," in *Men in Feminism,* ed. Alice Jardine and Paul Smith (New York: Methuen, 1988), 62–70.

3 See Robert James Waller, *The Bridges of Madison County* (New York: Warner, 1992), 117, 141, 82, and 105 respectively.

4 Ibid., 106.

5 Ibid., 111.

6 Thanks to the bulging clipping files in the Cinema Study Center at the Museum of Modern Art, I was able to read reviews of *Bridges* in over thirty daily newspapers and in more than twelve mass market magazines.

7 I am indebted to Tania Modleski for the concept that Hollywood films "arouse and contain" the various anxieties of their audiences. See Modleski, *Feminism without Women: Culture and Criticism in a "Postfeminist" Age* (New York: Routledge, 1991), 77.

8 Christine Holmlund, "Sexuality and Power in Male Doppelganger Cinema: The Case of Clint Eastwood's *Tightrope," Cinema Journal* 26.1 (1986): 31–42.

9 Adam Knee, "The Dialectic of Female Power and Male Hysteria in *Play Misty for Me,"* in *Screening the Male: Exploring Masculinities in the Hollywood Cinema,* ed. Steven Cohan and Ina Rae Hark (New York: Routledge, 1993), 87–102.

10 Robin Wood, *Hollywood from Vietnam to Reagan* (New York: Columbia University Press, 1986), 233.

11 Frank Krutnik, *In a Lonely Street: Film Noir, Genre, Masculinity* (New York: Routledge, 1991), 75.

12 Ibid., 107.

13 Sigmund Freud, "A Special Type of Object Choice Made by Men" (1910), in *The Standard Edition of the Complete Psychological Works of Sigmund Freud,* trans. and ed. James Strachey (London: Hogarth Press, 1974), 11:168.

14 As the trajectory from *Bonnie and Clyde* to *Body Heat* to *Basic Instinct* indicates, the sexually desirable women in many of these narratives have become progressively more threatening over the years. See Krin Gabbard and Glen O. Gabbard, "Phallic Women in Contemporary Cinema," *American Imago* 50.4 (1993): 421–39.

15 Christine Holmlund, "Aging Clint," paper delivered at the Society for Cinema Studies conference, Dallas, March 1996.

16 In "The Dialectic of Female Power," Knee discusses the inability of Eastwood's character to express himself in *Play Misty for Me*, in spite of his job talking on the radio. Dennis Bingham, in *Acting Male: Masculinities in the Films of James Stewart, Jack Nicholson, and Clint Eastwood* (New Brunswick, N.J.: Rutgers University Press, 1994), points out the unusually prolix character of Eastwood's McBurney in *The Beguiled* and of his John Wilson in *White Hunter, Black Heart*. In general, however, Eastwood's characters tend to be laconic or simply inarticulate.

17 Among many illustrations of the contradictions in popular constructions of masculinity, I cite Jonathan Goldberg's comments on Arnold Schwarzenegger's descriptions of the pleasures of bodybuilding. See Goldberg, "Recalling Totalities: The Mirrored Stages of Arnold Schwarzenegger," *Differences* 4.1 (1992): 172–204. When Schwarzenegger celebrates the "pump" and its attendant sensation of continuous orgasms all over his body, Goldberg observes, "This sounds like female orgasms" (175).

18 Gary Giddins, "Birdman of Hollywood," in *Faces in the Crowd* (New York: Oxford University Press, 1992), 41.

19 See Michael Rogin's *Blackface, White Noise: Jewish Immigrants in the Hollywood Melting Pot* (Berkeley: University of California Press, 1996).

20 For the most persuasive critique of *Bird*, see Stanley Crouch, "Bird Land," *New Republic*, 27 February 1989, 25–31.

21 Bingham, *Acting Male*, 189. As one reader of this essay has suggested, however, Callahan could just as easily be saying that he is doing it for the one and only person whose approval he requires—himself.

22 Bruce Ricker, conversation with the author, 30 July 1995.

23 Recorded in New York on August 11, 1980, *Once in Every Life* was released on the now defunct Bee Hive label. The personnel includes well-established jazz musicians Joe Wilder (trumpet), Frank Wess (tenor sax, flute), Billy Taylor (piano), Al Gafa (guitar), Victor Gaskin (bass), and Keith Copeland (drums).

24 Bob Blumenthal, "Clint Eastwood: Bridging Jazz and Film," *Jazz Times*, September 1990, 30.

25 The program is in the jazz on video collection at the Library of Congress. I thank Larry Appelbaum for bringing it to my attention.

26 Michael Cuscuna, conversation with the author, 12 December 1995.

27 Daniel Okrent, "The Greatest Record Ever Made," *Esquire*, June 1990, 46.

28 Ibid., 46.

29 "The Struggles of Johnny Hartman," *Our World*, October 1950, 20.

30 John S. Wilson, "Hartman Singing in 'Voice of Jazz,'" *New York Times*, 21 May 1982, 36.

31 Writing about Sinatra as a movie actor, Keir Keightley has said that "Sinatra's persona is continuously being masculinized in order to be re-feminized, and feminized in order to be re-masculinized." See Keightley, "Singing, Suffering, Sinatra: Articulations of Masculinity and Femininity in the Career of Frank Sinatra, 1953–1962," paper delivered at the annual meeting of the Society for Cinema Studies, Syracuse University, March 1994. Much the same can be said of Sinatra's singing career.

32 The 1966 version of "Girl Talk" is available on the compact disc, Johnny Hartman, *Unforgettable* (Impulse! IMPD-152). The song was originally issued on a pop album by ABC/Paramount, a company in the same family of labels as the more jazz-oriented Impulse!.

33 Krin Gabbard, *Jammin' at the Margins: Jazz and the American Cinema* (Chicago: University of Chicago Press, 1996), 101–37.

34 In 1998, the Carnegie Hall Jazz Band, another of New York's repertory jazz orchestras, scheduled an entire evening devoted to the music for Clint Eastwood's films.

35 I have also argued that the recent and largely unprecedented appearance of jazz in television commercials, often as the signifier of affluence and sophistication, is strong evidence that jazz has acquired real cultural currency. See the introduction to my anthology *Jazz among the Discourses* (Durham, N.C.: Duke University Press, 1995), esp. 1–2.

36 Dietz and Schwartz wrote "I See Your Face before Me" in 1937 for the show *Between the Devil*. Frank Sinatra recorded "I See Your Face before Me" on his classic LP, *In the Wee Small Hours* (1955). Johnny Hartman recorded the song twice, first on his Bethlehem LP, *Songs from the Heart* (1955), and subsequently on the 1980 Bee Hive album that Eastwood used for *Bridges*.

37 Advertisement for *The Bridges of Madison County* soundtrack CD, *The Nation*, 26 June 1995, 917.

38 The choice of the song may actually have been dictated by the dialogue. Kincaid's one-liner in the movie is taken from a more prolix passage in the novel: "I have one thing to say, one thing only, I'll never say it another time, to anyone, and I ask you to remember it: In a universe of ambiguity, this kind of certainty comes only once, and never again, no matter how many lifetimes you live" (Waller, *Bridges*, 117).

39 Armond White, "Eastwood's Jazz Substitutes for *Madison* Drama," *City Sun* [New York], 2–8 August 1995, 23.

40 Ibid.

41 Amiri Baraka [LeRoi Jones], *Blues People: Negro Music in White America* (New York: Morrow, 1963), 155.

42 See Joshua Berrett, "Louis Armstrong and Opera," *Musical Quarterly* 76.2 (1992): 216–41; and Lewis Porter, *Lester Young* (Boston: Twayne, 1985), 33–35.

43 Blumenthal, "Clint Eastwood: Bridging Jazz and Film," 197.

44 Johnny Otis, *Listen to the Lambs* (New York: Norton, 1968), and *Upside Your Head! Rhythm and Blues on Central Avenue* (Hanover, N.H.: University Press of New England, 1993).

45 Frank E. Dobson, "Poise, Authority, and Privilege: Race in Eastwood's *White Hunter, Black Heart*," paper delivered at the annual meeting of the Society for Cinema Studies, New York, March 1995.

46 Eastwood chose to cast Morgan Freeman in the role of Ned in *Unforgiven* even though the part had not been written for a black actor. When asked why he did not then have the script rewritten to acknowledge Freeman/Ned's color, Eastwood said, "It's just hipper not to mention it" (Bingham, *Acting Male,* 241). One wonders if Eastwood also understands how much the film is in fact changed by showing Ned's crucifixion/lynching at the hands of Little Bill (Gene Hackman) and his lackeys, thus justifying their eventual slaughter. With the hip white hero avenging racist violence at the end, the horror of his killing spree is substantially undermined.

47 White, "Eastwood's Jazz Substitutes," 23.

48 Eric Lott, *Love and Theft: Blackface Minstrelsy and the American Working Class* (New York: Oxford University Press, 1993).

49 Ibid., 53.

50 Molly Haskell, *From Reverence to Rape: The Treatment of Women in the Movies,* 2nd ed. (Chicago: University of Chicago Press, 1987), 163.

51 Jim Mullen, "Hot Sheet," *Entertainment Weekly,* 29 December 1995 and 5 January 1996, 148.

CASE STUDY: PORGY AND BESS

"It Ain't Necessarily So That It Ain't Necessarily So": African American Recordings of *Porgy and Bess* as Film and Cultural Criticism

ARTHUR KNIGHT

The latest revival underway will transfer the property from the stage to the screen; Samuel Goldwyn is making a motion picture which he believes to be the supreme achievement of his career—and at last those last corners of the world where the opera is only known as a memorable name, there too it will be a visual and audible and emotional experience.—Lawrence D. Stewart

In March 1961 Duke Ellington, in a trio with bassist Aaron Bell and drummer Sam Woodyard, recorded a version of "Summertime"—though it might be more accurate to say they mauled "Summertime." All three players attack their instruments aggressively. Woodyard, who may well be using his namesake location instead of a trap set, starts by setting up a semi-steady pounding more than a rhythm, and he maintains this pattern remorselessly. Bell joins with his own stop-and-start bass line, which has a remote relation, at best, to the chordal structure of the tune, and which does nothing to hint at the flowing languorousness usually associated with the song. When Ellington joins, he initially does a nearly one-fingered rendition of the melody, which, instead of resolving (at "hush little baby, don't you *cry*") he leaves emphatically open (playing, in effect, "hush little baby, don't you/don't you/don't you/don't you" and then starting the chorus over). From here Ellington virtually demolishes the song by pulling out snatches of the melody, repeating them maddeningly, warping them past dissonance to full-blown discord, and avoiding even hints of resolution.

After about three minutes and ten seconds, which seems like a long time in the context of this treatment, Ellington and his compatriots, fatigued perhaps by their destructive labor, seem to give in to the tune's rhythmic, melodic, and harmonic tugs. Woodyard and Bell quieten, and Ellington plays lush chords in the song's standard tempo. Near the end of the chorus, he repeats again, seeming now to lapse into the convention of the big finish. He pauses: Is this a return to the song's conventional form? A sort of apology for what's come before? On cue, all three players assault their instruments with renewed vigor and in harmonic and rhythmic combinations designed for maximum ugliness and noise. It sounds, in fact, as if Ellington may be crawling up under the lid of the piano. This trio's relationship with "Summertime" ends beyond resolution, beyond reconciliation.[1]

For listeners who know Ellington and for those who know "Summertime," the experience of listening to this recording is bewildering. This version seems like an act of hatred—one out of keeping both with Ellington's elegant and gracious performing persona and his usual modes of making and arranging music, and one that doesn't sort in any obvious way with the song's revered place in both the canon of American popular song and the canon of jazz standards. If "Summertime" worked in comparatively straight versions for Billie Holiday in 1936 and John Coltrane in 1960, among many, many others, why wouldn't Ellington let it work for him?[2] Alternatively, given what seems to be an antipathy to the song, why not simply leave it alone? What had "Summertime" ever done to Duke Ellington? Plenty, as it turns out.

Ellington recorded "Summertime" at the crest of a flood of recordings of *Porgy and Bess,* which had started in late 1957 after Samuel Goldwyn announced he had purchased the film rights for George and Ira Gershwin's and DuBose Heyward's show. With Goldwyn's announcement, *Porgy and Bess*'s career entered a new phase. After two decades of increasing success as a stage musical and supplier of popular song standards, *Porgy and Bess* was approaching legitimation as opera, the high cultural form Gershwin had always believed it occupied. And now it had received the imprimatur of Hollywood's highest-class and most successful independent producer and would be, presumably, a worldwide hit. *Porgy and Bess* was suitable for La Scala, where it had been performed by a U.S. touring company in 1954, *and* for Hollywood superproduction.[3] As was common in the period, the U.S. music recording industry responded to this development by proliferating products that could capitalize on the publicity for the "presold" Broadway and Hollywood (and, in this instance, quasi-high-cultural) commodity.[4] The flow of recordings, both of the score, more or less complete, and selected songs from the show, began in earnest in 1958, a year in advance of the release of Goldwyn's film (which was delayed by a fire on the set), and subsided in the early sixties, when the film's release had run its international course. A significant current in this flood was made of recordings by performers recognized—then and now—as masters of jazz, including Ellington doing "Summertime" but also including Ella Fitzgerald and Louis Armstrong as well as Miles Davis and Gil Evans performing the majority of the score.[5]

How did these jazz recordings make sense and function culturally in their moment of production and initial reception? This question is especially intriguing because of what, in the late fifties, was a more than two-decade-long vexed relationship between many African Americans and *Porgy and Bess*. I will delineate this relationship in more detail below, but for the moment, suffice it to say that by 1957 for many African Americans the cultural and representational politics of *Porgy and Bess* were complex enough to make African American performances of the score, whether by jazz, pop, or classical musicians, not obviously attractive. Indeed, part of the African American discomfort with *Porgy and Bess* stemmed from its apparent "obviousness" as a "choice" for black performers. In other words, this unease stemmed from the fact that *Porgy and Bess* was a traditional black show, created and controlled by and mostly profiting whites. It didn't help that the show was an artifact of the late Jazz Age and that the Scottsboro Boys era was struggling toward the movement for civil rights. By threatening to reify the most worrisome aspects of the show—its "negative" or "stereotypical" representations—the Goldwyn film compounded and focused African American qualms about *Porgy and Bess*. Compounding this unease still further was the marketplace "common sense" of the tie-in between African American musicians and musical styles and the film, along with the suspicion that this tie-in could only amplify and make more "natural" *Porgy and Bess*'s "obviousness" as a representation of African America.

One potential way that the late-fifties and early-sixties jazz recordings of *Porgy and Bess* could work, then, was as film criticism. Following African American traditions of Signifying, these recordings could use the music of *Porgy and Bess* both to criticize the film of *Porgy and Bess*, and the history of the productions leading up to it, and to remake better *Porgy and Besses*. Even as the opera seemed on the verge of congealing into a high-class hypercommodity, available everywhere, relentlessly repeatable, revered, and, hence perhaps beyond effective African American renovation, these recordings could attempt to keep *Porgy and Bess* open and alive to critical reperformance. The jazz recordings *could* do this work. But did they? Did the jazz recordings—specifically those by Armstrong and Fitzgerald and Davis and Evans—do this critical work and, if they did, how? under what conditions? and with what effects?

The Porgy *Perplex:* Porgy and Bess *and Its African American Receptions before the Film*

The story that would become *Porgy and Bess* originated—and came to George Gershwin's attention—with white, southern author DuBose Heyward's 1925 best-selling novel *Porgy*. Heyward's novel supplied the plot, the setting, and the characters that would remain much the same—but for the shift to performance media and three crucial narrative alterations—in the other versions of the work. Set about fifteen years in the past on "Catfish Row," a poor all-black section of Charleston, South Carolina, *Porgy* tells the story of an unlikely and passionate summer-long love affair between Porgy, a middle-aged paraplegic beggar, and Bess, a slightly younger, drug-addicted street woman. Ultimately, Porgy murders Bess's possessive, violent, and vengeful former lover, Crown, and is jailed for refusing to identify the body for the police. When he's released, Porgy returns to find Bess gone, lured away to Savannah by unnamed men, and he ends the story defeated and alone. Heyward's novel was highly regarded by many black critics, most notably W. E. B. Du Bois, Countee Cullen, and Sterling Brown.[6]

In 1927, DuBose and Dorothy Heyward's hit dramatic adaptation of the novel, still titled *Porgy*, was also championed by black critics, especially James Weldon Johnson.[7] This adaptation introduced the three key alterations in the *Porgy/Porgy and Bess* story. First, the resolutely sad and undramatic ending of the story, which has Porgy in his goat cart grieving the loss of Bess "alone in an irony of morning sunlight,"[8] gives way to a more active, romantic ending in which Porgy, depicted now as young instead of middle-aged, departs in quixotic pursuit of Bess. Second, Bess has been lured to New York—north rather than south—by a specific character, Sportin' Life, an urban emigrant to the north back for a visit.[9] Third, the vague period of the novel's setting—a relatively recent past made distant and "golden" by the looming presence of the modernization of the twenties—becomes concrete: "the present."[10]

The play became the basis for the *Porgy and Bess* libretto, with Gershwin's music replacing the African American vernacular music that Heyward had alluded to in the novel and that the Heywards had incorporated in their drama. Like its antecedents, the 1935–36 premiere run of *Porgy and Bess* garnered favorable attention from African American critics, and the black press followed the brief national tour—which included controversy over desegregating Washington, D.C.'s National Theater—with interest.

Now, however, there were dissenting voices. Both Hall Johnson, the African American choirmaster, and Duke Ellington criticized the show, though in measured terms, complaining that Gershwin's music did not match the story's subject. Still, even as they criticized the musical-narrative conception of *Porgy and Bess,* Johnson and Ellington praised the singing of the performers. Both especially praised John "Bubbles" Sublett, a jazz dancer and the only "untrained" voice in the cast, whom Gershwin had asked to interpolate his own dance and rhythmic breaks into his performance of Sportin' Life's "It Ain't Necessarily So."

The explicit problem of *Porgy and Bess* for Johnson and Ellington was musical inauthenticity. In Johnson's words, Gershwin's music for *Porgy and Bess* wasn't "real Negro" music.[11] Ellington was more emphatic: "It was not the music of Catfish Row or any other kind of Negroes."[12] Lurking behind this criticism was another problem that Johnson and Ellington left implicit: *Porgy and Bess* took up room in a cultural marketplace with a limited and shrinking number of places for "black works" and black workers, especially relative to the Harlem Renaissance era of less than ten years before. Moreover, insofar as *Porgy and Bess* was a success, whether critical or popular, it would set standards for "black works" in that marketplace. As "entertainers" working to make a living for themselves and their collaborators in that marketplace, Johnson and Ellington were acutely attuned to these problems with *Porgy and Bess.*

Porgy and Bess was, as it turned out, a modest, mixed critical success and minor commercial failure during its original run. Its uncertain genre—was it a musical or an opera? was it "folk" or not?—seemed to confuse critics, and its 124-performance run did not recoup its investors' money. However, the show's generic confusion piqued the interest of at least some critics, and for those willing to align *Porgy and Bess* with opera, 124 performances was an unparalleled popular success for a new work in this elite form.[13] Beginning in the early 1940s, and spurred in part by George Gershwin's untimely death in 1937, increasingly frequent and successful revivals of *Porgy and Bess* capitalized on the qualified success of the premiere production until, by the early 1950s there was a small *Porgy and Bess* industry.

As *Porgy and Bess* grew more successful, more African American critics debated the show's merits, and in this process an interesting change occurred: Johnson's and Ellington's original criticisms of the show's music were forgotten and replaced with concerns over the "images" of blacks the show conveyed. Even in his glowing review of the novel, W. E. B. Du Bois had recognized "the old and ever young" potential to mistake a representation for a representative, the potential for a reader, and by extension a spectator, to take the figures of *Porgy* to stand for all African Americans.[14] *Porgy and Bess* had compounded this potential—to a fault. Following the play, *Porgy and Bess* proposed to be set in "the present" (i.e., 1935), yet it used a milieu the novel had portrayed as recently—but resolutely—past; thus *Porgy and Bess* envisioned African America as timeless, progressless, romantically primitive.[15] *Porgy and Bess* didn't just depict a small section of black Charleston at a specific moment; it depicted an ostensibly contemporary Charleston whose black denizens couldn't imagine, let alone *be*—despite Sportin' Life's travels—the very types of professional, cosmopolitan "Negro" representing "them" on Broadway or on national and international tours. Because of these (mis)representations, language, characterization, and narrative replaced music as the locus of mounting black critical concern. So, for example, when the *Chicago Defender* announced, in a front-page headline in 1942, "Offensive 'Darky' Songs At Last Get Long-Awaited Boot Out of [Washington, D.C.] Schools," it explained the ban of "I Got Plenty o' Nuttin'" not in terms of its music but rather in terms of the lyric, which "contained phrases offensive to colored students."[16]

The shift from music to image criticism only exacerbated a critical problem Johnson and Ellington had avoided in their initial critiques of *Porgy and Bess*—namely the collaboration of African American performers in the realization of the show. As we saw in Johnson's and Ellington's criticisms of the premiere production, even in its initial moment, black criticism of *Porgy and Bess* existed in a complex, and qualifying, relationship with pleasure and pride in the achievements and excellence of the show's black performers. And performers—ranging from Ann Brown, Todd Duncan, and John Sublett in the thirties to Leontyne Price, William Warfield, and Cab Calloway in the fifties—remained a node of ambivalence for black critics and a crucial peg of acceptance for black celebrants of *Porgy and Bess*.

It was hard for African American critics not to say, in effect, "I don't appreciate the image or character or story of Porgy, but I can't deny the power of Duncan's voice." However, there is a subtle but important distinction between saying, "The music is bad (or inauthentic), but the performers perform it well" and saying, "The story, etc. are bad, but the performers perform the music well." The former statement, which reflects Johnson's and Ellington's position, places all value in the performer; the critical upshot is, "These performers should have better and more work opportunities." The latter statement leaves room for value in the musical text that occasions the performance, and insofar as it may be argued that the "image" (story, etc.) supplies the occasion for the musical text, this statement leaves room for value to seep back into the image of *Porgy and Bess;* the critical upshot here is muddled and uncertain, at best. And indeed, in 1954 when the *Defender* considered the U.S. and world tour of the work, its critic focused his ire entirely on a narrative that was "dangerous propaganda," "corroborat[ing] and verif[ying] the stereotyped conception of Negroes." In contrast, he thought the music the best part of the production, "a welcome relief from the tendency to over-do Negro folk songs."[17]

Goldwyn's announcement that he would adapt *Porgy and Bess* to film brought African American critical ambivalence about the show to a state of crisis: Once the "image" of *Porgy and Bess* was recorded, rather than theatrically and therefore evanescently performed, how would fine critical distinctions between text and performance/performer hold up? Now that a specific performance of the music would be technologically married to the image, would the show and its performers prove so separable? Would this single filmed performance haunt African Americans—via publicity images, rerelease of the film, screenings on TV—in ways and to an extent that stagings of the show never could? Did the opportunity for black performers to once more, and more widely than ever, demonstrate their excellence warrant the dangers? And what kinds of choices did those performers really have? Harry Belafonte publicly refused to play Porgy, though it's not clear he was ever offered the role. But in a move that could be seen as emblematic of both the bind of *Porgy and Bess* and black ambivalence about the work, Belafonte's friend Sidney Poitier accepted the role, saying to the mainstream press, "My reservations were washed away by Mr. Goldwyn in his plan for *Porgy and Bess*" while conveying to *Ebony* that he was "still cautious about *Porgy and Bess*" and wouldn't know if he was "artistically satisfied" with his work in the film until after he saw the finished product and judged its "social" merits.[18]

The jazz recordings of *Porgy and Bess* were made and initially marketed and consumed in this charged atmosphere. It was an atmosphere in which an African American performer would likely be damned by many black critics for *doing,* and damned by agents and record companies for *not doing, Porgy and Bess.* Presuming that not doing a version of the work (or at least some of its best-known songs) was not a possible—or even necessarily a desirable—option for Ella Fitzgerald and Louis Armstrong and Miles Davis and Gil Evans, the musicians whose versions I will turn to shortly, then the challenge becomes: How to protect oneself—and "the race"—from *Porgy and Bess* via *Porgy and Bess?* How to do *Porgy and Bess* without doing *Porgy and Bess?* How to undo *Porgy and Bess* through *Porgy and Bess?*

The Signifying Complex

For performers like Fitzgerald, Armstrong, Davis, Evans, and Ellington the challenge of addressing apparently unyielding, unwieldy, pre-given material under complex sociocultural circumstances was not new. Rather, this challenge was common to the circumstances for expression that African Americans—and sympathetic collaborators, like Evans, who, not incidentally, was white—had long and often found themselves in.[19] Consequently, techniques for meeting—and making knowledge, pleasure, critical points, and/or material profit from—this challenge were fundamental to the black music-making practices, loosely grouped under the name jazz, that these performers were all schooled in and dedicated to. For these performers, the answer to questions of how to engage *Porgy and Bess* was as simple and as complex, as obvious and as unguaranteed as Ralph Ellison's famous formulation, "change the joke and slip the yoke."[20]

Crucial among African American expressive techniques for changing the joke is Signifying. Drawn as an aesthetic category out of African American vernacular performance practices, especially competitive, improvisatory language games, Signifying is at once a set of formal devices, a way of deploying those devices, and a set of criteria for judging the success of such deployments. For Henry Louis Gates Jr., whose literary-critical formulations of Signifying have been most influential in bringing the concept into wider view and use, Signifying can be usefully distilled into "repetition and revision, or repetition with a signal difference."[21] Critical to Signifying is at once marking continuity—repetition—and marking a break—signaling difference. Just as important is that these formal devices be used fluidly in dialogic, polyvocal, responsive, and generative performance. And just as important as that is the sense of purpose underlying Signifying, which *must* revise. To Signify, a performance must be recognizable—at least to some of its audience—as different, and meaningfully so, from its antecedents. Signifying can pay homage, parody, ironize, and/or criticize, but it cannot just affirm, just repeat. Signifying, which is based in *performance*, has as a key quality the potential to flicker between implicit and explicit, between ironic and parodic, between extensive, encouraging (constructive) and restrictive, discouraging (destructive) critical modes. At one extreme, then, a Signifying performance can be a call—an invitation—for a response; but at the other extreme, Signifying can attempt to end the Signifying—and signifying—process. In other words, Signifying can say, to someone culturally trained and positioned to hear, "your turn" or "shut up."

Duke Ellington's 1961 "Summertime" is a clear instance of a Signifying performance that says, "stop—now." Recorded after almost a quarter century of theatrical stagings of *Porgy and Bess* and after the Goldwyn film adaptation had run in North America and Europe and was being released across Scandinavia (a significant market for jazz), the Ellington "Summertime" has clear antecedents. The critical Signifying of Ellington's version was almost certainly motivated by the whole history of *Porgy and Bess,* but the Ellington recording's unprettiness, spareness (just a trio, playing for under four minutes), and directness seem meant to criticize specifically the most recent, present, and enduring antecedent—the film, which was very pretty, very lush (and epic), and profoundly indirect. This splintery "Summertime" wishes to "revise" the song, the film it comes from, and the entire idea of *Porgy and Bess* that the film comes from.

I want to pursue a similar line of interpretation for the relation of the Armstrong-Fitzgerald and Davis-Evans recordings to the Goldwyn film. They Signify on the film, if very differently from one another and the Ellington "Summertime." However, both of these recordings present a problem that the Ellington piece does not: The Armstrong and Fitzgerald and Davis-Evans recordings of *Porgy and Bess* were both released shortly before the film was released in 1959. Indeed, Armstrong and Fitzgerald made their recording in 1957, shortly after Goldwyn announced plans for the film, and Evans and Davis made theirs in 1958, which would have coordinated well with the initially scheduled release of the film. In other words, both these recordings present a problem of antecedence.

Antecedence, as considered above in discussing Ellington's "Summertime," is a crucial idea in at least Gates's definition of Signifying, and it is one that seems integral to the category of criticism. Can a text Signify on what comes after? How can a Signifying work "repeat with a signal difference" what hasn't been said yet in the first place? Is it possible to be critical in advance?

The answer to this last question is, "of course"—though we often call such advance criticism uninformed or censorious. However, for people, like African Americans, who are relatively powerless—who, for example, have had little access to or influence over the production, distribution, exhibition, and mainstream reception of Hollywood films—advance criticism is inseparable from "politics" in a capitalist society characterized by mass reproducible forms organized in a highly commercial manner. Still, how can Signifying take place in advance? The accelerating logic of the commodity, the market, and the tie-in require that we examine the possibility of advance, preventative Signifying.

The traditions that undergird more formal(ized) notions of Signifying provide some guidance here. In the language game of Signifying, the Signifying performer not only responds to what came before but also works to anticipate and shape what will—or can—follow; so antecedent is not all. When Signifying performance enters the domains of recording and mass culture, in which antecedent and author and authority get wildly altered if not erased, things get complex: The temporal order in which audiences might encounter the components of Signifying performance(s) is less certain than it is "live," for "antecedent" and "Signifying" recorded objects not only come to exist simultaneously (as written texts do) but also, as market pressures increase, come to be made simultaneously. Such conditions urge thinking of Signifying as much discursively as textually.[22] Preventative Signifying, then, might Signify on a discourse, which the marketplace for commodities produces in quantity, in order to prevent the creation of— or at least the untroubled consumption of—a specific text.

When Goldwyn had announced plans for his film in 1957, he activated a discourse. This discourse included the history of *Porgy and Bess* productions and of mainstream theatrical and film representations more generally, of course, but it also included elements that allowed certain predictions about how Goldwyn's *Porgy and Bess* was likely to appear and sound—e.g., the facts that his film would use Otto Preminger as its director and Dorothy Dandridge as its female lead, both of whom had filled the same roles in the film of *Carmen Jones* three years earlier. The Armstrong-Fitzgerald and Davis-Evans recordings got made and released in the shadow of this discourse, so we need to imagine them paired and existing in material proximity with the film, even though these performers and many of their listeners couldn't have seen the film. Certainly Verve and Columbia, the corporations that released these recordings, hoped for such a connection and even hoped that their records would come out of the shadows and fully into the discursive world of the Goldwyn film.

It Ain't Necessarily "It Ain't Necessarily So": The
Armstrong-Fitzgerald and Davis-Evans Recordings

At the time they recorded *Porgy and Bess,* neither Louis Armstrong nor Ella Fitzgerald was much seen as an oppositional, political artist—perhaps just the reverse, especially in the case of Armstrong. For many African Americans—at least many African American performers—Armstrong, particularly in his recorded legacy, was a musical force to be reckoned with and Signified in the positive sense of the term, but Armstrong's grinning image, which was prominently visible in mainstream popular culture, was unacceptable and required Signifying revision of the most critical sort.[23] Under such conditions, could Armstrong Signify? Fitzgerald was widely revered for her extraordinary tone and inventive phrasing, but she was also in the midst of cementing her popular appeal through her canonizing "songbook" recordings. She was less flamboyantly and comically genial than Armstrong, but her performances were generally interpreted as conveying joy in and embrace of her material, not—in contrast to, say, Billie Holiday—danger, tragedy, or resistance.[24] Could Fitzgerald Signify? Or, more precisely, could she Signify critically as well as in homage? These were live questions in 1958, so before considering how the Armstrong-Fitzgerald recording might Signify on the film, we should consider how it doesn't Signify, how it is straight.

The general pattern of the Armstrong-Fitzgerald *Porgy and Bess* is almost reverent. It uses more than half of the opera's twenty-four songs, even incorporating a few bits of recitative, and includes two songs—"The Buzzard Song" and "Oh, Doctor Jesus"—that had been cut in the original production and were only just starting to be restored to new productions.[25] This quantity of music required that the recording be a double LP set. Its track listing hews strictly to the "dialect" orthography of the show and the published score. And it places the songs mostly in their original sequence, beginning and ending with the same songs the show does—namely with "Summertime" and "Oh Lawd, I'm On My Way"—and thus strongly suggesting the show's narrative arc. All of these marks of respect are emphasized and made explicit by the clearest marker of the recording's reverence: an extensive liner note by Lawrence Stewart, who was Ira Gershwin's assistant, and who provides a thorough history of the "opera"'s creation and productions, a full summary of the story, and a comprehensive explanation of where the various songs figure in the narrative.

The arrangements, by sometime Hollywood orchestrator, composer, and conductor Russell Garcia, "jazz up" the score in a way that is akin to the popular practices of arrangers like Nelson Riddle. Garcia's arrangements take liberties with the score that no operatic performance would but that a Broadway revival might. So, while Garcia's arrangements are not reverent in the ways the recording's packaging is, they are fully within ordinary popular music practice of the day, which is to say, they don't seem serious or heavy, but they never risk humor or irreverence, either.

Consider, as an example of the Armstrong-Fitzgerald recording at its straightest, the closing number, "Oh Lawd, I'm on My Way." In the show, Porgy and the chorus sing this song as he departs Catfish Row on his romantic attempt to journey to New York and find Bess. Here Armstrong's voice is enveloped by syrupy string arrangements and augmented with a bland, homogeneously harmonized, "heavenly" Swingles Singers-style chorus, which strongly implies that heaven is the afterlife and not, as might be inferred, New York—or at least the effort to make an active life on earth. Armstrong neither plays his horn nor scat sings in the course of this finale, devices he might have been able to use to cut some of its overwhelming sweetness, and so the Armstrong-Fitzgerald *Porgy and Bess* ends with whimper—potentially affirming the worst of the stereotypes that black critics saw in the show and feared in the film—instead of any sort of Signifying bang.

However, there are elements of the Armstrong-Fitzgerald recording that do work across the grain of the show and against expectations of the anticipated film. Most obviously, Armstrong and Fitzgerald sing *all* the parts, so the story and the specific—and, in the view of the show's black critics, stereotyped and demeaning—characters get subsumed in their performing personae. The musical "story" laid on top of the show's story becomes the story of the performers' range of professional achievement. (Amplifying this identification, Armstrong uses Fitzgerald's name in several of his ad libs.) Because Armstrong's and Fitzgerald's personae could be read as congruent with rather than in any opposition to the show's characters, this casting choice is not an obviously Signifying one, but by yoking together all the characters with just two voices, this casting subtly complicates the show's types *and* Armstrong's and Fitzgerald's types. Armstrong sings both the crippled, (perhaps) docile Porgy and the serpentine Sportin' Life, among others (though he never sings the arch villain, Crown); Fitzgerald sings the promiscuous, passionate Bess and the firm and righteous Maria, among others. Moreover, especially in the first half of the recording, many of the songs sung solo in the show are rearranged as duets—or trios, when we add Armstrong's trumpet—so that characters' voices and performers' personae (and genders) get further interarticulated and nuanced, even if these effects are then somewhat flattened by the recording's overly arranged and Armstrong-centered finale.

The effects I am suggesting here—along with instances of Armstrong and Fitzgerald "improving" through direct improvising—are fully evident on their recording of "It Ain't Necessarily So." Armstrong opens the song with a trumpet solo. He states the song's melody with only slight variations (most evident in phrasing), but he also plays emphatically in contrast to Garcia's bright but uninteresting orchestrations. What would be unmistakable here to any jazz fan—and, indeed, to many casual listeners and pop music fans in the fifties—is that this is Armstrong's "sound." This sonic signature, honed, refined, and reformed in live and recorded performances for over three decades, asserts Armstrong's undeniable presence in—and, for those inclined to hear this way, dominance of—this music.

After Armstrong's opening, Fitzgerald sings the first chorus. "It Ain't Necessarily So" is Sportin' Life's song in the show, and thus "belongs" to a male villain—associations Fitzgerald's gendered and very "pure" (tonally clear and articulated) sound immediately complicate. Her most obvious critical revision of the song—and this is true of her treatment of the material from *Porgy and Bess* generally—is her consistent correcting of the lyric's diction. Though she does stop short of "correcting" the title, Fitzgerald refuses the "dialect" written into the lyric and, instead, opts for an *intensely* precise delivery. Not for Fitzgerald, "De' tings dat yo' li'ble / to read in de Bible," but rather, "The things that you're liable / to read in the Bible." Building from Armstrong's mild play with the melody, Fitzgerald performs her own more noticeable embellishments on the melody and her own rhythmic alterations. After completing her chorus, she then improvises her own hornlike scat line, escaping Gershwin's melody and any sense of the show's character altogether. Following Fitzgerald's solo, Armstrong takes a vocal chorus that, while not nearly as crisp or overwhelmingly precise as Fitzgerald's, responds by following her lead, correcting much of the lyric's diction and ending with improvised scat singing. The song goes on to end with the pair singing in duet, taking a piece that in the show is sung by a heretical individualist, and making it shared and much more carefully framed—less overtly "provocative" property and, hence, more subtly provocative in the context of U.S. racial-cultural politics.

Because we'll return to "It Ain't Necessarily So" again with the Davis-Evans recording and the Goldwyn film, it's worth recalling that this song was the one place in the original production of the show and in some of its most famous revivals where an African American musician contributed directly to the score. In 1935, George Gershwin had cast the singer

21 A typical promotional still from *Carmen Jones* (1954). [Author's collection]

and dancer John Sublett so that he could interpolate his own music and dance into the opera, and in several revivals Cab Calloway inserted his own characteristic improvisations. In a sense, then, Armstrong and Fitzgerald have simply accepted Gershwin's initial invitation to a potentially Signifying performer. However, Armstrong and Fitzgerald take that invitation to improvise and expand it out to encompass much more of the score than Gershwin would have permitted and much more of it than anyone could imagine the film would ever permit.

In at least partial deference to its extensive liner notes, which take up three sides of the gatefold LP sleeve, the Armstrong-Fitzgerald recording did not carry an artist photo. Its cover was simply a photo of the work's title set as a mosaic. There are several ways to interpret this: It suggests the simultaneous fragmentation and unification created by imposing Armstrong's and Fitzgerald's voices on the many voices of the show's characters. It also suggests an unwillingness to impose too close a connection of Armstrong and Fitzgerald with the characters of *Porgy and Bess*. Additionally, it suggests an unwillingness to compete with the imminent—and perhaps immanent—images from the Goldwyn film, images that some critics were predicting would look a lot like the images from Preminger's 1954 black-cast musical *Carmen Jones*, which had been a commercial success.

Carmen Jones had a mixed reception among African American critics, but in his very critical review, James Baldwin had seen in the film's
image of blacks a prophecy: "Carmen Jones is one of the first and most explicit—and far and away the most self-conscious—weddings of sex and
color which Hollywood has yet turned out. (It will most certainly not be
the last.)"[26] Ultimately, Baldwin decided that Carmen Jones reflected the
"deeply disturbed" aspect of America's sexual fixation on blacks, and he
hoped that this revelation would be all for the good. When Baldwin reviewed Goldwyn's Porgy and Bess, he was dismayed to find nothing had
changed:

> These [images of] Negroes seem to speak to [the mainstream, white
> audience] of a better life—better in the sense of being more honest,
> more open, and more free: in a word, more sexual. This is the cruel-
> est fantasy of all, hard to forgive. It means that Negroes are penal-
> ized, and hideously, for what the general guilty imagination makes
> of them. This fantasy is at the bottom of almost all violence against
> Negroes. It is the reason they are not to be mixed in buses, houses,
> schools, and jobs; they are to remain instead in Catfish Row, to have
> fish fries and make love. It is a fantasy which is tearing the nation to
> pieces and it is surely time we snapped out of it.[27]

The Armstrong-Fitzgerald recording's lack of an artist portrait is a small
refusal of this fantasy.

Porgy and Bess, however, was also Armstrong and Fitzgerald's third collaboration for Verve records in a sixteen-month stretch, and they were pictured on their previous records. Consequently, they were easily visible to
anyone flipping through record shop racks for Porgy and Bess. These existing images of "Ella and Louis" also work against the fantasy Baldwin identifies. The photo of the pair on the cover of their first record is (apparently)
neither posed nor candid. It seems to capture two working musicians in
repose, perhaps midsession. These two musicians were also, of course,
international stars, but here they are shorn of all star trappings: they wear
ordinary, comfortable clothes and sit on folding chairs in a linoleum and
acoustic tiled room. The photos on the cover of the second record catch
the two performers at work—though at the work of reading music, rather
than singing or playing, which emphasizes their professionalism and lit-
eracy rather than their "naturalness" as musicians. In all of these photos,
Armstrong and Fitzgerald are regular and kind of neighborly looking, if
your neighborhood is Queens instead of Catfish Row. These photos also
show that—very unlike the images critics knew to expect from the film—

22 *Ella and Louis* record cover (1957). [Author's collection]
23 *Ella and Louis Again* record cover (1958). [Author's collection]

this "Bess" and "Porgy" are not young or conventionally beautiful. To re-turn to Baldwin's criticisms of the film, Armstrong and Fitzgerald may also speak—both through their instruments and their image(s)—of a better life, but their recording and the images that surrounded it "battle with the white man's image of the Negro,"[28] struggle not to allow that better life to be distilled into a fantasy of an alluring and alarming black sexuality.

Nevertheless, it is hard to imagine the Armstrong-Fitzgerald *Porgy and Bess* snapping anyone out of any fantasy. Its Signifying is of the gentle, inviting, mildly corrective sort, mingled with homage. Nothing makes this clearer than the end of the recording. First, Fitzgerald's voice dis-appears; Armstrong sings the last three songs alone. Next, Armstrong's horn disappears; he doesn't play on the last two songs. Last, to return to where I began my analysis of the Armstrong-Fitzgerald recording, the ar-rangement's banal heavenly chorus gets the last words. The Armstrong-Fitzgerald *Porgy and Bess* may Signify preventatively in relation to the forth-coming film by complicating the film's likely images by rubbing them against the very different images of the two performers, and it may Sig-nify preventatively by setting a high, and specifically African American inflected, standard of musicianship.[29] That said, the arrangements in gen-eral and the last couple of songs in their entirety set such a contrastingly low standard that Goldwyn may well have been reassured that he could do better.

As many jazz fans would have expected in 1958, such timidity was not forthcoming from the Miles Davis and Gil Evans recording, which brags in its liner notes, fully visible to the potential purchaser on the back cover of the LP sleeve, that it "do[es] a *job* on" the original music of *Porgy and Bess*.[30] And to be sure, especially relative to the Armstrong-Fitzgerald recording, it does.

The general musical design of the Davis-Evans recording takes a num-ber of steps to defamiliarize the opera. Unsurprisingly, Evans's arrange-ments dispense with vocals altogether, and they also spread the vocal melody line well around the unusual instrumentation of the (all brass, reeds, and woods) "orchestra," refusing to assign "characters" to specific instruments.[31] Consequently, Davis's trumpet variously is and isn't Porgy *and* Bess and many of the other characters; and the same can be said of the ensemble, both as a unit and in its individual parts.[32] Like the Armstrong-Fitzgerald recording, the Davis-Evans recording adds the relatively unfa-miliar "Buzzard Song" and "Oh Doctor Jesus," as well as an Evans original, but the single-LP Davis-Evans recording cuts thirteen of the original show's twenty-three songs.[33]

The most significant omission of the Davis-Evans recording is Porgy's "I Got Plenty o' Nuttin'." It is hard to imagine Davis playing this song in any form, but leaving this familiar tune—the same song that African Americans had lobbied, in 1942, to remove from the Washington, D.C., public school music curriculum—out of the recording substantially alters the overall flavor of the LP and further alters whatever vestigial sense of Porgy's character the recording calls forth. Any interested party would have predicted in 1958 that the Goldwyn film would include the song and, thus, would include Sidney Poitier on his knees singing, "I got plenty o' nuttin' and nuttin's plenty for me"—perhaps the most viscerally unappealing prospect of the film adaptation for black critics.

These alterations of (re)presentation and arrangement are amplified by Davis-Evans's similarly radical rearrangement of the order of the show's songs. Instead of the familiar opening of "Summertime," they begin with a shocking—very brassy, very loud, quite dissonant, and initially nearly a-rhythmic—arrangement of the foreboding "The Buzzard Song." The arrangement's dynamics, combined with the fact that this song had been left out of the 1935 production and the '42 revival and, hence, was not widely known, give the record a disorienting start.[34]

The rest of the record's order seems set by "feel" more than by the show's sequence, although as the recording draws to a close it does start to hew more to the show's order. However, as soon as it has begun to establish a sense of the original sequence, it stops—and not with the proper end of the show, "Oh Lawd, I'm on My Way." Rather, Davis and Evans end their record with the song Sportin' Life uses to exit (taking Bess with him), "There's a Boat Dat's Leavin' Soon for New York." It makes some sense to understand this choice as Davis's nod to his adopted home town—the world capitol of jazz, the place the recording was made, and, arguably, the home of *Porgy and Bess*. Beyond that, the effect of ending the recording with this gesture north and in the voice of the raffish villain, rather than with the hero, is provocative, championing New York over the nostalgia of Catfish Row *or* a "Heavenly Land." To emphasize this provocation, the track listing on the Davis-Evans recording corrects the dialect, something it does not do for any of the other song titles, so the song's title becomes, "There's a Boat *That's* Leaving Soon for New York." However, to avoid simply replacing the old ending of *Porgy and Bess* with a new triumphalism or sentimentality, Davis and Evans orchestrate the song so it just dwindles away, losing momentum and force until it is just gone.

The Davis-Evans recording of "It Ain't Necessarily So" is a good indicator of how of a piece these estrangement techniques are to their conception of their *Porgy and Bess.* As they do often on this record, they unfold the piece slowly, in both tempo and melody. At the start, they make this snappy, insouciant tune almost mournful and brooding, which is not at all in keeping with anyone else's "Sportin' Life" and was definitely not what audiences were expecting from Sammy Davis Jr., the performer slated to play the role in the film. Partly because of the tempo, but also because the melody is left unstated for the song's opening, it takes a while for even a knowledgeable listener to figure out which song this is, and even after Davis and the ensemble do state the melody, they do so only in small fragments, withholding the satisfaction of resolution and refusing to affirm fully the listener's memory of the song. (Recall that, in contrast, Armstrong states the melody of this song immediately and completely in his solo.) Still, after a period of disorientation, the tune *does* start to swing, and Davis *does* finally complete the melody in a solo right near the end of tune. By about three-fourths of the way through, then, this "It Ain't Necessarily So" does start to get to where it's expected to go. But forecasting their ending for "There's a Boat That's Leaving Soon," here too Davis and Evans choose to conclude with a diminuendo, with going affectively low instead of to the high they seemed headed for and that the original song so strongly encourages.

Again and again on their record, Davis and Evans make choices that work against the grain of the show and expectations of the film. If, as I've argued, the Armstrong-Fitzgerald recording ends with a metaphorical whimper when judged in terms of Signifying, the Davis-Evans recording ends many of its songs as well as the entire recording with a carefully orchestrated descent into silence, a literal musical whimper. But in the context of all Davis and Evans's other choices, this (repeated) whimper Signifies. The song that Evans wrote for this record, an up-tempo number built on the chord changes of the show's lament, hints at their Signifying message. The original lament is titled "Gone, Gone, Gone." The new, inverted version is given the title "Gone," which at once suggests, in the hip language of the day, approval and, in more ordinary usage, a desire in relation to *Porgy and Bess:* Would that it were. . . . Following this allusive, Signifying titling strategy, Davis and Evans might have usefully retitled their "It Ain't Necessarily So" "It Ain't Necessarily It Ain't Necessarily So." Indeed, the phrase "It Ain't Necessarily" seems implicitly to preface everything in this recording, including the title of the work: "(It Ain't Necessarily) Porgy and Bess."

Cementing this Signifying, the image chosen for the cover of the record plays provocatively with the possibilities for, pleasures of, and potential

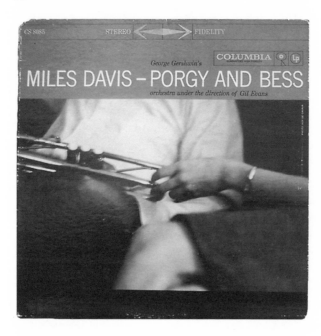

24 Miles Davis/
Gil Evans *Porgy
and Bess* record
cover (1959).
[Author's
collection]

for protest in uncertainty and ambiguity that the music creates. In this image, a man and woman sit next to one another. The man is apparently Davis, since he holds a trumpet loosely on his lap and is nattily, if casually, dressed. However, since the photo is cropped to show both figures from just below the knee to just about the shoulder, we can't be certain of either figure's identity. Sensually colored and cropped and choreographed for maximum suggestiveness (e.g., the woman's skirt is above her knee and she lightly touches the trumpet with one hand), this picture hints of love and romance and perhaps, to recall James Baldwin's critique of the film, of people who are "more sexual."

But if this fully functional Porgy is "the man with the horn," as Davis was coming to be known, then who is his Bess? More importantly, on the racialist terrain of the United States in 1958, what race is his Bess? While the man in the image is clearly, by U.S. standards, "black," the woman's skin, which is a warm tan color, is less legible.[35] So the cropping of the image is strategic. It doesn't allow recourse to other standard U.S. modes of racial identification (e.g., facial features, hair). It seems to suggest that "it ain't necessarily so" that love and romance and sex adhere to the lines enforced by the dominant social order, and, moreover, it hints, that isn't just the case in 1958 but—at least if this Bess should turn out to be what would be called black—has long been the case; otherwise this Bess wouldn't have the skin color she does. If the viewer-listener decides this Bess is white, the same issues are broached from a more directly confrontational angle. In either case, the interracial relations that *Porgy and Bess* is simultaneously founded upon and elides—a history of whites and blacks (like Evans and Davis) co-laboring to create, if not equally collaborating on or benefiting from, a show that stages and spectacularizes black sociocultural isolation—are brought to the fore. Here the "social commentary" that Duke Ellington felt was missing from *Porgy and Bess* back in 1935 and that Baldwin would find missing from the film is reinserted—though it remains in the elusive domain of (most) Signifying, more direct than the gentle Signifying homage of the Armstrong-Fitzgerald recording, but also not necessarily visible or audible to a mainstream audience as preventative criticism.

Necessarily "It Ain't Necessarily So":
The Goldwyn Porgy and Bess

But what, finally, about the delayed, absent antecedent of what I have been arguing is a kind of preventative Signifying? What about the Goldwyn film? The questions we might most like to ask—for example, did this Signifying have any effect on the production or its reception?—are impossible to answer with certainty, but then part of the history and point of Signifying is a certain uncertainty.[36] Given the overlapping of the production and distribution of the recordings with the preproduction and production of the film—as well as the film's elaborate division of labor (for example, many of the actors' singing voices were dubbed)—it seems unlikely that the Signifying recordings had much effect on the film. I've found no evidence that, for example, Otto Preminger, André Previn (the film's musical director), or any of the performers were aware of the recordings—though some of them probably were.

According to his son, Goldwyn was interested in re-creating the 1935 production, which was the *Porgy and Bess* he was familiar with. (That Goldwyn's original choice of director was Rouben Mamoulian, who directed the premieres of both the dramatic and operatic *Porgy/Porgy and Bess,* supports this claim.) In his re-creation project, Goldwyn both succeeded— the film is, like a number of other fifties adaptations of stage musicals, quite "true" to the source—and failed—the film seems dutifully wooden. Aside from a slight reordering of two songs, the restoration of two of the four songs that were cut from the '35 production, and the refusal of recitative, the film made few changes in the show's libretto. Most of the action takes place on a vast soundstage Catfish Row, and Preminger chose to use a predominantly long-take, long-shot style, so the pacing seems stately and the performers distant in the wide-screen compositions; despite the available space on the set, there is little dancing. André Previn's arrangements are updated but still primarily symphonic, and the voices are a mixture of operatically trained (for Poitier and Dandridge, among others) and popular (e.g., Pearl Bailey and Sammy Davis Jr.).

"It Ain't Necessarily So" can again serve as a representative example, this time in Sammy Davis's version. The scene, which takes place at a neighborhood picnic to a nearby island, uses the film's only natural setting—a flat, open field, backed by scrubby woods. The "wholesome" setting of nature and community are meant to contrast with Sportin' Life, but here Davis just seems out of place and constrained in his ability to dance; having Sportin' Life leap from a felled tree trunk to the bare earth conveys Davis's energy but not the character's aspirant urbanity. Davis delivers the song with oily insinuation, using crisp enunciation combined with abrupt shifts in dynamics, and he steers a middle path through the dialect, not applying it as thickly as the lyric suggests but also not drawing attention, as Fitzgerald does, to his corrections. Most disappointing in the number, especially compared with the Armstrong-Fitzgerald recording, is the scripted (by Gershwin) "scat singing" assigned Davis in call and response with the chorus. At this moment in the show when the 1935 and the world-touring productions opened themselves to direct African American input, Davis is confined to a bit of dance and to the scat singing sections Gershwin wrote—"Wa-doo—Zim bam boodle-oo / Hoodle ah da wa da—Scatty wa"—which sounds like a poor imitation of Cab Calloway from twenty-five years past.

As it turned out, Goldwyn's *Porgy and Bess* was exactly what African American critics feared—a widely distributed, dangerously fantastic image of African Americans that "the white man [could] cling . . . to" under the names of art and entertainment "in order not to revise his image of himself."[37] But ultimately Goldwyn's *Porgy and Bess* also turned out to be perhaps somewhat less than many critics had feared. At least relative to Goldwyn's probable eight-to-twelve-million-dollar investment, the film was a popular, commercial failure. Can this qualified failure be traced in any way back to the Armstrong-Fitzgerald and Davis-Evans recordings? Not in any direct way that I have found. Jazz critics often mentioned the film dismissively when they reviewed jazz recordings of *Porgy and Bess,* but this seems to be a reflex rather than informed judgment, and it may also have been shaped by the general critical failure of the film. In terms of their influence, these recordings are probably best seen as of a piece with late-fifties African American debate about the merits of adapting the show to film, and insofar as their Signifying is subtle, they could be understood—especially the Armstrong-Fitzgerald recording—to be in favor of—because they attempt to capitalize on—the adaptation. Moreover, while comparative statistics are not available, despite its "failure" the Goldwyn film, along with its soundtrack recording, almost certainly sold in greater numbers than either of these records, though both are said to have done well.

Yet the Signifying possibilities of these recordings did not end in the narrow window of the film's release. They continued (and continue) to be listened to and rereleased. You can still easily purchase the Armstrong-Fitzgerald and Davis-Evans recordings. Since 1972, however, the Goldwyn film has been available for viewing only at the Library of Congress. It was withdrawn from circulation for complex rights reasons, which were not eased by the fact that Ira Gershwin reportedly did not care for it. And, according to Norman Granz, who produced the Armstrong-Fitzgerald recording, Ira Gershwin was intimately acquainted with their version: "Every night when I finished doing something [with the Armstrong-Fitzgerald recording] I would go back and see Ira Gershwin," Granz has said. "Ira and I would play it, and he was overwhelmed."[38] So perhaps Armstrong and Fitzgerald's gentle Signifying homage had some preventative effect after all. At any rate, the Armstrong-Fitzgerald and Davis-Evans recordings went from potentially supplying alternative soundtracks to—and also images and implicit narratives for—the film to replacing it.

From where Duke Ellington sat at his piano bench recording his 1961 "Summertime," this belated victory for black Signifying performances must have looked awfully like a defeat. And the withdrawal of the film might not have made him feel that much better. After all, by 1972 *Porgy and Bess* was fully established in the operatic, Broadway, pop, and jazz canons—boosted there in large part by the flurry of activity spurred by the Goldwyn film. In 1964, Ellington was still seething: "*Porgy and Bess*, those people in alleys, waking up, dusting those carpets out of the window and beating their brooms in time and all that bullshit. You want to know about America, we're going to make a cultural exchange, we send you *Porgy and Bess*, this is the complete image of our Negro."[39]

Ellington would have been distressed to hear Sidney Poitier's 1980 assertion that, despite critical feelings about the story, African Americans "stood ready to acknowledge and applaud the genius in the music" or Donald Bogle's 1988 claim that "the music . . . always works with a black audience, [and] 'Summertime' . . . is now thought of as a black song."[40] Ellington had perhaps seen this coming, and his "Summertime" seems meant to cap—if not silence—the glut of *Porgy and Bess*es, which largely because they were (are) recordings instead of (more) evanescent live performances, contributed to the canonization of *Porgy and Bess*, even as they attempted to keep its cultural status contingent. In contrast to the Armstrong-Fitzgerald and Davis-Evans recordings, the Ellington "Summertime" emphatically separates capitalizing from Signifying—by making itself nearly unconsumable. (Underlining the fact that such issues were on his mind, Ellington would shortly make another aggressive trio record, pointedly titled *Money Jungle*.) Toward this end, Ellington's 1961 "Summertime" is not just Signifying on *Porgy and Bess* or the Goldwyn film; it is also meta-Signifying, Signifying on the very possibility of preventative, critical Signifying on and via the recording as commodity. As you might expect, this recording is hard to come by. But not as hard to come by as the Goldwyn *Porgy and Bess*.

Notes

Thanks to Mark Tucker and David LaRussa for their cheerful support, comments, and many loans of material. Thanks to Pam Wojcik and Martha Howard for their multiple readings of this work and their invaluable editing. And many thanks to Krin Gabbard for his valuable suggestions and for helping me keep the facts straight.

The quotation in my title is from Sun Ra. See John Szwed, *Space Is the Place: The Lives and Times of Sun Ra* (New York: Pantheon, 1997), 296. The Lawrence D. Stewart epigraph comes from the liner note to the Louis Armstrong and Ella Fitzgerald recording, *Porgy and Bess*, reissued as Verve 8274752, np.

1 Duke Ellington, *Piano in the Foreground*, Columbia COL474930-2.
2 In fact, Ellington had let "Summertime" work more conventionally for him. In the 1940s he had an unchallenging arrangement of the song in his band's book, apparently in support of vocalist Al Hibbler, which they recorded for a radio transcription service, and which can be heard in various broadcast versions (e.g., *Live from the Hurricane Club, NYC* [27 June 1943], source unknown). In the early fifties he did a "latin" instrumental arrangement; this version strayed much further from ordinary renderings of "Summertime" than the forties arrangement, but seems meant to highlight the soloist more than to do violence to the song (e.g., *Happy Birthday Duke! April 29th Birthday Sessions*, vol. 2 [29 April 1952], LaserLight 15784]). The orchestra did commercially record a version of this arrangement in 1956, which was included on *Duke Ellington Presents* for Bethlehem Records and then on the same company's version of *Porgy and Bess*, which was sold under Mel Torme's and Francis Faye's names. Live recordings of the Ellington band made from radio transcriptions in the 1960s show the band

sometimes performing a wildly cacophonous arrangement of "Summertime" seemingly based on the trio recording.

3 Throughout this essay, my understanding of the general production history of *Porgy and Bess* is indebted to Hollis Alpert, *The Life and Times of "Porgy and Bess"* (New York: Knopf, 1990).

4 As my epigraph shows, this connection was in the minds of those marketing these recordings, and this strategy was clear to critics at the time. See, for example, John S. Wilson, "Four More Approaches to *Porgy*," *High Fidelity Magazine*, June 1959, 92.

5 Other jazz artists to record *Porgy and Bess* in this period and in something near its entirety were Ralph Burns (1958), Rex Stewart and Cootie Williams (1959), Bob Crosby's Bobcats (1959), an ad hoc band of "*Porgy and Bess* All Stars" (1959), Mundell Lowe (1959), Hank Jones (1959), the Oscar Peterson Trio (1959), and the Modern Jazz Quartet (1963). Many more recorded songs from the show. For example, beside Coltrane's "Summertime," contained on his successful *My Favorite Things* LP, Nina Simone had her first hit in 1958 with a version of "I Loves You, Porgy," and, in an entirely different vein, Sun Ra recorded "Summertime" and several other tunes from the show.

6 W. E. B. Du Bois, "*Porgy*, by DuBose Heyward," *Crisis*, March 1926, reprinted in W. E. B. Du Bois, *Writings*, ed. Nathan Huggins (New York: Library of America, 1986), 1215; Countee Cullen, review of *Porgy*, *Opportunity*, December 1925, 379; Sterling Brown, "Our Literary Audience," *Opportunity*, February 1930, reprinted in *Within the Circle: An Anthology of African American Literary Criticism from the Harlem Renaissance to the Present*, ed. Angelyn Mitchell (Durham, N.C.: Duke University Press, 1994), 69–78.

7 James Weldon Johnson, *Black Manhattan* (1930; reprint, New York: Arno Press, 1968), 211–12. When, in the early 1930s, word circulated that Al Jolson wished to play Porgy in the then widely rumored Gershwin musical adaptation, the black press, extending Johnson's approbation, defended the play vehemently from this minstrelizing; see for example, "Al Jolson Given the Lead in 1933 Edition of *Porgy*," *Chicago Defender*, 9 December 1933, 8.

8 DuBose Heyward, *Porgy* (1925; reprint, London: Jonathan Cape, 1928), 221.

9 Sportin' Life is adapted from the character of Sportin' Life (the name *Porgy and Bess* will readopt) in the novel, but in the novel, Sportin' Life is driven from Catfish Row well before the story's conclusion and has nothing to do with Bess's disappearance.

10 DuBose Heyward, *Porgy*, 11; Dorothy Heyward and DuBose Heyward, *Porgy: A Play in Four Acts* (New York: Doubleday, Page, 1927), n.p. Alpert, in *The Life and Times of "Porgy and Bess,"* 38–39, argues that the novel is set before World War I and, based on comparisons between the history of Charleston and events depicted in the novel, makes the case that Heyward was probably thinking of it as set about 1911.

11 Hall Johnson, quoted in Alpert, *The Life and Times*, 122.

12 Duke Ellington quoted in Edward Morrow, "Duke Ellington on Gershwin's *Porgy*," *New Theatre*, December 1935, 5–6, reprinted in *The Duke Ellington Reader*,

ed. Mark Tucker (New York: Oxford University Press, 1993), 114–17. Ellington's manager's press agent protested that Ellington was misquoted by Morrow and published an apology to Gershwin (see Richard Mack, "Duke Ellington—In Person," *Orchestra World*, May 1936, n.p., reprinted in Tucker, 117–18), but Mark Tucker argues that while Morrow's questions may have been leading (and considerable portions of Morrow's own editorializing have been misattributed to Ellington over the years) the critical quotations seem to reflect Ellington's feelings. Ellington would never again be so publicly unguarded with his critical comments. It's also worth noting that, while Ellington was not a fan of "Gershwin's *Porgy*," he was at least somewhat familiar with its source material, having played a song setting of the story, written by Fields and McHugh, in 1932 (with Ethel Waters doing vocals).

13 For comparison, both *Show Boat* and *The Green Pastures* had each run for more than five hundred performances and toured much more widely and successfully just a few years earlier. In contrast, the Virgil Thompson–Gertude Stein oratorio *Four Saints in Three Acts* ran for forty-eight performances earlier in 1935.

14 Du Bois, "Porgy" 1215.

15 Beginning with the 1950s revival of *Porgy and Bess*, the program notes did place the action in "The Past." The original libretto for *Porgy and Bess* has never been published, but the revised libretto (not noted as such) can be found in Stanley Richards, ed., *Great Musicals of the American Theatre*, (Radnor, Pa.: Chilton, 1975), 1:75–113.

16 *Chicago Defender*, 14 March 1942, 1.

17 Dean Gordon Hancock, "'Dangerous Propaganda' Says This Critic of Planned Tour," *Chicago Defender*, 17 April 1954, 10. The *Defender* thought *Porgy and Bess* important enough to pair this critical piece with a second, much less prominently headlined piece by George Daniels, "Amusing Art, People the World Over Should See, Says Another."

18 Goldwyn press release quoted in Alpert, *The Life and Times*, 262; Lerone Bennett Jr., "Hollywood's First Negro Movie Star," *Ebony*, May 1959, 106. See also Sidney Poitier, *This Life* (New York: Knopf, 1980), 205–15.

19 For Miles Davis one of Gil Evans's crucial characteristics was that "the question of race never entered; it was always about music. He didn't care what color you were. He was one of the first white people I met that was like this" (Davis with Quincy Troupe, *Miles: The Autobiography* [New York: Touchstone, 1990], 122). I should note here that in this essay I won't even try to untangle how important or unimportant white producer-impresarios, like Norman Granz of Verve and George Avakian, who signed Davis to Columbia, were in initiating and shaping the 1958 recordings; rather, I'll (too) simply integrate them into the Signifying collective.

20 Ralph Ellison, "Change the Joke and Slip the Yoke," *Shadow and Act* (1958; New York: Vintage, 1964), 45–59.

21 Henry Louis Gates Jr., *The Signifying Monkey: A Theory of African-American Literary Criticism* (New York: Oxford University Press, 1988), xxiv. My ideas about Signifying, and my choice not to follow Gates's orthography—Signifyin(g)—

have also been influenced by Robert Walser, " 'Out of Notes': Signification, Interpretation, and the Problem of Miles Davis," in *Jazz among the Discourses*, ed.
Krin Gabbard (Durham, N.C.: Duke University Press, 1995), 165–88.

22 Walser ponders some of these same problems, but settles back on concerns with
"forebears" and "intertextuality" (Walser " 'Out of Notes,'" 169–73). See also
Ingrid Monson's analysis of Coltrane's "My Favorite Things," which was made
when the *Sound of Music* was just becoming a Broadway hit and well before it was
filmed (Monson, *Saying Something: Jazz Improvisation and Interaction* [Chicago:
University of Chicago, 1996], 106–21).

23 Miles Davis's stern visage in performance and very different use of the trumpet
were seen and heard by many to be doing this work. As it happened, a couple
months after Armstrong recorded *Porgy and Bess*, he directly criticized President Eisenhower's hesitation during the Little Rock school desegregation crisis.
This was an anomaly for Armstrong—one that he was roundly criticized for,
never repeated, and that was largely forgotten by the time of the release of the
Armstrong-Fitzgerald recording. Leonard Feather does a careful job of laying
out the complexities of Armstrong's multifaceted image and its reception in
From Satchmo to Miles (1972; reprint, New York: Da Capo, 1984), 13–42. In his
recent obituary of Lester Bowie, Gary Giddens takes Bowie's appreciation of
Armstrong as a mark of Bowie's iconoclasm: "You can't imagine how refresh-
ing it was to encounter a young avant-gardist in the early '70s who understood
and loved all of Armstrong, not just the '20s classics" (Giddens, "Weatherbird:
Lester Bowie 1941–1999," *Village Voice*, 14 December 1999, 162).

24 See Feather, *From Satchmo to Miles*, 87–96, and Martin Williams, "Ella and Her
Critics" (1966), in *Jazz Heritage* (New York: Oxford University Press, 1985), 40–
43.

25 Since the opera is through-sung, it is difficult to determine exactly how many
songs (a word Gershwin used freely to refer to his "arias") it contains. A conservative count of songs in the '35 production would be twenty-three (three songs,
not including the overture/introduction, were cut and are now restored in most
recordings and many productions). The Armstrong-Fitzgerald recording (all references are to Verve 8274752) consists of fourteen songs, twelve from the original production.

26 James Baldwin, "Life Straight in De Eye," *Commentary*, January 1955, reprinted
as "*Carmen Jones:* The Dark Is Light Enough" in *Notes of a Native Son* (1955; New
York: Bantam, 1964), 40.

27 James Baldwin, "On Catfish Row," *Commentary*, September 1959, reprinted in
The Price of the Ticket: Collected Nonfiction, 1948–1985 (New York: St. Martins,
1985), 180. (Baldwin claims to like *Porgy and Bess* as a show and to have great
respect for Heyward's novel [179].)

28 Ibid., 180.

29 The Armstrong-Fitzgerald recording may even be attempting to Signify preventatively by treating the show respectfully, in contrast to what many would expect
from Hollywood—though film adaptations of stage musicals, under the sway
of Rogers and Hammerstein, had become increasingly "accurate" in the 1950s.

30 All references are to Miles Davis, *George Gershwin's Porgy and Bess* (orchestra under the direction of Gil Evans), Columbia 1274. The liner notes are by Charles Edward Smith.

31 Rex Stewart and Cootie Williams's version, *Porgy and Bess Revisited* (1959) did this.

32 Davis did sometimes play flugelhorn instead of trumpet on the record, but since the distinction between Davis's use of the two instruments eludes even expert listeners, I just refer to the trumpet.

33 The Davis-Evans recording contains twelve songs (not counting the Evans composition), ten from the '35 production; see note 25.

34 This disorientation still works. Martha Howard, who had heard more versions of this argument than she probably cared to and had heard the Davis-Evans recording, still reported to me that one day, expecting something like the ordinary opening of most versions of *Porgy and Bess*, she had popped a cassette of the record in her car's tape player and was so startled she nearly drove off the road.

35 This Bess-that-ain't-necessarily-Bess could be played in this photo by the actress cast as the film's Bess, Dorothy Dandridge, whom Baldwin describes as "taffy-colored"; "*Carmen Jones*" 40.

36 Gates argues that "indirection" is central to Signifying; Gates, *The Signifying Monkey*, 103, 122–23.

37 Baldwin, "On Catfish Row," 180.

38 Granz is quoted in William Ruhlman's liner essay for *The Complete Ella Fitzgerald and Louis Armstrong on Verve* (Verve 314 537 284–2).

39 This passage is from a 1964 interview with Carter Harman that Ellington requested not be published while he was alive. It is quoted in Stuart Nicholson, *Reminiscing in Tempo: A Portrait of Duke Ellington* (Boston: Northeastern University Press, 1999), 329.

40 Poitier, *This Life*, 205; Donald Bogle, *Blacks in American Films and Television* (New York: Fireside, 1989), 167.

"Hollywood Has Taken on a New Color": The Yiddish Blackface of Samuel Goldwyn's *Porgy and Bess*

JONATHAN GILL

No matter how black things seem, if you have courage, a darkness can be overcome. — Samuel Goldwyn

It is necessarily so—there really was a crippled black beggar who lived in
a Charleston, South Carolina slum, begging from a goat cart and satisfied
with "plenty o' nuthin'." His story, with some embellishments made to his
love life, was published as *Porgy* in 1925 by DuBose Heyward, and appeared
on stage, in a version co-written with Heyward's wife, Dorothy, in 1927.
Captivated by the story, George Gershwin and his brother Ira turned the
drama into an opera in 1935, and after more than two decades of touring
America and the world to almost unanimous acclaim, the story became a
Hollywood film, with Sidney Poitier and Dorothy Dandridge leading the
black cast. So why is the first thing that appears on the screen, as Gershwin's overture begins, the name of Samuel Goldwyn? How is that Goldwyn
could call himself the "sole creator" of the movie, making the official name
of the film *Samuel Goldwyn's Porgy and Bess*, even putting his name alone
on the front cover of the soundtrack?[1]

To ask these questions is to ask to whom *Porgy and Bess* belongs, and in
the larger sense who has the right to represent African American culture.
He may have started out a penniless Jewish immigrant working in an up-
state New York glove factory, but Goldwyn eventually became one of the
founding fathers of the American film industry, the creator of Hollywood,

25 Samuel Goldwyn in 1942. [Author's collection]

and the first and for a time the only independent movie producer, whose films had won twenty-six Oscars, largely as the result of his autocratic, manipulative, domineering nature. Goldwyn's control over his pictures was legendary. He was often quoted as saying, "I make my pictures to please myself,"² but something other than mere pleasure was obviously at work: "He took all the risks, made all the decisions, personally cast the films . . . in many cases directed the directors, supervised all of the publicity, even told the exhibitors how to run the show. Every film he made, in all respects, was his."³ Is it any surprise, then, that Goldwyn chose to end his career—he was in his late seventies when he made *Porgy and Bess*—with a story whose challenges to racial and musical authenticity make it the supreme example of American self-fashioning, a film Harold Cruse would call "the most contradictory cultural symbol ever created in the Western world"?⁴

In *Porgy and Bess*, the last word on contradictions comes from Sportin' Life, a dapper bootlegger and confirmed cynic who apparently spends his free time rewriting the Bible. When all of Catfish Row—except for Porgy—goes for a picnic and religious retreat on nearby Kitiwah Island, Sportin' Life, played in the film by Sammy Davis Jr., can hardly contain his scorn

at the preacher's homily, and offers a gleeful counter-sermon: David striking down Goliath? Jonah finding a "home-in" some whale's "abdomen"?
Pharaoh's daughter fishing Moses from a stream? "It ain't necessarily so,"
Sportin' Life sings. Yet the words Ira Gershwin used to express of this
heretic's view of Methuselah's quality of life at age nine hundred deserve
special attention: "But who calls dat livin' / When no gal'll give in / To no
man what's nine hundred years?"[5] While Ira Gershwin clearly meant the
incorrect use of the relative pronoun "what" to convey Sportin' Life's less-
than-perfect grammar, to mistake an adjectival subordinate clause, requiring introduction by "that" or "who," for a noun clause, which requires an
introductory "what," is less a feature of black English than the Yiddish English that was the native tongue of the Gershwins. This lapse in the opera's
masquerade in black suggests that when the blackface mask that George
and Ira Gershwin—and Samuel Goldwyn—wear in Porgy and Bess slips, it
is not a white person underneath, à la Uncle Remus, as Philip Furia suggests, but a Jew.[6] If this was only implicit in the 1935 opera, recall that the
film role of Sportin' Life was played by a real, live Jew—Davis had converted in the mid-1950s while recuperating from an automobile accident,
and was observant enough to refuse to work when filming was scheduled
for Yom Kippur. Indeed, the repertoire of imagery and characterization
surrounding Davis's Sportin' Life—this diminutive interloper from New
York is compared to a buzzard, prowling the roofs of Catfish Row inappro-
priately dressed in tails and spats, hair "conked" to control its natural curls,
and told that church picnics are "not for your kind"—further suggest that
he is Catfish Row's only Jew.

Sportin' Life's "what," the kind of affective borrowing that linguists call
a morpho-syntactical loan translation, functions as a half-buried gesture,
evidence of the constitutive role that Yiddishkeit plays in the Gershwins'
music, and in many of Hollywood's representations of African American
culture. If standard blackface was evidence, in Ann Douglas's terms, that
"a distinctively modern art meant undoing dispossession, making inventive use of one's buried or censored cultural and linguistic origins," what
we are dealing with here is the use of someone else's buried or censored
origins.[7] To pay attention to Sportin' Life's "what" questions the traditional
understanding of Porgy and Bess's racial economy—that it is a white version of black culture—and means recognizing the complicated collaboration between whites, blacks, and Jews that made modern American popular music possible. This is particularly true for the film version of Porgy
and Bess, the "darkest" of African American works, in which the producer,
both directors, the screenwriter, and even one member of the cast were

Jewish. Sportin' Life's "what" signals the claims of a whole range of races and cultures on the masking joke that American culture has always been.

The Real American Folk Song

The Gershwins themselves must take some responsibility for the lack of nuance in traditional discussions of the racial and ethnic sources of *Porgy and Bess*. In the constant and inescapable negotiations in the early part of the century surrounding the meaning of Americanness, the brothers inevitably opted for a sanitized, nonracial, nonethnic position. Early in his career, George Gershwin's entry in a contest for a new national anthem was the bland "O Land of Mine, America." Among the brothers' first collaborations was "The Real American Folk Song (Is a Rag)" but that tune made no mention of ragtime's African American origins. In their 1927 collaboration *Strike up the Band,* their "Typical Self-Made American" is "a Mason and an Elk and Woodman" who "upholds the country's laws / Because because because because."[8] George persisted in calling *Porgy and Bess* simply "American" music, and his definitive statement of ethnic affiliation was equally patriotic: "My people are Americans."[9] If, as Michael Rogin writes of *The Jazz Singer,* "the black-inspired music of urban Jews was a declaration of war against the racial hierarchy of Protestant, genteel culture,"[10] the Gershwins wanted no place on the front lines.[11]

Early writings about the Gershwins offer precisely the same assimilationist scenario. In David Ewen's 1943 biography, Papa and Mamma Gershwin speak perfect English, while in real life their thick Yiddish accents proved a lifelong embarrassment to their children. So too does Ewen transform the secondhand piano that the family bought in 1910 into a brandnew instrument. Ewen admits that the Gershwins "had that deeply ingrained respect for culture which had always been a hereditary trait of their race"—but nowhere does Ewen tell what race that is.[12]

Such an account is deeply, and no doubt purposefully misleading. The household that the Gershwins grew up in was not religious—of three sons, only Ira was given a barmitzvah—but it was in every other way Jewish. George and Ira's father, Moishe Gershovitz, was the grandson of a rabbi, and came to America as part of the mass Jewish exodus from Russia in the years following Czar Alexander III's pogroms. Later known as Morris, he settled in New York's Lower East Side, then known to many as "Jewtown," and married a Jewish woman, Rose Bruskin. Their first son, Izzy, assumed that his given name was Isidore or Ira until the age of thirty-two, when he discovered upon receiving a passport that his true name was in fact Israel.

Morris and Rose's second child, born in 1898 across the street from a synagogue in a Jewish section of Brooklyn known as East New York, was listed
on his birth certificate as "Jacob Gershvine"—he was to be called George.

George and Ira were exposed early to the thriving world of Yiddish
theater in turn-of-the-century New York. The family frequented many of
the dozens of Lower East Side venues presenting Jewish vaudeville and
operetta, and Yiddish actors could be found almost nightly at card games
at the Gershwin home. Among George's first professional efforts was a collaboration in 1915 with the composer Sholom Secunda, and a year later,
George's first piano rolls included two Yiddish tunes. Nonetheless, aside
from plans George had in the late 1920s to write an opera based on Saul
Anski's play *The Dybbuk*—he went as far as signing a contract with the
Metropolitan Opera, and even composed some fragments—the Gershwins limited their professional interest in the Yiddish language and its
theatrical traditions to hit-and-run affect. A "Romantic Verse" preserved
in one of Ira's college diaries rhymes "watsis" with "matsis,"[13] and one of
his lyrics in *Of Thee I Sing* (1931) rhymes "quinces" with "blintzes," while
the famous melody " 'S Wonderful," from *Funny Face* (1927), strongly resembles the traditional Yiddish song "Noach's Tieve," according to Secunda. In *Girl Crazy* (1929), Ira created the character of Gieber Goldfarb,
a Jewish taxicab driver from New York who is transplanted to a small western town; there, disguised as an Indian, he escapes from a tight situation by speaking Yiddish. Finally, the original production for the Union
Square demonstration scene in *Let 'Em Eat Cake* (1933) included a man
holding a sign in Yiddish: "Arbeiters fun China Farainent Aich!"—meaning "workers from China unite!" All this play with Yiddish, even if it was
only affect, meant that the Gershwins were identified with Jewish culture
almost reflexively, especially when it came to *Porgy and Bess*. Oscar Levant claimed *Porgy and Bess* was "a glorious paean to American Jewish
music," in which Serena's prayer to Dr. Jesus might be described as "can-
torial chant," and Sportin' Life's cynicism could be called "Talmudic skepticism"; Virgil Thomson's ruthless review of the opera criticized its "gefilte
fish orchestration."[14]

To think of *Porgy and Bess* as "Jewish" seems preposterous today, but it
is important to recall that while an earlier generation of Jews in the American entertainment industry largely consisted of businessmen of German
origin, publishing sheet music of the most benign ditties possible, the new
cast of gefilte-fish-eating Eastern-European Jews wrote, joked, and sang
their way to fame in blackface masks that depended on an offensive visual
shock for its entertainment. It is hard to find a single important early-

twentieth-century Jewish entertainer who did not have an early career that involved black culture or its representation. Just as the popularity of blacks in blackface was waning—not coincidentally, along with African American dialect writers—Eddie Cantor, Al Jolson, Sophie Tucker, and many others were putting on the burnt cork. It is not at all clear why the first Americans to truly appreciate and popularize—and, no doubt, exploit—African American music were Jews. Certainly, the years of mass Jewish immigration from Eastern Europe to the northern cities of America coincided with the arrival of African Americans fleeing Jim Crow in search of freedom and jobs; perhaps Jews and blacks in New York, Philadelphia, Boston, Chicago, and many other cities found commonalities based in their shared suffering and marginalization—that, at any rate, is the traditional answer.

The affinities between the blues, on the one hand, and a melancholia judaica on the other, were apparent to George Gershwin's first biographer, Isaac Goldberg, who asserted "a common Oriental ancestry in both Negro and Jew."[15] Whether or not Goldberg's genetics were correct, he certainly represents the orientalist aspect of white America's fascination with Jews in blackface, an imaginative project in which a "primitive" sense of the world—deep emotions, expressive cries, an animalistic sense of rhythm and feeling—come more naturally to the "darker" races. Jews and blacks, as well as Asians, Hispanics, Hawai'ian, and even southern Europeans constituted the unofficial focus of the American entertainment industry's interest. Blackface offered whites, African Americans, and Jews a single dramatic device to portray them all because it offered, as Rogin notes, "access to allegedly black qualities—intense emotionality and the musical expression that results from it."[16]

The Gershwins played along with these orientalist fantasies. George's first publicly performed composition, "Piano Solo" (1914), by "George Gershwin," according to the program, was a tango. His sister Frances performed in a 1917 vaudeville act in which, as she wrote in a letter at the time, "a girl sings Let's all be Americans now. Then Honey sings Mississippi. And a boy and girl sings and dances Honalua Hickie Bula Boo."[17] Jolson's "Swanee" was George's version of a "Far Eastern one-step" called "Hindustan,"[18] and in 1922 George and Ira's "Mischa, Jascha, Toscha, Sascha" told the story of three "Temp'ramental Oriental Gentlemen" who were "born right in the middle / Of darkest Russia."[19] In 1920, the same year that Henry Ford began reprinting the notorious anti-Semitic forgery known as *The Protocols of the Elders of Zion,* Gregory Mason of Columbia University complained of "the insidiousness of the Jewish menace to our artistic integrity," and warned his readers of "Jewish tastes and standards, with

their Oriental extravagance"—as opposed to "Anglo-Saxon sobriety and restraint."[20] This essentialist fiction comforted anti-Semites claiming jazz
was Jewish music, not, according to Ford's *Dearborn Independent,* because
of genetics alone but because of "the organized eagerness of the Jew to
make alliance with the Negro."[21]

Whether it was a common genetic background or a global aesthetic conspiracy that made the African American and the Jew part of the same dark
other in America, any study of *Porgy and Bess* would be foolish to ignore
the very real history of the Gershwins' contact with African Americans in
the "Syncopated City," as Ira called Manhattan in the original version of
"Fascinatin' Rhythm." Among George's earliest musical memories was a
classical piece, Anton Rubenstein's "Melody in F," heard at an arcade on
125th Street, which in 1904 was already becoming the most important
street in the biggest black community in America. In fact, the Gershwins
lived in Harlem from 1904 to 1907, and made their home there again a
decade later, when George often heard James Reese Europe's orchestra at
a nightclub on 135th Street. During this time George studied with the pianist Luckey Roberts, and by 1916, according to the recollection of Eubie
Blake, he had gained a reputation among Harlem pianists. Also around
1916 George was friends with Will Vodery, who got him his first job, performing at Fox's City Theater on 14th Street. Al Jolson reportedly heard
"Swanee" for the first time when Gershwin played it for him at Bessie
Bloodgood's Harlem whorehouse, and in his later years, when he was famous and wealthy, Gershwin continued to associate publicly and privately
with African Americans. Willie "The Lion" Smith," who attended the premiere of *Rhapsody in Blue,* recalled a party at which he performed together
with Gershwin, James P. Johnson, and Fats Waller. Gershwin first met
James Rosamonde Johnson, who performed in the premiere of *Porgy and
Bess,* at a party attended by James Weldon Johnson and Paul Robeson. After
the premiere, Gershwin hosted a party honoring the pianist Art Tatum.

Much of this activity can be written off as racial slumming, common
among white Manhattanites between the wars. Consider a letter George
wrote to Ira in 1918: "Dear Iz—from the plantation [:] Give ah run down
to de plantation un tell seamble Ginsberg that—I sen my love un kisses
un also tell 'im that I'm in the city of Baltimo' . . . in fect how's all my
ren's. Hah? Tell me right away in a letter. Garuss everybody for me."[22] However, if George's biographers tend to whitewash his Jewishness, they also
take a cue from his friends (and enemies) in emphasizing his affinity with
African Americanness. Gershwin's friend Oscar Levant wrote that George
"found a natural outlet through his Negroid characters,"[23] and Ewen wrote

of *Porgy and Bess* that George was "writing the folk music of a race, and writing it with such authenticity that, in its final form, it seemed to be the work not of an American born and raised in city streets but that of several generations of Negroes who had passed these melodies down from father to son."[24] George not only "felt as though he were one of them," according to Joan Peyser, a later biographer, he even looked like one of them.[25] His physical appearance was invariably described by his contemporaries using racial code: "dark," "swarthy," "lank," with a "low-slung, Neanderthal jaw."[26] One journalist wondered openly in the *Charleston News and Courier* whether George himself might play the role of Crown.[27]

This portrayal of George as somehow darker than white reaches a climax, not surprisingly, in accounts of the making of *Porgy and Bess*, which was largely written in the summer of 1934 on an island near Charleston. If George was to have achieved an authentic version of Jewish music in preparation for *The Dybbuk* by traveling to Eastern Europe, so too did he now root himself in a small, isolated Gullah community fittingly known as Folly Beach. This scenario, which DuBose Heyward describes as "more like a homecoming than an exploration,"[28] is dutifully repeated in every account of the creation of *Porgy and Bess*, and once again the Gershwins played along, encouraging the racial fantasizing behind such accounts. George fancied his time at Folly Beach as a return to nature, in the company of African Americans all but indistinguishable from their natural surroundings: "I am fascinated by the beaches, the black bambinos, the crabs and turtles," he wrote to a friend.[29] In a letter to his mother the composer exulted in the primitiveness of the place, but he nonetheless found a four-room house with a screen porch and piano, and brought along his set of paints and his golf clubs. The only sign of civilization that Gershwin was willing to recognize was, as he tellingly wrote to Ira, "a Jewish delicatessen."[30] Folly Beach appealed "to the primitive man in me," Gershwin wrote to another friend,[31] as if he had traveled backwards along his genetic heritage, to that point where Jew and black were racially equivalent. One journalist found Gershwin walking along deserted beaches "bare and black above the waist."[32] One of George's neighbors—this supposedly remote, primitive place also hosted a summer colony of rich Charlestonites—noted that "he used to take off his shirt and walk up and down the beach, and in the evenings we would walk and sing spirituals. He loved to walk on the beach; he got burned nearly black by the sun."[33]

On Folly Beach, Gershwin not only looked black, he sounded black, even blacker than black, according to Heyward's account: "At a Negro meeting on a remote sea-island George started 'shouting' with them, and eventually to their huge delight stole the show from their champion 'shouter.' " [34] Gershwin's status as America's foremost composer of black music was confirmed at rehearsals, when he found that his African American singers, who had been trained to sing classical music, were lacking in "authentic" African American diction. Even one of Gershwin's more recent biographers notes that "Gershwin amazed them often by demonstrating how they were to interpret their parts." [35]

Internalizing the Mask

On the opera's opening night, James Rosamond Johnson whispered in Gershwin's ear: "George, you've done it—you're the Abraham Lincoln of Negro music." [36] Yet there was a sense at the premiere, primarily among African American musicians, that the Gershwins were trying to pass, and failing—that the music was simply not black enough. Even Johnson, who played the part of the lawyer Frazier and served as the assistant choral director, found only "eighty percent of its musical idioms . . . negroid." [37] Gershwin biographies have Duke Ellington going even further in a statement that has become part of the Ellington lexicon, though the passage was almost certainly misattributed: "No Negro could possibly be fooled by *Porgy and Bess.* . . . [T]he times are here to debunk such tripe as Gershwin's lampblack Negroisms." [38] Whoever put these words in Ellington's mouth failed to understand that the Gershwins' role playing in *Porgy and Bess* was simply that—playing—and that as such the opera has as much in common with the type of Modernist self-conscious masking developed by Pound and Eliot as it did with late-nineteenth-century verismo opera. At any rate, would not a work that openly attempted to accurately represent an "authentic" African American experience fail, given the impossibility of determining what such an experience consists of? *Porgy and Bess* is certainly not "real" black music, nor, despite the racial play that surrounds its creation and even made its creation possible, does it attempt to be. Yet neither is the opera a "real" white version of black music, or even a "real" Jewish version of a white version of black music, any more than *The Dybbuk* would have captured any definitive, comprehensive version of Jewishness.

Gershwin told Isaac Goldberg:

> I am a man without traditions. What I'd like to do would be to write an opera of the melting pot, of New York City itself, which is the symbolic and actual blend of the native and immigrant strains. This would allow for many kinds of music, black and white, Eastern and

Western, and would call for a style that should achieve, out of this diversity, an artistic and aesthetic unity. Here is a challenge to a librettist, and, what is to my liking, to my own music. I'd rather fail at this than achieve a passable duplication of an already consecrated style.[39]

This early claim for his music as simply "American"—which seemed to evade Gershwin's awareness of his heritage and traditions—in fact addressed quite directly the problem of what a black person is, what a white person is, what a Jew is, what, in short, an American is. Given this aim, perhaps the most obvious context in which to view and hear *Porgy and Bess* is not verismo opera, or even Modernist poetry, but blackface minstrelsy, which since before the Civil War was asking the very same question provoked by Sportin' Life's Yiddish grammar: what is the difference between a who and a what? That such questions are framed by race is an American inevitability abundantly clear in Ewen's notion that Gershwin's artistic maturity might be understood in terms of a racial emancipation: "In his earlier works, Gershwin had been the slave of jazz: it dominates his thoughts, his feelings. In *Porgy and Bess* Gershwin was its master, using it with sparing economy to serve his artistic purpose."[40]

Jewish music and jazz in general are often considered the essential "ethnic" presences in the Gershwins' music, but the actual traditions of blackface minstrelsy—in addition to those of jazz, blues, or ragtime—have their place as well. In fact, *Porgy and Bess* was not the Gershwins' first try at the blackface genre. In 1922 George presented *Blue Monday,* a segment of the Broadway revue *George White's Scandals* telling of a doomed love affair between two young Harlemites. The show, arranged by the black composer Will Vodery and conducted by the white "King of Jazz" Paul Whiteman, was performed by an all-white cast in blackface. *Blue Monday* was real blackface, meaning a music that featured white performers playing blacks, but it is not often recognized that blacks in blackface are an equally valid and traditional form of minstrelsy, and it is in this context that *Porgy and Bess* may be considered a form of blackface minstrel show, attacking traditional notions of racial identity by imitating imitation. Duke Ellington claimed that Gershwin indulged in "negroisms," but what else is there but negroism on stage? In blackface, African Americans, condemned throughout modernity as incapable of originality and innovation, undermine what Michael North calls the white "false concept of originality"[41] by playing playing, by reinventing the drama of invention. Any proper understanding of blackface minstrelsy must recognize how no race, class, ethnic group, gender, or nationality is "safe" within its conventions—not in the simple doubling represented by blacks in blackface, and even less so in the multiple doublings of a New York Jewish man putting words into the mouth of an educated, northern, African American woman playing an illiterate, southern, African American woman. For the Jew to black up—and here we must recognize how Gershwin in *Porgy and Bess* one-ups Al Jolson in *The Jazz Singer* by internalizing the mask—is not merely to comment on race relations in America, but to enter white society by playing whites playing blacks. The Jew's perceived intermediate racial position between white and black allowed whites to consider Jewishness as a guarantee of jazz's blackness. This is why Benny Goodman, not Duke Ellington, was crowned king of swing, and why George Gershwin was considered, in Heyward's words, "the only white man in America" who could out-shout that champion black shouter on Folly Beach.[42] No wonder Gershwin joked that Todd Duncan, the original operatic Porgy, was more Jewish than him, and that he was more black than Duncan.[43]

If for whites the Jewish aspect of jazz endowed the music with an authentic blackness, Jews also profited from the deal. For Jews, masquerading in blackface authorized the whiteness of Jewish culture; blackface became a way to explore Jewishness. It may have been this process of projecting blackness or it may have been a sense of racial insecurity that led Irving Berlin—the composer of "White Christmas" was a Jew born Isidore Balin—to claim in a 1920 interview that the Russian-Jewish immigrants already dominating popular music in America were of "pure white blood."[44] Either way, blackface became a way for the Gershwins to represent themselves, as Jews, and Sportin' Life's discourse might be considered a midrash, which is always a dangerous enterprise, if taken seriously. After all, the original words for "It Ain't Necessarily So" were, according to the process in which Ira Gershwin used "dummy lyrics" so that singers could practice the rhythm of the lyrics while the final version was being polished, "An Order of Bacon and Eggs"[45]—a forbidden meal for any Jew who takes the letter of the law seriously.[46] Moreover, while there are plenty of reasons to doubt Bible stories, Sportin' Life—or rather, the Gershwins—are playing a much more dangerous game. Goliath did not lie down and die, as the lyrics tell us, but was knocked down and killed; Jonah did not live in the whale, but was only trapped for three days in a great fish; Pharaoh's daughter did not fish Moses from the water, but sent one of her servants; finally, Methuselah did not live 900 years, but 969 years, not an easy fit for the lyric's meter, but a fact of crucial importance, because Methuselah died in the same year that God sent the flood to annihilate all of mankind with the exception of Methuselah's grandson, Noah, and his family. The

Gershwins, assimilated, nonobservant Jews, rewrote these stories in order to prove them false; "It Ain't Necessarily So" itself is not necessarily so. As such, the Gershwins in *Porgy and Bess* were toiling over their identities as Jews in the only way possible on stage: not only outside the faith, but in the mask of the other, so as to overcome the totalizing racial imperatives of American culture. When, to borrow a phrase from Gertrude Stein, another writer fleeing Americanness and Jewishness, there is no there there, the self's voice is only heard in the song of the other. According to Ira Gershwin, through Porgy, "plenty o' nuthin'" is more than enough.

"How Can They Say I'm Anti-Negro?"

It is no wonder that this opera, which was too Jewish for some audiences, too black for others, and too white for the rest, took almost twenty-five years to make it to the silver screen, and why it was withdrawn from circulation after just over a decade. Although the touring version, wounded by critical and popular failure, petered out after a few months (but not before desegregating Washington, D.C.'s National Theater in March 1936), the wildly successful international tours in the 1940s and 1950s convinced Hollywood that here was a musical prophet who was finally ready to be honored in his own country, and inspired Goldwyn to take on the role of producer one last time.

No one will ever know much about Goldwyn's early years, and he liked it that way, offering a fiction that is so general as to be the only truth: "My early boyhood was spent in Europe."[47] In fact, since there was no birth certificate or other form of official documentation, neither the birth date nor even the real name can be confirmed for the child born to Avraham and Hannah Gelbfisz in Warsaw around the time Czar Alexander III's campaign against the Jews ignited pogroms throughout Eastern Europe can be confirmed. Judge Learned Hand's ruling in granting Goldwyn's 1923 legal battle for his studio to bear his own name—"a self-made man may prefer a self-made name"—speaks volumes.[48] Was Samuel Godfisch born on August 27, 1882, as Alvin Marill claims, or was it a year earlier, as Arthur Marx attests? Or is A. Scott Berg correct in writing that it was in July of 1879 that Schmuel Gelbfisz was born? Or was it Shmuel ben Avraham, as Michael Freedland insists? Nor is it clear exactly when this boy fled Poland for Germany, England, perhaps Canada, and eventually America, where he became an American citizen officially named Samuel Goldfish in 1902. Whatever his name, this boy worked as a laborer, foreman, salesman, and eventually partner in a Gloversville, New York glove factory before marrying into a family involved in vaudeville, and starting a film company, hiring Cecil B. DeMille, and helping establish Hollywood by shooting his first film, *The Squaw Man*, there in 1914. After forming Paramount with Adolph Zukor, in 1918 he took the name Goldwyn and moved to California for good, becoming an early independent producer before forming Metro-Goldwyn-Mayer in 1924. He worked with Warner Brothers and United Artists for almost two decades, making dozens of hits before being "included out" of their future plans, as he put it. Undeterred, Goldwyn went on to make such classics as *The Little Foxes* (1941), *The Best Years of Our Lives* (1946), *Wuthering Heights* (1954), and *Guys and Dolls* (1955).

Although Goldwyn was raised as an Orthodox Jew, speaking Hebrew at the Hasidic religious school known as cheder until the age of eleven—he spoke Yiddish to his family, and Polish to his gentile neighbors and employers—he never again went to schul after coming to America, and raised the children of his second wife, Francis, to follow her Catholicism. There is no record of Goldwyn's response to Sammy Davis Jr.'s refusal during the filming of *Porgy and Bess* to work on Yom Kippur, other than going to work himself, as he always did on the Sabbath and on Jewish holidays; but the irony must have been unmistakable. For Goldwyn, as for so many figures in the entertainment industry in the early years of the century, Jewish culture and black culture were inseparable, so it is not clear whether Goldwyn's Jewishness complicates or simplifies what Donald Bogle calls "the blackface fixation"—in which a black actor plays a white version of blackness, as opposed to some more "valid representation."[49] Goldwyn struck it rich with *Potash and Perlmutter* (1923), a film version of the 1905 play about the misadventures of two squabbling Jewish men—indeed, the film was so successful that Goldwyn went on to make two sequels, *In Hollywood with Potash and Perlmutter* (1924) and *Partners Again* (1926). As with most figures in the early-twentieth-century entertainment industry, however, Jewish theater meant blackface, and Goldwyn made a national star of Eddie Cantor—born Edward Iskowitz—by featuring him in blackface routines in six films in the 1930s. Who better than Goldwyn to produce the masterpiece of the man that Isaac Goldberg, speaking confidently and with some authority for the rest of his country, considered its "foremost writer of American-Negroid music."[50]

By 1957, *Porgy and Bess*'s status as an international hit had overcome the doubts of dozens of producers and directors wary of making an all-black film. Among the ninety offers that the Heyward and Gershwin estates entertained for the film rights were those of Joseph Mankiewicz, Louis B. Mayer, and Harry Cohn (who suggested a blackface film in which Al Jolson would play Porgy, Rita Hayworth would play Bess, and Fred Astaire would play Sportin' Life), so Dorothy Heyward and Ira Gershwin were even willing to accept Goldwyn's low bid of $650, 000 in May of 1957, so much did they trust his taste.[51] Goldwyn had, after all, attended the October 1935 premiere of *Porgy and Bess* in New York and loved it, eventually becoming close friends with George and Ira, working with the brothers on *The Goldwyn Follies* in the months before George's tragically early death in 1937, keeping George's autographed portrait in his office, and never tiring of calling Gershwin the nation's greatest composer; he promised the Gershwins and Dorothy Heyward that he would "preserve the integrity of *Porgy and Bess*."[52] By 1957 Goldwyn knew *Porgy and Bess* would be his last film, his last chance to black up, and he was unconcerned about spending $15 million to split the difference between artistic integrity and racial integration.

If the original production of the opera in 1935 posed no problems other than allowing the Gershwins to let their natural blackness show, and training the black cast members how to shed their whiteness, Goldwyn's task of assembling the professional filmmakers, writers, actors, and singers in 1959 to re-create Catfish Row was more troublesome. After an unsuccessful attempt to recruit Langston Hughes and Elia Kazan—an African American and a Jew—as writer and director, Goldwyn settled on N. Richard Nash (born Nathan Richard Nusbaum) and Rouben Mamoulian, two Jews with plenty of experience with African American culture. Mamoulian had directed all-black casts three times in addition to the original stage version of *Porgy* in 1927 and the opera in 1935. Nonetheless, while casting was getting under way in late 1957 an advertisement appeared in the *Hollywood Reporter* in which the Council for the Improvement of Negro Theater Arts objected to the plot of *Porgy and Bess* as racist, false, and disparaging, as the product of a producer who acted like he was part of some "master race."[53] Perhaps Goldwyn's opponents had read an article called "The Best Advice I Ever Had," which appeared with Goldwyn's byline in *Reader's Digest* in June 1956, when all of Hollywood was trying to hook *Porgy and Bess*, in which Goldwyn recalled the counsel offered by his uncle back in the "Europe" of his boyhood: "No matter how black things seem, if you have courage, a darkness can be overcome."[54]

Goldwyn responded to the accusation of racism by asserting his Jewishness, a time-honored though always suspect gesture of cross-identification: "I'm Jewish. I ran away from Hitler. How can they say I'm anti-Negro?"[55] While it is true that Goldwyn's portrayals of blacks on screen were certainly as racist as the rest of his peers in Hollywood in the 1920s and 1930s, he had more recently begun to repair his reputation, taking the bold step of putting integrated jazz bands on screen in *A Song Is Born* (1948), and contributing to the NAACP. Of course, the latter gesture absolved him of racism no more than his contributions to Jewish philanthropies—he gave $100,000 each year to United Jewish Welfare Fund, and was elected president of the United Jewish Appeal, for whom he raised $9 million—made him Jewish.

Goldwyn would have accomplished far more by listening to his director, since agitation over questions of race were dwarfed by concerns in the early stages of the film about Goldwyn's objections to Mamoulian's insistence on authenticity; Mamoulian wanted to shoot on location wherever possible, even if it meant filming on Charleston's Cabbage Row, which Heyward used as his model for the Catfish Row of *Porgy*. The appointment of Otto Preminger to replace Mamoulian in 1958 further inflamed cast members who trusted Mamoulian's treatment of black characters. Preminger assented to Goldwyn's insistence that location shots be limited to the dock scenes and the picnic on Kitiwah Island, and eventually ended up shooting these scenes not in South Carolina but in California, on the relatively nearby San Joaquin River.

Objections that arose over scenes shot on the vast soundstage Goldwyn constructed in Hollywood show that Preminger was in a no-win situation in questions of authenticity. Goldwyn's publicly distributed "Production Notes" bragged about the "careful 'aging'" given the sets, but in fact Catfish Row appears curiously sanitary. So too, the "infinite pains" taken with the costumes "to make them appear used and worn" cannot hide the artifice inevitable and even proper to Hollywood costume conventions of the day.[56] It is no wonder, then, that Preminger avoided the sense of intimacy that close-ups would have afforded; the glacial, rigid, even mechanical pans and the cold camera angles that scan the vast soundstage from a distance insulate the viewer from the insulation.

Preminger's attitudes on race were as suspect as his taste in costumes, sets, locations, and camera angles, according to many potential cast members. Was it because or in spite of his *Carmen Jones*, another all-black musical with a mannerist approach to race relations and a strong urge to overcome some darkness? Leigh Whipper, who had been selected to play the role of the crab man, spoke not only personally but as the president of the Negro Actors Guild of America when he claimed that Preminger "had no respect for my people," although it is not clear how much he represented "his people," since other members of the Guild publicly denounced Whipper's statement, and rightly so.[57] Born to an upper-class Jewish family in Vienna, Preminger had no formal Jewish education; he learned about

Judaism at state-supported Catholic schools, where he was the victim of a brutal anti-Semitic beating as a child. The example of his father, a government prosecutor who had been raised religious and whose career was destroyed because he refused to convert, also seems to have had an influence on Preminger, who was himself denied the opportunity to run the Vienna State Theater at the age of twenty-six because he too refused to convert. Preminger's arrival in 1935 in the United States was, as with Goldwyn, a matter of choice. Preminger's family, on the other hand, were actually fleeing Hitler's police when they arrived in America three years later. Preminger quickly gained a reputation as a headstrong, stubborn director. Like Goldwyn, he was one of the first independent directors, and like Goldwyn, his interests in Judaism and African American culture were keen. If a gritty, historical realism inspired the representations of Jewishness in his films, a sense of "fantasy"—it is the word he used to describe his *Porgy and Bess*—dominated his representations of African Americans. Although Preminger claimed to have no patience for the "racial nonsense" in which Hollywood loved to indulge, the quadruple equivocation in his statement that "certainly as far as I know, as far as I am aware (you can never tell), I have no prejudices" is revealing.[58]

As we have seen, casting had always been an issue with the stage version of *Porgy and Bess*, ever since DuBose Heyward suggested that Al Jolson perform the title role in blackface instead of Gershwin's first choice of Paul Robeson, but Preminger's involvement in the film brought such conflicts to a newer, uglier level, once again around the issue of authenticity: how should blackness be represented, and who should do the representing? The *Hollywood Reporter* advertisement in late 1957 implored actors to avoid casting sessions, and although it was unclear if this organization was the legitimate representative of many black actors, or simply a single person with a vendetta against Goldwyn, none of Goldwyn's choices for the leads—he wanted Harry Belafonte to play Porgy, Lena Horne in the role of Bess, and Nat King Cole, of all people, to play Sportin' Life—signed up. Belafonte, who had worked with Preminger on *Carmen Jones* five years earlier, and was perhaps the best-known black actor in America, refused the role of Porgy, claiming that playing a crippled beggar was below his dignity. Goldwyn's second choice for Porgy was the "ebony saint," Sidney Poitier. If Poitier, like Belafonte, had steadfastly refused to play toms, coons, mulattoes, mammies, or bucks—the most frequent choices for blacks actors throughout most of Hollywood's history, according to Donald Bogle's famous formulation—he had not risen above those "sterile paragons of virtue completely devoid of mature characterization or of any political or social reality."[59] It was only under Goldwyn's infamous personal pressure—one understands by reading between the lines that Goldwyn personally put Poitier's future in Hollywood on the line—that this "model integrationist hero"[60] agreed to play an uneducated character for whom "plenty o' nuthin'" was enough.

Like Belafonte, Horne found the role beneath her dignity, so Goldwyn looked to another elegant, light-skinned star: Dorothy Dandridge, who also had appeared in *Carmen Jones*. Dandridge also had to be coerced into playing a drug-addicted siren of the slums who can't help loving the murderous Crown, played by Brock Peters. As Blevins Davis noted, Dandridge's Bess was "so refined it was laughable,"[61] and not just in a class sense; like Goldwyn, she struggled her entire life to overcome some darkness. At one point Dandridge, who had a reputation in Hollywood for her attraction to white men, told Preminger that she could not work with Peters because "he's so black."[62] However scurrilous the rumors, on screen Dandridge avoids Peters wherever possible, squirming out of his embraces and flinching at his kisses.

Normative Us, Deviant Them

When the film finally opened in June 1959, press reception ranged from mixed to hostile. While boosters of the film bragged that Dandridge was eventually nominated for a Golden Globe in the category of best actress in a musical, it is worth remembering how limited her competition was in 1959. The film's achievements at the Academy Awards were similarly disappointing, with nominations for best costume design and best sound recording, and an Oscar for best score. The latter is perhaps the biggest shock, since compared to Gershwin's original orchestrations, the score is pure schmaltz, at least in comparison to the "gefilte fish" original. The 105-piece orchestra and choir go through the motions without the spontaneity and volatility of Gershwin's own arrangements; one wonders whether it was the strength of the original compositions or Goldwyn's still-towering influence in the industry that guaranteed *Porgy and Bess* its only Oscar.

Beneath the surface of the critical reception of the film in 1959 was the accusation that Gershwin, Goldwyn, and Preminger had no right to make a film about African Americans, and that such a work could only be undermined by the artifice that is natural to blackface aesthetics. *Esquire* called *Porgy and Bess* "folkery-fakery,"[63] while the *Los Angeles Tribune* called the film "a smear, a stereotype, a disgrace, an embarrassment to Negroes."[64] Is it any wonder that box office receipts failed to bring the production out of the red? The fact that the film was hardly shown at all in the segregated South contributed yet another example of how *Porgy and Bess* pleased no one by trying to please everyone: it was too white for blacks and too black for whites.

Nor have recent scholars recognized the inevitability of artifice in *Porgy and Bess,* and in any film dealing with race. Donald Bogle rejects the misrepresentation and falsification of the story and its characters as negative idealization, yet seems unaware that idealization is the name of the game in Hollywood, and in American race relations as a whole. Bogle, who once worked as a story editor for Preminger, dismisses as racist and as aesthetically inferior anything but "valid representations" of African Americans, but seems bound by a set of prescriptive typologies no less rigid, inaccurate, and even racist than the tom, the coon, the mulatto, the mammy, or the buck. Whether by *valid* Bogle means the validity conferred on the representers by virtue of their race, in which black is a normative "us" and white is a deviant "them," or the validity conferred on the characters represented by virtue of their moral qualities, in which black is a normative good and white is a deviant bad—seems hardly to matter. The real Porgy was, by all accounts, less heroic yet more "valid" than the one dreamed by the profoundly Jewish imaginations of its composer, lyricist, and producer.

Fittingly, of all the Jews involved in the film it is the most religious of them all, Sammy Davis Jr., who challenges the racial conventions of Ira Gershwin's lyrics. Whereas Cab Calloway's soundtrack performance follows the copyrighted lyrics of "It Ain't Necessarily So," which read "when no gal'll give in," Davis can be heard and seen undoing the contraction so indicative of blackface, singing "when no gal will give in." It was just such a display of "precise, cultivated accents that are miles away from the Negro slums of South Carolina"[65] that offended critics who no doubt liked their fantasy slums dirty, their imaginary blacks as black as possible. Mamoulian had called *Porgy and Bess* "a specifically Negro contribution to American music and acting" and sought to honor that contribution by relying on the natural dignity and authenticity conferred by location shots,[66] but James Rosamonde Johnson, the choir director in 1935, still claimed that he had worked on "an opera about Negroes rather than a Negro opera."[67] Perhaps Preminger's ignorance as to the nuances of American race relations actually helped him to recognize that any production of *Porgy and Bess* would be a "fantasy."

How different was Preminger's attempt "to take the terror, fright and

26 Sammy Davis Jr.
[Author's collection]

oppression out of ghetto living"—the words are those of Dorothy Dandridge, and note that she uses a term that had only recently stopped describing Jewish neighborhoods[68]—from the insistence of Pearl Bailey, in
the role of Maria, that none of the female actresses wear handkerchiefs
on their heads, and that the writers delete a tasteless remark about water-
melons? Bailey, wary of the brand of fantasy that Preminger advocated,
having appeared in *Carmen Jones,* signed on to the project only after threats
from Goldwyn, but clearly used her position to engage in some fantasizing of her own. The same goes, except the other way, for Carol Easton, who
finds "a basic dishonesty" in the production values,[69] as if the sets could
have been made a bit shabbier, the costumes a bit more ragged, the actors
trained to speak and sing like "real" African Americans; perhaps more
conscientious, harder-working scriptwriters might have also included ex-
pletives and background noise. So too, denying the Jewish content of the
blackface mask enables Ed Guerrero to claim that Hollywood exercised a
total and unequivocal subordination, marginalization, and devaluation of
African Americans. When Guerrero argues that white attempts to represent blackness are always bad and can only be opposed by black counter-

efforts, he is reproducing and authorizing the aesthetic and racial bipolar syndrome that he deplores, replacing "one grand, multifaceted illusion" with another,[70] without realizing the necessarily illusory status of the entire project.

If the type of "white Negroism" on display in the stage version of *Porgy and Bess* is a phenomenon peculiar to Jewish American culture, as Jeffrey Melnick has argued,[71] how much more so is the affective borrowing that Goldwyn puts into Sammy Davis Jr.'s mouth. Yet this is not the same kind of musical miscegenation—the phrase was coined by Isaac Goldberg in the *American Mercury* a month before the premiere of *The Jazz Singer* in 1927[72]—that simultaneously terrified and seduced Virgil Thomson, himself no stranger to musical miscegenation, having collaborated with Gertrude Stein on the all-black *Four Saints in Three Acts:* "I don't mind his being a light composer, and I don't mind his trying to be a serious one. But I do mind his falling between two stools."[73] What we have in the film version of *Porgy and Bess* is not so much Cruse's "contradiction"— the etymology suggests voices singing against each other—as a claim for Jewishness not between light and serious, black and white, but including them. This is neither highbrow nor lowbrow, but "He-brow," as Ira Gershwin once put it.[74]

Racial Bipolar Syndrome

In tracking the mutually reflexive racial and musical gestures of Goldwyn's revisions to *Porgy and Bess,* it is important to keep in mind the history that separates the opera and the film. Ultimately Goldwyn's *Porgy and Bess* reflects both the progress and the problems that America had made in terms of race relations since 1935, the racial imagery that had been both dismantled and reinforced, for better and for worse. If the 1935 stage version of *Porgy and Bess* was written in the shadow of those great shocks to race relations in the Depression, the Scottsboro Boys trial at home and the Nuremburg laws abroad, by the time the film version premiered in June 1959 much had changed for both African Americans and Jews. Felix Frankfurter was appointed to the Supreme Court, Gwendolyn Brooks won the Pulitzer Prize, and Ralph Bunche won the Nobel Prize. The army was desegregated and Israel was founded. But if much had changed for the better for Jews and African Americans from the *Porgy and Bess* of the Depression to the *Porgy and Bess* of the cold war, much had also changed between them, for better and for worse. Although Jews were crucial participants in the Civil Rights movement of the 1950s, with the Anti-Defamation League supporting the NAACP in Brown v. Board of Education in 1954, and Jews marching with Martin Luther King Jr. in Montgomery in 1955, tensions between the two groups were also on the rise.

In the late 1950s Goldwyn's aesthetics—inasmuch as the man who is quoted as saying "an oral contract isn't worth the paper it's written on" can be said to have an aesthetics—answered the American demand for fantasy disguised as reality. As early as the early 1920s an advertisement for Goldwyn Pictures asked, "Why do you enjoy this picture or that one so much? Have you stopped to think why? . . . All the characters seemed just like real people."[75] Yet what does Goldwyn's rejection of Mamoulian's liberal realism for Preminger's less racially particularist fantasy signal almost four decades later? Whether Goldwyn dropped the singing of many of the cast members, including both Poitier and Dandridge, in favor of the dubbed voices of Robert McFerrin and Adele Addison, because they were not good enough or because they were not black enough, in the end Goldwyn found black singers who were good enough to dub the parts. Then again, since Goldwyn allowed Loulie Jean Norman, who was white, to dub Diahann Carroll's Clara, perhaps he felt that the race of the performer had little to do with the racial content of the performance—perhaps Norman, like Gershwin, could sing blackness better than Carroll.[76]

The Jewishness of *Porgy and Bess,* and of all forms of modern American blackface, suggests a position not in between but outside the racial choices of "white, yellow, or black," as the opera's "Red-Headed Woman" puts it; the "new color"[77] that Gershwin saw Hollywood taking on as early as 1936 was not a color at all, however, but a recognition that the Jew is not so much a color or a lacuna in the American system of racial meanings, but a means of circulation; it is through the Jew that white and black rhyme. After all, in *Porgy and Bess* we have an opera, written in the nonstandard English of African Americans and interpreted by the nonstandard English of the American Jewish immigrant, that becomes in the jargon of the music world a "standard," best known first through black actors directed and produced on stage and screen in the 1930s, 1940s, and 1950s, and finally through jazz musicians of every complexion in the 1960s. How fitting that the film version of *Porgy and Bess* is not only unavailable on video but out of public circulation in any venue; when Goldwyn's rights to the film expired in 1972, the legal owners refused to rerelease or distribute the film in any format, including for television. How fitting that this most representative work of the American identity, an encyclopedic drama of

American self-fashioning, in which plenty o' nuthin' is plenty indeed, is so obscure, yet so accessible; it can only be experienced in one place, one viewer at a time, but for free, for anyone willing and able to visit the Library of Congress. Apologies to Sir William Harcourt, but who can experience the all-American Yiddish blackface of Goldwyn's *Porgy and Bess* and fail to admit that we are all schvartzes now?

Notes

1   Hollis Alpert, *The Life and Times of "Porgy and Bess"* (New York: Knopf, 1990), 265.
2   Ibid., 257.
3   Alvin Marill, *Samuel Goldwyn Presents* (South Brunswick, N.J.: A. S. Barnes, 1976), 17.
4   Harold Cruse, *The Crisis of the Negro Intellectual* (1967; New York: Quill, 1984), 103.
5   Ira Gershwin, *The Complete Lyrics of Ira Gershwin* (New York: Knopf, 1993), 238.
6   Philip Furia, *Ira Gershwin: The Art of the Lyricist* (New York: Oxford University Press, 1996), 142.
7   Ann Douglas, *Terrible Honesty: Mongrel Manhattan in the 1920s* (New York: Farrar, Straus, & Giroux, 1995), 376.
8   Gershwin, *The Complete Lyrics*, 91.
9   Edward Jablonski, *Gershwin* (New York: Doubleday, 1987), xiv.
10 See Michael Rogin, *Blackface, White Noise: Jewish Immigrants and the Hollywood Melting Pot* (Berkeley: University of California, 1996), 73–120.
11 While the plot and characters of *Porgy and Bess* are the work of DuBose Heyward, and to a lesser extent his wife Dorothy, the opera's lyrics, which this essay focuses on as the central text of the work, are largely those of Ira Gershwin, although the two writers did collaborate on "I Loves You Porgy," "I Got Plenty o' Nuthin'," and "Bess You Is My Woman Now."
12 David Ewen, *The Story of George Gershwin* (New York: Henry Holt, 1943), 12.
13 Deena Rosenberg, *Fascinating Rhythm: The Collaboration of George and Ira Gershwin* (New York: Dutton, 1991), 16.
14 Joan Peyser, *The Memory of All That: The Life of George Gershwin* (New York: Simon & Schuster, 1993), 248 and 253, and Rosenberg, *Fascinating Rhythm*, 298 and 301.
15 Isaac Goldberg, *George Gershwin: A Study in American Music* (New York: Simon & Schuster, 1931, New York: F. Unger, 1958), 41.
16 Rogin, *Blackface, White Noise*, 102. It is worth noting that the character of Porgy in DuBose Heyward's 1925 novel of the same name, on which the opera was based, has "something Eastern" about his look" (2).
17 Jablonski, *Gershwin*, 24.
18 Ibid., 30.

19 Ira Gershwin, *The Complete Lyrics*, 28.

20 Jablonski, *Gershwin*, 59.

21 *The International Jew: The World's Foremost Problem* (Dearborn, Mich., 1920–22; repr. Los Angeles: Christian Nationalist Crusade, n.d.), 3:70.

22 Peyser, *The Memory of All That*, 49.

23 Oscar Levant, *A Smattering of Ignorance* (New York: Doubleday, Doran: 1940), 182.

24 Ewen, *The Story of George Gershwin*, 154.

25 Peyser, *The Memory of All That*, 45.

26 Charles Schwartz, *Gershwin, His Life and Music* (New York: Bobbs-Merrill, 1973), 123.

27 Rouben Mamoulian saw something different in George's appearance: He looked "like a patriarch. I would look at him and all but see a long white beard and a staff in his hand." See Merle Armitage, ed., *George Gershwin* (New York: Longmans, Green, 1938), 55.

28 Armitage, *George Gershwin*, 39.

29 Edward Jablonski, *Gershwin Remembered* (Portland, Oreg.: Amadeus, 1992), 900.

30 Rosenberg, *Fascinating Rhythm*, 272.

31 Robert Kimball and Alfred Simon, *The Gershwins* (New York: Atheneum, 1973), 177.

32 Jablonski, *Gershwin*, 275.

33 Jablonski, *Gershwin Remembered*, 99.

34 Armitage, *George Gershwin*, 39.

35 Alpert, *The Life and Times of "Porgy and Bess*," 103.

36 Jablonski, *Gershwin Remembered*, 106.

37 Alpert, *The Life and Times of "Porgy and Bess*," 122.

38 Edward Morrow, "Duke Ellington on Gershwin's *Porgy*," *New Theatre*, December 1935, 5–6, reprinted in Mark Tucker, ed., *The Duke Ellington Reader* (New York: Oxford University Press, 1993), 117.

39 Goldberg, *George Gershwin*, 275.

40 Ewen, *The Story of George Gershwin*, 162.

41 Michael North, *The Dialect of Modernism: Race, Language, and Twentieth-Century Literature* (New York: Oxford University Press, 1994), 182.

42 Armitage, *George Gershwin*, 39.

43 Jablonski, *Gershwin*, 281.

44 Ian Whitcomb, *Irving Berlin and Ragtime America* (London: Century, 1987), 15.

45 Ira Gershwin, *The Complete Lyrics*, 237.

46 Ira Gershwin used this example in an offhand way when explaining the way in which his job consisted of "fitting words mosaically to music" (237).

47 Carol Easton, *The Search for Samuel Goldwyn: A Biography* (New York: Morrow, 1975), 14.

48 *Simpson's Contemporary Quotations*, compiled by James B. Simpson (New York: Houghton Mifflin, 1988), entry 6310.

49   Donald Bogle, *Toms, Coons, Mulattoes, Mammies, and Bucks: An Interpretive History of Blacks in American Films* (1973; reprint, New York: Continuum, 1994), 27.

50   Peyser, *The Memory of All That*, 237.

51   Some of these suggestions were not in fact so far-fetched—DuBose Heyward had wanted Al Jolson to play Porgy in the earliest proposals for a musical version of his play, with a score by Jerome Kern and Oscar Hammerstein. Moreover, a 1943 production in Nazi-occupied Denmark used an all-white cast—before being shut down by the Gestapo (Alpert, *The Life and Times of "Porgy and Bess,"* 140).

52   Ibid., 250.

53   Arthur Marx, *Goldwyn: A Biography of the Man behind the Myth* (New York: Norton, 1976), 343.

54   Marill, *Samuel Goldwyn Presents*, 17.

55   Alpert, *The Life and Times of "Porgy and Bess,"* 266. Goldwyn's claim about running from Hitler is, of course, an outright fabrication, although he did extend help in the 1930s and 1940s to relatives fleeing the murderous surge of anti-Semitic activity in Eastern Europe.

56   "Production Notes," 6–7. These "Production Notes" were presumably distributed to journalists at the time of the film's release. A copy is contained in the press clippings file on *Porgy and Bess* at the Motion Picture Division of the Library of Congress.

57   Alpert, *The Life and Times of "Porgy and Bess,"* 265.

58   Gerald Pratley, *The Cinema of Otto Preminger* (New York: A. S. Barnes, 1971), 110, 144, and 35.

59   Ed Guerrero, *Framing Blackness: The African American Image in Film* (Philadelphia: Temple University Press, 1993), 72.

60   Bogle, *Toms, Coons*, 175.

61   Alpert, *The Life and Times of "Porgy and Bess,"* 287.

62   A. Scott Berg, *Goldwyn: A Biography* (New York: Knopf, 1989), 486.

63   Easton, *The Search for Samuel Goldwyn*, 282.

64   Michael Freedland, *The Goldwyn Touch: A Biography of Samuel Goldwyn* (London: Harap, 1986), 245.

65   Alpert, *The Life and Times of "Porgy and Bess,"* 277.

66   Freedland, *The Goldwyn Touch*, 243.

67   Schwartz, *Gershwin*, 245.

68   Alpert, *The Life and Times of "Porgy and Bess,"* 273.

69   Easton, *The Search for Samuel Goldwyn*, 280.

70   Guerrero, *Framing Blackness*, 2.

71   Jeffrey Melnick, *Ancestors and Relatives: The Uncanny Relationship of African Americans and Jews* (Ph.D. diss., Harvard University, 1994), 553.

72   Rogin, *Blackface, White Noise*, 99.

73   Virgil Thomson, *The Virgil Thomson Reader* (Boston: Houghton Mifflin, 1981), 25.

74   Ira Gershwin, *Complete Lyrics*, 30.

75 Easton, *The Search for Samuel Goldwyn*, 100e.

76 Cab Calloway appears on the separately released soundtrack in the role of Sportin' Life instead of Davis because Davis was under an exclusive recording contracts with Decca. The differences are startling: Calloway takes enormous musical liberties with the role, which may have been a matter of style, or due to the fact that Davis had to work under Goldwyn's constant observation.

77 Jablonski, *Gershwin Remembered*, 148.

CONTEMPORARY COMPILATIONS

Picturizing American Cinema: Hindi Film
Songs and the Last Days of Genre
COREY K. CREEKMUR

The dullest and most stale devices of operetta were transplanted into the cinema, and the plague of the "song hit" infected the world's film industries. In the last years of silent films, such theme-songs had already begun to be tacked on to a few individual films, to gain increased propaganda for them by means of records and other means of publicity. The germ of the theme-song spread with terrible rapidity, became an epidemic, and systematically disintegrated the sound film.—Kurt London, *Film Music*, 1936

With the coming of the talkies the Indian motion picture came into its own as a definite and distinctive piece of creation. . . . This was achieved by music. . . . It gives us musical entertainment which even the best of Hollywood pictures cannot.—N. R. Desai, Indian Film Distributor, 1938

In order to encourage critical discussion of the contemporary film soundtrack within an international frame, whether defined by the freedom of postcolonial cultural exchange or by the rapacious expansion of neocolonial global capitalism—both evident, for instance, in the marketing category of "world" music—this essay draws upon the important but still underinvestigated example of the popular Hindi-language cinema produced by the prolific film industry of Bombay (now Mumbai) known as Bollywood.[1] Drawing upon suggestions made by Paul Willemen regarding the possibility of a "comparative studies in cinema" and by Ashish Rajadhyaksha, in his challenging reevaluation of Indian silent cinema in relation to the influential discourse on early American and European cinema,

I argue that Bombay cinema is not appropriately or even usefully represented as a unique or exotic case radically distinct from Western norms; popular Indian cinema can serve to challenge central and overgeneralized claims of (implicitly Western) film theory and history.[2] Influential theories of cinema spectatorship, for instance, need not be "adjusted" to account for the unusual and specific "case" of India; to the contrary, Bombay cinema, precisely because it is a mainstream cinema and thus unexceptional, even what one might call emphatically conventional, demands that theories of spectatorship must adequately account for it, if those theories are to remain broadly convincing and generally applicable to "cinema" as an international form of popular entertainment. I am, therefore, neither attempting to explain or understand Bombay cinema on "its own terms" nor blindly analyze it through Western models. Rather, I am seeking what Willemen has described, employing Bakhtin's notions of "creative understanding" and "necessary alterity" as "not simply a matter of engaging in a dialogue with some other culture's products, but of using one's understanding of another cultural practice to re-perceive and rethink one's own cultural constellation at the same time." Willemen asks, rejecting the sufficiency of "simple curiosity" as an answer: "If the critical study of, say, Chinese or Indian cinemas is not also aimed at modifying our Euro-American notions of cinema, then why study these cultural practices at all?"[3]

For practical purposes I must reduce an argument that obviously deserves more subtle elaboration to two rather obvious but crucial points: First, the popular Indian cinema simply cannot be treated as an "exception" to dominant modes, given its centrality in the lives of millions of consumers around the world. However, a curious logic has often allowed one of the world's largest film industries, catering to both a massive native and growing diasporic audience, to be persistently represented as a curious, unusual, and even marginal case, even as an ironically popular, highly commercial form of "third world" cinema within the discipline of film studies. (Though of course for decades Indian cinema was represented almost exclusively in the West by the work of Satyajit Ray, with a vast, and presumably more vulgar, cinema known only as a rumor.) Second, and more significantly, Bombay cinema, despite its own recourse at times to claims of cultural specificity and signs of regressive nationalism or religious communalism, has always been necessarily defined through an explicitly modern, colonial and postcolonial dialog with the West, a fact that could be supported by internal evidence from hundreds of film examples, including the explicit address of many recent Bombay films, including the blockbusters *Dilwale Dulhania Le Jayenge* (1995) and *Pardes* (1997), to anticipated NRI

27 Raj Kapoor in *Shree 420* (1955). [Author's collection]

(non-resident Indian) spectators located around the world through, among other things, emigration narratives and the increased prevalence of English words and phrases accommodating a younger diasporic audience that may not speak fluent Hindi.[4] Indeed, the advertising tag-line for *Pardes*, featuring sequences in California and Las Vegas, was "American Dreams, Indian Soul."

I hardly mean to suggest that Bombay cinema does not employ very distinctive features, or that modern Indian cinema, to secure an explicitly Westernized modernity, fully abandons significant ties to Indian cultural history and representational practices, though the occasional attempt to locate the "purity" or "essence" of Indian cinema outside of modern history now surely seems misguided. Nevertheless, the still-common representation of popular Indian cinema in the West as a kind of curiously commercialized folk ritual produced for naive and overly emotional spectators seriously misrepresents cinema's role in the construction of modern India and of "Indianness" itself as an increasingly international and commercialized cultural identity—perhaps articulated in its "classic" form by the hit song "Meera Joota Hai Japani" sung by Mukesh for Raj Kapoor's 1955 *Shree 420*: "My shoes are Japanese, My pants are English, My red hat is Russian, but my heart is Indian." The song's continued echo is evident when heard in Africa in Mira Nair's diaspora drama *Mississippi Masala* (1992) and when quoted in the opening pages of Salman Rushdie's *The Satanic Verses* (1988) in the mouth of Gibreel Farishta as he falls from the sky toward England. While the song asserts a "Hindustani" interior despite the outward signs of postwar commerce, this now-classic assertion of a "pure" Indian heart of course derives from an impure movie and a pop song, two of the twentieth century's most successful cultural and commercial imports; the song's widespread appeal has obviously been supported by its ongoing, mass dissemination through film, record, radio, television, and video cassette as much as through its proud declaration of national identity.

Though the dominance of Hindi cinema throughout India is often challenged, there seems little question that modern Indian identity, often and perhaps especially outside India itself, is often secured by the knowledge and experience of Bombay films and Bombay film songs. Certainly the most common, and often apologetic or embarrassed claims for the "exceptional" status of Bombay cinema focus upon its extensive—if not excessive—use of musical sequences in virtually every film. Even Satyajit Ray, India's internationally celebrated Bengali art-film director and, again, often the single representative of "Indian cinema" for the West, was motivated to write an appreciative but skeptical essay on "those songs."[5] "Those songs," which the industry describes as "picturized" when provided with visual elaboration, are frequently identified as both the sentimental core of contemporary Indian popular culture and as the perhaps embarrassing element that continually prevents much of the world from accepting and appreciating Hindi cinema. (And the songs certainly contribute to the notorious three-hour length of most Hindi films, which Western viewers do not often recognize as a bonus for the price of their tickets.)

However—to retrieve my focus on a possible comparative analysis of the contemporary film soundtrack—I argue that the use of popular music in Hollywood cinema has been, for almost forty years, unconsciously moving toward a model established by Hindi cinema when the first Indian sound film, *Alam Ara* (1931), featured seven songs; while *The Jazz Singer* (1927) had already suggested that the future American cinema might *often* be musical, *Alam Ara* effectively demanded that the Indian cinema should *always* be so. (The first Tamil sound feature, *Kalidas*, produced in Bombay a few months later, more decisively signaled the future by featuring almost fifty songs, though these were not picturized in the contemporary sense.) I should make it absolutely clear that I cannot demonstrate the direct influence of Bombay upon Hollywood, for which there is virtually no evidence: I might more precisely claim that Bombay cinema has unwit-

28 Advertisement for *Alam Ara* (1931), India's first sound film.
[Author's collection]

tingly anticipated current Hollywood practice rather than influenced it. At present, popular Indian cinema remains almost entirely unknown in the United States, for film critics and scholars as well as average (non-NRI) filmgoers. Screenings of Indian films in the United States and the Asian groceries that stock Indian videotapes in most major American cities both cater almost exclusively to NRI consumers, and Bombay producers have not courted (or really needed) a non-Asian American audience. In its explicit commercial appeal and strong reliance on a star system, Bombay cinema might be justifiably compared to the internationally popular Hong Kong cinema of recent decades, which, however, unlike Bombay cinema, developed a cult following and critical commentary in the United States leading to Hollywood's recent assimilation of Hong Kong stars, directors, and especially stylistic features. While prominent American directors have indulged their desire to transport Hong Kong conventions into their films, the virtually unknown cinema of Bollywood in fact has offered the stylistic model that Hollywood doesn't seem to know it has been seeking for decades even as it moves ever closer to it.

The American Film Song (after the Hollywood Musical)

In order to see the relation between American film and its unrecognized and indirect model in Hindi cinema, the current model of the Hollywood soundtrack must be examined. Two recent American films including the kind of self-reflexive moments more expected than exceptional in postmodern commercial cinema can serve as a point of departure. In each instance characters within the narratives, employing their own home recording equipment, mimic the extradiegetic work of the music supervisors for their films. During one of the last sequences in *Boogie Nights* (1997), when down-and-out porn stars Dirk, Reed, and Todd enter the surreal Hollywood home of Rahad Jackson to pull off a shady drug deal, Rahad informs them that he compiles his own mix tapes because he "doesn't like to be told what to listen to, when to listen to it, or anything." Across a lengthy scene that transforms nervous comedy into violent mayhem, what Rahad has titled "My Awesome Mix Tape #6" blends Night Ranger's "Sister Christian," "Jessie's Girl"—by Rahad's buddy "Ricky" Springfield—and "99 Luftballoons" by Nena, though a tense moment derives from the cassette's suddenly silent auto-reversal, a dramatic pause highlighted by a cut to an extreme close-up of the tape. In *Romy and Michele's High School Reunion* (1997), to inaugurate the road trip that will take the main characters from Los Angeles back to Tucson and toward a reconciliation with their unresolved adolescent traumas, Michele pops a home-recorded cassette into their borrowed car's tape deck: "I taped all the nostalgic songs from high school to get us in the mood," she announces, generously including the film's audience as well as Romy in her carefully selected and sequenced soundscape. Michele's choices, which might easily be swapped for one of Rahand's "awesome" tapes, include Kenny Loggins's "Footloose," "Turning Japanese" by The Vapors, and Culture Club's "Karma Chameleon," songs that encourage and perhaps ironically comment upon the willful rewriting of their pedestrian lives that the pair are about to undertake.

Both of these late 1990s films, like many others, evoke memories, images, and especially the sounds of the relatively recent pop cultural past, and so the actual soundtracks these films produced—in both cases a successful single disc quickly supplemented by an additional collection of "more songs from" each film—might serve in turn as nostalgic collections for the many consumers who, unlike do-it-yourselfers Rahad or Michele, are quite happy to purchase prepackaged sequences of earlier hits. The freedom of musical choice or at least of individualized song sequencing that Rahad and Michele enjoy is of course not fully replicated through the passive consumption of the soundtracks to their films, but the fact that these soundtracks were released in the era of the compact disc implicitly encourages the expanded consumer options of random shuffling and alternative sequencing, the technical possibilities that may function as quotidian manifestations of "progress" and "personal choice," if not manifestations of the concept of "freedom" itself under late capitalism. Just a decade earlier, such opportunities for individual musical control were clearly more limited by Harold's LP's in *The Big Chill* (1983), another film in which a character seeks to construct the musical soundtrack of his everyday life, though in the now-faded era of twelve-inch vinyl, cardboard dust jackets, turntables, and tone arms. (*The Big Chill* was also apparently the first film to spawn a follow-up soundtrack featuring "more hits" after the huge success of its initial release.) Most significantly, the otherwise distinct Rahad, Michele, and Harold each attempt to construct "soundtracks" for their own lives by choosing and sequencing pop songs within films that appear to have assembled their own soundtracks in much the same cut-and-paste way. Although the actual construction of these soundtracks was in large measure determined by the semi-invisible corporate affiliations linking the film and music subsidiaries of contemporary entertainment conglomerates, for the characters and filmmakers alike, the apparent goal appears to be the same: the collecting and effective sequencing of an "awesome" pop soundtrack that subtends personal memories and expresses individual meanings even as it also functions as both advance advertising and franchise income for the film's conglomerate owners.

While the long-neglected film soundtrack has finally received extended critical attention, most of this work remains concentrated on the non-diegetic "background" score characteristic of the classical Hollywood cinema.[6] Many recent studies of film music only gesture—often dismissively—toward the standard contemporary film soundtrack, which typically maintains an instrumental score while emphasizing a more sonically and commercially prominent selection of discrete pop songs, whether new or old (and often both), frequently including highlighted title and end-credit numbers.[7] Indeed, the dominance of the pop music soundtrack in contemporary cinema, featuring specific songs rather than a unified score, can be illustrated by simply noting the now-common practice of selecting compelling film titles from the large store of preexistent, fondly recalled pop-rock oldies: among others, recall *Peggy Sue Got Married* (1986), *Blue Velvet* (1986), *Stand by Me* (1986), *La Bamba* (1987), *You Can't Hurry Love* (1988), *Sea of Love* (1989), *Pretty Woman* (1990), *Love Potion No. 9* (1992), *When a Man Loves a Woman* (1994), *It's My Party* (1996), *One Fine Day* (1996), and *Addicted to Love* (1997). For all of these movies, the already familiar title provides the first draw for the audience, promising at the very least the chance to hear an old favorite once more, though perhaps in a new version by an up-and-coming performer. In many cases, the familiar song even summarizes the plot or announces the "high concept" of the film: the narrative merely reiterates the well-known message of the song. In fact, the use of the exact same songs in trailers for different films unashamedly declare the fundamental sameness of many recent Hollywood features: for instance, The Eurythmics' "Would I Lie to You" is heard in the trailers for *Liar Liar* (1997) and *Krippendorf's Tribe* (1998) as well as *Romy and Michele's High School Reunion,* three films explicitly about—lying.[8]

However, magazines such as *Soundtrack!, Music from the Movies,* and *Film Score Monthly,* as well as websites directed toward the avid collectors of film soundtracks, proudly ignore the pervasive construction of film song sequences through collage, and prestige record labels like Varese Sarabande have emerged to market the instrumental scores of mainstream films to connoisseurs who disdain the assemblages of pop tunes from these same films—the soundtracks that more vulgar consumers increasingly send up the best-selling charts. For example, K. J. Donnelly, discussing *Batman* (1989), memorably describes the film's soundtrack as "a cohabitation of [Danny] Elfman's score with Prince's songs" and recalls that "*Batman* was the first film to institute the release of two soundtrack

LPS, a strategy that has become more common since."[9] Like many of the explicitly popular guides to film music, Marshall Crenshaw's useful *Holly-wood Rock* "lists all the songs performed in each film" included in the volume but bluntly emphasizes that "songs merely appearing on the sound-track are not listed."[10] However, since many of the most memorable and successful songs in contemporary cinema "merely" appear on their film's soundtracks, stubbornly maintaining the standard formal distinction between nondiegetic instrumental scores, diegetic performed numbers, and what might be tentatively distinguished as "soundtrack songs" misrepresents—whatever aesthetic criteria are at stake—the dominant formal construction and commercial practices of contemporary, soundtrack-song-saturated cinema.[11]

For the most part, those critics who have grudgingly acknowledged compilation soundtracks have emphasized the origins of this shift in the rise of rock and roll as the dominant form of popular music, and in the corporate-industrial links that increasingly define entertainment monopolies. For instance, Gary Marmorstein's breezy history of film music, *Hollywood Rhapsody,* concludes with discussions of the "movie song" and the "rock and roll soundtrack" in order to explicitly mark a narrative of creative decline motivated by corporate greed: "Instead of commissioning original new songs that might enhance a film story, or at least showcase the talent of one of its stars, most movie studios are using generic or nostalgic rock music to promote the recordings of their subsidiaries (or, in the case of Columbia Pictures and Sony Music, their music-parents)."[12] Mark Evans, apparently spotting and dreading the shape of things to come as early as 1975, hardly concealed his disgust when he summarized "recent trends" in film music: "Producers have used noise, allowed rock albums to be inserted in a soundtrack at deafening levels of amplification, or dispensed with music altogether." After noting the influential example of *The Last Picture Show* (1971), which collected period country and western songs by Hank Williams and Eddy Arnold, among others, Evans reconsidered the teleology of this apparent musical degeneration: "Strangely enough, such 'compiled scores' were first used during the silent film era; perhaps film scoring has come full circle."[13] However, it's clear from most accounts of the arrival of the compilation score that the historical conjunction of a growing youth audience with the dominance of rock and roll due to "declining musical standards" is largely to blame. The continual and increased production of compilation soundtracks is also, again, commonly understood to be the effect of ever more intricate relationships between ever more concentrated entertainment conglomerates such as Time Warner, which view all their products as tie-in commodities and a means of advertising across media and markets.

Although many successful film soundtracks from the 1950s onward—aside from those linked to films explicitly identified as musicals—often featured a single, isolatable "theme song" with vocals (such as *Breakfast at Tiffany's* [1961] "Moon River" or *High Noon's* [1952] "Do Not Forsake Me, Oh My Darlin'"), the increased identification of popular music with a youth market via rock and roll generated the first notable soundtracks constructed out of a *sequence* of discrete pop songs. Commonly marketed and consumed on 45 rpm discs and jukeboxes, or via the radio format of top-forty "singles," rock and roll encouraged its reception through individual "hit" songs until ambitious rock groups like the Beatles and the Who composed "concept albums" beginning in the mid-1960s that emphasized an overall musical and thematic (even narrative) coherence, leading to the designation of works such as The Who's *Tommy* as "rock operas." The first major films that relied upon compilation soundtracks were therefore produced for and often by the increasingly film-literate youth of the 1960s whose musical tastes did not include older soundtrack hitmakers like Andy Williams or Tex Ritter: *The Graduate* (1967), highlighting five Simon and Garfunkel songs, and especially *Easy Rider* (1969), with its mix of different performers such as Steppenwolf and Jimi Hendrix, remain the best known and most successful models, though the rapid appearance of other hippie films such as *The Strawberry Statement* (1970), *The Magic Christian* (1970), and *Zabriskie Point* (1970) quickly confirmed a dominant pattern. When *Midnight Cowboy* (1969) took the previously recorded but obscure Harry Nillson song "Everybody's Talkin'" as its theme song, the possible gap between the production of a pop song and its appropriation for a film soundtrack was illuminated: songs only needed to be chosen, not composed, for films. Creative insertion and clever juxtaposition replaced original integration as the goal of music-filled films.

Many later films, following the influential lead of *American Graffiti* (1973), then constructed their entire musical soundtracks out of already well-known, previously successful pop recordings.[14] While its setting in the recent past of the early 1960s motivated its inclusion of period songs—setting the model for many later historical re-creations like *Dazed and Confused* (1993), *Forrest Gump* (1994), or *The Wedding Singer* (1998)—*American Graffiti's* success in resurrecting half-forgotten oldies may have established the now-common practice of including at least a few old favorites on the soundtracks of films set in the present. *Pretty Woman* (1990) therefore relies upon Roy Orbison's familiar title recording (actually "Oh

Pretty Woman") from 1964—rather than Van Halen's hit 1982 remake
"(Oh) Pretty Woman"—in order to comfortably introduce new songs by
Christopher Otcasek and Go West, which respectively introduce the film's
two main characters, while an updated mix of David Bowie's 1975 hit
"Fame," retitled "Fame 90," has it both ways as a new version of an old hit.
Sleepless in Seattle (1993)—which would successfully replicate its soundtrack strategies with its virtual remake *You've Got Mail* (1998)—mined
the prerock era to include pop chestnuts by Louis Armstrong and Gene
Autry that could now rub shoulders with current "adult contemporary"
stars Harry Connick Jr. and Celine Dion. While most compilation soundtracks now take advantage of the historically unprecedented assumption
that almost all "popular" music is implicitly "youth" music, the unantici-
pated survival of rock and roll as a successful style for almost half a century has allowed the categories of "golden oldies" and "classic rock" to be
mined for nostalgic re-creation rather than for their original significance
as youthful and rebellious cultural expression. Although their temporal coordinates and connotations obviously remain distinct, a soundtrack song
by either Frank Sinatra or Nirvana now functions to evoke and encapsulate
fondly recalled pasts for audiences.

Alongside the transformation of the film soundtrack, the success of
MTV and the music video format continued to emphasize popular film
songs as isolatable aesthetic objects or commodities, while the best-selling
compilation soundtracks for recent films have become an increasingly
effective means of producing synergetic revenue for the works they once
presumably summarized. A multidirectional marketing tool, the film
soundtrack, previously considered a souvenirlike reminder of an already
enjoyed film, now serves simultaneously as preview, tie-in, *and* supple-
ment, and in some cases soundtracks, whose success was once assumed
to derive *only* from a film's popularity, have sold well *despite* their affiliation with box-office flops: *Less Than Zero* (1987), *Boomerang* (1992), and
Above the Rim (1994) might stand for increasingly frequent examples. Contemporary film soundtracks are again often guided by demands obscure
to most audiences: since most entertainment companies are linked by intricate corporate ties, what might appear as aesthetic choices (choosing
and placing songs that best serve the meaning or mood of a film) are very
often straightforward marketing decisions, designed to showcase musical
acts on a media conglomerate's roster or to reinvigorate songs already in
its catalog, thereby promoting subsidiary but, at least to the public eye,
distinct products.[15]

The industrial and commercial contexts for the creation and current success of the compilation soundtrack have recently been explicated by Jeff Smith's illuminating study *The Sounds of Commerce*. In sections devoted specifically to the compilation soundtrack and the role of the music supervisor in the film production process, Smith persuasively demonstrates how the compilation soundtrack—which at first might seem to undermine the standard coherence of film scores due to its emphasis on isolated songs—has in practice served many of the traditional soundtrack's conventional functions.[16] In addition to its helpful historical survey, Smith's book effectively argues for the creative possibilities of the compilation score, despite the form's commonly being scorned or ignored by musicians and critics.

However, despite its impressive sweep and accumulation of information, Smith's study remains, with a few exceptions, focused upon American cinema and music, though Smith is clearly aware that the corporate changes he chronicles are global in their commercial reach and transnational in their capital holdings. Smith's extended analysis of the rock songs structuring the Danish film *Breaking the Waves* (1996) thus strikes an odd note in his text, since it only serves his structural but not clearly his industrial claims. But this curious selection, of an international "art film" co-production that nevertheless compiles its soundtrack in the mode of recent commercial Hollywood cinema, actually serves to highlight the fact that film scholars have, for over thirty years, not only neglected the compilation soundtrack's use in various kinds of cinema, from the underground classic *Scorpio Rising* (1963) to the art film remake *City of Angels* (1998), but that film studies has also consistently ignored the presence and function of popular music in international cinema.

Latin American, African, Arab, Eastern European, and even British musicals (such as the Jessie Matthews vehicles produced in the 1930s) have not played a significant part in studies of the genre, and even Cantopop's important function in Hong Kong movies remains largely ignored in the growing body of work on that internationally popular cinema.[17] Although the sustained study of popular music in national cinemas may eventually solicit the expert knowledge of area specialists, the ever-expanding international music industry clearly encourages musical production, marketing, and consumption to exceed national, cultural, and linguistic boundaries: film scholarship, while attentive to the identity claims made by national cinemas, has not apparently been listening very attentively to what Robert Burnett calls "the global jukebox," the international music industry whose relatively cheap products, including film soundtracks, cross borders far more easily and efficiently than films.[18] Our recently increased understanding of music in Hollywood cinema is certainly a sign of progress, but like many forms of information, this gain might also reveal some of the remaining gaps in our knowledge. For example, we might come to recognize that what looks relatively new in American movies looks rather conventional in Bombay.

The Hindi Film Song (Despite the Hollywood Musical)

In their groundbreaking history of Indian cinema, Erik Barnouw and S. Krishnaswamy noted that "the Indian sound film, unlike the sound films of any other land, had from its first moment seized *exclusively* on music-drama forms," an emphasis they attributed to India's "river of music, that had flowed through unbroken millennia of dramatic tradition."[19] In his more focused study, *Cassette Culture: Popular Music and Technology in North India*, ethnomusicologist Peter Manuel similarly but less carefully claims that "virtually all commercial Indian films have been musicals."[20] Manuel's actual point is the irrefutable fact that Indian popular cinema as a whole has been suffused with music and musical performance, but his casual use of the common genre term *musical* will certainly strike film scholars as immediately curious. Indeed, although the popular Indian film critic Chidananda Das Gupta claims that "India is one of the few countries in the world where every film is a musical," even he quickly qualifies his assertion in order to clarify that "Indian films are overloaded with songs, but very few are 'musicals' in the Western sense."[21] William O. Beeman more emphatically asserts that "no separate musical 'genre' can be said to have developed in Indian film, because music was a constant factor in all productions," so "it would be a mistake to consider Indian film, with song and dance as integral elements, to be in any way the Indian equivalent of the Western musical."[22] More recently Vinay Lal has written that Indian "popular films, some of them immensely long, were once divided into two categories, 'mythological' and 'social,' although at another level they all appear to belong to a genre more commonly associated with American cinema, the 'musical,'" though a footnote warns that Lal uses "the word 'musical' advisedly, and in a rather colloquial way, for as a genre the American 'musical' has certain formal elements which are lacking in its Indian counterpart."[23] M. Madhava Prasad, after acknowledging the larger and important claim that "the question of genre has been a notoriously difficult one for critics of Indian cinema," then remarks that "incipient generic distinctions are undermined by the expansive identity of the 'social,'" the latter itself another admittedly imprecise term: "The only element that is exclusive to the social and thus critical to its identification as a genre is its

29 Madhuri Dixit performs "Ek Do Teen" in *Tezaab* (1988). [Author's collection]

contemporary reference." Prasad nevertheless reidentifies the 'social' as a version of another, more familiar generic form: "With a few exceptions, these socials are usually musicals. The musical, which is an intermediate form in which cinema's links with the stage are worked out, and in which pre- and extra-cinematic skills and languages are put on display, has become a marginal form in Hollywood, whereas in the Hindi cinema the continuing dominance of the musical-social is a symptom of the continued dependence of the cinema on the resources of other cultural forms."[24] By relating the "musical-social" to Hollywood's "marginal form" but emphasizing their differences, Prasad tends to reinforce Barnouw and Krishnaswamy's earlier admonition that "the role of music reminds us that Indian cinema is not really comparable to cinema elsewhere."[25] Finally, in their recent introduction to popular Indian cinema, K. Moti Gokulsing and Wimal Dissanayake betray a continual uncertainty about which adjective should modify which noun: popular Indian films, they claim, "are largely melodramatic, often musicals."[26] Emphasizing that "Indian popular films are, as already noted, basically melodramas," the authors immediately renegotiate this claim by deciding, a few pages later, that "Indian popular films are generally melodramatic musicals which are non-naturalistic in the West-ern sense."[27] Their later identifications of popular films as "mostly roman-tic musicals" or "both romantic musicals and melodramas"[28] only empha-size the insecurity and instability lurking behind any such bold declarative statements.

As Prasad notes, the problem of genre may be general rather than spe-cific in discussions of Indian cinema, as Sanjeev Prakash also suggests when he says "it would be unfair to say that there are no clear genres" in Indian cinema, but recognizes that, "to the uninitiated observer, music and dance in the Indian popular cinema are so pervasive and overpower-ing as to set to naught all attempts to study genres, thematic development or stylistic nuance."[29] Broadly, as Ashish Rajadhyaksha and Paul Willemen note in their invaluable *Encyclopedia of Indian Cinema*, "a great deal more work needs to be done on the problems of defining, analyzing and peri-odizing genres in Indian Cinema."[30] As they emphasize, "many [Indian] films deliberately combine, as in a menu, elements from what in the West would be regarded as different genres," and so conventional Indian genres such as mythologicals, saint films, and stunt films are also thoroughly but implicitly musical forms, with the "musical" itself an uncommon— because redundant—designation serving almost all Bombay cinema. In short, there may be no distinguishable "musicals" in Bombay cinema pre-cisely because all of its products are so thoroughly musical. Typical block-buster "masala" or "omnibus" films such as the record-breaking *Sholay* (1975), given their standard three-hour running times, effectively cover the generic bases, mixing action, romance, comedy, melodrama, and—most consistently—elaborate sequences that "picturize" an average of five to six songs. Since, however, the presence of songs is not motivated generically, Indian films are often thought to risk narrative logic and overall coherence. As Manuel says, summarizing a common view, musical sequences, since they conventionally appear in almost all Hindi films, "may be dramatically functional . . . [but] more often the songs are more-or-less gratuitous in-sertions into the plot, to be enjoyed for their own sake."[31] Asha Kasbekar, on the other hand, finds that "critical studies of popular Indian Cinema tend to concentrate on the structural complexities of film plots and often ignore the extra-narrative texts that are provided by the songs. However, the plot of a film is deliberately engineered so as to provide openings for a song-and-dance number at regular intervals."[32] Indeed, the assumption that Bombay films are constructed as plots that get "interrupted" by songs, or, in the preferred terms of contemporary film theory, that the films are narratives disrupted by spectacle, may simply have things backwards. The

Hindi composer Vanraj Bhatia reinforces this perspective: "Film music is . . . more important than the film. Unlike the films of the West in which music plays a subservient role as a prop for the visuals, the Indian film finds its major strength in its music — many a bad film has been saved from oblivion by the popularity of its songs." As Bhatia says, "The most dramatic moments in our films are often those where all action stops and the song takes over." [33]

I have not quoted these frequently contradictory accounts simply to demonstrate an inconsistent use of terms or an unresolved debate regarding the designation of Indian genres, especially in relation to the Hollywood musical. These comments, in fact, seem more significant as a whole for their persistent attempts to make and then qualify analogies rather than for potentially successful clarifications by specific critics. Indeed, I think that the confusion surrounding the proper terms for comparing virtually all Hindi films to a single waning genre of the classical Hollywood cinema misrepresents the larger extent to which the song-dominated Hindi cinema *as a whole* resembles the increasingly song-dominated American cinema *as a whole* that has developed, through the compilation soundtrack, in the wake of the decline of a more delimited musical genre: again, the Bombay cinema provides an unacknowledged model for the body of American cinema which has, in effect, displaced the musical genre by effectively and persistently incorporating it. Critics of popular Indian cinema appear to stumble over generic terms and remain unable to clarify affiliations with Hollywood models because they wish to characterize the overriding element (picturized song sequences) that links almost all popular Indian films with a more specific form of classical Hollywood cinema. But while what seems plausible to say for Bombay films — "they're all musicals, they're all melodramas" — seems initially questionable to claim about the apparently more varied and heterogeneous Hollywood cinema, in fact it seems more and more convincing to declare the great majority of Hollywood films to be melodramas, which is then also to say, recalling the original meaning of that term, that most Hollywood films are musical — if not musicals.

More precisely, the common musical components of otherwise diverse films suggest their fundamental basis in the mode of melodrama, essentially defined as "a dramatic narrative in which musical accompaniment marks the emotional effects." This broad use of the term, according to Thomas Elsaesser's groundbreaking 1972 essay on film melodrama, "is still perhaps the most useful definition, because it allows melodramatic elements to be seen as constituents of a system of punctuation, giving expressive color and chromatic contrast to the story-line, by orchestrating the emotional ups and downs of the intrigue."[34] In this expansive elaboration, however, the inherent musical elements of melodrama (the melos directing the drama) have already become metaphors, whereas the contemporary Hollywood cinema, if any single dominant feature marks it, has been sure to punctuate its products with pop music. Although *Boogie Nights* might be, based upon a balance of elements, identified as a drama with comic moments (there are laughs tempering the pain), and *Romy and Michele's High School Reunion* recognized as a comedy with dramatic moments (there is pain beneath the laughter), their common soundtracks, even featuring those mix tapes which might as well be traded, work toward collapsing those differences. If a number of recent films (and of course their compilations soundtracks), including one with the actual title, have chronicled "the last days of disco," then Hollywood as a whole appears to be experiencing the last days of genre.

Recently, in an extremely persuasive and far-reaching essay, Linda Williams has argued that the recent identification and analysis of a distinct melodramatic *genre* has deflected the recognition of American cinema's fundamental melodramatic *mode,* which actually subtends most genres. For Williams, therefore, melodrama "is not a specific genre" but "is the fundamental mode of popular American motion pictures."[35] Arguing brilliantly against critical commonplaces which assert Hollywood's realist aesthetic, define melodrama in terms of excess, or associate melodrama exclusively with feminine emotion, Williams emphasizes "not that melodrama is a submerged, or embedded, tendency within realist narrative—which it certainly can be—but that it has more often itself been the dominant form of popular moving-image narrative." Recalling the often-neglected theatrical debts of Hollywood narratives, Williams concludes that "the basic vernacular of American moving pictures consists of a story that generates sympathy for a hero who is also a victim and that leads to a climax that permits the audience, and usually other characters, to recognize that character's moral value."[36] (It is hard not to recognize this "American" story as a perfect summary of the major 1970s films of Bollywood's superstar Amitabh Bachchan.) In related work, Rick Altman, revising his own groundbreaking work on the concept of genre in American cinema, has recalled the commercial imperative that always encouraged Hollywood films to be marketed and consumed as texts that combine genres or cross generic boundaries: "At every turn, we find that Hollywood labors to identify its pictures with multiple genres, in order to benefit from the increased interest that this strategy inspires in diverse demographic groups."[37]

In an earlier essay that in part motivated Williams's recent project, Altman also emphasized the intermediary role that popular theatre—theatrical melodrama as a mode—played in the transformation of novels into films, though film critics have most often bypassed that middle ground in their desire to demonstrate affinities between the novel and narrative cinema. It seems to me that Williams and Altman have accurately identified a perspective on American popular cinema that might crucially redirect our critical understanding of that enormous body of material. Williams, in fact, while concentrating on early cinema and especially the crucial figure of D. W. Griffith, also demonstrates the melodramatic underpinnings of a number of recent American films, including *Philadelphia* (1993), though she does not mention the "melodramatic" function of that film's compilation soundtrack, which places Bruce Springsteen and Neil Young alongside Sade and, in the film's emotional highpoint, Maria Callas.

In fact, a brief aside in Williams's discussion seems to acknowledge the importance of a topic she otherwise neglects. As a few persistent critics have attempted to remind the recent formulators of the melodramatic genre, music originally identifies the "melos" of melodrama. Seeking a clearer understanding of the complex feelings generated by the temporal and rhythmic elements of melodrama (such as a chase or rescue), Williams recognizes that "the best way to understand what we feel is to draw an analogy to music":

> The sustained play with hurry-up and slowdown is much like the approach to the end of a romantic symphony. Romantic music is the musical form that was adopted by what film historians have called the classical but I am calling the melodramatic cinema. Nineteenth-century symphonic music begins in an original key area, a home base (or tonic) out of which the variations and digressions into new keys and rhythms occur. It then returns in the final movement, with much fanfare, and sometimes considerable delay, to the tonic. Melodramatic narrative does much the same. Primed by the beginning tonic of the original theme—the register of the original space of innocence—the narrative wants to return to this point of origin and teases us throughout all subsequent development with the haunting threat of its loss.[38]

Although she soon moves away from her musical analogy, Williams claims that "this teasing delay of the forward moving march of time has not been sufficiently appreciated as key to the melodramatic effect. . . . The original patterns—whether of melody, key, rhythm, or of physical space and time—thus take on a visceral sort of ethics. They are *felt* as good."[39] While embedded within a wide-ranging essay, I think that the link Williams draws between melodrama and music to explain the pervasive and fundamental mode in American cinema gets to the heart of the matter, and I am even willing to suggest that Williams's exclusive focus upon the European Romantic tradition in music and the classical American cinema may unnecessarily limit the relevance of her claims for comparative cinema studies. Setting aside her reference to the distinctive structure of the Romantic symphony, Williams unintentionally moves us closer to understanding some of the pleasures and conventions—indeed, the pleasurable conventions, deeply tied to the "felt ethics" she emphasizes throughout her essay—of most Bombay cinema.

In yet another aside in what was one of the key texts for the recent reevaluation of film melodrama, Peter Brooks's *The Melodramatic Imagination*, he had already written "Not only is the very existence of melodrama as a distinct genre originally linked to its use of music, music is inherent to its representations, as to those of the cinema, its inheritor in this convention."[40] Williams in effect takes up this reminder, but only extends it a bit further herself. My sense is that the daring revision of contemporary film studies and American film history Williams proposes might be more completely developed though concentrated attention to the musical soundtracks that accompanied earlier Hollywood films—work that scholars like Gorbman, Kalinak, and Flinn have already undertaken—and which in their permutation as compilations now dominate popular cinema. As Peter Brooks also notes, "Through the film and the pervasive exploitation of background music, we have become so accustomed to music used toward the dramatization of life that it is difficult for us to recapture its radical effect, to measure its determination of our reading of the representations before us."[41] Insofar as the musical sequences in Bombay films remain unfamiliar to Western viewers—especially when they appear in the midst of action scenes and are performed by macho stars like the legendary Amitabh Bachchan—these moments, despite their adherence to conventions, might "recapture" the "radical effect" of musical dramatization that continues to define Bombay as well as Hollywood cinema.

Picturizing American Cinema (beyond Genre)

Now the mainstream Hollywood film regularly promises what Bombay has routinely delivered for fifty years: a collection of prominent, popular songs in virtually every film released. As Michel Chion has recently noted (though with reference to the voice), "radio has been showing up again and again as a subject" in recent cinema, justifying the inclusion of numerous pop songs in films as otherwise diverse as *Good Morning Vietnam* (1987), *Radio Days* (1987), and *Do the Right Thing* (1989).[42] In contemporary Hollywood, pop songs pervade, as one would expect, in biopics dealing with pop musicians (such as *Sweet Dreams* [1985], *La Bamba* [1986], *Great Balls of Fire!* [1989], *The Doors* [1991], *What's Love Got to Do with It?* [1993], and *Selena* [1997]) and occasional dance-dominated musicals (*Saturday Night Fever* [1977], *Flashdance* [1983], *Footloose* [1984], and *Dirty Dancing* [1987]) that generally, unlike earlier examples, rely upon prerecorded songs by singers and musicians not visible in the films. But the much more widespread compilation soundtrack marks—or more accurately blurs—all currently popular film genres, whether or not musical production or performance is a central focus of the narratives. All of the following examples, selected from the tip of Hollywood's iceberg, feature extensive pop soundtracks (in addition to more conventional scores) constructed for films that do not obviously call for such musical saturation. The conventional genre terms I have chosen in order to identify these films seem less compelling than the more pervasive convention of the compilation soundtrack that links these titles:

Action films: *Top Gun* (1986), *The Rock* (1996), *Armageddon* (1998)

Urban social dramas: *Colors* (1988), *Boyz in the Hood* (1991), *Juice* (1992), *Philadelphia* (1993), *Above the Rim* (1994), *Dangerous Minds* (1995)

Teen comedies: *Fast Times at Ridgemont High* (1982), *Wayne's World* (1992), *Reality Bites* (1994)

Contemporary film noir: *Goodfellas* (1990), *A Rage in Harlem* (1991), *True Romance* (1993), *Pulp Fiction* (1994), *Devil in a Blue Dress* (1995), *Casino* (1995), *Jackie Brown* (1997)

Romantic comedies: *Pretty in Pink, Cocktail* (1988), *When Harry Met Sally* (1989), *Pretty Woman* (1990), *Singles* (1992), *Four Weddings and a Funeral* (1994), *My Best Friend's Wedding* (1997), *You've Got Mail* (1998), *Notting Hill* (1999)

Romantic dramas: *City of Angels* (1998), *The Horse Whisperer* (1998)

Horror films: *Christine* (1983), *Scream* (1996), *I Know What You Did Last Summer* (1997)

Science fiction: *Freejack* (1992), *The Crow* (1994), *The X-Files* (1998), *The Matrix* (1999)

Contemporary adaptations of literary classics such as *Romeo and Juliet* (1996), *Great Expectations* (1998), or animated features like *Cool World* (1992) and *Space Jam* (1996), not to mention Disney's recent animated films (the real upholders of the model of the Hollywood musical), have also contributed to making the (live action) musical genre's earlier and somewhat distinctive function of foregrounding popular music increasingly unnecessary or redundant. If Bombay in some sense never needed the musical, with popular music supplied in abundance in all its films, then Hollywood may no longer need the musical, since popular music is now supplied in abundance in the majority of its films as well. As in Bombay, the regular and conventional use of popular music potentially overrides the genre distinctions that otherwise distinguish these films by narrative elements or iconic markers. Virtually all of the recent films I've mentioned in this essay feature at least one sequence in which diegetic sound is drained away so that a prominent song can overwhelm the visuals, so that even if songs are no longer performed in many contemporary films, key sequences of the films are constructed to emphasize or (we might finally appropriate the vivid Bollywood verb) "picturize" popular songs. K. J. Donnelly, for instance, has accurately described the sequence employing Prince's song "Party Man" in *Batman* as an instance in which "musical logic dominates visual and narrative logic" to the extent that "the song is articulating and creating the dynamics of the action in a way reminiscent of song sequences in film musicals."[43] There is plenty of evidence that this logic is at work in the construction of contemporary films: the director's comments on the DVD version of Wes Anderson's *Rushmore* (1998), for example, often acknowledge that sequences throughout the film were planned to follow the 1960s British Invasion songs which had already been selected for the soundtrack.

Aside from the sheer presence of music, the most distinctive characteristic of Hindi film music, and perhaps of Indian sound practice, is the regular and acknowledged use of a relatively small number of playback singers to perform the hundreds of songs produced annually by the film industry. In this case at least, the exceptional status of Indian cinema seems reaffirmed, and here the name of Lata Mangeshkar might be ritually invoked as the most legendary of Bombay's exceptions to any other cinema's standard figures.[44] Her career, stretching from 1947—the year of India's Independence—to the present has virtually defined the national female voice through more than five thousand recorded film songs in multiple languages.[45] Among other effects, the use of playback singers, whose voices have sometimes but not exclusively been associated with specific

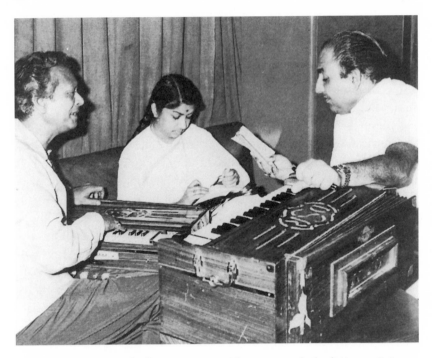

30 Naushad (Hindi-Urdu film composer) with superstar playback singers Lata Mangeshkar and Mohammed Rafi. [Author's collection]

film stars, has split stardom between the screen and soundtrack. Mangeshkar's stardom does not fully overlap with, but coexists alongside and now often exceeds the fame of the female stars who appropriate her voice. The popular live musical shows of Indian performers produced for diasporic audiences in Europe and the United States emphasize this split in celebrity too, since they commonly feature either the heretofore invisible singers and musicians who record for the Bombay industry, *or* major film stars, who lip-synch and dance in person to the prerecorded backing tracks from their most popular films. Although the Bombay song sequence, unlike many of the interpolated songs of current Hollywood practice, would commonly be identified as "diegetic," given their elaborate mouthing on screen, the conventional use of playback singers always underlines the split between image and sound which, as critics of the musical have demonstrated, Hollywood even in its most unrealistic genres worked to obscure: Bombay cinema, in other words, allows the playback singer Asha Bhosle (Lata's similarly legendary sister) a fame that Hollywood could never accord the frequent vocal dubber Marni Nixon. (The recent Britpop band

31 Advertisement for live show of Indian film stars in Ft. Lauderdale, Florida (1998). [Author's collection]

Cornershop's hit single "Brimful of Asha" is at least one piece of evidence for this claim.) Most importantly and aside from the impact upon stardom, the acknowledged use of playback singers as a recording practice itself encourages Bombay film songs to be consumed as discrete units of construction. Although they provide the music for diegetic performances, Bombay songs are recognized to also be nondiegetic sound, music whose source is elsewhere even as it supports visual responses in the story space, a seeming contradiction that in fact illuminates recent Hollywood practice.

Although some Hollywood films seek to imply diegetic sources for the songs on their compilation scores, most announce their sonic distance from and origins outside the space of the narrative; this is especially the case when popular songs are well known before they appear in a film, even if their reappropriation serves additional purposes. When, for example, Gene Autry's recording of "Back in the Saddle Again" comments on a widower's reentry into dating in *Sleepless in Seattle,* the age and familiarity of the song also affirm its still separate status as an aesthetic and even commercial entity. While, therefore, the playback singer has no obvious equivalents in Hollywood practice, the gap that playback singing holds wide open for Indian audiences has also become more visible in contemporary American film.

Although the many formal implications of this increasingly acknowledged gap between sound and image deserve further attention, I want to emphasize that Bombay and Hollywood also suggest an ongoing conceptual merger in current soundtrack marketing rather than film style, where significant formal differences actually remain vivid. Bombay film songs can be and are commonly marketed as works by their singers and, notably, their composers and lyricists, whose names are as well known to fans as those of the actors who visualize the songs. The ease with which songs can be extricated from films perhaps explains a common but initially curious element in the marketing of Indian soundtrack albums. Although, for example, the CD packaging of soundtracks to the recent blockbuster films *Dilwale Dulhania Le Jayenge* (1997), *Pardes* (1997), *Dil to Pagal Hai* (1997), and *Dil se . . .* (1998) all feature images of current megastar leading man Shah Rukh Kahn, none use his or his equally famous female co-stars' names on their covers. Credits for music and lyrics are featured, however, and song titles are all accompanied by the names of their singers, or "artistes." While at one level it's unnecessary to provide the names of instantly recognizable film superstars, I want to emphasize that the explicit separation of image and sound announced in the on-screen credits of Hindi films is extended even more fully into the marketing of film music—which is, more or less, Indian popular music—where stars may still provide visual appeal but are not confused with or nominally associated with the musical content of the songs otherwise linked to their films. Compilation albums of film songs by single playback singers, male-female duos, or composers are also common, emphasizing the organizational link provided by musical talent rather than the sequences established by the films in which hit songs appear. This pattern has now extended to video and DVD compilations, such as the recent *Lata Mangeshkar: The Queen of Melody*, which may feature a singer—who, again, does not appear on screen—as the significant link between diverse films, stars, and visual styles.

Accepting significant cultural differences in style and content, this dominant model for the marketing of Hindi soundtracks resembles in form the relatively recent phenomenon of major pop musicians producing albums that at once serve their fans and the consumers of a particular film soundtrack, groups that might but need not fully overlap. Prince's *Batman* soundtrack, Madonna's *I'm Breathless* (of songs "inspired by" *Dick Tracy*), and Björk's *Selmasongs–Music from the Motion Picture "Dancer in the Dark"* all suggest not just a full merging of corporate interests but a full breakdown in typical distinctions between a musician's work—having a certain status in their own artistic and commercial development—and a sound-track album of music serving the demands of a film. Such examples, along with the now common fact that at any given moment approximately a fifth of the best-selling albums on the American pop charts are film sound-tracks, eventually demonstrate a curious logic. As the film and music industries become increasingly intertwined, with all of their products simultaneously seeking to market each other through both intricate and bluntly obvious cross-references, the once-presumed links between a film and its songs have shifted unexpectedly: once again, the film soundtrack no longer necessarily functions as a secondary object, a souvenir, of the enjoyed film. In India, virtually all popular music is film music, and many songs become popular in spite of or irrespective of their films. For the entertainment industries centered in Hollywood, the situation in Bombay is still a marketing dream, but one which, nonetheless, promises eventual realization: in the future, all popular American music could be film music too. And while it's not absolutely necessary for profits, if the consumers of this music also happen to go to see the movies that include those songs— Hollywood may be dreaming—so much the better.

Notes

Thanks to Pam and Arthur for encouragement and patience, to Philip Lutgendorf, Ashish Rajadhyaksha, and Neepa Majumdar for opening my eyes and ears to Indian cinema, and to Rick Altman and the Sound Research Seminar for regular (super) sonic ideas.

1   Hereafter, the terms *Indian popular cinema, Bombay cinema, or Hindi cinema* will be used to represent the largest popular, commercial cinema industry in India and, it is often claimed, the world. Although widely used by fans and the industry itself, the term *Bollywood* is somewhat controversial, and clearly retains derisive overtones. It is also important to acknowledge the existence of other popular "Indian cinemas," including the equally large Tamil and Telegu industries. For a brief overview of India's regional cinemas, see K. Moti Gokulsing and Wimal Dissanayake, *Indian Popular Cinema: A Narrative of Cultural Change* (Stoke on Trent: Trentham Books, 1998), 123–31. The best brief overviews of Indian cinema are provided by Ashish Rajadhyaksha, "Indian Cinema: Origins to Independence," and "India: Filming the Nation," in *The Oxford History of World Cinema*, ed. Geoffrey Nowell-Smith (New York: Oxford University Press, 1996), 398–409 and 678–89. Recently, British film criticism and film studies pedagogy have taken more notice of Bombay cinema. See Heather Tyrrell, "Bollywood in Britain," *Sight and Sound* 8.8 (1998): 20–22, and Asha Kasbekar's "An Introduction to Indian Cinema," in *An Introduction to Film Studies*, 2nd ed.,

ed. Jill Nelmes (London: Routledge, 1999), 381–415. While Indian cinema and culture have a more visible presence in England than in the United States, this seems a poor excuse for the consistent neglect of Hindi cinema by American film critics and teachers.

2 See Paul Willemen, "The National" and "The Third Cinema Question" in *Looks and Frictions: Essays in Cultural Studies and Film Theory* (London: BFI, 1994). I am referring here specifically to Rajadhyaksha's brilliant lectures for a course on Indian silent cinema at the University of Iowa in 1988, but also see Rajadh-yaksha, "Neo-Traditionalism: Film as Popular Art in India," *Framework* 32–33 (1986): 21–67; and "The Phalke Era: Conflict of Traditional Form and Modern Technology," in *Interrogating Modernity: Culture and Colonialism in India*, ed. Tejaswini Niranjana, P. Sudhir, and Vivek Dhareshwar (Calcutta: Seagull Books, 1993), 47–82.

3 Willemen, "The National," 214. See also the important first footnote to "The Third Cinema Question," 203, which specifically criticizes the tendency to iden-tify national exceptions to mainstream definitions, rather than to recognize such "exceptions" as important challenges to the definitions themselves: as Willemen insists, if "Indian melodrama" does not fit general Western defini-tions of "melodrama," the latter rather than the former should be put into ques-tion.

4 Here one might also cite the now virtually obligatory references to Bombay films, stars, and songs throughout the English-language fiction of such inter-nationally prominent diasporic Indian writers as Salman Rushdie (*The Satanic Verses*) or Shashi Tharoor (*Show Business*), and especially in the work of the younger generation that includes Vikram Chandra (*Red Earth and Pouring Rain*), Ameena Meer (*Bombay Talkie*), and Ardashir Vakil (*Beach Boy*). Another version of a cross-cultural phenomenon is discussed in Amit Rai, "An American Raj in Filmistan: Images of Elvis in Indian Films," *Screen* 35.1 (1994): 51–77.

5 Satyajit Ray, "Those Songs," in *Our Films, Their Films: Essays* (New York: Hy-perion, 1994), 72–75. Ray's essay was originally published in 1967. Though he presents himself as a fan of film songs, Ray admits, "If I were asked to find room for six songs in a story that is not expressly a 'musical', I would have to throw up my hands and give up. If I were forced, I would either revolt or go berserk. And yet six songs per film, per *every* film, is the accepted average, and at no point in the history of Indian films has there been an uproar against it except from a tiny highbrow minority who write about it in snickering terms in the pages of little magazines whose readership would barely fill a decent-sized cinema" (73).

6 Actually, as Rick Altman has noted, film music has always received a fair amount of attention despite protests to the contrary, whereas most other aspects of film sound have been neglected. See Rick Altman, "Introduction: Sound's Dark Cor-ners," in *Sound Theory Sound Practice*, ed. Rick Altman (New York: Routledge, 1992), 173. Nonetheless, ongoing attention to film scores by film studies schol-ars is a recent phenomenon. For more on the literature on film scoring, see Knight and Wojcik's introduction and Altman's essay in this volume.

7 In a recent edition of his book on film composers, Tony Thomas, for example,

makes the bizarre claim that "with the emergence of rock-and-roll . . . more and more film scores emerged with pop-orientated [*sic*] music, often using rock or folk musicians on the soundtrack. The folly of that method became apparent and within a few years it ceased." See Tony Thomas, *Music for the Movies*, 2nd ed. (Los Angeles: Silman-James Press, 1997), 13.

8   See Laura Morgan, "Same Old Song," *Entertainment Weekly*, 19 November 1999, 29.

9   See K. J. Donnelly, "The Classical Film Score Forever? *Batman, Batman Returns*, and Post-Classical Film Music," in *Contemporary Hollywood Cinema*, ed. Steve Neale and Murray Smith (New York: Routledge, 1998), 144–45.

10 Marshall Crenshaw, *Hollywood Rock: A Guide to Rock 'n' Roll in the Movies*, ed. Ted Mico (New York: Harper Perennial, 1994), 8. Likewise, Mark Thomas McGee insists that "performers of the music must be onscreen for the music to rate an entry" in *The Rock and Roll Movie Encyclopedia of the 1950s* (Jefferson, N.C.: McFarland, 1990), x. Linda J. Sandahl, however, includes approximately fifty compilation soundtracks (along with a smaller number of single-artist soundtracks) in her *Encyclopedia of Rock Music in Film: A Viewer's Guide to Three Decades of Musicals, Concerts, Documentaries, and Soundtracks, 1955–1986* (New York: Blandford, 1987), 179–200. The chapter on "Soundtrack Rock" in another popular guide is brief but especially insightful: see David Ehrenstein and Bill Reed, *Rock on Film* (New York: Delilah Books, 1982), 64–73.

11 For example, Kristin Thompson's otherwise illuminating *Storytelling in the New Hollywood: Understanding Classical Narrative Technique* (Cambridge, Mass.: Harvard University Press, 1999), which demonstrates narrative continuities between classical and contemporary Hollywood cinema, pays scant attention to the use of pop songs in some of the films she analyzes (especially *Desperately Seeking Susan*), though Thompson generally chooses to analyze recent films that feature more conventional scores. The familiar opposition in film studies between "diegetic" sound (with an ostensible source within the world of the narrative, whether visible or not) and "nondiegetic" sound (lacking a source in the story space) generally assumes a distinction that recent films increasingly blur by often suggesting but not fully clarifying that all of a film's "soundtrack" songs may be diegetic, with sources in, for instance, the urban or suburban landscapes of contemporary youth culture: all of the songs in *Desperately Seeking Susan*, for example, have possible diegetic sources, though the songs are not always acoustically realistic. The contemporary pop soundtrack has not been entirely neglected by scholars, but given the pervasiveness of the practice I'm describing, the topic remains surprisingly marginal within recent criticism. For an exception, in addition to Donnelly's "The Classical Film Score Forever?", see Kevin J. H. Dettmar and William Richey, "Musical Cheese: The Appropriation of Seventies Music in Nineties Movies," in *Reading Rock and Roll: Authenticity, Appropriation, Aesthetics*, ed. Dettmar and Richey (New York: Columbia University Press, 1999), 311–26.

12 Gary Marmorstein, *Hollywood Rhapsody: Movie Music and Its Makers, 1900 to 1975* (New York: Schirmer Books, 1997), 402. Marmorstein's overview is often

useful but contains errors that rock fans will find laughable; for instance, he misquotes the opening line of Elvis Presley's "Jailhouse Rock" as "Once [sic] threw a party in the country jail" (391), and rearranges the songs of *Saturday Night Fever* when he refers to "the title sequence, in which the title tune [sic] plays over a high-heeled John Travolta strutting along a Bay Ridge avenue" (399). Illuminating studies of the ever-narrowing entertainment industry include: Ben H. Bagdikian, *The Media Monopoly*, 5th ed. (Boston: Beacon Press, 1997); Jon Lewis, "Money Matters: Hollywood in the Corporate Era," in *The New American Cinema*, ed. Lewis (Durham, N.C.: Duke University Press, 1988), 87–121; and Thomas Schatz, "The Return of the Hollywood Studio System," in *Conglomerates and the Media*, ed. Erik Barnouw et al. (New York: New Press, 1997), 73–106. Although neglected by critics, in the music industry trade journal *Billboard*, compilation soundtracks receive a great deal of regular attention: see, for example, J. R. Reynolds, "Soundtrack Boom Offers Exposure for R&B Acts," *Billboard*, 1 February 1997, 1, 67–68; Catherine Applefeld Olson, "Soundtracks: The Reel Thing: Soundtrack Sales Stronger Than Ever, as Film and Music Learn to Get Along," *Billboard*, 26 April 1997, 17, 19, 24, 26; Chris Morris, "Soundtracks Offer Sweet Relief to Retail," *Billboard*, 26 April 1997, 1, 97.

13   Mark Evans, *Soundtrack: The Music of the Movies* (New York: Hopkinson & Blake, 1975), 202–3. The book seems written under the restrictive weight of its short introduction by legendary Hollywood composer Miklos Rozsa, who muses that "although the quality of film music today has declined, the public's nostalgia for the film music of the Golden Age of the movies is at a high peak" (n.p.). Evans also quotes Rozsa's hopelessly square judgment that rock and roll is "the most God-awful noise mankind has invented since leaving the jungle. It is thrown into every film. They say, 'The kids like it. Play for the kids.' If the kids like sex, violence, and horror, we do not help them change their values; we are merely playing down for the dollar" (208). Although Rozsa sounds like every clichéd antirock parent in 1950s exploitation films, his recognition of the shifting demographics and commercial imperatives of film music are at least hard to deny.

14   On the importance of *Easy Rider*'s songs, see Lee Hill, *Easy Rider* (London: BFI, 1996), 28, though Hill seems to greatly underestimate the soundtrack's impact on later Hollywood practice. According to David Ehrenstein and Bill Reed, many of the songs in *Easy Rider* "substitute for plot, dialogue, and characterization," demonstrating "rock music's ability to fill in gaps where narrative imagination flagged." However, they claim, "After *American Graffiti*, the sound of rock in the movies would no longer mean that the action would have to come to a halt" (67, 70). On the equally influential soundtrack for *The Graduate*, see Susan Knobloch, "*The Graduate* as Rock 'n' Roll Film," *Spectator* 17.2 (1997): 61–73. According to Roy M. Prendergast, *The Graduate* shoulders some of the blame for later practice: "Matters became worse in 1968 with the success of the film *The Graduate*, which contained a string of Simon and Garfunkel pop tunes. Now, it seemed, not one pop tune was enough; there must be a *collection* of pop tunes which, incidentally, create a nice record album. It so happened, as we have seen in the past, that the concept of a series of pop tunes used to accompany the vari-

ous surrealistic montage sequences in *The Graduate* worked very well aesthetically, but the success of the picture and the accompanying soundtrack created a host of musical imitators." See Roy M. Prendergast, *Film Music: A Neglected Art,* 2nd ed. (New York: Norton, 1977), 148. Ehrenstein and Reed, conversely, judge *The Graduate* the "watershed film . . . which took the integration of rock sounds with storytelling onto a new and more ambitious level." See *Rock on Film,* 66. Although these three films are the most commonly cited for their creative and influential integration of rock songs, Ehrenstein and Reed usefully identify a number of other significant though less often recalled examples, including Hal Ashby's *Shampoo* (1975) and *Coming Home* (1977). The revised version of Manvell and Huntley's *The Technique of Film Music* (first published in 1957) includes a brief but interesting discussion of the "exclusively pop score" featuring "a surprising choice of groups" used in Michaelangelo Antonioni's *Zabriskie Point* (1968); see Roger Manvell and John Huntley, *The Technique of Film Music,* rev. ed. by Richard Arnell and Peter Day (New York: Hastings House, 1975), 260–63.

15 A number of filmmakers have expressed their dismay and capitulation to the demands of corporate marketing regarding soundtrack choices. Director Penelope Spheeris, for example, notes that she had no control over the selection of songs for the soundtrack and Warner Bros. album for *Wayne's World.* See Jonathan Romney and Adrian Wootton, eds., *Celluloid Jukebox: Popular Music and the Movies since the 50s* (London: BFI, 1995), 133–35.

16 Jeff Smith, *The Sounds of Commerce: Marketing Popular Film Music* (New York: Columbia University Press, 1998). Other recent studies complement Smith's more rigorous book in some ways. See Russell Lack, *Twenty-Four Frames Under: A Buried History of Film Music* (London: Quartet Books, 1997), esp. 207–31 on pop music, and John Mundy, *Popular Music on Screen: From Hollywood Musical to Music Video* (Manchester: Manchester University Press, 1999), which treats pop compilation soundtracks briefly in its final chapter. R. Serge Denisoff and William D. Romanowski, *Risky Business: Rock in Film* (New Brunswick, N.J.: Transaction Publishers, 1991), is valuable for its wealth of detailed information, though it does not take a distinct critical perspective on the material it accumulates.

17 See, however, Steven Teo's fascinating discussion of Hong Kong's "sing-song girl" films of the late 1950s and early 1960s in *Hong Kong Cinema: The Extra Dimensions* (London: Routledge, 1997), 29–39. As Teo reports, most Mandarin films in this period, "regardless of genres, featured a tune or two" (29), often in *chaqu,* "inserted musical sequences" which "tended to have a life of their own" (30). Teo clarifies that *chaqu* were eventually differentiated from "full-fledged" musicals (*gechang pian*) and opera films (*xiqu*) (31). I should also note that the late John Kobal's unjustly ignored history of the film musical also includes a valuable chapter on (also ignored) European musicals: see John Kobal, *Gotta Sing, Gotta Dance: A History of Movie Musicals,* rev. ed. (London: Spring Books, 1983), 44–87. There are a few (English-language) exceptions worth noting, though none has effected the needed (re)examination of the musical as an international genre or of popular film music as a comparative topic. See, for ex-

ample: David Martinez, "Chasing the Metaphysical Express: Music in the Films of Wong Kar-Wai," in *Wong Kar-Wai*, ed. Jean-Marc Lalanne, David Martinez, Ackbar Abbas, and Jimmy Ngai (Paris: Éditions Dis Voir, 1997), 29–35; Yeh Yueh-yu, "A Life of Its Own: Musical Discourses in Wong Kar-Wai's Films," *Post Script* 19.1 (1999): 120–36; and Viola Shafik, *Arab Cinema: History and Cultural Identity* (Cairo: American University in Cairo Press, 1998), 101–20.

18 See Robert Burnett, *The Global Jukebox: The International Music Industy* (London: Routledge, 1996); for additional accounts of the increasingly global music-entertainment industry, see Pekka Gronow and Ilpo Saunio, *An International History of the Recording Industry*, trans. Christopher Moseley (London: Cassell, 1998); Michael Chanan, *Repeated Takes: A Short History of Recording and Its Effects on Music* (London: Verso, 1995), 151–78; Keith Negus, *Music Genres and Corporate Cultures* (London: Routledge, 1999), 152–72; and Andre Millard, *America on Record: A History of Recorded Sound* (Cambridge: Cambridge University Press, 1995), 331–45. For a less neutral account of the concentration of entertainment media into a few conglomerates, see Ben H. Bagdikian, *The Media Monopoly*, 5th ed. (Boston: Beacon Press, 1997).

19 Erik Barnouw and S. Krishaswamy, *Indian Film*, 2nd ed. (New York: Oxford University Press, 1980), 69, 72.

20 Peter Manuel, *Cassette Culture: Popular Music and Technology in North India* (Chicago: University of Chicago Press, 1993), 41.

21 Chidananda Das Gupta, *Talking about Films* (New Delhi: Orient Longman, 1981), 30. See also Das Gupta, *The Painted Face: Studies in India's Popular Cinema* (New Delhi: Roli Books, 1991), 59–69.

22 William O. Beeman, "The Use of Music in Popular Film: East and West," *India International Centre Quarterly* 8.1 (1981): 85, 82. Nonetheless, in Narendra Sharma's survey he claims that in the second decade of sound film, "the film song emerged as a star item in the film. It no longer was a mere functionary. On the film song depended the popularity of the film, that is its repeat value and box-office returns. . . . [F]or the most part, films had to be musicals!" See Narendra Sharma, "Half a Century of Song," *Cinema Vision India* 1.4 (1980): 58. Obviously, the use of the term *musical* is implicitly at stake in these discussions.

23 Vinal Lal, "The Impossibility of the Outsider in the Modern Hindi Film," in *The Secret Politics of Our Desires: Innocence, Culpability and Indian Popular Cinema*, ed. Ashis Nandy (London: Zed Books, 1998), 228, 254.

24 M. Madhava Prasad, *Ideology of the Hindi Film: A Historical Construction* (Delhi: Oxford University Press, 1998), 135–36.

25 Barnouw and Krishnaswamy, *Indian Film*, 279.

26 Gokulsing and Dissanayake, *Indian Popular Cinema*, 23.

27 Ibid., 27, 29.

28 Ibid., 93, 96.

29 Sanjeev Prakash, "Music, Dance and the Popular Films: Indian Fantasies, Indian Repressions," in *Indian Cinema Superbazaar*, ed. Aruna Vasudev and Phillipe Lenglet (New Delhi: Vikas Publishing House, 1983), 114.

30 Ashish Rajadhyaksha and Paul Willemen, *Encyclopaedia of Indian Cinema*, rev. ed. (London: BFI and Oxford University Press, 1999), 13.

31 Manuel, *Cassette Culture*, 41.

32 Kasbekar, "An Introduction to Indian Cinema," 385.

33 Vanraj Bhatia, "Stop the Action, Start the Song," *Cinema Vision India* 1.4 (1980): 33. This was a special issue of "India's first professional Cinema quarterly" (now defunct) devoted to the Indian film song. Other useful material on Indian film songs includes Alison E. Arnold, "Hindi filmi git: On the History of Commercial Indian Popular Music" (Ph.D. diss., University of Illinois, Urbana-Champaign, 1991); Alison E. Arnold, "Popular Film Song in India: A Case of Mass-Market Musical Eclecticism," *Popular Music* 7.2 (1988): 177–88; Bhaskar Chandavarkar, "Indian Film Song," in *70 Years of Indian Cinema*, ed. T. M. Ramachandran (Bombay: CINEMA India-International, 1985); Anupama Chandra, "Music Mania," *India Today*, 15 November 1994, 180–97; Anupama Chandra and Kavita Shetty, "Hitting the Right Notes," *India Today*, 30 November 1993, 52–53; Partha Chatterjee, "When Melody Ruled the Day" and "A Bit of Song and Dance," in *Frames of Mind: Reflections on Indian Cinema*, ed. Arnua Vasudev (New Delhi: UBSPD, 1995), 51–65, 197–218; Darius Cooper, "The Hindi Film Song and Guru Dutt," *East-West Film Journal* 2.2 (1988): 49–65; Carlo Coppola, "Politics, Social Criticism and Indian Film Songs: The Case of Sahir Ludhianvi," *Journal of Popular Culture* 10.4 (1977): 897–902; Sanjeev Prakash, "Music, Dance and the Popular Films: Indian Fantasies, Indian Repressions," in *Indian Cinema Superbazaar*, ed. Aruna Vasudev and Philippe Lenglet (New Delhi: Vikas Publishing House, 1983), 114–18; Ashok Ranade, "The Extraordinary Importance of the Indian Film Song," *Cinema Vision India* 1.4 (1980): 4–11; Madan Gopal Singh, "Jottings on the Indian Film Song: If Music Be the Food of Love . . ." *Cinemaya* 39–40 (1998): 4–9; Teri Skillman, "Songs in Hindi Films: Nature and Function," in *Cinema and Cultural Identity: Reflections on Films from Japan, India, and China*, ed. Wimal Dissanayake (Lanham: University Press of America, 1988), 149–58; Teri Skillman, "The Bombay Hindi Film Song," in *Yearbook for Traditional Music 1986* (New York: International Council for Traditional Music, 1986), 133–44. Also see the special issues of *CinemaVision India* 2.2 (1983): "Mortal Men, Immortal Melodies: The Golden Age of Hindi Film Music," and *Cinema Vision India* 1.4 (1980): "The Rise of the Indian Film Song."

34 Thomas Elsaesser, "Tales of Sound and Fury: Observations on the Family Melodrama," in *Home Is Where the Heart Is: Studies in Melodrama and the Woman's Film*, ed. Christine Gledhill (London: BFI, 1987), 50. See also Ravi Vasudevan, "The Melodramatic Mode and Commercial Hindi Cinema: Notes on Film History, Narrative and Performance in the 1950s," *Screen* 30.3 (1989): 29–50.

35 Linda Williams, "Melodrama Revised," in *Refiguring American Film Genres: Theory and History*, ed. Nick Browne (Berkeley: University of California Press, 1998), 42.

36 Ibid., 58.

37 Rick Altman, *Film/Genre* (London: BFI, 1999) 57. Altman demonstrates this

point with examples from the 1930s to 1988's *Cocktail*. He also discusses the history of the category of melodrama within film studies: see 69–77. Williams bases some of her argument upon Altman's earlier essay emphasizing the common neglect of theatrical versions of popular novels by film critics: see Altman, "Dickens, Griffith, and Film Theory Today," *South Atlantic Quarterly* 88.2 (1989): 321–59.

38 Williams, "Melodrama Revised," 73.

39 Ibid., 74.

40 Peter Brooks, *The Melodramatic Imagination: Balzac, Henry James, Melodrama, and the Mode of Excess* (1976; reprint, New York: Columbia University Press, 1984), 48. For a fascinating essay that develops these ideas in another national context, see Caryl Flinn, "Music and the Melodramatic Past of New German Cinema," *Melodrama: Stage, Picture, Screen*, ed. Jacky Bratton, Jim Cook, and Christine Gledhill (London: BFI, 1994) 106–18.

41 Brooks, *The Melodramatic Imagination*, 49.

42 Michel Chion, *The Voice in Cinema*, trans. Claudia Gorbman (New York: Columbia Univesity Press, 1999), 167. Chion's comments are part of his epilogue for the English translation of his book, originally published in 1982.

43 Donnelly, "The Classical Film Score Forever?", 148.

44 In addition to Neepa Majumdar's illuminating essay in this volume, see the two hagiographic biographies: Raju Bharatan, *Lata Mangeshkar: A Biography* (New Delhi: UBSPD, 1995), and Harish Bhimani, *In Search of Lata Mangeshkar* (New Delhi: Indus, 1995). I am grateful to Ashish Rajadhyaksha for bestowing these instruments of worship upon an incipient fan.

45 In addition to the (often debated) total numbers, one can gauge her impact by perusing the celebratory sets *50 Glorious Years* (Gramaphone Company of India, 1996 and 1997), two volumes of five CDS each, in which her voice dominates the collection of "Independent India's Greatest Hits." Among her hundreds of recordings, a helpful overview is available through the five-CD set *Lata Mangeshkar: The Nightingale*, in the "Legends" series (Gramaphone Company of India/RPG, 1997).

Popular Songs and Comic Allusion in Contemporary Cinema

JEFF SMITH

Consider the following scene from *Con Air* (1997). The plot of this Jerry Bruckheimer action film concerns the escape attempt of several barbarous inmates, who stage a daring skyjack during a simple prison transfer operation. When Cyrus "The Virus" Grissom (John Malkovich) and his cohorts succeed in gaining control of the plane (a second time), they celebrate by singing and dancing to the Lynyrd Skynyrd classic "Sweet Home Alabama." The film's reluctant hero, Cameron Poe (Nicolas Cage), looks on and wonders whether he will ever return to his home. A former special forces officer, Poe had hoped to serve the brief remainder of his sentence and return to his wife and child in Alabama. At the same time, however, the film's most vicious murderer, a cannibalistic serial killer named Garland "the Marietta Mangler" (Steve Buscemi), points out a second irony in the use of "Sweet Home Alabama." Watching the inmates' celebration, Garland observes: "Define irony. A bunch of idiots dancing on a plane to a song made famous by a band that died in a plane crash."

While this example from *Con Air* is characteristic of the ways pop songs frequently function in films, it is somewhat unusual to the extent that it "bares the device" of such musical allusion.[1] Garland serves as a kind of diegetic auditor in the film, reminding spectators of the ironic function of the Skynyrd tune. In this sense, the character also serves as a surrogate for the film's narration. By explaining the reference for us, Garland invites us to admire the cleverness of the allusion as well as its self-consciousness. As this example implies, the use of songs as ironic commentary may be viewed as a particular configuration of postmodern culture, where a very self-conscious mode of textual address is situated within a larger network of intertextual references.

As this example from *Con Air* also indicates, the use of popular music in such ironic modes has become an ever more important part of cinematic signification. In fact, within the film industry, music supervisors commonly refer to such locutions as "joke cues," and they must be identified as such when requesting copyright clearance from the song's publisher or the recording artist's record label.[2] Moreover, in a recent interview, singer/songwriter Michael Penn, who scored the film *Boogie Nights* (1997), claimed that the music in *Boogie Nights* was "not only integral to the vibe of the movie" but also functioned as "commentary, whether it's just sort of a stupid pun or some real undercurrent of what's happening on screen."[3]

As these examples indicate, contemporary cinema is marked by a more general tendency to use pop songs as a resource for humorous allusions, one that comments on the situations depicted in a film either through its lyrical content or through an extramusical system of pop culture references. But what does it mean to describe a song as a pun? What specific textual operations are necessary for a pop song to function as a form of ironic commentary? What features of the film text does the music comment on? What accounts for the current prevalence of musical allusion and to what extent is this specific practice informed by larger economic, cultural, and historical contexts?

These issues can be approached by categorizing forms of popular musical allusion and by placing them within a broader historical and theoretical framework. Despite the innovative character of the present techniques, comic uses of popular music have a long history in American cinema. Chuck Berg notes, for example, that certain silent film accompanists, known as "film funners," established reputations based on their ability to use music as a form of ironic commentary. According to Berg, "such a performer often became a distinct feature of the house for which he played and was sure of an audience of his own which came largely 'to see what he would do with the pictures.'"[4] Similarly, in a study of African American exhibition sites in Chicago, Mary Carbine points out that the improvised accompaniment of ragtime bands during the silent era sometimes worked as a form of wry wit for both audiences and performers alike.[5] Such uses of music, however, became less and less common once silent film accompaniments began to be standardized, and broader notions of appropriateness and restraint gradually eliminated the kinds of musical spoofing practiced by the "film funners."[6]

As cinema entered the sound era, the use of music as ironic commentary or wordplay was mostly confined to animated shorts, especially those produced by Warner Bros. and MGM. According to Daniel Goldmark, the time pressures associated with animation production encouraged the use of specific compositional shortcuts in order to produce the requisite six-minute score that was expected each week. In the case of Carl Stalling, the easiest way for him to meet those demands was to use the titles of musical works as a quick and dirty means of matching music to onscreen actions. As director Chuck Jones put it, "If there was a lady dressed in red, he'd always play 'The Lady in Red.' If somebody went into a cave, he'd play 'Fingal's Cave.' If we were doing anything about eating, he'd do 'A Cup of Coffee, a Sandwich and You.'"[7] Over time, Stalling's compositional shorthand evolved into a highly personal and idiosyncratic style that strung together very brief snippets of popular songs as accompaniment to the cartoon's progression from gag to gag. In *Mouse-Warming* (1952), for example, Stalling's six-minute score borrows melodies from more than a dozen different sources, and rapidly moves from theme to theme, using the associational elements of each piece's title to create a semantic correlation between music and visual gag.[8]

The referentiality of Stalling's work, however, was generally not typical of scores composed for classical Hollywood features, and as such, the use of musical irony generally took on a less specifically comic tone. Instead, as Claudia Gorbman notes, when music functioned ironically in classical Hollywood films, it typically did so by adopting an anempathetic relation to the narrative. In such instances, the music appears to be unaware of or indifferent to the dramatic situation depicted onscreen. The emotional power of anempathetic music comes from its very emotionlessness, the sense that it remains blissfully ignorant of the human calamities it accompanies.[9]

The use of songs toward more overtly comic ends, such as puns or as ironic commentary, was relatively rare in feature films during the classical Hollywood studio era. There are some well-known exceptions to this, of course, such as the use of "It's a Most Unusual Day" to accompany Roger Thornhill's ensnarement in international intrigue in Alfred Hitchcock's *North by Northwest* (1959). A more interesting, if somewhat less famous, example occurs in Paramount's *The Big Broadcast* (1932). When Bing Crosby and Leslie McWhinney (Stuart Erwin) contemplate suicide after being dumped by their fiancées, the radio in Bing's darkened apartment suddenly plays "I'll Be Glad When You're Dead, You Rascal You."

Such exceptions notwithstanding, it was not until the advent of New

Hollywood that the comic use of musical allusions returned with any sort of frequency. Directors like Martin Scorsese and George Lucas had grown up listening to early rock and roll, and they were among the earliest to use rock recordings as the basis of their scores. Yet while examples of musical allusion crop up in films such as *The Last Picture Show* (1971) and *Mean Streets* (1973), the film that most systematically exploited this strategy was Lucas's *American Graffiti* (1973).[10] Other commentators have noted some of these comic allusions, the most famous being the use of Frankie Lymon and the Teenagers' "Why Do Fools Fall in Love?" to accompany Curt's vision of the blonde in the T-Bird. There are several others, however. Fats Domino's "Ain't That a Shame" accompanies a later glimpse of the blonde, but in this instance the song ironically underscores the fact that Curt (Richard Dreyfus) is trapped in a car with the Pharaohs. Similarly, Bobby Freeman's "Do You Wanna Dance?" underscores John's impromptu race with Bob Falfa (Harrison Ford) down a city street, a juxtaposition that humorously equates a lover's plea with a driver's dare.

Although each of the examples above seems to demonstrate an especially apt correspondence of music and narrative, Lucas himself noted that the process of selecting music was more open than one might imagine: "Walter Murch did the sound montages, and the amazing thing we found was that we could take almost any song and put it on almost any scene and it would work. You'd put a song down on one scene, and you'd find all kinds of parallels. And you could take another song and put it down there, and it would still seem as if the song had been written for that scene. All good rock and roll is classic teenage stuff, and the scenes were such classic teenage scenes that they sort of meshed, no matter how you threw them together."[11] That the songs themselves were virtually interchangeable is not only attributable to Lucas's depiction of "classic teenage stuff," but also attests to music's oft-noted ability to transform the meaning of any event it accompanies.

Following the enormous success of both the film and soundtrack album, *American Graffiti* emerged as one of the dominant models for using popular music in films. Its use of pop records both as a network of intertextual references and as a source of authorial commentary would influence several directors and screenwriters who subsequently adopted Lucas's technique of writing songs directly into the script. More importantly, *Graffiti* also presaged the growing influence that economic and industrial factors would have on developments in film scoring. These include the resurgence of film and music cross-marketing campaigns, the boom in soundtrack album sales, and the emergence of music supervisors as significant parts of the production process. Taken together, all of these factors helped to create an environment in which popular musical allusions would flourish as a specific scoring technique.

Economic Motivations for the Use of Popular Songs as Comic Allusions

In the 1970s, the success of soundtrack albums, such as *American Graffiti* and *Saturday Night Fever* (1978), encouraged a new cycle of film and music cross-promotions.[12] As a 1979 *Billboard* article noted, such cross-promotions depended on several components, among them: "Commercially viable music. Timing. Film cooperation on advance planning and tie-ins. Music that's integral to the movie. A hit movie. A hit single. A big-name recording star. A big-name composer."[13] Certainly, some ingredients were more important than others, but promoters believed that the absence of one or two spelled the difference between a campaign's overall success or failure.

Perhaps more importantly, these cross-marketing campaigns were also early manifestations of the industry's current interest in corporate synergy. In fact, several historians have argued that the term itself was coined by record executive Danny Goldberg to specifically describe the principle behind the cooperative ventures of film and record companies. For Goldberg, the concept of synergy held that a well-coordinated marketing campaign could use a soundtrack album to generate advance interest in its accompanying film, and vice versa. In theory, such a campaign would yield hits both at box offices and on record charts. These film and music cross-promotions exemplified the fiscal benefits of synergy as a more thoroughgoing corporate principle, one which enabled companies to spread risk, maximize resources, access multiple profit centers, and activate different divisions of a diversified conglomerate.

In the early eighties, MTV emerged as still another ancillary market for films based on its success in promoting such titles as *Flashdance* (1983), *Footloose* (1984), and *Top Gun* (1986). As a specific cultural form, music video offered certain promotional advantages through its ability to function as a "music trailer." Like a more conventional movie trailer, the video not only supported an individual song, but also gave audiences an idea of the film's premise, stars, genre, and visual style. By the mid-eighties, the industry had developed a concise formula for effective cross-promotion, which R. Serge Denisoff and George Plasketes describe as "movie + soundtrack + video = $$$."[14]

While all of these factors have encouraged the production and exploitation of soundtrack albums, the growth of this market since 1975 has been nothing short of remarkable. In the last decade alone, annual sales of soundtrack albums have quadrupled. By 1995, the soundtrack album had become an important enough commodity that most major record labels had specific divisions devoted to their production and exploitation. Moreover, in 1997, the combined sales of the top five soundtracks of the year —
Space Jam, Men in Black, Gang Related, The Preacher's Wife, and *Evita* —
topped the $14 million mark.[15]

The growing demand for popular recordings in film, television, and advertising has driven up licensing revenues at a comparable rate. EMI-Capitol Music, for example, has seen its master licensing business nearly quintuple since 1989. Likewise, according to one label executive, the costs of using a particular recording over a film's opening credits are now five to ten times higher than what they were ten years ago.[16] Although several factors govern the price tag on an individual song, including its narrative importance, its prominence on the soundtrack, and the length of the musical excerpt used, synchronization fees for a popular title can run anywhere from $150,000 to $750,000. In all of these ways, the increased use of popular music in films has greatly enhanced the value of publishers and record labels' back catalogs.

Yet while the demand for licensed music is higher than ever, so is the competition to get songs and recordings into feature films. Publishers and record labels must be ever more proactive in their efforts to place songs in films. To get filmmakers interested in their holdings, publishers frequently offer them a catalog sampler, which contains up to twelve CDs worth of material broken down into various categories.[17] Says Scott James of MCA Publishing, "Our sampler goes to music supervisors, music heads, advertisers, merchandisers—anyone who has a need for music." Catherine Farley, the director of special products and licensing at the All American Group, takes a similarly assertive stance. To promote the licensing of masters from All American's urban music label, Street Life, Farley sends all of the label's new releases to African American filmmakers in the hopes that one will ultimately use the music in a film.

Perhaps more importantly, because of their involvement with almost every aspect of a soundtrack's preparation, music supervisors have emerged as some of Hollywood's most important deal makers. While some music supervisors perform mostly administrative tasks, several others actively participate in creating a soundtrack's overall concept by taking part in scoring sessions, negotiating licensing arrangements, and in some cases, even organizing "casting calls" for songwriters and performers. For these reasons, music supervisors are often targeted by publishers who attempt to involve themselves in the preparation of temp tracks. Publishers do this in the hope that once their song is included in the temp track, the director will ultimately become attached to it and will be much more reluctant to cut it from the final release print. Having placed a song in this way, publishers are consequently in a much better negotiating position and can ask for higher licensing fees from the project's music supervisor.

The growing awareness of pop music's economic function in the film industry has altered production practices in other ways as well. In a reversal of the fifties vogue for title songs, the late eighties and early nineties saw dozens of films taking their titles from preexisting popular songs. Although this practice goes back to the halcyon days of the studio system, the current emphasis on pop song titles began in the mid-eighties with films like *Peggy Sue Got Married, Blue Velvet,* and *Stand By Me.* It reached its apex in 1991 when several films in various stages of production attempted to cash in on the trend, among them *Only the Lonely, Rich Girl, Love Potion No. 9, Back in the U.S.S.R., Delirious, There Goes My Baby, Rescue Me, My Girl, Ramblin' Rose, Frankie and Johnny, Poison Ivy,* and *My Own Private Idaho.*[18] The practice is still common, as evidenced by such recent titles as *Fools Rush In, Addicted to Love,* and, of course, *Boogie Nights.*

For distributors, a well-known song title has a number of advantages as a built-in marketing hook. First, a popular song title gives any film some measure of name recognition. Secondly, a particular title may have a nostalgic resonance for certain audience members. Paramount president David Kirkpatrick described the practice thus: "It puts them [audience members] in a place that's comfortable, so there is an immediate sort of interest or draw toward the movie in question."[19] Although some production executives deny that the strategy is employed with that much forethought, they nonetheless acknowledge that their marketing teams will typically come up with a list of fifty possible titles for a film and that one or two of these is usually a song title.

As film and music cross-marketing grows more standardized, directors and screenwriters have also become increasingly aware of pop music's potential as a tool of cinematic expression. For this reason, it should surprise no one that directors like John Hughes, Quentin Tarantino, and Paul Thomas Anderson frequently write songs directly into their scripts. In doing so, these directors attempt to match the associations of a particular song with the mood and meanings of the scene it accompanies. Some directors even take this process a step further by selecting songs for certain sequences even before the script is written. Describing his own approach to the score, Tarantino says, "One of the things that I do as a filmmaker is if I start to seriously consider the idea of doing a movie, I immediately try to find out what would be the right song to be the opening credit sequence even before I write the script."[20]

Yet while the packaging of pop songs for films and soundtrack albums has become an integral part of the production process, the economic impetus for the practice does not dictate the kinds of narrative functions that the music itself performs. Put another way, economic considerations can explain the presence of popular music in films, but not the ways in which it is actually used. For the most part, the use of pop music conforms to the same sorts of dramatic functions served by orchestral scores; it underlines character traits, suggests elements of character development or point of view, reinforces aspects of the film's setting, and supports the film's structure by bridging spatial and temporal gaps between sequences.

It is within this larger network of narrative functions that one must situate the musical pun. What differentiates the latter from these other dramatic functions, however, is the pun's status as a specific form of humor. As such, the narrative functions of the musical pun must be understood in terms of its relation to theories of film comedy. Can the use of popular songs as ironic commentary in films be properly understood as a kind of wordplay? Under what conditions do we understand songs functioning as musical puns?

Musical Puns and Theories of Film Comedy

At first glance, it would seem that the notion of songs as puns poses several problems when weighed against current theories of film comedy. Even a cursory comparison shows that there are many differences between musical puns as I have described them here and the more conventional comic devices associated with cinema, such as verbal jokes and sight gags. The relation between musical puns and comedy can be assessed according to three criteria, namely the musical pun's perceptual saliency, its narrative function, and its bisociative qualities.

As one might expect, music in the cinema usually occupies a different perceptual register than do jokes or sight gags. In order to preserve the intelligibility of dialogue, music and ambient sound tend to be mixed much lower than speech, and thus they often are comprehended by spectators only as part of an overall sound design. Consequently, many spectators pay no specific attention to the music of a film, and will notice these musical puns only as part of a subsequent viewing when their attentions are less directed toward following the narrative.

In contrast, the same sound mixing conventions that subordinate music and ambient sound serve to foreground verbal jokes. In *Tomorrow Never Dies*, for example, James Bond (Pierce Brosnan) offers up one of his trademark double entendres in a verbal exchange with M (Dame Judi Dench). When Bond says that he is in the midst of taking language lessons to learn something of the "Danish tongue," M trumps his double entendre by remarking that she always knew James was a "cunning linguist." Spectators might say that they do not "get the joke"—few seemed to in the crowded Manhattan theater in which I saw the film—but this is a far cry from not having heard it. Similarly, framing and editing usually foreground sight gags, such that they can hardly go unnoticed by spectators. In this respect, musical puns are probably closer in their perceptual difficulty to some of the sight gags that appear in Jacques Tati's films. As Kristin Thompson points out in her analysis of *Play Time* (1967), Tati does not always foreground or center his sight gags, and sometimes stages several gags simultaneously, making it "literally impossible to see all of them in one viewing."[21]

Despite this perceptual difficulty, though, musical puns, verbal jokes, and sight gags all share something in terms of their narrativity. One of the most hotly debated issues in theories of film comedy is the question of the extent to which gags and jokes are narrativized, and much of this debate has been framed in terms of whether or not gags function as moments of pure spectacle.[22] While the specifics of this debate fall outside the scope of this essay, my contention here is that musical puns, like gags and verbal jokes, can function as "throwaways" in the sense that they engage a brief affective response but may be forgotten as soon as they are heard.

This is not to say, however, that musical puns have no bearing on a film's narrative. Rather, because they are frequently motivated as source music, musical puns may serve a concomitant function by contributing to a film's diegetic effect. Because of its close connection to its historical and social context, popular music is an especially effective means of denoting particular time periods or suggesting a particular sociocultural milieu. As such, it can serve as a kind of cultural shorthand for establishing setting or reinforcing the traits of a character.

Such narrative functions, however, are related more to the overall style of the music than they are to specific titles or lyrical content. More often than not, the humor derived from the use of musical allusion comes from the ironic juxtaposition of the lyrics or title of a particular song and the situation depicted in the narrative. As a resource for humor, the linguistic element of popular songs neither advances the film's narrative nor contributes much to our understanding of the diegesis. It is within this more limited sense that musical puns may exhibit a tension with cinematic narrative that is more generally characteristic of verbal jokes and sight gags.

A more significant similarity between sight gags, verbal jokes, and musical puns is that they are all bisociative. Building on ideas derived from Henri Bergson and Sigmund Freud, Arthur Koestler defines bisociation as the movement between two associative chains of logic, each of which represents a distinct interpretive frame. According to Koestler, humor arises from the juxtaposition of these two associative chains to create two incongruous ways of seeing something, such as a person, sentence, or situation.[23] Bisociation thus requires that within the realm of humor its object must be both A and Non-A at the same time. Similarly, Michael Mulkay notes that jokes are designed to display both congruity and incongruity simultaneously. Jokes may evoke two incongruous chains of associative logic, but they must do so in a manner in which the connection between these different frames of reference remains perfectly understandable. Humor that fails to make this connection falls under the rubric of the non sequitur rather than the joke proper.

Puns offer the clearest examples of the bisociative process, one in which the two frames of reference are connected by a principle of aural similarity. For example, in the Marx Brothers' "Password Routine" from *Horsefeathers* (1932), Chico offers several such puns using the names of fish suggested by Groucho. Thus, when Groucho suggests that the password may be "sturgeon," Chico confuses this with the word "surgeon," and replies, "Ah, you crazy. Sturgeon he's a doctor, cuts you open whenna you sick." Later, Chico will confuse the words "haddock" and "headache" when he suggests that he sometimes takes aspirin for a "haddock." In each of these instances, Chico's malapropism bisociatively connects two distinct chains of association, one related to species of fish and one related to medical terminology. Each pun produces humor through the audience's recognition of the aural similarity of the two terms and the way in which this similarity gives rise to the semantic incongruities of Chico's statements.

While the sight gag typically does not rely on the pun's principle of linguistic resemblance, it is often marked by a similarly bisociative logic. In his taxonomy of sight gags, Noël Carroll notes that all of his examples display a "double (or multiple) aspect." According to Carroll, "Sight gags seem to presuppose the possibility of visually interpreting the image in two or more ways."[24] Perhaps more importantly, Carroll echoes Koestler's definition of bisociation by arguing that the humor of the sight gag arises from the incongruity of these multiple interpretations and the multiple frames of reference they presuppose. Mutual interference gags, for example, are events that can be viewed as two or more distinct—and in some instances, mutually exclusive—series of actions that interpenetrate one another. The overlapping elements of each series of actions create two different but nonetheless plausible interpretations of the same event. One of the two usually proves to be the "correct" interpretation, but for the gag to work, the audience must see how both could be plausible relative to the actants' different points of view.[25]

Carroll offers comparable analysis of the other kinds of gags in his taxonomy. Object analog gags are ones in which the same object is viewed under two seemingly incongruous aspects, one literal and one metaphorical. Mimed metaphors are gags in which the same action is staged in a way that it produces visual similes between dissimilar sets of objects. Switch movement gags are actions or gestures that take on different meanings based on their visual similarity and their association with seemingly incongruous forms of activity, such as boxing and dancing.[26] In each of these sight gags, an object, action, or event produces two seemingly incompatible but nonetheless explicable interpretations. The humor of the gag arises from its juxtaposition of two associative chains of logic and two incongruent frames of reference.

Musical puns are also bisociative, albeit in ways that are subtly different from linguistic puns and sight gags. While some musical puns in films involve the play of aural similarities characteristic of a linguistic pun, they more commonly juxtapose two different ways of interpreting the song's title: that of the original scenario described or implied in the lyrics of the song and the more immediate situation represented in the cinematic text. These two frames of reference must be sufficiently different to create the incongruity upon which the pun is based; if the narrative frames of reference mirror one another, then the juxtaposition lacks the incongruity necessary to the bisociative process. Yet, while different, each frame of reference must also be associatively elicited by some linguistic element of the title. This is important since the spectator must recognize the title's relevance to the narrative situation depicted in the film to activate the two interpretive possibilities presupposed by the pun's play of meaning.

Musical puns in film require a certain detachment of a song's title from its original context and a concomitant recontextualization of the title in terms of the film's narrative. Consider the opening of *The Big Chill* (1983), which uses Marvin Gaye's classic recording of "I Heard It through the

Grapevine" in a bisociative manner. For those viewers familiar with the song, the first frame of reference evoked by the title relates to the scenario of infidelity described in the song's lyrics. Told in the first person, the lyrics represent the perspective of the cuckolded lover and express the emotional anguish caused by his partner's romantic betrayal. As such, the title refers to the network of gossip that has informed the narrator of his lover's perfidy, the "grapevine" that informally circulates information about the affair. The second frame of reference is provided by the narrative situation depicted in the film. The film's opening sequence also refers to the "grapevine" as an informal information system, but in this instance the news that travels from person to person is that of a friend's suicide rather than a lover's infidelity. Thus, while both frames of reference draw upon the colloquial notion of a "grapevine," they also rely on the pronominal ambiguity of the "it" of the song's title to evoke two incongruent narrative scenarios. Using the scenario depicted by the song's lyrics, the "it" refers to the news of an illicit affair; using the alternate scenario provided by the film's sound and image tracks, the "it" refers to the news of a tragic death.

Not coincidentally, the song's impact on the scene in the film is also twofold. On the one hand, the specifically musical features of the song—its modality, its minor key harmonies, Gaye's emotive performance—neatly underline the solemnity of the funeral preparations and the sudden sorrow each character experiences upon learning of Alex's death. At the same time, however, for viewers familiar with the song, the wordplay associated with the title adds a secondary frisson of pleasure in our recognition of its unexpected aptness to the scene it accompanies.

I do not mean to suggest here that audiences actively listen and comprehend song lyrics during the course of a film. Indeed, a spectator's attention is mostly directed toward the film's narrative and not toward the decipherment of often unintelligible rock lyrics. However, if the song is already well-known, then the matter of song lyrics becomes more a question of recognition rather than cognition. Instead of deciphering lyrics, viewers simply apply what they already know—a title or chorus—to the specific dramatic context that is depicted in the film. Thus one need not have a thorough understanding of the song's lyrics, but simply the minimal information supplied by the song's title. Not surprisingly, this system of musical allusion places a certain premium on well-known songs. After all, if the song is unfamiliar to the audience, then they will fail to grasp the specific way in which the song's title relates to the scene it accompanies.

Musical puns that are motivated as source music are bisociative in another way. When the allusion functions as part of the diegesis, the pun associated with the song's title generates two seemingly incongruous forms of textual motivation. On the one hand, the use of a song as source music enables the audience to motivate it realistically. In films, songs are commonly heard coming from boom boxes, jukeboxes, radios, and stereos, and the placement of the musical allusion within the diegesis allows the pun to arise "naturally" out of the action the song accompanies. At the same time, however, insofar as the song can function as an expressive device, it can also be motivated as a form of authorial commentary. Since each of these categories of motivation maintains its own logic, the resulting tension between them produces a certain incongruity with respect to our understanding of its textual function. Here again, a certain frisson of pleasure may be produced by the fact that the song simply happens to be playing in the background of the scene, but is also a perfectly apt or ironic comment on the action depicted within the film. In such instances, some of the humor of the musical pun derives from the improbable coincidence implied by the juxtaposition of these two kinds of textual motivation.

Musical Puns in Contemporary Cinema: Examples and Analysis

Having sketched out the theoretical context for the use of pop songs as musical puns in films, I now turn to some examples culled from contemporary mainstream films. At the outset, I should point out an axiom common to all of the examples I will discuss, namely lexical ambiguity. Although the musical pun derives its humor from incongruity, this incongruity itself is made possible by a semiotic ambiguity evident in the phrasing of a song title or lyric. This ambiguity may take on several forms, but its play of meaning commonly falls into one of four categories: pronominal ambiguity, syntactic ambiguity, semantic ambiguity, or the juxtaposition of the literal and figurative.

The aforementioned example from *The Big Chill* offers a good example of the first category. The lack of a clear referent for the word *it* in the title "I Heard It through the Grapevine" renders it a somewhat empty signifier. Virtually any scenario can provide the "it" heard by the subject of the title. Song titles that contain this type of pronominal ambiguity offer certain advantages to directors and music supervisors in that they are often applicable to several dramatic contexts. Not surprisingly, films that deal with gender issues sometimes make use of this type of pun as a means of extending the text's thematic implications. In *The Long Kiss Goodnight* (1996), for example, the film's soundtrack periodically comments on the heroine's transformation from *femme* to *femme fatale*. This is most evident during the moment when Sam (Geena Davis) finally makes herself over as Charlie, a change signified by a montage of Sam cutting her hair and dying it blonde. The soundtrack ironically underlines this transformation through the choice of Santana's cover of "She's Not There." Playing on the ambiguity of the pronoun "she," the song's double meaning comments on both the narrative and thematic implications of Sam's metamorphosis. On the one hand, the "she" of the song title refers to Samantha herself and Charlie's rejection of her previous incarnation as wife, mother, and PTA member. On the other hand, the "she" of the title refers more broadly to the absence of femininity in Charlie and her emergence as a phallic heroine more generally associated with the action film. This is later concretized in the film's climactic chase scene, in which Charlie tells her pursuers to "Suck my dick!" just before she crashes her runaway truck into a wall.

If *The Big Chill* and *The Long Kiss Goodnight* offer examples of the first category, then *Bound* (1996) offers a good instance of the second: syntactic ambiguity. In an early scene set in a Chicago bar, a couple of women approach and proposition one of the film's protagonists, a tough ex-con named Corky (Gina Gershon). The sexual orientation of the characters in this scene is ironically underlined by a piece of music emanating from the bar jukebox, namely Aretha Franklin's recording of "(I Never Loved a Man) The Way I Love You." In this case, the shift between lyrics and film as frames of reference simply recontextualizes the implied meaning of the title. The scenario of normative heterosexual romance implied in the song's lyrics suggest that the title of Aretha Franklin's recording might be more properly phrased "I Never Loved a(ny other) Man (The Way I Love You)." In the film, however, the setting of the lesbian bar recontextualizes the title such that it might be rephrased as "I Never Loved a(ny) Man (The Way I Love You)." This recontextualization not only effects a shift from the particular to the general (i.e., one hypothetical man becomes all men), but it also effects a shift in the gender of the unspecified pronoun "you." Where the lyrics imply a male object in the title, the film suggests one that is female.

A third category of ambiguity concerns a more generalized semantic ambiguity that develops when the title is unmoored from its original lyrical context. A good example of this type comes from *A Very Brady Sequel* (1995). In several scenes where Marcia and Greg amorously ogle one another, Luther Vandross's recording of "If Loving You Is Wrong" plays nondiegetically on the soundtrack. Although the unspecified "you" seems to hint at a pronomial ambiguity, the key term of the song's title is the word *wrong*, which ambiguously suggests some unnamed taboo. Here again, the

32 Lisa Kudrow and Mira Sorvino as title characters in *Romy and Michele's High School Reunion*. [Author's collection]

cinematic signifier serves to recontextualize the meaning of the original lyrics by suggesting a taboo different from the one described there. Where the original lyrics describe the narrator's desire for a married woman, the scene the song accompanies in *A Very Brady Sequel* broadly hints at desires of a more incestuous nature. In doing so, the song literalizes a subtext that was only hinted at in the television series upon which the film was based.

This example also points up the importance of audience foreknowledge. Early on, the song is excerpted such that the cues accompanying Greg and Marcia's first stirrings of desire work as an instrumental theme. Without lyrics, the song functions largely as background music. Later, we will hear a slightly longer, vocalized excerpt of the song that makes the connection between song and scene more explicit. What makes this progression interesting is the extent to which it foregrounds the importance of the song's familiarity. Those who know the song get the joke on the first hearing. Others will get it later when the song's lyrics make the joke more obvious.

The fourth type of musical pun involves the juxtaposition of figurative and literal meanings of a term. In such instances, playing the song in a dramatic context may literalize some aspect of the song's title or vice versa. A brief sequence from *Romy and Michele's High School Reunion* (1997) offers a paradigmatic example of this kind of comic allusion. As the titular char-

acters page through their high school yearbook, the pictures they view motivate a series of brief flashbacks. These epigrammatic comic vignettes not
only introduce us to the major characters who will appear at the reunion,
but also delineate the social tensions that prompt Romy and Michele to
claim they invented Post-It notes. The last of these flashbacks depicts those
on the lowest rung of the class's social ladder, the geeks who take part in the
school's science fair. Accompanied by Thomas Dolby's "She Blinded Me
with Science," the sequence shows Toby photographing Heather (Janeane
Garafolo) and Sandy (Alan Cumming) for the school's yearbook. Not only
does the sequence play off the song's reference to science, but the flash of
Toby's camera momentarily whites out the screen, literalizing the metaphorical "blind"-ness of the song's title.

A rather more complex example of this type of allusion occurs early in
Wes Craven's Scream (1996). After the gruesome prologue in which Casey
(Drew Barrymore) is savagely stabbed by an assailant garbed in a "Grim
Reaper" costume, the scene shifts to the bedroom of Sidney (Neve Camp-
bell), the film's virginal heroine. As Sidney works at her computer, her
boyfriend Billy (Skeet Ulrich) sneaks into her room through the window.
During a conversation about their relationship, an acoustic cover of "Don't
Fear the Reaper" plays softly in the background, an ironic comment on the
brutality we have just seen in the opening sequence. More importantly,
however, the allusion to the Blue Öyster Cult classic recasts the song's title
by literalizing its meaning. While the title itself invokes the Reaper as a
popular symbol for death, the film presents us with an actual person, who
not only dresses as the Grim Reaper but also unleashes homicidal ven-
geance on the other characters of the film. The irony here, of course, is that
Billy himself proves to be one of the film's dual slashers and is, in fact, the
"Reaper" to be feared.

The juxtaposition of literal and figurative meanings is also evident in
a brief sequence from The Big Lebowski (1998), but in this case the film
inverts the relationship seen in the previous two examples. Rather than
literalize the figurative, this sequence recasts the literal as metaphor. The
sequence in question is one in which Dude (Jeff Bridges) is sent to a doctor
by Maude Lebowski (Julianne Moore), a zany performance artist seeking
to conceive a child. Although the exam is ostensibly for a punch in the jaw,
Dude later learns that he was surreptitiously being checked as a prospec-
tive sperm donor. The brief sequence concludes with the doctor asking
Dude to remove his undergarments, presumably for a prostate check. As
Dude hitches down his shorts, the familiar skiffle-style intro of Creedence
Clearwater Revival's "Lookin' out My Back Door" sneaks into the sound-

track and provides a sound bridge to the next sequence in which Dude sings along to the song on his car radio. Of course, the sequence offers an elaborate pun on the more scatological implications of the term "back door," namely the orifice probed in the elided prostate exam. More to the point, however, the sequence inverts the relationship seen in earlier examples. In John Fogerty's song, the "back door" of the title is the door to the narrator's back porch. *The Big Lebowski* thus recontextualizes the meanings of the original lyric by encouraging us to focus on the possibly prurient connotations of the song's title.[27]

In sum, while musical puns often function in films as a resource for humor, they also serve or reinforce other narrative functions more generally associated with film music. As the examples above indicate, musical puns sometimes reinforce thematic implications, comment on characters or situations, cover ellipses between sequences, or foreshadow later narrative developments. Yet as the examples also indicate, the use of musical puns in films is usually done in a rather piecemeal fashion. While most of these films contain several popular recordings, only a few in each film actually function as musical puns.

This is not to say that musical puns only operate in an isolated fashion. Rather, as I noted earlier, *American Graffiti* offers perhaps the best example of a film that uses musical puns systematically. For a contemporary counterpart to *Graffiti*, one might look to the Paul Thomas Anderson film, *Boogie Nights*. A paean to the heyday of filmed pornography, the film charts the rise and fall of the fictional porn star Dirk Diggler (Mark Wahlberg), whose claim to fame rests on the enormity of his thirteen-inch penis. As is true of many films, Anderson's soundtrack uses period tunes to reinforce the film's time scheme, in this case the seventies and early eighties. The shift from disco to lite metal, from the Ohio Players to Night Ranger, corresponds with the film's depiction of changes in clothing, hairstyles, and more broadly, the porn industry's shift from film to video.

Besides contributing to the film's setting, the musical soundtrack serves several other narrative functions. Chief among these is the use of songs to cover ellipses and to unify the numerous party sequences. Befitting the film's multicharacter structure, a device that itself is a throwback to prominent seventies directors like Robert Altman, Anderson typically uses these sequences as occasions to crosscut among several disparate lines of action. In the first of three party sequences at the home of director Jack Horner (Burt Reynolds), Anderson uses five songs to tie together the various subplots that develop within the scene. These include Dirk's introductions to Reed Rothchild (John C. Reilly), Buck (Don Cheadle), the Colonel (Robert

Ridgley), and Scotty J (Philip Seymour Hoffman); Becky and Buck's argument about his cowboy garb; Maurice's (Luis Guzman) attempt to convince Amber (Julianne Moore) to help him get a film role; Little Bill's (William H. Macy) finding his wife having sex in the driveway; and the Colonel's discovery that his date has overdosed on cocaine.

This strategy of using music to cover ellipses will also be important to the film's montage sequences ("Machine Gun" covers the montage of Dirk's rise to fame), and to later sequences, especially those after Dirk has left Jack's production unit. For example, Roberta Flack's "Compared to What" covers the sequence illustrating several characters' emotional disintegration just after Dirk's departure. During this sequence we see Jack making a film with his new star, Johnny Doe; Buck unsuccessfully applying for a loan; Amber and Rollergirl's drug-induced babbling; Todd (Thomas Jane) making several trips to buy cocaine for Dirk and Reed; and lastly, Reed and Dirk's efforts to retrieve their master tapes from a recording studio. Anderson also uses music to signify action taking place off-screen. For example, in an early scene where Rollergirl offers to fellate Dirk at the disco, the orgasmic vocalizing heard in the recording used to accompany the scene, the Chakachas' "Jungle Fever," serves as an aural objective correlative for the elided money shot.

In addition, *Boogie Nights'* score plays a third function by reinforcing certain character traits of the film's protagonist. In fact, like more classically oriented scores, *Boogie Nights* achieves this by drawing an analogy between the film's central character and the score's overall concept.[28] According to trade press, the concept for *Boogie Nights* involved putting together a compilation of " '70s and '80s one hit wonders." [29] To be sure, several of the artists included on the soundtrack had successful or even legendary careers, among them War, the Commodores, the Beach Boys, and Marvin Gaye. Yet for every Marvin Gaye classic, there are four tunes by less successful artists, such as the Emotions, Hot Chocolate, Sniff 'n' the Tears, and Apollo 100. The notion of a "one-hit wonder" is particularly important here since it is not only an apt assessment of star Mark Wahlberg's recording career, but it also summarizes Dirk's belief that "everyone is blessed with one special thing." In his case, it just happens to be a gargantuan penis.

Given this overall concept, it should not surprise anyone that several of the musical puns in *Boogie Nights* make bisociative references to Dirk's colossal member. Peter Lehman has written about the use of penis-size jokes in Hollywood cinema, and although his comments refer specifically to dialogue, they are nonetheless pertinent to my discussion of *Boogie Nights* for several reasons.[30] First, Lehman points out that, like the musical pun, penis-size jokes usually function as throwaways, as isolated moments of humor within a larger narrative structure. Second, like musical puns, penis-size jokes frequently appear in films generally not defined as comedies. These similarities are important insofar as they reinforce the earlier argument that musical puns generally do not advance the film's narrative but nonetheless serve other narrative functions more or less secondarily.

Yet while such similarities support the more general analogy between musical puns in film and verbal humor, they should not cause us to overlook some significant differences. Lehman indicates one of those differences when he cites a *Variety* review of the film *Thinkin' Big* (1988), which asks, "Can a full-length film be constructed from jokes about penis size?" Lehman uses this question to launch into a discussion of the types of films that make extensive use of penis-size jokes and the implicit judgments of taste that such commentary entails. For Lehman, films that make wholesale use of such jokes tend to be dismissed as vulgar teen comedies, while more prestigious films use penis-size jokes only at isolated moments in order to preserve their aura of respectability.[31]

Yet Lehman's generalization seems a bit hasty when it comes to the critically acclaimed *Boogie Nights*. The film not only features several humorous reaction shots of characters' gawking at Dirk's penis, but as noted earlier, many of the musical puns in the film work as references to the character's "one special thing." This is not to say that the film is constructed entirely out of penis-size jokes—the claim made for *Thinkin' Big*—but rather that the penis-size jokes in *Boogie Nights* function thematically and are more than just isolated moments in the film. Perhaps what saves the film's pretense toward critical esteem is the peculiar form of these jokes. By couching them in the context of the film score's role as narration, they function largely within the guise of authorial commentary. As such, the jokes seem clever rather than crass, subtle rather than smutty.

Melanie's recording of "Brand New Key" offers possibly the clearest instance of the musical pun functioning as a penis joke. The song appears in the scene in which Dirk auditions for Jack by having sex with Rollergirl in the director's living room. Before disrobing, Rollergirl puts a tape containing the song on Jack's stereo. As she climbs atop Dirk, we hear Melanie intone:

> I've got a brand new pair of roller skates
> You've got a brand new key
> I think that we should get together
> And try them on to see

Although the song functions partly as a signature tune for Rollergirl, it also takes on a more specifically pornographic tone within this dramatic context. Like the example from *The Big Lebowski*, it does so by transforming the literal meaning of the song's lyrics to bring out the somewhat salacious subtext of the song. Within the film, the notion of "trying on" the roller skates refers quite specifically to the audition, while the phrase "brand new key" functions allusively as a metaphorical signifier for Dirk's member. Moreover, the visual image suggested by the lyrics—that of a key turning the size adjustment knob of a roller skate—serves as an apt metaphor for the act of sexual intercourse. As is typical of the musical pun, the song's cinematic context brings out the bisociative implications of its title, and recasts "Brand New Key" as an extended metaphor comparing sex to roller skating.

While the preceding example works by juxtaposing the literal and figurative senses of language, some of the film's other musical puns exploit the principle of pronomial ambiguity. The use of Hot Chocolate's "You Sexy Thing" during the first of Jack's parties not only offers a good example of this type of pun, but also illustrates the way in which musical allusions give rise to several possible interpretations. As the music begins over a shot of Scotty J, it initially offers a simple ironic comment on the schlubby, slightly overweight production assistant. A little later, as the song continues under an iris shot of Dirk that signifies Scotty's point of view, the lyrics specifically underline both Scotty's desire for Dirk and the apparent impossibility of such a relationship ("I believe in miracles"). By underlining Scotty's sexual orientation, the song foreshadows a later development when Scotty, drunk from a New Year's party, tries to kiss Dirk and confesses his attraction to him. This example, of course, is quite similar to the one in *Bound*, and it similarly uses pronomial ambiguity to alter the gender of the song's putative object. Although the song's original lyrics are presumably addressed to a female, the neutered gender of the pronouns "you" and "thing" allows them to also function in the film in relation to Dirk. At a third level, however, the ambiguity of these same terms also allow the title to function as an offhand reference to Dirk's organ. After all, it is Dirk's "sexy thing" that not only provides the character with his raison d'être, but also furnishes the film with its central enigma (just how big is it?).

The appearance of ELO's "Livin' Thing" over the closing credits complements the Hot Chocolate example heard earlier. The song sneaks in at the tail end of the film's closing scene, a rather glib reference to *Raging Bull* (1980) in which Dirk rehearses dialogue for his upcoming scene in front of a mirror, unzips his pants, and finally displays his much talked about penis to the audience. Dirk's schlong thus becomes the "livin' thing" of the title, replacing the more generalized notion of desire hinted at by the song's lyrics. As a final comment on Anderson's protagonist, the ELO tune serves as a helpful reminder of the extent to which his "gift" controls virtually every aspect of his life. Put another way, with no other discernible talent, Dirk's member functions synecdochally as a symbol for Dirk himself, so much so that the two become almost interchangeable.

Interestingly, several other songs that appear on the film's accompanying soundtrack albums take on a pornographic resonance in light of the film's larger dramatic context. For example, although the Emotions' "Best of My Love" appears as source music in the film's opening sequence at a disco, it retrospectively works as yet another reference to Dirk's penis size. Similarly, although in the film Three Dog Night's recording of "Mama Told Me Not to Come" serves to reinforce the disapproval of Dirk's mother, it retrospectively plays on the double meaning of the word *come* to function as what seems to be a parental prohibition against sex. Finally, although the Beach Boys' majestic "God Only Knows" accompanies a montage of the characters' newfound success toward the end of the film, it retrospectively seems like an ode to Dirk's "one special thing." The song's chorus affirms, "God only knows where I'd be without you." Playing on the ambiguity of the pronoun "you," it provides the ultimate comment on Dirk's career as an actor.

Conclusion

As the use of popular music in film grows, so does the use of popular songs in the form of musical puns. There are several factors that help to account for this trend, such as the burgeoning emphasis on soundtracks as marketing tools, the rise of music supervisors within the production team, and the verdant proclivity among directors to write songs directly into the script. By now the practice has become so common that it not only appears in the films themselves, but also in the trailers used to advertise the films. The trailer for *Con Air*, for example, uses Phil Collins's recording of "Something in the Air Tonight" in precisely this fashion. Using the ambiguity of the word *something*, the trailer transforms the generalized sense of anticipation into a specific "thing," namely the plane that is the setting for much of the film's action. Similarly, television advertisements for Jim Carrey's *Liar, Liar* (1997) recasts the implications of the Eurythmics' recording of "Would I Lie to You." Although the song is actually about a woman's breakup with her lover, the title is used here to underline the film's central premise (i.e., that under the spell of his son's birthday wish, Carrey's character is inexplicably unable to tell a lie).

Like other musical puns in films, those used in trailers and advertisements rely on the bisociative implications of a song's title to create their play of meaning. Typically, this bisociation takes the form of some lexical ambiguity, such as the song title's use of indefinite pronouns or the shift in meaning from the figurative to the literal. The use of popular songs in specific dramatic situations enables a shift in the title's meaning away from the context provided by the song's lyrics and toward the context provided by the film's strategies of representation. These two contexts provide two incongruous frames of reference for interpreting the film's title, and the humor of the pun derives from the juxtaposition of these seemingly incompatible but nonetheless understandable hermeneutic potentialities.

As *The Hollywood Reporter* points out in a recent issue devoted to film music, "A film's composer handles the score, but supervisors are responsible for every other bit of music that turns up in a film—from a snatch of something on a car radio to the tune behind an MTV-ready montage sequence to an original hit-in-waiting over end credits."[32] The use of popular songs as musical allusions remains an important weapon in the supervisor's arsenal. Describing the "Brand New Key" sequence from *Boogie Nights,* Chuck Crisafulli writes, "It's a moment of giddy fun, wherein music and picture work together perfectly on screen."[33] At their best, musical allusions not only serve conventional dramatic functions but also provide viewers with moments of postmodern pleasure.

Notes

1 The notion of "baring the device" comes, of course, from Russian Neoformalism. For a more complete discussion of this concept, see Kristin Thompson, *Breaking the Glass Armor: Neoformalist Film Analysis* (Princeton: Princeton University Press, 1988).

2 I learned this in a conversation with Margot Corr, the music supervisor on actor/director Stanley Tucci's last two projects, *Big Night* (1996) and *The Impostors* (1998). Corr told me that the reason for identifying joke cues to publishers and record companies is that some artists frown on comical uses of their work.

3 Quoted in Chris Willman, "A Little 'Nights' Music," *Entertainment Weekly,* 14 November 1997, 90.

4 Charles Merrell Berg, *An Investigation of the Motives for and the Realization of Music to Accompany the American Silent Film, 1896–1927* (New York: Arno Press, 1976), 244.

5 See Mary Carbine, " 'The Finest Outside the Loop': Motion Picture Exhibition in Chicago's Black Metropolis, 1905–1928," *Camera Obscura* 23 (May 1990): 12.

6 For more on the development of professional standards for silent film accompanists, see Tim Anderson, "Reforming 'Jackass Music': The Problematic Aesthetics of Early American Film Music Accompaniment," *Cinema Journal* 37.1 (1997): 3–22.

7 Quoted in Daniel Goldmark, "Carl Stalling and the Quick Cue: Popular Music in the Warner Bros. Cartoons, 1936–1958," paper presented at the Cinema and Popular Song Conference, Iowa City, Iowa, 3 April 1999.

8 See ibid. For more on music in animated shorts, see also Roy M. Prendergast, *Film Music: A Neglected Art*, 2nd ed. (New York: W. W. Norton, 1992), 180–209; and Scott Curtis, "The Sound of Early Warner Bros. Cartoons," in *Sound Theory/Sound Practice*, ed. Rick Altman (New York: Routledge, 1992), 191–203.

9 Claudia Gorbman, *Unheard Melodies: Narrative Film Music* (Bloomington: Indiana University Press, 1987), 23–24.

10 For more on the music of *American Graffiti*, see my *The Sounds of Commerce: Marketing Popular Film Music* (New York: Columbia University Press, 1998).

11 George Lucas, quoted in Dale Pollock, *Skywalking: The Life and Films of George Lucas* (New York: Harmony Books, 1983), 127.

12 For more on the economic and industrial context for this current cycle, see my *The Sounds of Commerce;* Alexander Doty's "Music Sells Movies: (Re)New(ed) Conservatism in Film Marketing," *Wide Angle* 10.2 (1988): 70–79; Justin Wyatt's *High Concept: Movies and Marketing in Hollywood* (Austin: University of Texas Press, 1994); and R. Serge Denisoff and William D. Romanowski's *Risky Business: Rock in Film* (New Brunswick, N.J.: Transaction Books, 1991).

13 Susan Peterson, "Selling a Hit Soundtrack," *Billboard*, 6 October 1979, ST-2.

14 R. Serge Denisoff and George Plaskettes, "Synergy in 1980s Film and Music: Formula for Success or Industry Mythology," *Film History* 4.3 (1990): 257–76.

15 David Browne, "Star-Ship Enterprise," *Entertainment Weekly*, 13 March 1998, 31.

16 Alan Waldman, "Going for a Song," *Hollywood Reporter*, 26 August 1997, S-12, S-66.

17 This practice is not unlike what early music publishers did in compiling volumes of mood music or in preparing handbooks for silent film musicians. Compilers such as J. S. Zamecnik, Giuseppe Becce, and Erno Rapee typically organized cues into groups based on considerations of setting, action, and mood.

18 See Larry Rohter, "In Movies, a Formula Is Born: Hitching One's Star to a Song," *New York Times*, 8 July 1991, C 11.

19 Ibid., C 11.

20 Quoted in *The Celluloid Jukebox: Popular Music and the Movies since the 50s*, ed. Jonathan Romney and Adrian Wootton (London: British Film Institute, 1995), 130.

21 Thompson, *Breaking the Glass Armor*, 256.

22 For an excellent overview of this debate, see Kristin Brunovska Karnick and Henry Jenkins's "Introduction: Funny Stories," in *Classical Hollywood Comedy*, ed. Karnick and Jenkins (New York: Routledge, 1995), 63–86.

23 Sigmund Freud, of course, discusses joke techniques in *Jokes and Their Relation to the Unconscious*. (See especially Chapters 1 and 2 of the Standard Edition, edited and translated by James Strachey [New York: W. W. Norton, 1960], 1–104.) I, however, do not want to be be too tightly bound to a Freudian conception of the joke in my analysis of the musical pun in cinema. For this reason, I have specifically chosen to use the terms brevity and bisociation rather than more psychoanalytically weighted terms, such as condensation and displacement. Arthur Koestler, *The Act of Creation* (London: Pan Books, 1966). For discussions of Koestler's concept of bisociation, see Michael Mulkay, *On Humor: Its Nature and Its Place in Modern Society* (New York: Basil Blackwell, 1988); Victor Raskin, *Semantic Mechanisms of Humor* (Boston: Reidel, 1985); Christopher P. Wilson, *Jokes: Form, Content, Use, and Function* (London: Academic Press, 1979); Harvey Sacks, "Some Technical Considerations in a Dirty Joke," in *Studies in the Organization of Conversational Interaction*, ed. J. Scheinken (New York: Academic Press, 1978), 249–70; and Jerry M. Suls, "Two-Stage Model for the Appreciation of Jokes and Cartoons," in *The Psychology of Humor*, ed. J. E. Goldstein and P. E. McGhee (New York: Academic Press, 1972), 81–100. I should note here that Andrew Horton also discusses Koestler's work in his introduction to *Comedy/Cinema/Theory* (Berkeley: University of California Press, 1991), but Horton mistakenly refers to Koestler's concept as "biosociation."

24 Noël Carroll, *Theorizing the Moving Image* (Cambridge: Cambridge University Press, 1996), 155.

25 Ibid., 144.

26 Ibid., 150–54.

27 Thanks to Mark Olsen for pointing this example out to me. While some might object I have overstated the prurient connotations of the song's title, I would remind readers that these implications of the term "back door" had long been fodder for blues and rock lyrics. Consider, for example, Willie Dixon's "Back Door Man" or Clarence Carter's delightfully nasty Christmas tune, "Back Door Santa."

28 For more on how the film score plays a particular character's point of view, see Fred Karlin's *Listening to Movies: The Film Lover's Guide to Film Music* (New York: Schirmer Books, 1994), 70–84.

29 Ray Bennett, "Sounds of Fall," *Hollywood Reporter*, 26 August 1997, S-77.

30 See Peter Lehman, "Penis Jokes and Their Relation to Hollywood's Unconscious," in *Comedy/Cinema/Theory*, ed. Horton, 43–59.

31 Ibid., 55–56.

32 Chuck Crisafulli, "Chasing Goosebumps," *Hollywood Reporter*, 13 January 1998, 3.

33 Ibid.

GENDER AND TECHNOLOGY

The Girl and the Phonograph;
or the Vamp and the Machine Revisited
PAMELA ROBERTSON WOJCIK

In the film *Little Voice* (Mark Herman, 1998), Jane Horrocks plays a girl nicknamed Little Voice, LV for short. She is a reticent, reclusive girl who has been almost entirely speechless since her father's death but who has an incredible secret vocal gift. Devoting her life wholly to her late father's record collection—clearly the collection of a gay man, though the film never acknowledges it as such—LV has learned to perfectly mimic her father's favorite stars: Shirley Bassey, Marilyn Monroe, Marlene Dietrich, and, most impressively, Judy Garland. LV's records not only fill the gap left by her father's death but also enable her to communicate with his beatific ghostly image, which appears throughout the film. LV's records substitute for her largely absent voice and keep her in a kind of perpetual childhood, removed from social and sexual contacts. When LV is forced to leave her private world of records and perform her impersonations on stage for a public audience, she has a total mental breakdown and accidentally burns her house down. Emphasizing the degree to which LV's records stand in for speech, at the end of the film, when LV discovers all her records destroyed in the fire, she emits a silent scream. Then, screaming out loud, she accuses her mother of killing her father with neglect and announces, "My name is Laura, not LV." Finally free from both her mother and her records, LV, who is consistently compared to a bird in a gilded cage, joins her new friend, Bill (Ewan McGregor), in letting his caged homing pigeons fly free.

Interestingly, in its tale of a girl's overly obsessive and inappropriate re-

33 Jane Horrocks as the title character in *Little Voice*. [Publicity still courtesy of Miramax.]

lation to phonograph records, a relation that has to be exorcised for the girl to mature and find her own voice, *Little Voice* also shows LV's mother using records for somewhat different purposes. LV's obsessive attachment to her records provides a protective sonic barrier between herself and her mother, Marie (Brenda Blethyn). But Marie, an aging on-the-prowl widow, none-theless has her own records that express her more directly sexual desires. For instance, to celebrate her romantic conquest of local celebrity Ray Say (Michael Caine), whom Marie calls "Elvis Breath," Marie and her friend Sadie (Annette Badland), play "Boogie Fever" and dance in the living room.

In an important and telling scene, a key battle between mother and daughter over the mother's promiscuous and drunken ways takes place through a duel of phonographs: upstairs, LV blasts Judy Garland's "That's Entertainment" while downstairs Marie and boyfriend Ray Say blare Tom Jones's "It's Not Unusual." Crosscutting shows Marie and Ray dancing together to their music, while LV listens intently to hers until a blown fuse stops both records. Then LV begins singing, perfectly imitating Garland's trembling voice in the dark of her bedroom. Thus, whereas LV's use of records signifies lack and functions as a fetishistic substitute for her lost father, Marie's records function to signal her promiscuity and insensitivity to LV's needs.

The Boy and the Phonograph

Within discourses on phonographs and gender, *Little Voice*'s emphasis on female uses of phonographs would seem to be an aberrant text. Most analyses of records and gender assume that phonograph culture is predominantly the province of men. For instance, in his essay "Sizing Up Record Collections: Gender and Connoisseurship in Rock Music Culture," Will Straw explores but doesn't challenge the "easy and intuitive acceptance of the idea that record collecting, within Anglo-American cultures at least, is among the more predictably male-dominated music-related practices."[1]

Straw acknowledges the stereotype of the straight male record collector as a nerd. Thus, for Straw, Nick Hornby's novel *High Fidelity* provides a literary touchstone. Hornby's narrator, the owner of a record shop, describes his customers:

> I get by because of the people who make a special effort to shop here Saturdays—young men, always young men with John Lennon specs and leather jackets and armfuls of square carrier bags—and because of the mail order: I advertise in the back of glossy rock magazines, and get letters from young men, always young men, in Manchester and Glasgow and Ottawa, young men who seem to spend a disproportionate amount of their time looking for deleted Smiths singles and "ORIGINAL NOT RERELEASED" underlined Frank Zappa albums. They're as close to being mad as makes no difference.[2]

Here, phonograph culture is decidedly male, decidedly young, and associated with homosocial bonding at the same time that it is maligned as a sort of nerdish obsession. Throughout the novel, Hornby details a male-centered phonograph record culture that is defined by collecting, expertise, and list making, and that is not only distinct from the world of women but somewhat incompatible with heterosexual coupling.

Focusing on phonograph technology rather than record collecting, Holly Kruse finds that early-twentieth-century audio technology is initially marketed to women; but, when the gramophone is marketed to women, it is sold primarily as an educational tool for children and as a decorative item for the home. In other words, the gramophone is gendered female only as a domestic object. By the 1920s, according to Kruse, educational discourse largely drops out and the phonograph is doubly articulated as, on the one hand, "masculine, serious, authentic" and, on the other, "feminine, frivolous, and domestic."[3] Keir Keightly argues that audio technology is fully gendered as masculine by the 1950s.[4] His essay on gender and hi-fidelity suggests that the gendering of audio technology as masculine is a postwar notion related to the development of the LP and hi-fi equipment. Analyzing the discourse around phonographs in magazines such as *High Fidelity, Playboy,* the *Saturday Review of Literature,* and *McCall's* between 1948 and 1958, Keightly finds hi-fi characterized as a key weapon in the battle between the sexes. Linked to excessive volume, do-it-yourself technology, and the creation of a separate listening space, hi-fi, according to Keightly, is defined as a private masculine escape from domesticity and as providing a fantasy of bachelorhood for married men. According to Kruse and Keightly, then, the phonograph is linked to contemplation and high art, and thus distinguished from feminine mass culture—the province of distraction—as associated with radio and TV. Women are increasingly distanced from phonograph culture and portrayed as confused by and hostile toward the technology.

The movie *Diner* (Barry Levinson, 1982) exemplifies this gendered division. In a famous scene from the film, Schrevie (Daniel Stern) yells at his wife Beth (Ellen Barkin) for misfiling his records. Schrevie is angry that a record by James Brown, for instance, is filed under the letter "J," and that Beth doesn't know who Charlie Parker is. Delineating both the husband's mania and the wife's painful shame, this scene sets out an opposition between the sexes around phonograph culture. Schrevie has a connoisseur's interest in categorizing his records, knowing the labels, and amassing knowledge. Linking record collecting to homosocial bonding, Schrevie complains that Beth, unlike his male friends, never asks him what's on the B-side.

While *Diner* does represent the masculine gendering of phonographs, there is, however, another way to read this scene. Instead of viewing it as proof of women's relative distance from phonographic culture, we might view it as a scene demonstrating how women's use of phonographs has been historically obscured and denied by the masculine discourse on phonographs. After all, it is not the case that *Diner* pits masculine use of phonographs against feminine nonuse. Instead, it privileges masculine use—associated with regimes of knowledge—over feminine use—associated with just wanting to hear the music. Rather than show Beth actively seeking out auditory pleasure—which she must do in order to upset Schrevie's system—the film aligns her use with decorative distraction: we see her paint her nails. It thus obscures and denigrates her use of phonographs.

In a commensurate example, *A Letter to Three Wives* (Joseph Mankiewicz, 1949) highlights the masculine gendering of hi-fi technology but also exposes fissures in that gendering. In the film, George (Kirk Douglas), a schoolteacher, is a high-culture snob and hi-fi aficionado who has a do-it-yourself hi-fi player built by his students. His wife Rita (Ann Sothern), writes soap operas for radio, a medium George dismisses as wasteful low culture. When his wife's boss, a radio sponsor, comes to dinner, she breaks one of George's records as she leaps up and switches on the radio-phonograph to hear one of her shows.

This scene perfectly demonstrates Keightly's claims about the masculinization of hi-fi culture and the way in which a high/low culture distinction gets gendered as male/female. However, what interests me in this example is the origin of the broken record. A recording of a Brahms' concerto in B Flat, recorded in Vienna before the war, it arrives earlier that day as a birthday present for George from Addie Ross (Celeste Holm), the town flirt who has run off with one of the three husbands of the film's title. In buying him a collectable, Addie recognizes George's serious interest in music, while George's wife, who forgets his birthday entirely, is negatively associated with radio and mass culture. Crucially, both of these scenes are presented in Rita's flashback when she tries to determine if her husband is the one who has run away with Addie. That the scene of domestic dissonance takes place around the site of the phonograph fits well with Keightly's discussion of hi-fi's role in the battle between the sexes. What, though, do we make of Addie's role in this battle? Unlike Beth, who can still be aligned with distraction, Addie partakes in serious masculine phonograph culture. She, however, is marked as sexually transgressive. Thus, even as the film mocks the woman who privileges radio over hi-fi, it also demonizes women's use of phonographs.

These examples suggest how complicated the gendering of phonograph culture is. They register what Rick Wojcik refers to as a "set of unstable relations between popular music, playback technology, and the listening subject."[5] Without denying that there is a thoroughly male-centered phonograph culture or that serious record collecting is predominantly a masculine activity, I believe we must complicate our understanding of how phonograph culture gets gendered. First, we can add a third term, as it were, to our understanding of gender and phonographs by considering a different stereotype, that of the gay male collector. Unlike the nerdish connoisseurship associated with heterosexual male collecting and hi-fi culture, the stereotypical gay male collector's interest in records is not defined by his interest in records or record players per se. Instead, the gay man's record collection reflects specific taste cultures stereotypically associated with gay culture, including disco and dance culture, and especially gay male fandom for female stars, such as opera diva Maria Callas, or Holly-wood stars such as Judy Garland and Barbra Streisand. This stereotype can be seen in the film *Philadelphia* (Jonathan Demme, 1993) in which AIDS patient Andrew Beckett (Tom Hanks) dramatically interprets the Maria Callas aria "La Mamma Morta" for his homophobic lawyer (Denzel Wash-ington).[6] In a different vein, *In and Out* (Frank Oz, 1997), in line with TV shows like *Northern Exposure,* uses the fact that closeted Howard Brackett (Kevin Kline) likes listening to Barbra Streisand albums as "proof" that he is gay.

The straight male stereotype and the gay male stereotype differ in a few key ways that suggest not only different use values for phonographs but also how the figure of the phonograph can be used as a shorthand for gender identification. At its most basic, the stereotype of the straight male record collector and/or hi-fi connoisseur revolves around commodi-ties—records, equipment—whereas the stereotype of the gay male collec-tor revolves around the specific music played. In each case, the phonograph functions as a fetish. In the straight stereotype it is perhaps a Marxist com-modity fetish, an end in itself, whereas the gay male stereotype fits a more Freudian notion of the fetish, insofar as the phonograph substitutes for a lack, the absent performer, and enables gay male identification with the performer.

Along with this difference, the two stereotypes also demarcate a dif-ferent emotional register for straight and gay men. The straight male's pleasure in phonographs is stereotypically the pleasure of collecting and amassing knowledge. Like sports, it enables the homosocial bonding of experts and sublimates the erotics of this bonding. The connoisseur is obsessive but curiously dispassionate. By contrast, the gay man's plea-sure, strongly associated with torch, involves deep emotionality—recall that Beckett, in *Philadelphia,* weeps as he translates Callas's words. Where the stereotypical straight male collector's relation to his records is largely cerebral, the gay man has a more embodied relationship to his records: he dances, lip-synchs, and sings along.

Obviously these stereotypes are reductive and limiting. My point in de-scribing them is not to promote them. Rather, I would suggest that com-paring these stereotypes points toward alternate ways we might envision masculine relations to phonograph culture. Taken together, they provide a helpful backdrop for differentiating a less obvious but no less prevalent set of stereotypes associated with women and phonographs. As these stereo-types suggest, the phonograph functions as an overloaded gender signifier. In films, the figure of the phonograph functions as the perfect synecdoche of the audiovisual and, as such, serves as a nexus for a host of stereotypes associated not only with ideology and imagery linked to popular music, but also with cinema's audiovisual regime.

The Girl and the Phonograph

As I have suggested, academic discussions have, for the most part, ignored or denied female use of phonographs. Most academic discussions of phonographs obscure female participation because they assume that woman = wife and that feminine = domestic. If, however, we look at magazines aimed at single women, we can find the germs of an alternative discourse. In a cursory examination of *Seventeen* magazine and *Cosmopolitan* between 1944 and 1960 (roughly the same period Keightly covers) I found young women routinely being hailed as phonograph users.

Sometimes phonographs are marketed to women as tools for typically feminine modes of mass cultural consumption. For instance, one mail order company entices women with the offer of "a talking picture of your favorite star."[7] Another promises that you can "Get Thin to Music" and shows a woman twisting in front of a phonograph.[8] Still, references to phonographs also appear in ads for unrelated products, suggesting not only that advertisers assume a female phonograph culture but also that the appeal of phonographs can be harnessed to other commodities. For instance, one company offers a "disc-jockey" blouse decorated with records; a dress company features a picture of a model holding a record to advertise its "Krush-No-Vel" fabric; and a shoe company features an image of a portable phonograph and compares shoes to records: "The disc crowd's in a spin about these new 'hits.'"[9]

At the same time, the magazines address women as serious record buyers. In its very first issue in September 1944, *Seventeen* introduced a monthly feature called "Music on a Platter," which offered reviews of classical, jazz, and pop vocal records. Initially, this column reflects the educational discourse Holly Kruse mentions and is placed in the "Your Mind" section of the magazine. But, by 1948, this column has moved to the "Having Fun" section, and been renamed "As We Heard Them." In a special reader issue in May 1950, a fifteen-year-old girl writes the column from Brooklyn. She describes the centrality of music to her life, starting with her radio alarm: "After school, I spend several hours each day doing my homework. I'm one of those people who likes to listen to music while I pore over my geometry. . . . I stack up all the singles the phonograph can handle without running berserk and settle down. . . . I find that music relaxes part of my mind while I concentrate on the work I'm doing with the other." She explains that she likes "hot music," folk, and show tunes equally and that she and her brother pool their money in a kind of partnership to buy records: "Music may not be a girl's best friend—but life wouldn't be nearly as much fun without it."[10]

These magazines also include enthusiastic references to phonographic technology. For instance, when the LP is introduced, *Seventeen* immediately recommends that its readers purchase a Long Playing Microgroove: "We're all for anything that makes recorded music cheaper, lovelier to listen to, easier to play and handle. . . . You need this machine."[11] *Cosmopolitan* doesn't include references to phonograph records until the introduction of the LP, but then jumps on the bandwagon and includes record reviews along with its coverage of movies, sheet music sales, and other aspects of popular culture. Starting in the 1950s, *Cosmopolitan* also routinely runs ads for mail order record clubs. A 1955 Christmas gift buying guide in *Cosmopolitan* features an ad for his-and-her phonographs (hers features "makeup case styling") amidst recommendations for LPs such as *Music for Tired Lovers* and Eartha Kitt's *Down to Eartha*, and books like *The High Fidelity Reader* and *The Fabulous Phonograph*.[12]

In these examples, women are hailed as viable consumers and listeners. They are envisioned as interested in technology, not afraid of it. In these magazines, the phonograph is something of a free-floating signifier: it is, alternately, a toy, a decorative item, a serious technology, a party machine, and a key to access a world of music. Thus, coincident with a masculine discourse about hi-fi technology, we find a flexible and positive feminine discourse about phonography. Yet this discourse has been historically obscured, not only by academic analyses but also by cinematic reframings of women's relation to phonography.

Diner and *A Letter to Three Wives* shore up heterosexual masculine dominance in phonography by invoking female use of phonographs, but they fail to show women actually using phonographs. In this, however, they are by no means typical. In fact, as I will indicate, cinema offers up numerous representations of women playing phonographs and other playback technologies. Thus, rather than view *Little Voice* as an aberrant text in the discourse on gender and phonographs, I propose we view it as the culmination of a long tradition of representation of women and phonographs that challenges the easy assumption of a male (straight or gay) centered phonograph culture.

What I will call the trope of the girl and the phonograph exists from at least the early 1930s to the present and in European and Australian cinema as well as in Hollywood. It thus precedes the introduction of the LP in 1948, and continues past the introduction of hi-fi technology into the digital age. This trope typically involves discreet scenes in a film in which a woman is shown playing a phonograph or other playback technology, such as cassette players. She is generally alone or in the company of another woman or women. Rather than being a passive listener, she often performs with the record—dancing, singing, or lip-synching. Unlike the married women and mothers in most discourses about gender and phonographs, the women in these scenes are often single. Therefore, domesticity is not at issue. Instead of domestic uses, the phonograph in these scenes signals a range of uses related to the woman's desire. These are not scenes of unmitigated pleasure, however. Instead, they represent female phonography as inappropriate or unhealthy behavior. These scenes displace a possible discourse about female pleasure in phonograph culture by using the trope of the phonograph as shorthand for female transgression and lack. Still, I will suggest that the persistence of this trope reflects more pliant female uses of and pleasures in the phonograph even as it seeks to contain them.

The Bad Girl and the Phonograph

The trope of the girl and the phonograph most typically betokens female desire with some accompanying transgression. In some teen films, for instance, the phonograph marks awakening sexual desire and a concomitant desire to cross class boundaries. In *Miss Annie Rooney* (Edwin L. Marin, 1942), for example, Shirley Temple's Annie Rooney listens to a divine arrangement of "Jitterbug Jukebox" on her "groan box" while reading *Pygmalion* and talking on the phone to her friend about her desire to meet a better class of boy. While Annie's family is poor, she falls in love with a boy from the other side of the tracks. Similarly, in *Pretty in Pink* (Howard Deutch, 1986) Molly Ringwald's Andy is a girl from the wrong side of the tracks who falls for a rich boy. Her difference from her fellow classmates is marked both by her eccentric taste in clothing and her job in a record store.

The visually striking New Zealand film *Heavenly Creatures* (Peter Jackson, 1994) provides a much darker instance of teen transgression. In this film, class fantasy fuels budding lesbian desire and then takes the form of a deadly family romance. When the wealthy, cosmopolitan Juliet Hulme (Kate Winslet) enters the all-girls high school in Christchurch, she and Pauline Parker (Melanie Lynsky) develop an instant rapport. Together they create an imaginary world peopled by "saints" from popular culture, such as Orson Welles. Mario Lanza's records play a key role in their relationship and provide much of the film's score. First, Juliet describes Lanza as "the world's greatest tenor." Then we see Pauline at home playing a well-worn Lanza record in rapt delight. She carries her Lanza record when she first visits Juliet's house, a mansion compared to the rather shabby boarding house her family runs. When Juliet's brother breaks Pauline's record, Juliet chooses one from her vastly superior collection of Lanza records and the girls dance to "Be My Love," knocking down Juliet's ineffectual academic father and driving him from the room. The girls' relationship is threatened when both sets of parents become increasingly concerned about the "unhealthy" attachment the girls have for each other. Then, in a subverted primal scene, Juliet discovers her glamorous mother in bed with another man and learns that her emasculated father has agreed to live as a "threesome." Finally, the Hulmes decide to divorce and send Juliet away to South Africa. Faced with the prospect of being separated from each other, the girls transfer their anger to Pauline's hapless mother and plot to kill her. In a bizarre family romance, they imagine a perfect future together with a re-formed and idealized Hulme family. They celebrate their decision to kill Pauline's mother by burning their Mario Lanza records in ritualistic fashion.

In a somewhat different vein, African American teenager Sarah Jane (Susan Kohner) attempts to transgress racial boundaries by passing as white in Douglas Sirk's *Imitation of Life* (1959). In a key scene showing Sarah Jane's growing resentment of the privilege accorded her white childhood friend, Sarah Jane looks out her bedroom window at her friend, Susie (Sandra Dee), riding her new horse, a graduation gift. Turning away from the window, Sarah Jane dances to provocative jazzy music playing on her portable phonograph. Executing sexy dance steps among numerous strewn records, she kicks a stuffed white lamb out of the frame. As in the examples above, Sarah Jane's transgression is yoked to her awakening sexual desire. This scene follows one in which her white boyfriend discovers her secret and it precedes her entry into the world of burlesque.

The trope extends beyond teen culture to include single postadolescent women. In *I'm No Angel* (Wesley Ruggles, 1933), for instance, Mae West's character, Tira, uses records as part of a seductive con. To hook a stage-door-johnny in a blackmail scam, Tira enacts a false seduction. She sorts through a collection of records ready-made for her "suckers" ("No One Loves Me Like That Frisco Man," "No One Loves Me Like That Memphis Man," ". . . Dallas Man," etc.) and chooses the appropriate one, like a vaudeville star inserting "local" material. Then, putting the record on her portable phonograph, Tira sings along with herself on record as she suggestively sprays perfume on her body, then sexily dances with the "Dallas man" until her fellow con artist enters the room to play the role of indignant husband.

In *The Miracle of Morgan's Creek* (Preston Sturges, 1944), Betty Hutton's Trudy Kockenlocker takes a break from her work in a retail record store and delights her male suitors, a group of soldiers on leave, by lip-synching to a basso profundo rendition of "The Bell in the Bay." This comedic scene stands in for Trudy's initial encounter with the soldiers she joins later at a going away party. That night, one of these soldiers will trick Trudy into a false marriage and abandon her, pregnant with sextuplets. Emphasizing the importance of the phonograph, when the soldiers leave the store, Trudy's would-be boyfriend Norval enters the store and asks to buy phonograph needles. However, this turns out to be just a ruse to talk to Trudy, as Norval—who is considered unfit for the army and therefore unworthy of Trudy's attentions—confesses that he does not even own a phonograph. The small-town hoyden Trudy has mastered the technology that Norval does not possess—mastery clearly marked as sexual. Not coincidentally, perhaps, at the end of the film when the "schnooks" and "gossips" of the town—as Trudy's sister Emmy (Diana Lynn) calls them—abandon Trudy, only Mr. Rafferty (Julius Tannen), who owns the phonograph shop, supports her.

While Trudy's scandalous pregnancy is played for laughs, the trope of the girl and the phonograph takes a melodramatic turn in *In This Our Life* (John Huston, 1942). Here, Bette Davis portrays a vivacious tramp, named Stanley, who steals her sister's husband away on the eve of her own wedding. In our first glimpse of the life Stanley leads with her now poor brother-in-law and lover Peter (George Brent), we see a close-up of a phonograph, then Stanley's high heel shoes, which she animates to dance along to a recording of "South American Way." When Peter arrives she explains that she bought the phonograph with dowry money given to her by her uncle. The phonograph becomes the object of an argument in which a horrified Peter explains how economically decadent and morally bankrupt the purchase is.

The similarly transgressive alcoholic nymphomaniac Marilee Hadley (Dorothy Malone) in *Written on the Wind* (Douglas Sirk, 1956) also has a memorable scene with a phonograph. Prior to this scene, Marylee is driven home by the police and discovered to be routinely picking up strange men and taking them to motels. Rather than express remorse, she retires to her room, where she performs a gleeful solo dance to Brown and Freed's "Temptation" as she strips down to a black merry widow, then puts on a pink negligee. In a memorable crosscutting sequence, we see Marylee's father, upset at her trampy ways, suffer a heart attack and collapse on the stairs. The power of the scene comes partly from Sirk's editing, but Malone's deliciously wicked and frenzied performance makes Marylee's dance, and the unabashed erotic energy it represents, seem responsible for her father's death.

In another instance, in *Pulp Fiction* (Quentin Tarantino, 1994), when Mia Wallace (Uma Therman) and Vincent Vega (John Travolta) return from a flirtatious dinner at Jack Rabbit Slim's, she puts on the reel-to-reel while he goes to the bathroom. As Urge Overkill's cover version of Neil Diamond's "Girl, You'll Be a Woman Soon" plays, Mia dances alone to the music. Upstairs in the bathroom, Vincent talks himself out of having an adulterous affair with her, while, downstairs, Mia overdoses on heroin.

These examples all involve sexually transgressive women. *Miss Annie Rooney* and *Pretty in Pink* show the relatively innocent transgression of class lines. *Heavenly Creatures* yokes Pauline and Juliet's transgressive lesbian desire to murderous impulses. *Imitation of Life* links Sarah Jane's sexual transgression to "passing." In *I'm No Angel*, *The Miracle of Morgan's Creek*, and *Written on the Wind*, the phonograph functions to signal real or potential promiscuity. In *Pulp Fiction* and *In This Our Life*, the trope signals real or potential adultery. The use of the phonograph in these examples parallel's Marie's use in *Little Voice* or Addie's link to phonographs in *A Letter to Three Wives*.

In all but the most innocent teen films, the woman is punished for her transgression. Pauline and Juliet are jailed and separated from each other. Sarah Jane is blamed for her mother's death. Tira finds herself involved in a possible murder. Trudy must cope with an illegitimate pregnancy. Marilee loses her father, her brother, and, finally, her one true love. Stanley dies in a car accident and Mia overdoses.

The Sad Girl and the Phonograph

In other films, the trope of the girl and the phonograph more closely parallels LV's use and is employed to mark some kind of lack as well as sexual desire. Sometimes, as in *Muriel's Wedding* (P. J. Hogan, 1994), playback technology has a compensatory function. Twice in the film, Muriel (Toni Collette) plays a cassette of ABBA performing "Dancing Queen." Both instances link to her pitiful wedding fever. The first time, Muriel has just been caught shoplifting a dress to wear to a friend's wedding and she plays the song in her bedroom in her parents' house. The second time, Muriel is in her Sydney flat and plays the song after her friend Rhonda (Rachel Griffiths) discovers her trying on wedding dresses in a desperate attempt to make herself into a bride. In both instances, Muriel sings along, flatly and just barely moving her lips. The music and the act of playing it is a consolation for depression. The song signifies her fantasy world and thus ABBA plays at her happiest moments as well as her bleakest. At her sham wedding, for instance, "Dancing Queen" plays as she walks down the aisle. And when she first meets Rhonda at an island resort, the two win a talent contest by lip-synching ABBA's "Waterloo" while dressed in full ABBA costumes and perfectly mimicking an ABBA video. As with the others, Muriel's desires transgress societal rules. Ultimately, however, Muriel has to give up her fantasy life and her unrealistic fantasies about weddings to become a mature woman, and, in doing so, she determines that she no longer needs to listen to her ABBA records.

In *Funny Lady* (Herbert Ross, 1975) the phonograph provides an ironic commentary on Fanny Brice's caustic mood. Fanny (Barbra Streisand) learns that her ex-husband, Nick Arnstein (Omar Sharif) has remarried, to an older wealthy woman. Depressed, she sits alone in her dressing room listening to a record of herself singing a torchy version of "More Than You Know." Then, she abruptly scratches the record and says, "What do you know?" She flips the record over to an ironically peppy version of "How Lucky Can You Get?" Listening to lyrics such as "If there's a man who'd leave me, I am happy to say / I haven't run into him yet," she looks at mementos of her relationship with Arnstein and plays "he loves me, he loves me not" with a yellow rose he has given her. Staring into space, she smokes a cigarette and then gulps a drink. She begins singing along with the record, altering the tone of the song to more accurately register her bitter disposition. Finally, she exits to an empty stage, where she continues singing a venomous version of the song in a classic Streisand angry solo.[13]

In a different example, in *Breakfast at Tiffany's* (Blake Edwards, 1961), Holly Golightly (Audrey Hepburn) puts on the phonograph as she describes to Paul (George Peppard) why Tiffany's is her fantasy ideal. As she explains it, Tiffany's represents security—"nothing bad can happen there"—a security lacking in her own life, which is filled with what she calls "the mean reds," days of being afraid without even knowing why. She says that if she could ever feel that same sense of security in real life, she would own furniture and give her cat a name. However, despite not wanting to be tied down by possessions, Holly does own a phonograph. In part, her party-and-date-driven lifestyle explains this, and the phonograph supplies a source for the numerous Mancini songs heard in the extended party

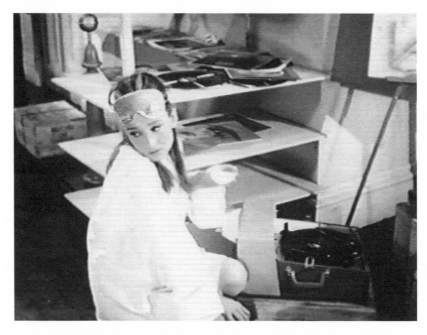

34 A sad girl and a phonograph. Audrey Hepburn explains "the mean reds" in
Breakfast at Tiffany's. [Video frame enlargement]

sequence later. The phonograph also establishes her as a source of noise
and disruption in Mr. Yunioshi's life (Mickey Rooney in a racist portrayal
that threatens to ruin the film). But, more importantly, the phonograph
seems to partially fill the lack Holly describes—as one of her only pieces
of furniture and as something that fills space sonically. In addition, as Jeff
Smith notes, the song Holly plays, "Sally's Tomato," a Latin-tinged jazz
ballad, provides an auditory link to the ethnic men who populate Holly's
life and, by extension, to her predatory gold digging desires toward those
men.[14] Thus, the lack of security Holly describes is connected, through the
trope of the phonograph, to her aberrant sexuality. In fact, the trope of the
phonograph strongly suggests a cause and effect relationship between her
lack of security and her aberrant sexuality.

Three phonograph scenes punctuate Fassbinder's remarkable *The Bitter
Tears of Petra Von Kant* (1972). Together, they underscore the film's claus-
trophobic narrative of frustrated lesbian desire and loss. In the first, Petra
(Margit Carstensen) puts on the Platters' "Smoke Gets in Your Eyes" as she
dresses and then slow dances with her love-struck assistant, Marlene (Irm
Hermann), before coldly pushing her away. In the second, Petra plays the
Walker Brothers' "In My Room" for her new crush, Karin (Hanna Schy-

35 A bad girl and a phonograph. Jeanne Moreau plots a murder in *The Bride Wore Black*. [Video frame enlargement]

gulla). When she puts on the record, she tells Karin that her records are the music of her youth: "They either make me very sad or very happy. It depends." As Karin dances alone, and Marlene types in the background, Petra describes her first love as her most perfect and explains that this love, her first husband, was killed. Continuing her monologue, she describes the burden of suffering: "People are terrible. They can bear anything. Anything." At the end of the film, another Platters record, "I'm the Great Pretender," plays as Marlene finally frees herself from Petra and exits.

One the most striking associations between the phonograph, sexuality, and lack occurs in Truffaut's *The Bride Wore Black* (1968). Julie (Jeanne Moreau) is a young bride whose husband is killed on the steps of the church immediately after the wedding ceremony. Bent on revenge, Julie stalks and kills the five men responsible for her husband's murder. Before each murder, Julie plays a 45 rpm mandolin record on her portable phonograph player. In a complicated flashback sequence, as Julie recalls her husband's death, we see the link between this record and her revenge. Scenes from Julie's childhood show her playing her phonograph for David, her husband-to-be, as Julie's adult voice-over narration describes her childhood dream of being married to David. Thus the phonograph shifts from being a sign of desire to a sign of revenge when the object of desire is taken away. As in *Funny Lady, Muriel's Wedding, Breakfast at Tiffany's,* and *The Bitter Tears of Petra von Kant,* the phonograph stands in for a complex of meanings linking female desire and lack.

Fetishizing the Phonograph

Given the frequency of this trope—and these examples are by no means exhaustive—we might ask why playback technology comes to signify transgressive female desire and lack. Kathryn Kalinak usefully highlights ways in which film music has been gendered and, in particular, how certain kinds of music signify transgressive female sexuality. She argues: "The classical Hollywood film score collaborated in the dominant ideology which punished women for their sexuality. Visual displays of female sexuality were accompanied by a nucleus of musical practices that carried implications of indecency and promiscuity through their association with so-called decadent forms such as jazz, blues, and ragtime."[15] Although she mentions links to popular song forms, Kalinak is describing traditional underscoring practice. She cites "a predilection for woodwind and brass instrumentation," the use of saxophones and muted horns, and "unusual harmonies," among other techniques, as musical cues to female transgression.

While Kalinak usefully points to ways in which film music has been gendered and, in particular, how it traditionally cues female transgression, her analysis cannot account for the trope of the girl and the phonograph. First, the phonograph typically elicits diegetic prerecorded song forms rather than nondiegetic scores.[16] Second, the particular kind of music played in these scenes varies widely. It encompasses a variety of musical styles and periods, including classical as well as popular music, and ranging from Mario Lanza to the Platters, from Mancini to the mandolin. Thus, no particular style of instrumentation can be said to dominate. And, third, the meaning of these scenes seems to depend more upon our understanding of how the woman employs the phonograph than on the specific song played. I am not denying that the specific music matters. Of course it does, and we can read these scenes individually in terms of how the song contributes to meaning. However, the music functions differently than if it were employed nondiegetically. The meaning exceeds the music here because the playback technology figures so prominently. The image of the woman using playback technology is as important as any cueing the music performs.

To some degree, we can view the trope of the girl and the phonograph as part of a larger tradition of conflating female sexuality and technology. In the essay "The Vamp and the Machine: Fritz Lang's *Metropolis*," which I've echoed in my title, Andreas Huyssen explores "why and how male fantasies about women and sexuality are interlaced with visions of technology." Through an examination of *Metropolis*, Huyssen finds corresponding views of an active and destructive female sexuality and the destructive power of technology: "The woman has appropriated the phallic power and activity of the machine and . . . she now turns this power violently against men."[17] Certainly, to some degree, the trope of the girl and the phonograph reflects some of this anxiety about women and technology, but the phonograph is hardly the menacing, out-of-control female robot Huyssen describes. Instead of viewing the phonograph as technology per se, or technology out of control, we need to consider the specificity of this technology, what "phallic power" it holds, and what it offers women.

In the context of classical cinema, the strongest "phallic power" of the phonograph might be auditory, the power to both listen to and produce sound. In Kaja Silverman's classic book on the female voice in cinema, she proposes that auditory power is gendered masculine in classic cinema.[18] Taking Laura Mulvey's famous analysis of visual pleasure into the realm of sound, Silverman claims that the woman in classic cinema is coded as inadequate or castrated in classic cinema not only through visual means but also sonically: "What this castration entails is her exclusion from symbolic power and privilege. That exclusion is marked as a passive relation to classic cinema's scopic and auditory regimes—as an incapacity for looking, speaking, or listening authoritatively, on the one hand, and what might be called a 'receptivity' to the male gaze and voice, on the other."[19] If woman is viewed as lacking in relation to auditory power, the phonograph might be seen as a kind of fetish object, providing a false auditory power. Of course, in psychoanalytic theory, the fetish "speaks as much to the desire to castrate woman as to deny her castration."[20] In other words, the fetish serves to inscribe lack where there is none, to simultaneously avow and disavow female lack.

By viewing the phonograph as a fetish, we can more clearly understand how the phonograph comes to be associated with sexual transgression and lack. It also opens up one reason why the trope of the girl and the phonograph so often entails a sadistic narrative of punishment. On the one hand, the woman, seen as lacking, presents a problem to be solved. On the other hand, the woman, seen as having the phallus, requires castration. Overall, many of the women in these films can be seen as masculinized and even castrating, wielding some inappropriate phallic power. Stars like Mae West and Barbra Streisand are constantly plagued by accusations that they are "masculine" and castrating. And, as I have suggested, many of the narratives—especially *The Miracle of Morgan's Creek, In This Our Life,* and *Written on the Wind*—explicitly contrast female transgression with male lack and do so around the figure of the phonograph.

According to Silverman, in line with Laura Mulvey, the fetish is projected onto women by patriarchal society and underpins dominant ideology about sexual difference. Looking for more specific textual agents, we might consider the importance of fathers in these narratives. In *Little Voice,* LV explicitly inherits her record collection from her father. *Miss Annie Rooney, Pretty in Pink, Written on the Wind,* and *The Miracle of Morgan's Creek* all feature girls being raised by single fathers. Stanley, from *In This Our Life,* has an ill, bedridden mother, a weak father, and a commanding paternalistic uncle. In *Muriel's Wedding,* Muriel has a nearly catatonic mother and a domineering philandering father. Sarah Jane is raised by her single mother in *Imitation of Life,* but her mother says she "favors her daddy" and attributes Sarah Jane's transgressive desire to "pass" to him. Holly Golightly from *Breakfast at Tiffany's* and Mia Wallace from *Pulp Fiction* both have much older father-figure husbands. The phonographic fetish in these films may signify some kind of unresolved Oedipal complex in which the woman identifies with her father through the phonograph, as LV does, for example. Recall the twisted family romance in *Heavenly Creatures,* in which the girls idealize the father and kill the mother. At the same time, the phonograph can be seen as a fetish through which the father projects his lack onto the daughter he creates.[21]

Consider the 1952 "Spinner Record" episode from *Dick Tracy.*[22] In it, Spinner Records serves as a cover for criminal activity. The custodian of the police vault has stolen items for Spinner and is being blackmailed by him. To cover up his tie to Spinner, the custodian pretends to be a record collector. However, as Dick Tracy investigates, he discovers that Spinner's daughter, Ginny, is the only record buyer in the house. She shares her hobby with a close female friend, Marge. Together, they purchase a Spike Dyke recording of "Cocktails for Two" from Spinner's female assistant. Seeking the seductive sounds of easy listening, the girls discover that the B-side has a secret backwards recording. Played slowly, the record reveals the sound of the custodian's voice, admitting his guilt.

Read psychoanalytically, we can see that the record in this comic strip functions to conceal the custodian's lack, not his daughter's. The custodian assumes the role of a record collector when, in fact, he has no records.

36a This Dick Tracy episode shows female camaraderie at the record store.

36b A warning to women.

36c And sadistic violence against women. ["Spinner Records" episode, Dick Tracy Weekly #27. Author's collection]

Then, through the records, the daughter discovers his admission of guilt. Moreover, the importance of the record is highlighted through two images of violence against women. First, Spinner hits his assistant when he learns that she sold the record. Then, looking for the record, Spinner beats young Marge, smashing her in the face with a record. Thus sadism enters the story and the women are punished for their ownership and knowledge of male lack—the record they possess, which Spinner lacks, and the proof of guilt it contains, the custodian's confession.

On the Flip Side

Taking the phonograph as a projected masculine fetish would suggest that the phonographic trope in these films exists only as a masculine projection that buttresses the male gendering of phonographs by positing women's relation to phonographs as simultaneously lacking and transgressive. In other words, the trope participates in a kind of sonic *fort/da* that represents female auditory power only in order to mute it. If, however, the trope of the girl and the phonograph is ultimately implicated in the gendered regimes of both classical cinema and phonography, it still necessarily elicits the woman's momentary pleasure in and use of playback technologies. What reverberates after watching these scenes is not necessarily the negative undertones, but the momentary feelings of release and freedom they awaken.

It may be that the threat posed by the trope of the girl and the phonograph is not just the woman's access to auditory power. Perhaps the true threat is the image of a woman using technology to give herself private, even solo, pleasure. If, in other words, the phonograph functions as a fetish, perhaps the flip side of that well-worn phallic substitute is a sex toy. All of these scenes show women actively engaged with playback technology. They point toward a variety of uses women might make of phonographs, and especially ways in which phonographs enable private modes of self-expression. The women in these films dance, sing, and lip-synch to records. They use records to seduce. They use records to cheer themselves up. Records spur memory and provide inspiration. Using the phonograph, the women become performers who make spectacles of themselves, often by themselves and for themselves. As often, the phonograph mediates a variety of homosocial and homosexual girl-girl relationships. These scenes point to a host of ways women might use phonographs, uses that are not intrinsically related to sexual transgression or lack, and uses that are not intrinsically "feminine" either. These uses are obscured by the more predictable cinematic discourse about female transgression and lack.

The persistent trope of the girl and the phonograph in cinema reminds us that we should not take for granted male dominance within phonograph culture or assume that men just naturally gravitate toward phonographs more than women do. Instead, we should recognize that the masculine discourse has been rigorously safeguarded through the creation of a negative cinematic discourse about female use of phonographs. And, when we get tired of listening to the same old tune about men and phonographs, we should flip the disk over to discover a different song, one that more accurately records women's phonographic experience.

Notes

Portions of this essay were presented at the Conference on Cinema and Popular Song at the University of Iowa in April 1999, the 1999 Society for Cinema Studies Conference, and the Gender Studies Forum at the University of Notre Dame. Thanks especially to Keir Keightly, Jeff Smith, Corey Creekmur, Arthur Knight, and Jim Collins for your comments. Thanks to Rick Wojcik for the Dick Tracy reference.

1   Will Straw, "Sizing Up Record Collections: Gender and Connoisseurship in Rock Music Culture," in *Sexing the Groove: Popular Music and Gender,* ed. Sheila Whiteley (New York: Routledge, 1997), 4.

2   Nick Hornby, *High Fidelity* (New York: Riverhead Books, 1995), 37. Stephen Frears's film adaptation of *High Fidelity* counters this homosocial model somewhat. In the film, many store customers, and some of the most vocal, are women.

3   Holly Kruse, "Early Audio Technology and Domestic Space," *Stanford Humanities Review* 3.2 (1993): 12.

4   Keir Keightly, " 'Turn It Down!' She Shrieked: Gender, Domestic Space, and High Fidelity, 1948–1959," *Popular Music* 15.2 (1996): 149–77.

5   Rick Wojcik, "Putting the 'Easy' in Easy Listening: Veiled Female Nudity and the Tijuana Brass," paper presented at "Approaches to American Mass Cultures Conference," University of Chicago, February 1994. In his analysis of easy-listening record covers, Wojcik suggests that the gendering of phonograph culture is less uniform than it may appear. He examines the taken-for-granted dominance of nude women on easy-listening covers and claims that while this art does offer obvious fantasies of bachelor-pad seductions, that use-value obscures other relations that the music promises, uses that are gendered as feminine.

6   On gay male opera fandom, see Wayne Koestenbaum, *The Queen's Throat: Opera, Homosexuality, and the Mystery of Desire* (New York: Vintage Books, 1994).

7 Hollywood Star Records advertisement, *Seventeen*, July 1948, 79.

8 Wallace Records advertisement, *Ladies Home Journal*, January 1950.

9 Cornibert Blouse advertisement, *Seventeen*, February 1948, 147; Evergrand Sales Corp. advertisement, *Seventeen*, October 1944, 17; Sandler of Boston advertisement, *Seventeen*, March 1950.

10 Ann Joy Levitt, "As You Heard Them: Popular Records," *Seventeen*, May 1950, 16.

11 "Here's Uninterrupted Record Music," *Seventeen*, September 1948, 36.

12 Paul Affelder, "Down to Eartha: The Best in Records," *Cosmopolitan*, December 1955, 6–7.

13 For more on Streisand's solos, see my essay "A Star Is Born Again, or How Streisand Recycles Garland," in *Falling for You: Essays on Cinema and Performance*, ed. Lesley Stern and George Kouvaris (Sydney, NSW: Power Publications, 1999), 177–208.

14 Jeff Smith, *The Sounds of Commerce: Marketing Popular Film Music* (New York: Columbia University Press, 1998), 85–86.

15 Kathryn Kalinak, *Settling the Score: Music and the Classic Hollywood Film* (Madison: University of Wisconsin Press, 1992), 120.

16 One exception might be the monothematic score for *Laura* (Otto Preminger, 1944), in which David Raksin's theme continuously shifts from diegetic sources to nondiegetic scoring, and plays once as a record on a turntable in Laura's house.

17 Andreas Huyssen, "The Vamp and the Machine: Fritz Lang's *Metropolis*," in *After the Great Divide: Modernism, Mass Culture, Postmodernism* (Bloomington: Indiana University Press, 1986), 68, 77.

18 Silverman defines "classic cinema" loosely as a textual model that identifies the male subject with mastering speech, vision, and hearing. Kaja Silverman, *The Acoustic Mirror: The Female Voice in Psychoanalysis and Cinema* (Bloomington: Indiana University Press, 1988), ix.

19 Ibid., 31.

20 Ibid., 22.

21 See Huyssen, "The Vamp and the Machine," 70–71, for a discussion of the importance of male fantasies of parthenogenesis in creating the female robot.

22 Chester Gould, *Dick Tracy Weekly* #26 and #27 (1952; reprint, Chicago, Ill.: Tribune Media Services, 1988).

Select Bibliography

Abel, Richard, ed. *French Film Theory and Criticism, 1907–1939*. Princeton, N.J.: Princeton University Press, 1988.

Allen, Robert C. *Horrible Prettiness: Burlesque and American Culture*. Chapel Hill: University of North Carolina Press, 1991.

Alpert, Hollis. *The Life and Times of "Porgy and Bess."* New York: Knopf, 1990.

Altman, Richard, and Mervyn Kaufman. *The Making of a Musical: Fiddler on the Roof*. New York: Crown Publishers, 1971.

Altman, Rick. *Film/Genre*. London: British Film Institute, 1999.

———. "The Silence of the Silents." *Musical Quarterly* 80.4 (1996): 648–718.

———, ed. *Sound Theory/Sound Practice*. London: Routledge 1991.

———. *The American Film Musical*. Bloomington: Indiana University Press, 1989.

———. "Dickens, Griffith, and Film Theory Today." *South Atlantic Quarterly* 88.2 (1989): 321–59.

———. "The Technology of the Voice." *Iris* 3.1 (1985): 3–20.

———, ed. *Genre: The Musical*. London: Routledge & Kegan Paul, 1981.

Anderson, Benedict. *Imagined Communities: Reflections on the Origin and Spread of Nationalism*. London: Verso, 1983.

Anderson, Gillian. *Music for Silent Films: 1894–1929*. Washington, D.C.: Library of Congress, 1988.

Anderson, Tim. "Reforming 'Jackass Music': The Problematic Aesthetics of Early American Film Music Accompaniment." *Cinema Journal* 37.1 (1997): 3–22.

———. "Which Voice Best Becomes the Property? Tie Ups, Intertexts, and Versioning in the Production of *My Fair Lady*." *USC Spectator* 17.2 (1997): 75–91.

Andrew, Dudley. *Mists of Regret: Culture and Sensibility in Classic French Film*. Princeton, N.J.: Princeton University Press, 1995.

———. "Family Diversions: French Popular Culture and the Music Hall." In *Popular European Cinema*, ed. Richard Dyer and Ginette Vincendeau, 15–30. New York: Routledge, 1992.

Aranda, Francisco. *Luis Buñuel: A Critical Biography*. Translated and edited by David Robinson. London: Secker & Warburg, 1975.

Armitage, Merle, ed. *George Gershwin*. New York: Longmans Green, 1938.

Arnold, Alison. "Hindi Filmi Git: On the History of Commercial Indian Popular Music." Ph.D. diss., University of Illinois at Urbana-Champagne, 1991.

——. "Popular Film Song in India—A Case of Mass Market Musical Eclecticism." *Popular Music* 7.2 (1988): 177–88.

Austin, Wade. "The Real Beverly Hillbillies." In *The South and Film*, ed. Warren French, 83–94. Jackson: University of Mississippi Press, 1991.

Babington, Bruce, and Peter William Evans. *Blue Skies and Silver Linings: Aspects of the Hollywood Musical*. Manchester: Manchester University Press, 1985.

Bagdikian, Ben H. *The Media Monopoly* 5th ed. Boston: Beacon Press, 1997.

Baker, Glenn A, ed. *Monkeemania*. London: Plexus, 1986.

Bakhtin, Mikhail. *Rabelais and His World*. Translated by Helene Iswolsky. Bloomington: Indiana University Press, 1984.

Baldwin, James. "On Catfish Row." *Commentary*, September 1959. Reprinted in *The Price of the Ticket: Collected Nonfiction, 1948–1985*. New York: St. Martin's, 1985.

——. "Life Straight in De Eye." *Commentary*, January 1955. Reprinted as "*Carmen Jones:* The Dark Is Light Enough" in *Notes of a Native Son*. New York: Bantam, 1964.

Bandy, Mary Lea, ed. *The Dawn of Sound*. New York: Museum of Modern Art, 1989.

Baraka, Amiri (as LeRoi Jones). *Blues People: Negro Music in White America*. New York: Morrow, 1963.

Barnouw, Erik, and S. Krishnaswamy. *Indian Film*. 2nd ed. New York: Oxford University Press, 1980.

Barrios, Richard. *A Song in the Dark: The Birth of the Musical Film*. Oxford: Oxford University Press, 1995.

Basile, Giusy. "Une esthétique neuve de la chanson à l'écran." In *René Clair, ou le Cinéma à la lettre*, ed. Noël Herpe and Emmanuelle Toulet, 139–52. Paris: Association Française de Recherche sur l'Histoire du Cinéma, 2000.

Basile, Giusy, and Chantal Gavouyère. *La Chanson française dans le cinéma des années trente: Discographie*. Paris: Bibliothèque Nationale de France, 1996.

Batteau, Allen W. *The Invention of Appalachia*. Tucson: University of Arizona Press, 1990.

Baxter, John. *Buñuel*. New York: Carroll & Graf, 1998.

Beeman, William O. "The Use of Music in Popular Film: East and West." *India International Centre Quarterly* 8.1 (1981): 77–87.

Beja, Morris, ed. *Perspectives on Orson Welles*. New York: G. K. Hall, 1995.

Bennett, Lerone, Jr. "Hollywood's First Negro Movie Star." *Ebony*, May 1959, 100–108.

Berg, A. Scott. *Goldwyn: A Biography*. New York: Knopf, 1989.

Berg, Charles Merrell. *An Investigation of the Motives for and the Realization of Music to Accompany the American Silent Film, 1896–1927*. New York: Arno Press, 1976.

Berrett, Joshua. "Louis Armstrong and Opera." *Musical Quarterly* 76.2 (1992): 216–41.

Bharatan, Raju. *Lata Mangeshkar: A Biography*. New Delhi: UBS Publishers' Distribution, 1995.

Bhatia, Vanraj. "Stop the Action, Start the Song." *Cinema Vision India* 1.4 (1980): 31–36.

Bhimani, Harish. *In Search of Lata Mangeshkar*. India: Harper Collins, 1995.

Bingham, Dennis. *Acting Male: Masculinities in the Films of James Stewart, Jack Nicholson, and Clint Eastwood*. New Brunswick, N.J.: Rutgers University Press, 1994.

Biskind, Peter. *Easy Riders, Raging Bulls: How the Sex-Drugs-and-Rock 'n' Roll Generation Saved Hollywood*. New York: Simon & Schuster, 1998.

Blacking, John. *How Musical Is Man?* Seattle: University of Washington Press, 1973.

Blumenthal, Bob. "Clint Eastwood: Bridging Jazz and Film." *Jazz Times*, September 1995, 28–32, 197.

Bodroghkozy, Aniko. "'We're the Young Generation and We've Got Something to Say': A Gramscian Analysis of Entertainment Television and the Youth Rebellion of the 1960s." *Critical Studies in Mass Communication*, June 1991, 217–30.

Bogle, Donald. *Toms, Coons, Mulattoes, Mammies, and Bucks: An Interpretive History of Blacks in American Films*. New York: Viking, 1973; New York: Continuum, 1994.

———. *Blacks in American Films and Television*. New York: Fireside, 1989.

Bordwell, David. *Narration in the Fiction Film*. Madison: University of Wisconsin Press, 1985.

Bourdieu, Pierre. *Distinction: A Critique of the Judgement of Taste*. Translated by Richard Nice. Cambridge, Mass.: Harvard University Press, 1984.

Bowers, Q. David. *Nickelodeon Theatres and Their Music*. Metuchen, N.J.: Scarecrow Press, 1999.

Bowlly, Al. *Modern Style Singing ("Crooning")*. London: Henri Selmer, 1934.

Briggs, Adam and Paul Cobley, eds. *The Media: An Introduction*. Harlow: Longman, 1998.

Bronson, Harold, ed. *Hey Hey We're the Monkees*. Los Angeles: Rhino, 1996.

Brooks, Peter. *The Melodramatic Imagination: Balzac, Henry James, Melodrama, and the Mode of Excess*. New York: Columbia University Press, 1984.

Brown, Royal S. *Overtones and Undertones: Reading Film Music*. Berkeley: University of California Press, 1994.

Brown, Sterling. "Our Literary Audience." *Opportunity*, February 1930. Reprinted in *Within the Circle: An Anthology of African American Literary Criticism from the Harlem Renaissance to the Present*, ed. Angelyn Mitchell, 69–78. Durham, N.C.: Duke University Press, 1994.

Brunschwig, Chantal, Louis-Jean Calvet, and Jean-Claude Klein. *Cent ans de chanson française*. Paris: Éditions du Seuil, 1981.

Bufwack, Mary. "*Coal Miner's Daughter, Honeysuckle Rose, The Night the Lights Went Out in Georgia*: Taking the Class out of Country." *Jump Cut* 28 (1983): 21–23.

Buhler, James, Carol Flinn, and David Neumeyer, eds. *Music and Cinema*. Middletown, Conn.: Wesleyan University Press, 2000.

Buñuel, Luis. *My Last Sigh*. Translated by Abigail Israel. New York: Random House, 1984.

Buñuel, Pedro Christian Garcia. "L'affair de *L'Age d'or.*" *Recordando a Luis Buñuel.* Zaragoza: Sansueña, Industrias Graficas, 1985.

Burnett, Robert. *The Global Jukebox: The International Music Industry.* New York: Routledge, 1996.

Byrne, Connie, and William O. Lopez. "*Nashville.*" *Film Quarterly* 29.2 (1975–1976): 13–25.

Cantaloube-Ferrieu, Lucienne. *Chanson et poésie des années 30 aux années 60.* Paris: A. G. Nizet, 1981.

Carbine, Mary. "'The Finest Outside the Loop': Motion Picture Exhibition in Chicago's Black Metropolis, 1905–1928." *Camera Obscura* 23 (May 1990): 9–14.

Carroll, Noël. *Theorizing the Moving Image.* Cambridge, Mass.: Cambridge University Press, 1996.

Chambers, Iain. *Urban Rhythms: Pop Music and Popular Culture.* New York: St. Martin's Press, 1985.

Chanan, Michael. *Repeated Takes: A Short History of Recording and Its Effects on Music.* New York: Verso Press, 1995.

Chandavarkar, Bhaskar. "Now It's the Bombay Film Song." *Cinema in India,* July–September 1989, 18–23.

———. "Indian Film Song." In *70 Years of Indian Cinema,* ed. T. M. Ramachandran. Bombay: CINEMA India-International, 1985.

Chandra, Anupama. "Music Mania." *India Today,* 15 November 1994, 180–97.

Chandra, Anupama, and Kavita Shetty, "Hitting the Right Notes." *India Today,* 30 November 1993, 52–53.

Chatterjee, Partha. "A Bit of Song and Dance." In *Frames of Mind,* ed. Aruna Vasudev, 197–218. New Delhi: UBSPD, 1995.

———. "When Melody Ruled the Day." In *Frames of Mind,* ed. Aruna Vasudev, 51–65. New Delhi: UBSPD, 1995.

Chauncey, George. *Gay New York: Gender, Urban Culture, and the Making of the Gay Male World, 1890–1940.* New York: Basic Books, 1994.

Chicago Recorded Music Workgroup. "What Are We Listening To? What Are We Talking About? Recorded Sound as an Object of Interdisciplinary Study." *Stanford Humanities Review* 3.2 (1993): 171–75.

Ching, Barbara. "The Possum, the Hag, and the Rhinestone Cowboy: Hard Country Music and the Burlesque Abjection of the White Man." In *Whiteness: A Critical Reader,* ed. Mike Hill, 117–33. New York: New York University Press, 1997.

———. "Acting Naturally: Cultural Distinction and Critiques of Pure Country." *Arizona Quarterly* 49.3 (1993): 107–25.

Chion, Michel. *The Voice in Cinema.* Translated by Claudia Gorbman. New York: Columbia University Press, 1999.

———. *Audio-Vision: Sound on Screen.* Edited and translated by Claudia Gorbman. New York: Columbia University Press, 1990.

Cinema Vision India 2.2 (1983): "Mortal Men, Immortal Melodies: The Golden Age of Hindi Film Music" [special issue].

Cinema Vision India 1.4 (1980): "The Rise of the Indian Film Song" [special issue].

Clarke, David B, ed. *The Cinematic City.* London: Routledge, 1997.

Coe, Jonathan. *James Stewart: Leading Man*. London: Bloomsbury, 1994.

Cohen, Phil, ed. *New Ethnicities, Old Racisms?* London: Zed Books, 1999.

Cohen, Sarah Blacher, ed. *From Hester Street to Hollywood: The Jewish-American Stage and Screen*. Bloomington: Indiana University Press, 1983.

Collins, Jim. "Toward Defining a Matrix of the Musical Comedy: The Place of the Spectator within the Textual Mechanisms." In *Genre: The Musical: A Reader*, ed. Rick Altman, 134–46. London: Routledge & Kegan Paul, 1981.

Condemi, Concetta. *Les Cafés-Concerts: Histoire d'un divertissement, 1849–1914*. Paris: Quai Voltaire, 1992.

Conway, Kelley. "The *Chanteuse* at the City Limits: Femininity, Paris, and the Cinema." Ph.D. diss., University of California, Los Angeles, 1999.

———. "Les 'goualeuses' de l'écran." In *Le cinéma au rendez-vous des arts: France, années 20 et 30*, ed. Emmanuelle Toulet, 162–71. Paris: Bibliothèque Nationale de Paris, 1995.

Cooper, Darius. "The Hindi Film Song and Guru Dutt." *East-West Film Journal* 2.2 (1988): 49–65.

Coppola, Carlo. "Politics, Social Criticism, and Indian Film Songs: The Case of Sahir Ludhianvi." *Journal of Popular Culture* 10.4 (1977): 897–902.

Corbett, John. *Extended Play: Sounding off from John Cage to Dr. Funkenstein*. Durham, N.C.: Duke University Press, 1994.

Coyle, Rebbecca, ed. *Screen Scores: Studies in Contemporary Australian Film Music*. Sydney: Allen & Unwin, 1999.

Crafton, Donald. *The Talkies: American Cinema's Transition to Sound, 1926–1931*. History of the American Cinema. Vol. 4. New York: Scribner's, 1997.

Creekmur, Corey. "The Space of Recording: The Production of Popular Music as Spectacle." *Wide Angle* 10.2 (1988): 32–40.

Crenshaw, Marshall. *Hollywood Rock: A Guide to Rock 'n' Roll in the Movies*. Edited by Ted Mico. New York: Harper Perennial, 1994.

Cripps, Thomas. *Making Movies Black*. New York: Oxford University Press, 1993.

———. "'Race Movies' as Voices of the Black Bourgeoisie: *The Scar of Shame*." In *American History/American Film: Interpreting the Hollywood Image*, ed. John E. O'Connor and Martin A. Jackson, 39–55. New York: Ungar, 1979.

———. *Slow Fade to Black: The Negro in American Film, 1900–1942*. 1977. Reprint, New York: Oxford University Press, 1993.

Crosby, Bing. *Call Me Lucky*. New York: Da Capo Press, 1953.

Crosby, Ted. *The Story of Bing Crosby*. New York: World Publishing Company, 1946.

Cullen, Countee. Review of *Porgy*, by DuBose Heyward. *Opportunity* (December 1925): 379.

Darby, William, and Jack Du Bois. *American Film Music: Major Composers, Techniques, Trends, 1915–1990*. Jefferson, N.C.: MacFarland, 1991.

Das Gupta, Chidananda. "Why the Films Sing." In *The Painted Face: Studies in India's Popular Cinema*, 59–69. New Delhi: Roli Books, 1991.

———. "Music: Opium of the Masses?" In *Talking about Films*, 29–39. New Delhi: Orient Longman, 1981.

Davenport, Guy. *Geography of the Imagination.* San Francisco: North Point Press, 1981.

Davis, Miles, with Quincy Troupe. *Miles: The Autobiography.* New York: Touchstone, 1990.

Dawidoff, Nicholas. *In the Country of Country: People and Places in American Music.* New York: Pantheon, 1997.

de la Colina, José, and Tomás Pérez Turrent. *Objects of Desire: Conversations with Luis Buñuel.* Edited and translated by Paul Lenti. New York: Marsilio Publishers, 1992.

Denisoff, R. Serge, and William D. Romanowski. *Risky Business: Rock in Film.* New Brunswick, N.J.: Transaction Books, 1991.

Denisoff, R. Serge, and George Plaskettes, "Synergy in 1980s Film and Music: Formula for Success or Industry Mythology." *Film History* 4.3 (1990): 257–76.

Dettmar, Kevin J. H. and William Richey. "Musical Cheese: The Appropriation of Seventies Music in Nineties Movies." In *Reading Rock and Roll: Authenticity, Appropriation, Aesthetics,* ed. Dettmar and Richey, 311–26. New York: Columbia University Press, 1999.

Deutsch, Didier C., ed. *Musichound Soundtracks: The Essential Album Guide to Film, Television, and Stage Music.* New York: Music Sales, Ltd., 1999.

Dickstein, Morris. *Gates of Eden: American Culture in the Sixties.* New York: Basic Books, 1977.

Dillaz, Serge. *La Chanson sous la IIIe République, 1870–1940.* Paris: Tallandier, 1991.

Dobson, Frank E. "Poise, Authority, and Privilege: Race in Eastwood's *White Hunter, Black Heart.*" Paper delivered at the Society for Cinema Studies Conference, New York, March 1995.

Donnelly, K. J. "The Classical Film Score Forever? *Batman, Batman Returns* and Post-Classical Film Music." In *Contemporary Hollywood Cinema,* ed. Steve Neale and Murray Smith, 144–45. New York: Routledge, 1998.

Doty, Alexander. "Music Sells Movies: (Re)New(ed) Conservatism in Film Marketing." *Wide Angle* 10.2 (1988): 70–79.

Douglas, Ann. *Terrible Honesty: Mongrel Manhattan in the 1920s.* New York: Farrar, Straus, & Giroux, 1995.

Du Bois, W. E. B. *The Souls of Black Folk.* New York: Vintage Books/Library of America, 1990.

———. "*Porgy,* by DuBose Heyward." *Crisis,* March 1926. Reprinted in W. E. B. Du Bois, *Writings,* ed. Nathan Huggins, 1215. New York: Library of America, 1986.

Durgnat, Raymond. *Luis Buñuel.* Berkeley: University of California Press, 1977.

Dyer, Richard. *Only Entertainment.* New York: Routledge, 1992.

———. *Heavenly Bodies: Film Stars and Society.* New York: St. Martin's, 1986.

———. "Entertainment and Utopia." In *Genre—The Musical: A Reader,* ed. Rick Altman, 175–89. New York: Routledge & Kegan Paul, 1981.

———. *Stars.* London: British Film Institute, 1979.

Early, Gerald, ed. *Lure and Loathing: Essays on Race, Identity, and the Ambivalence of Assimilation.* New York: Viking Penguin, 1993.

Easton, Carol. *The Search for Samuel Goldwyn: A Biography.* New York: Morrow, 1975.

Ehrenstein, David, and Bill Reed. *Rock on Film.* New York: Delilah Books, 1982.

Ellison, Curtis W. *Country Music Culture: From Hard Times to Heaven.* Jackson: University of Mississippi Press, 1995.

Ellison, Ralph. *Shadow and Act.* New York: Vintage, 1964.

Elsaesser, Thomas. "Tales of Sound and Fury: Observations on the Family Melodrama." In *Home Is Where the Heart Is: Studies in Melodrama and the Woman's Film,* ed. Christine Gledhill, 43–69. London: British Film Institute, 1987.

Engel, Lehman. *The American Musical Theater.* Rev. ed. New York: Collier Books, 1975.

Ennis, Philip H. *The Seventh Stream: The Emergence of Rock 'n' Roll in American Popular Music.* Middletown, Conn.: Wesleyan University Press, 1992.

Erenberg, Lewis A. "Things to Come: Swing Bands, Bebop, and the Rise of a Postwar Jazz Scene." In *Recasting America: Culture and Politics in the Age of Cold War,* ed. Lary May, 221–45. Chicago: University of Chicago Press, 1989.

———. *Steppin' Out: New York Nightlife and the Transformation of American Culture, 1890–1930.* Chicago: University of Chicago Press, 1981.

Evans, Mark. *Soundtrack: The Music of the Movies.* New York: Hopkinson & Blake, 1975.

Ewen, David. *The Story of George Gershwin.* New York: Henry Holt, 1943.

Eyman, Scott. *The Speed of Sound: Hollywood and the Talkie Revolution, 1926–1930.* New York: Simon & Schuster, 1997.

Feather, Leonard. *From Satchmo to Miles.* 1972. Reprint, New York: Da Capo, 1984.

———. "Sixty Years of Jazz: An Historical Survey." *The Encyclopedia of Jazz.* New York: Da Capo Press, 1960.

Feiler, Bruce. *Dreaming Out Loud: Garth Brooks, Wynonna Judd, Wade Hayes, and the Changing Face of Nashville.* New York: Avon Books, 1998.

Feuer, Jane. *The Hollywood Musical,* 2nd ed. Bloomington: Indiana University Press, 1993.

Fiedler, Leslie A. *The Return of the Vanishing American.* New York: Stein & Day, 1969.

Flinn, Caryl. "Music and the Melodramatic Past of New German Cinema." In *Melodrama: Stage, Picture, Screen,* ed. Jacky Bratton, Jim Cook, and Christine Gledhill, 106–18. London: British Film Institute, 1994.

———. *Strains of Utopia: Gender, Nostalgia, and Hollywood Film Music.* Princeton, N.J.: Princeton University Press, 1992.

Fordin, Hugh. *MGM's Greatest Musicals: The Arthur Freed Unit.* 1975. Reprint, New York: Da Capo Press, 1996.

Forster, Arnold, and Benjamin R. Epstein. *The New Anti-Semitism.* New York: McGraw-Hill, 1974.

Fox, Aaron. "The Jukebox of History: Narratives of Loss and Desire in the Discourse of Country Music." *Popular Music* 11.1 (1992): 53–72.

Fredrickson, George M. *The Black Image in the White Mind.* New York: Harper & Row, 1971.

Freedland, Michael. *The Goldwyn Touch: A Biography of Samuel Goldwyn.* London: Harap, 1986.

Freud, Sigmund. "A Special Type of Object Choice Made by Men." In *The Standard*

Edition of the Complete Psychological Works of Sigmund Freud, trans. and ed. James Strachey, 11:163–76. 1910. Reprint, London: Hogarth Press, 1974.

———. *Jokes and Their Relation to the Unconscious.* Edited and translated by James Strachey. New York: W.W. Norton, 1960.

Friedwald, Will. *Jazz Singing: America's Great Voices from Bessie Smith to Bebop and Beyond.* New York: Scribner's, 1990.

Frith, Simon. *Performing Rites: On the Value of Popular Music.* Cambridge, Mass.: Harvard University Press, 1996.

———. *Sound Effects.* New York: Pantheon, 1981.

Frith, Simon, Andrew Goodwin, and Lawrence Grossberg, eds. *Sound and Vision: The Music Video Reader.* London: Routledge, 1993.

Frith, Simon, and Andrew Goodwin, eds. *On Record: Rock, Pop and the Written Word.* New York: Pantheon, 1990.

Furia, Philip. *Ira Gershwin: The Art of the Lyricist.* New York: Oxford University Press, 1996.

Gabbard, Krin. *Jammin' at the Margins: Jazz and American Cinema.* Chicago: University of Chicago Press, 1996.

———, ed. *Representing Jazz.* Durham, N.C.: Duke University Press, 1995.

———, ed. *Jazz among the Discourses.* Durham, N.C.: Duke University Press, 1995.

Gaines, Jane. "Fire and Desire: Race, Melodrama, and Oscar Micheaux." In *Black American Cinema,* ed. Manthia Diawara, 49–70. New York: Routledge, 1993.

———. "*The Scar of Shame:* Skin Color and Caste in Black Silent Melodrama." *Cinema Journal* 26.4 (1987): 3–21.

Garga, B. D. *So Many Cinemas: The Motion Picture in India.* Mumbai [Bombay]: Eminence Designs, 1996.

Gates, Henry Louis, Jr. *The Signifying Monkey: A Theory of African-American Literary Criticism.* New York: Oxford University Press, 1988.

Gershwin, Ira. *The Complete Lyrics of Ira Gershwin.* New York: Knopf, 1993.

Giddins, Gary. *Faces in the Crowd: Players and Writers,* 39–51. New York: Oxford University Press, 1992.

———. *Jazz and American Pop.* New York: Oxford University Press, 1981.

Gilroy, Paul. *The Black Atlantic: Modernity and Double Consciousness.* Cambridge, Mass.: Harvard University Press, 1993.

Gitlin, Todd. *The Sixties.* New York: Bantam, 1993.

Givanni, June, ed. *Remote Control: Dilemmas of Black Intervention in British Film and TV.* London: British Film Institute, 1995.

Goffman, Erving. *Frame Analysis: An Essay on the Organization of Experience.* Cambridge, Mass.: Harvard University Press, 1974.

Gokulsing, K. Moti, and Wimal Dissanayake. *Indian Popular Cinema: A Narrative of Cultural Change.* Stoke on Trent: Trentham Books, 1998.

Goldberg, Isaac. *George Gershwin: A Study in American Music.* New York: Simon & Schuster, 1931; New York: F. Unger, 1958.

Goldberg, Jonathan. "Recalling Totalities: The Mirrored Stages of Arnold Schwarzenegger." *Differences* 4.1 (1992): 172–204.

Goldmark, Daniel. "Carl Stalling and the Quick Cue: Popular Music in the Warner

Bros. Cartoons, 1936–1958." Paper presented at the Cinema and Popular Song Conference. Iowa City, Iowa, April 1999.

Goostree, Laura. "The Monkees and the Deconstruction of Television Realism." *Journal of Popular Film and Television*, summer 1988, 50–58.

Gorbman, Claudia. *Unheard Melodies: Narrative Film Music.* Bloomington: Indiana University Press, 1987.

Green, J. Ronald. "'Twoness' in the Style of Oscar Micheaux." In *Black American Cinema*, ed. Manthia Diawara, 26–48. New York: Routledge, 1993.

Green, Stanley. *Encyclopedia of the Musical Film.* Oxford: Oxford University Press, 1981.

Gronow, Pekka, and Ilpo Saunio. *An International History of the Recording Industry.* Translated by Christopher Moseley. London: Cassell, 1998.

Grout, Donald J. *A History of Western Music.* New York: W. W. Norton, 1973.

Guerrero, Edward. *Framing Blackness: The African American Image in Film.* Philadelphia: Temple University Press, 1993.

Gupta, Sunil, ed. *Disrupted Borders: An Intervention in Definitions of Boundaries.* London: Rivers Oram Press, 1993.

Haas, Dominique. "*L'Âge d'or.*" *L'Avant-Scène du Cinema*, November 1983.

Hamm, Charles. *Irving Berlin, Songs from the Melting Pot: The Formative Years, 1907-1914.* New York: Oxford University Press, 1997.

———, ed. *Irving Berlin: Early Songs.* 3 Vols. Music of the United States of America. Madison: A-R Editions, 1994.

———. *Yesterdays: Popular Song in America.* New York: W.W. Norton, 1979.

Hansen, Miriam. *Babel and Babylon: Spectatorship and American Silent Film.* Cambridge, Mass.: Harvard University Press, 1991.

Hanson, Cynthia A. "The Hollywood Musical Biopic and the Regressive Performer." *Wide Angle* 10.2 (1988): 15–23.

Harper, Phillip Brian. *Are We Not Men?: Masculine Anxiety and the Problem of African-American Identity.* New York: Oxford University Press, 1996.

Harris, Charles. *After the Ball: Forty Years of Melody.* New York: Frank-Maurice, 1926.

Haskell, Molly. *From Reverence to Rape: The Treatment of Women in the Movies.* 2nd ed. Chicago: University of Chicago Press, 1987.

Hemming, Roy, and David Hadju. *Discovering Great Singers of Classic Pop.* New York: Newmarket Press, 1991.

Heyward, Dorothy, and DuBose Heyward. *Porgy: A Play in Four Acts.* New York: Doubleday, Page, 1927.

Heyward, DuBose. *Porgy.* 1925. Reprint, Mattituck, N.Y.: Amereon Ltd., 1988.

Hill, Lee. *Easy Rider.* London: British Film Institute, 1996.

Hilmes, Michele. *Radio Voices: American Broadcasting, 1922–1952.* Minneapolis: University of Minnesota Press, 1997.

Hindley, Geoffrey, ed. *The Larousse Encyclopedia of Music.* Secaucus, N.J.: Charwell Books, 1977.

Hitchcock, H. Wiley, and Stanley Sadie, eds. *New Grove Dictionary of American Music.* New York: Grove Press, 1986.

Hoberman, J. "Is 'The Jazz Singer' Good for the Jews?" *Village Voice,* 7–13 January 1981, 32.

Holmlund, Christine. "Aging Clint." Paper delivered at the Society for Cinema Studies Conference, Dallas, March 1996.

———. "Sexuality and Power in Male Doppelganger Cinema: The Case of Clint Eastwood's *Tightrope.*" *Cinema Journal* 26.1 (1986): 31–42.

Horton, Andrew. *Comedy/Cinema/Theory.* Berkeley: University of California Press, 1991.

Huyssen, Andreas. *After the Great Divide: Modernism, Mass Culture, Postmodernism.* Bloomington: Indiana University Press, 1986.

Institute of Contemporary Arts. *Black Film/British Cinema.* London: ICA Documents 7, 1988.

Jablonski, Edward. *Gershwin Remembered.* Portland, Oreg.: Amadeus Press, 1992.

———. *Gershwin.* New York: Doubleday, 1987.

Jameson, Fredric. *The Political Unconscious: Narrative as a Socially Symbolic Act.* Ithaca, N.Y.: Cornell University Press, 1981.

Jenkins, Henry. *What Made Pistachio Nuts? Early Sound Comedy and the Vaudeville Aesthetic.* New York: Columbia University Press, 1992.

Jennings, John J. *Theatrical and Circus Life.* St. Louis: M.S. Barnett, 1882.

Johnson, James H. *Listening in Paris: A Cultural History.* Berkeley: University of California Press, 1995.

Johnson, James Weldon. *Black Manhattan.* 1930. Reprint, New York: Arno Press, 1968.

Johnson, Victoria E. "Polyphony and Cultural Expression: Interpreting Musical Traditions in *Do the Right Thing.*" *Film Quarterly.* 47.2 (1993): 18–29

Kagan, Norman. *American Skeptic: Robert Altman's Genre-Commentary Films.* Ann Arbor, Mich.: Pierian Press, 1982.

Kalinak, Kathryn. *Settling the Score: Music and the Classical Hollywood Film.* Madison: University of Wisconsin Press, 1992.

Karlin, Fred. *Listening to Movies: The Film Lovers Guide to Film Music.* New York: Wadsworth, 1994.

Karnick, Kristin Brunovska, and Henry Jenkins, eds. *Classical Hollywood Comedy.* New York: Routledge, 1995.

Kasbekar, Asha. "An Introduction to Indian Cinema." In *An Introduction to Film Studies,* 2nd ed., ed. Jill Nelmes, 381–415. London: Routledge, 1999.

Kassabian, Anahid. *Hearing Film Music: Tracking Identification in Contemporary Hollywood Film Music.* New York: Routledge, 2000.

Kasson, John F. *Rudeness and Civility: Manners in Nineteenth-Century America.* New York: Hill & Wang, 1990.

Keightly, Keir. "Turn it Down! She Shrieked: Gender, Domestic Space, and High Fidelity, 1948–1959." *Popular Music* 15.2 (1996): 149–77.

———. "Singing, Suffering, Sinatra: Articulations of Masculinity and Femininity in the Career of Frank Sinatra, 1953–1962." Paper delivered at the Society for Cinema Studies Conference, Syracuse, March 1994.

Keil, Charles, and Steven Feld. *Music Grooves*. Chicago: University of Chicago Press, 1994.

Kernfeld, Barry, ed. *The New Grove Dictionary of Jazz*. 2 vols. New York: Macmillan, 1988.

Kesey, Ken. *Ken Kesey's Garage Sale*. New York: Viking, 1973

Keyssar, Helen. *Robert Altman's America*. New York: Oxford University Press, 1991.

Kimball, Robert, and Alfred Simon. *The Gershwins*. New York: Atheneum, 1973.

Klein, Jean-Claude. *La Chanson à l'affiche: Histoire de la chanson française du café-concert à nos jours*. Paris: Editions du May, 1991.

———. *Florilège de la chanson française*. Paris: Bordas, 1990.

Knee, Adam. "The Dialectic of Female Power and Male Hysteria in *Play Misty for Me*." In *Screening the Male: Exploring Masculinities in the Hollywood Cinema*, ed. Steven Cohan and Ina Rae Hark, 87–102. New York: Routledge, 1993.

Knight, Arthur. *Dis/Integrating the Musical: African American Musical Performance and American Musical Film, 1927–1959*. Durham, N.C.: Duke University Press, forthcoming.

———. "Star Dances: African American Constructions of Stardom, 1925–1965." In *Classic Hollywood; Classic Whiteness*, ed. Daniel Bernardi. Minneapolis: University of Minnesota Press, forthcoming.

———. "*Jammin' the Blues*, or the Sight of Jazz, 1944." In *Representing Jazz*, ed. Krin Gabbard, 11–53. Durham, N.C.: Duke University Press, 1995.

Knobloch, Susan. "*The Graduate* as Rock 'n' Roll Film." *Spectator* 17.2 (1997): 61–73.

Kobal, John. *Gotta Sing, Gotta Dance: A History of Movie Musicals*. Rev. ed. London: Spring Books, 1983.

Koestenbaum, Wayne. *The Queen's Throat: Opera, Homosexuality and the Mystery of Desire*. New York: Vintage Books, 1994.

Koestler, Arthur. *The Act of Creation*. London: Pan Books, 1966.

Kovacs, Steven. *From Enchantment to Rage: The Story of Surrealist Cinema*. Cranbury, N.J.: Associated University Press, 1980.

Kresh, Paul. "Is There Any Music at the Movies?" In *Film Music: From Violins to Video*, ed. James L. Limbacher, 32–42. Metuchen, N.J.: Scarecrow Press, 1974.

Kruse, Holly. "Early Audio Technology and Domestic Space." *Stanford Humanities Review*. 3.2 (1993): 1–14.

Krutnik, Frank. *In a Lonely Street: Film Noir, Genre, Masculinity*. New York: Routledge, 1991.

Kuenzli, Rudolf E., ed. *Dada and Surrealist Film*. New York: Willis Locker & Owens, 1987.

Kushner, Tony. "Immigration and 'Race Relations' in Postwar British Society." In *Twentieth-Century Britain: Economic, Social and Cultural Change*, ed. Paul Johnson, 411–26. London: Longman, 1994.

Lacan, Jacques. *Écrits*. Paris: Éditions du Seuil, 1966.

Lack, Russell. *Twenty-Four Frames Under: A Buried History of Film Music*. London: Quartet Books, 1997.

Lacombe, Alain, and François Porcile. *Les Musiques du cinéma français*. Paris: Bordas, 1995.

Lacombe, Nicole, and Alain Lacombe. *Fréhel*. Paris: Belfond, 1990.

Lal, Vinal. "The Impossibility of the Outsider in the Modern Hindi Film." In *The Secret Politics of Our Desires: Innocence, Culpability and Indian Popular Cinema*, ed. Ashis Nandy, 228–59. London: Zed Books, 1998.

Langer, Susanne K. *Philosophy in a New Key: A Study in the Symbolism of Reason, Rite, and Art*. New York: Mentor Books, 1948.

Lastra, James. *Sound Technology and American Cinema*. New York: Columbia University Press, 2000.

Leaming, Barbara. *Orson Welles: A Biography*. New York: Penguin, 1985.

Leary, Timothy. *The Psychedelic Experience: A Manual Based on the Tibetan Book of the Dead*. New York: Citadel, 1995.

Lee, Martin A., and Bruce Shlain. *Acid Dreams — The Complete Social History of LSD: The CIA, the Sixties, and Beyond*. New York: Grove Weidenfeld, 1985.

Lees, Gene. *Singers and the Song*. New York: Oxford University Press, 1987.

Leppert, Richard, and Susan McClary, eds. *Music and Society: The Politics of Composition, Performance and Reception*. Cambridge: Cambridge University Press, 1987.

Levant, Oscar. *A Smattering of Ignorance*. New York, Doubleday, Doran 1940.

Levine, Lawrence W. *Highbrow/Lowbrow: The Emergence of Cultural Hierarchy in America*. Cambridge, Mass.: Harvard University Press, 1988.

Levinson, Jerold. "Film Music and Narrative Agency." In *Post-Theory: Reconstructing Film Studies*, ed. David Bordwell and Noel Carrol, 248–82 . Madison: University of Wisconsin Press, 1996.

Lewis, Jon. "Money Matters: Hollywood in the Corporate Era." In *The New American Cinema*, ed. Lewis, 87–124. Durham, N.C.: Duke University Press, 1988.

Limbacher, James L. *Keeping Score: Film and Television Music, 1980–1988; With Additional Coverage of 1921–1979*. Metuchen, N.J.: Scarecrow Press, 1991.

Lipstadt, Deborah. *Denying the Holocaust: The Growing Assault on Truth and Memory*. New York: Plume Books, 1994.

London, Kurt. *Film Music: A Summary of the Characteristic Features of Its History, Aesthetics, Technique, and Possible Developments*. Translated by Eric S. Bensinger. London, 1936.

Lott, Eric. *Love and Theft: Blackface Minstrelsy and the American Working Class*. New York: Oxford University Press, 1993.

Lynn, Loretta, with George Vecsey. *Coal Miner's Daughter*. New York: Warner Books, 1977.

Macklin, F. Anthony. "*Nashville*: America's Voices." *Film Heritage* 11.1 (1975): 6–10.

Malone, Bill. *Country Music USA*. Austin: University of Texas Press, 1985.

Mancini, Henry, and Gene Lees. *Did They Mention the Music?* Chicago: Contemporary, 1989.

Manuel, Peter. *Cassette Culture: Popular Music and Technology in North India*. Chicago: University of Chicago Press, 1993.

Manvell, Roger, and John Huntley. *The Technique of Film Music*. Revised and enlarged by Richard Arnell and Peter Day. New York: Hastings House, 1975.

Marill, Alvin. *Samuel Goldwyn Presents*. South Brunswick, N.J.: A. S. Barnes, 1976.

Marks, Edward. *They All Sang: From Tony Pastor to Rudy Vallee.* New York: Viking, 1935.

Marks, Martin Miller. *Music and the Silent Film: Contexts and Case Studies, 1895–1924.* New York: Oxford University Press, 1997.

Marmorstein, Gary. *Hollywood Rhapsody: Movie Music and Its Makers, 1900 to 1975.* New York: Schirmer Books, 1997.

Marre, Jeremy, and Hannah Charlton. *Beats of the Heart: Popular Music of the World.* New York: Pantheon, 1985.

Martinez, David. "Chasing the Metaphysical Express: Music in the Films of Wong Kar-Wai." In *Wong Kar-Wai,* ed. Jean-Marc Lalanne, David Martinez, Ackbar Abbas, and Jimmy Ngai, 29–35. Paris: Éditions Dis Voir, 1997.

Marx, Arthur. *Goldwyn: A Biography of the Man Behind the Myth.* New York: Norton, 1976.

Mast, Gerald. *Can't Help Singin': The American Musical on Stage and Screen.* Woodstock, N.Y.: Overlook Press, 1987.

Mayne, Judith. "Walking the *Tightrope* of Feminism and Male Desire." In *Men in Feminism,* ed. Alice Jardine and Paul Smith, 62–70. New York: Methuen, 1988.

McClary, Susan. *Feminine Endings: Music, Gender, and Sexuality.* Minneapolis: University of Minnesota Press, 1991.

McCracken, Allison. "'God's Gift to Us Girls': Crooning, Gender, and the Re-Creation of American Popular Song, 1928–1933." *American Music* 17. 4 (1999): 365–95.

McGee, Mark Thomas. *The Rock and Roll Movie Encyclopedia of the 1950s.* Jefferson, N.C.: McFarland, 1990.

McGilligan, Patrick. *Jack's Life.* New York: W. W. Norton, 1994.

Melnick, Jeffrey. *Ancestors and Relatives: The Uncanny Relationship of African Americans and Jews.* Ph.D. diss., Harvard University, 1994.

Millard, Andre. *America on Record: A History of Recorded Sound.* New York: Cambridge University Press, 1995.

Miller, Jonathan. *The Body in Question.* London: Jonathan Cape, 1978.

Mitra, Sumit. "O Indisputable and Indispensable Queen." *Cinema Vision India* 2.2 (1983): 38–45.

Modleski, Tania. *Feminism without Women: Culture and Criticism in a "Postfeminist" Age.* New York: Routledge, 1991.

Monson, Ingrid. *Saying Something: Jazz Improvisation and Interaction.* Chicago: University of Chicago Press, 1996.

Morrow, Edward. "Duke Ellington on Gershwin's Porgy." *New Theatre,* December 1935, 5–6. Reprinted in *The Duke Ellington Reader,* ed. Mark Tucker, 114–17. New York: Oxford University Press, 1993.

Mulkay, Michael. *On Humor: Its Nature and Its Place in Modern Society.* New York: Basil Blackwell, 1988.

Mundy, John. *Popular Music on Screen: From Hollywood Musical to Music Video.* Manchester: Manchester University Press, 1999.

Murch, Walter. "Restoring the Touch of Genius to a Classic." *New York Times,* 6 September 1998, sec. 2: 1+.

Naremore, James. *The Magic World of Orson Welles*. 2nd ed. Dallas: Southern Methodist University Press, 1989.

Negus, Keith. *Music Genres and Corporate Cultures*. London: Routledge, 1999.

Nericcio, William Anthony. "Of Mestizos and Half-Breeds: Orson Welles' *Touch of Evil*." In *Chicanos and Film: Essays on Chicano Representation and Resistance*, ed. Chon A. Noriega, 53–65. New York: Garland Press, 1992.

Nichols, Bill. *Blurred Boundaries: Questions of Meaning in Contemporary Culture*. Bloomington: Indiana University Press, 1994.

Nicholson, Stuart. *Reminiscing in Tempo: A Portrait of Duke Ellington*. Boston: Northeastern University Press, 1999.

Noble, Peter. *The Negro in Films*. London: Skelton Robinson, n.d. [1948].

North, Michael. *The Dialect of Modernism*. New York: Oxford University Press, 1994.

Null, Gary. *Black Hollywood: The Negro in Motion Pictures*. Secaucus, N.J.: Citadel Press, 1975.

O'Brien, Lucy. *She Bop: The Definitive History of Women in Rock, Pop and Soul*. London: Penguin, 1996.

Ortega y Gasset, José. *The Dehumanization of Art and Other Essays*. Princeton N.J.: Princeton University Press, 1968.

Orvell, Miles. *The Real Thing: Imitation and Authenticity in American Culture, 1880-1940*. Chapel Hill: University of North Carolina Press, 1989.

Ostransky, Leroy. *The Anatomy of Jazz*. Seattle: University of Washington Press, 1960.

Otis, Johnny. *Upside Your Head! Rhythm and Blues on Central Avenue*. Hanover, N.H.: University Press of New England, 1993.

———. *Listen to the Lambs*. New York: Norton, 1968.

Perry, George. *Alfred Hitchcock*. London: Macmillan, 1975.

Peterson, Richard A. *Creating Country Music: Fabricating Authenticity*. Chicago: University of Chicago Press, 1997.

Peyser, Joan. *The Memory of All That: The Life of George Gershwin*. New York: Simon & Schuster, 1993.

Pleasants, Henry. *The Great American Popular Singers*. New York: Simon & Schuster, 1974.

Poitier, Sidney. *This Life*. New York: Knopf, 1980.

Porter, Lewis. *Lester Young*. Boston: Twayne, 1985.

Prakash, Sanjeev. "Music, Dance and the Popular Films: Indian Fantasies, Indian Repressions." In *Indian Cinema Superbazaar*, ed. Aruna Vasudev and Phillipe Lenglet, 114–18. New Delhi: Vikas Publishing House, 1983.

Prasad, M. Madhava. *Ideology of the Hindi Film: A Historical Construction*. Delhi: Oxford University Press, 1998.

Pratley, Gerald. *The Cinema of Otto Preminger*. New York: A. S. Barnes, 1971.

Prendergrast, Roy M. *Film Music—A Neglected Art: A Critical Study of Music in Films*. 2nd ed. New York: W. W. Norton, 1992.

Rai, Amit. "An American Raj in Filmistan: Images of Elvis in Indian Films." *Screen* 35.1 (1994): 51–77.

Rajadhyaksha, Ashish. "Indian Cinema: Origins to Independence" and "India: Filming the Nation." In *The Oxford History of World Cinema*, ed. Geoffrey Nowell-Smith, 398–409 and 678–89. New York: Oxford University Press, 1996.

———. "The Phalke Era: Conflict of Traditional Form and Modern Technology." In *Interrogating Modernity: Culture and Colonialism in India*, ed. Tejaswini Niranjana, P. Sudhir, and Vivek Dhareshwar, 47–82. Calcutta: Seagull Books, 1993.

———. "Neo-Traditionalism: Film as Popular Art in India." *Framework* 32/33 (1986): 21–67.

Rajadhyaksha, Ashish, and Paul Willemen, *Encyclopedia of Indian Cinema*. Rev. ed. London: British Film Institute and Oxford University Press, 1999.

Ranade, Ashok. "The Extraordinary Importance of the Indian Film Song." *Cinema Vision India* 1.4 (1980): 4–11.

Raskin, Victor. *Semantic Mechanisms of Humor*. Boston: Reidel, 1985.

Ray, Satyajit. *Our Films, Their Films: Essays*, 72–75. New York: Hyperion, 1994.

Rearick, Charles. *The French in Love and War: Popular Culture in the Era of the World Wars*. New Haven, Conn.: Yale University Press, 1997.

Reuben, Bunny. "Hindi Screen Acting: An Assessment of Three Generations." *Star and Style* 3.4 (1970): 16–17.

Rifkin, Adrian. *Street Noises: Parisian Pleasure, 1900–40*. Manchester: Manchester University Press, 1993.

Rogin, Michael. *Blackface, White Noise: Jewish Immigrants in the Hollywood Melting Pot*. Berkeley: University of California Press, 1996.

———. "'Make My Day!': Spectacle as Amnesia in Imperial Politics." *Representations* 29 (winter 1990): 99–123

Romney, Jonathan, and Adrian Wootton, eds. *Celluloid Jukebox: Popular Music and the Movies since the 50s*. London: British Film Institute, 1995.

Rosenbaum, Jonathan. "Orson Welles' Memo to Universal." *Film Quarterly* 46.1 (1992): 2–11.

Rosenberg, David, ed. *The Movie That Changed My Life*. New York: Penguin, 1991.

Rosenberg, Deena. *Fascinating Rhythm: The Collaboration of George and Ira Gershwin*. New York: Dutton, 1991.

Ross, Andrew, and Tricia Rose, eds. *Microphone Fiends: Youth Music and Youth Culture*. New York: Routledge, 1994.

Roszak, Theodore. *The Making of a Counterculture: Reflections on the Technocratic Society and Its Youthful Opposition*. New York: Doubleday, 1969.

Rothmuller, Aron Marko. *The Music of the Jews: An Historical Appreciation*. New York: A. S. Barnes, 1954.

Rutherford, Jonathan, ed. *Identity: Community, Culture, Difference*. London: Lawrence & Wishart, 1990.

Sacks, Harvey. "Some Technical Considerations in a Dirty Joke." *Studies in the Organization of Conversational Interaction*, ed. J. Scheinken, 249–70. New York: Academic Press, 1978.

Sadie, Stanley, ed. *The New Grove Dictionary of Music and Musicians*. 5th ed. New York: Macmillan, 1980.

Sandahl, Linda J. *Encyclopedia of Rock Music in Film: A Viewer's Guide to Three De-*

cades of Musicals, Concerts, Documentaries, and Soundtracks, 1955–1986. New York: Blandford, 1987.

Sanjek, David. "Blue Moon of Kentucky Rising over the Mystery Train: The Complex Construction of Country Music." *South Atlantic Quarterly* 94. 1 (1995): 29–55.

Schatz, Thomas. "The Return of the Hollywood Studio System." In *Conglomerates and the Media*, ed. Erik Barnouw et al. New York: New Press, 1997.

Schwartz, Charles. *Gershwin: His Life and Music.* New York: Bobbs-Merrill, 1973.

Self, Robert. "Invention and Death: The Commodities of Media in Robert Altman's *Nashville*." *Journal of Popular Film* 5 (1976): 273–88.

Shafik, Viola. *Arab Cinema: History and Cultural Identity.* Cairo: American University in Cairo Press, 1998.

Sharma, Narendra. "Half a Century of Song." *Cinema Vision India* 1.4 (1980): 56–61.

Sharma, Sanjay, Ashwani Sharma, and John Hutnyk, eds. *Dis-orienting Rhythms: The Politics of the New Asian Dance Music.* London: Zed Books, 1996.

Siefert, Marsha. "Image/Music/Voice: Song Dubbing in Hollywood Musicals." *Journal of Communication* 45.2 (1995): 44–64.

Silverman, Kaja. *The Acoustic Mirror: The Female Voice in Psychoanalysis and Cinema.* Bloomington: Indiana University Press, 1988.

Singh, Har Mandir, ed., *Hindi Film Geet Kosh.* 4 vols. Kanpur, India: Satinder Kaur, 1988, 1984, 1980, 1986 respectively.

Singh, Madan Gopal. "Jottings on the Indian Film Song: If Music Be the Food of Love . . ." *Cinemaya* 39–40 (1998): 4–9.

Sitney, P. Adams, ed. *The Avant-Garde Film: A Reader of Theory and Criticism.* Anthology Film Archives Series 3. New York: Anthology Film Archives, 1987.

Skillman, Teri. "Songs in Hindi Films: Nature and Function." In *Cinema and Cultural Identity: Reflections on Films from Japan, India, and China,* ed. Wimal Dissanayake, 149–58. Lanham: University Press of America, 1988.

———. "The Bombay Hindi Film Song." In *Yearbook for Traditional Music 1986,* 133–44. New York: International Council for Traditional Music, 1986.

Slobin, Mark. "Some Intersections of Jews, Music, and Theater." In *From Hester Street to Hollywood: The Jewish-American Stage and Screen,* ed. Sarah Blacher Cohen, 29–43. Bloomington: Indiana University Press, 1983.

———. *Tenement Songs: The Popular Music of the Jewish Immigrants.* Urbana: University of Illinois Press, 1982.

Smith, Jeff. *The Sounds of Commerce: Marketing Popular Film Music.* New York: Columbia University Press, 1998.

———. "Unheard Melodies? A Critique of Psychoanalytic Theories of Film Music." In *Post-Theory: Reconstructing Film Studies,* ed. David Bordwell and Noel Carrol, 230–47. Madison: University of Wisconsin Press, 1996.

Smith, Paul. *Clint Eastwood: A Cultural Production.* Minneapolis: University of Minnesota Press, 1993.

Smulyan, Susan. *Selling Radio: The Commercialization of American Broadcasting, 1920–1934.* Washington, D.C.: Smithsonian Institution Press, 1994.

Spoto, Donald. *The Dark Side of Genius: The Life of Alfred Hitchcock.* New York: Ballantine, 1984.

Stanford Humanities Review 3.2 (1993): " 'And the Walls Come A-Tumblin' Down': Music in the Age of Postdisciplinarity" [special issue].

Stember, Charles Herbert et al. *Jews in the Mind of America*. New York: Basic Books, 1966.

Stevens, Jay. *Storming Heaven: LSD and the American Dream*. New York: Harper & Row, 1987.

Stowe, David W. *Swing Changes: Big-Band Jazz in New Deal America*. Cambridge, Mass.: Harvard University Press, 1994.

Studlar, Gaylyn. *This Mad Masquerade: Stardom and Masculinity in the Jazz Age*. New York: Columbia University Press, 1996.

Suls, Jerry M. "Two Stage Model for the Appreciation of Jokes and Cartoons." In *The Psychology of Humor*, ed. J. E. Goldstein and P. E. McGhee, 81–100. New York: Academic Press, 1972.

Susman, Warren. *Culture as History: The Transformation of American Society in the Twentieth Century*. New York: Pantheon Books, 1984.

Swain, Joseph P. *The Broadway Musical: A Critical and Musical Survey*. New York: Oxford University Press, 1990.

Szwed, John. *Space Is the Place: The Lives and Times of Sun Ra*. New York: Pantheon, 1997.

Taylor, John. *A Dream of England: Landscape, Photography and the Tourist's Imagination*. Manchester: Manchester University Press, 1994.

Teo, Steven. *Hong Kong Cinema: The Extra Dimensions*. London: Routledge, 1997.

Thomas, Helen, ed. *Dance in the City*. New York: St. Martin's, 1997.

Thomas, Rosie. "Sanctity and Scandal: The Mythologization of Mother India." *Quarterly Review of Film and Video* 11.3 (1989): 11–30.

———. "Indian Cinema—Pleasures and Popularity." *Screen* 26.3–4 (1985): 116–32.

Thomas, Tony. *Music for the Movies*, 2nd ed. Los Angeles: Silman-James Press, 1997.

———, ed. *Film Score: The View from the Podium*. S. Brunswick, N.J.: A. S. Barnes, 1979.

Thompson, Kristin. *Storytelling in the New Hollywood: Understanding Classical Narrative Technique*. Cambridge, Mass.: Harvard University Press, 1999.

———. *Breaking the Glass Armor: Neoformalist Film Analysis*. Princeton: Princeton University Press, 1988.

Ticchi, Cecelia, ed. *Reading Country Music: Steel Guitars, Opry Stars, and Honky Tonk Bars*. Durham, N.C.: Duke University Press, 1998.

———. *High Lonesome: The American Culture of Country Music*. Chapel Hill: University of North Carolina Press, 1994.

Toll, Robert C. *The Entertainment Machine: American Show Business in the Twentieth Century*. New York: Oxford University Press, 1982.

Truffaut, François. *Hitchcock*. New York: Simon & Schuster, 1985.

Tyrrell, Heather. "Bollywood in Britain." *Sight and Sound* 8.8 (1998): 20–22.

Vallee, Rudy. *My Time Is Your Time*. New York: Ivan Obolensky, 1962.

———. *Vagabond Dreams Come True*. New York: E. P. Dutton, 1920.

Vasudevan, Ravi. "The Melodramatic Mode and Commercial Hindi Cinema: Notes on Film History, Narrative and Performance in the 1950s." *Screen* 30.3 (1989): 29–50.

Vincendeau, Ginette. "The *Mise-en-Scène* of Suffering: French *Chanteuses Réalistes.*" *New Formations* 3 (1987): 107–28.

———. "French Cinema in the 1930s: Social Text and Context of a Popular Entertainment Medium." Ph.D. diss., University of East Anglia, 1985.

Waller, Robert James. *The Bridges of Madison County.* New York: Warner, 1992.

Walser, Robert. "'Out of Notes': Signification, Interpretation, and the Problem of Miles Davis." In *Jazz among the Discourses,* ed. Krin Gabbard, 165–88. Durham, N.C.: Duke University Press, 1995.

Watson, Ben. *Frank Zappa: The Negative Dialectics of Poodle Play.* New York: St. Martin's, 1995.

Weiss, Elizabeth, and John Belton, eds. *Film Sound.* New York: Columbia University Press, 1985.

Wenders, Wim. *Emotion Pictures.* London: Faber & Faber, 1989.

Werbner, Pnina, and Tariq Modood, eds. *Debating Cultural Hybridity.* London: Zed Books, 1997.

Whitcomb, Ian. *Irving Berlin and Ragtime America.* London: Century, 1987.

Whiteley, Sheila, ed. *Sexing the Groove: Popular Music and Gender.* New York: Routledge, 1997.

Wide Angle 10.2 (1988): "Film/Music/Video" [special issue].

Willemen, Paul. *Looks and Frictions: Essays in Cultural Studies and Film Theory.* London: British Film Institute, 1994.

Williams, Linda. "Melodrama Revised." In *Refiguring American Film Genres: Theory and History,* ed. Nick Browne. Berkeley: University of California Press, 1998.

Williams, Martin. *Jazz Heritage.* New York: Oxford University Press, 1985.

Williams, Raymond. *Marxism and Literature.* Oxford: Oxford University Press, 1977.

Willis, Paul, with S. Jones, J. Canaan, G. Hurd. *Common Culture: Symbolic Work at Play in the Everyday Cultures of the Young.* Milton Keynes: Open University Press, 1990.

Wilson, Christopher P. *Jokes: Form, Content, Use, and Function.* London: Academic Press, 1979.

Wojcik, Pamela Robertson. "A Star Is Born Again, or How Streisand Recycles Garland." In *Falling for You: Essays on Cinema and Performance,* ed. Lesley Stern and George Kouvaris, 177–208. Sydney, NSW: Power Publications, 1999.

[Wojcik], Pamela Robertson. "Mae West's Maids: Race, 'Authenticity,' and the Discourse of Camp." In *Camp: Queer Aesthetics and the Performing Subject, a Reader,* ed. Fabio Cleto, 393–408. Ann Arbor: University of Michigan Press, 1999.

———. "Home and Away: Friends of Dorothy on the Road in Oz." In *The Road Movie Book,* ed. Steven Cohan and Ina Rae Hark, 271–86. New York: Routledge, 1997.

———. *Guilty Pleasures: Feminist Camp from Mae West to Madonna.* Durham, N.C.: Duke University Press, 1996.

Wojcik, Rick. "Putting the 'Easy'' in Easy Listening: Veiled Female Nudity and the Tijuana Brass." Paper presented at Approaches to American Mass Cultures Conference, University of Chicago, February 1994.

Wolfe, Tom. *The Electric Kool-Aid Acid Test*. New York: Bantam, 1969.

Wood, Michael. "*Nashville* Revisited: The Two Altmans." *American Review* 24 (1976): 102–19.

Wood, Robin. *Hollywood from Vietnam to Reagan*. New York: Columbia University Press, 1986.

Wyatt, Justin. *High Concept: Movies and Marketing in Hollywood*. Austin: University of Texas Press, 1994.

Young, Christopher. *The Films of Doris Day*. Secaucus N.J.: Citadel Press, 1977.

Yueh-yu, Yeh. "A Life of Its Own: Musical Discourses in Wong Kar-Wai's Films." *Post Script* 19.1 (1999): 120–36.

Contributors

RICK ALTMAN is Professor of Cinema and Comparative Literature at the University of Iowa. He is best known for his work on American film genres (*Genre: The Musical*, 1981; *The American Film Musical*, 1987; *Film/Genre*, 1999) and film sound ("Cinema/Sound," *Yale French Studies* 60 [1980]; *Sound Theory/Sound Practice*, 1992; "The State of Sound Studies," *IRIS* 27 [1999]), as well as the performances of his troupe, The Living Nickelodeon.

PRISCILLA BARLOW is a doctoral student at the University of Chicago. Her dissertation, "Best Sellers to Blockbusters: Film and the Popular Novel 1910–1927," employs an intertextual approach to examine cinema spectatorship, film adaptation, and mass media.

BARBARA CHING is Assistant Professor of English at the University of Memphis. Her book *Wrong's What I Do Best: Hard Country Music and Contemporary Culture* is forthcoming.

KELLEY CONWAY is Assistant Professor in the Department of Communication Arts at the University of Wisconsin, Madison. She is currently at work on a book about the realist singer in French film and culture.

COREY K. CREEKMUR is Associate Professor in the Department of English and in the Department of Cinema and Comparative Literature at the University of Iowa, where he also serves as the director of the Institute for Cinema and Culture. He is the coeditor of *Out in Culture: Gay, Lesbian, and Queer Essays on Popular Culture* (Duke University Press), and the author of *Cattle Queens and Lonesome Cowboys: Gender and Sexuality in the Western* (Duke University Press) and a forthcoming study of the musical genre.

KRIN GABBARD is Professor of Comparative Literature at the State University of New York, Stony Brook. He is the author of *Jammin' at the Margins: Jazz and the American Cinema* (1996) and *Psychiatry and the Cinema* (1999), and the editor of *Jazz among the Discourses* and *Representing Jazz* (both Duke University Press, 1995). He is currently writing a book on music and masculinity in the movies.

JONATHAN GILL teaches at Columbia University. He is currently working on a book about black-Jewish relations in America from 1654 to 1967 called *Blacking Up, Jewing Down.*

ANDREW KILLICK is Assistant Professor of Ethnomusicology at Florida State University. His research extends to various traditions in European, Korean, and American popular music, musical theater, and film. He is now working on a book on the Korean Opera form *changgeûk.*

ADAM KNEE holds a doctorate in cinema studies from New York University and has taught at universities in the United States, Australia, and Thailand. He has published numerous articles on a wide range of film topics, including race, masculinity, and genre.

ARTHUR KNIGHT teaches in the English Department and the American Studies, Film Studies, and Literary and Cultural Studies Programs at the College of William and Mary. His book on the African American film musical is forthcoming from Duke University Press.

JILL LEEPER is completing a dissertation on representations of the freakish body at the University of Rochester. She teaches at Indiana University–Purdue University at Indianapolis.

NEEPA MAJUMDAR is a Ph.D. candidate at Indiana University, Bloomington. She is writing a dissertation on stardom in Indian popular cinema.

ALLISON MCCRACKEN is a doctoral candidate in American Studies at the University of Iowa. She is currently completing her dissertation on crooning and American culture, 1920–1940.

MURRAY POMERANCE is Chair and Professor in the Department of Sociology at Ryerson University. His fiction has appeared in the *Paris Review, New Directions,* and elsewhere. He is the author of *Magia D'amore* (1999), coeditor of *Bang Bang, Shoot Shoot! Essays on Guns and Popular Culture* (1999), and *Closely Watched Brains* (2001), and editor of *Ladies and Gentlemen, Boys and Girls: Gender in Film at the End of the Twentieth Century* (2001).

PAUL B. RAMAEKER is a Ph.D. candidate at the University of Wisconsin, Madison. He is currently completing his dissertation on visual style in the Hollywood cinema of the 1970s and '80s.

JEFF SMITH is Assistant Professor in the Program of Film and Media Studies at Washington University in St. Louis. He is author of *The Sounds of Commerce: Marketing Popular Film Music* (1998).

PAMELA ROBERTSON WOJCIK is Associate Professor in the Department of Film, TV, and Theatre at the University of Notre Dame. She is author of *Guilty Pleasures: Feminist Camp from Mae West to Madonna* (Duke University Press, 1996) and is currently writing a book called *Typecasting: Film Acting and Identity*.

NABEEL ZUBERI is Lecturer in Film, Television, and Media Studies at the University of Auckland in Aotearoa/New Zealand. His recent work includes *Sounds English: Transnational Popular Music* (2001). His current research is on different forms of mediation in the South Asian diaspora.

Index

Mullen, Jim, 312

Mulvey, Laura, 449–450

Murch, Walter, 227–228, 231–232, 410

Muriel's Wedding, 1, 444–445, 448, 450

Muse, Clarence, 269, 276–277, 285–287, 291

Music: and ethnicity, 234–236; Jewish, 186–198; meaning of, 185–188, 199–200; motifs, 234. *See also* Bhangra; Classical music; Classical Hollywood film score; Country music; Easy listening; Jazz; Mariachi; Mutual implication; Popular music; Swing

Musicals, 6–7, 162, 164–166, 186–188, 209; in Indian cinema, 387–390, 395

Music supervisor, 13, 386, 410, 412–413

Music video (MTV), 7, 13, 76, 178, 248, 252, 385, 411

Mutual implication, 226, 230, 232

My Beautiful Laundrette, 246, 257

My Darling Clementine, 4

My Girl, 413

My Own Private Idaho, 413

Nadel, Norman, 193

Nair, Mira, 377

Najma, 245

Naremore, James, 233, 236, 238

Naseeb, 163–166, 177

Nash, N. Richard, 360

Nashville, 204–214, 218, 221

Nelson, Ozzie, 125

Nericcio, William, 240–241

Nesmith, Michael, 74, 79–80, 83–84, 89–90, 92

Nice, The, 83

Nichols, Bill, 250

Nicholson, Jack, 10, 76, 85, 87–88, 90, 95, 204

Nickelodeons, 19–23, 26, 29

Niehaus, Lennie, 307

Night Ranger, 423

Nightmail, 250, 253

Nilsson, Harry, 92, 384

Nirmal, 251, 255

Nirvana, 385

Nixon, Marni, 396

Norman, Loulie Jean, 367

North, Michael, 356

North by Northwest, 409

Ohio Players, 423

Oliver!, 11, 188, 192–194, 196

Olson, Christopher, 57

One Fine Day, 382

Only the Lonely, 413

Orbison, Roy, 384

Orvell, Miles, 203

Otcasek, Christopher, 385

Otis, Johnny, 309–310

Out of the Past, 298

Paint Your Wagon, 300–301

Pale Rider, 311–312

Pangborn, Frank, 121

Pardes, 376–377, 398

Paris la nuit, 136–137

Parker, Charlie, 302, 309, 311, 436

Pechan, Chirag, 253

Peggy Sue Got Married, 382, 413

Penn, Michael, 408

Pepe le Moko, 147–148, 151

Perry, George, 53

Peters, Brock, 363

Peterson, Wolfgang, 310

Le petit theatre de Jean Renoir, 137

Peyser, Joan, 354

Phantom Lady, 4

Philadelphia, 392, 438

Phonograph: records and players, 14; as fetish, 438, 449–452; and gender, 435–453; representations of, 433–434, 441–452. *See also* Playback technology

Piaf, Edith, 135–137, 142, 156

Picturized songs, 163, 167, 378, 389, 395–397. *See also* Indian cinema; Playback singers

Library of Congress Cataloging-in-Publication Data

Soundtrack available : essays on film and popular music /
edited by Pamela Robertson Wojcik and Arthur Knight.

p. cm.

Includes bibliographical references and index.

ISBN 0-8223-2800-3 (cloth : alk. paper)

ISBN 0-8223-2797-x (pbk. : alk. paper)

1. Motion pictures and music.   2. Motion picture
music—History and criticism.   3. Popular music—
History and criticism.   I. Wojcik, Pamela Robertson.
II. Knight, Arthur.

ML2075 .S68   2001

781.5'42'09—dc21   2001033706